Microsoft® Office 2010
Inside Out

Ed Bott
Carl Siechert

PUBLISHED BY
Microsoft Press
A Division of Microsoft Corporation
One Microsoft Way
Redmond, Washington 98052-6399

Library of Congress Control Number: 2010933006

Printed and bound in Canada.

Microsoft Press books are available through booksellers and distributors worldwide. For further information about international editions, contact your local Microsoft Corporation office or contact Microsoft Press International directly at fax (425) 936-7329. Visit our Web site at www.microsoft.com/mspress. Send comments to mspinput@ microsoft.com.

Acquisitions Editor: Juliana Aldous
Developmental Editor: Devon Musgrave
Project Editor: Valerie Woolley
Editorial Production: Publishing.com
Technical Reviewer: John Pierce; Technical Review services provided by
   Content Master, a member of CM Group, Ltd.

Body Part No. X16-88505

To Judy Bott and Jan Siechert,
for their patience, support, and love.

Contents at a Glance

Table of Contents

Part 1: Office Fundamentals

What do you think of this book? We want to hear from you!

Microsoft is interested in hearing your feedback so we can continually improve our books and learning resources for you. To participate in a brief online survey, please visit:

microsoft.com/learning/booksurvey

Part 2: Word

Part 3: Excel

Part 4: OneNote

Part 5: PowerPoint

Part 6: Outlook

Part 7: Sharing and Collaborating

What do you think of this book? We want to hear from you!

Microsoft is interested in hearing your feedback so we can continually improve our books and learning resources for you. To participate in a brief online survey, please visit:

microsoft.com/learning/booksurvey

Acknowledgments

Anyone who has written a book knows that it's a team effort and that surpassing a high quality bar sometimes takes longer than anyone expects. We've been blessed to work with a remarkably talented and patient team.

We put extra pressure on our longtime collaborator Curtis Philips of Publishing.com, who performed the editing, layout, and production tasks for this book. Our delays didn't seem to faze him or his team of experts, which included technical editor John Pierce and proofreader Andrea Fox. They each made invaluable improvements to the manuscript.

If you need PowerPoint expertise in a hurry, you can't do better than Deanna Reynolds, whose contributions to Part 5 provided a huge assist just when we needed it the most.

The penguin photographs scattered throughout the book were provided by Carol and Bruce Wagner, who will probably use this exposure as an excuse to take yet another trip abroad. (It doesn't take much.)

Whenever we had questions about Office, the go-to guy was Scott Massey of Waggener Edstrom, who quickly connected us to the developers, testers, product planners, and technical experts who were able to help us track down authoritative answers. (There are far too many people on the Office team to thank individually, so instead we offer a collective thank you.)

Our friends at Microsoft Press—including product planner Juliana Aldous, content development manager Devon Musgrave, project editor Valerie Woolley, associate publisher Steve Weiss, and publisher Ben Ryan—provided their usual support and guidance.

Our good friend and literary agent Claudette Moore (whom we like to call "The Hammer") worked overtime to give us the encouragement and assistance we desperately needed at various times during this book's development. And her assistant, Ann Jaroncyk, provided additional encouragement by ensuring that the checks found their way to our bank accounts.

Carl's colleagues at LittleMachineShop.com—Chris Wood, Cheryl Kubiak (that's her on page 238), Roger Proffitt, Connie Manz, and Luis Ocampo—endured his extended absences and grouchier-than-usual demeanor. Their support, along with that of our long-suffering wives, made it possible to bring you this book and keep a bit of our sanity.

Many, many thanks to all.

Ed Bott and Carl Siechert
August 2010

Book Support and Resources

Additional Resources

The authors have set up a website for readers of *Microsoft Office 2010 Inside Out* and *Windows 7 Inside Out*. At the site, you can find updates, corrections, links to other resources, and more useful tips. In addition, you can discuss Office 2010 and Windows 7 with the authors and with other readers. We hope you'll join us at *w7io.com*.

Errata and Book Support

We've made every effort to ensure the accuracy of this book and its companion content. If you do find an error, please report it on our Microsoft Press site at *Oreilly.com*:

1. Go to *http://microsoftpress.oreilly.com*.

2. In the Search box, enter the book's ISBN or title.

3. Select your book from the search results.

4. On your book's catalog page, under the cover image, you'll see a list of links.

5. Click View, Submit Errata.

You'll find additional information and services for your book on its catalog page. If you need additional support, please e-mail Microsoft Press Book Support at

mspinput@microsoft.com

Please note that product support for Microsoft software is not offered through the addresses above.

We Want to Hear from You

At Microsoft Press, your satisfaction is our top priority, and your feedback our most valuable asset. Please tell us what you think of this book at

http://www.microsoft.com/learning/booksurvey

The survey is short, and we read *every one* of your comments and ideas. Thanks in advance for your input!

Stay in Touch

Let's keep the conversation going! We're on Twitter (*http://twitter.com*): @MicrosoftPress, @EdBott, and @CarlSiec.

Conventions and Features Used in This Book

This book uses special text and design conventions to help you find the information you need more easily.

Text Conventions

Convention	Meaning
Abbreviated commands for navigating the ribbon	For your convenience, this book uses abbreviated commands. For example, "Click Home, Insert, Insert Cells" means that you should click the Home tab on the ribbon, then click the Insert button, and finally click the Insert Cells command.
Boldface type	**Boldface** indicates text that you type.
Initial Capital Letters	The first letters of the names of tabs, dialog boxes, dialog box elements, and commands are capitalized. Example: the Save As dialog box.
Italicized type	*Italicized* type indicates new terms.
Plus sign (+) in text	Keyboard shortcuts are indicated by a plus sign (+) separating key names. For example, Ctrl+Alt+Delete means that you press the Ctrl, Alt, and Delete keys at the same time.

Design Conventions

INSIDE OUT   This Statement Illustrates an Example of an "Inside Out" Heading

These are the book's signature tips. In these tips, you get the straight scoop on what's going on with the software—inside information about why a feature works the way it does. You'll also find handy workarounds to deal with software problems.

Sidebar

Sidebars provide helpful hints, timesaving tricks, or alternative procedures related to the task being discussed.

TROUBLESHOOTING

This statement illustrates an example of a "Troubleshooting" problem statement.

Look for these sidebars to find solutions to common problems you might encounter. Troubleshooting sidebars appear next to related information in the chapters. You can also use "Index to Troubleshooting Topics" at the back of the book to look up problems by topic.

Cross-references point you to locations in the book that offer additional information about the topic being discussed.

CAUTION

Cautions identify potential problems that you should look out for when you're completing a task or that you must address before you can complete a task.

Note

Notes offer additional information related to the task being discussed.

PART 1

Office Fundamentals

Inside Office 2010

BECOMING proficient in Microsoft Office isn't easy. You have to master a minimum of four programs and as many as seven, depending on which edition of Office is installed on your PC. You have to use both sides of your brain (the analytical and the artistic), sometimes in the same program at the same time. And you're expected to remember the ins and outs of a program you might use only once every few weeks or months.

It's little wonder that most of us are comfortable with one or two Office programs and flail around in frustration when we need to use one of the others. When you're using a program that's less familiar to you, you're so busy trying to figure out how to accomplish basic tasks that you don't even think about time-saving strategies and advanced features and capabilities.

That's where we come in. We wrote this book from scratch, with the goal of delivering exactly what you need to become productive with the five core applications in Office 2010—Word, Excel, OneNote, PowerPoint, and Outlook. We provide a cram course in each program, covering the core features and technologies and suggesting productivity-enhancing expert tips to help you work smarter.

We're pretty certain that most of our readers have at least a passing familiarity with Office, so we won't waste your time with tedious history lessons and tutorials. In this introductory chapter, we offer a whirlwind tour of what's new and what's changed from your previous Office edition, along with a basic road map to this book. Fasten your seatbelts!

What's New? What's Changed?

Did you skip an Office upgrade? If your new copy of Office 2010 replaced Office 2003 or earlier, then you missed the single biggest change in Office 2007: the ribbon. In Office 2010, this interface element is now a part of every program in the Office family, without exception. The ribbon replaces the drop-down menus and icon-laden toolbars from earlier Office editions with tabs that stretch horizontally across the top of the program window. Figure 1-1, for example, shows the Insert tab from Word 2010.

Figure 1-1 The ribbon interface combines menus and toolbars into a single horizontal arrangement.

The ribbon isn't only about turning menus on their side. Other additions to the Office interface allow you to choose formatting options from a gallery and preview their effect on your live data before committing to a change. In all Office programs, paste options allow you to adjust formatting on the fly rather than using Undo in a series of trial-and-error attempts.

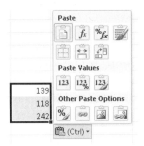

If you're already familiar with the ribbon from Office 2007, you'll notice incremental improvements in this upgrade. In a welcome change from Office 2007, the ribbon is also customizable; using the dialog box shown in Figure 1-2, you can remove command groups from the ribbon, create your own custom command groups and tabs, rename existing groups and tabs, and save your custom settings for reuse on a different Office 2010 installation.

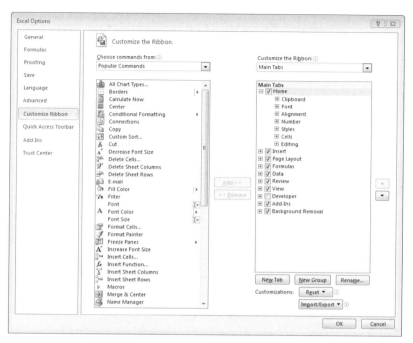

Chapter 1

Figure 1-2 If you don't like the default ribbon in an Office program, change it by adding, removing, and rearranging tabs and individual commands.

With one exception, clicking a tab on the ribbon displays a horizontal strip of commands and options related to that task. The exception is the File tab, which always appears in the first position on the left side; clicking File opens the new Office Backstage view, which occupies the entire program window and consolidates multiple tasks into a single location without forcing you to open multiple dialog boxes. Click any of the options that appear, menu-style, along the left side of the window to fill Backstage view with the details for that task. Figure 1-3, for example, shows the Print tab in Word 2010, with a neatly arranged group of settings (accessible only through dialog boxes in previous Office editions) and a Print Preview pane.

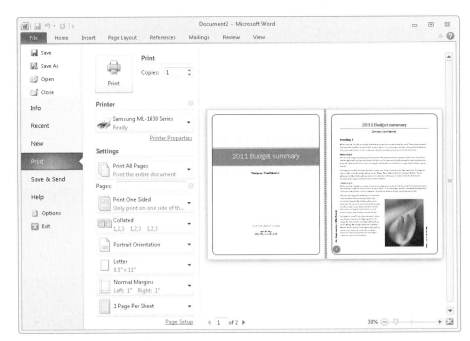

Figure 1-3 Clicking the File tab opens Backstage view, which consolidates common options and previews in a single location.

For a detailed look at the Office 2010 ribbon, Backstage view, Live Preview, and other interface elements, see Chapter 3, "Using and Customizing the Office Interface."

All of the Office programs we cover in this edition (with the exception of OneNote) include significant improvements for inserting and editing graphics. The picture-editing tools are especially noteworthy, providing options you can use to crop a photo, remove distracting background elements, and add artistic effects without having to leave the document window. In Figure 1-4, you can see an original image on the left; the image on the right is the result after applying the Pencil Grayscale effect.

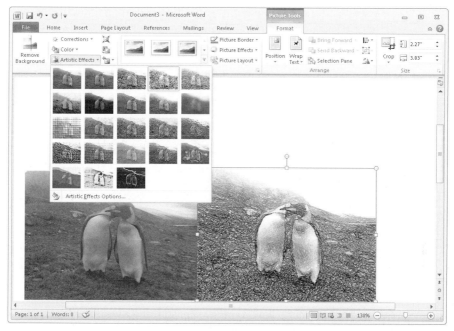

Figure 1-4 Image-editing tools available throughout Office 2010 allow you to crop and transform pictures without leaving the document window.

You'll find comprehensive instructions on how to insert and edit photos, screen shots, Smart-Art graphics, and other visual elements in Chapter 6, "Working with Graphics and Pictures."

A Field Guide to Office 2010 Editions

If you want to install Office on a new PC or upgrade an earlier Office version on an existing PC, you have an impressive—and potentially confusing—array of options. Through traditional retail distribution channels (in brick-and-mortar stores or online), you can choose from three editions:

- **Office Home and Student** includes Word, Excel, OneNote, and PowerPoint. You can install and activate a retail copy of this edition on up to three PCs in a single household for personal, nonbusiness use. The license agreement specifically prohibits using this edition "in any commercial, nonprofit or revenue-generating activities, or by any government organization."

- **Office Home and Business** replaces the previous Office Standard edition. It includes all the programs from the Home and Student edition and adds Outlook. Under the license agreement, if you purchase a retail copy of this edition you can install and activate it on one computer (the "licensed device") and install another copy on a portable device "for use by the single primary user of the licensed device."

- **Office Professional** is the top-of-the-line Office edition, intended for consumers and small businesses. It includes the programs in the Home and Business edition and adds Publisher and Access. The licensing terms are similar to those of the Home and Business edition. The same package is available for purchase by students and faculty through academic resellers (at a significantly discounted price) as **Office Professional Academic**.

For instructions on how to install and activate a retail copy of Office 2010, see Chapter 2, "Installing and Updating Microsoft Office 2010."

What's in Office Starter Edition?

If you buy a new Windows PC, the computer manufacturer might have installed Office 2010 Starter Edition. This free edition is not a trial copy; it contains no "time bomb" that causes it to stop working after a few months. It is also considerably more limited than any retail Office edition. It includes only two programs, Word Starter and Excel Starter, both of which allow you to create, edit, and save documents in their respective formats but lack access to advanced features.

What makes Office 2010 Starter Edition most interesting is that it contains the installation code for all three retail editions. If you decide you want to upgrade to one of those editions, you can purchase a product key card that allows you to unlock and activate your preferred edition. The discounted price (compared to the full packaged Office product) includes a single license and does not allow you to install that Office edition on another PC.

For more details on Office Starter edition and how to convert it to a full-featured edition, see "Upgrading from Office 2010 Starter Edition" on page 30.

Finally, businesses that have volume-license agreements with Microsoft can choose from two available Office editions:

- **Office Standard** includes Word, Excel, OneNote, PowerPoint, Outlook, and Publisher.

- **Office Professional Plus** is the high-end enterprise offering, containing the same set of programs as Office Standard and adding Access, Microsoft Communicator, SharePoint Workspace (formerly Groove Workspace), and InfoPath.

INSIDE OUT   How to check which Office edition is installed on a Windows PC

If you're not certain which Office edition is installed on your PC, here's how to check.

Open Microsoft Word (you can use another Office program if you prefer; the steps are the same as those listed here). Click File, and then click Help. At the right side of the window you'll see a block of information like the one shown here.

Product Activated

Microsoft Office Professional Plus 2010

This product contains Microsoft Access, Microsoft Excel, Microsoft SharePoint Workspace, Microsoft OneNote, Microsoft Outlook, Microsoft PowerPoint, Microsoft Publisher, Microsoft Word, Microsoft InfoPath.

Change Product Key

About Microsoft Word

Version: 14.0.4760.1000 (32-bit)
Additional Version and Copyright Information
Part of Microsoft Office Professional Plus 2010
© 2010 Microsoft Corporation. All rights reserved.
Microsoft Customer Services and Support
Product ID: 02260-000-0000002-00026
Microsoft Software License Terms

In addition to information about your edition and the programs in it, this display also allows you to see whether your installation has been activated and whether you're running a 32-bit or 64-bit copy. Links at the bottom provide access to support resources and allow you to read the license agreement associated with your edition.

Note

In this book we do not cover Access, Publisher, and other programs found only in the Professional and enterprise editions of Office. Stand-alone programs such as Project and Visio, which are part of the Office family but aren't included in any packaged Office edition, are also outside the scope of this book's coverage.

Word 2010

In Office 2010, Word is arguably misnamed. Yes, it still allows you to process words: entering and editing blocks of text, checking your spelling and grammar, specifying typefaces and fonts, and formatting paragraphs as headings and body text. But in Office 2010, Word adds a significant new set of design and page-layout tools that make it suitable for medium-strength desktop publishing jobs. We cover the full range of Word features in the four chapters devoted to Word in this book.

The Navigation pane, an optional interface element that appears at the left side of the Word editing window when enabled, is much improved. As in previous versions, you can use headings in your document to quickly move between sections. The new Search Document box at the top of the Navigation pane allows you to search efficiently, especially in long documents. Figure 1-5 shows search results using the page browser; an alternate view allows you to see the same results organized as snippets of text so that you can see them in context.

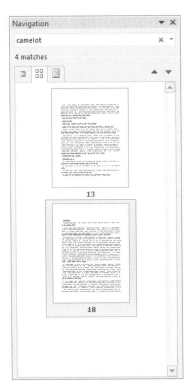

Figure 1-5 When you use the Navigation pane to search for a word or phrase, you can view the results as thumbnail pages (shown here) or as text snippets.

In addition to the picture-editing tools available throughout Office, Word 2010 offers an assortment of text effects for fine typography. If you use OpenType fonts (the standard for Windows), you can precisely control ligatures and kerning. You can also create visual effects such as shadows, reflections, gradients, bevels, and glows, as illustrated in Figure 1-6. These effects (which can be cringe-inducing if used carelessly) are not limited to WordArt graphics but can be used with ordinary text—meaning they can be included in styles, spelling reviews, and so on.

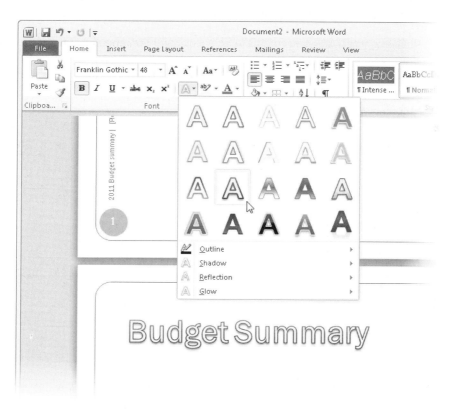

Figure 1-6 Use the Text Effects gallery to add shadows, reflections, and other visual pizzazz to ordinary text.

Like its Office-mates, Word also includes an assortment of new document recovery features that allow you to roll back to one of five previous AutoSaved versions or recover from an unexpected crash. You can also restore a draft version of a document even if you close Word without saving it.

Excel 2010

Shockingly, many Office users have no idea that Excel can be used for something other than budgets and simple lists. If your only exposure to Excel is the monthly ritual of adding your department's numbers to the corporate budget template, we have some surprises for you. In the four chapters we devote to Excel, we cover the fundamentals of formulas, formatting, and filtering data; we also help you unlock the magic of PivotTables, which sound intimidating but are easy to master and incredibly useful once you learn how they work.

The most obvious improvements in Excel 2010 are related to data analysis and presentation. Most professional number crunchers use charts and visualizations to help other people understand the impact of a mass of raw numbers. The new sparklines feature embeds graphic representations of data trends directly within those numbers (and updates them automatically as the numbers change), as shown in Figure 1-7.

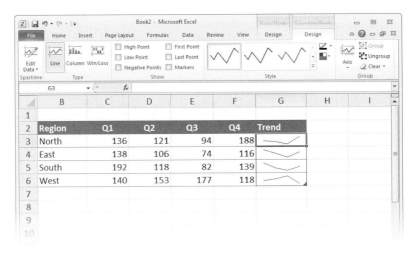

Figure 1-7 Using sparklines allows you to visualize trends and patterns alongside the data in an Excel worksheet.

For cutting large data sets into manageable workloads, Excel 2010 offers several useful tools: Use PivotTables, for example, to quickly and easily create crosstabs and summaries of even very large data sets with just a few clicks. In traditional lists or PivotTables, you can create search filters to help find relevant items.

OneNote 2010

Although OneNote has been a part of Office since the 2003 release, many experienced Office users are unlikely to have spent even a minute with it. That's because OneNote was previously included only with the Home and Student and Ultimate editions of Office.

In Office 2010, OneNote has been given a big promotion and is now one of the core programs installed with every retail and enterprise Office edition. If you've never seen OneNote, we strongly recommend that you spend some time with this incredibly useful and versatile free-form note-taking program.

If you're already familiar with OneNote, you'll appreciate some of the subtle improvements in this upgrade. For starters, you can dock OneNote in a narrow window that automatically arranges itself on the side of your monitor. In that configuration, you can take full advantage of the new Linked Notes feature, which automatically creates a link to the current Word document, PowerPoint presentation, or web page (Internet Explorer only), as in Figure 1-8.

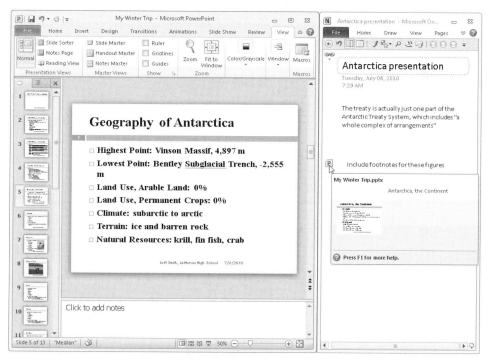

Figure 1-8 OneNote can dock itself alongside another Office program or your web browser and create automatic links between the notes you create and the source material.

Your familiarity with Word will pay off in OneNote 2010 as well: You can now apply formatting for headings and body text in OneNote by using the same keyboard shortcuts that work in Word. OneNote 2010 includes the Format Painter found in other Office programs, allowing you to copy formatting from one location to another. It also offers greatly improved tools for searching and organizing information in your notebooks. That capability is invaluable when your collection of notebooks becomes too big for you to find random bits of information by simply flipping through pages.

In this book, we devote three chapters to OneNote. If you're new to the program, we recommend that you start at the beginning and read all the way through to learn some of the subtleties of this unusual but powerful program.

PowerPoint 2010

Most audiences groan when they realize you're about to launch into a PowerPoint presentation. But slide shows don't have to be deadly or dull—in fact, as we demonstrate, they don't even have to be slide shows, in the traditional sense. Using PowerPoint 2010, you can create photo albums and web-based presentations that don't include a single bullet point.

At the top of the new-features list in PowerPoint 2010 is a set of tools that allows you to embed video clips into a slide, format the video container, and even trim a lengthy clip so that only the relevant section plays. Figure 1-9 shows these tools in action.

Figure 1-9 New video-editing tools in PowerPoint 2010 allow you to embed, trim, and format video clips.

If you already have a solid background in building presentations with PowerPoint, we'll show you the subtle (and, in some cases, dramatic) changes in familiar tools. You can now open multiple presentations in separate windows, for example, making it easier to copy slides in one presentation for use in another. You can also divide complex presentations into sections for easier management. We'll also demonstrate how to use the improved set of animations and the slide transitions shown here:

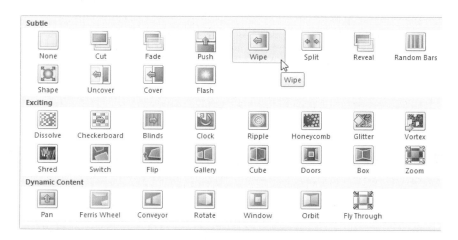

Outlook 2010

For many Office users (especially those in corporations that live and die by e-mail), Outlook is the first program they open in the morning and the last one they shut down at night. In between, Outlook helps you juggle e-mail, meetings, appointments, tasks, and contact information for friends, family, clients, coworkers, and anyone else. In Office 2007, the Outlook user interface was a half-step behind the other core members of the Office family, using the menus and toolbars from Office 2003 and earlier editions. In Office 2010, Outlook has caught up, shifting the extensive collection of Outlook commands, options, and settings to the ribbon interface used by other Office programs.

First and foremost, Outlook is an e-mail client program that helps you compose, send, receive, and manage messages using most standard e-mail protocols. You can combine multiple accounts into a single set of folders. One noteworthy change for any Outlook user in a corporate setting is support for up to 15 Microsoft Exchange accounts in a profile; previously, each Exchange account required a separate profile.

If e-mail overload is an issue, you'll want to read our explanation of Outlook's new conversation view, which groups messages into threads. New conversation management tools allow you to clean up a conversation by removing redundant messages. A new Ignore button lets you automatically delete conversations (including future responses) in which you're an uninterested bystander trapped on the Cc line.

Another new tool in Outlook 2010 gives you the capability of creating Quick Steps, which automate repetitive message-handling tasks. These "macros" appear by default as buttons on the Message tab and can also be assigned to keyboard shortcuts, as shown in Figure 1-10.

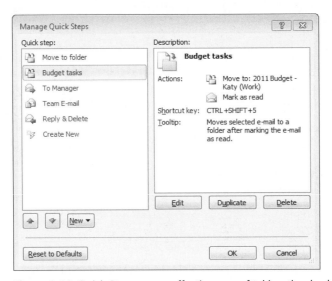

Figure 1-10 Quick Steps are an effective way of taking the drudgery out of routine message-management tasks.

Outlook 2010 also recognizes the increasing importance of keeping track of interactions with friends, family, and coworkers over time. The new People pane appears at the bottom of every e-mail message and contact; it integrates a complete message history for the message sender or contact, along with connections to social networking sites, RSS feeds, status updates, meetings, and so on.

Sharing and Collaborating on Office Files

As in previous versions, Office 2010 includes a full set of features designed to help you collaborate with other people on documents, workbooks, presentations, and notebooks. Some collaboration features are self-contained; in Word, Excel, and PowerPoint, for example, you can embed comments and track revisions within a saved file and then share that file via e-mail.

But most of the Office 2010 applications also permit real-time collaboration using files stored on the free Windows Live SkyDrive service or on a corporate SharePoint server. In fact, all of the document-centric programs in Office 2010—Word, Excel, PowerPoint, and OneNote (but not Outlook)—allow you to view and edit documents from a browser by using Office Web Apps. You'll find more details about these tools and techniques in the final three chapters of this book, which collectively make up the "Sharing and Collaboration" section.

CHAPTER 2

Installing and Updating Microsoft Office 2010

Now it's time to dive in: let's get Microsoft Office 2010 set up and running on your computer. With program delivery methods that are new to Office 2010, installing Office is easier than ever before. Nonetheless, you need to be aware of some gotchas in the purchase and setup processes. In this chapter we help you to select an appropriate Office edition, install it properly, and configure it to ensure problem-free performance.

Choosing an Office Edition

With five different Office 2010 editions available, selecting the best one for your purposes might appear to be a difficult or confusing choice. In the earlier versions of Office, that was certainly the case, given the scattershot collection of programs in each of the many editions. One edition might have had all the programs you wanted except one, but invariably it seemed the edition that included the missing program excluded another you wanted.

The lineup has been simplified in Office 2010, and, most significantly, each edition is a superset of the next lower edition. In other words, as you can see in Table 2-1, there's a straight progression from each edition to the next, and clear differentiation between them.

> **CAUTION**
>
> Microsoft does not offer an easy or inexpensive upgrade path that would, for example, let you purchase Office Home and Business and then later upgrade to Office Professional for the difference in price. (You can purchase Office programs individually, but that turns out to be an expensive way to upgrade.) Therefore, you should evaluate your requirements carefully and decide exactly which programs you need before you select an Office edition.

Table 2-1 **Office 2010 Edition Comparison**

Edition	Word	Excel	OneNote	PowerPoint	Outlook	Publisher	Access	More*
Office Home and Student	✔	✔	✔	✔				
Office Home and Business	✔	✔	✔	✔	✔			
Office Standard	✔	✔	✔	✔	✔	✔		
Office Professional	✔	✔	✔	✔	✔	✔	✔	
Office Professional Plus	✔	✔	✔	✔	✔	✔	✔	✔

* The additional programs included in Office Professional Plus are Microsoft Outlook 2010 with Business Contact Manager, Microsoft InfoPath 2010, Microsoft Communicator, and Microsoft SharePoint Workspace 2010. This edition also provides support for integrated solution capabilities such as enterprise contact management, electronic forms, information rights management, and policy management.

There's one other factor you must consider before making your selection: licensing. Table 2-2 summarizes the differences among the editions. (For information about volume licensing programs, visit the Microsoft Volume Licensing home page at *w7io.com/10202*.)

Table 2-2 **Licensing and Availability of Office 2010 Editions**

Edition	Licensing and Availability
Office Home and Student	Available only through retail channels. Licensed only for noncommercial use. Each boxed copy can be installed on up to three PCs in a single household; a product key card is valid for a single installation.
Office Home and Business	Available through retail channels and via volume licensing programs. Each boxed copy can be installed on one computer and on one portable device for use by the same person; a product key card is valid for a single installation.
Office Standard	Available only through volume licensing programs.
Office Professional	Available through retail channels and via volume licensing programs. Each boxed copy can be installed on one computer and on one portable device for use by the same person; a product key card is valid for a single installation.
Office Professional Plus	Available only through volume licensing programs.

INSIDE OUT
Ease deployments with the Office Environment Assessment Tool

If it's your job to install Office 2010 on several computers, you'll find the Office Environment Assessment Tool to be useful for evaluating your needs. For each computer, the tool detects which version and edition of Office is already installed (it recognizes all versions going back to Microsoft Office 97), identifies any add-ins in use by Office (you can use this information to determine if an Office 2010–compatible version is available—or necessary), and points out potential upgrade problems. In addition, it compiles a list of installed third-party programs that might be incompatible with Office 2010. You can download the Office Environment Assessment Tool at *w7io.com/10201*.

System Requirements for Office 2010

In general, system requirements for the latest version of Office are nearly the same as those for Office 2007, and they're not much more rigorous than those for Office 2003. Most new computers meet the requirements, and if your computer already has Office 2007 installed, Office 2010 will almost certainly work satisfactorily. And if your computer runs Office 2003, it might have enough muscle to handle Office 2010. The specific minimum hardware requirements for Office 2010 are as follows:

- 256 MB memory

- 500 MHz processor

- 1.5–3.5 GB available disk space (depends on Office edition)

- 1024 × 768 resolution display

In addition, Microsoft suggests (but doesn't require) the use of a graphics processor unit (GPU) that's separate from the CPU. One that's DirectX 9.0 compliant and has at least 64 MB of video memory speeds up graphics-rendering tasks, such as displaying charts in Excel or playing video and performing slide transitions in PowerPoint. (PowerPoint in particular benefits from GPU rendering.)

INSIDE OUT   Check for DirectX compatibility

Windows includes a diagnostic program that tells you at a glance which version of DirectX your GPU is using. To use it, in the Start menu search box (or in the Run dialog box if you're using Windows XP) type **dxdiag** and then press Enter. On the Display tab, shown here, the DirectX Diagnostic Tool shows the DirectX version in use.

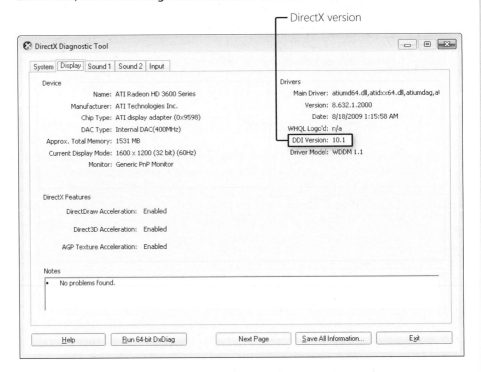

To determine the amount of video memory, you need to visit a different dialog box. In Windows 7, right-click the desktop and choose Screen Resolution. In the dialog box that appears, click Advanced Settings. The Adapter tab in the next dialog box that appears shows the relevant value as Dedicated Video Memory. Starting from Display in Control Panel, follow similar steps to find this value in Windows XP or Windows Vista.

To run a 32-bit version of Office 2010, your computer must have one of the following operating systems:

- Windows 7 (32-bit or 64-bit)

- Windows Vista SP1 (32-bit or 64-bit)

- Windows XP SP3 (32-bit)

- Windows Server 2008 R2 (64-bit)

- Windows Server 2008 (32-bit or 64-bit)

- Windows Server 2003 R2 with MSXML 6.0 (32-bit or 64-bit)

The 64-bit version of Office 2010 requires one of these operating systems:

- Windows 7 (64-bit)

- Windows Vista SP1 (64-bit)

- Windows Server 2008 R2 (64-bit)

- Windows Server 2008 (64-bit)

Choosing Between 32-Bit and 64-Bit Versions

All editions of Office 2010 (except Starter) are available in 32-bit and 64-bit versions. (Retail boxed copies include both versions, but if you're purchasing Office online you must make your selection at the time of download.)

The future of computing is 64 bit, and the 64-bit version of Office offers some distinct advantages. Most importantly, it enables access to much more memory, which allows you to work with extremely large files (for example, Excel files larger than 2 GB).

However, there is little to be gained if your files are not humongous, and the 64-bit version has its own limitations. First, it can be installed only on 64-bit operating systems, as detailed in the previous section. Many add-ins for Office are not compatible with the 64-bit version, and you're more likely to encounter other compatibility problems, such as issues with Visual Basic for Applications (VBA) macros and with certain ActiveX controls in Internet Explorer. Furthermore, with some hardware configurations, graphics rendering can be slower on the 64-bit version. It is for these reasons that Microsoft recommends the 32-bit version for most users, and it's that version that's usually installed by default when you order a new computer with Office preinstalled.

For a technical discussion of the issues surrounding 64-bit versions of Office, see the Tech-Net article at *w7io.com/10203*.

Setting Up Office

Setting up Office is generally a straightforward process that requires little input from you and in which you're aided by plenty of on-screen guidance. In this section we describe three methods for procuring and installing Office:

- Installing from retail media (sometimes referred to as *full packaged product*), such as a boxed copy you can buy at a bricks-and-mortar store or from an online merchant that ships merchandise

- Using Click-to-Run, which is a service that allows you to purchase Office online and begin using it almost immediately

- Upgrading from Office Starter, a reduced-functionality Office edition that's included on many new computers

In addition, we explain the process of upgrading from an earlier version of Office.

INSIDE OUT Install Office throughout your organization

Microsoft provides tools and information that make it easier to install multiple copies of Office. You can push customized versions of Office to computers over the network, for example. The Microsoft Office 2010 Resource Kit provides details; you can download the Resource Kit from *w7io.com/10204* or view the content online at *w7io.com/10205*. Note that much of the information pertains primarily to use of volume-licensed editions of Office.

Installing from Retail Media

Installing a full version of Office 2010 from a retail boxed copy (or from its online equivalent, a downloaded executable installation file) is similar to the one used for previous versions of Office and other programs—except with fewer steps and less interaction required.

Start the installation by running the Setup program on the installation DVD (or by running the downloaded installation file). If you want to take the shortest path to a completed installation, in the first dialog box that appears, enter your product key and click Continue; review the license terms, click the acceptance check box, and click Continue; click Install Now (see Figure 2-1); wait a bit and, upon completion, click Close. Type a few characters and five clicks—and you're done.

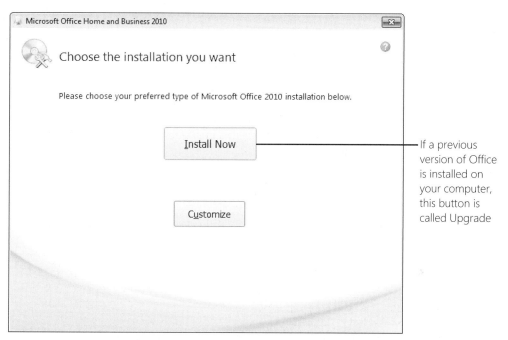

Figure 2-1 Your first big setup decision comes when this dialog box appears. And if you click Install Now (or Upgrade, which appears in its place if an earlier version of Office is already installed on your computer), it's your last decision as well.

> **Note**
>
> **The product key determines which edition will be installed. For the three retail editions (Home and Student, Home and Business, and Professional), the installation files are essentially the same. This bit of knowledge can be handy for avoiding multiple downloads (if you're installing different editions on different computers, for example) and for finding a usable installation file or DVD if you need to reinstall Office and you can't find your original copy.**

You can be selective about which Office components you install, determine what to do with any Office programs installed from a previous version (if you take the default path, the setup program removes the previous version and replaces it with Office 2010), and specify where the program files will be stored. To take any of these actions, click Customize in the dialog box shown in Figure 2-1. Setup then displays a dialog box similar to the one shown in Figure 2-2.

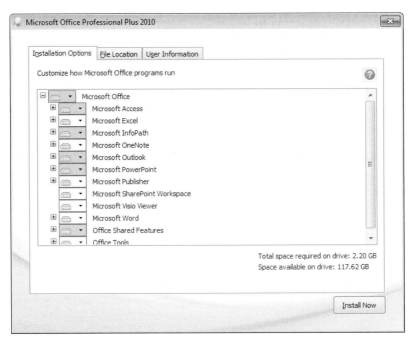

Figure 2-2 To save space on your hard drive, you can choose to not install Office components you don't plan to use.

For details about preserving previously installed Office programs, see "Upgrading from an Earlier Office Version" on page 32.

The Installation Options tab shows a hierarchically organized list of Office components. Click the plus sign next to an item to see a list of that item's subcomponents. When you click a component's name, a brief description of the component appears near the bottom of the dialog box.

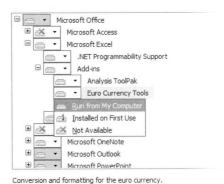

Conversion and formatting for the euro currency.

A button with a white background indicates that all subcomponents are set the same way as the displayed component; a gray background indicates that one or more subcomponents have an installation setting that's different from the displayed component. For each component, you can select one of three settings by clicking the arrow next to the component's name:

- **Run From My Computer**   Select this option to install the component (but not any of its subcomponents) on your computer's hard drive.

- **Installed On First Use**   If you select this option, the component won't be installed on your computer until you attempt to use the component. At that time, Office will need access to your Office DVD or the installation file from which you ran Setup.

- **Not Available**   Select this option for each component you don't plan to use or install.

For items that contain subcomponents, a fourth option is available: Run All From My Computer. Choosing this option is equivalent to expanding the item and selecting Run From My Computer for each subcomponent.

On the File Location tab, you can specify the folder where you'd like to store the Office program files. Unless you have unique requirements, it's best to use the default location—a subfolder of Program Files or Program Files (x86)—because it inherits appropriate protections that allow access by all users while preventing inadvertent (or malicious) changes to the Office program files.

The User Information tab provides a place to enter your name, your initials, and the name of your organization. Office uses this information to enter your name in a document's properties (to identify you as the author, for example), to tag review comments with your initials, to put your organization's name in a predefined header or footer in printed documents, and other similar purposes. If you don't perform a custom installation, Office asks for this information the first time you run an Office program.

After you've made your settings on each tab of this dialog box, click Install Now (or Upgrade if you have an earlier Office version installed) to complete the process.

Installing from the Web with Click-to-Run

When you purchase Office 2010 online directly from Microsoft, Microsoft uses Click-to-Run to download and install Office. This method uses virtualization in a way that lets you begin using Office programs almost immediately as they are streamed to your computer. During this process, you need to remain connected to the Internet to run Office programs, but upon completion a cached version of Office is fully installed and you can use it offline.

Click-to-Run offers other advantages over traditional online program delivery: You get the most-up-to-date version of Office, and you don't need to download or install patches immediately following installation. Click-to-Run is ideal for installing Office on computers that don't have an optical drive, which is the case with many notebook and netbook computers.

CAUTION

Click-to-Run is designed for use only with high-speed (download speeds greater than 1 Mbps) Internet connections. With slower connections, using virtualized Office while it's streaming to your computer is painfully slow—to the point that it's completely unusable. If you have dial-up or another type of slow connection, you should instead obtain a complete installation file by selecting that option for download, if available. Better yet, purchase an Office disc.

To install using Click-to-Run, after you complete the purchase click the Download Now button. In the Security Warning dialog box that appears, click Save. Save the file to a folder on your computer, and don't change the file name. When the download of this small file (under 2 MB) is complete, click Run to launch it, which installs and runs the Click-to-Run service. Alternatively, click Close in the Download Complete dialog box, and then double-click the desktop icon for the new file.

Because this file is downloaded from the Internet—the source of most viruses and other malicious files—you'll see a security warning asking if you want to run the file. After confirming that the publisher is indeed Microsoft Corporation, click Run. Depending on your User Account Control settings, you might also be asked if you want to allow the program to make changes to your computer; click Yes.

TROUBLESHOOTING

You get an error message about drive Q

After launching the downloaded program file, you might see a message about setting up Office on Q. Click-to-Run versions of Office require exclusive use of drive Q, a virtual drive that the setup program creates. If your computer already has a drive Q—even if it's empty and unused—this error occurs.

The solution is to change the drive letter for your existing drive Q to another letter. You'll find instructions for doing that in Windows 7 at *w7io.com/10207*. The steps for changing a drive letter in Windows Vista or Windows XP are nearly the same once you find your way into the Disk Management console. You can do this in any version of Windows (including Windows 7) by right-clicking Computer (or My Computer) and choosing Manage; you'll find Disk Management under Storage.

After a short time, the Microsoft Office Click-to-Run Bootstrapper program launches PowerPoint, as shown in Figure 2-3.

Figure 2-3 A pop-up notification by the taskbar informs you that the download is in progress.

You need to accept the license agreement, enter your user name and initials, and specify your update settings. Upon completing those simple tasks, you'll find that you're running a fully functional version of PowerPoint (opened to an introductory slide show). Furthermore, you'll find shortcuts for your other new Office programs on the Start menu. Although it might take considerable time—hours, in some cases—to finish downloading the entire Office package, you can go ahead and run any of these programs immediately; code needed for programs and features you use jumps to the head of the queue.

You don't need to stay connected continuously until the download is complete. If you need to disconnect, Click-to-Run picks up where it left off the next time you connect to the Internet. You can check the status of the download at any time by opening the Click-to-Run Application Manager in Control Panel. (In Windows 7 or Windows Vista, simply open Control Panel and begin typing **click-to-run** in the search box; click Click-to-Run Application Manager when it appears.)

When the Click-to-Run download is complete, a pop-up notification appears.

> **Note**
>
> A Click-to-Run Office installation is not the same as one installed from retail media. Although you no longer need an Internet connection to run Office after the download is complete, it periodically uses your Internet connection to check for updates and download them. Moreover, Office continues to run in a virtualized version. As part of the virtualization process, Office uses a virtualized drive Q, which you can see if you open Computer in Windows Explorer. You don't need to (in fact, you shouldn't) access this drive directly, but in case you start wondering what it is and where it came from—now you know.

Upgrading from Office 2010 Starter Edition

Many computers sold through retail channels come with Office 2010 Starter edition prein-stalled. This edition contains only Word Starter 2010 and Excel Starter 2010, feature-limited versions of Word and Excel. A computer with Office Starter edition also has on its hard drive all the files needed to upgrade to a full version of Office—one that not only unlocks the additional features of Word and Excel but also includes OneNote, PowerPoint, and Outlook.

> **Note**
>
> In the past, new computers often included Microsoft Works as a low-end productiv-ity suite. Office 2010 Starter edition replaces Microsoft Works in this role, and it offers some distinct advantages. Because Starter is a subset of the full Office editions, every-thing you learn about Office Starter applies to Office as well, so there's no extra train-ing or difficult transition needed after you upgrade. Furthermore, Office Starter creates and edits documents using standard Word and Excel file formats, so all your documents continue to work seamlessly after the upgrade without requiring any conversion.

One of the hallmarks of Office Starter edition is the omnipresent task pane, which also includes an advertisement. As shown in Figure 2-4, the task pane (perhaps as an inducement to upgrade so that you can recover this bit of screen real estate) includes a link for upgrading to a full version.

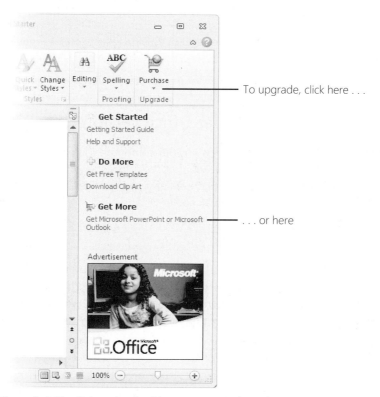

To upgrade, click here . . .

. . . or here

Figure 2-4 The link under Get More starts you along the upgrade path.

You can also initiate the upgrade process by clicking Purchase on the Home tab or by clicking Purchase on the Info tab in Backstage view. All of these methods open a page in your web browser (you'll need to have an active Internet connection) where you can learn about the various upgrade editions and pricing. From that page, follow links to purchase and unlock the upgrade edition.

As an alternative to purchasing an upgrade online, you can purchase a product key card from a retailer or computer manufacturer. Click any of the purchase links described above, and then follow the instructions for entering information from the product key card you purchased.

Chapter 2

INSIDE OUT Enter your product key to upgrade a trial edition

If you have a product key card and a trial version of a full Office 2010 edition is already installed on your new computer, you can enter your product key without starting Office. In Control Panel, open Programs And Features, and then select Microsoft Office 2010 in the list of installed programs. Click Change, select Enter A Product Key, and then click Next.

Upgrading from an Earlier Office Version

If you have an earlier version of Office on your computer, you probably want to upgrade it to Office 2010 as part of the installation process. However, you might prefer to keep the older version in addition to Office 2010—at least until you become familiar with the newer version. Or you might need to keep an earlier version handy for compatibility testing.

CAUTION

Outlook 2010 and SharePoint Workspace (the successor to Microsoft Office Groove 2007) can't coexist with earlier versions of these programs. Therefore, if you choose to include one or both of these programs in your installation, you won't have the option to preserve the old version of that program; it's replaced by the Office 2010 version.

With a Click-to-Run installation, keeping an old version is easy. Because Click-to-Run is designed, in part, to be a showcase for trial editions of Office, it leaves your old programs in place. You'll find both old and new versions on your Start menu, and you can run either version—or both simultaneously if you're so inclined.

When you install from a boxed copy or a downloaded installation file, the default action is to replace old program versions with the Office 2010 version. If you want to keep some or all of the older programs installed, you must choose a custom installation by clicking Customize in the setup dialog box similar to the one shown earlier in Figure 2-1. The customization dialog box, similar to the one shown in Figure 2-2, has an additional tab that's not present when no previous Office version is detected: Upgrade. See Figure 2-5.

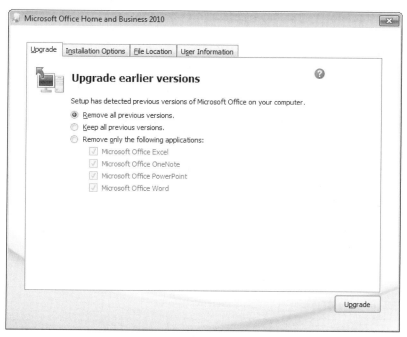

Figure 2-5 If you choose to keep only some older programs, remove the check mark next to the programs you want to keep. (Yes, it's somewhat counterintuitive, so read the text carefully before you click Upgrade.)

When you no longer need your older version—or, heaven forbid, you decide not to use Office 2010—you can uninstall either one. In Control Panel, open the program management application (in Windows 7 and Windows Vista it's called Programs And Features; in Windows XP it's Add Or Remove Programs). Select the Office version you want to remove and then click Uninstall (in Windows XP, click Remove).

Using Office Anytime Upgrade

If you have a retail edition of Office installed (that is, Home and Student, Home and Business, or Professional), you might've noticed a feature called Office Anytime Upgrade. This feature, which you can find on the Start menu in the Microsoft Office\Microsoft Office 2010 Tools folder, provides a convenient way to purchase an edition with more programs and capabilities. The entire process, from payment through installation, can be handled online.

Check the offering carefully, however. At the time of this book's publication, purchasing through Anytime Upgrade does not provide any credit for the edition you already own.

To take a look, open the aforementioned Start menu item. (With Windows 7 and Windows Vista, the easiest way to do that is to type **upgrade** in the Start menu search box, and then click Office Anytime Upgrade.) As shown below, Office Anytime Upgrade also provides a convenient way to enter a product key; this capability is most useful if Office 2010 is preinstalled on your computer and you have a product key card.

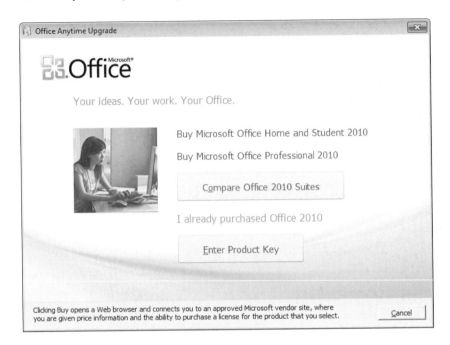

Customizing Your Office Installation

After Office 2010 is installed, you might want to change some choices you made during installation. For example, you might want to install a program or component that was omitted during the original installation. You can make such changes in the program management application in Control Panel. To begin the customization process:

- In Windows 7 or Windows Vista, type **program** in the Start menu search box, and then click Programs And Features (under Control Panel in Windows 7; under Programs in Windows Vista). Select your Office 2010 program, and then click Change.

- In Windows XP, open Control Panel and double-click Add Or Remove Programs. Select your Office 2010 program, and then click Change.

In the dialog box that appears, select Add Or Remove Features, and then click Continue. (The other options in this dialog box are Repair, Remove, and Enter A Product Key.) The dialog box shown next is reminiscent of the one shown earlier in Figure 2-2. Use it to specify which components you want to install.

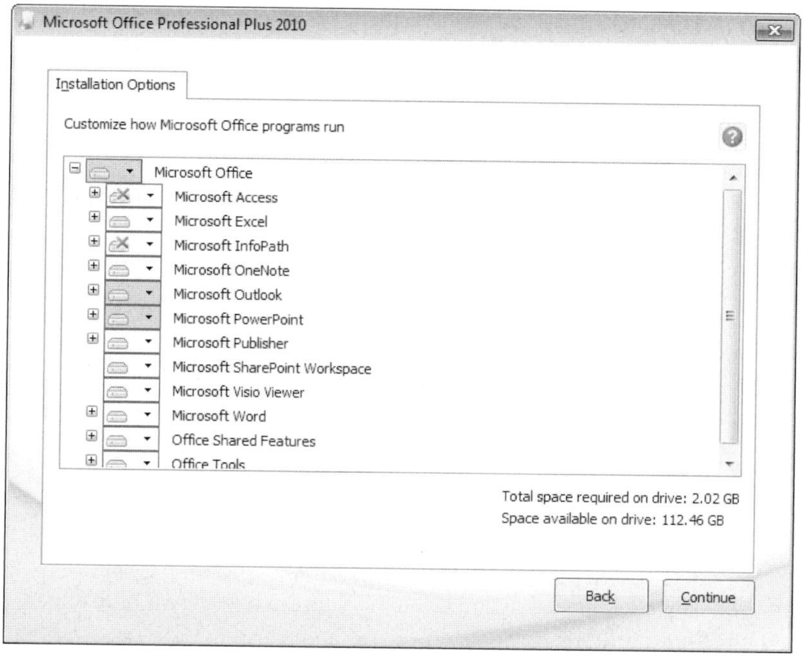

Chapter 2

Note

If you're using a Click-to-Run version of Office 2010, when you click Change in Control Panel, the Click-to-Run Application Manager offers to repair your Office installation; no other options are available.

Validating and Activating Your Copy of Office

One step in the installation process is to enter the product key for your copy of Office 2010. (In some cases, the setup program is able to perform this step automatically, so you don't need to type the key.) Although the setup program verifies that the product key you provide is a valid key, one more step is required: activation. Activation associates your valid product key with your computer. You must activate each copy of Office you install.

Note

Activation occurs automatically if, during setup, you leave the Attempt To Automatically Activate My Product Online check box selected (its default state).

If Office activation isn't performed automatically, you can use Office for up to 30 days before you're required to activate or Office is no longer fully functional. (You can view documents but not edit them, for example.) In this state, the title bar is bright red and includes a message about the activation problem, like this:

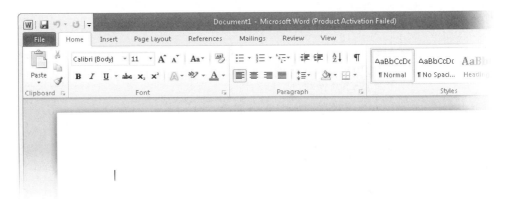

Until you activate Office, a dialog box similar to the one shown here appears each time you start an Office program.

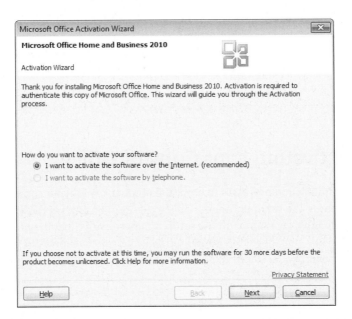

Simply click Next and, in a few moments, the activation wizard reports its success or suggests alternative methods to complete the activation process. You might be asked to enter your product key, for example.

TROUBLESHOOTING

You can't find your product key

Can't find your product key? Microsoft Knowledge Base article 823570 (*w7io.com/823570*) helps you to find it or, if necessary, obtain a new one.

You can check your activation status at any time by clicking the File tab in any Office program and then clicking Help. Figure 2-6 shows a system that has been activated; on a system that has not yet been activated, "Product Activation Required" appears prominently on a colored background near the top of the window.

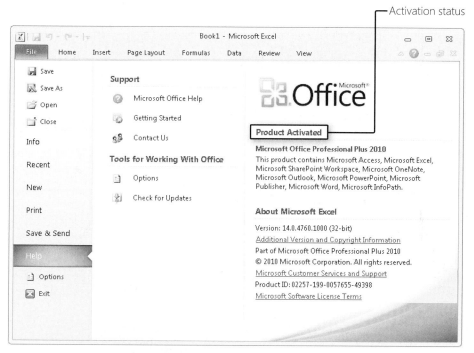

Activation status

Figure 2-6 Click Help in Backstage view to see which edition of Office is installed, which programs it includes, its version number, and the activation status.

Note

The activation process for volume-licensed copies of Office is not the same as the process described in this book for retail copies. Volume activation can be done using either of two methods: Multiple Activation Key (MAK) or Key Management Service (KMS). For details about these methods, see "Volume Activation for Microsoft Office 2010" on TechNet (*w7io.com/10206*).

Keeping Office Up to Date

As they say, nothing lasts forever. Your nice, shiny Office installation will undoubtedly need updates soon—perhaps to address new security exploits, to update junk mail filtering rules, or to fix a newly discovered bug.

With a Click-to-Run version of Office, you're all set. By default, updates are downloaded and installed automatically. If you want to confirm this setting, click the File tab in any Office program, and then click Help. As shown in Figure 2-7, clicking Update Options lets you disable updates—but you really shouldn't do that!

Figure 2-7 The Update Options button on the right side of the Help tab appears only on Click-to-Run versions of Office 2010.

In non–Click-to-Run versions of Office, the Help tab in Backstage view includes a Check For Updates button. There's no particular reason to use that button however, as it's merely a shortcut to Windows Update—the standard part of Windows that manages the download and installation of updates to Windows and Microsoft applications, including Office.

To open Windows Update without traipsing through Backstage view, find it on your computer's Start menu (hint: in Windows 7 and Windows Vista, type **update** in the Start menu search box). In Windows Update, click Change Settings to review your current update settings. We concur with Microsoft's recommendation: select Install Updates Automatically (Recommended). With that setting in place, important updates are downloaded and installed automatically. Optional updates—ones that might add features or functionality but are not critical to your computer's security—are installed only at your specific direction. You do that by opening Windows Update, clicking the optional updates link if it appears, selecting the updates to install and clicking OK, and then clicking Install Updates.

INSIDE OUT   Which version is installed, 32-bit or 64-bit?

Part of keeping Office up to date is installing and maintaining current versions of Office add-ins. Because most add-ins run on either 32-bit Office or 64-bit Office (but not both), you need to know which you have before you download add-in files. However, once Office is installed, it's not easy to tell whether you're using the 32-bit or 64-bit version because the outward differences are few. One way to tell is to click the File tab in any Office program and then click Help; next to the version number under "About Microsoft program" you'll find either "(32-bit)" or "(64-bit)."

That method can be tedious, especially if you have several machines to check. A value in the registry provides another way to determine which is installed. In the HKEY_LOCAL_MACHINE\SOFTWARE\Wow6432Node\Microsoft\Office\14.0\Outlook key, a value named Bitness is set either to x86 (for 32-bit Office) or x64 (for 64-bit). (That's on computers running a 64-bit version of Windows. On systems with a 32-bit version of Windows, you can find the Bitness value if you omit \Wow6432Node from the aforementioned registry path. But that's hardly necessary, because a system running 32-bit Windows can run only a 32-bit version of Office.) A simple script or batch program can read this value and tell you which version is installed, and you don't even have to open an Office application.

Saving and Restoring Settings and Data

You've probably developed a routine for regularly backing up your documents and other files. (If you haven't, you should!) Without a reliable backup, data you have created or purchased can disappear in an instant due to hardware failure, a power surge, theft, fire, or any of countless other calamities. A good backup also provides a source for moving information to a new computer or replicating it on your other computers.

Documents and other data usually get top mindshare when you establish backup procedures. But aside from Office documents, consider the other Office-related settings stored on a computer, which include:

- Ribbon customizations

- Quick Access Toolbar customizations

- Themes

- Templates

- E-mail signatures

- E-mail account profiles

- Add-ins

- Default file locations for templates

- Default file format

- Display preferences (rulers, scroll bars, and so on)

- AutoCorrect lists

- Custom dictionaries

- Building blocks

- Window positions

This is only a partial list of the settings that Office 2010 relies on and maintains. Although most of these settings can be re-created without too much difficulty, doing so is time consuming. It would be better to have the ability to save these settings and restore them when needed. Unfortunately, the settings are scattered about: some are stored in the Windows registry and many are stored in files (in a variety of formats) in various folders. Therefore, backing up the numerous settings manually is close to impossible.

Office 2003 included a Save My Settings wizard for the purpose of managing these settings, but Office 2010 includes nothing comparable. Windows Easy Transfer, which is a tool included with Windows 7 for moving documents and settings from one computer to another, can back up and restore Office settings. However, at the time of this book's publication, it supports only Office 2007 and earlier versions; by the time you read this it might support Office 2010. Still, Windows Easy Transfer is a rather clumsy tool for just saving and restoring Office settings.

The best option we've found is a program called Office Settings Backup Wizard 2010, from Computer Network Consultants (*settingsbackup.com*). Settings Backup Wizard, shown in Figure 2-8, provides comprehensive settings backup, and it can be configured to save settings automatically at scheduled times. Although the program is not free, it can be a real timesaver.

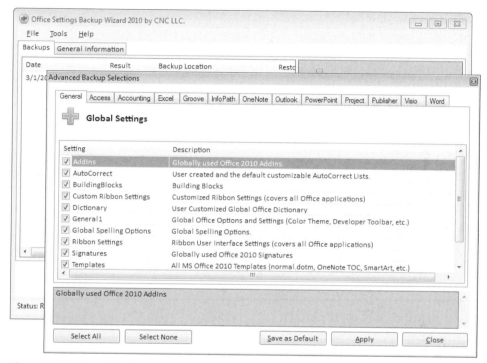

Figure 2-8 Settings Backup Wizard provides granular control that lets you selectively save or restore the myriad settings associated with Office.

For information about ribbon settings, see "Saving and Reusing Custom Ribbon and Toolbar Settings" on page 65.

Using and Customizing the Office Interface

F you switch quickly between the different programs in the Office 2010 family, the first thing you'll notice is the striking similarity in their basic design. All the programs in the Office 2010 family share a broad set of interface elements and tools. The layout of each program window contains the same elements in the same positions: a ribbon filled with commands at the top of the window, using the window's full width, and a much smaller Quick Access Toolbar just above it. When you dig deeper into each program, you'll see more common elements, including a customizable status bar along the bottom of most program windows, galleries of design and formatting tools that allow you to instantly pre-view their effects in your document, a mini-toolbar containing useful formatting options, and various help tools.

In some cases, these common features are literally identical, as is the case if you use the SmartArt feature to create a diagram for use in a Word document or in a PowerPoint pre-sentation. In other cases, the common features are more or less similar, with important differences that become obvious as you begin to look more closely. You'll notice these dif-ferences immediately if you compare the options available for checking spelling in a Word document with the much simpler set of tools in PowerPoint and Excel.

Our goal in this chapter is to introduce the interface elements that are common to all Office programs and explain how to use each one. We also describe the best ways to cus-tomize and personalize the Office interface. Our starting point is the single biggest change of all, the new Microsoft Office Backstage view.

Managing Programs and Documents in Office Backstage View

Just below the title bar in every Office program, you'll see a white File heading on a brightly colored background. This can't-miss target is available at the left side of the ribbon in every Office program.

As you might guess from the name, the list of choices available when you click File is very much like the list of functions found on the File menu in Office 2003 and earlier editions. (In Office 2007, these options were buried, confusingly, beneath a glowing orb containing the Office logo. In Office 2010, the location of the File menu is much more obvious.)

INSIDE OUT   Use color coding to tell which program is which

In the default Silver theme, with one exception, every tab name in every Office program is unobtrusive: black text on a gray background. The nonconformist is the File heading, which sits at the left of the tab bar and stands out with white type on a bold-colored background. Each Office program has its own designated color: Word is blue, Excel green, OneNote purple, PowerPoint orange, and Outlook yellow. That color scheme is consistent throughout a program's design. The green Excel icon on the Windows taskbar matches the green logo in the program's title bar, and the green background behind the File heading is echoed in the highlights on the list of options directly beneath it.

Click File, and the contents of the program window are replaced by the new Office Backstage view, shown in Figure 3-1.

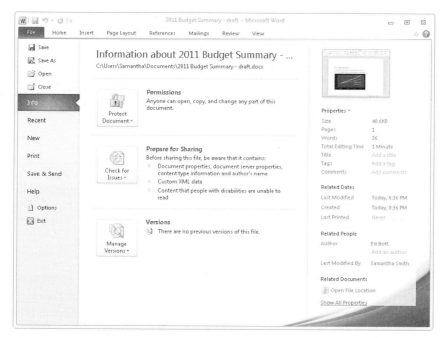

Figure 3-1 Click File to open Office Backstage view, which consolidates information and tasks related to the current file in a series of tabs arrayed along the left side.

The basic arrangement of Office Backstage view is similar in each of the five programs we cover in this book. The choices available along the left side vary slightly, depending on the program.

Backstage View in Word, Excel, and PowerPoint

For Word, Excel, and PowerPoint, the choices along the left side of Backstage view are identical, although the details on each tab vary from program to program.

Save, Save As, Open, Close

A group of four indented options—Save, Save As, Open, and Close—allow you to perform core file-management tasks for the current document. The indentation indicates that these options don't use the Backstage view area to the right; instead, if necessary, the program opens a common Save As or Open dialog box and allows you to interact with the Windows file system.

The other indented choice in Backstage view is Options, which also opens a separate dialog box rather than displaying its choices in Backstage view. For more on this choice, see "Adjusting Program Options" on page 67.

Info

Click Info to view a thumbnail of the current document and to inspect its properties and details such as file size, the date it was created, when it was last modified, and any tags added by the program itself (author name, for example) or by a person who worked on the file. This section also contains tools to help you work with multiple versions, restrict access and editing permissions, and check for the presence of confidential information before sharing.

For an in-depth discussion of how to create and save files and view or change their properties using Office 2010, see Chapter 4, "Managing Office Files." For details on how you can prevent unwanted access to or restrict editing of documents in shared locations, see "Protect documents from unwanted access or copying" on page 822. To learn more about how to prevent embarrassing disclosures of information in shared documents, see "Inspecting and Removing Personal and Confidential Information" on page 821.

Recent

Click Recent to display a list of files you've created or opened recently using the current program. You can pin any document to this list to prevent it from being automatically removed. All shortcuts on the Recent list are displayed with pinned items listed first (in alphabetical order by file name) and unpinned items below them (in the order in which they were opened). In the Options dialog box, under the Display heading, you'll find an option to specify how many documents are visible in this list. (The default setting is 20, but you can enter any number from 0 to 50.) At the bottom of this tab is another check box, Quickly Access This Number Of Recent Documents, which lists recently opened documents on the menu on the left, just above Info.

INSIDE OUT   Use the Recent list to copy an existing document

The conventional way to copy an existing document is to open it, make your changes, and save the altered document under a new name. If you use that technique, however, you risk accidentally overwriting the original document with your changes if you click Save instead of Save As. A safer alternative is to right-click the document's entry on the Recent list and then click Open A Copy. The newly created document is identical to the original, but if you inadvertently click Save, you are prompted to enter a file name and location.

New

Click New for options that allow you to create a new document, workbook, or presentation. You can begin with a blank slate or use an existing document or template as your starting point. Although it isn't immediately obvious, all three of the document-centric Office programs include a collection of useful templates that are worth exploring. Figure 3-2, for example, shows the many variations on standard calendars available in PowerPoint. The New tab also includes a search box to help you explore the enormous collection of categorized templates available online at Office.com.

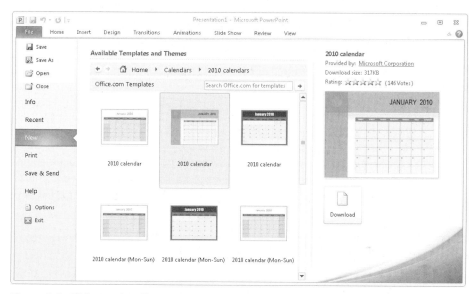

Figure 3-2 Click New in Office Backstage view and browse through a broad selection of templates for Word, Excel, and PowerPoint (shown here).

For a full discussion of how to find, use, and manage Office templates, see "Using Templates to Streamline Document Creation" on page 97.

Print

Click Print for access to local and network printers. From this information-rich tab, you can adjust printer settings, preview all or part of a document, and adjust options for the current print job, such as the number of copies to be printed. You'll notice some subtle per-program differences in available options; you have direct access to headers and footers in PowerPoint, for example, but must click Page Setup to reach the equivalent settings in Word and Excel.

INSIDE OUT Use the Print option to convert documents, too

The Print tab in Backstage view isn't limited to physical printers. You'll also find virtual printers here that allow you to "print" a document without using a single sheet of paper. If you've set up the Windows Fax feature, you can click Fax to save an image of the printout in the background in Tagged Image File Format (TIFF) and send it to a remote fax device. Use the Microsoft XPS Document Writer to save to files in the XML Paper Specification (XPS) format, which can be viewed using the XPS Viewer in Windows Vista and Windows 7. The Send To OneNote 2010 driver creates a resizable image of what your printout would look like and then pastes it into the OneNote notebook you designate (a topic we cover more fully in "Filling a Notebook with Text, Pictures, Clippings, and More" on page 495). Third-party programs can add entries here as well, as Adobe's Acrobat does in creating a virtual printer for the Adobe PDF format.

Save & Send

Click Save & Send to access options for sending all or part of a document via e-mail and saving files in file storage locations on the web or on a local network. This tab, shown in Figure 3-3, also includes shortcuts for saving a file in PDF or XPS format or sending it as an Internet Fax.

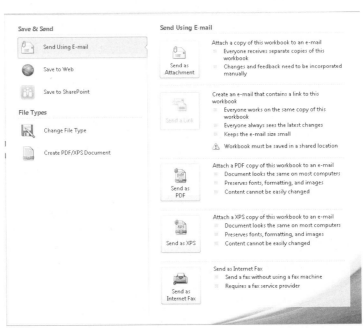

Figure 3-3 Options on the Save & Send tab in Office Backstage view allow you to send documents via e-mail and save them in alternate formats or locations.

For a more detailed discussion of options included on the Save & Send tab, see "Sharing Your Work in PDF and Other Formats" on page 95 and "How SharePoint and Office Work Together" on page 864.

Help

The final tab, Help, provides access to the usual assortment of online reference information (which we cover later in this section), plus links to technical support, program options, and product information such as the installed version and activation status.

For the ins and outs of installing, updating, and activating Office, see Chapter 2, "Installing and Updating Microsoft Office 2010."

Backstage View in OneNote and Outlook

In OneNote and Outlook, the options available in Office Backstage view are different, primarily because these programs aren't predicated on creating and saving individual files.

Both programs include a trio of tabs in common with their Office-mates: Info, Print, and Help.

In OneNote, the Info tab includes buttons that allow you to adjust settings for any open notebook and to view sync status. The contents of the Info tab in Outlook vary depending on whether you click File in the main Outlook window or after opening an individual item. In the main Outlook window, this tab provides access to e-mail account settings, cleanup tools, automatic replies, and rules and alerts, as shown in Figure 3-4. The Info pane for an individual item includes options appropriate to that item, including the option to view properties, set permissions, and move an item to another folder.

For a full discussion of how to manage e-mail account settings in Outlook, see "Setting Up Mail Accounts" on page 707.

Print options in Outlook are dramatically simpler than in the three document-centric programs, and OneNote print options are downright spartan, with only two buttons, Print and Print Preview, on the tab. The Help tab offers information and settings similar to those found in the other programs.

In the main Outlook window, Backstage view also includes an Open tab that provides basic tools for opening calendars and data files and for importing files, settings, and RSS feeds. This option is not available in the Info pane for a window containing an Outlook item.

OneNote includes Open, New, and Save As tabs that are designed to handle the program's unique file-management challenges, which can't be handled in the Windows Open and Save As dialog boxes. Figure 3-5 shows the Save As tab, with its range of options for saving pages, sections, or entire notebooks in a variety of formats.

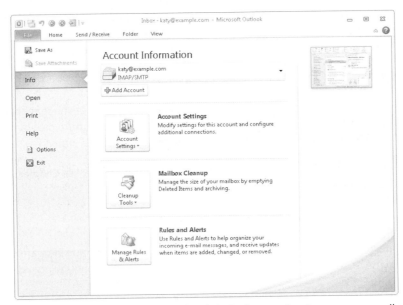

Figure 3-4 In Outlook, click the Info tab in Backstage view to manage e-mail accounts and mailboxes.

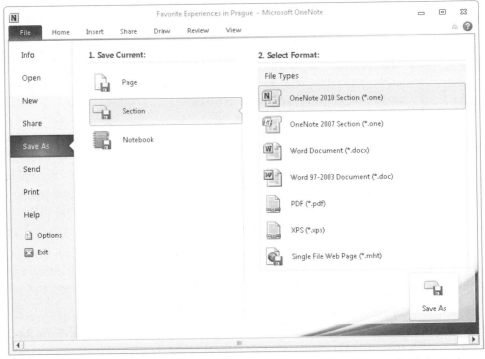

Figure 3-5 Because of OneNote's unique file-management needs, the tabs available in Backstage view offer different options than you'll find elsewhere in Office.

To learn how best to work with OneNote notebooks, sections, and pages, see "What's in a OneNote Notebook?" on page 490.

The Share tab in OneNote allows you to control who can access a notebook stored in a shared network folder. The Send tab is for inserting or attaching notebook pages to e-mail messages and blog pages.

Using and Customizing the Ribbon

An archeologist looking at the evolution of Microsoft Office would no doubt divide its timeline neatly into two eras: The Menu-Toolbar Era lasted from the early 1990s through Office 2003. The emergence of Office 2007 marked the dawn of the Ribbon Era.

In this section, we introduce these common features and explain how to use each one. We also describe the best ways to customize and personalize the Office interface.

Using the Ribbon

Without question, the ribbon marked a radical change in appearance for the Office interface. If your time with Office began in 2006 or earlier, you learned how to navigate through the program by using drop-down menus that were essentially lists of commands under a group of headings: File, Edit, View, and so on.

Despite the visual differences between the ribbon and the old-style menus, their basic functionality isn't all that different. Tabs on the ribbon function in much the same way as the top-level menu choices do, and commands are arranged into groupings in a manner that's like cascading menus. One benefit of this big switch was that it created an opportunity to reorganize the overall menu structure into a more modern arrangement. For example, many of the commands on the Edit and Format menus in Office 2003 are consolidated, logically, on the Home tab in Office 2010.

The key to using the ribbon effectively is to understand how it's organized and learn how it works. As we noted earlier, the ribbon is divided into tabs, each with its own heading. Every program contains a default set of tabs that are available at all times. Figure 3-6 shows the References tab from Word 2010, which contains 20 or so visible commands organized into six groups.

Figure 3-6 This tab is divided into six groups, each labeled along the bottom and separated from other groups by vertical dividers.

When a program window is maximized on a large monitor, you can see a mix of large icons, small icons, and labels designed to make it easier to see these groupings at a glance. But something interesting happens to the ribbon when you resize a program window. The order of groups (and of commands within each group) remains the same, but the labels alongside some commands disappear, and some commands are moved to drop-down menus to accommodate the horizontal space available. In a narrow window, the choices available on the Reference tab are the same, but the groups are compressed, as shown here.

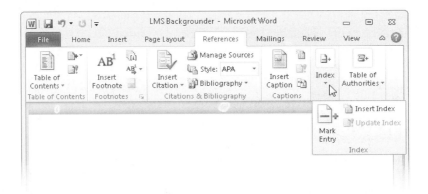

In addition to the default tabs, context-sensitive tabs appear at the right side of the ribbon when needed. If you insert a picture into a Word document and click to select the picture, the Picture Tools tab appears at the end of the ribbon, identified by a distinctive color-coded group name in the title bar, as shown in Figure 3-7.

For details on how to create custom tabs or change the layout of built-in tabs, see "Personalizing the Ribbon" on page 57.

In the lower right corner of some command groups, you might see a button that looks like a tiny arrow pointing down and to the right. These dialog box launchers enable access to settings that aren't available through the ribbon itself. Clicking the dialog box launcher below the Picture Styles command group (shown in Figure 3-7), for example, opens the Format Picture dialog box.

Every Office program includes an enormous selection of tabs, most of them dedicated to groups of features that are specific to that program. A handful of default main tabs are available in multiple programs and are described in Table 3-1.

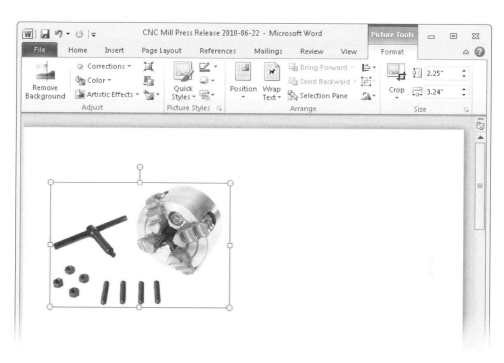

Figure 3-7 Tabs containing task-specific tools appear as needed at the right side of the ribbon.

Table 3-1 Features, Tools, and Commands Available on Common Ribbon Tabs

Tab Name	Contents
Home	Basic editing and formatting tools, as well as the Clipboard and find/replace functions. Outlook has seven task-specific Home tabs to cover individual item types (e-mail messages, contacts, appointments, and so on).
Insert	Insert and edit tables, charts, shapes, text boxes, and all types of images. This tab also provides access to tools for inserting symbols and creating and editing hyperlinks.
Review	Basic proofing (spelling, grammar) and reference (dictionary, thesaurus) tools, language tools, and commands to add sticky-note comments. This tab also includes file-comparison and change-tracking options.
View	Switch between views (Normal, Reading, Outline), show rulers and grid-lines, zoom a document, arrange and switch between windows, and view or record macros.
Developer	Normally hidden, this tab contains tools for working with Visual Basic code and macros and managing add-ins. Tools for building custom forms in Outlook are here, as is access to document templates and the Document Panel.
Add-Ins	If you install a third-party add-in or template that creates its own custom tabs, they appear here.

Most Office programs also share dedicated Tools tabs for working with equations, tables, pictures, SmartArt diagrams and charts, and ink objects (which must be created on a tablet or touch-enabled PC but can be viewed and edited on any Windows computer). The Drawing Tools tab contains tools for inserting, arranging, formatting, and resizing shapes and text boxes. A set of Background Removal tools appears on its own tab if you select a picture and click the Remove Background option on the Picture Tools tab.

INSIDE OUT   Auto-hide the ribbon

When you want to use as much screen real estate as possible for your document, the ribbon can feel like a space hog. For those occasions, the solution is simple: click the small, upward-facing arrow at the far right of the row of tab names, just to the left of the Help button. (You can also right-click any part of the ribbon and then click Minimize The Ribbon on the shortcut menu, double-click the heading for the active tab, or press Ctrl+F1 to achieve the same effect.) Minimizing the ribbon hides its contents, leaving only the tab names behind in an arrangement that looks surprisingly like the old-style Office menu bar. Click any tab name to show the contents of that tab so you can use those groups of commands. Click anywhere in the document to hide the ribbon again. Click the downward-facing arrow or double-click any tab name to expand the ribbon to its normal height.

Galleries and Live Previews

If the ribbon were merely menus turned on their side, it would be mildly interesting but not worth more than a few seconds' thought. What makes the ribbon much more interesting in everyday use is its ability to help you pick from collections of defined formatting options called *galleries* and see the effects of those changes on your document using Live Preview.

Some live previews are supremely simple. The Fonts list in all Office programs, for example, displays each font name in the font it represents; when you hover the mouse pointer over a font name, the current text selection changes to that font. Move the mouse away, and the font returns to its current setting; click the font name to apply it. The same is true of font attributes, colors (for fonts or backgrounds), tables (in Excel), styles (in Word and Excel), and transitions in PowerPoint, among other elements.

After inserting a picture into a document, you can use the Quick Styles gallery on the Picture Tools tab to apply a preset border and shadow to it, as in the example in Figure 3-8.

Figure 3-8 Pointing to an option in the Quick Styles gallery allows you to preview borders, rotation, and shadow effects.

For a complete discussion of the many options available for manipulating pictures and graphics in Office programs, see Chapter 6, "Working with Graphics and Pictures."

You can see a similarly compelling effect using the galleries that apply themes (collections of colors, fonts, and effects) to an entire document, workbook, or presentation. The Themes galleries are on the Page Layout tab in Word and Excel and on the Design tab in PowerPoint.

In some (but not all) galleries, you can tweak an existing entry or create a new one from scratch and save the result as a custom entry in the list. If this option is available, you see a Save option in the gallery itself, and any custom items you create appear in a separate section of the gallery. Figure 3-9 shows a custom theme saved to the Word Themes gallery.

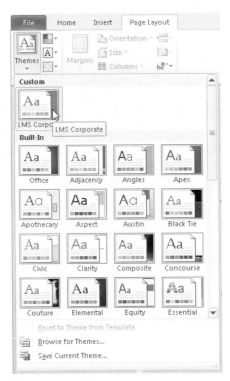

Figure 3-9 When you use the Save Current Theme option at the bottom of this gallery, your new theme is saved in the Custom section at the top.

INSIDE OUT   Add a gallery to the Quick Access Toolbar

Although the most obvious use of the Quick Access Toolbar is to save shortcuts to individual commands, you can also use this slim strip of screen real estate to save shortcuts to entire galleries. The gallery appears on the Quick Access Toolbar as an icon with a small black arrow to its right; click the icon to display the gallery's contents in a visual list, just as it would appear had you switched to the appropriate tab and unfurled the gallery directly. To add a gallery to the Quick Access Toolbar, right-click the main command button for the gallery, and then click Add To Quick Access Toolbar. If you right-click within the gallery itself, the command is Add Gallery To Quick Access Toolbar. The effect is the same either way.

If you find Live Preview annoying or distracting, you can turn it off on a program-by-program basis. Click File, and then click Options. On the General tab, under the User Interface Options heading, clear the Enable Live Preview option.

Personalizing the Ribbon

One of the most vociferous complaints about the ribbon when it first appeared in Office 2007 was its inflexibility. Customization options required specialized tools and a programmer's skills. In Office 2010, that situation is dramatically changed. Within each program, the ribbon can be extensively customized.

The starting point for all ribbon customizations is the dialog box shown in Figure 3-10. Right-click any empty space on the ribbon, and then click Customize The Ribbon on the shortcut menu. You can also click File, click Options, and then select the Customize Ribbon tab. This example is taken from OneNote, but the overall appearance and general operation of the Customize The Ribbon page are the same in all five Office programs.

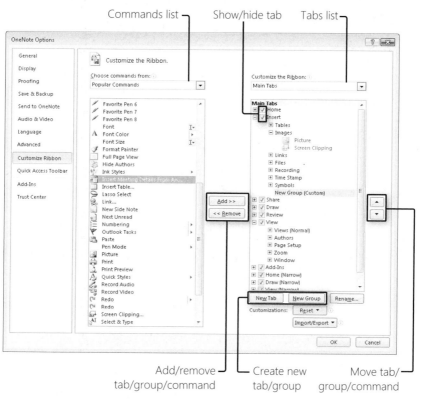

Figure 3-10 Use the customization options to create new tabs and hide existing ones, organize commands into new groups, and otherwise personalize the ribbon.

The Choose Commands From list above the left column allows you to control which items are shown in the list beneath it. You can choose Popular Commands to show a filtered list, show all commands, or restrict the display to commands that are not available on any default tab. Use one of the tabs options (All Tabs, Main Tabs, Tool Tabs, and so on) if you want to copy an existing tab or group.

The Customize The Ribbon list allows you to filter the choices shown in the column on the right. You can choose All Tabs, Main Tabs, or Tool Tabs.

Here's what you can and can't do with the ribbon in all Office programs:

- You *can* change the left-to-right order in which default and custom tabs appear on the ribbon. If you want to move PowerPoint's Slide Show tab to the third position, after Home and Insert but before Design, you can do that. To move a tab, select its entry in the Tabs list and drag it up or down; alternatively, you can use the Move Up and Move Down arrows on the right, or right-click and then click Move Up or Move Down on the shortcut menu.

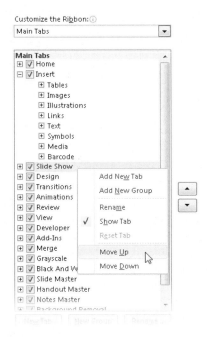

- You *cannot* change the left-to-right order of the contextual tabs that appear when you select a particular type of object or switch to a different editing mode. The move options appear dimmed and are unavailable for the shared Background Removal tab, for example, for the Blog Post tab in Word, and for any of the options in the Tool Tabs group for any program.

- You *can* hide individual tabs. The Developer tab is hidden as part of the initial configuration in all programs. You can banish any other tab as well by clearing its check box in the Tabs list. If you're confident that you will never use Word's Mail Merge feature, you can banish the Mailings tab. A hidden tab is not deleted, and it can be restored at any time.

- You *can* change the order of groups within any tab, including default and contextual tabs. You can, for example, move the Themes group from the left side of the Page Layout tab in Word or Excel to the far right or to any position in the middle. To do so, select the group and use the Move Up or Move Down button, or right-click and use the equivalent choices on the shortcut menu.

- You *can* remove groups from any tab, including built-in tabs. Right-click the group and click Remove. You can also move groups from one tab to another by using the Move Up and Move Down buttons.

- You *cannot* remove commands from a default group, nor can you rearrange the order of commands within such a group.

- You *can* create one or more custom tabs for each program. Each new custom tab starts with one new custom group, which you can fill with individual commands. You can also add groups from any existing tab to a custom tab. Figure 3-11 shows the settings for a custom tab in Word, assembled from existing groups and individual commands. Figure 3-12 shows the resulting custom tab in Word.

- You *can* add one or more custom groups to any tab, including default, custom, and contextual tabs. You can then fill those groups with any commands available in the current program and position the custom group anywhere on the tab. Use the New Group button to create a group; click Rename to change the default label that appears beneath the group.

- You *can* rename any default tab or group. The new name can contain punctuation and other special characters and has no practical restrictions on its length. Select the item from the Tabs list, and then click the Rename button to enter its new name.

Chapter 3

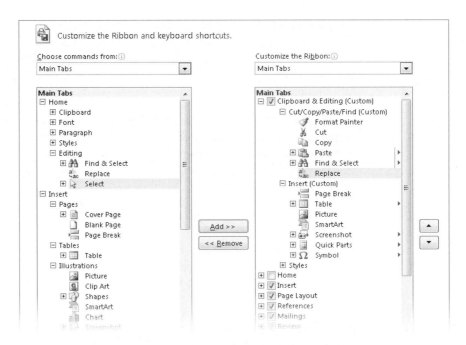

Figure 3-11 The custom tab at the top of the Tabs list on the right is assembled from individual commands and existing groups picked from the list on the left.

Figure 3-12 This custom tab is the result of the settings shown in Figure 3-11. Note that we've hidden the Home tab.

- You *cannot* change the name of a command in a default group, nor can you change the icon associated with a command.

- You *can* rename a command within a custom group. The Rename dialog box also gives you the option to choose an alternative icon for the command.

- You *can* use small icons without labels for all commands within a custom group. To do so, right-click the group name in the Tabs list and choose Hide Command Labels.

Chapter 3

INSIDE OUT   ## A roundabout way to rearrange commands

As we note here, the option to rearrange commands is not available within default groups on a built-in tab. But you can accomplish the same goal if you're willing to make it a multistep process. Start by creating a custom tab using the same name as the one you want to clone (your copy is identified by the Custom label after it). Rename the default custom group that's created to match the name of the first group you want the tab to contain. Next, choose All Tabs from the list above the left column. In that list, select the first command from the first group on the tab you want to clone, and then click Add. Continue clicking Add until you've created a clone of the existing group. Repeat this process for each additional group and tab, and then use the basic customization tools to remove unwanted commands and adjust the order of other commands. Hide or remove the built-in tab or group and move your custom clone to its position.

If you find that you've made a mess of the ribbon and you want to start over, click the Reset button beneath the Tabs list. The two options here allow you to reset changes for a single tab or remove all customizations. Beware, though: the latter option resets the Quick Access Toolbar as well!

And one final word on the subject: Just because you can tweak the ribbon doesn't mean you should. Using a nonstandard, heavily customized layout means that you're likely to be unproductive, at least briefly, whenever you sit down to work with a PC that uses an unmodified ribbon. You'll also have to remember to save your customizations in a safe place so that you can apply them if you replace your PC or reinstall Office.

We describe the import/export feature in "Saving and Reusing Custom Ribbon and Toolbar Settings" on page 65.

Customizing the Quick Access Toolbar

The Quick Access Toolbar consists of a single row of small icons, with no labels allowed. In its default configuration, it includes only a few shortcuts (Save, Undo, and Redo for Word, Excel, and PowerPoint, slightly different options for OneNote and Outlook), but you can add as many more as you like, with each icon associated with a single command.

INSIDE OUT   Make the Quick Access Toolbar go away

There's no check box or button to hide the Quick Access Toolbar, but you can achieve almost the same result by leaving it in its default position above the ribbon and removing all commands. With no commands assigned to the Quick Access Toolbar, you'll see a tiny separator line and arrow to the right of the program icon in the title bar. It's almost, but not quite, invisible.

By default, this tiny toolbar is located on the title bar, just to the right of the program icon and above the ribbon. If you plan to add more than a few shortcuts to the Quick Access Toolbar, we recommend that you exercise your option to move it below the ribbon. (Click the arrow to the right of the Quick Access Toolbar to see the Show Below The Ribbon option at the bottom of a list of frequently used commands.) In that configuration, the commands are easier to see and are less likely to crowd out the title of the current window.

Note

Any commands you add to the Quick Access Toolbar are reflected in the current program window only. If you want the same arrangement of shortcuts on the Quick Access Toolbar in different programs, you must make those changes in each Office program individually. Likewise, the setting to position the Quick Access Toolbar above or below the ribbon must be applied separately in each program.

Personalization options for the Quick Access Toolbar are severely limited. You can add separator lines to arrange commands into groups, and you can move commands to suit your fancy, but that's about it. You can't resize the toolbar itself or the icons on it; you can't add text labels; and you can't add a second row or create submenus. If you add more icons than will fit in the width of the program window, you need to click the double-headed arrow at the end of the toolbar to see the overflow.

The simplest customization option for the Quick Access Toolbar is to choose from a short list of 10 to 12 popular commands, as picked by the designers of Office. To expose this list, click the arrow to the right of the Quick Access Toolbar. A check mark indicates that the corresponding command is on the toolbar already. Click the command to toggle the selection.

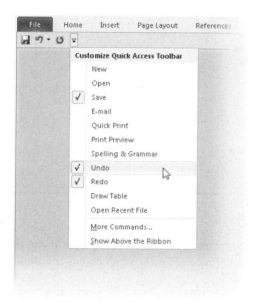

You can also add individual commands directly to the Quick Access Toolbar by right-clicking on the command in the ribbon and choosing Add To Quick Access Toolbar. If you use this option or the short list, the new command appears at the end of the Quick Access Toolbar.

Chapter 3

To add commands that aren't readily available, or to rearrange the order of commands, you need to open the dialog box shown in Figure 3-13. Right-click the Quick Access Toolbar or the ribbon, and then click Customize Quick Access Toolbar. Or click the arrow to the right of the Quick Access Toolbar and select More Commands. (You can also reach this location from Office Backstage view: click File, click Options, and then select the Quick Access Toolbar tab.)

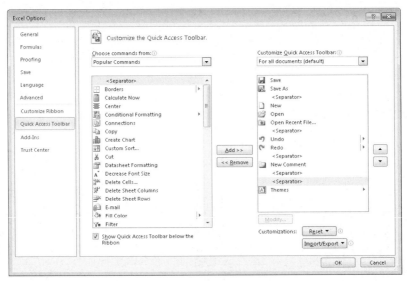

Figure 3-13 Pick commands from the list on the left and add them to the Quick Access Toolbar. Separators help group related commands together.

You work with items in this dialog box using the same tools and techniques as for personalizing the ribbon, except with fewer options. Filter the list of commands on the left to locate those you want to add. Use the Move Up and Move Down buttons to change the order of commands, and use the Separator item liberally to arrange commands in groups that are easier to remember and locate.

To remove all your customizations and start fresh, click the Reset button at the bottom of the dialog box, and then click Reset Only Quick Access Toolbar. As for the second option, Reset All Customizations, we offer the same caution here as we did with respect to the ribbon. This option is an all-or-nothing choice, resetting every change you've made to both the ribbon and Quick Access Toolbar. If you're experimenting, you'll want to back up your settings regularly so that you can restore them easily after a full reset.

Saving and Reusing Custom Ribbon and Toolbar Settings

The right customizations can have a positive effect on your productivity and on your aching muscles. Arranging commonly used commands in a convenient location can help you eliminate unnecessary mouse movements and clicks. If you invest more than a few minutes customizing a layout, save your settings in a backup location. Later, you can use that settings file to restore your custom ribbon and Quick Access Toolbar arrangements on a new PC or after reinstalling Office. You can also share the saved settings with other people and, as we explain in the Inside Out sidebar at the end of this section, you can modify the saved settings to quickly share some customizations between Office programs.

You'll find the Import/Export button at the bottom of the customization dialog boxes for the ribbon and the Quick Access Toolbar. The available options and results are the same in either place.

INSIDE OUT   Move your settings from Word to Excel? Yes, but . . .

The export option saves your custom settings as an XML file. The import option uses that file to restore settings. Given the similarities between Office programs, you might be tempted to try exporting settings from one Office program and importing them in another. Surprisingly, it works—if you follow some common-sense guidelines and keep your expectations reasonable.

You'll be most effective if you stick with commands that are shared among Office programs. That's actually pretty easy: the custom tab shown in Figure 3-12 was created in Word but works reasonably well in Excel, with three commands in the Insert group missing after the import step is complete.

The secret is to open the saved .exportedUI file in a text editor such as Notepad and edit a property in the first line of the file. The program you used to export the settings is identified in a custom tag at the top of the XML file. To import the file to a different program, you need to change that tag to reflect the target. So, look for this tag:

```
<mso:cmd app="Word" dt="0" />
```

Replace "Word" with "Excel." Save the settings file, being sure to preserve the .exportedUI extension, and import it into Excel. You now have a good base for beginning your customization of each program's unique features.

Chapter 3

Click Export All Customizations to save an XML file containing details about all additions and modifications to the ribbon and the Quick Access Toolbar. You'll be prompted to save the file in your Documents folder using the Exported Office UI File format (with the .exportedUI file name extension). The default file name is *ProgramName* Customizations, where *ProgramName* is the program you're currently using: Word, Excel, and so on.

To replace the settings on another Office installation with the settings you saved in the Exported Office UI file, open either the Quick Access Toolbar or Ribbon customization dialog box, click Import/Export, choose Import Customization File, and browse to the file you saved previously. Note that the saved settings eliminate any existing customizations you made to the ribbon or Quick Access Toolbar; you can't use the Import/Export feature to merge settings from two machines.

Using and Customizing the Status Bar

On any list of common interface elements in Office, it's easy to miss the status bar that runs along the bottom of the program window in Word, Excel, PowerPoint, and Outlook (but not in One Note). That's understandable. After all, this thin strip of screen real estate is a mere 20 pixels high. By default, the status bar displays information about the current document on its left side: page number and word counts in Word, slide number and theme name in PowerPoint, number of items and number of unread items in the current Outlook folder, and so on.

On the right side of the status bar you'll find controls that allow you to interact with the current document. The Zoom slider at the right side of the status bar allows you to make the contents of the current editing window (or the Reading Pane in Outlook) larger or smaller, as shown in Figure 3-14.

Figure 3-14 Click the percentage at the left of the slider to open the Zoom dialog box; the Fit Slide To Current Window button at the right is found only in PowerPoint.

Just to the left of the slide control are buttons that let you change the view: from Normal to Slide Sorter in PowerPoint, for example, or from Print Layout to Outline view in Word.

The status bar is actually more interesting and useful than it first appears, for two reasons. First, many options on the status bar are clickable. In Word, for example, you can click the Page indicator to open the Find And Replace dialog box, or click Words to open a dialog box containing additional statistics, such as the number of paragraphs, characters, and lines.

Second, you can customize the information displayed on the status bar by right-clicking the status bar and clearing or selecting items on the list of available options. Figure 3-15 shows the customization options available for Excel.

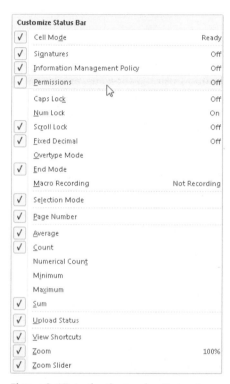

Figure 3-15 In the Customize Status Bar menu, the check marks indicate items that are currently available for display on the status bar.

Adjusting Program Options

Clicking Options in Office Backstage view in any program opens a tabbed dialog box that gives you access to a sometimes overwhelming set of options for that program. Many of the options are program-specific, but others represent shared features or similar ways of handling the same general task. In this section, we concentrate on the most useful common features you're likely to find in these dialog boxes.

Without exception, the first tab in the Options dialog box for each program is General. Here, you'll find options to disable the Mini toolbar and Live Preview—which some Office users find more annoying than helpful.

The General tab is also where you set the default font for Excel workbooks (shown here) and OneNote documents.

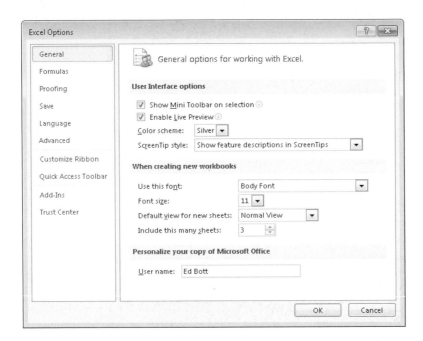

Several of the options available on the General tab actually apply to all Office programs when selected. If you choose the Blue or Black color scheme in lieu of the default Silver, the new theme is applied to all Office programs. Similarly, when you change the values in the User Name box in Excel, your changes are also reflected in Word and PowerPoint.

The Proofing tab contains settings for the spelling check feature used in Word, Excel, OneNote, and PowerPoint. (Outlook uses the same spelling check engine as Word; thus, any customizations you make in that program are reflected in the e-mail editor.) This tab is also where you'll find settings that control how AutoCorrect works. Although this feature is most commonly associated with Word, the core features are actually available in Excel, Power-Point, and OneNote as well.

For an explanation of how AutoCorrect can save you time and keystrokes and how to use it in Word and elsewhere, see "Entering Boilerplate and Other Oft-Used Text" on page 116.

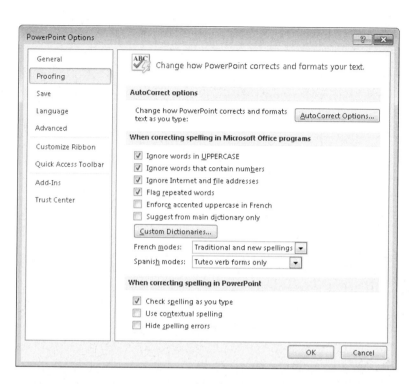

If you look at only one of the tabs in the Options dialog box, the Save tab should be it. In Word, Excel, and PowerPoint, this is where you assign a default document format, configure how often the program should automatically save your work, and specify default locations for your files and for AutoRecover files. In OneNote, the tab is called Save & Backup, and the backup procedures are much different but still worth paying close attention to, as shown next.

Customize how documents are saved.

Save documents

Save files in this format: Word Document (*.docx)   ▾

☑ Save AutoRecover information every   10   ◦   minutes

☑ Keep the last Auto Recovered file if I close without saving

AutoRecover file location: \AppData\Roaming\Microsoft\Word\   Browse...

Default file location: C:\Users\Ed Bott\Documents\   Browse...

Offline editing options for document management server files

Save checked-out files to: ⓘ

◦ The server drafts location on this computer

◉ The Office Document Cache

Server drafts location: C:\Users\Ed Bott\Documents\SharePoint   Browse...

Preserve fidelity when sharing this document: 📄 Penguin Social Behavior ▾

☐ Embed fonts in the file ⓘ

☐ Embed only the characters used in the document (best for reducing file size)

☑ Do not embed common system fonts

OK   Cancel

For more information on how to configure AutoRecover and why it can help you breathe a sigh of relief, see "Backup and Recovery Options" on page 103. For details on how to configure OneNote's automated backup options, see "Backing Up and Recovering Notebooks" on page 543.

Finally, every program has an Advanced tab in its Options dialog box. There, you'll find a mix of essential and esoteric settings, most of them specific to the current program. We discuss these options in more detail in the chapters dedicated to each program.

Finding Help and Support Options

All the programs in Office provide multiple opportunities for you to find help and reference information. The Microsoft Office Help viewer is available at any time with a press of the F1 key or a click of the blue circle with a white question mark, found in the top right corner of the ribbon.

Unlike in most Windows programs, the Help system in Office 2010 assumes by default that you have an always-on connection to the Internet, which ensures that you receive up-to-date assistance. Although you can treat Office Help like a book and read it from cover to cover (figuratively speaking), it's most useful if you navigate to the place in the program where you need assistance and then press F1. If you do that from the Visual Basic for Applications (VBA) Editor in Word, for example, the Help viewer displays Word VBA Help and

How-To, including a complete object library reference for Office 2010 and a full language reference for VBA.

Two bits of unexpectedly useful information are available at almost any time. When you're working in the program window, you can point to any command on the ribbon or the Quick Access Toolbar and see a description of the command and, if available, its keyboard shortcut, as shown here.

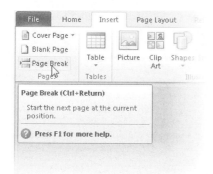

In addition, options within some dialog boxes are marked with faint white circles containing an equally faint lower-case "i" (for Information); allow the mouse pointer to rest over the icon, and you'll see a balloon explaining the feature, in a format similar to that used with balloon tips on commands.

Using Keyboard Shortcuts

Most Windows shortcuts work equally well in Office programs, both for managing windows and for text editing. In Word, Excel, and PowerPoint, for example, you can press Ctrl+N to start a new blank document, workbook, or presentation. Ctrl+F6 switches between open windows in the current program. Ctrl+B, Ctrl+I, and Ctrl+U apply bold, italic, and underline formatting to the current selection.

For a full list of keyboard shortcuts associated with text formatting, see "Applying Text Formatting" on page 123.

As we noted in the previous section, you can find the keyboard shortcuts for some commands by using the ScreenTip that appears when you allow the mouse pointer to hover over a command on the ribbon or Quick Access Toolbar. In Excel, OneNote, PowerPoint, and Outlook, those shortcuts are fixed and cannot be changed, nor can you add custom keyboard shortcuts.

The single exception to this rule is Word, which allows you to attach keyboard shortcuts to any command. (We discuss this option in more detail in "Our Favorite Word Tweaks and Tips" on page 335.

If you're an Office veteran and a fast touch typist, you're likely to miss the old-style menus, which made it possible to use the Alt key to pull down menus and make selections without having to move your hands off the keyboard. The good news is that those accelerators are still available in Office 2010. Virtually every object in the Office 2010 user interface is accessible via a keyboard sequence. Tap the Alt key to see which keys are attached to each onscreen object, as shown in Figure 3-16.

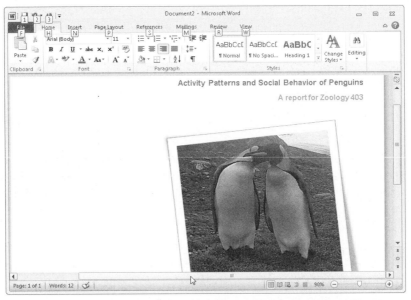

Figure 3-16 Tapping Alt displays keyboard shortcuts associated with objects on the ribbon and Quick Access Toolbar. Tapping H here shows shortcut keys for commands on the Home tab.

In some cases, the keyboard shortcut for a command might require multiple keystrokes in sequence. If you tap Alt, then H, then F in Word, you'll see the options shown here:

Press F to move to the Fonts list, S to choose a font size, G or K to make the current selection larger or smaller, and so on.

INSIDE OUT   Many old keyboard shortcuts still work

If your muscle memory is hard-wired with ancient menu sequences from Office 2003 and earlier versions, you're in for a pleasant surprise. Many of those old sequences still work. If you're editing a document in Word 2010 and press Alt+E, for example, Word recognizes that as the accelerator key for the Edit menu in Word 2003 and displays the ScreenTip shown here:

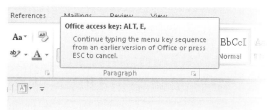

Press E (the accelerator for the Replace option on the old Edit menu), and Word dutifully pulls up the Find And Replace dialog box with the Replace tab highlighted, just as your muscles remember.

Arranging and Switching Between Document Windows

The three document-centric programs in the Office family—Word, Excel, and PowerPoint—each let you work with multiple documents in separate windows. You can also open a single document, worksheet, or presentation in multiple windows; this technique is especially useful with long documents, when you want to compare content in widely separated parts of the same file.

To facilitate the process of managing multiple windows, the View tab in all three programs is stocked with window-oriented commands. New Window opens the current document in a new window, appending a window number to the document's name in the title bar, with the original document identified as *Document*:1 and the new window labeled *Document*:2. The Arrange All command tiles all open document windows for the current program on the main monitor. Use the Switch Windows option to select from the list of open windows.

Word and Excel have an additional set of window controls on the View menu specifically intended to make it easier to compare the contents of multiple windows. If two and only two windows are open in the current program, you can click View Side By Side to automatically arrange them for comparison. If more than two windows are open, Word or Excel asks which document you want to compare with the current one. Synchronous scrolling is enabled by default when you view two windows side by side; with this option on, you can use the mouse wheel or scroll bars to move through both documents at the same pace.

CHAPTER 4

Managing Office Files

ANYONE who uses Microsoft Office 2010 for any length of time will develop opinions about the features, user interface elements, and design decisions. When Office users get together, that's what they're most likely to argue about. And yet all those things are merely a means to an end: the document.

In this chapter, we examine the data files that Office creates and uses. We explain which file formats each Office program supports; how to create, open, and save document files; how to convert documents to different file formats; and how to organize your documents so that you can easily find them later. In addition, we describe the features built in to Office that help you to avoid losing data.

Three of the programs included with Office—Word, Excel, and PowerPoint—use a traditional document-centric model. Each document—a Word document, an Excel workbook, or a PowerPoint presentation—is contained in a single file that you can open, move between folders, attach to an e-mail message, and so on. Many of the techniques described in this chapter apply primarily to document files of this type.

The other two Office programs described in this book, OneNote and Outlook, use a data store rather than discrete document files. The data store in OneNote, which is called a *notebook,* can include numerous pages, subpages, and sections, for example. An Outlook message store contains your collection of e-mail messages, contacts, appointments, and tasks. In these programs, you generally don't need to concern yourself with individual document files. Nonetheless, each program is capable of opening multiple stores simultaneously and of saving part of a store (a OneNote page or an Outlook message, for example) as a separate document file. You'll find the details of working with data stores in the OneNote and Outlook sections of this book. But don't head back there just yet; you'll find plenty of information in this chapter that you can use to understand and better use files in those programs.

> **Note**
>
> Throughout this chapter—indeed, throughout this book—you might be confused about our use of the term *document*. In its narrowest definition, it refers to a Word data file (as opposed to a data file for Excel or PowerPoint: workbook and presentation, respectively). However, *document* can also refer generically to user-created files from any program—files that are stored by default in your Documents library or Documents folder. You'll find both definitions in use here.

Which File Formats Does Office 2010 Support?

If you're creating documents for use only on your own computer, you don't need to worry too much about file formats. Create a workbook in Excel 2010, for example, save it in the default format (without even being aware what the default format is), and you can reopen it without a hitch. Historically, however, one of the pain points for Office users has been exchanging documents with other users. Office file formats have evolved over the decades as new document features are supported. When you share a document with people who don't have the same version of Office as you, the document might not look the same when they open it—or they might not be able to open it at all. Compatibility becomes even more problematical when you need to share documents with someone who doesn't have any version of Microsoft Office and uses a different suite of programs (or none at all).

Office 2010 addresses compatibility issues by supporting several different popular file formats for reading and saving. Additional formats are available for export; Office 2010 can save documents in these formats, but you cannot open or edit such files in Office programs. Conversely, to provide compatibility with some of your long-archived files, a handful of formats can be imported; to save changes to these files, you must use one of the newer formats.

Note, however, that when you save a document in a format other than the default Office format, you might see a warning similar to the following one. This lets you know that not all Office 2010 features are supported by the selected file format and that you can expect some loss of fidelity when you open the document in its native program—or even when you reopen it in Office 2010.

For more information about file compatibility, see "Checking for Compatibility with Earlier Office Versions" on page 88.

The following tables show the document file types supported by Word (Table 4-1), Excel (Table 4-2), OneNote (Table 4-3), PowerPoint (Table 4-4), and Outlook (Table 4-5).

Table 4-1 **Supported File Formats in Word 2010**

Type	Extension	Description
Word Document	.docx	This XML-based format is the default format for Word 2010 and Word 2007. This document type cannot contain VBA macro code. For more information, see "Understanding the Office 2010 Default Formats: Office Open XML" on page 85.
Word Macro-Enabled Document	.docm	This format is similar to the one above, except that it can contain VBA macro code.
Word 97-2003 Document	.doc	This ubiquitous format is the native format used by versions of Word prior to Word 2007.
Word Template	.dotx	This is the default format for templates used in Word 2010 and Word 2007. This document type cannot contain VBA macros. For more information, see "Using Templates to Streamline Document Creation" on page 97.
Word Macro-Enabled Template	.dotm	This format is similar to the one above, except that it can contain VBA macro code. Although a template in this format can contain macro code, by default a document created from a macro-enabled template is saved as .docx, which is stripped of macro code.
Word 97-2003 Template	.dot	This is the template format used by versions of Word prior to Word 2007.
PDF	.pdf	This export-only format lets you create documents that can be viewed on nearly any computer. For more information, see "Sharing Your Work in PDF and Other Formats" on page 95.

Chapter 4

Type	Extension	Description
XPS Document	.xps	This export-only format provides a cross-platform alternative to PDF. For more information, see "Sharing Your Work in PDF and Other Formats" on page 95.
Single File Web Page	.mht or .mhtl	This format, which stores all components of a web page in a single file for easy portability, can be viewed in most modern web browsers.
Web Page	.htm or .html	HTML is the standard language of the web. Unlike the preceding format, a traditional HTML document contains only text and commands; other page elements, such as pictures and style sheets, are stored in separate files. Word saves these related files in a subfolder with the same name as the .htm file.
Web Page, Filtered	.htm or .html	Saving a document in this format creates a standard HTML file (and a subfolder with additional files, if necessary) with Office-specific tags removed. This can cause the loss of document features that are supported in Office but not by standard HTML.
Rich Text Format	.rtf	This format is widely supported by word-processing programs, including the WordPad program included with all versions of Windows.
Plain Text	.txt	This lowest-common-denominator format contains only unformatted text.
Word XML Document	.xml	This format uses XML tags that correspond to an XML schema, making it useful for some custom data interchange applications.
Word 2003 XML Document	.xml	This uses the Word 2003 implementation of XML documents.
OpenDocument Text	.odt	This XML-based format was originally developed for use with the OpenOffice.org office suite, and it has gained some adherents who didn't like the proprietary nature of earlier binary Office formats.
Works 6–9 Document	.wps	This is the format used by Microsoft Works for word-processing documents.
WordPerfect 5.x	.doc	This import-only format lets you read documents created in WordPerfect; to make changes, you must save in a different format.
WordPerfect 6.x	.wpd or .doc	This import-only format lets you read documents created in more recent WordPerfect versions; to make changes, you must save in a different format.

Table 4-2 **Supported File Formats in Excel 2010**

Type	Extension	Description
Excel Workbook	.xlsx	This XML-based format is the default format for Excel 2010 and Excel 2007. This workbook type cannot contain VBA macro code or Microsoft Excel 4.0 macro sheets. For more information, see "Understanding the Office 2010 Default Formats: Office Open XML" on page 85.
Excel Macro-Enabled Workbook	.xlsm	This format is similar to the one above, except that it can contain VBA macro code.
Excel Binary Workbook	.xlsb	This format provides extremely fast performance for opening and saving data files. File sizes are larger than comparable .xlsx files, and this format is less secure.
Excel 97-2003 Workbook	.xls	This is the native format used by Excel 97, Excel 2000, Excel 2002, and Excel 2003.
Microsoft Excel 5.0/95 Workbook	.xls	This format was widely used in the mid-1990s.
Microsoft Excel 4.0 Workbook	.xlw	This import-only format dates to the early 1990s.
Excel Template	.xltx	This is the default format for templates used in Excel 2010 and Excel 2007. This workbook type cannot contain VBA macros or Microsoft Excel 4.0 macro sheets. For more information, see "Using Templates to Streamline Document Creation" on page 97.
Excel Macro-Enabled Template	.xltm	This format is similar to the one above, except that it can contain VBA macro code. When you save a workbook created from a macro-enabled template that includes macro code, Excel prompts you to save the workbook as macro-enabled.
Excel 97-2003 Template	.xlt	This is the template format used by earlier versions of Excel.
Excel Add-In	.xlam	This format is used for supplemental programs that run code. It supports the use of VBA projects and Excel 4.0 macro sheets.
Excel 97-2003 Add-In	.xla	This is the add-in format used by earlier versions of Excel.
Microsoft Excel 4.0 Macro	.xlm, .xla	This import-only format lets you open old macro sheets and convert them to VBA.

Chapter 4

Type	Extension	Description
PDF	.pdf	This export-only format lets you create documents that can be viewed on nearly any computer. For more information, see "Sharing Your Work in PDF and Other Formats" on page 95.
XPS Document	.xps	This export-only format provides a cross-platform alternative to PDF. For more information, see "Sharing Your Work in PDF and Other Formats" on page 95.
Single File Web Page	.mht or .mhtl	This format, which stores all components of a web page in a single file for easy portability, can be viewed in most modern web browsers.
Web Page	.htm or .html	This format uses a standard HTML file along with supporting files (such as pictures and style sheets) in a like-named subfolder.
Text (Tab Delimited) Unicode Text Text (Macintosh) Text (MS-DOS)	.txt	Each of these formats creates a plain-text file in which each cell in a row is separated by a tab character. The difference among the four variants is the character encoding.
CSV (Comma Delimited) CSV (Macintosh) CSV (MS-DOS)	.csv	These formats are similar to the preceding format, except that a comma separates each cell value.
Formatted Text (Space Delimited)	.prn	This plain-text file uses spaces to align columns of data.
DIF (Data Interchange Format)	.dif	This is a text file format that dates back to the 1980s; it's designed for moving data between different spreadsheet programs.
SYLK (Symbolic Link)	.slk	This is another format for exchanging data between different spreadsheet programs.
XML Data	.xml	This format can be used in custom data interchange applications.
XML Spreadsheet 2003	.xml	This format uses XML tags that correspond to an XML schema, making it useful for some custom data interchange applications.
OpenDocument Spreadsheet	.ods	This XML-based format was originally developed for use with the OpenOffice.org office suite.
Access Database	.mdb, .mde, .accdb, .accde	These import-only formats let you use data from an Access database.
Query File	.iqy, .dqy, .oqy, .rqy	These import-only formats let you use data from a SQL Server database.
dBase File	.dbf	These import-only formats let you use data from a dBase database.

Table 4-3 **Supported File Formats in OneNote 2010**

Type	Extension	Description
OneNote Package	.onepkg	This format combines all the sections of a OneNote notebook into a single portable file.
OneNote Table Of Contents	.onetoc2	This file provides an entry point to a notebook.
OneNote 2010 Section	.one	Each section in a notebook is saved in a separate file; this is the section format used in OneNote 2010.
OneNote 2007 Section	.one	This is the section format used in OneNote 2007.
Word Document	.docx	You can save a page or a section as a Word 2010 document in the default Office Open XML format.
Word 97-2003 Document	.doc	You can save a page or a section in the native format used by versions of Word prior to Word 2007.
PDF	.pdf	This export-only format lets you create documents that can be viewed on nearly any computer. For more information, see "Sharing Your Work in PDF and Other Formats" on page 95.
XPS Document	.xps	This export-only format provides a cross-platform alternative to PDF. For more information, see "Sharing Your Work in PDF and Other Formats" on page 95.
Single File Web Page	.mht or .mhtl	This export-only format, which stores all components of a web page in a single file for easy portability, can be viewed in most modern web browsers.

For details about working with the OneNote data store, see "Creating and Opening One-Note Files" on page 491.

Chapter 4

Table 4-4 **Supported File Formats in PowerPoint 2010**

Type	Extension	Description
PowerPoint Presentation	.pptx	This XML-based format is the default format for PowerPoint 2010 and PowerPoint 2007. This presentation type cannot contain VBA macro code or Action settings. For more information, see "Understanding the Office 2010 Default Formats: Office Open XML" on page 85.
PowerPoint Macro-Enabled Presentation	.pptm	This format is similar to the .pptx format, except that it can contain VBA macro code.
PowerPoint 97-2003 Presentation	.ppt	This is the native format used by PowerPoint 97, PowerPoint 2000, PowerPoint 2002, and PowerPoint 2003.
PowerPoint Template	.potx	This is the default format for templates used in PowerPoint 2010 and PowerPoint 2007. This presentation type cannot contain VBA macros or Action settings. For more information, see "Using Templates to Streamline Document Creation" on page 97.
PowerPoint Macro-Enabled Template	.potm	This format is similar to the .potx format, except that it can contain VBA macro code. Although a template in this format can contain macro code, by default a presentation created from a macro-enabled template is saved as .pptx, which is stripped of macro code.
PowerPoint 97-2003 Template	.pot	This is the template format used by earlier versions of PowerPoint.
Office Theme	.thmx	An Office theme incorporates a set of colors, fonts, and effects that you can use to apply a consistent look to Word documents, Excel workbooks, and PowerPoint presentations.
PowerPoint Show	.ppsx	This format automatically opens as a slide show. It cannot contain macros.
PowerPoint Macro-Enabled Show	.ppsm	This format automatically opens as a slide show. It can contain macros.
PowerPoint 97-2003 Show	.pps	This is the slide show format used by earlier PowerPoint versions.
PowerPoint Add-In	.ppam	This macro-enabled format is for a presentation designed to be run as a supplemental program.
PowerPoint 97-2003 Add-In	.ppa	This is the add-in format for earlier PowerPoint versions.

Type	Extension	Description
PowerPoint XML Presentation	.xml	This Office 2003 format uses XML tags that correspond to an XML schema, making it useful for some custom data interchange applications.
PowerPoint Picture Presentation	.pptx	In this format, each slide in a presentation is a picture.
PDF	.pdf	This export-only format lets you create documents that can be viewed on nearly any computer. For more information, see "Sharing Your Work in PDF and Other Formats" on page 95.
XPS Document	.xps	This export-only format provides a cross-platform alternative to PDF. For more information, see "Sharing Your Work in PDF and Other Formats" on page 95.
Windows Media Video	.wmv	This export-only format lets you save your presentation in a standard video format.
GIF Graphics Interchange Format	.gif	This export-only format lets you save your slides in a standard graphics format.
JPEG File Interchange Format	.jpg	This export-only format lets you save your slides in a standard graphics format.
PNG Portable Network Graphics Format	.png	This export-only format lets you save your slides in a print-quality graphics format.
TIFF Tag Image File Format	.tif	This export-only format lets you save your slides in a standard graphics format.
Device Independent Bitmap	.bmp	This export-only format lets you save your slides in a standard graphics format.
Windows Metafile	.wmf	This export-only format lets you save your slides in a standard graphics format.
Enhanced Windows Metafile	.emf	This export-only format lets you save your slides in a standard graphics format.
Outline/RTF	.rtf	This format preserves presentation text in a standard word-processing format.
OpenDocument Presentation	.odp	This XML-based format is used by the OpenOffice.org office suite.
Web Page	.htm,.html, .mht, mhtl	These import-only formats open a web page as a presentation.
Outlines	.txt, .rtf, .doc, .docx, .docm, .wpd, .wps	These import-only formats open a presentation using the text in standard word-processing document formats, including those used by Word, WordPerfect, and Microsoft Works.

Chapter 4

Table 4-5 **Supported File Formats in Outlook 2010**

Type	Extension	Description
All Outlook Items		
Outlook Message Format – Unicode	.msg	This is the default format for Outlook items stored outside the data store. It uses Unicode character encoding, which supports characters in any language.
Outlook Message Format	.msg	This format is similar to the preceding one, except it uses traditional character encoding.
Outlook Template	.oft	This is the format for templates used in Outlook.
Text Only	.txt	This format uses only plain, unformatted text.
Messages		
HTML	.htm or .html	This is the standard format for web pages. Supporting files, such as images and style sheets, are stored in a subfolder.
MHT Files	.mht or .mhtl	This format, which stores all components of a web page in a single file for easy portability, can be viewed in most modern web browsers.
Calendar Items		
iCalendar Format	.ics	This is a widely supported open standard format for sending meeting requests and tasks over the Internet.
vCalendar Format	.vcs	vCalendar is an earlier format for sending meeting requests.
Rich Text Format	.rtf	This format is widely supported by word-processing programs.
Contacts		
vCard Files	.vcf	This is a standard format for electronic business cards.
Rich Text Format	.rtf	This format is widely supported by word-processing programs.
Tasks		
Rich Text Format	.rtf	This format is widely supported by word-processing programs.

Additional formats are supported for exporting or importing data between Outlook data files and other databases. For more information, see "Importing and Exporting Outlook Data" on page 792.

Understanding the Office 2010 Default Formats: Office Open XML

By default, the three document-centric programs in Office—Word, Excel, and PowerPoint—use documents stored in the Office Open XML (OOXML) format. This XML-based format, which was introduced with Office 2007, offers several advantages over the binary formats used in Office 2003 and earlier versions. Most notably:

- **Smaller files**   Each document file (a .docx, .xlsx, or .pptx file, for example) is actually a container file in the ZIP archive format. The document parts—including the document text, embedded images, formatting commands, and so on—are saved as individual files within the container. Zip compression technology reduces the file size as much as 75 percent. Office automatically unzips the container when you open a document and rezips it when you're done.

  This not only means you need less disk space to store documents, but it facilitates sending documents as e-mail attachments and reduces the time needed to move files to and from network or Internet locations.

- **More robust files**   Because the document file contains discrete files within a ZIP archive, you should be able to open and work with the document even if some component parts are missing or damaged.

- **Better control over personal information**   With the older binary formats, some notoriously embarrassing incidents arose in which snoops were able to find personal information and earlier edits to a document. The Open XML formats support the use of the document inspector (see Figure 4-1), which identifies potential privacy problems (and other issues) and lets you remove personally identifiable information such as author names, document revisions, file paths, and so on. For more information about the document inspector and privacy concerns, see "Inspecting and Removing Personal and Confidential Information" on page 821.

Chapter 4

INSIDE OUT   Dig into an Open XML document

If you're curious about the structure and content of an Open XML document, it's easy to take a look inside. Start by changing the file name extension to .zip, and then open the file as a compressed folder in Windows Explorer. In the root of the compressed folder, you'll see a document named [Content_Types].xml. This file, which you can view in a web browser, identifies the parts of the document. The files that make up these parts are located within subfolders of the compressed folder.

"How To: Manipulate Office Open XML Formats Documents" provides an introductory tour of the structure and content of the files within a document file; you can find this article in the MSDN library at *w7io.com/10402*.

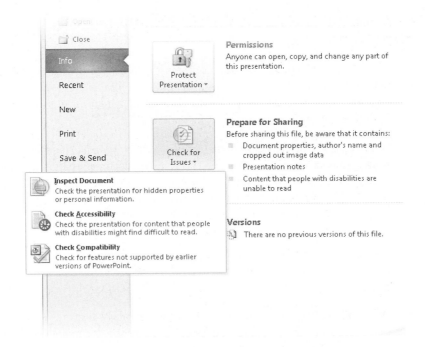

Figure 4-1 On the Info tab in Backstage view, a summary of potential privacy issues appears next to Check For Issues. Click the button and choose Inspect Document for details and removal.

Setting a Default File Format

As noted earlier, Office 2010 uses Open XML as the default format for documents you create and save in Word, Excel, and PowerPoint. "Default," in this case, merely means that when you save a document for the first time, that format is preselected in the Save As dialog box. (When you open a document in a different format, Office uses the file's original format as the default choice when you resave it.)

You might want to select a different format as the default choice, particularly if you frequently share documents you create with people who don't have Office 2010 or Office 2007. Changing the default format is easy, but it's not particularly intuitive. Here's how:

1. In Backstage view, click Options.

2. In the Options dialog box, click Save.

3. Next to Save Files In This Format, select the format you want to use by default.

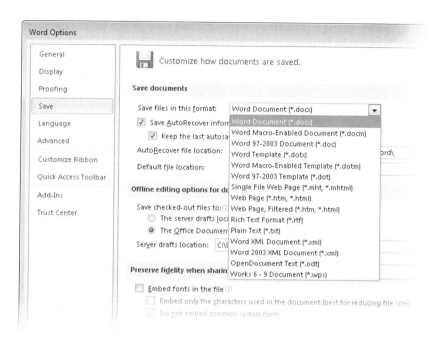

You need to separately specify your choice in Word, Excel, and PowerPoint.

> **Note**
>
> In some countries, the first time you run an Office 2010 program it asks you to choose between two default formats: Office Open XML or OpenDocument (ODF). (OpenDocument formats were developed for the OpenOffice.org office suite. Selecting ODF as your default format provides compatibility with other programs, but it doesn't support all features of Office 2010.) Your choice in this dialog box sets the default for all three programs: Word, Excel, and PowerPoint.

Using Office 2010 Formats with Earlier Office Versions

Microsoft offers a free compatibility pack for earlier versions of Office that enables users of those versions to read, modify, and save Word, Excel, and PowerPoint documents in the Office Open XML format—the default format used by Office 2010. If you regularly exchange documents with someone who hasn't upgraded to Office 2010 (or Office 2007, which also supports Office Open XML formats natively), the compatibility pack provides an excellent solution. It also lets users of the older Office versions enjoy the benefits of Open XML formats described earlier in the chapter.

The Microsoft Office Compatibility Pack for Word, Excel, and PowerPoint File Formats works with any of these earlier Office versions:

- Microsoft Office 2000 with Service Pack 3

- Microsoft Office XP with Service Pack 3

- Microsoft Office 2003 with Service Pack 3

To download the Microsoft Office Compatibility Pack for Word, Excel, and PowerPoint File Formats, visit *w7io.com/10401*. For more details about installing, using, and troubleshooting the compatibility pack, see Microsoft Support article 924074 (*w7io.com/924074*).

Checking for Compatibility with Earlier Office Versions

Not surprisingly, the newest version of Office has features that were not part of earlier Office versions—features as varied as new numbering formats in Word, sparklines (in-cell graphs) in Excel, and reflection shape effects in PowerPoint.

If you exchange documents with users who don't have Office 2010, you'll want to know if your documents will appear the same when those users open your files in their Office programs. Each Office 2010 program includes a compatibility checker that identifies items in your document that won't work properly with earlier Office versions. The compatibility checker runs automatically when you save a document in one of the downlevel formats such as Word 97–2003 Document (.doc), Excel 97–2003 Workbook (.xls), and PowerPoint 97-2003 Presentation (.ppt). If the compatibility checker finds incompatible items in your document, it displays a dialog box that identifies each problem, similar to the one shown in Figure 4-2. When a dialog box like this appears, click Continue to proceed with the save operation (with full knowledge of the limitations and consequences) or click Cancel to return to the Save As dialog box without saving.

You can also run the compatibility checker on demand at any time. As shown earlier in Figure 4-1, on the Info tab in Backstage view, click Check For Issues, and then click Check Compatibility.

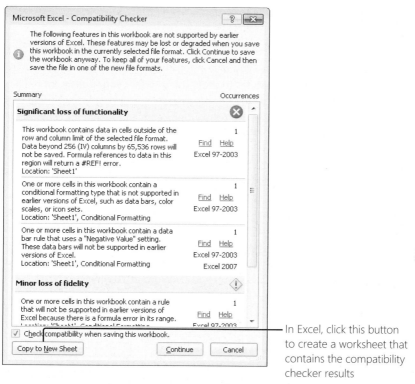

In Excel, click this button to create a worksheet that contains the compatibility checker results

Figure 4-2 For each compatibility issue, the compatibility checker provides details about the issue and explains which Office versions are affected.

When you work with a document in one of the Office 97–2003 formats, Office 2010 uses *compatibility mode,* as indicated in the program's caption. In compatibility mode, commands and features that are not supported by the older document format are unavailable.

You can easily restore full functionality to a document if you're working in compatibility mode. On the Info tab in Backstage view, click the Convert button. The Save As dialog box then appears so you can save the document in an Office 2010 format.

Chapter 4

INSIDE OUT **What are the new, incompatible features in each program?**

It'd be nice to know before you save a document—or even before you run the compatibility checker—which features to avoid using so that your document remains compatible with old Office versions. Although some details are lacking, you can find much of this information in Help. Open Help for your program and search for *compatibility mode*.

Opening and Saving Documents

When you open or save a document from within an Office program, you use an Open or Save As dialog box similar to the one you've seen in countless other programs. But these dialog boxes have evolved over the years, sprouting new features along the way, and they also have some features unique to Office—so you might want to take a fresh look. Figure 4-3 shows the Open dialog box used by Word 2010 on Windows 7.

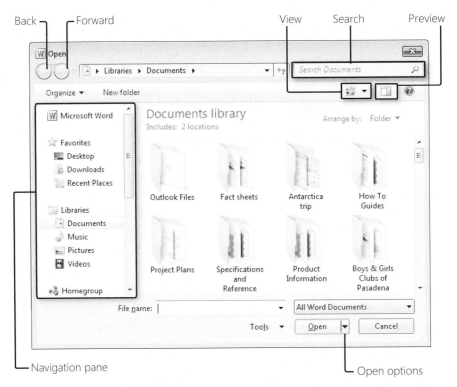

Figure 4-3 The Open dialog box in Windows 7 has a search box (not available in Windows XP) and a better Navigation pane than the one in Windows XP or Windows Vista.

You get to the Open dialog box by clicking File, Open. In Word, Excel, and PowerPoint (but not OneNote or Outlook), you can get there even faster by using either of its keyboard shortcuts, Ctrl+O or Ctrl+F12.

> **Note**
>
> In this chapter, we discuss opening and saving documents on your computer and your network. For information about working with documents in the cloud, see "Storing and Using Office Documents on Windows Live SkyDrive" on page 842, and "How SharePoint and Office Work Together" on page 864.

Here are some notable features of the Open dialog box that many users don't know about:

- **Back and Forward buttons**   As you browse between folders, these buttons let you retrace your steps, just like the similar buttons in your web browser.

- **Search box**   In Windows 7 and Windows Vista, entering text in the search box filters the window contents to include only documents in the current folder and its subfolders that contain that text. If you're working in a folder that's automatically indexed by Windows, such as your libraries (Windows 7 only) or your Documents folder, the filtering is almost instantaneous. You can further narrow your search with the use of search filters. Using search filters in Windows Vista requires you to learn the filter syntax; in Windows 7, however, click in the search box to select common filters as well as a history of your recent searches.

- **View button**   Click this button to easily switch between details view (which includes date, file size, and other details), small icons, large icons, and other views.

- **Preview button**   Click this button (available only in Windows 7) to open a preview pane in which you can view the file that's selected in the file pane. You can open the preview pane in Windows Vista with a little extra effort: click Organize, Layout, Preview Pane.

- **Navigation pane** As its name suggests, you use the Navigation pane to move between the libraries (Windows 7 only), drives, and folders on your computer and your network. Be aware that you can customize the Navigation pane in various ways to speed navigation: add or remove libraries, add or remove favorites (simply drag a folder to the Favorites icon), or even change it to the Windows XP–style hierarchy, for example.

- **Open options** Naturally, clicking Open opens the selected file for editing. But if you click the arrow by the Open button, you'll see additional options, as shown here:

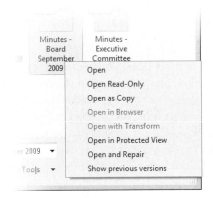

- **Open Read-Only** When you open a document in read-only mode, Office doesn't prevent you from making changes. However, to save any changes, you must save the document with a new name, preserving the original unedited document.

- **Open As Copy** This option creates a copy of the document, inserting the word *Copy* and a number before the file name, and then opens the copy.

- **Open In Protected View** Protected View is designed primarily for potentially risky files, such as documents you download from the Internet or a message attachment from a sender identified as unsafe. In Protected View, you're prevented from editing or saving the document unless you explicitly enable these features after the document opens. For more information about Protected View, see "How Office 2010 Protects You" on page 818.

- **Open And Repair** If your file doesn't open properly, try this option, which attempts to repair corrupted files or, if that's not possible, extract the valid data.

- **Show Previous Versions**   This option opens a folder-like view of earlier saved versions of the selected folder or file. Previous Versions is a feature of Windows 7 (all editions) and Windows Vista (Business, Enterprise, and Ultimate editions only) that uses volume shadow copies to periodically preserve copies of your files.

Note also that the Open dialog box (and the Save As dialog box) are, in effect, small Windows Explorer windows. That means you can right-click a folder or file to display a menu of available actions, and you can use all the other Windows Explorer knowledge you've acquired to move, rename, delete, and otherwise manipulate files—all without leaving Office.

For details about searching, working with the Navigation pane, using libraries, and managing files, we shamelessly recommend *Windows 7 Inside Out* (Microsoft Press, 2009) or, if you use Windows Vista, *Windows Vista Inside Out Deluxe Edition* (Microsoft Press, 2008).

You use the Save As dialog box, shown in Figure 4-4, to save a document for the first time or to save it with a new name or in a different file format.

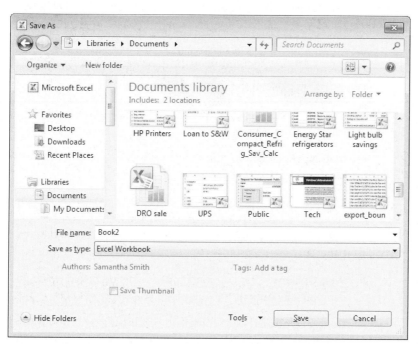

Figure 4-4 When you save a document, you can specify properties such as Authors and Tags.

The upper part of the dialog box looks and works like the Open dialog box. The lower section includes a place for you to enter a file name for the document, specify a file format (select from the Save As Type list; for information about the various formats, see "Which File Formats Does Office 2010 Support?" on page 76), and set other options that vary depending on the file format you select. If you select the default format or one of the other Office Open XML formats, you'll see options similar to those in Figure 4-4, including:

- **Authors**   Office initially populates this field with the name of the user who created the document. (This name is set when you install Office; you can change it by clicking File, Options, and then changing User Name on the General tab.) Click this name to add other names to the file properties; separate multiple author names with semicolons.

- **Tags**   You can use tags to categorize your documents. Create keywords that identify the topic, type of document (for example, How To), or other criteria. To enter a tag, click Add A Tag and type; separate multiple tags with semicolons. For more information, see "Organizing Office Documents Using File Properties and Details" on page 99.

- **Title**   Use this field to enter a document title, which, like the Authors and Tags properties, can be useful for identifying and finding documents. (If, as shown in Figure 4-4, this option doesn't appear, drag the border of the dialog box to increase its width.)

- **Save Thumbnail**   Select this option if you want to create a thumbnail image of the document. This image appears in Windows Explorer (and in the Open and Save As dialog boxes) in place of the standard document icon.

- **Tools**   Click Tools to display a menu of additional options (not all options are available in all Office programs):

    - **Map Network Drive**   Click this to assign a drive letter to a shared network drive.

    - **Save Options**   This command is equivalent to clicking File, Options, and then clicking the Save tab. For information about the options on this tab, see "Setting a Default File Format" on page 86, and "Backup and Recovery Options" on page 103.

    - **Web Options**   This command opens a dialog box in which you can set various compatibility options for web pages you create in Office.

    - **General Options**   This command opens a dialog box in which you can set security-related options for encryption, password protection, and macro handling.

    - **Compress Pictures**   This command opens a dialog box in which you can specify options for compressing pictures to reduce the file size.

To open the Save As dialog box, click File, Save As. Alternatively, press F12. Table 4-6 provides a quick reference chart of keyboard shortcuts for working with the Open and Save As dialog boxes.

Table 4-6 Keyboard Shortcuts for Opening and Saving Documents

Action	Keyboard Shortcut
Display the Open dialog box	Ctrl+O or Ctrl+F12
Display the Save As dialog box	F12 (or, if the document has not been saved before, Ctrl+S)
Open the selected folder or file	Enter
Move to the parent of the current folder	Backspace
Save a document	Ctrl+S

Sharing Your Work in PDF and Other Formats

At times you'll want to share your document in a format that ensures document fidelity on a wide variety of computer platforms and in a form that is not easily modified. That is, you want anybody to be able to view your document and have it look identical to what you've created in Office—and you don't want them to inadvertently make changes to the document. Office 2010 supports two such formats:

- Adobe Portable Document Format (PDF) is a good format for this purpose because of its ubiquity. Adobe Reader and other programs that can display PDF files are available for most versions of Windows, Macintosh, Linux, UNIX, and mobile devices.

- The XML Paper Specification (XPS) format has some advantages for sharing read-only documents (XPS can more closely match the appearance of your original Office document), but it is not as widely known or supported as PDF. An XPS viewer program is included with Windows 7 and Windows Vista. Users of Windows XP can get XPS-viewing capabilities by installing Internet Explorer 8 or a viewer such as the free one from Microsoft (*w7io.com/10403*). Other options for Windows as well as for other operating systems can be found at *w7io.com/10404*.

Both formats solve the most common problems with document sharing. With most other formats, if the document recipient doesn't have the same fonts installed that you used to create a document, it won't look the same. Likewise, any linked images will be missing from the recipient's document. PDF and XPS formats can include embedded fonts and images to preserve document fidelity.

Using the Save As dialog box, described in the preceding section, you can select PDF or XPS as the document type. Word, Excel, and PowerPoint offer another path that you might find easier to use.

1. In Backstage view, click the Save & Send tab.

2. Under File Types, click Create PDF/XPS Document, and then click the Create PDF/XPS button.

This brings you to the now-familiar Save As dialog box, but with some additional options available, as shown here.

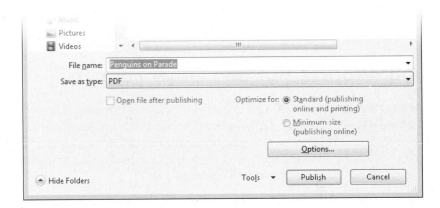

- **Open File After Publishing**   If this option is selected, the PDF or XPS document opens in the program registered for that document type (typically, Adobe Reader for PDF and XPS Viewer for XPS). If you don't have a viewer program installed, this option is unavailable.

- **Optimize For**   Choosing Standard produces high-resolution files suitable for use by a commercial printer, but the files can be quite large. Choosing Minimum Size produces files that are smaller and are usually good enough for viewing on a computer screen.

- **Options**   In the Options dialog box, you can specify which parts of a document to include in the output, whether to create bookmarks in the output file, and certain options specific to PDF or XPS. The options are slightly different for each program, but they're generally similar to the Options dialog box for PowerPoint, shown next.

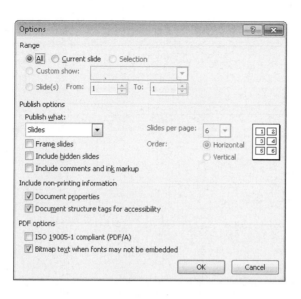

Using Templates to Streamline Document Creation

By default, when you open Word, Excel, or PowerPoint, you're faced with a blank document, workbook, or presentation into which you can begin typing, formatting, and so on. Similarly, after launching an Office program, you can create a new blank document by opening Backstage view, clicking New, and clicking Create. (On the New tab, Blank Document, Blank Workbook, or Blank Presentation is selected by default.)

But why start with a blank slate? Office can use a *template* to start a new document. Templates can be real time savers and help to enforce a uniform appearance to your documents. Templates can contain text, pictures, styles, and macros, all in place for easy reuse.

Office includes a number of templates for various common document types, such as letters, budget worksheets, and sales presentations. In addition, hundreds more templates are available as free downloads from Office.com. And you can easily create your own templates by saving a file in a template format.

You can see how templates work by going to the New tab in Backstage view, as shown in Figure 4-5.

Chapter 4

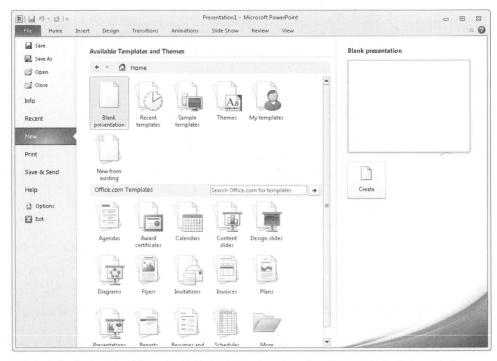

Figure 4-5 A preview of the selected template appears on the New tab in Backstage view.

The top part of the New tab provides access to templates stored on your computer. This section includes Recent Templates (templates you have used recently), Sample Templates (samples included with Office), and My Templates (templates you have saved and templates you have downloaded from Office.com). The last option in the top part, New From Existing, creates a new document from an existing document, incorporating everything stored in that document.

The lower part of the New tab leads to downloadable templates from Office.com. (You'll need to be connected to the Internet to view these templates or use them for the first time.) You can browse templates by category, or you can use a search term such as *blue* or *Thanksgiving*.

Note that you can explore the available templates in much the same way you might explore a website. Back and Forward buttons let you retrace your steps, and a Home button takes you directly back to the template home, shown in Figure 4-5.

After you select the template you want, click Create (or, in the case of Office.com templates, click Download) to open a new document based on the template.

INSIDE OUT   Set a location for templates you save

You can save a document as a template in any folder. However, only templates stored in a designated template folder appear when you click My Templates. By default the template folder is the AppData\Roaming\Microsoft\Templates folder within your profile folder. You can change this default location by following these steps:

1. In Word (oddly, this doesn't work in Excel or PowerPoint), open Backstage view and click Options.

2. In the Word Options dialog box, click Advanced.

3. Scroll all the way to the bottom, and then click File Locations.

4. In the File Locations dialog box, select User Templates, and then click Modify.

5. Browse to the folder you want to use for templates, and then click OK in each dialog box.

The change you make here determines the template location for Excel and PowerPoint as well as Word.

If you have many templates and you want to organize them, use subfolders of the template folder. Each subfolder appears as a separate tab in the New dialog box that appears when you click My Templates.

You can also designate a second template location. In the File Locations dialog box (step 4 in the procedure), the Workgroup Templates setting specifies a folder intended for shared templates (as opposed to your own personal templates), but it can be directed to any folder.

Organizing Office Documents Using File Properties and Details

In addition to the content of a document, files in the Office Open XML document format (as well as many other file formats) can contain other details about the document in the form of *metadata*. Metadata can include properties such as the name of the document author; the number of pages, paragraphs, lines, words, and characters in the document; the date and time it was last printed; and much more.

To view the properties of a document in Office, open Backstage view. Document properties are displayed along the right side of the Info tab, beneath the thumbnail representation of the document window, as shown in Figure 4-6. (Tip: Click the thumbnail to immediately return to the document and tab that were displayed before you entered Backstage view.)

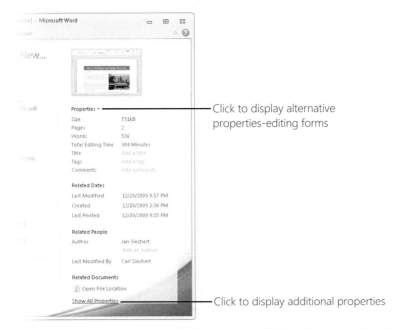

Figure 4-6 You can edit most properties by simply clicking the property's value and typing.

Some properties, such as the number of words and editing time, are generated automatically by Office and can't be edited. The others can be edited here on the Info tab; simply click and type. As noted earlier, some properties can be set when you use the Save As dialog box to save a document. You can display and edit a more comprehensive list by clicking Properties on the Info tab. Doing so offers two choices:

- **Show Document Panel**   This option displays a pane at the top of the document window that includes some of the most common editable properties, as shown next.

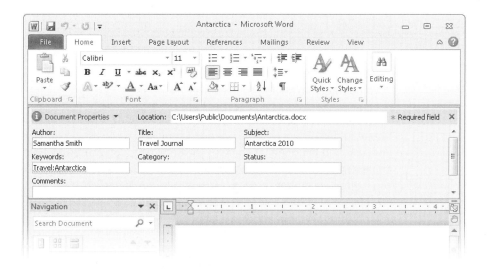

- **Advanced Properties**   This option displays a multitabbed properties dialog box that provides access to more properties than you thought possible. And if that's not enough, you can create your own custom properties. (You can reach this same dialog box by clicking Document Properties, Advanced Properties in the upper left corner of the document panel.)

INSIDE OUT   Be consistent in your tag usage

Tags (which appear under Keywords on the document panel) are most effective in your searches when you use them consistently. For example, in the preceding example, you'd want to be sure that you always use the word *Travel* instead of using that word and *Travels* interchangeably.

The easiest way to enforce this consistency is to enter your tags in the Save As dialog box rather than the Keywords box in the document panel or the Tags box on the Info tab in Backstage view. That's because when you begin typing a tag name in the Save As dialog box, a list of previously used tags that begin with the letters you type appears; you can simply select one of those to ensure that the current document is tagged identically to others you've tagged.

Chapter 4

Finding Office Files

Why bother entering properties such as a title, author, and tags? The benefit of using tags and other properties to specify details about your document is that it simplifies finding that document the next time you need it.

The time-honored method for organizing documents is to save them in a hierarchical structure of folders. Then, to retrieve a document, you navigate through the folder structure until you find the one that contains the document you want. This system is often difficult to implement. (For example, do you create folders by project? By date? By type of document?) You'll often encounter situations where it would be perfectly logical to save a document in any of several folders—so which do you choose? And will you remember the location when you go to retrieve the document later?

The use of tags, categories, and other editable fields—as well as system-maintained properties such as the modification date—makes the folder structure and file location much less important. With the search capabilities built in to Windows 7 (and, to a lesser degree, in Windows Vista), it's easy to search across multiple folders and drives to find a specific document based on its content, author, tags, title, and other properties.

To use properties to find a document, use the search box in the Open dialog box. (For details about the Open dialog box, see "Opening and Saving Documents" on page 90.) In the search box, you can type some words that appear in your document, and you can use one or more properties as filters. In Windows 7, commonly used filters appear when you click in the search box; click a filter name (for example, Authors), and then select from the list that appears. To use filters in Windows Vista, or to use other filters in Windows 7, type the filter name followed by a colon and then type the filter text. You can use any property as a filter, including the system-maintained properties such as the number of slides in a presentation.

INSIDE OUT   Display properties in the Open dialog box

If you choose Details view, each file shown in the Open dialog box occupies one line in a list. You can add properties of your choosing to the display for each file by right-clicking a column heading (such as Name or Date Modified) and then clicking the names of other properties you want to display. To sort on the contents of any column, click the column heading.

Keep in mind that searches look in subfolders as well as the current folder, so if you start your search in the Documents library or Documents folder, your search scope can include all files in your carefully organized folder structure—and all those disorganized ones as well.

Filter your documents to narrow the possibilities and open the preview pane, and you can quickly find the document you want.

All of the search and display options that we describe for the Open dialog box also work in Windows Explorer, allowing you to find that document you're looking for without opening an Office program.

INSIDE OUT   Windows XP users: Install Windows Search

Search capabilities in Windows have come a long way since the much-derided search puppy showed up in Windows XP. If you still use Windows XP, all is not lost (pun intended), however. Installing Windows Search 4.0, a free program from Microsoft, brings many of the modern search capabilities to your older operating system. For more information, visit *w7io.com/10405*.

Backup and Recovery Options

Throughout this chapter, we focus on saving documents. It's wise to periodically save a document you're working on by pressing Ctrl+S, but unfortunately, that doesn't always happen. To prevent accidental loss of your documents, Office 2010 includes AutoRecover and autosave, options that can save your bacon (as well as your document) in situations when Office closes before you save the file. This can occur if you experience a power outage, a program closes unexpectedly (put another way: crashes), or you close the Office program without first saving your document.

When AutoRecover is enabled, it automatically saves a copy of your document at an interval you set. (Note that it saves a copy; it does not overwrite your previously saved file.) Autosave saves a copy of the document you're working on if you close the Office program without saving.

To review AutoRecover and autosave settings, open Backstage view and click Options. In the Options dialog box, click Save, as shown here.

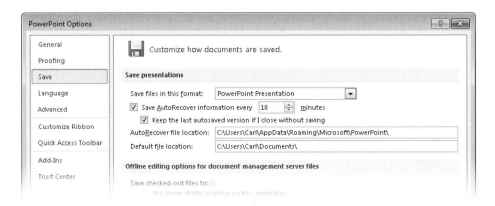

To enable AutoRecover, select Save AutoRecover Information Every and specify a time interval. While you're here, check the AutoRecover File Location box and specify a different location if you like. Lastly, to avoid mistakes of your own making, select Keep The Last Autosaved Version If I Close Without Saving; this option is available only when AutoRecover is enabled.

Disaster happens. How do you get your document back? Read on...

Restoring Previous Versions Saved by AutoRecover

To open a previous version of the document you're currently working on, click File to open Backstage view. On the Info tab, saved versions appear by the Manage Versions button, as shown here.

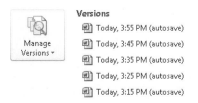

Click any version to open it. Note that a message appears at the top of the document window, informing you that this is not the last-saved or most recent version of the document. Click the Restore button to replace the last-saved version with the currently displayed version—the one you selected from the versions list.

> **Note**
>
> If you're using Word (but not Excel or PowerPoint), you can compare the currently displayed document and the last-saved version by clicking Compare. This opens a new document that shows the differences between the versions. For more information about document comparison, see "Reviewing Tracked Changes" on page 287.

Restoring Discarded Documents Saved by Autosave

If you close Office without saving your document and you've enabled autosave, Office saves your document for four days in the C:\Users*username*\AppData\Microsoft\Office\ UnsavedFiles folder. You can open a document directly from that folder (by double-clicking it in Windows Explorer, for example), or you can open it from within Office, using either of two methods:

- In Backstage view, click Recent. In the lower right corner of the Recent tab, click Recover Unsaved Documents (in Word), Recover Unsaved Workbooks (Excel), or Recover Unsaved Presentations (PowerPoint).

- On the Info tab in Backstage view, click Manage Versions, and then click Recover Unsaved Documents (in Word), Recover Unsaved Workbooks (Excel), or Recover Unsaved Presentations (PowerPoint).

Regardless of how you retrieve the document, Office displays a message informing you that it's an unsaved file and prompting you to use Save As to give it a file name and location.

Chapter 4

CHAPTER 5

Entering, Editing, and Formatting Text

S ERIOUSLY? An entire chapter about entering and editing text? Don't you just click in a document and type? At its most basic level, yes. You can enter and usedit text in Office 2010 programs in much the same way you would in the simplest text editor, such as Notepad. But as you would expect, Office offers much more, including various shortcuts to expedite text entry and rich formatting capabilities. In this chapter, we describe the features and techniques common to all Office programs for entering and editing text, using fonts, and formatting text.

Entering and Selecting Text

You might assume that as the core functionality of word processors and other productivity programs like the ones in Office 2010, features for entering, selecting, and editing text have fully matured and that there's nothing new in this area. Although that's largely true, Office 2010 incorporates a number of small but meaningful enhancements to the genre. And many of the less well-known techniques that are not new to Office might be new to you.

First, let's take a brief look at some basic procedures. These techniques apply not only to all Office programs, but also to most dialog boxes and other programs in which you enter or edit text.

To enter text, place the insertion point where you want the text…and type. (The *insertion point* is a flashing vertical line that indicates where the text you type will be inserted. Don't confuse it with the *mouse pointer*, a nonflashing cursor that takes on different shapes as you point at different objects, which indicates where your next mouse action will occur.) To position the insertion point, move the mouse pointer to the place you want to enter text and then click. Alternatively, you can move the insertion point by using the keyboard shortcuts shown in Table 5-1.

Table 5-1 **Keyboard Shortcuts for Moving the Insertion Point**

Action	Keyboard Shortcut
Move one character left or right	Left Arrow or Right Arrow
Move one word left or right	Ctrl+Left Arrow or Ctrl+Right Arrow
Move up or down one line	Up Arrow or Down Arrow
Move to beginning of previous or next paragraph	Ctrl+Up Arrow or Ctrl+Down Arrow
Move to beginning or end of current line	Home or End
Move up or down one screen	Page Up or Page Down
Move to top of previous or next page or slide	Ctrl+Page Up or Ctrl+Page Down
Move to beginning or end of a document	Ctrl+Home or Ctrl+End

To perform other tasks with text, you must first select it. When text is selected, the insertion point disappears and the selected text is highlighted with a blue background. Your editing now affects the selection; for example, you can apply text formatting to the selection or copy the selection to the Clipboard. If you type, your typing replaces the selection.

Select text by holding down Shift and using the keyboard shortcuts shown in Table 5-1 to extend the selection. To select text using the mouse, click where you want to begin the selection, and then drag to the end of your selection. You can also employ a couple of mouse shortcuts: double-click to select an entire word, or triple-click to select an entire paragraph. If you don't release the mouse button after the final click, you can drag to extend the selection by words or paragraphs. (Word offers additional keyboard and mouse shortcuts for selecting text. For details, see "Use Word tricks for selecting text" on page 215.)

INSIDE OUT   Enable precise selection

When you select text in Word or PowerPoint with the mouse, once you drag beyond a word boundary, the selection extends by a word at a time. For most routine editing tasks in ordinary text, that's a handy feature that forgives a little sloppiness in your mouse handling. Some users find this behavior annoying, however, and you might encounter situations where it's undesirable.

To configure Word or PowerPoint so that selections begin and end precisely where you drag instead of observing word boundaries, click File to open Backstage view, click Options, and then click Advanced. Under Editing, clear When Selecting, Automatically Select Entire Word.

The final topic in our tour of text editing basics is deleting text. With the keyboard, it's easy: use any of the keyboard shortcuts in Table 5-2, and your text is gone. (If you change your mind, you can restore the deleted text; for details see "Using Undo, Redo, and Repeat" on page 115.)

Table 5-2 Keyboard Shortcuts for Deleting Text

Action	Keyboard Shortcut
Delete one character to the left of the insertion point	Backspace
Delete one word to the left of the insertion point or selection	Ctrl+Backspace*
Delete the selection or one character to the right of the insertion point	Delete
Delete one word to the right of the insertion point	Ctrl+Delete*

* Does not work in Excel

To remove text using the mouse, select the text to delete, right-click, and choose Cut. Note that doing so moves the text to the Clipboard, enabling you to subsequently paste the text elsewhere. Unless you're using the Office Clipboard, the text you delete replaces the current Clipboard contents. The Backspace and Delete keys do not move text to the Clipboard. For details about Clipboard operations, see "Using the Clipboard with Office Programs" on page 129.

> **Note**
>
> One simple but powerful addition to the text-editing capabilities of Office 2010 programs is Paste Options. This enhancement to the basic cut, copy, and paste operations for moving or copying a selection provides a preview of the available paste formats. For details see "Using Paste Options" on page 130.

> **What About Speech Input?**
>
> Versions of Office earlier than Office 2007 included rudimentary speech recognition capabilities that you could use to dictate text and edit documents. This feature is no longer included in Office because speech recognition is now part of Windows. Windows 7 and Windows Vista both include speech recognition capabilities that use your spoken words to work with all programs—not just Office. You can use this feature to dictate text, to issue commands, to switch between applications (making it easier to bring in text from other programs), and to perform nearly any computer task without touching your keyboard or mouse.
>
> To learn about speech recognition capabilities in Windows 7, see *w7io.com/10501*. For information about speech recognition in Windows Vista, visit *w7io.com/10502*. If you use Office 2010 with Windows XP, you need to find a third-party program to enable speech recognition.

Chapter 5

Entering Symbols and Other Special Characters

Not all of the text characters you need to insert in a document are represented by a key on the keyboard. This is often the case for letters used in languages other than your own, math symbols, unusual punctuation marks, and many more situations. You can enter such characters in any of the following ways:

- **Insert Symbol**   On the Insert tab of any Office program, click Symbol.

- **AutoCorrect**   Type a character sequence associated with an AutoCorrect entry.

- **Character code**   If you know the ASCII character code or the Unicode character code, use a keyboard shortcut to convert those values to a character.

Each of these methods is described in detail next.

> **Note**
> Word offers additional ways to enter certain symbols with little or no effort, including inserting fraction characters and dashes, and lets you define your own shortcut keys for symbols you use often. For details, see "Inserting Special Characters" on page 200.

Entering Characters with Insert Symbol

A simple visual way to find and insert nonkeyboard characters is with Insert Symbol. Click the Insert tab, and then click Symbol. In Word, OneNote, and Outlook, a gallery of recently used symbols appears, as shown next.

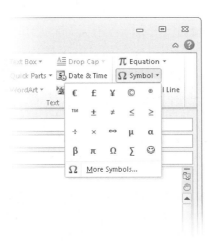

If the symbol you want is in the gallery, simply click it, and Office "types" it at the insertion point. If you need a different symbol, click More Symbols, which takes you to a Symbol dialog box similar to the one shown in Figure 5-1. (Clicking Symbol in Excel or PowerPoint takes you directly to this dialog box, bypassing the gallery view.)

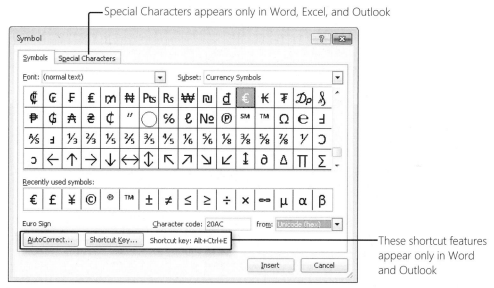

Figure 5-1 shown with the annotation "Special Characters appears only in Word, Excel, and Outlook" pointing to the Special Characters tab, and "These shortcut features appear only in Word and Outlook" pointing to the AutoCorrect and Shortcut Key buttons.

Figure 5-1 The Symbol dialog box from Word, shown here, includes some elements that are not available in all Office programs.

Hundreds of characters are available in the Symbol dialog box. Although you can scroll through the entire list, you can save some time by selecting a subset from the list in the upper right corner. In Word, Excel, and Outlook, the Special Characters tab offers a short list of symbols commonly used in typesetting applications, such as dashes, fixed-width spaces, and "curly" quotation marks.

Leaving Normal Text in the Font box inserts a character without any formatting; it inherits the formatting of the paragraph, word, or cell in which you insert the character. Select a font if you want the selected character to appear in a font that's different from the target area or if you need symbols from a special symbol font, such as Webdings or Wingdings.

Once you find the character you want, click to select it, and then click Insert. The dialog box remains open so that you can insert additional characters; click Close when you finish.

Chapter 5

Additional Symbol dialog box features in Word and Outlook make future entry of a particular character easier:

- **AutoCorrect**   To define an AutoCorrect string that Office automatically changes to the selected character whenever you type the string, click AutoCorrect. For more information, see the next section.

- **Shortcut Key**   If a shortcut key for the selected character has been defined, it appears near the bottom of the Symbol dialog box. Within a document you can press the shortcut key (or key sequence) to insert the character without visiting the Symbol dialog box. To define or change the shortcut key for the selected character, click Shortcut Key, which opens a dialog box like the one shown next.

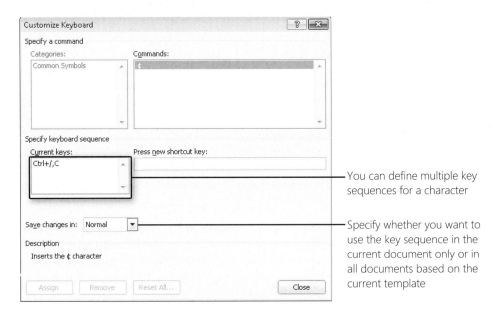

You can define multiple key sequences for a character

Specify whether you want to use the key sequence in the current document only or in all documents based on the current template

Entering Characters with AutoCorrect

AutoCorrect is a feature that automatically replaces a character sequence that you type with another sequence you specify. The replacement occurs as you type. The feature was initially introduced to Word as a tool for automatically correcting common typing errors, such as typing **teh** for "the." But it's also a convenient way to enter commonly used characters and symbols that would otherwise require a visit to the Symbol dialog box; you type a mnemonic character sequence, and Office automatically replaces it with a character.

Many common symbols already have AutoCorrect definitions. For example, typing **-->** changes to a right arrow symbol (➜) and typing **(tm)** changes to a trademark sign (™). From the Symbol dialog box in Word or Outlook, you can select a character and then click AutoCorrect to open an AutoCorrect dialog box in which you can specify the mnemonic sequence you want to use to invoke the selected character. With other Office applications, you get to the AutoCorrect dialog box by clicking File, Options, Proofing, AutoCorrect Options.

INSIDE OUT   See which keys are already assigned as symbol shortcuts in Word

If you open the Customize Keyboard dialog box from the Symbol dialog box, you can specify a shortcut key (or remove an existing shortcut key) only for the symbol that is selected when you click Shortcut Key. By taking a different path to this dialog box, you can review the shortcut keys assigned to many common symbols.

In Word (but not Outlook), click File to open Backstage view, and then click Options, Customize Ribbon. Click the Customize button (next to Keyboard Shortcuts). In the Categories list in the Customize Keyboard dialog box, scroll down and select Common Symbols. Then select items in the Common Symbols box to see the shortcut keys, if any, assigned to each symbol.

INSIDE OUT   Select the character before you open the AutoCorrect dialog box

When you get to the AutoCorrect dialog box to enter the mnemonic sequence in the Replace box, you also need to enter the character you want to insert in the With box. The easiest way to do that is to insert the symbol in your document (choosing Insert, Symbol, for example), select the symbol, and then open AutoCorrect. Doing it that way prepopulates the With box with the current selection.

While you have the AutoCorrect dialog box open, scroll through the list on the AutoCorrect tab to see which characters already have definitions.

For details about AutoCorrect, see "Entering Boilerplate and Other Oft-Used Text" on page 116.

Chapter 5

Entering Characters with Character Codes

You might've noticed the Character Code box in the Symbol dialog box. (See Figure 5-1.) Each character and symbol is identified by a unique numeric code called a *Unicode character code*. Each of the most common letters and symbols—essentially the ones that have been in every Western-language font since the dawn of the computer age—can alternatively be identified by its *ASCII character code*. (ASCII, which stands for American Standard Code for Information Interchange, is an older character-encoding system that uses a single byte to represent each character. That provides for a maximum of 256 characters, a limitation that led to the development of the Unicode system, which supports thousands of unique characters.)

Once you know the code for a character, you can use that knowledge to insert the character using the keyboard. Simply use the key combinations shown in Table 5-3.

Table 5-3 Key Combinations for Entering Symbols and Other Characters

Action	Keys	Notes
Insert a character using its ASCII character code	Alt+0 *code*	Hold down Alt as you type a zero followed by the code as a decimal value (up to three digits) on the numeric keypad.
Insert a character using its Unicode character code	*code*, Alt+X*	
Replace the character to the left of the insertion point with its Unicode character code	Alt+X*	Use this to learn a character's code without opening the Symbol dialog box.

* Does not work in Excel or PowerPoint

Inserting a Character: An Example

As you've seen in this section, Office offers several methods for entering symbols and characters. You'll undoubtedly use different methods depending on how often you use a particular character and which method you find easiest to use. For example, to enter a copyright symbol (©), you could use any of these techniques:

- Choose Insert, Symbol. Scroll until you find © on the Symbols tab, select it, and click Insert.

- Choose Insert, Symbol. Scroll until you find © on the Special Characters tab, select it, and click Insert.

- Type **(c)**. A predefined AutoCorrect entry changes this sequence to a copyright symbol.

- In Word or Outlook (but not Excel, OneNote, or PowerPoint), press **Ctrl+Alt+C**, the predefined shortcut key for the copyright symbol.

- Hold down the Alt key and, on the numeric keypad, type **0169**, the decimal ASCII character code for the copyright symbol.

- In Word, OneNote, or Outlook, type **a9** (the Unicode character code for the copyright symbol), and then press Alt+X.

Expert Text Editing Techniques

In the following sections, we describe some features that can make it faster and easier to produce letter-perfect text. Some, such as the undo and redo features, are used by practically everyone—but even those familiar features have some capabilities you might not be aware of. Other features, such as the ability to enter mathematical equations, are used by few people, but because they make quick work of complex tasks, they're good to know about for those rare occasions when you do need them.

Using Undo, Redo, and Repeat

As in most Windows-based programs, if you make an error in an Office program you can undo your last edit by pressing Ctrl+Z. (Table 5-4 shows the keyboard shortcuts for undo, redo, and repeat operations.) But Office goes further; while you work in an Office program, it retains a history of each edit you make. You can view this history by clicking the arrow next to the Undo button, a default resident of the Quick Access Toolbar, as shown next.

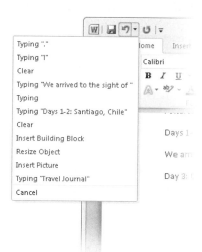

To undo one or more edits, click the earliest edit you want to undo. Office undoes that edit and all subsequent edits (you can't selectively undo a single edit except for the most recent one), reverting your document to the state it was in when you made that edit. If you go too far (or if you change your mind again), you can restore the undone edits by pressing Ctrl+Y or clicking the Redo button, which appears by default to the right of the Undo button on the Quick Access Toolbar.

If you don't have any undone edits, you can use the alternate function of the Redo button and keyboard shortcut: Repeat. The Repeat command performs the same edit again, but the edit is applied to the current selection or at the current location of the insertion point. For example, you could type a word, move the insertion point to a different place, and then press Ctrl+Y to type the word again. Similarly, you could format some selected text (italicize it, for example), select some different text, and click Repeat to italicize the new selection.

Table 5-4 **Keyboard Shortcuts for Undo, Redo, and Repeat**

Action	Keyboard Shortcut
Undo the last edit	Ctrl+Z
Redo or repeat an edit	Ctrl+Y*

* In Word, you can use F4 as an alternative for Ctrl+Y.

Entering Boilerplate and Other Oft-Used Text

Earlier in this chapter, we explained how to use AutoCorrect to insert a symbol or other character. AutoCorrect, of course, can handle more demanding tasks. One of these tasks is to replace a short mnemonic character sequence with a bigger chunk of text, such as boilerplate text for a proposal or contract, or even a commonly used phrase, such as "To whom it may concern:". Follow these steps to define an AutoCorrect entry:

1. Enter the text you want to be able to reuse, and then select it.

2. Click File and then, in Backstage view, click Options.

3. In Outlook (but not other Office 2010 programs), click Mail and then click Spelling And Autocorrect.

4. Click Proofing, and then click AutoCorrect Options to display a dialog box similar to the one shown in Figure 5-2.

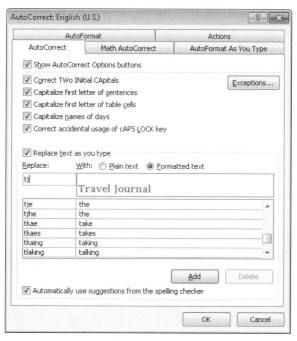

Figure 5-2 In Word (shown here) and Outlook, you can preserve formatting as part of the AutoCorrect entry.

5. In the Replace box, type the mnemonic text you want to use as an abbreviation for the full text.

6. If you're using Word or Outlook, select Plain Text or Formatted Text, depending on whether you want the text to inherit the formatting from the place where you use it or to always retain its current formatting.

7. Click Add.

While you're in the AutoCorrect dialog box, review the other options on the AutoCorrect tab; these options vary a bit between Office programs.

To use AutoCorrect in your document, simply type the mnemonic text you specified. The moment you follow that text with a space or punctuation mark, or you press Enter, Office replaces the mnemonic text with the full text.

If you then move the mouse pointer or the insertion point to someplace within or immediately after the corrected text, a small blue bar appears below the beginning of the inserted text. Click the bar or press Shift+Alt+F10 to display the AutoCorrect Options menu, shown next. There's always an option to undo the AutoCorrect action; other menu options vary depending on the type of replacement that's made.

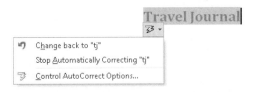

AutoCorrect entries that you create in Excel, OneNote, or PowerPoint are available in all Office programs. Plain text AutoCorrect entries that you make in Word or Outlook are also available in all programs, but formatted entries you make in Word are available only in Word, and formatted entries you make in Outlook are available only in Outlook.

INSIDE OUT   Copy your AutoCorrect entries to another computer or profile

Office saves unformatted AutoCorrect entries in AutoCorrect List files, which have an .acl file name extension. (The file name varies depending on the language you use.) To use your AutoCorrect entries on another computer (or to share them with another user on your computer), locate these files in the %AppData%\Microsoft\Office folder. (You can type the path in Windows Explorer exactly as shown here, and the %AppData% environment variable automatically expands to the full path. In Windows 7, that path is C:\Users*username*\AppData\Roaming\Microsoft\Office by default, but it might not be the same on your computer.) Copy the two .acl files to the comparable folder on another computer or in another user's profile.

Formatted AutoCorrect entries in Word are stored in the Normal.dotm template file, which is stored by default in %AppData%\Microsoft\Templates. You can copy this file to another computer or profile, but be aware that the template includes styles, macros, and other items. You can't extract and copy only the AutoCorrect entries, and if you copy the entire file, you also replace the styles and other items in the template file you overwrite.

Word and the message editor in Outlook offer another feature for inserting frequently used elements. Called AutoText, this feature provides additional capabilities for storing formatting, page breaks, graphics, and other elements as part of a building block. For details, see "Using Building Blocks" on page 330.

Entering Hyperlinks

On the web, everyone is familiar with *hyperlinks*—text or graphics that open another web page when you click them. But hyperlinks don't exist only on web pages, and they don't link only to other web pages. You can insert hyperlinks in any Office document, and the links' targets can be files or documents stored on your computer as well as web pages.

To insert a hyperlink, select the text or graphic you want to use as a clickable region. Then, on the Insert tab, click Hyperlink. Alternatively, use the keyboard shortcut for Insert Hyperlink, Ctrl+K. The Insert Hyperlink dialog box appears.

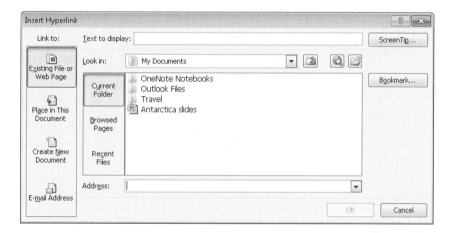

This small dialog box is packed with options and features. Start by making a selection under Link To:

- **Existing File Or Web Page**   Click to create a link to another document, file, or web page. Then, under Look In, click Current Folder (to link to a file on your computer), Browsed Pages (to link to a web page that you visited recently), or Recent Files (to link to a file you recently used).

  Alternatively, you can browse to a file location by using the Windows Explorer–like controls to the right of Look In, or you can browse to a web location by clicking the Browse Web button, which opens your web browser. When you find the page you want, switch back to the Insert Hyperlink dialog box without closing your browser; the page's URL appears in the Address box.

- **Place In This Document**   Click to link to a heading or bookmark (Word), cell (Excel), or slide (PowerPoint) in the current document.

- **Create New Document**   Click to create a new document and link to it.

- **E-Mail Address**   Click to create a hyperlink that opens a new, preaddressed message window in your default mail program.

The Insert Hyperlink dialog box includes other options you might want to customize:

- **Text To Display**   If you select text or graphics before you open the Insert Hyperlink dialog box, it appears here. Otherwise, Office suggests the text that forms the clickable link in your document; you can override that suggestion by typing your own text.

- **ScreenTip**   ScreenTip text appears when you hover the mouse pointer over the hyperlink in the document; you can use the ScreenTip to provide a description of the link destination or other assistive text.

- **Bookmark**   To specify a location within the targeted web page or document, click Bookmark and choose a heading, bookmark, cell, or slide.

- **Target Frame**   In Word, you can specify what kind of window the linked page or document will appear in.

To edit a hyperlink in a document, right-click it. The shortcut menu includes options to open, edit, or remove the hyperlink.

> **Note**
>
> In place of the Hyperlink command, OneNote has a Link command, which provides comparable capabilities. The dialog box is not at all like the Insert Hyperlink dialog box in other Office programs, however. For details about links in OneNote, see "Using Links for Quick Connections" on page 530.

Entering Mathematical Equations

Although Office cannot solve the world's complex mathematical problems, it can present them in an eye-pleasing fashion. Office includes a powerful equation editor that supports the use of symbols and layouts that'll make you look like a genius.

To insert an equation in your document, click the Insert tab. If you then click the arrow next to Equation, you'll see a gallery of common equations that you can use as is, or you can use them as a starting point for building an equation of your own. Click an equation from the gallery, or (in Word only) click More Equations From Office.com to see additional predefined options.

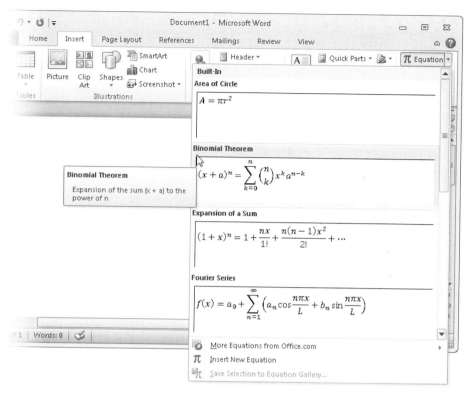

If you prefer to start with a clean slate, click Insert New Equation or, more simply, click directly on Equation on the Insert tab instead of clicking the arrow next to it.

When you have inserted an equation—using one from the equation gallery or by starting fresh—you can click anywhere within it to select the equation or a part of it. The ribbon then sprouts an Equation Tools tab, as shown in Figure 5-3.

The Tools group on the Equation Tools Design tab shown in Figure 5-3 has commands for inserting a new equation (it can be inserted within an existing equation or it can replace the existing equation, depending on the selection) and formatting it. Click the arrow button in the lower right corner of the Tools group to open the Equation Options dialog box.

Chapter 5

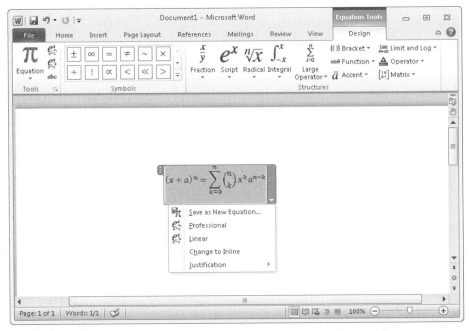

Figure 5-3 A shortcut menu for equations appears when you click the arrow to the right of the equation (Word only) or right-click the equation.

The Symbols group provides a gallery of math symbols to insert in your equation. Click the arrow below the scroll bar to expand the size of the symbols gallery; you can then click the title bar of the expanded gallery to switch to different subsets of symbols, as shown next.

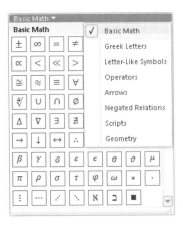

Lastly, the Structures group on the Equation Tools Design tab shown in Figure 5-3 provides galleries of components to insert in an equation, such as integrals, fractions, radicals, and so on.

INSIDE OUT   Use AutoCorrect in equations

You might've noticed the Math AutoCorrect tab in the AutoCorrect dialog box shown earlier in Figure 5-2. Math AutoCorrect provides similar functionality within a math region (the frame that encompasses an equation). Type a mnemonic character sequence, and Office automatically replaces it with the associated symbol or word. For example, type **\le**, and Office changes it to $\le$, the symbol for less than or equal to. You can review the predefined mnemonic sequences and add your own by opening AutoCorrect (for details about how to do this, see the steps in "Entering Boilerplate and Other Oft-Used Text" on page 116) and clicking Math AutoCorrect. Math AutoCorrect is not available in Excel.

Applying Text Formatting

One of the most essential feature sets for enhancing the appearance of your documents—the ability to format text—is also among the easiest to understand and implement. In short, you select the text you want to format and then choose one of several readily accessible tools for applying the format. Figure 5-4 shows how it's done.

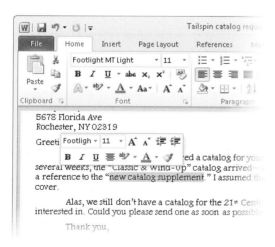

Figure 5-4 In all Office programs except Excel, a Mini toolbar appears above the selected text; point at it to keep it from fading away. To display the Mini toolbar in Excel, right-click the selection.

> **Note**
>
> As an alternative to applying formatting directly to selected text, *styles* provide a way to apply multiple attributes simultaneously. (They also make it easier to maintain a consistent look throughout your documents.) The style galleries appear in the Styles group on the Home tab in Word and Excel. For details about styles in Word, see "Giving Your Documents a Consistent Appearance" on page 224. For Excel, see "Formatting Cells and Ranges" on page 376.

Applying Character Formatting

After you select text (for details, see "Entering and Selecting Text" on page 107), you can apply formatting such as font (typeface), size, bold, italic, underline, highlighting, and text color by clicking options on the Mini toolbar that appears or in the Font group on the Home tab. (In OneNote, which has fewer text-formatting capabilities, look in the Basic Text group on the Home tab.) If you prefer to use the keyboard, Table 5-5 shows shortcuts for common formatting tasks.

Table 5-5 **Keyboard Shortcuts for Formatting**

Action	Keyboard Shortcut
Make text bold	Ctrl+B
Make text italic	Ctrl+I
Make text underlined	Ctrl+U
Decrease text size	Ctrl+Shift+<*
Increase text size	Ctrl+Shift+>*
Decrease text size by 1 point	Ctrl+[**
Increase text size by 1 point	Ctrl+]**
Remove character formatting	Ctrl+Spacebar**

  * Does not work in Excel

** Does not work in Excel or OneNote

INSIDE OUT Apply formatting to part of an Excel cell

In Excel, formats normally apply to all content in the selected cell. You can selectively format text within a cell by selecting the part you want to format in the formula bar.

Additional text formatting options are available in the Font dialog box, which you can open by clicking the Font dialog box launcher (the arrow in the lower right corner of the Font group on the Home tab) or by pressing its keyboard shortcut, Ctrl+Shift+F.

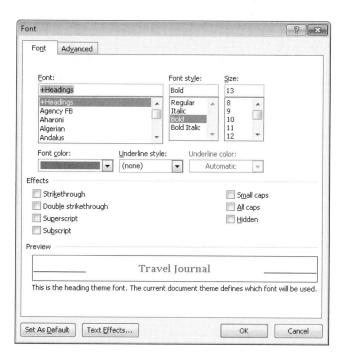

Not surprisingly, Word offers the most options for text formatting. For information about the advanced, Word-only features (such as ligatures and other features of OpenType typography), see "Applying Advanced Text-Formatting Capabilities" on page 307.

Applying Paragraph Formatting

To apply formats that control layout, such as alignment (left aligned, centered, indented, and so on) or line spacing, you use options in the Paragraph group on the Home tab. (Comparable functions are found in the Alignment group on the Home tab in Excel and in the Basic Text group in OneNote.) Commands for rotating text and for setting up bulleted lists or numbered lists are here too.

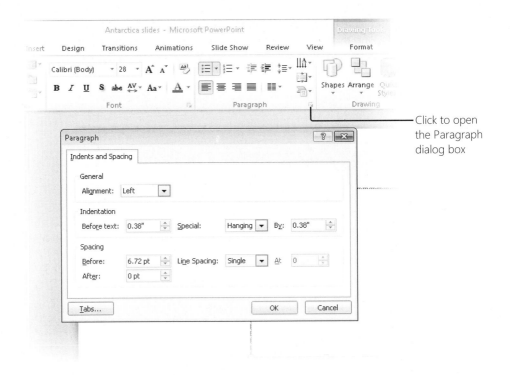

Click to open the Paragraph dialog box

Table 5-6 shows keyboard shortcuts for common paragraph alignment tasks. Note that none of these shortcuts work in Excel.

Table 5-6 Keyboard Shortcuts for Aligning Paragraph Text

Action	Keyboard Shortcut
Left align	Ctrl+L
Center	Ctrl+E*
Right align	Ctrl+R
Justify (align left and right)	Ctrl+J**
Increase left indent	Ctrl+M***
Decrease left indent	Ctrl+Shift+M***

   * Does not work in OneNote

 ** Does not work in OneNote or Outlook

*** Does not work in OneNote or PowerPoint

Using and Managing Fonts

Office shows a sample of each font when you open the Font list on the Home tab or the Mini toolbar, as shown in Figure 5-5.

Figure 5-5 Fonts in the current theme are grouped at the top of the fonts list.

Modern computers are likely to have scores of fonts installed, which makes for a long list to choose from when you want to specify a font. You can ease the selection process by focusing on the fonts at the top of the list, under the Theme Fonts heading. Among other elements, a *theme* incorporates a pair of fonts (one for headings and one for body text) that work well together.

To select theme fonts, open the Page Layout tab (in Word or Excel), Design tab (PowerPoint), or Options tab (Outlook). Then, in the Themes group, click Fonts. Select one of the existing themes or create your own.

The new theme fonts you select immediately apply to all text in your document except that which has had explicit nontheme formatting applied. For more information, see "Using Office Themes" on page 185.

> **Note**
>
> In Windows 7, Fonts in Control Panel has an option to hide a font. A font that's hidden does not appear in your programs' fonts list—except in Office programs. Office uses its own control for listing fonts. Whenever an Office program lists fonts, whether in the ribbon, the Mini toolbar, or the Font dialog box, the list includes all fonts installed on your system. If the long list of fonts annoys you, the only way to shorten the list is to delete from your system the fonts you don't use; to delete fonts, visit Fonts in Control Panel.

Copying Formatting

After you get one part of your document looking just the way you want it to, you'll often find it easy to copy its formatting to another place in your document (or in another Office document) instead of going through the formatting steps again. In Office programs, you can copy and paste formats with the Format Painter in much the same way that you copy and paste content with the Clipboard.

To copy text formatting, begin by placing the insertion point within the text that has the format you want to reuse. Then click Format Painter (in the Clipboard group on the Home tab).

To apply the formatting, click the text that you want to "paint." (If you want to apply the formatting to more than one word, drag across the text you want to reformat.)

The Format Painter ordinarily works only for the first click or drag after you click Format Painter. The mouse then returns to its normal function. If you want to copy formatting from one bit of text to several places, double-click the Format Painter button. The Format Painter then applies the format to each place you subsequently click, until you click Format Painter again or press Esc.

You can also copy formatting by using the keyboard. Position the insertion point or selection in the text with the format you want to copy, and then press Ctrl+Shift+C, the keyboard shortcut for copying formatting. To apply the copied formatting, position the insertion point or selection in the text you want to change, and then press Ctrl+Shift+V.

The formatting copied with Ctrl+Shift+C remains available for pasting until you copy a different format. It's not a one-shot deal (like the Format Painter), and although this feature works much like the Clipboard, the copied formatting is not displaced when you copy something to the Clipboard.

Using the Clipboard with Office Programs

The Clipboard—an intermediate storage location that facilitates copying and moving text and other objects—has been a part of Windows since the earliest days. It continues to work in Office programs the same way it works throughout Windows:

- To copy, you select the item to copy, use the Copy command (or its keyboard shortcut, Ctrl+C) to copy to the Clipboard, and then use the Paste command (or press Ctrl+V) to insert the item in a new location. (Table 5-7 shows Clipboard-related keyboard shortcuts.)

- To move, use the Cut command (or press Ctrl+X) to remove the item from your document and place it on the Clipboard, and then use the Paste command to insert the item elsewhere.

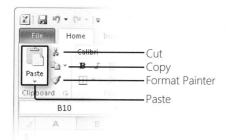

Table 5-7 Keyboard Shortcuts for Copying and Moving Text and Formatting

Action	Keyboard Shortcut
Copy the selection	Ctrl+C
Cut the selection	Ctrl+X
Paste the Clipboard contents	Ctrl+V
Display Paste Special dialog box to select format for pasted item	Ctrl+Alt+V
Copy formatting only	Ctrl+Shift+C
Paste formatting only	Ctrl+Shift+V

The Clipboard in Windows holds only a single item. When you copy or cut something to the Clipboard, it remains there until you copy or cut something else; the original content is then lost. By default, Office programs rely on the Windows Clipboard, but Office also includes the more capacious Office Clipboard. For details, see "Managing Multiple Clippings with the Office Clipboard" on page 133.

INSIDE OUT Move and copy without using the Clipboard

Word (and Outlook, which uses Word as its message editor) has some additional tricks that make it easy to copy or move selected text and graphics. These are one-time actions that do not affect the Clipboard, unlike normal copy, cut, and paste operations.

- To move the selected item, press F2, place the insertion point at the target location, and press Enter. This is comparable to the standard mouse technique of dragging the selection to a new place.

- To copy the selected item, press Shift+F2, place the insertion point at the target location, and press Enter. You can do the same thing with the mouse by holding the Shift key as you drag the selection to the new location.

You might find these shortcut keys easier to manage than the standard Ctrl key shortcuts. And because these methods don't use the Clipboard, the previous Clipboard contents remain in place, ready to be pasted again. Remember, however, that these techniques work only in Word and in Outlook messages.

For information about copying formats (rather than text or other content) from one part of a document to another, see the previous section, "Copying Formatting."

Using Paste Options

The designers of Office 2010 gathered data from countless people to see how they use Office, as a means of identifying areas for improvement. A surprising finding was that the most common action that users perform after pasting something from the Clipboard is to immediately choose Undo. For a variety of reasons, more often than not the paste operation produced results other than what the user wanted or expected. Office 2010 addresses this problem through the use of Paste Options, which uses Live Preview to show the paste results and lets you select other paste options without first using Undo.

To use Paste Options, select the document matter you want to replace with the Clipboard content or place the insertion point where you want the content to be inserted. Then do any of the following:

- On the Home tab, click the arrow below the Paste button (in the Clipboard group) to display Paste Options, as shown in Figure 5-6.

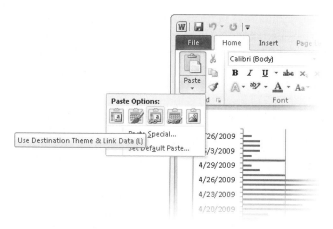

Figure 5-6 Available paste options depend on Clipboard content.

● Right-click the selection or where you want the content to be inserted. Paste Options similar to those shown in Figure 5-6 appear as part of the shortcut menu.

● Press Alt, H, V to display Paste Options.

Regardless of how you get there, as you hover over each of the options (or use the Left Arrow or Right Arrow key to move the highlight between options), Office displays the Clipboard content in the document exactly as it will appear when you complete the paste operation by clicking an option or pressing Enter. Options vary depending on the content on the Clipboard and the capabilities of the target location; the choices can be numerous, as you can see in the Excel example shown next.

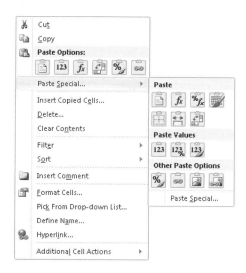

Options typically include Use Destination Theme and Use Destination Styles (options that paste text but pick up formatting from the destination document), Keep Source Formatting (an option that retains the formatting from the original copy location), and Keep Text Only (which pastes unformatted text, making this option essentially the same as typing the text).

After you paste—whether you use Paste Options or just press Ctrl+V—if you're not pleased with the result you have another chance to correct it. The Paste Options button appears near the end of your pasted text. Click it, press Ctrl, or press Alt+Shift+F10 to open the Paste Options menu with choices as before.

If the Paste Options button is in your way, press Esc to make it disappear.

Setting Default Paste Options

For each of several different paste scenarios, each Office program maintains a set of default actions for paste operations. The default action takes place if you simply click the Paste button or press Ctrl+V. You can specify the default actions for each program as follows:

- In Word, click the arrow below the Paste button on the Home tab, and click Set Default Paste.

- In Word, Excel, or PowerPoint, click File, Options. In the Options dialog box, click Advanced, and then scroll to the Cut, Copy, And Paste section.

- In OneNote, click File, Options. In the Options dialog box, click Advanced, and then scroll to the Editing section.

- In Outlook, click File, Options. In the Options dialog box, click Mail, and then scroll to the Other section.

Word, shown next, offers the most options for controlling paste behavior, but you'll find similar options for each Office program.

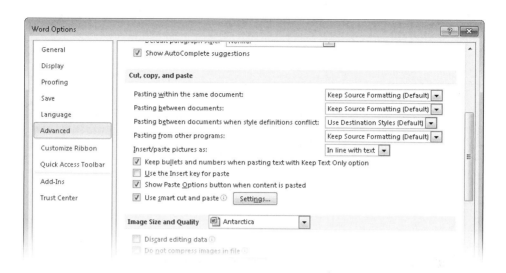

The Clipboard-related options for Word, in fact, are so numerous that some are tucked away in a dialog box that appears when you click Settings, as shown next.

Managing Multiple Clippings with the Office Clipboard

The Clipboard in Windows holds a single item. When you copy or cut something, the current Clipboard content is discarded and replaced with the new content. Office programs include the Office Clipboard, which can store up to 24 items that you copy or cut. You can select any of these 24 items and paste it into your document.

To enable the Office Clipboard, click the arrow in the lower right corner of the Clipboard group on the Home tab or press Alt, H, F, O to display the Clipboard task pane. Figure 5-7 shows the task pane after several items have been copied to it.

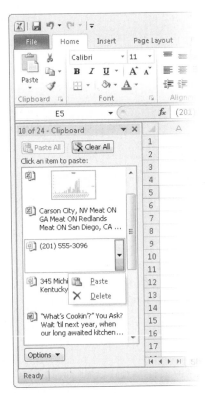

Figure 5-7 To paste an item from the Office Clipboard, click it. Alternatively, point to the item, click the arrow next to it, and click Paste.

By default, the Office Clipboard collects items you copy only while the Clipboard task pane is shown. (You can change this behavior with an options setting.) While your Office program is running and the task pane is open, it collects items you copy from any program—not just Office programs. After you copy or cut 24 items to the Office Clipboard, the oldest item is discarded. You can also delete individual items; as shown in Figure 5-7, click the item's menu arrow and then click Delete.

> **Note**
>
> Paste Options uses only the most recently added Clipboard content. Pasting any other item from the Office Clipboard uses the simple Paste command. (In most cases, that's equivalent to selecting Keep Source Formatting in Paste Options.)
>
> If that doesn't produce the result you want, simply press the Ctrl key or click the Mini toolbar that appears after you paste. Paste Options then appears, and you can try different options with Live Preview to correct the problem.

You can modify how the Office Clipboard works with a few settings, which you access by clicking Options at the bottom of the Clipboard task pane.

If you select Show Office Clipboard Icon On Taskbar (the default setting), an icon appears in the Windows notification area—but only when an Office 2010 program is running. The taskbar icon provides easy access to Office Clipboard controls.

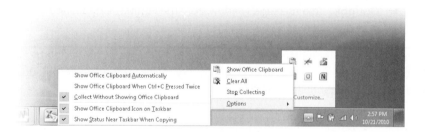

> **Note**
>
> The Office Clipboard retains all the clipped items between Office sessions, but these items are accessible (and new items are added) only when an Office program is running. In addition, the Clipboard task pane must be open in at least one Office program or the Collect Without Showing Office Clipboard option must be selected.

Finding and Replacing Text and Formatting

Searching for text in a document is a basic function of all Office programs, whether you're trying to locate a particular passage in a lengthy report or you need to find all occurrences of a newly obsolete product name. All Office programs have the ability to quickly find text. A related feature allows you to replace occurrences of one text string with another, either en masse or one at a time as you review each occurrence.

The implementation of the Find command in each Office program is slightly different:

- **Word**   Press Ctrl+F or, in the Editing group on the Home tab, click Find, which opens the Search tab in the Navigation pane. (If you prefer to use the traditional Find dialog box, click the arrow next to Find and choose Advanced Find.)

- **Excel**   Press Ctrl+F or, in the Editing group on the Home tab, click Find & Select, Find.

- **OneNote**   Press Ctrl+E or click in the search box. (To limit your search to the current page, press Ctrl+F.)

- **PowerPoint**   Press Ctrl+F or, in the Editing group on the Home tab, click Find.

- **Outlook**   In a message window, click the Format Text tab, and then, in the Editing group, click Find.

In each case, your initial search options are fairly simple, as suggested by the Find dialog box from PowerPoint shown in Figure 5-8. Type the text you want to find, specify any search options, and click Find Next.

Figure 5-8 To search again for a term you previously used, click the arrow in the Find What box.

The Find dialog box remains open until you click Close, so you can click Find Next repeatedly to search through your entire document. Even with the dialog box open, you can continue to work in your document—something you can't do with many other dialog boxes in Office programs. If the Find dialog box gets in your way, close it. You can continue your search without it; simply press Shift+F4 to repeat the last search.

To find text and replace it with different text, the process is similar: Press Ctrl+H or, in the Editing group (on the Home tab in Word, Excel, and PowerPoint; on the Format Text tab in Outlook), click Replace. (In Excel, you click Find & Select, Replace.) The dialog box that appears is similar to the one shown in Figure 5-8, with a few additions, as shown in the following example from Word.

Click Find Next to locate the next occurrence of your search text. Then click Replace to replace that occurrence, or click Find Next to skip to the next one without making a change. If you're certain that you want to change all occurrences, click Replace All, which quickly does the deed with no further review. (Remember that, as with all edits, you can use Undo if you take this action in error.)

Table 5-8 shows the keyboard shortcuts for finding and replacing text.

Table 5-8 **Keyboard Shortcuts for Finding and Replacing Text**

Action	Keyboard Shortcut
Open the Find tool	Ctrl+F
Repeat find	Shift+F4
Find and replace text and formatting	Ctrl+H

Word (Figure 5-9) and Excel (Figure 5-10) also have the ability to search for text that's formatted a certain way and to (optionally) replace that formatting with new formatting. For details about the additional find and replace features in Word, see "Searching Within a Document" on page 210. For more information about similar capabilities in Excel, see "Finding, Editing, Moving, and Copying Data" on page 465.

Figure 5-9 Word has additional options for searching and replacing text that are exposed when you click More. The Format button leads to options for finding and replacing text formats.

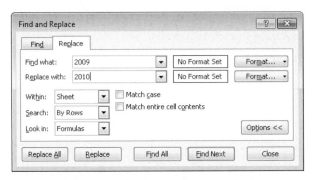

Figure 5-10 In Excel, click Options to customize how searches operate and to search for formatting information.

Checking Spelling

While the appearance of your document is important, spelling errors can make your document (and you) look bad no matter how attractive it is in other ways. To avoid such errors, each Office program includes a feature to check the spelling of each word in a document. You can use this feature to check the spelling of individual words, or you can check the entire document, perhaps as part of your final review.

Correcting a Single Word

By default, in Word, OneNote, PowerPoint, and Outlook (but not Excel), the spelling checker works as you type to identify words that might be misspelled. Office programs indicate potential spelling errors with a squiggly red underline. You don't need to act on it right away; the underline remains in place until you fix the error or tell Office to ignore it. (Don't worry; the red underlines don't appear when you print your documents.)

To review a word that has a squiggly red underline, right-click the word. At the top of the shortcut menu, Office offers its best guesses at what you meant to type, as shown in Figure 5-11.

Figure 5-11 Spelling suggestions and options appear at the top of the shortcut menu when you right-click a word that has a squiggly red underline.

To replace the misspelled word, simply click the correct word from the choices presented. If the correct choice doesn't appear, you have several other options. Although the options vary a bit from one Office program to another, they include the following:

- **Ignore** If the word is correct as typed, click Ignore. Office removes the underline and won't mark this word again, although it will mark other instances of the word.

- **Ignore All** Choose this option, and Office deems correct all occurrences of the word in this document. In this situation, however, you might prefer to choose the next option.

- **Add To Dictionary** Office adds the word you typed to its spelling dictionary, which means it won't be marked as wrong in this document or any other. Be sure you're right before you choose this option. (You can edit the dictionary if necessary. For details, see "Using Custom Dictionaries" on page 142.)

- **AutoCorrect** Choose this option when you've made a typographical error (such as transposing two letters) that you're likely to make again. The submenu that appears repeats the list at the top of the menu; select one of those words, and thereafter any time you make the same typographical error, Office immediately corrects it. If the correct word is not in the list, choose AutoCorrect Options from the submenu. This opens the AutoCorrect Options dialog box (shown earlier in Figure 5-2), in which you can type the word you want to appear each time you type the word you mistakenly typed.

- **Language** In Office programs other than Excel, you can specify the language used in your document. And in Word, PowerPoint, and Outlook, you can specify the language for specific parts of a document. (You might use a foreign word or phrase in your text, for example, or you might include an entire section of text that is translated into another language.) Choose this option to specify the language of the flagged word if it's not the same as the default language for the document. Office then uses the spelling dictionary for that language to check this word. (For more information, see "Setting Language and Regional Options" on page 145.)

- **Spelling** Choose this option to open the interactive Spelling dialog box, which we describe later in this chapter.

- **Look Up** This Word-only option provides a link to an online dictionary as well as other references.

Correcting Spelling Throughout a Document

To review spelling throughout your document, click the Review tab. In the Proofing group (Spelling in OneNote), click Spelling (Spelling & Grammar in Word and Outlook). Or, more simply, press F7. Office begins scanning your document from the beginning, and when the first error is found, a dialog box similar to the one shown in Figure 5-12 appears.

Figure 5-12 Office shows the misspelled word in context, highlighted in a bold red font.

Here you'll see options similar to those on the shortcut menu shown earlier in Figure 5-11: Ignore Once (same as Ignore), Ignore All, Add To Dictionary, and AutoCorrect. To make a correction, select a replacement in the Suggestions box and click Change (or click Change All to correct all occurrences in the document). If the correct word doesn't appear in the Suggestions box, type the correction directly in the Not In Dictionary box, and then click Change. Office then resumes its search for the next misspelled word.

As part of its spelling review, Word also checks the grammar in your document. For information about the additional options for checking spelling in Word, see "Checking Grammar and Spelling" on page 242.

Setting Options for Spelling Correction

You might find that Office is too aggressive in finding errors in the type of documents you produce or that it misses some errors. You can set options to control how the spelling checker works. To do so, in the dialog box shown in Figure 5-12, click Options. Alternatively, in any Office program, click File to open Backstage view, click Options, and then click Proofing. A dialog box like the one shown in Figure 5-13 appears.

Chapter 5

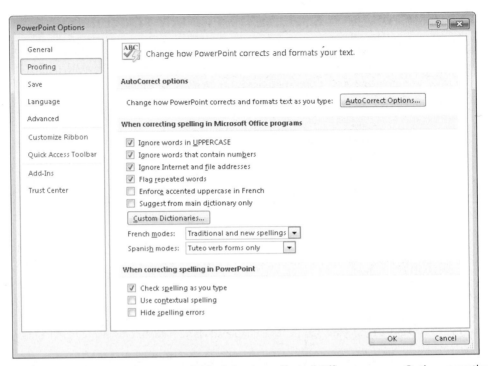

Figure 5-13 Options in the center of this dialog box affect all Office programs. Options near the bottom affect only the program in which you open this dialog box.

Using Custom Dictionaries

The standard dictionary included with Office includes hundreds of thousands of standard words, plus proper names for many common companies, products, and people. But your documents undoubtedly include words that are correctly spelled but not included in the standard dictionary. These words might include specialized terms used in your business (medical terms, for example) or uncommon proper names (Bott and Siechert come to mind).

For these terms, Office uses custom dictionaries. Some custom dictionaries, such as for industry-specific terms, are available from third-party suppliers. But you can also build your own. In fact, when you choose Add To Dictionary during a spelling review, you're adding the word to a custom dictionary, not to the standard dictionary for your language.

To work with custom dictionaries, open the Options dialog box and click Proofing, as shown in Figure 5-13. Then click Custom Dictionaries to open the dialog box shown next.

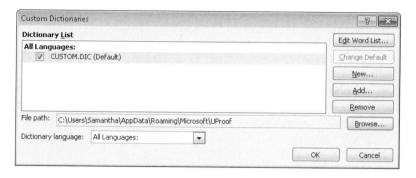

Click New to create a new dictionary file, or click Add to add another existing dictionary file to the list. (You can use multiple custom dictionaries.) A dictionary file is a plain-text file with each word on its own line. It should have a .dic file name extension, although that's not required. By default, dictionary files are stored in %AppData%\Microsoft\UProof (C:\Users*username*\AppData\Roaming\Microsoft\UProof on a Windows 7 system with default configuration), but you can store them in any folder.

To assign a language to a dictionary, select the dictionary name and then make a selection in the Dictionary Language list. If you specify a language, Office uses the dictionary only when checking words that are tagged as being in that language.

To view or modify the words in a custom dictionary, select the dictionary name and then click Edit Word List. This leads to a dialog box similar to the one shown next.

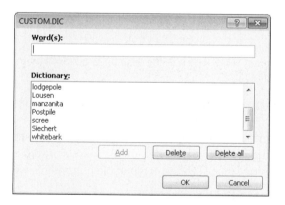

To enter a new word, type it in the Word(s) box and click Add. To delete a word from the dictionary, select it and click Delete.

Chapter 5

Using the Thesaurus and Other References

If you're unable to come up with the perfect word, the thesaurus might help. To use the thesaurus in an Office program, select the word you want to look up, and then press Shift+F7. Alternatively, in the Proofing group on the Review tab, click Thesaurus. (Although this option doesn't appear on the ribbon in OneNote, the Shift+F7 keyboard shortcut works.) Office then opens the Research task pane, shown in Figure 5-14.

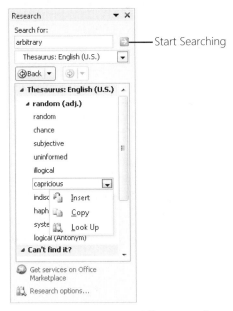

Figure 5-14 To look up a different word, type it in the Search For box, and then press Enter or click the green Start Searching button.

If the thesaurus offers a word that's better than your original, point to it, click the arrow next to it, and choose Insert. The word replaces your original typing. If the suggested word is close but not quite what you're looking for, click it; Office then looks up that word in the thesaurus. Perhaps the first suggestions were better; the Back and Forward buttons let you step through your lookup history, much like the comparable buttons in a web browser.

Click the arrow next to the name of the current reference book (Thesaurus: English (U.S.) in Figure 5-14) to see the names of other available references. These can include dictionaries, thesauruses for other languages, sites with financial and company data, and general reference sites. To add or remove items from this list and to search for additional services, at the bottom of the Research task pane, click Research Options.

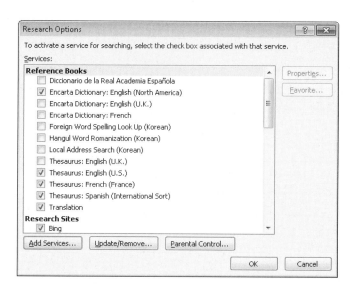

Setting Language and Regional Options

As mentioned earlier in this chapter, each Office document has a language assigned to it, and Office uses that designation to determine which dictionaries to use for checking spelling and grammar, which reference books to use, and which language to use as the source when translating documents to another language. Language settings also affect sort order and regional options such as date format and page size. (These systemwide options are set in the Region And Language dialog box in Control Panel.)

To set the default language used by new documents you create and to set other options related to language, in the Language group on the Review tab, click Language, Language Preferences. (This option doesn't appear on the ribbon in Excel, but you can get to the same place by clicking File, Options, Language.)

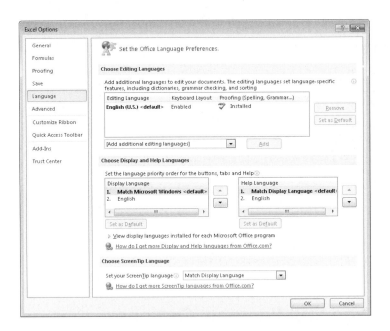

If you plan to work in a language that doesn't appear in the Editing Language list, select it from the drop-down list immediately below, and then click Add. If the keyboard layout and proofing dictionaries for the new language are not yet configured, links in those columns lead to more information.

Note that you can also specify the language for the user interface in Office, for Help text, and for ScreenTips. Not all languages are included in each Office edition, however.

To set the proofing language for selected text within a document, in the Language group on the Review tab, click Language, Set Proofing Language. In the dialog box that appears, select the language.

Translating Text to Another Language

Office includes several tools for language translation. Bear in mind that this is strictly computer translation, and the results are unlikely to be as good as that done by a native-speaking human translator. However, it can be useful for rough translation. Office programs offer two translation tools: one that works in the Research task pane and a Mini Translator that pops up in a document window.

To use the first method on selected text, in the Language group on the Review tab, click Translate, Translate Selected Text. The Research task pane opens, where you can select a target language, as shown next. Click Insert to replace the selection, or scroll down for additional options.

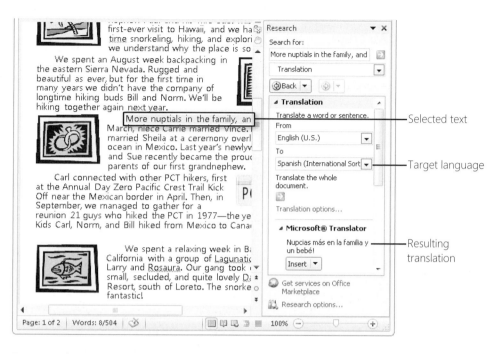

Selected text

Target language

Resulting translation

To set up the Mini Translator (not available in Excel), on the Review tab click Translate, Mini Translator. After you select a language, you simply point at a word or selected text, and the Mini Translator appears in a Mini toolbar, as shown next. (Like the formatting Mini toolbar, it fades away unless you point at it.)

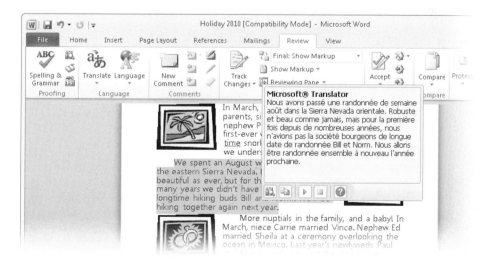

CAUTION

Be aware that the Mini Translator works only when you have an active Internet connection, and it sends your text over the Internet in unencrypted format.

You can use the translated text in your document by clicking the Copy button, which places the translation on the Clipboard. Alternatively, click the Expand button to display the text in the Research task pane, where you can use the Insert button to replace the selected text with the translated version.

To stop using the Mini Translator, click Translate, Mini Translator again to turn it off.

Working with Graphics and Pictures

Working with Drawing Layers in Office
Documents 150
Inserting Pictures into Office Documents 162
Making Your Pictures Look Great. 163
Finding and Using Clip Art 172
Capturing and Inserting Screenshots 174

Adding Shapes and Text Boxes. 175
Displaying Data Graphically with Charts 179
Adding SmartArt to Documents 180
Applying Text Effects with WordArt 182
Drawing with Ink 183
Using Office Themes 185

E FFECTIVE communication of ideas often requires much more than verbal skills. With Office 2010, you can easily add pictures and other types of graphics that make your documents more visually appealing while at the same time supplanting the proverbial thousand words.

We begin our exploration of the picture-handling capabilities of Office, naturally, with a picture. Figure 6-1 shows the Insert tab on the ribbon in PowerPoint. The Insert tabs in Word, Excel, and Outlook (and, to a lesser degree, OneNote) are quite similar, and this tab is the starting point in each program for adding graphics and pictures to a document.

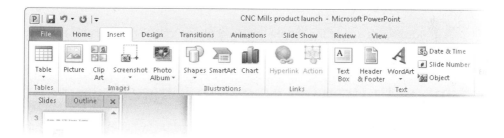

Figure 6-1 The Insert tab for each Office program has a few program-specific options (such as Photo Album in this example from PowerPoint), but most options are found in all Office programs.

In this chapter, we describe how to insert and modify each of the following types of graphical objects:

- **Picture** This option includes photographs, of course, but can also be used to insert a file saved in any of numerous picture file formats. (See "Inserting Pictures into Office Documents" on page 162.)

- **Clip Art**   Clip art comprises photographs, illustrations, and even audio and video clips that are typically offered as part of a library of stock files from which you can choose. (See "Finding and Using Clip Art" on page 172.)

- **Screenshot**   This option captures any open window (even those that are covered by other windows) or part of your screen and inserts it in your document. (See "Capturing and Inserting Screenshots" on page 174.)

- **Shapes**   This option provides line illustrations in a wide variety of shapes that you can further customize. (See "Adding Shapes and Text Boxes" on page 175.)

- **SmartArt**   SmartArt is a collection of templates for drawings, diagrams, flow charts, organizational charts, and so on. (See "Adding SmartArt to Documents" on page 180.)

- **Chart**   Office supports a large number of ways to display numeric data as an image for easier interpretation and analysis. (See "Displaying Data Graphically with Charts" on page 179.)

- **Text Box**   As you would expect, a text box holds text, which gives you greater flexibility in placement and formatting vis-à-vis surrounding text. (See "Adding Shapes and Text Boxes" on page 175.)

- **WordArt**   WordArt provides a number of effects (such as skewing, stretching, rotating, shading, coloring, and distorting) that can be applied to text for use in logos, titles, and similar display purposes. (See "Applying Text Effects with WordArt" on page 182.)

Toward the end of the chapter we describe two other ways to apply art, colors, and shapes to your documents: ink (drawn with a stylus) and Office themes.

Working with Drawing Layers in Office Documents

Before we dive into the specifics of inserting pictures, shapes, SmartArt, and other graphical elements, it helps to understand how Office manages those objects. In this section, we explain the concept of layers in Office documents, how to select graphical elements, and how to manipulate those graphics in ways that are common to all Office programs.

Although the finished product from Office is two-dimensional—whether it's printed on a sheet of paper or displayed on a flat-screen monitor—a graphics-laden document has a layer for each graphic, arranged in a virtual three-dimensional stack. It's as though you took a blank sheet of paper, wrote some text on it, and then started laying printed photographs and graphics clipped from a magazine atop the sheet. You'd soon have a stack of clippings, with some obscuring part or all of the ones behind them.

In Word and Outlook you can, in effect, peel the text off the page and lay it in front of the stack of graphics. PowerPoint can also place a slide's text in front of the stacked graphics, but the implementation is slightly different; in PowerPoint, slide text (with a transparent background) is itself stored in a placeholder (a type of graphics container), so placing the text in front of other graphics is simply a matter of bringing that layer to the front. Graphics in Excel always remain in front of text and numbers in cells, so you need to be sure that you move your graphics to a place where they don't cover important data.

Selecting Graphics and Pictures

To work with a graphic or picture after it is placed in a document—whether you want to move it, resize it, adjust its colors, or whatever—you must select it. The simplest way to select an object is to click it. A selected object is shown with a frame, as you can see in Figure 6-2.

Figure 6-2 A selected picture or graphic has a frame with handles.

Selecting Text Boxes and WordArt

When you click a text box or a WordArt object, the frame initially appears as a dashed line, as shown in Figure 6-3. With the frame in this state, you'll also notice the appearance of an insertion point or a text selection, for this is the way you edit the text in such objects. To work with the object itself rather than the text it contains, move the mouse pointer to the dashed line, where it changes to a four-headed arrow, and click. The insertion point or text selection disappears, and the frame becomes a solid line. To return to text editing, click the text inside the frame. Alternatively, once an object is selected, you can toggle between text selection and object selection by pressing Enter and Esc. Table 6-1 shows other keyboard shortcuts for selecting objects.

Figure 6-3 To select a text object with a dashed frame, point to the frame and click.

Table 6-1 Keyboard Shortcuts for Selecting Graphics and Pictures

Action	Keyboard Shortcut
Select an object when another object is selected	Tab or Shift+Tab
Select all objects	Ctrl+A
Open the Selection And Visibility pane	Alt+F10
Selecting Text in WordArt and Text Boxes	
Select an object when text in the object is selected	Esc
Select text when the object is selected	Enter

Working with Multiple Graphics and Pictures

Selecting objects becomes more complicated when your document contains several objects, especially if they are stacked one in front of another. When objects are stacked, clicking selects only the front-most one. If objects further back are not completely covered, you can click an uncovered part to select that object. Alternatively, after you select an object, you can press Tab to cycle the selection through the objects back to front (or Shift+Tab to cycle from front to back).

A complex document with many graphics and pictures becomes much easier to manage when you use the Selection And Visibility pane (see Figure 6-4), which you can display in any of the following ways:

- On the Home tab, in the Editing group, click Select, Selection Pane.

- If an object is already selected, under Picture Tools or Drawing Tools, click the Format tab. Then, in the Arrange group, click Selection Pane.

- Press Alt+F10.

The Selection And Visibility pane lists all objects on the current page, worksheet, or slide. To select an object, simply click its name.

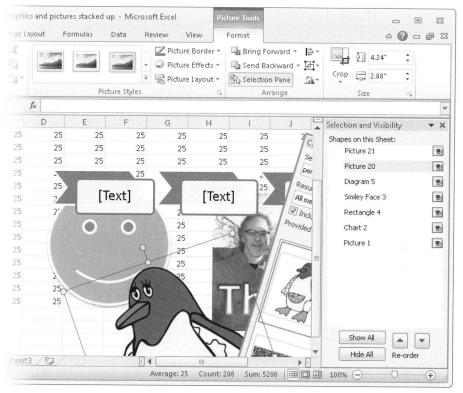

Figure 6-4 The Selection And Visibility pane, shown on the right side of this cluttered screen, lets you select individual objects—no matter how deeply they're buried.

The default object names aren't particularly helpful in determining which object is which, so in a document with many objects that you manipulate often, you might want to take the time to give each object a more meaningful name. To do so, click the object name, click it a second time to enter edit mode, and then type the new name.

The Selection And Visibility pane has another handy trick: the ability to hide objects. Click the icon to the right of an object's name to hide it or to make it visible again. (Note that objects in Word with Wrap Text set to In Line With Text can't be hidden.)

To select multiple objects, hold Ctrl as you click each one. This works whether you click the objects directly or click their names in the Selection And Visibility pane.

Positioning Objects

To move a selected object (or multiple selected objects), move the mouse pointer over the object until it becomes a four-headed arrow, and then drag. (For some types of objects, such as SmartArt, WordArt, or text boxes, you must point at the object's border frame. For other objects, you can point to any part of the object.)

> **Note**
>
> Word and Outlook support a positioning style called In Line With Text, which is not available in Excel or PowerPoint. Inline objects move as part of the text flow, and therefore can't be moved by dragging or using the Layout dialog box, described next. To position an object using these features, you must first select a different text wrapping style by right-clicking the object and choosing Wrap Text.

For more precise positioning, right-click the object and choose Size And Position (Word, PowerPoint, and Outlook) or Size And Properties (Excel). Then:

- In Word or Outlook, the Layout dialog box appears. Click the Position tab, where you'll find options for aligning the object with margins and other page landmarks as well as for specifying a precise location on a page. For details, see "Adding Pictures and Graphics" on page 237.

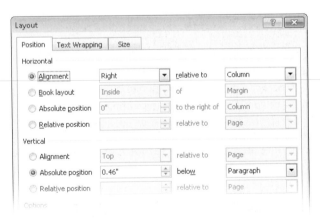

- In PowerPoint, the Format Shape dialog box appears. In the left pane, click Position, whereupon you'll see options for specifying the position relative to the upper left corner or center of the slide. For more information, see "Adding Graphics and Video Clips" on page 601.

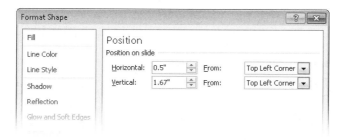

- In Excel, the Format Shape dialog box appears. In the left pane, click Properties. Although you can't enter dimensions to identify a precise location, options here allow you to specify whether and how an object's position and size change when you change the width and height of underlying cells.

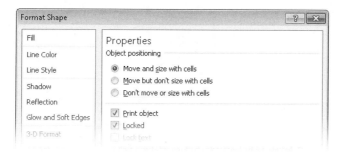

Aligning and Evenly Distributing Objects

In many cases, you won't want to fiddle with precise positioning of individual elements. Instead, you want to quickly align one or more objects, or you want to evenly space several objects on a page or slide. Office offers a quick path to each goal. To find that path, select the object (or objects); then, under Picture Tools, Drawing Tools, Chart Tools, or SmartArt Tools, click the Format tab. In the Arrange group, click Align to display an array of options, as shown in Figure 6-5.

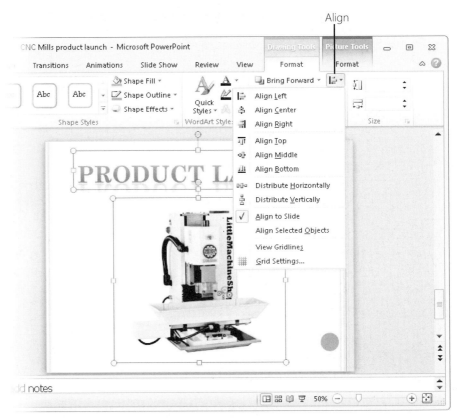

Figure 6-5 Regardless of how carelessly you place objects, you can whip them back into this arrangement with just two steps: click Align Center (to center each object horizontally) and click Distribute Vertically (to evenly space each object vertically).

Changing the Z-Order of Stacked Objects

As we explained earlier in this chapter, graphics and pictures are layered one in front of another in a virtual stack. You'll sometimes need to change the order so that one object doesn't improperly obscure another. For example, if you place a caption for a picture in a text box, you'll want the text box to be in front of the picture.

To move an object forward or back in the stack, select the object and, under Picture Tools, Drawing Tools, Chart Tools, or SmartArt Tools, click the Format tab. In the Arrange group, click either Bring Forward or Send Backward, which moves the object forward or backward one position in the stack. (Clicking the arrow next to these buttons exposes an additional command that moves the object all the way to the front or back of the stack.)

Alternatively, you can move items within the stack by using the Selection And Visibility pane, shown earlier in Figure 6-4. Select the item to move, and then click a Re-Order arrow to move the item up (toward the front of the stack) or down (toward the back) in the list of shapes.

Resizing and Rotating Graphics and Pictures

The techniques for changing the size or the orientation of pictures are similar to those for positioning objects. You can directly manipulate objects by clicking and dragging, or for more precise control, you can enter specific values in a dialog box.

To resize an object using the mouse, select the object and then drag one of the sizing handles (shown earlier in Figure 6-2). Your results might not match your expectations unless you use these techniques:

- To maintain the object's aspect ratio, use one of the corner sizing handles and hold down the Shift key as you drag. (For pictures, it's not necessary to hold Shift to maintain the aspect ratio. But it doesn't hurt, and that way you can use a consistent technique for all object types.)

- To keep an object centered in the same location as you change its size, hold down Ctrl as you drag.

- To maintain the aspect ratio and the center location, hold Ctrl and Shift as you drag.

To resize using the keyboard, select the object and then hold Shift as you press an arrow key. Hold Ctrl+Shift to enlarge or reduce in smaller increments.

You can achieve greater precision when you resize by entering dimensions in the Size group on the Format tab or in a dialog box. Right-click the object, and choose Size And Position (Word, PowerPoint, and Outlook) or Size And Properties (Excel). In the resulting dialog box, you can specify the dimensions or enter a scaling factor, which calculates the size as a percentage of the object's current size or original size. Figure 6-6 shows the Format Shape dialog box in PowerPoint; you'll find similar options in the other Office programs.

You'll sometimes want to rotate graphics and pictures in a document. This might be required because your camera doesn't automatically rotate pictures when you shoot in portrait orientation. Or you might want to tilt an item slightly as an artistic effect.

Chapter 6

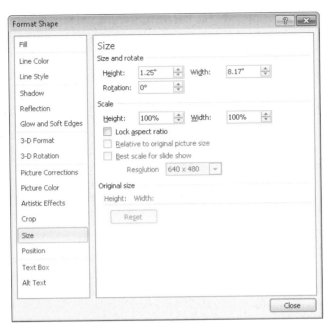

Figure 6-6 As you change the height and width, the scaling values change to match—and vice versa.

To rotate a graphic or picture with the mouse, select it and then point to the rotate handle (shown earlier in Figure 6-2). Drag in either direction around the center of the object, and it rotates in that direction.

You'll find that the image "snaps" into position at each 90-degree mark when you rotate it using the mouse. If your intent is to rotate an image 90 degrees, an easier method is to use the Rotate tool, which is in the Arrange group on the Format tab (under Picture Tools or Drawing Tools).

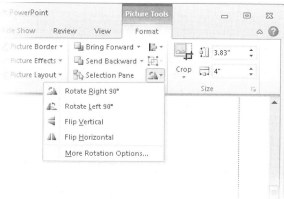

Rotate the selected object with the keyboard by holding the Alt key as you press the Left Arrow (for counterclockwise rotation) or Right Arrow key. Each keypress rotates the object 15 degrees. Press Ctrl+Alt with an arrow key to rotate 1 degree at a time.

The last command on the Rotate menu, More Rotation Options, opens the Layout dialog box (Word) or Format Shape dialog box (shown earlier in Figure 6-6), where you can specify a rotation angle with one-degree precision.

INSIDE OUT   Use the Mini toolbar

When you right-click an object, a Mini toolbar that includes the most commonly used tools on the Format tab appears.

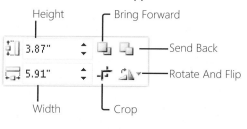

Office also supports three-dimensional rotation of graphics and pictures. For more information, see "Adding Shapes and Text Boxes" on page 175 and "Applying Picture Styles" on page 167.

INSIDE OUT   Specify dimensions using your preferred unit of measure

By default, Office displays measurements using the units associated with your computer's Region And Language settings, which turns out to be inches in the United States and millimeters in other countries. Nevertheless, in any Office dialog box, you can enter dimensions using any of the following units:

- Inches: in or "

- Centimeters: cm

- Millimeters: mm

- Points (a printer's measurement equal to 1/72 inch): pt

- Picas (a printer's measurement equal to 12 points, or 1/6 inch): pi

- Pixels (normally 1/96 inch; dots per inch [dpi] can be changed in Control Panel): px

To use one of these units, type the numeric value followed by one of the abbreviations in the list above. (If you don't specify the unit, Office assumes you're using the default unit.) As soon as you move to a different field in the dialog box, Office converts the dimension you entered to the default unit.

To change the default unit of measure in Word, Excel, or OneNote, click File, Options. In the Options dialog box, click Advanced, and then scroll to Display (Other in OneNote). Under that heading, you'll find the list of available units of measure. Note that your setting in one Office program doesn't affect the other programs. If you want to change the default setting for all programs (not just Office), visit Region And Language in Control Panel.

Grouping Objects

When you have several related objects properly positioned in relation to each other, you'll want to group them. Doing so makes it easier to move or manipulate all the component objects as one, and it prevents inadvertently modifying part of the graphic or picture.

A simple example of the benefit of grouping is a logo that comprises two objects: a design saved as a picture and a slogan in a text box. After resizing and moving the objects individually until they're in proper position, select them both. Then, on the Format tab, click the Group button (see Figure 6-7), and then click Group.

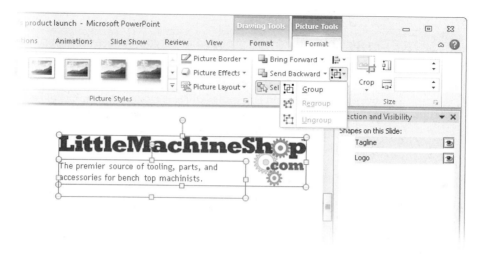

Figure 6-7 Choosing Group causes the selected objects to be combined into a single object, as shown in Figure 6-8.

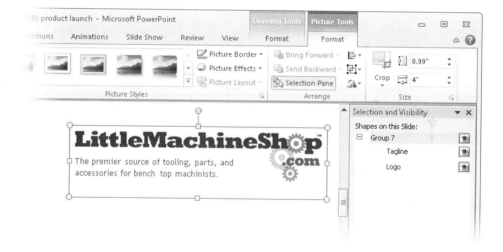

Figure 6-8 After grouping, the grouped objects share a single selection frame. Note that the Selection And Visibility pane shows the objects within the group.

TROUBLESHOOTING

Grouped objects remain grouped after you choose Ungroup

After you choose the Ungroup command, it might appear that the objects remain grouped. For example, if you drag one of the formerly grouped objects, all objects move together. The problem is that Office leaves all objects selected after you choose Ungroup. The solution is simple: Click outside any of the grouped objects, which clears the selection. You can then select individual objects.

Inserting Pictures into Office Documents

In the context of Office, "picture" refers to much more than photographs. Regardless of composition, a picture is a file in any of many popular graphics formats, including JPEG, Portable Network Graphics (.png), Graphics Interchange Format (.gif), Windows Bitmap (.bmp), Windows Metafile (.wmf), and Encapsulated PostScript (.eps).

To insert a picture, click the Insert tab, and in the Illustrations group (Images in PowerPoint), click Picture. The Insert Picture dialog box appears, which has all the same features as the familiar File Open dialog box. Navigate to the picture you want, select it, and click Insert. Note that you can select and insert multiple pictures simultaneously; hold Ctrl as you click to select each picture.

Also note the arrow next to the Insert button, which exposes two additional insert options.

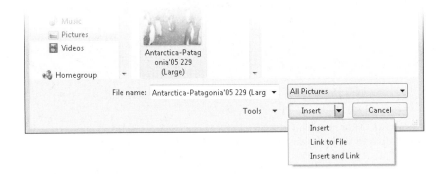

Choosing Link To File commands Office to insert a link to the picture file's location instead of embedding the picture file in the Office document. This results in a smaller document file size, but more importantly, it means the document will always show the current version of the picture file. If you change the file in its original location, you'll see the updated version the next time you open the Office document. If the file is not available at the linked location (if, for example, it has been renamed or deleted, or if it's on a server drive that's not currently available), a red X appears instead of the picture.

Insert And Link embeds the picture file in the document *and* includes a link to the original file. When you open a document, if the linked file is available, Office displays it; if not, Office displays the embedded version.

That's all there is to it. After you insert a picture, you can select it, move it, resize it, and work with it in various ways, as described in the next section, "Making Your Pictures Look Great."

INSIDE OUT Choose a better default wrapping style for pictures in Word

When you insert a picture or screenshot in Word, by default it is placed at the insertion point. A graphic positioned this way (which is called In Line With Text) acts like any other letter or symbol in the text stream: when you type to the left of the graphic, it shifts to the right until it no longer fits and then wraps to the next line. In-line graphics work best in layouts that have text above and below each picture (like most of the screen illustrations in this book, for example) but not beside them. Place each picture in its own paragraph to use this style.

You can be much more creative in your layouts by setting pictures so that text "wraps" around them. To change the wrapping style for a picture, right-click it and choose Wrap Text. For details, see "Adding Pictures and Graphics" on page 237.

If you find yourself frequently changing the wrapping style, you should change the default. To do that, click File, Options. In the Word Options dialog box, click Advanced. Under Cut, Copy, And Paste, locate Insert/Paste Pictures As, and select an option.

Making Your Pictures Look Great

Programs in Office 2010 include picture editing tools that rival many stand-alone programs for editing digital images. Using just the tools in Word, Excel, PowerPoint, or Outlook, you can apply artistic touches such as blurs, paint strokes, and mosaic effects. A number of predefined picture styles include borders, reflections, 3-D effects, and perspective tilting. You can automatically outline the subject of a photo and remove the background. Other tools let you overlay text in creative ways. And then there are the more mundane tasks: making color corrections; adjusting brightness, contrast, and sharpness; and resizing photos. A new cropping tool even makes it easier to see what you're removing from the image.

Chapter 6

A complete description of the picture-editing capabilities of Office could fill a chapter—or a book—so we don't explain every option in detail. Fortunately, with the start we provide here, you'll find that these features are easily discoverable. And the Live Preview capability provided by most of the picture-editing tools makes them intuitive to use as well.

For information about two other common tasks that apply to other types of graphics as well as pictures, see "Resizing and Rotating Graphics and Pictures" on page 157.

Cropping Pictures

You're an exceptional photographer if each picture you take is perfectly composed. For those pictures that aren't perfect, you'll want to crop to remove unnecessary background or to better fit the space in your document. Earlier Office versions had cropping capabilities, but they were difficult to use because you couldn't really see what you were doing. In Office 2010, you can see exactly what's included and what's excluded before you commit.

To crop a picture, select it, click the Format tab (under Picture tools), and in the Size group, click Crop. Cropping handles appear on your picture; drag a handle to adjust the cropping. Alternatively, you can drag the picture. Either way, note that the area to be cropped out remains visible but shaded. To crop equally from both sides of a picture, hold Ctrl as you drag one of the side cropping handles. To crop equally from all four sides, hold Ctrl and drag one of the corner handles. Press Esc or click outside the picture when you're done.

As shown in Figure 6-9, you can also crop to a particular aspect ratio (that is, the ratio of width to height). This is useful when you want an image to perfectly fill a screen or a particular size of photo paper or picture frame, for example. Click the arrow by the Crop button, and then click Aspect Ratio and select the ratio you want.

Note that when you drag a cropping handle, the aspect ratio is not maintained; you get free-form dragging just as if you used the normal Crop command. You'll sometimes find that getting the best results when cropping to a particular aspect ratio requires an iterative process of resizing and cropping. Those iterations might also include choosing the Fill or Fit command on the Crop menu. Both commands maintain (or restore, if necessary) the original picture's aspect ratio, but they crop the image to fit the current picture shape and size.

Figure 6-9 To maintain the aspect ratio after you make a selection, drag the picture instead of dragging the cropping handles.

For more precise cropping control, right-click the picture and choose Format Picture. In the left pane of the Format Picture dialog box, click Crop, and then enter the dimensions.

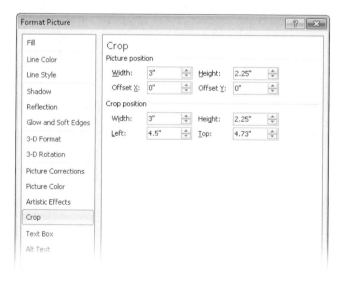

If you find rectangular cropping to be too dull, you might enjoy experimenting with the Crop To Shape command on the Crop menu. With it, you can get some truly strange (and sometimes wonderful) effects by using predefined shapes as crop outlines. (Figure 6-10 shows an example of the former.) Most shapes can be modified in various ways after you apply them. For more information about working with shapes, see "Adding Shapes and Text Boxes" on page 175.

Figure 6-10 Drag the shape handles (in this example, the diamonds along the left and bottom edges) to adjust the shape.

Adjusting Colors and Applying Artistic Effects

Features in Office for correcting picture colors and applying special effects range from the essential to the bizarre. Yet they're generally easy to understand, and, best of all, with Live Preview you're able to see how a particular setting looks with *your* picture. You don't need to rely on a thumbnail of a sample picture or try to guess how numeric settings translate to visual images.

The tools for adjusting color are on the Format tab (under Picture Tools) in the Adjust group. Select a picture, click the Format tab, and then click Corrections to see a gallery of options for adjusting the picture's sharpness, brightness, and contrast. As shown in Figure 6-11, clicking Color displays a gallery for adjusting saturation and tone, as well as for applying a color tint to the picture. To see how a setting will look, simply hover the mouse pointer over it, and the setting is temporarily applied. When you find the one you like, click it.

The third gallery in the Adjust group, Artistic Effects, works in an identical fashion. The effects include an assortment of filters and simulated techniques, such as pencil sketch, paint brush, looking through frosted glass, and so on. Most defy description, so the best way to learn about them is to open the gallery and point.

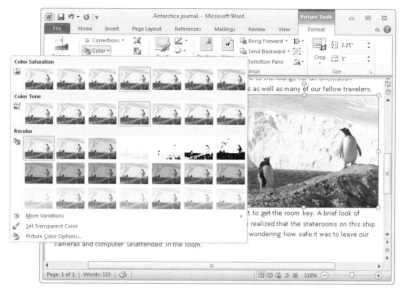

Figure 6-11 The current settings have a bold outline in the gallery.

At the bottom of each gallery is a command that leads to an options dialog box. You can get to the same dialog box by right-clicking the picture and choosing Format Picture, or by clicking the dialog box launcher in the lower right corner of the Picture Styles group on the Format tab. In the Format Picture dialog box, click Picture Corrections, Picture Color, or Artistic Effects. You can view and edit numeric values that correspond to the gallery settings, and you can make precise adjustments to the settings. In addition, Presets buttons on each tab provide another gallery view. One difference here: To see the effect on your picture, you must click the thumbnail in the gallery; pointing to it does nothing.

Applying Picture Styles

The Picture Styles group on the Format tab contains tools for adding a border to your picture and for applying effects such as shadows, reflections, glows, and three-dimensional rotation. The Picture Styles group also includes a Quick Styles gallery, which contains preconfigured combinations of each of these settings.

To use the Quick Styles gallery, select one or more pictures, and then point to one of the visible thumbnails. If none of those suit your fancy, you can scroll down in the gallery or, better yet, click the More button, the arrow at the bottom of the scrollable window. Figure 6-12 shows an example. When you find a suitable option, click it to apply the settings.

Figure 6-12 The Quick Styles gallery makes it easy to try different effects.

To make your own settings—or to adjust the ones made by a Quick Styles preset—click Picture Border (where you can select a color, line width, and line style) or Picture Effects (where you can choose shadows, reflections, glows, softened edges, bevels, and three-dimensional rotation from galleries). Each of these options can be viewed and fine-tuned in the Format Picture dialog box. Click the dialog box launcher in the Picture Styles group, and then click Line Color or Line Style to set up a border, or click Shadow, Reflection, Glow And Soft Edges, 3-D Format, or 3-D Rotation to make settings that correlate to the Picture Effects galleries.

Another option in the Picture Styles group, the Picture Layout gallery, embeds your selected pictures into SmartArt objects. With this feature, you can make some professional-looking presentation materials with just a few clicks. For more information, see "Adding SmartArt to Documents" on page 180.

Removing the Picture Background

Another feature new to Office 2010 is one that automatically removes the background from a picture, leaving only the picture subject visible. To use this feature, it helps to have a picture with the subject in sharp focus, and with good contrast. Yet you can sometimes get surprisingly good results even with less-than-perfect pictures.

To remove the background from a picture, select the picture, click the Format tab, and in the Adjust group, click Remove Background. Office quickly makes its best guess at cropping and masking the background, which it identifies with a magenta overlay. As shown in Figure 6-13, this initial attempt isn't always perfect.

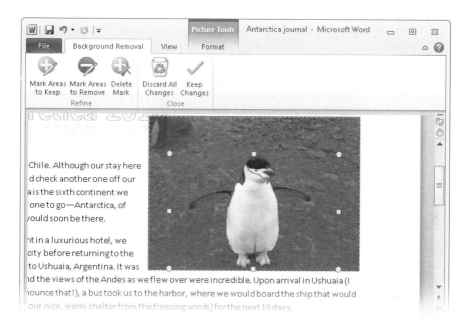

Figure 6-13 Initially, Office didn't include this penguin's wings, which are closer in color to the background than to the rest of the penguin.

If the initial results aren't quite right, click Mark Areas To Keep, and then click the additional areas to include (such as the penguin's wings in Figure 6-13). Click Mark Areas To Remove and then click any unwanted areas that Office left in. If a single click merely deposits a mark but doesn't include or exclude the area of interest (as indicated by the colored mask), try dragging through the area. When you're done, click Keep Changes. In our example, we zoomed in, and then it took just a drag along the length of each wing to produce this result.

INSIDE OUT   Adjust the cropping area

You'll find that with some photos, automatic background removal doesn't work well, and the initial results mistakenly include or exclude several areas. Before you start making manual corrections, the first thing you should do is adjust the cropping indicators to more closely match the final outline you want. When you change the cropping, Office modifies the background selection and, in our experience, often does a much better job with your assistance here.

Undoing Picture Edits

As you experiment with the picture formatting features in Office, not every shot is going to be a keeper. Mistakes that you recognize right away, of course, can always be undone in the usual manner: click Undo on the Quick Access Toolbar, or press Ctrl+Z. But you might decide much later to revert to the original photo settings.

Doing so is quite simple: Select the picture, click the Format tab, and in the Adjust group, click Reset Picture (to restore the background, remove borders and other picture styles, and restore the original colors) or Reset Picture & Size (to do all of the foregoing, plus remove any cropping and restore the picture's original size).

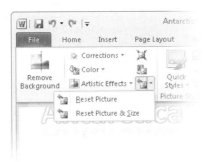

TROUBLESHOOTING

Changes to pictures can't be undone, or edits disappear

A setting buried deep in Office options can lead to some head-scratching moments if it's not set properly. The symptoms can be either of the following:

- After making various picture edits, as described in the following sections, you decide you don't like the changes and want to restore the original picture—but the Reset button is unavailable.

- Each time you open a document containing a picture inserted with the Link To File or Insert And Link command, all the artistic effects and other edits you've added are gone, and the original picture file appears.

These seemingly opposite symptoms can arise from the same root cause: the Discard Editing Data setting. To review the setting, click File, Options. In the Options dialog box, click Advanced, and scroll to Image Size And Quality. Unless reducing the file size of your Office document is paramount, clear Discard Editing Data.

What About Office Picture Manager?

Office 2010 includes a program called Microsoft Office Picture Manager, which you'll find on the Start menu in the Microsoft Office 2010 Tools subfolder of the Microsoft Office folder. Office Picture Manager provides a way to manage your pictures as stand-alone files outside Office documents. With Office Picture Manager, you can convert picture files from one format to another (by using its Export command, not Save As). Compared with the tools built in to the primary Office programs, Office Picture Manager has slightly better options for color correction (but no live previews) and a few additional tools, such as red-eye removal.

Nonetheless, Office Picture Manager is a relic from earlier Office versions, and there's little reason to use it because better options are readily available. Windows Live Photo Gallery (available as a free download from Microsoft at *download.live.com*) provides all the functionality of Office Picture Manager and more. Another program we recommend is IrfanView (*irfanview.com*), which offers unsurpassed viewing capabilities and file conversions, among other features.

Finding and Using Clip Art

The term "clip art" comes from the days when graphic artists would purchase printed catalogs of stock art, from which they would "clip" (literally cut out) an item to be pasted into camera-ready artwork. Although the methods have changed radically, clip art lives on—now in the form of an online catalog of line art, illustrations, photographs, audio clips, and video clips.

For more information about working with video, see "Adding Graphics and Video Clips" on page 601.

To find and insert clip art, follow these steps:

1. Click the Insert tab, and click Clip Art. The Clip Art task pane appears.

2. Under Search For, type a word or two that describes what you're looking for.

3. Click the arrow by Results Should Be, and select the types of media you want to include in your search.

4. To include Microsoft's online catalog in the search, select Include Office.com Content. If you don't select this box, Office looks only at your local collection, which includes a handful of clip art included with Office 2010, plus any items you've added to your collection.

5. Click Go. To learn more about a displayed result, hover the mouse pointer over it.

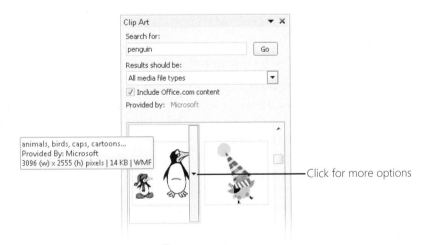

Click for more options

6. To insert an item in your document, click it. For other options, click the arrow along its right side.

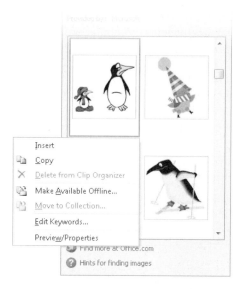

Choose Make Available Offline if you want to reuse the clip in the future. Office stores the clip in a collection, which is a database file stored on your computer. You can organize your clip collection into folders (you're asked to select a folder or create a new one when you choose Make Available Offline), which can be useful for managing large collections.

Although the search capabilities of the Clip Art task pane don't rely on the organizational structure of your collections, if you feel compelled to tidy them up, Office 2010 includes for that purpose a program called Microsoft Clip Organizer. You can find it on the Start menu by clicking All Programs, Microsoft Office, Microsoft Office 2010 Tools. Clip Organizer is also useful if you want to add items to your collections from files on your computer, a scanner, or a camera. Other than that, there's seldom reason to venture into Clip Organizer.

INSIDE OUT   Edit clip art

A limitation of stock art is that it might not precisely fit your artistic concept. Many clip art images can be modified, however. For example, you can right-click an illustration and choose Edit Picture. Office warns that the picture is not editable, but then offers to convert it to an editable format. Click Yes, and get creative. Similarly, imported photographs can be modified with any of the techniques and effects described earlier in "Making Your Pictures Look Great" on page 163.

Chapter 6

Capturing and Inserting Screenshots

You'll sometimes find it useful to insert a representation of a window (or part of a window) clipped from your computer's screen. For example, you might want to include part of a web page in a document, or if you're documenting computer procedures for your office, you might want to show a program window.

To insert a screenshot, first be sure that the window you want to capture is not minimized to the taskbar. (It's okay if it's covered by other windows, including the Office window you're working in.) Then click the Insert tab, and in the Illustrations group, click Screenshot. Thumbnail images of each window appear, as shown in Figure 6-14.

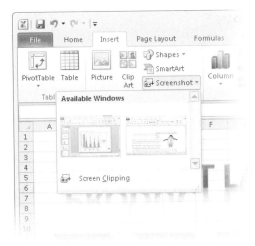

Figure 6-14 Available windows include all windows and dialog boxes that are not minimized, except for the Office window in which you're working.

Click a thumbnail to insert an image of the entire window. If you want to show only part of the screen, you can crop the window image after you insert it, or you can click Screen Clipping. When you click Screen Clipping, the Office window disappears from view, exposing the underlying screen—whatever it may contain. Use the mouse to drag across the area you want to capture, creating a rectangular clipping area. When you release the mouse button, Office immediately inserts an image of the area you outlined.

> **Note**
>
> Although OneNote doesn't have the ability to capture and insert entire windows, you can grab screen clippings in OneNote. On the Insert tab, in the Images group, click Screen Clipping. For more information, see "Screen Clippings" on page 504.

INSIDE OUT   Capture the Office window

Ironically, the new screenshot feature in Office 2010 doesn't let you capture an image of the Office program itself. Workarounds abound, but the simplest is to press Alt+PrtScn (which copies the current window to the Clipboard) and then press Ctrl+V to paste the Clipboard content into your document.

Inserted screenshots are handled by Office programs exactly like pictures. When you select a screenshot, Picture Tools appears on the ribbon. The Format tab contains the same tools and features, and you can apply to a screenshot any of the changes described earlier in "Making Your Pictures Look Great" on page 163.

Unlike pictures that you insert, however, screenshots don't exist elsewhere as an image file. In Word, OneNote, PowerPoint, and Outlook (but not Excel), it's easy to create such a file. Simply right-click the image and choose Save As Picture.

Adding Shapes and Text Boxes

Office includes a variety of shapes that can be inserted as line illustrations. Shapes include arrows and other symbols to use in diagrams, various polygons, boxes for callouts and other text, and some that'll leave you wondering what possible use they could have. Although the unadorned shapes are not much to look at, Office includes a full range of effects, colors, shading, and other customizations that can add some pizzazz to your document.

The tools for inserting and customizing shapes also work on text boxes. A text box is, in fact, merely a rectangular shape that can contain text.

To insert a shape, click the Insert tab, and in the Illustrations group, click Shapes. A gallery of predefined shapes appears. (If you're inserting a text box, you can bypass the Shapes gallery by clicking Text Box, which is in the Text group on the Insert tab.)

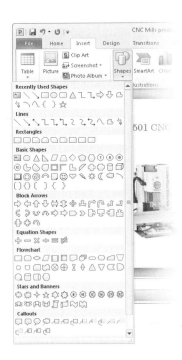

Click a shape, and then drag in the document to create a container for the shape. Don't worry if the size or position isn't quite right; you can easily change move, resize, or rotate the shape by selecting it and dragging its handles. (For details, see "Positioning Objects" and "Resizing and Rotating Graphics and Pictures" earlier in this chapter.) To modify a shape, select the shape and look for shape handles, which appear as yellow diamonds.

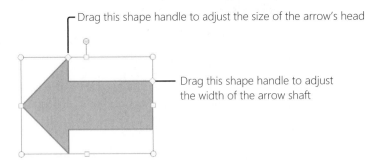

Drag this shape handle to adjust the size of the arrow's head

Drag this shape handle to adjust the width of the arrow shaft

For more fine-grained control, on the Format tab, in the Insert Shapes group, click Edit Shape, Edit Points (or right-click the shape and click Edit Points). Each point that defines the shape appears as a black square, which you can drag in any direction. To add a new point, hold down Ctrl and click anywhere on the shape's outline; Ctrl+click an existing point to remove it. When you click a point to select it, two additional handles appear; together, these three points define the point and the line segment on either side of it. You can drag the point or one of its handles to get different effects. To change the type of point, hold Shift (for a smooth point), Ctrl (straight point), or Alt (corner point) as you drag a handle.

The real fun begins when you apply shape styles. Select a shape, click the Format tab (under Drawing Tools), and click the More button in the Shape Styles group to see a gallery of predefined styles, as shown in Figure 6-15. Like the Picture Styles gallery, this one uses Live Preview; as you point to a thumbnail, its formatting appears in your document as well. Click a gallery item to apply the formatting.

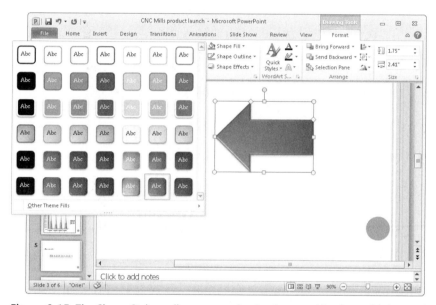

Figure 6-15 The Shape Styles gallery can apply pleasing combinations of colors and effects with a single click.

The Shape Styles gallery displays colors and styles that conform to the currently selected theme; changing the theme also changes the gallery contents. (For more information, see "Using Office Themes" on page 185.) If none of the options in the Shape Styles gallery tickles you, use the tools on the right side of the Shape Styles group on the Format tab:

- **Shape Fill**   Options here let you fill the shape with a color (either solid or as a gradient), a picture from a file on your computer, or a texture (from a gallery that includes various fabrics, stones, wood grains, and other materials).

- **Shape Outline**   Select a color, line weight, and line style for the shape's outline.

- **Shape Effects**   Available effects are similar to the ones you can apply to pictures: shadows, reflections, glows, soft edges, bevels, and three-dimensional rotation, each of which is displayed in a Live Preview gallery.

All the settings available on the Format tab—and more—can also be configured in the Format Shape dialog box. To view it, click the dialog box launcher (the arrow in the lower right corner of the Shape Styles group on the Format tab) or right-click a shape and choose Format Shape.

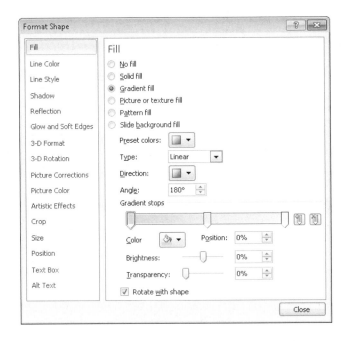

INSIDE OUT   Copy and move graphics and formatting

To copy or move a selected graphic or picture, you can use the Clipboard as you would with ordinary text. The usual keyboard shortcuts (Ctrl+X for Cut, Ctrl+C for Copy, and Ctrl+V for Paste), Home tab commands, and menu commands do the job.

But—just as you can with text—you can copy all the formatting for a graphic or picture, which is handy when you need to apply extensive (but consistent) styles and formats to many pictures. Use the Format Painter or use keyboard shortcuts: Ctrl+Shift+C to copy formatting, and Ctrl+Shift+V to paste formatting. For more information, see "Copying Formatting" on page 128.

Displaying Data Graphically with Charts

Data charts have been a key feature of Excel since its earliest appearance back in 1985. The chart capabilities and features increased dramatically over the years, of course, but full-featured charting remained primarily an Excel feature, with lesser charting capabilities available in other Office programs. With Office 2010, however, the full range of charting features is available in Word, PowerPoint, and Outlook, as well as Excel.

To insert a chart in a document, click the Insert tab and then click Chart. The Insert Chart dialog box appears, in which you can select from an astonishing gallery of chart types. (Because charting remains a central part of Excel, there isn't a single Chart tool on the Insert tab. Instead, each chart type appears in its own gallery. You can, however, open Insert Chart by clicking the dialog box launcher in the Charts group on the Insert tab.)

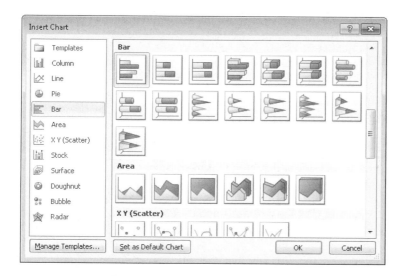

Select a chart type (you can change it later) and click OK. A worksheet then opens in a new window in Excel; this is where you enter the data for your chart. You can then switch back and forth between entering data in the Excel window and viewing and formatting the resulting chart in your document window. (If you're inserting a chart in Excel, the data and the chart appear in different parts of the same window.)

To change the appearance of your chart, select the chart and click the tabs under Chart Tools:

- Use the Design tab to change overall settings, such as chart type, data orientation, and styles.

- On the Layout tab, you can modify specific chart elements, such as titles, axes, and legends.

- The Format tab is the place to manage shape styles, position, and size—settings we cover elsewhere in this chapter. (See "Adding Shapes and Text Boxes" on page 175; "Positioning Objects" on page 154; and "Resizing and Rotating Graphics and Pictures" on page 157.)

For details about displaying data with charts, including descriptions of features on the Design and Layout tabs, see Chapter 13, "Charts and Data Analysis."

Adding SmartArt to Documents

SmartArt graphics provide an easy way to create graphical lists, process diagrams, organizational charts, and similar diagrams that meld shapes, text, and pictures into compelling visuals.

To insert SmartArt, click the Insert tab, and click SmartArt. A dialog box appears, in which you can select from an array of layouts, as shown in Figure 6-16. Select one and click OK.

The next step is to enter text into the SmartArt graphic. If the Text pane isn't displayed, select the graphic and click the arrow at the center of the left side of the frame. Within the Text pane, shown in Figure 6-17, use the keyboard shortcuts shown in Table 6-2. Alternatively, right-click an item in the Text pane, and choose from the menu. Tools in the Create Graphic group on the Design tab under SmartArt Tools provide a third (and sometimes best) method for organizing the text in a SmartArt graphic.

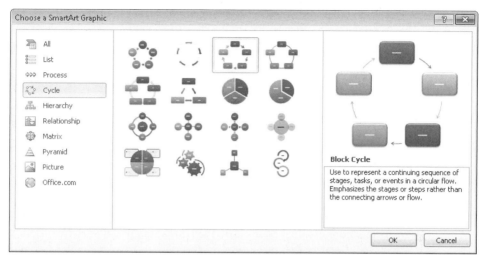

Figure 6-16 When you select a graphic, a larger visualization and a description of the graphic's use appear in the right pane.

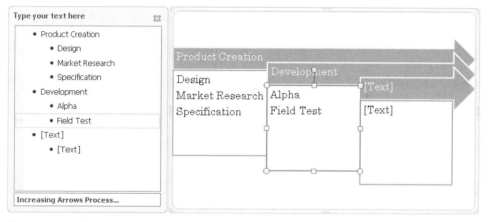

Figure 6-17 Although you can enter text directly into the graphic, it's usually easier with the aid of the Text pane.

Table 6-2 Keyboard Shortcuts for Text Entry in SmartArt Graphics

Action	Keyboard Shortcut
Go to next entry	Down Arrow
Go to previous entry	Up Arrow
Create new entry	Enter
Delete entry	Delete (you must first delete any text)
Demote current entry	Tab
Promote current entry	Shift+Tab

Chapter 6

The Design tab under SmartArt Tools includes galleries in which you can select a different SmartArt design (in the Layouts group), a different color scheme (in the SmartArt Styles group), or a different style (a predefined configuration of fill, outline, and effects settings for shapes and text in the SmartArt graphic).

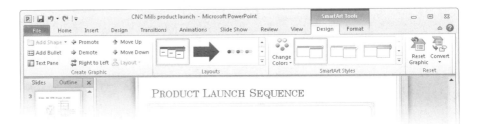

You'll find more granular controls on the Format tab under SmartArt Tools. You can modify shapes individually or en masse (a SmartArt graphic is an assemblage of individual shapes) by using the tools and techniques described earlier in this chapter for individual shapes. (See "Adding Shapes and Text Boxes" on page 175.) In addition, you can format text using all the options available for WordArt, as described in the next section.

Applying Text Effects with WordArt

A fixture in Word for many years, WordArt has changed significantly (for the better) in recent editions. It's now easier to use, more flexible, and can create attractive text effects—instead of the funhouse-mirror style distortions that typified its output in earlier editions. Moreover, you can now use WordArt in Excel, PowerPoint, and Outlook as well as Word.

To convert existing text to WordArt, first select the text. Then (whether you have text selected or not) click the Insert tab, and in the Text group, click WordArt. A gallery of colorful styles appears. Click one, and you'll see your text (or placeholder text, if you didn't have any selected) in the new style. When the selection frame is a dashed line, you can select and enter text. (Use the Esc and Enter keys to switch between text entry and formatting modes.) You also specify a font, font size, and effects such as bold and italic while you're in text entry mode; use the usual text formatting tools on the Home tab or the Mini toolbar.

With your text in place, you can proceed to modify other aspects of its appearance. Select the WordArt object and then click the Format tab (under Drawing Tools). Here, in the WordArt Styles group, you can select a different predefined lettering style from the gallery. (If a Quick Styles button appears, click it to display the gallery.) The three tools to the right of the gallery offer additional customization options similar to those available for shapes:

- Click Text Fill to select coloring options for the letters. You can select a color (solid or gradient). Or go crazy: use a picture from a file or a texture cropped to the shape of the letters.

- Click Text Outline to specify the color, line weight, and style of the letter outlines.

- Click Text Effects (see Figure 6-18) to add shadows, reflections, and other effects. Each item on the Text Effects menu leads to a gallery submenu with Live Preview.

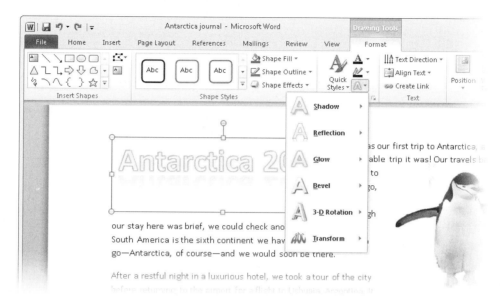

Figure 6-18 You'll find the funhouse-mirror effects in the Transform gallery.

All the settings and effects available on the Format tab, along with additional options, can be viewed and configured in the Format Text Effects dialog box. To open it, click the Word-Art Styles dialog box launcher.

Drawing with Ink

On tablet PCs and other computers equipped with pen input, you can use your stylus to add "ink" to a document. You might find this convenient for taking notes, marking up corrections, or inserting free-hand drawings.

When the stylus gets close to the display, Ink Tools appears on the ribbon and below it, the Pens tab, which is shown in Figure 6-19. In the Write group, you select a tool—pen, highlighter, or eraser—and your stylus acts as that tool. To use your stylus in its other role—as a mouse replacement that you can use to select text and objects, position the insertion point, and so on—click (or, more accurately, tap) Select Objects.

Figure 6-19 In the Pens group you specify the color and thickness for each pen and then select your favorites, which remain visible without you having to open a gallery.

Ink is stored as an object similar to any other graphic. Click to select it, and you'll see the familiar selection frame along with its sizing and rotate handles. When selected, the Format tab under Drawing Tools becomes available, although most of its tools and effects can't be applied to ink.

The inking feature has a couple of nonobvious tricks that assist in converting your scrawl into usable data:

- If you click Convert To Shapes (in the Ink Art group on the Pens tab) before you begin drawing, when you draw a shape that resembles a circle, rectangle, or other standard shape from the Shapes gallery, Office instantly and automatically converts it from ink to a normal shape object. With this capability, you can sketch out organization charts, flow charts, and similar diagrams and not have it appear like it was created by a six-year-old.

- You can convert handwritten text into typed characters. Right-click the ink object that contains your handwriting, and choose Copy Ink As Text. The text is now on the Clipboard, and you can paste it into your document. The handwriting-to-text conversion isn't perfect (although we've seen it correctly interpret scratchings that we had trouble reading), so be sure to proofread it carefully.

Using Office Themes

The final section of this chapter deals not with individual graphic objects but with a feature that can change the overall appearance of your document with just a few clicks. That feature is document themes. A *theme* is a collection of formatting options that include a set of colors, a set of fonts (one for headings and one for body text), and a set of effects (such as line styles and fill effects).

A theme in PowerPoint also includes backgrounds. For more information about themes in PowerPoint, see "Applying Themes" on page 611.

Selecting a theme causes all these theme elements to be applied to a document. (You can override theme settings for any part of a document, and those parts won't be affected by theme changes.) Themes are consistent across all Office programs. You can, for example, apply a theme to a Word document and apply the same theme to an Excel worksheet and a PowerPoint presentation, giving them a consistent look and feel.

To apply a theme to the current document, click the Page Layout tab (in Word and Excel) or the Design tab (PowerPoint) and then click Themes, as shown in Figure 6-20. Point to a theme to see a live preview of your document, and click a theme to apply its settings.

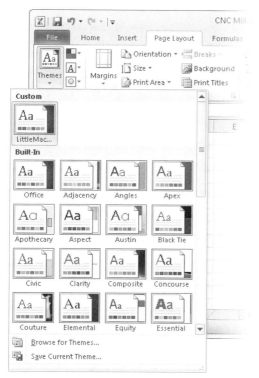

Figure 6-20 The Custom section appears only if you have saved one or more themes.

Chapter 6

To see what components constitute a theme (and to change them to your liking), use the other buttons in the Themes group on the Page Layout (or Design) tab.

- **Colors** A theme includes a dozen (usually complementary) colors that are applied to different document elements. You can select one of the 40-odd built-in color collections, or you can click Create New Theme Colors to make a custom collection.

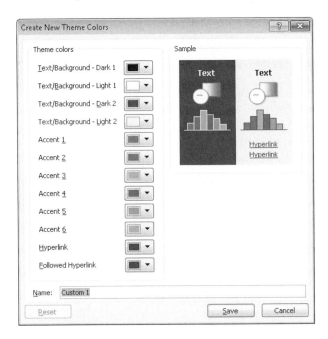

- **Fonts** A theme comprises two fonts: one for headings and one for body text. Select a built-in pairing, or click Create New Theme Fonts to mix your own. Office differentiates between headings and body text based on the paragraph style (Word), cell style (Excel), or placeholder type (PowerPoint).

- **Effects** Select one of the built-in line and fill effects combinations. You can't create your own variation.

After you've made your selections and customizations in each of these three areas, you might want to save this combination as a new custom theme. To do that, click Themes, Save Current Theme. Each theme is stored in its own file, so it's easy to copy the theme file to other computers, thereby enabling consistent appearance throughout an organization. Theme files are stored by default in %AppData%\Microsoft\Templates\Document Themes (C:\Users*username*\AppData\Roaming\Microsoft\Templates\Document Themes on a Windows 7 computer with default settings), but you can store them in any folder.

If your custom theme doesn't appear in the Themes gallery after it's been copied to a computer, click Themes, Browse For Themes to locate it.

PART 2
Word

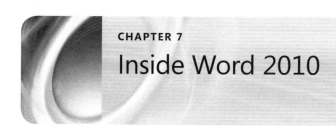

CHAPTER 7

Inside Word 2010

F UTURISTS have long predicted the "paperless office," a prognostication that obviously has not come to pass. Much of the paper that we continue to spew out comes from word-processing programs, a core computer task going back even further than the personal computer revolution that began in the early 1980s. In the early days, of course, a "word processor" processed only words and text. A modern word-processing program like Word 2010 melds text and graphics in ways that used to be possible only with high-end desktop-publishing programs.

Should the paperless office ever become a reality, computer users' reliance on Word won't diminish, because it's also ideal for creating online documents, including blog posts and documents distributed in PDF, XPS, and other electronic formats.

In this chapter, our focus is on how you build and format documents—regardless of the final output medium. We cover the basics of creating a document, searching and navigating in a document, adding commonly used elements such as pictures and lists, and formatting to improve a document's appearance and readability.

In the three chapters that follow, we cover more complex formatting tasks, explain Word's features for reviewing and sharing documents, and wrap up our Word coverage with a compendium of advanced topics.

What's in a Word Document?

A "document" in Word can be any in a wide range of items, including letters of correspondence, brochures, reports, books, forms, certificates, and other items that typically end up being printed on paper. In addition, Word is an ideal tool for producing documents that usually appear only on-screen, such as blog posts and web pages. There's not much in common among these disparate document types, although most contain primarily text, perhaps embellished with some pictures or other graphics.

With its printer-centric roots, a Word document consists of one or more pages. Page sizes are normally based on paper sizes used in desktop printers, although you can define a page as any size up to 22 inches (558.7 mm) square.

In this section, we assume that you are using the standard Word 2010 Document (.docx) format. For a description of other available formats, see Table 4-1, "Supported File Formats in Word 2010," on page 77.

Figure 7-1 shows a brochure/data sheet for a new product. In the figure, you can see some features that can be incorporated into Word documents, such as pictures and other graphics, text wrapped around irregular shapes, multiple-column layouts, tables, and bulleted lists. We explain how to implement each of these features (and many more) in this and the following three chapters.

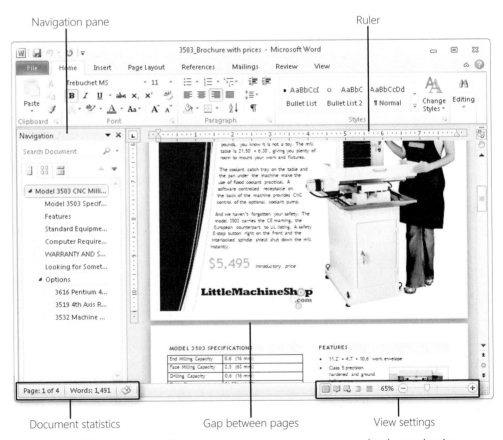

Figure 7-1 In Print Layout view, the document's on-screen appearance closely matches its printed output.

Chapter 7

The Word window shown in Figure 7-1 shows a couple of optional (but very useful) components. The Navigation pane is handy not only for navigating within a document (for more information, see "Navigating Within a Document" on page 203), but also for organizing documents (see "Using Outlines to Plan, Organize, and Edit Documents" on page 245). The Navigation pane is also the primary search interface in Word (see "Searching Within a Document" on page 210). The other nonstandard element shown in the figure is the ruler along the top and left edges of the document workspace. The ruler allows you to see and adjust margin, indent, and tab settings (see "Setting Page Layout Options" on page 221; "Formatting Paragraphs" on page 219; and "Using Tabs" on page 198).

To display or hide these items, visit the View tab, shown in Figure 7-2.

You can also display or hide the ruler by clicking
View Ruler, the button at the top of the scroll bar

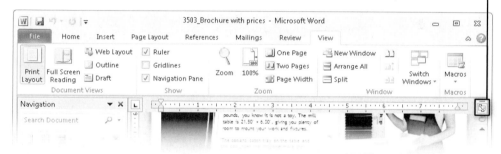

Figure 7-2 Options for displaying rulers and the Navigation pane are in the Show group on the View tab.

INSIDE OUT   Work with documents in Compatibility Mode

To maintain compatibility with earlier versions of Word, Word uses Compatibility Mode. If you and the people with whom you exchange documents work exclusively in Office 2010 (and you use default settings for saving documents), your documents are stored in Office Open XML format, which has a .docx file name extension. Compatibility Mode never enters the picture.

If you exchange documents with users of earlier Word versions (or you open documents that you created in an earlier version), you might see "[Compatibility Mode]" in the title bar of the Word window. This indicator appears in documents saved in the older binary format (.doc extension) used by Word 2003 and earlier versions. Similarly, it occurs with .docx files saved in Word 2007, which doesn't support all the features of Word 2010 (particularly text effects and OpenType typographic features). For more information about file formats and compatibility between versions, see "Which File Formats Does Office 2010 Support?" on page 76.

You enter Compatibility Mode automatically whenever you open a document that you saved with compatibility features maintained, or when you open a document created in an earlier Word version. In Compatibility Mode, you're likely to notice some changes other than the title bar notice:

- Some features are unavailable. (For example, in the Font group on the Home tab, Text Effects is unavailable. And in the Illustrations group on the Insert tab, Screenshot is unavailable.)

- Other features are noticeably different in their implementation. (For example, if you select a picture and then click the Format tab under Picture Tools, the Adjust group contains different options than you see when a file is not in Compatibility Mode, and the Picture Styles group is replaced with less-capable Shadow Effects and Border groups.)

- You might see some artifacts that Compatibility Mode doesn't fully address, such as minor layout changes.

Disabling these features in Compatibility Mode ensures that you won't incorporate elements in your document that can't be properly rendered when the document is opened in an earlier Word version. If you don't plan to use a document in the old Word version again, it's easy to upgrade the current document to pure Word 2010 format. Click File, and on the Info tab, click Convert.

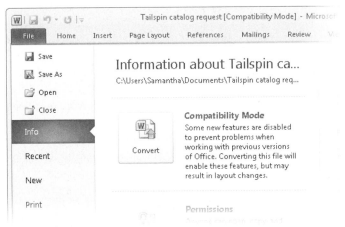

If, on the other hand, you need to share a document with someone using an older version, be sure to use a compatible format. When you save a document in Compatibility Mode, it maintains its original format. To convert a Word 2010 document (such as a new one you create), when you save the document, do this: Click File, Save As, and then select Word 97-2003 Document in the Save As Type box.

A number of advanced settings can be made to ensure compatibility with particular Word versions. To work with these settings, click File, Options. In the Options dialog box, click Advanced, and then scroll all the way to the bottom. In the drop-down lists, select which documents you want to affect and which version of Word you want to ensure compatibility with. Each version has its own collection of predefined compatibility settings; you can review or modify the individual settings by clicking Layout Options.

Working in an Appropriate Document View

By default, documents in Word are displayed in Print Layout view, which closely approximates the appearance of ink on paper. Within the document area of the Word window, you see a white background (or other color if you change the page color) scaled to represent a single sheet of paper. In Print Layout view, document content is laid out just the way the document will print, faithfully rendering margins, line breaks, page breaks, and graphics positioning. For most purposes, Print Layout view is best, and it's therefore a good default.

INSIDE OUT   Set the page color

You can set the background color for your pages by clicking the Page Layout tab and then, in the Page Background group, clicking Page Color and selecting a color. The color you select doesn't print, but choosing a color in this way is useful in two situations:

- You're going to print on colored paper. (Your on-screen document looks more like the finished product.)

- You're creating a document for on-screen use, whether as a Word document or another file format, such as PDF, XPS, or HTML. When you save in any of these formats, the background color is preserved as part of the document.

Print Layout view is one of five available document views. The others are covered in the following sections.

Full Screen Reading View

Full Screen Reading view, shown in Figure 7-3, is unique in that it fills the screen and omits the usual window trappings (borders, scroll bars, and so on) except for a single narrow toolbar at the top.

Click here for navigation options

Figure 7-3 Full Screen Reading view provides a convenient way to read and review documents. By default, you can't type text in this view, so inadvertent edits are unlikely.

As its name suggests, Full Screen Reading view is designed primarily for reading documents, not editing them. (If you do want to edit text in this view, click View Options, Allow Typing.) Full Screen Reading view works much like an e-book reader, in that it reformats text to properly fit the screen pages at a legible size. (If you prefer to see the print layout, click View Options, Show Printed Page.) Other commands on the View Options menu let you adjust the text size, display one page or two, and configure reviewing options. (For information about these options, see "Tracking and Highlighting Changes Made to a Document" on page 285.)

As with any good e-book reader, you can highlight passages, insert comments similar to sticky notes, look up a highlighted word or phrase in a dictionary or other online research tool (for more information, see "Using the Thesaurus and Other References" on page 144), or translate text (see "Translating Text to Another Language" on page 146). Commands for all these options are on the Tools menu.

To page through a document in this view, press the Page Down or Page Up key, or click the arrows in the title bar or near the bottom corners of the screen. For additional navigation options, such as jumping directly to a heading or other landmark, click the screen number at the center of the title bar.

To leave Full Screen Reading view, click Close or press Esc. Doing so doesn't close Word altogether; rather, it returns you to a "normal" Word window with your document displayed in Print Layout view.

> **Note**
>
> By default, e-mail attachments open in Full Screen Reading view. If you find this behavior annoying, you can change it in either of two ways:
>
> - In Full Screen Reading view, click View Options, Don't Open Attachments In Full Screen to remove the check mark by the command.
>
> - In any other view, click File to open Backstage view and then click Options. On the General tab, under Start Up Options, clear Open E-Mail Attachments In Full Screen Reading View.

Web Layout View

Web Layout view shows how your document would appear as a web page. Text wrapping is determined by window width rather than page (paper) width. There are no margins around the edge of the page (because there is no "page"), and there are no headers or footers. Text wrapping and positioning of pictures and graphics observe the limited capabilities of the HTML language and rendering by web browsers. Although this view is useful mainly for working with documents to be viewed online, because of the way it wraps text to fit the window it's occasionally handier than Print Layout view for the phase in document preparation where you're more interested in what the words say than how they're laid out on the page. Unlike Draft view, pictures and graphics are displayed.

Outline View

Outline view displays your document's headings as a hierarchical outline and shows tools specifically for working in this view on the Outlining tab. For more information, see "Using Outlines to Plan, Organize, and Edit Documents" on page 245.

Draft View

Draft view shows only the text in the body of your document. Headers, footers, pictures, and other graphics are not displayed, and line breaks might not accurately match how the document will print. (Line break fidelity depends on the window width and zoom level. Lines break at the margin or the window width, whichever is narrower.) In years past, when computers were much less powerful than those available now, Draft view was commonly used instead of Print Layout view, which could be dreadfully slow. With modern computers, there's seldom reason to invoke Draft view unless your goal is to focus exclusively on text content. If you also want to see in-line graphics while working on text, use Web Layout view.

Switching Views and Zooming

To switch between views, click an option in the Document Views group on the View tab, shown in Figure 7-2. Easier yet, click one of the buttons in the lower right corner of the Word window, each of which corresponds to a document view. (See Figure 7-1.) If you prefer keyboard shortcuts, use the ones in Table 7-1.

Table 7-1 Keyboard Shortcuts for Selecting a Document View

Action	Keyboard Shortcut
Switch to Print Layout view	Ctrl+Alt+P
Switch to Outline view	Ctrl+Alt+O
Switch to Draft view	Ctrl+Alt+N

INSIDE OUT Show more in Print Layout view

By design, Print Layout view shows an accurate representation of each page, including its margins and any headers or footers. This information can occupy a lot of vertical space, leaving less room on the screen for the document content you're working on. You can hide this space by pointing to the gap between pages and double-clicking when the mouse pointer appears as shown here.

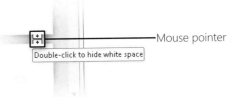

Mouse pointer

To again display the header and footer area, double-click the (now thinner) page separator.

Another factor in choosing a view that works best for you is zoom level, or magnification. Your ideal zoom percentage might vary depending on your screen size and resolution, your visual acuity, your manual dexterity (for precise mouse positioning), the fonts you choose, and the type of work you're doing (for example, you might need to zoom way in while editing a picture, and then zoom back out to work on text).

You adjust the zoom percentage using the slider in the lower right corner of the Word window, next to the document view buttons. For more precise control, click the View tab and then click Zoom to display the dialog box shown in Figure 7-4.

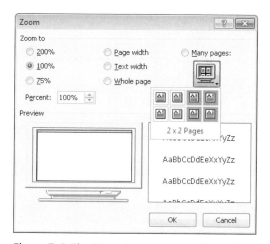

Figure 7-4 The Many Pages option adjusts the zoom level to precisely fit the selected number of pages in the window.

The Zoom group on the View tab (shown earlier in Figure 7-2) also provides options for quickly returning to 100 percent scaling or to certain preset zoom levels that scale to fit one or two pages in the window or fit the page width to the window width. With these presets (other than 100 percent), the zoom level automatically adjusts when you change the window size. Note that these presets generally have no effect except in Print Layout view.

Creating and Editing Documents

In this section, we take a look at some document editing techniques that are used only in Word. The nature of text-centric documents produces some unique requirements, and in this section we discuss the solutions provided by Word 2010.

The process of starting a new document is essentially the same in all Office programs. For details, see "Using Templates to Streamline Document Creation" on page 97. Likewise, the methods for opening existing documents and saving documents are the same in Word as they are in other Office programs. For details, see "Opening and Saving Documents" on page 90. For information about basic editing techniques that apply to all Office programs, see Chapter 5, "Entering, Editing, and Formatting Text."

Using Tabs

Tabs are fixed locations that you can use to align lines of text. To insert a tab, press the Tab key; the insertion point advances to the next tab stop. You can set the positions of tabs and set other options, such as alignment type, by using the ruler or the Tabs dialog box.

To set tabs using the ruler, follow these steps:

1. If the ruler is not visible, click the View Ruler icon at the top of the vertical scroll bar, or select Ruler in the Show group on the View tab.

2. Click the box at the left end of the ruler until it displays the tab alignment type you want.

Left-aligned tab   Text starts at the tab position.

Center-aligned tab   Text is centered on the tab position. (Text automatically re-centers as you type.)

Right-aligned tab   Text ends at the tab position. (Characters shift to the left as you type.)

Decimal-aligned tab   Numbers with a decimal point align the decimal point at the tab stop. (Numbers or text without a decimal point or period are right-aligned.)

Bar   This is not a tab stop; rather, it inserts a vertical line at the tab position as a column divider.

3. Click the ruler where you want to set the tab stop. If you don't click precisely where you want the tab stop, you can drag the tab-stop marker along the ruler.

The Tabs dialog box lacks the ability to show your tab stops in position, but it offers one feature not available via the ruler: the ability to specify leader characters. (In the typesetting world, a leader is a repeated character to the left of a tab stop—often a row of periods.) To use the Tabs dialog box to set one or more tab stops:

1. On the Home tab, click the Paragraph dialog box launcher (the arrow in the lower right corner of the Paragraph group). Then, in the Paragraph dialog box, click Tabs.

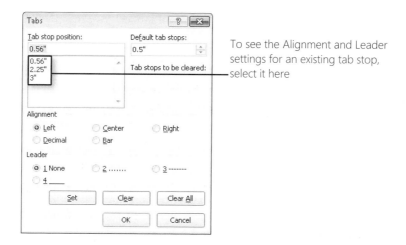

To see the Alignment and Leader settings for an existing tab stop, select it here

2. In the Tab Stop Position box, enter the position, as measured from the left margin.

3. Under Alignment, select one of the five alignment types.

4. Under Leader, select periods, hyphens, underlines, or no leader character. The leader character fills the gap between the tab stop and any text to its left.

5. Click Set.

6. To set additional tab stops, repeat steps 2 through 5. Click OK when you're done.

By default, left-aligned tabs are set every one-half inch. However, if you set any tab stops yourself, all default stops to the left of your tabs are ignored.

Tab stops are included in a paragraph style. This means that each time you press Enter (to start a new paragraph) at the end of a paragraph with tab stops set, the following paragraph will have the same tab-stop settings. More importantly, it means you can store tab stops as part of a paragraph style in a template.

To remove a tab stop using the ruler, simply drag the marker off the ruler. Using the Tabs dialog box, you can remove a tab stop by selecting it and clicking Clear.

INSIDE OUT   Don't use tabs for the wrong reasons

It's easy to spot a document created by someone who's not proficient in using Word. Press Ctrl+* or click Show/Hide ¶ (in the Paragraph group on the Home tab) to display formatting characters, and if the page is littered with right arrows (→)—the symbol for tab characters—it has been created in a way that makes editing difficult and inefficient.

Tabs provide the best way to align text from a single line with text in other lines. Word has better tools for other types of tabular text. Where each clump of text might consist of more than one line, don't fall for the amateur mistake of trying to use tabs and line breaks; instead use a table. (For details, see "Creating a Table" on page 253.) And if you want to set up snaking columns of text (as in a newspaper, where when the text reaches the bottom of the first column it continues in the next column), using tabs would be a nightmare; instead, use columns. (For details, see "Formatting Columns and Sections" on page 248.)

Tabs are also a poor solution for indenting text from the left margin and for indenting the first line of a paragraph. Both of these tasks are better accomplished with paragraph formatting; see "Formatting Paragraphs" on page 219.

Inserting Special Characters

Office 2010 offers several tools for inserting symbols that don't correspond to a key on your keyboard, such as math symbols, arrows, and letters used in foreign languages. Tools that work in all Office programs include the Symbol option on the Insert menu, AutoCorrect, and entering character codes. For details about these tools, see "Entering Symbols and Other Special Characters" on page 110.

Word adds a few additional methods to the mix:

- In the Symbol dialog box (to open it, on the Insert tab, click Symbol, More Symbols), the Special Characters tab offers easy access to characters often used in documents, such as dashes and trademark symbols. (By visiting that tab, you can quickly learn the keyboard shortcuts for characters you use often.)

- Additional AutoCorrect options enable automation beyond the ability to replace one character string with another. To view and modify AutoCorrect options, click File, Options, click the Proofing tab, and click AutoCorrect Options. In addition to the options on the AutoCorrect tab, be sure to review the options on the AutoFormat As You Type tab, shown next. Options here automate the entry of characters such as fractions and dashes; other options automate the formatting of lists, paragraphs, and other elements.

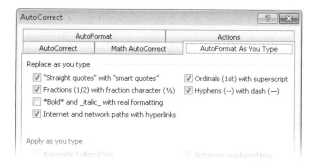

Changing Case

Not everyone has the foresight to correctly capitalize text while typing. Fortunately, Word offers two methods for the common task of switching between uppercase (capital) and lowercase letters in existing text. With both methods, you begin by selecting the text in which you want to correct the capitalization.

The first method is to click Change Case, which you'll find in the Font group on the Home tab. A menu of capitalization styles appears.

The other method is to press Shift+F3, which cycles through lowercase, uppercase, and either sentence casing (if the selection ends with a period) or capitalizing each word.

Changing case using these methods actually changes the characters, just as if you pressed (or didn't press) the Shift key. You can also change case with a character format, which changes the appearance of each letter but not the underlying text. For details, see "Formatting Text" on page 216.

Controlling Line Breaks and Hyphenation

As you type text, word processing programs ordinarily move to the next line when you reach the right margin, breaking the line at the last space before the word that would go beyond the margin. Sometimes you'll want to force a new line in specific places; in other cases you might want to prevent a line from breaking, such as between words in a proper name or in the middle of a phone number. Table 7-2 shows the keys for controlling breaks.

Table 7-2 **Break Characters**

To Insert	Press
Line break	Shift+Enter
Page break	Ctrl+Enter
Column break	Ctrl+Shift+Enter
Nonbreaking space	Ctrl+Shift+Spacebar
Nonbreaking hyphen	Ctrl+Shift+Hyphen
Optional hyphen	Ctrl+Hyphen

Inserting a nonbreaking space or hyphen ensures that the line won't end at that character; instead, the word preceding the nonbreaking character moves down to the next line. An optional hyphen is normally invisible, but if it falls near the end of a line, Word inserts a hyphen and a line break at that point.

Word has two other characters for managing line breaks: a no-width optional break and a no-width non break. These work like spaces and nonbreaking spaces, respectively, except that they don't occupy any space. By default, no shortcut key exists for these characters. To enter them, go to the Special Characters tab in the Symbol dialog box. (If you use them often, select one in that dialog box and click Shortcut Key to assign your own shortcut key.)

You manage hyphenation by clicking Hyphenation (in the Page Setup group) on the Page Layout tab. Hyphenation is turned off by default. If you choose Automatic, Word hyphenates your entire document without further intervention. If you choose Manual, Word asks about each word it proposes to hyphenate. You can accept Word's suggestion (indicated by a flashing cursor) by clicking Yes; move the insertion point to your preferred break and click Yes; or click No to prevent hyphenating the word.

Inserting the Date, Time, and Document Properties

You'll often want to include the current date in a document, such as when you're typing a letter. The simplest way to do this is to let AutoText take over. Begin typing the date (spelled out or in m/d/y format), and after you type the fourth character, a pop-up tip offers to complete the date if you would be so kind as to press Enter. Fair enough.

If you want additional formatting options, or if you want to enter the date in a way that can be updated to the current date when you use the document at another time, click Insert, Date & Time (in the Text group). Doing so displays a dialog box showing the current date and time formatted in various ways.

If you've been diligent about maintaining document properties (details such as the document title and author), you might find it useful to include some of these properties in your document text. To do so, on the Insert tab click Quick Parts, Document Property, and then click the name of the property to include. If you select a property that hasn't yet been defined in this document, Word enters a placeholder where you can type the property value. There's a real advantage to entering properties using the Quick Parts feature instead of typing the property value as ordinary text in your document: If you later change the property value, all occurrences of it in your document update automatically.

For more information about document properties, see "Organizing Office Documents Using File Properties and Details" on page 99.

Navigating in Word Documents

Naturally, the same techniques for browsing through a document in virtually any Windows-based program—scroll bars, Page Up and Page Down keys, and so on—work in Word 2010. But finding your way around a long document in these ways can be tedious, to say the least. Fortunately, Word includes a host of its own navigation features that make it easier to go directly to a particular location in a document.

Navigating Within a Document

A welcome addition to the navigation toolkit in Word 2010 is the Navigation pane, shown earlier in Figure 7-1. To display the Navigation pane, select its check box on the View tab, or press Ctrl+F.

The Navigation pane has three tabs near its top:

- The left tab shows each of the headings in your document, and you can jump directly to any heading by clicking it in the Navigation pane. (For information about what defines a heading, see "Formatting Paragraphs" on page 219.)

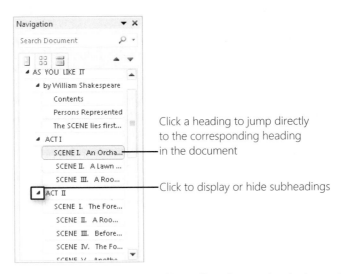

Click a heading to jump directly
to the corresponding heading
in the document

Click to display or hide subheadings

You can expand or contract this outline view so that it shows the headings you want
without you having to scroll a long way to find a particular heading: Click the triangle
at the left edge of a parent heading to expand or contract its subheadings. To expand
or contract the entire outline to a particular heading level, right-click any heading
and choose Show Heading Levels.

The headings tab is not just for navigation, however. With it, you can add, remove,
promote, and demote headings, and you can reorganize your document by dragging
headings in the Navigation pane. For details, see "Using Outlines to Plan, Organize,
and Edit Documents" on page 245.

- The middle tab shows a thumbnail image of each page in your document. You can
skip immediately to a document page by clicking its thumbnail.

Chapter 7

- The right tab shows search results. For details about using the Navigation pane for searching, see "Searching Within a Document" on page 210.

As an infomercial huckster might say, "But wait. There's more!" In addition to browsing by heading and by page, a less apparent feature of the Navigation pane lets you browse by other elements in a document, including graphics, tables, and reviewer comments. Click the magnifier icon next to Search Document to display a list of browse targets.

Choose Tables, for example, and on the left tab each heading under which a table resides is highlighted. On the center tab, only pages that contain a table appear as thumbnails. And in the document itself, every table is highlighted. You can move to the next or previous table by clicking the arrow buttons to the right of the tabs. To return to the normal Navigation pane views, click the X that replaced the magnifier you clicked earlier.

Similar functionality is available without using the Navigation pane. Click Select Browse Object (the round button near the bottom of the vertical scroll bar) to display a list of object types by which you can browse, as shown in Figure 7-5. Use the arrow keys or mouse to highlight an option, and then press Enter or click to select it. Thereafter, clicking Next or Previous (the double arrows above and below Select Browse Object) or pressing Ctrl+Page Down or Ctrl+Page Up jumps to the next or previous occurrence of the selected object type. (The default is to browse by page.)

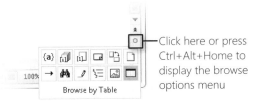

Click here or press
Ctrl+Alt+Home to
display the browse
options menu

Figure 7-5 You can choose to browse by field, endnote, footnote, comment, section, or page (top row). The bottom row browse options include heading, graphic, or table, plus shortcuts to the Go To and Find dialog boxes.

Word offers another way to navigate by object with its Go To command, which opens the Find And Replace dialog box to the Go To tab. You can display this dialog box, shown in Figure 7-6, in any of the following ways:

- In the Navigation pane, click the magnifier icon next to Search Documents and choose Go To from the menu that appears.

- On the Home tab, click the arrow next to Find (in the Editing group) and click Go To.

- Click Select Browse Object and click Go To (the arrow icon).

- Press Ctrl+G or F5.

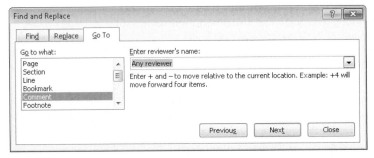

Figure 7-6 The interface is old school, but Go To offers some navigation capabilities not available in the Navigation pane.

Go To offers some additional object types that aren't available in the Navigation pane or in Select Browse Object. And unlike those methods, it's designed for going directly to a specific occurrence of an object as well as browsing from one to the next. For this reason, Go To has a couple of additional navigation tricks. For some types of objects (such as pages, sections, and lines), you can enter a number to go directly to a numbered item (for example, select Graphic and type **4** to go to the fourth picture or graphic, counting from the beginning of the document). If you precede the number with a plus or minus sign, you jump forward or back the specified number of objects; for example, select Line and type **+10** to advance ten lines. For other object types (such as bookmarks), Go To provides a list of valid destinations to which you can go.

INSIDE OUT   Jump to your last edit location when you open a document

When you open a document, you can pick up where you left off the last time you worked on the document. Press Shift+F5 to go to the location of the last edit when the document was closed.

You'll sometimes want to move around in a document while you're typing or editing text—when it might not be convenient to take your hand off the keyboard and reach for the mouse. Rest assured that Word has plenty of keyboard shortcuts for navigating around a document. Some of them are common to all Office programs, and you'll find them listed in Table 5-1 on page 108. Table 7-3 supplements the list with shortcuts that are unique to Word.

Table 7-3 **Keyboard Shortcuts for Navigating in Word**

Action	Keyboard Shortcut
Open the Navigation pane	Ctrl+F
Display the list of browse objects	Ctrl+Alt+Home
Go to the next object of the selected type	Ctrl+Page Down
Go to the previous object of the selected type	Ctrl+Page Up
Go to a page, section, bookmark, graphic, or other location	Ctrl+G or F5
Cycle through the locations of your last four edits	Ctrl+Alt+Z or Shift+F5
Go to top of current screen	Ctrl+Alt+Page Up
Go to bottom of current screen	Ctrl+Alt+Page Down

INSIDE OUT   Scroll using a stylus

If you have a computer with a stylus or touch capability, you have yet another way to move through a document: Click Pan, the hand-shaped icon near the top of the vertical scroll bar. The mouse (or stylus) pointer changes to a hand, and you can drag in any direction to scroll in a document, which is often easier than trying to use scroll bars. To return to normal pointer functionality, click Pan again.

Working with Multiple Document Windows

It's not just hard-driving multitaskers who sometimes need to have several document windows open simultaneously. For example, while you're working on a new document, you might want to have one or more reference documents open, or you might want to have an earlier, similar document open so that you can copy text and pictures from it.

Each document you open—whether you open it from Windows Explorer, a desktop shortcut, or the File menu in Word—appears in its own window. The standard Windows tools for arranging windows (easiest: right-click the taskbar and choose an arrangement) and for switching between windows (press Alt+Tab or click the taskbar button) apply to Word windows, of course. However, when you use these tools, you typically end up resizing or switching among all your open windows, including those for your web browser, e-mail program, games, and so on. Word has a few tricks for working exclusively with open Word windows without disturbing any of your other windows.

You'll find the window-management commands in the Window group on the View tab, shown earlier in Figure 7-2. These commands act as follows:

- **New Window**   Opens a new window that also contains the current document. To differentiate the windows, the caption (title bar) for each window shows a colon and a number after the file name.

- **Arrange All**   Places all open Word windows on the primary monitor, splitting the space equally among them so all are visible.

- **Split**   Splits the current window into two panes; see the following tip for details.

- **View Side By Side**   If two Word windows are open, this displays them side by side, each filling half the screen, so that you can easily compare the documents. (If more than two Word windows are open, Word asks which one you want to display next to the current window.) The feature is intended for comparing different versions of a document, but it also provides a quick and easy way to arrange windows containing different documents.

- **Synchronous Scrolling**   When this option is selected, scrolling in either side-by-side window scrolls both windows together. (Again, this feature is most useful for comparing versions of a document.) This option is available only when View Side By Side is selected.

- **Reset Window Position**   Restores the position of side-by-side windows so each occupies half the screen. This option is available only when View Side By Side is selected, and it has an effect only if one or both windows have been resized.

- **Switch Windows**   Displays a menu of all open Word windows, allowing you to quickly switch to another.

INSIDE OUT   Use a split-screen view of a document

When you're editing a document, it's often useful to look at two different parts of a document simultaneously. You might want to refer to a picture or table in one part of your document while you enter a textual description in another part, for example. You can click New Window (in the Window group on the View tab) to open the same document in a second window, but sometimes it's more convenient to split a single document window into two panes. You can split a window horizontally by using whichever method is easiest for you:

- On the View tab, click Split, and then click where you want the split to be.

- Drag the Split tool, the horizontal line at the top of the vertical scroll bar (just above View Ruler), down to the desired location.

- Press Ctrl+Alt+S, use the Up Arrow or Down Arrow key to move the split where you want it, and then press Enter.

You can then work in either part of the window. The panes scroll independently, and you can set each one to a different zoom level or document view. To switch to the other pane, click in it or press F6. (You might need to press F6 several times. Once you figure out the sequence, you can alternate between F6 and Shift+F6 to switch directly between the two panes.)

To remove the split, click Remove Split (in the Window group on the View tab), drag the pane divider to the top or bottom of the pane, or press Ctrl+Alt+S.

Naturally, Microsoft hasn't forgotten lovers of keyboard shortcuts when it comes to managing windows. Table 7-4 shows the ones that are unique to Office.

Table 7-4 **Keyboard Shortcuts for Working with Windows**

Action	Keyboard Shortcut
Move to the next or previous Word window	Ctrl+F6 or Ctrl+Shift+F6
Move to the next or previous pane (applies to panes in a split document, task panes, the ribbon, and status bar tools)	F6 or Shift+F6
Maximize or restore the current window	Ctrl+F10
Split the current window or remove the split	Ctrl+Alt+S

Searching Within a Document

Our discussion of the Navigation pane in the preceding sections touches on various items you can look for to quickly reach various locations in a document. But we haven't yet explored the topic of searching for text, which can also serve as a sort of navigational aid.

The easiest way to search for a particular text string is to type the text in the Search Document box at the top of the Navigation pane. (Press Ctrl+F to go directly there, regardless of whether the Navigation pane is already displayed.) As you enter your search text, Word immediately searches the document and displays its results, as shown in Figure 7-7. When you press Enter, Word selects the first occurrence of your search text.

Enter your search text here

Word displays each occurrence in context on this tab . . .   . . . and highlights all occurrences in the document

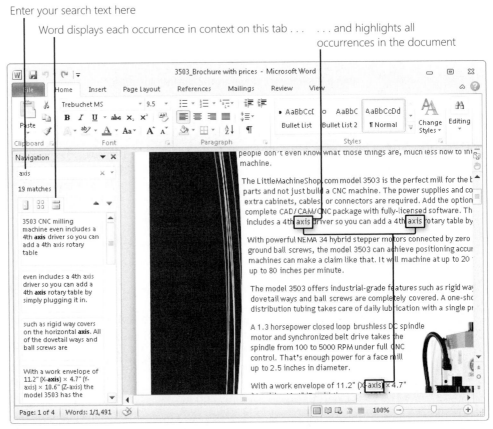

Figure 7-7 Search results in the Navigation pane are refined as you type each character in the search box.

To go to a particular search result, simply click the item in the Navigation pane. Note that the other tabs work as they do with object searches, described earlier in this chapter. On the left tab, each heading above each occurrence of the search text is highlighted, so you can see at a glance which parts of the document contain the text. The center tab is filtered so that it shows thumbnail images only of pages that include the search text.

As an alternative to clicking a search result, you can click the up or down arrow to the right of the tabs to go to the previous or next occurrence of the search text.

INSIDE OUT   Set find options

You can customize the way Navigation pane searches work by clicking the arrow at the right end of the Search Document box and choosing Options. The Find Options dialog box enables the use of wildcards (? for a single character, * for one or more characters) and lets you narrow (Match Case or Find Whole Words Only, for example) or widen (Sounds Like, Ignore Punctuation Characters, or Find All Word Forms, for example) your search.

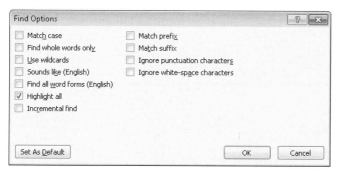

Sounds Like looks for your search word and its homonyms (words that sound the same but are spelled differently, such as *bread* and *bred*). It's great (grate?) for finding commonly confused words such as *there* and *their*.

Find All Word Forms uses a lexicon of related terms to include in search results. For example, with this option selected, a search for "buy" will find all occurrences of *buy*, *buying*, and *bought*.

Note that with some of these options selected, Word doesn't begin searching until you press Enter after entering your search text.

Searching for Nonstandard Characters

Searching in Word is not limited to letters, numbers, and other symbols. You'll often want to search for line-ending codes, perhaps to eliminate repeated line breaks or to find an occurrence of text that is at the end of a paragraph, for example. Table 7-5 lists the special characters and other items you can search for and the character string you enter to find them.

Table 7-5 Search Strings to Find Special Characters

Item to Find	Search String
Manual line break	^l (lowercase letter L)
Paragraph break	^p
Column break	^n
Manual page break	^m
Section break	^b
Tab character	^t
White space (space or tab)	^w
Nonbreaking space	^s
Nonbreaking hyphen	^~
Optional hyphen	^-
En dash (–)	^=
Em dash (—)	^+
Caret (^)	^^
Section symbol (§)	^%
Paragraph symbol (¶)	^v
Any character	^?
Any letter	^$
Any digit	^#
Endnote mark	^e
Footnote mark	^f
Field	^f
Graphic	^g

Including Formatting in Your Search Criteria

You might've noticed the Advanced Find command, either on the menu in the Navigation pane or on the Find menu in the Editing group on the Home tab. Selecting this command opens the Find And Replace dialog box and displays the Find tab. Longtime Word users will recognize this as the Find interface from earlier (pre–Navigation pane) versions of Word, but it continues to offer one capability that's not available in the Navigation pane: search for formatting.

You might want to use this feature to find an instance of a word in a heading or that's in boldface text, for example. To do that, on the Find tab in the Find And Replace dialog box, click More to expose additional options. Enter the text you want to find in the Find What box, and then click Format to specify the formatting you're looking for.

INSIDE OUT   Search for highlighted text

Highlighting text can be useful for students and others who want to mark important passages and for content authors who want to mark a section for later review. Because highlighting isn't treated like other character formats, you might conclude that the only way to return to the highlighted sections is to visually scan your pages. Fortunately, that's not the case.

To go to the next highlighted section, choose Advanced Find. Don't enter any text in the Find What box; just click Format (if the Format button doesn't appear, first click More), choose Highlight, and click Find Next.

Repeating a Search

If you use Advanced Find, you can leave the Find And Replace dialog box open even as you work in your document. You can go to the first search result, make some edits, and then click Find Next in the still-open Find And Replace dialog box to go to the next search result. (Note, however, that you might encounter some limitations while the dialog box is open. For example, you can't move text by dragging and dropping.)

Similarly, the Navigation pane can stay open while you switch back and forth between document and task pane, making it easy to go to the next result. Although the search results and highlights in the Navigation pane disappear when you edit in the document, they reappear when you click either of the arrows (the Previous Search Result or Next Search Result button) to the right of the tabs.

If you do close the Find And Replace dialog box or the Navigation pane, however, you can still go to the next result from your previous search: Simply press Ctrl+Alt+Y.

Searching and Replacing

A common editing task is to replace all occurrences of a certain word or phrase with another. To do that, press Ctrl+H to open the Find And Replace dialog box to the Replace tab, as shown in Figure 7-8.

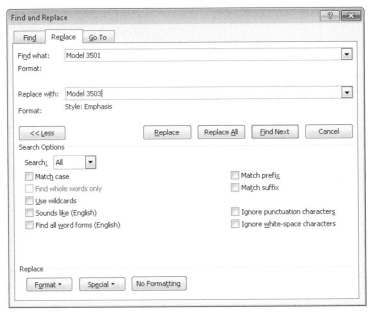

Figure 7-8 For a straight replacement of one bit of text with another, you can hide the clutter of this busy dialog box by clicking Less.

Clicking More displays additional options that let you refine your search, search for text formatted in a certain way, and apply formatting to the replacement text. If the insertion point is in the Find What box when you click Format, Word searches for text that has the formatting your specify. If it's in Replace With, Word applies the formatting when it replaces text.

Making Your Documents Look Good

An important part of "processing" words is formatting them to be legible and visually compelling. As with so many other tasks in Office, formatting can be done in several ways. In the next few pages, we describe how to apply formats directly to characters, paragraphs, and pages.

Direct formatting is the most obvious and most intuitive way to apply formatting, but as you'll see in the next section, "Giving Your Documents a Consistent Appearance" on page 224, the use of styles, themes, and templates offers more powerful ways to format a document. Nonetheless, the principles of direct formatting apply to those methods as well.

To apply formatting, you select the text you want to format and then apply the format.

> **Note**
>
> You can also apply formats without selecting text. Place the insertion point in a word, and any character formats you choose are applied to the entire word. Any paragraph formats you choose apply to the entire paragraph.

INSIDE OUT   Use Word tricks for selecting text

All the usual techniques you know for selecting text in other Windows-based programs (for an overview, see "Entering and Selecting Text" on page 107) work equally well in Word. Because manipulating text is one of its core functions, Word offers additional features for quickly and easily selecting text.

Touch typists and others who prefer keyboard shortcuts have an alternative to holding the Shift key as they use arrow keys to extend the selection. Press (and release) F8. Then use the arrow keys or other methods to extend the selection. Press Esc to cancel the F8 extend mode.

F8 is also handy for quick selections: Press it a second time to select a word, a third time to select a sentence, a fourth time to select a paragraph, and a fifth time to select the entire document. Press Shift+F8 to reduce the size of the selection.

Have you ever tried to make a vertical selection? Doing so is useful, for example, in tabular text, where you want to select text in one column to format it. The trick for doing that is to hold Alt or Ctrl+Alt as you drag, or press Ctrl+Shift+F8 and then use arrow keys to extend the selection.

Other tricks for mouse users: Double-click to select a word, triple-click to select a paragraph. Click in the left margin to select a line, or double-click in the left margin to select a paragraph.

To make multiple selections (which allows you to apply formatting to many different parts of a document simultaneously), hold the Ctrl key as you click and drag to make each selection. If you accidentally select something you didn't want to select, keep holding Ctrl and click the wrong selection again; that selection is cleared, while the rest of your selections remain.

Formatting Text

In Chapter 5, we showed how to format text by selecting the text and then choosing options on the Home tab or the Mini toolbar (or using keyboard shortcuts) to apply a font, point size, and basic formats such as bold and italic. For details, see "Applying Character Formatting" on page 124.

INSIDE OUT   Deal with fonts that aren't installed on your computer

A document that was created on a different computer might use fonts that are not installed on your computer. If you open such a document, Word does its best to find a similar font on your system to use for display and printing.

And if you're not happy with Word's best? Specify your own substitute fonts. Click File, Options. On the Advanced tab, under Show Document Content, click Font Substitution. In the dialog box that appears, Word lists all the fonts that are used but not installed. To specify a different font, select a missing font and then choose from the Substituted Font list.

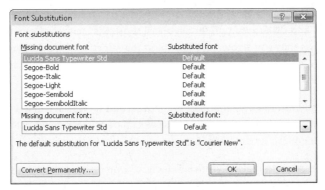

If you subsequently open the document on a computer where the original font is installed, Word uses that font. To change all occurrences in the document so that the substitute fonts are always used, click Convert Permanently.

Word supports several additional character formats that you can apply to text. Although some can be controlled from the Home tab, others require a visit to the Font dialog box, which you can launch by clicking the arrow in the lower right corner of the Font group on the Home tab or by pressing Ctrl+Shift+F. (Many of these formats can also be applied with shortcut keys, as shown in Table 7-6.)

Table 7-6 **Keyboard Shortcuts for Formatting Characters**

Action	Keyboard Shortcut
Open the Font dialog box	Ctrl+Shift+F
Change to Symbol font	Ctrl+Shift+Q
Increase font size	Ctrl+Shift+ >
Decrease font size	Ctrl+Shift+ <
Increase font size by 1 point	Ctrl+]
Decrease font size by 1 point	Ctrl+[
Turn bold on/off	Ctrl+B
Turn italics on/off	Ctrl+I
Turn underlining on/off	Ctrl+U
Turn word underlining (not spaces) on/off	Ctrl+Shift+W
Turn double-underlining on/off	Ctrl+Shift+D
Turn superscript on/off	Ctrl+Shift+Plus
Turn subscript on/off	Ctrl+ =
Turn small caps format on/off	Ctrl+Shift+K
Turn all caps format on/off	Ctrl+Shift+A
Turn hidden text on/off	Ctrl+Shift+H
Clear all manual character formatting	Ctrl+Spacebar

Most options in the Font dialog box need no further explanation, but some people are unfamiliar with the following:

- **Small Caps**   In this format, capital letters appear as they always do, but lowercase letters appear as smaller versions of the capitals—LIKE THIS.

- **All Caps**   As you would expect, in this format all letters appear as capital letters. The important thing to note is that the character codes do not change; Word merely changes the way lowercase letters are displayed. This difference means that if you turn off the All Caps format (or change to a style that doesn't have All Caps turned on), all the text reverts to its previous capitalization. Conversely, if you actually change case (by using the Change Case option in the Font group on the Home tab, or by using the Shift+F3 shortcut), the original capitalization is lost.

- **Hidden**   Text with this format disappears altogether except when you select Show/Hide ¶ (in the Paragraph group on the Home tab) or press Ctrl+*. Hidden text is handy for notes to yourself that you don't want to include in printed documents. (By default, hidden text doesn't print, even when it's displayed on the screen. To change this setting, click File, Options. On the Display tab, under Printing Options, select Print Hidden Text.)

CAUTION

Don't rely on hidden text to retain your deepest, darkest secrets. Anybody who has access to your document file can display the hidden text.

In this chapter, we describe text formatting through the selection of fonts and basic attributes. Word can do much more, however, including gradient fills, reflections, and other effects. For details, see "Applying Text Effects with WordArt" on page 182 and "Applying Advanced Text-Formatting Capabilities" on page 307.

Highlighting Text

You can highlight text—that is, apply a background color much as you would with a highlighter felt pen on a paper document—by clicking the Text Highlight tool in the Font group on the Home tab. (Optionally, click the arrow next to the tool to select a different pen color.) The mouse pointer changes to a highlighter pen, and you can then highlight various passages by dragging over them. Click the tool again or press Esc to turn off the highlighter pen. (Alternatively, you can highlight text by selecting it and then clicking the Text Highlight tool on the Home tab or on the Mini toolbar.)

Although you apply highlighting in the same fashion as character formats (such as bold or a point size), it is not a character format. Highlighting can't be included in a character or paragraph style, and it is not removed when you click Clear Formatting (in the Font group on the Home tab) or press Ctrl+Spacebar. To remove highlighting, click the arrow by the Text Highlight tool and choose No Color.

Highlighting can be copied just like other formats. For details, see "Copying Formatting" on page 128.

You can choose to hide highlighting on-screen and in printed documents without removing it. (Click File, Options. On the Display tab, under Page Display Options, clear Show Highlighter Marks.)

Although you can't include highlighting in a style, you can use the Shading tool (in the Paragraph group on the Home tab) to achieve a similar effect. Shading can be included in character and paragraph styles.

Formatting Paragraphs

Options for managing paragraph formatting appear on the Home tab and on the Page Layout tab (in the Paragraph group on both tabs).

The basics of paragraph formatting are the same in Word as in other Office programs; for more information, see "Applying Paragraph Formatting" on page 125.

On either tab, clicking the arrow in the lower right corner opens the Paragraph dialog box, shown in Figure 7-9. Here you can precisely set indents from the margins and line spacing.

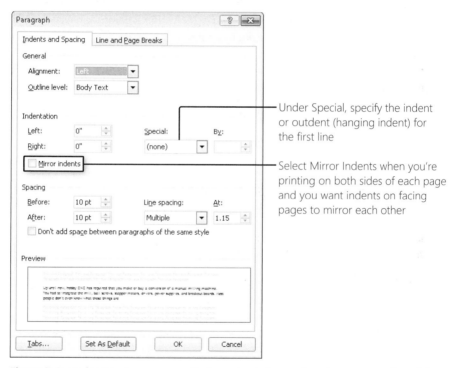

Under Special, specify the indent or outdent (hanging indent) for the first line

Select Mirror Indents when you're printing on both sides of each page and you want indents on facing pages to mirror each other

Figure 7-9 Under Spacing, you specify the space between lines in a paragraph and the amount of space above and below each paragraph.

As an alternative to the ribbon tools and the Paragraph dialog box, you can set indents by using the ruler, shown in Figure 7-10. Simply drag the indent markers to relocate them. To move the left indent and first indent simultaneously, drag the box below the left indent marker. Note that indents can extend into the page margins (notice the right indent in the figure); because indents are measured from the margin, the numeric values under Indentation in the Paragraph dialog box are negative in this case.

Figure 7-10 The colored background in the ruler indicates the page margins.

Standard line spacing settings (single, double, and so on) are readily made with the Line And Paragraph Spacing tool on the Home tab or by using keyboard shortcuts (see Table 7-7). Additional options are available only in the Paragraph dialog box. The Single option accommodates the largest font or graphic in each line, plus a bit of extra space. (If you have different point sizes in each line, the spacing within a paragraph will vary.) The 1.5 Lines, Double, and Multiple options are multiples of the Single line spacing value. With the At Least option, you specify a spacing value in points; Word uses the lesser of this value or the size needed to accommodate the largest font or graphic in a line. The Exactly option spaces all lines precisely at the height you specify, regardless of their content.

Table 7-7 **Keyboard Shortcuts for Formatting Paragraphs**

Action	Keyboard Shortcut
Left align	Ctrl+L
Switch between centered and left-aligned	Ctrl+E
Switch between right-aligned and left-aligned	Ctrl+R
Switch between justified (aligned left and right) and left-aligned	Ctrl+J
Increase left indent to next 0.5 inch	Ctrl+M
Reduce left indent to next 0.5 inch	Ctrl+Shift+M
Create a hanging indent	Ctrl+T
Reduce the hanging indent	Ctrl+Shift+T
Set line spacing to Single	Ctrl+1
Set line spacing to Double	Ctrl+2
Set line spacing to 1.5 Lines	Ctrl+5
Add or remove space before (12 pt)	Ctrl+0
Clear all manual paragraph formatting	Ctrl+Q

You also specify the space before (above) and after (below) each paragraph in the Paragraph dialog box. Note that the space after one paragraph is not added to the space before the following paragraph; instead, Word always uses the larger of the two values. The Paragraph dialog box also includes an option to suppress the space before and after paragraphs of the same style. This is handy, for example, with a bulleted list. You might want space before and after the list to set it off from other text, but not have space between each bullet item.

TROUBLESHOOTING

Text or graphics get clipped

If you set line spacing to Exactly, you might find that tops and bottoms of some letters don't appear. Of course, the problem could be that you're using text that's too big to fit in the allotted space; increase the line spacing or reduce the point size of the text.

That's not always the case, however. Because of a change in the way Word 2010 handles fonts, you might need to set a compatibility option to eliminate the clipping. Click File, Options, and click the Advanced tab. Scroll all the way to the bottom, and click the arrow to expand Layout Options. Then select Don't Center "Exact Line Height" Lines.

If your in-line graphics are being clipped, you have two alternatives: use a line spacing option other than Exactly, or change the graphic's text-wrapping style. (For details, see "Adding Pictures and Graphics" on page 237.)

Note

The default paragraph spacing in Word 2010 is different from previous versions of Word. In previous versions, the default was Single spacing, with no space after. In Word 2010, the default line spacing is Multiple 1.15 (that is, 15 percent more than Single) with a blank line after each paragraph. If you prefer the old, tighter spacing, on the Home tab click Change Styles, Style Set, Word 2003.

Paragraph formatting is associated with the paragraph mark at the end of each paragraph. (The paragraph mark is normally hidden, but you can display it and other formatting marks by pressing Ctrl+*.) You can demonstrate this by selecting and copying a paragraph mark and then pasting it elsewhere; the paragraph that ends with the newly pasted mark uses the same paragraph styling as the paragraph from which it was copied.

Setting Page Layout Options

Options on the Page Layout tab determine the page size, orientation, and margins for a document—settings you can also make via the Page Setup dialog box, shown next.

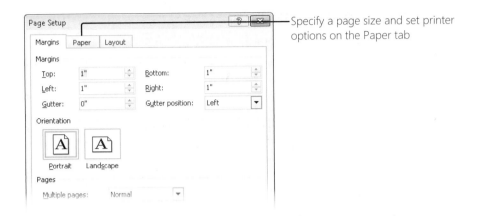

Specify a page size and set printer options on the Paper tab

To quickly adjust the page margins, use the ruler. As shown earlier in Figure 7-10, the "live" area within the margins is indicated by a white background in the ruler. To move a margin, drag the edge of the colored area.

Also on the Page Layout tab, options in the Page Background group provide access to some interesting, but seldom used, features. You can select or create a "watermark"—some text or a picture that prints as a background on each sheet. Watermarks are often used to identify proprietary information (with a message like "CONFIDENTIAL" or "DO NOT COPY"), but the feature makes it easy to use a picture (which can be optionally washed out so it doesn't interfere with text) as a background. Clicking Page Borders opens the Borders And Shading dialog box, wherein you can define a rectangular frame to surround each page.

For information about multicolumn and other complex layouts, see "Formatting Columns and Sections" on page 248.

Adding Headers, Footers, and Page Numbers

A header or footer is a block of text at the top or bottom of each page. Some headers and footers are constant throughout a document—perhaps showing your company name or a document's date. Headers and footers can also incorporate variable text; this can be as simple as a page number, or it can vary depending on the page content. (For example, notice the headers in this book. The ones on left-hand pages include a page number, the chapter number, and the chapter title; headers on right-hand pages include heading text, which changes throughout the chapter.)

You'll want to decide whether to use different headers and footers on left and right pages (something to consider only if your document will be printed on both sides of the paper), and whether you want to use a different header and footer (or none at all) on the first page of the document. You can make those settings on the Layout tab of the Page Setup dialog box, but it's simpler to just go directly to the Insert tab and click Header or Footer. Either way, a gallery appears, from which you can select a predefined or a blank header or footer.

After you make your selection, you're working in the header and footer area of the document. Many of the predefined headers and footers have content controls, which are defined areas where you can type. Many content controls are linked to document properties. For example, many headers and footers use the Title property to incorporate the document title into the document. If you've already defined the title, it appears in place when you insert a header or footer that uses it. If you haven't yet defined the title, placeholder text appears, as shown in Figure 7-11.

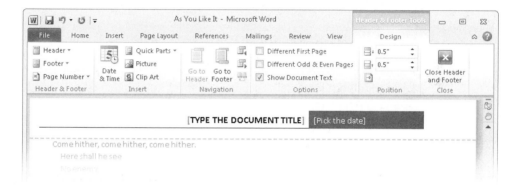

Figure 7-11 Typing over the document title placeholder not only fixes the header but sets the Title property. Headings update automatically if you change the value of the Title property.

INSIDE OUT   Prevent content controls from updating

To convert the text in a content control to static text—regardless of whether it comes from a property setting or you typed it—right-click it and choose Remove Content Control.

To work in the header and footer area, double-click it. To switch back to the body of your document, double-click it or click Close Header And Footer on the Design tab under Header & Footer Tools (see Figure 7-11). While working in the header and footer area, use tools in the Navigation group to jump back and forth between header and footer and to jump to the previous or next footer in a document with multiple sections. Each section has its own header and footer. If you want to use the same one in successive sections, go to the section *after* the one whose header and footer you want to continue; then click Link To

Previous. (For more information about sections, see "Formatting Columns and Sections" on page 248.)

Editing in the header and footer area is the same as editing in the document body: click and type.

Also on the Design tab, you can select a different header or footer; insert the date, time, picture, or other items; specify whether to use different headers on the first, odd, and even pages; and specify the distance between the header or footer and the edge of the page.

Giving Your Documents a Consistent Appearance

In the preceding pages, we explain how to apply formatting directly. Although this technique is useful for short documents, if you try to directly format a longer document you'll discover the shortcomings of this method. First, it's tedious; you need to make a lot of individual settings separately. Second, it's difficult to maintain consistency throughout a document. And third, it's difficult to modify your document if you decide to implement a different design.

Word has three related features that overcome the weaknesses of direct formatting:

- **Themes** An Office *theme* is a set of theme colors, theme fonts, and theme effects. Switching to a different theme changes all those components at once—as long as the document uses styles that rely on theme fonts and colors. For information about selecting and modifying themes, see "Using Office Themes" on page 185.

- **Styles** A *style* is a collection of formatting settings that can be applied to characters, paragraphs, lists, or tables. A character style, for example, might specify a font, size, font style, and color. A paragraph style typically includes character formatting information (font, size, and so on) as well as formats that apply strictly to paragraphs, such as line spacing, indents, borders, and tab stop settings. You can apply a style—and all the formatting steps it includes—with a simple selection in the Quick Style gallery.

  Word 2010 includes a number of predefined styles—indeed, several sets of predefined styles—that you can use right away, or you can define your own styles.

- **Templates** A *template* is a file in which you can store styles. Each document you create is based on a template. Word uses the template called Normal.dotm by default, but you can select a different template (one that's included with Word, one you download, or one you create yourself) when you create a new document. When you create a new document, Word copies all the styles (along with AutoText entries and any text, pictures, or other document elements) into the new document.

Understanding how themes, styles, and templates work together is an essential part of Word mastery. It might seem daunting because Word offers numerous choices—dozens of predefined themes, countless styles (and style sets, which are collections of styles), and over 50 sample templates—and on first appearance you might think these all work independently. That's not the case.

A template brings its own collection of styles, so once you apply styles to a document, if you select a different style set (or change templates), your document instantly changes to reflect the formatting for the like-named styles in the new style set or template. And if the styles are defined to use theme fonts and theme colors, when you change themes, you get the fonts and colors from the new theme. You can make these changes in any order, and through the use of galleries and Live Preview, you can easily see how each change in styles affects the document.

As an example, Figure 7-12 shows a document that was created using the Adjacency Report template, one of the samples included with Word 2010. The screen on the right shows the same document, with the Modern style set and Black Tie theme applied.

Figure 7-12 Changing the style set added paragraph borders and backgrounds; changing the theme applied different fonts, colors, and a page background.

Using these formatting techniques instead of direct formatting is a trait of advanced Word users—yet once you understand the concepts, you'll find that using styles, themes, and templates is actually much easier than direct formatting. Using styles and themes allows you to provide consistency throughout a document, and by saving and using templates, you can employ a consistent appearance from one document to another and throughout your organization.

INSIDE OUT   Use PowerPoint slide backgrounds to fill shapes

A consistent appearance among all your company's documents lends a professional air, but you can go a step further by incorporating similar graphic elements in your Word documents and PowerPoint presentations. You can do that by using slide backgrounds from your PowerPoint presentations to fill shapes in your Word document.

To use these backgrounds, be sure to select the same theme in your Word document and in the PowerPoint presentation whose designs you want to echo. Select the shape you want to format and then, under Drawing Tools, click the Format tab. In the Shape Styles group, click the More button to open the gallery. At the bottom of the gallery, click Other Theme Fills to display a gallery of fills that mirror elements in the Power-Point template.

The Adjacency Report template, used to create the document shown in Figure 7-12, uses these fills as page backgrounds. Changing the theme selected a different, more visible, background.

Applying Styles

The simplest way to apply a style is to make a selection in the Quick Style gallery, which occupies most of the Styles group on the Home tab, as shown in Figure 7-13. As you point to different options in the gallery, Live Preview shows how each option looks in your document.

CAUTION

As noted earlier, if you apply a paragraph style when no text is selected, Word applies the style to the paragraph that contains the insertion point. Likewise, if all or parts of more than one paragraph are selected, Word applies the paragraph style to each paragraph that is fully or partially selected. However, if less than one full paragraph is selected, Word applies only the character formats from the paragraph style and does not apply any paragraph formats. For more information, see "Understanding Linked Styles" on page 313.

Figure 7-13 The current style of the selection is highlighted in the gallery.

Handy as it is, the Quick Style gallery has some drawbacks. It doesn't show all available styles in a template, and it can be a bit cumbersome to use. Fortunately, as with so many operations in Office, alternative methods abound. You can apply styles with any of these techniques:

- Press Ctrl+Shift+S to open or switch to the Apply Styles task pane, which normally appears as a floating window. Begin typing the name of the style you want, and when the full name appears, press Enter to apply the style. The task pane remains open, so you can switch to it at any time by clicking it or pressing Ctrl+Shift+S.

—Styles

- Open the Styles task pane, shown in Figure 7-14, by clicking the dialog box launcher in the Styles group on the Home tab; by pressing Ctrl+Alt+Shift+S; or by clicking Styles in the Apply Styles pane. To apply a style, simply click it. Note that when you point to a style name, a ScreenTip shows a textual description of the style's attributes. If you prefer a more visual approach, select Show Preview, which displays each style name as the style is formatted. The Styles task pane has additional tricks and capabilities; for details, see "Tools for Working with Styles" on page 231.

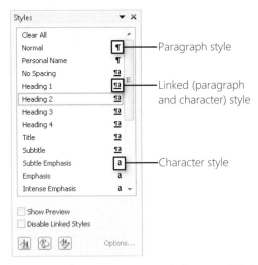

Figure 7-14 The Styles pane includes a symbol that identifies each style's type.

- Use a keyboard shortcut to apply a style to the current selection. Table 7-8 shows predefined shortcuts for applying styles, and you can define your own shortcuts for applying other styles. To do that, open the Modify Style dialog box (for details, see "Creating a New Style" on page 233) and click Format, Shortcut Key.

Table 7-8 Keyboard Shortcuts for Applying Styles

Action	Keyboard Shortcut
Open the Apply Styles task pane	Ctrl+Shift+S
Open the Styles task pane	Ctrl+Alt+Shift+S
Apply the Normal paragraph style	Ctrl+Shift+N
Apply the Heading 1 style	Ctrl+Alt+1
Apply the Heading 2 style	Ctrl+Alt+2
Apply the Heading 3 style	Ctrl+Alt+3
Apply the List Bullet style	Ctrl+Shift+L

INSIDE OUT   Show style names in Draft and Outline views

If you use Draft view or Outline view to work in your document, it's sometimes difficult to see which styles are in use. To overcome this difficulty, click File, Options. In the Word Options dialog box, click the Advanced tab and scroll down to Display. Next to Style Area Pane Width In Draft And Outline Views, enter 1".

Now you'll see a pane along the left side of your document that shows the style for each paragraph. To adjust the width of this pane, simply drag the line that separates it from the document content.

Making Global Changes to Your Document

Having applied styles to the paragraphs and text in your document, you can now experience the magic of themes and style sets.

You can select a different theme by choosing from the Themes group on the Page Layout tab. As you point to each theme, Live Preview shows its effect on your document. To remove theme settings and revert to settings in the template, click Themes again and choose Reset To Theme From *TemplateName* Template.

To select a new style set, in the Styles group on the Home tab, click Change Styles, Style Set. A menu of predefined style sets appears, and again Live Preview shows the result. (Note that you can also select the Colors and Fonts theme elements from the Change Styles menu. These are the same choices you see on the Page Layout tab.) Commands at the bottom of the Style Set submenu restore the Quick Styles from the template or from the current document. (Although a new document gets its styles from a template, you can subsequently modify those styles and keep the changes only in the document, without updating the template.)

You can also make global changes by modifying your existing styles or by applying a different style to certain paragraphs. When you modify a style, all instances of that style in your document are updated to use the new attributes. For more information, see "Creating a New Style" on page 233.

INSIDE OUT   Prevent formatting changes

If your intent is to enforce a uniform look throughout your organization's documents, having the freedom to select different themes and style sets works against this goal. To limit formatting changes in a document, click Restrict Editing on the Review tab. In the Restrict Formatting And Editing pane, click Settings (under Formatting Restrictions). In the Formatting Restrictions dialog box, shown next, select the styles you want to allow, and select options to prevent changing style sets and themes. Click OK. Back in the Restrict Formatting And Editing pane, click Yes, Start Enforcing Protection.

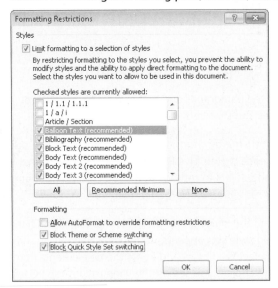

Restrictions you impose this way protect only the current document. Through the Manage Styles dialog box, you can impose additional restrictions, and you can apply these restrictions to the current document or to the current template, which then enforces the restrictions on any new documents created from the template. For more information about Manage Styles, see the following section, "Tools for Working with Styles."

INSIDE OUT   Change all occurrences of one style to another

You might have a need to change all instances of a style to another. This is often the case when you import text from a document that uses different styles, for example. You can use search and replace to find and replace each one, but there's a simpler way to select all occurrences of a style. In the Quick Style gallery, right-click the style of interest and choose Select All *xx* Instance(s). (Alternatively, in the Styles task pane, click the arrow to the right of a style name to find this command.) With all instances selected, you can then apply another style, apply direct formatting, or even delete all paragraphs formatted with that style.

Tools for Working with Styles

In addition to the tools for applying styles, Word offers several tools for examining formatting and styles, including these:

- **Reveal Formatting**   Press Shift+F1 to display this task pane, which shows all the formatting attributes applied to the current selection. Each of the blue underlined headings in this task pane is a link to the dialog box in which you can change that particular attribute.

Under Selected Text, select Compare To Another Selection to open a second sample text box. Select some other text, and Reveal Formatting lists the formatting differences between the two selections.

- **Style Inspector** In the Styles task pane, click Style Inspector (the second button at the bottom of the pane) to open the task pane shown next. In its first and third boxes, Style Inspector shows which styles have been applied at the paragraph and character level. The second and fourth boxes identify any direct formatting that has been applied. A button next to each of these boxes clears that formatting from the selection.

- **Manage Styles** The Manage Styles dialog box, which you open by clicking the third button at the bottom of the Styles task pane, is the place to make a variety of style-related settings, including these:

  - On the Set Defaults tab, specify the format for text and paragraphs that don't have any style applied, for which Word uses the built-in Normal style. (A common gripe about earlier versions of Word was the difficulty of changing the default style of 10-point Times New Roman. Although Manage Styles is deeply buried, once you find it you'll see that changing the default formatting is easy.)

  - The Edit tab includes a complete list of styles from the current document; select any one and click Modify to make changes to the style.

  - To limit the formatting changes that users can make, visit the Restrict tab.

- On the Recommend tab, you can identify certain styles as "recommended" and specify the order in which they appear in the Styles or Apply Styles panes. (To show recommended styles or other styles, click Options in the Styles pane, shown earlier in Figure 7-14.)

- To copy styles from one document or template to another, click Import/Export to open the Organizer dialog box.

> **Note**
>
> To add a style to the Quick Style gallery, open the Styles pane, click the arrow to the right of the style name, and click Add To Quick Style Gallery. To remove a Quick Style from the gallery (but not delete the style from the document), right-click the gallery entry and choose Remove From Quick Style Gallery.

Creating a New Style

When the template you're using doesn't have a style you need, create a new one. You can do this in either of two ways:

- Use any combination of styles, themes, and direct formatting to create an example of the style you want. Then right-click it, point to Styles, and choose Save Selection As A New Quick Style. Word displays a dialog box in which you can give the new style a name, which appears in the Quick Style gallery, the Styles pane, and the Apply Styles pane. By default, the new style is stored in your document, but it is not added to the template from which the document was created. To add it to the template, you need to modify the style, which you can do by clicking Modify in the Create New Style From Formatting dialog box.

- Create a new style "from scratch." In the Styles pane, click New Style (the first button at the bottom of the pane). A dialog box similar to the one shown in Figure 7-15 appears.

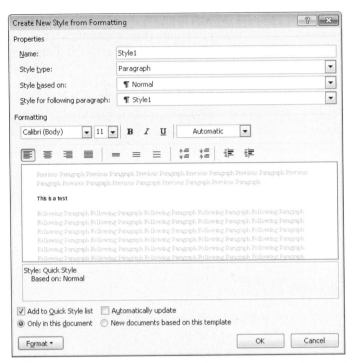

Figure 7-15 Basic character and paragraph formatting options are in this dialog box. Click Format for additional options.

Some items in this dialog box require a bit of explanation:

- **Style Type** Your choice here determines which options are available elsewhere in the dialog box (see Table 7-9 for details), so it should be your first stop after you give the style a name. For more information about the Linked style type, see "Understanding Linked Styles" on page 313.

- **Style Based On** If you want to make a style that's similar to another one, you can save time by selecting that style here. You won't need to repeat its settings, and you ensure that the two styles stay in sync. That is, if you make changes to the base style, those changes appear in the new style automatically. If you want to be sure that the new style does *not* change when you update another style, select No Style here.

- **Style For Following Paragraph** This feature adds a bit of automation to your document when you enter text by setting the style for the next paragraph when you press Enter in a paragraph that uses this style. It's typically used for heading styles, so that the paragraph following a heading is automatically formatted as body text.

- **Font**   Select one of the first two entries, which include the word *Body* or *Headings*, if you want changes to the font theme to affect this style. Note that if you click Format, Font to select font details, the two theme options are identified as +Body and +Headings.

- **Font Color**   To enable theme colors to affect this style (and other style colors you can set, such as the colors for underlines, borders, and shading), in the Font Color box select an option under Theme Colors. To prevent theme influence, select an option under Standard Colors.

- **Automatically Update**   If you select this check box, whenever you apply direct formatting to a paragraph that uses this style, Word automatically updates the style (and thereby updates all paragraphs in the document that use the style). We don't recommend this option, as too often it makes changes you don't expect.

  If you don't select Automatically Update, you can update a style by right-clicking the paragraph and choosing Styles, Update *StyleName* To Match Selection.

Table 7-9 Formatting Options Available for Each Style Type

	Character	Paragraph	Linked	Table	List
Font	✔	✔	✔	✔	✔
Paragraph		✔	✔	✔	
Tabs		✔	✔	✔	
Borders and Shading	✔	✔	✔	✔	
Banding				✔	
Language	✔	✔	✔		
Frame		✔	✔		
Numbering		✔	✔		✔
Shortcut Key	✔	✔	✔		✔
Text Effects	✔	✔	✔	✔	
Table Properties				✔	

If you prefer to use a dialog box similar to the one shown in Figure 7-15 to make changes to a style, you can do so by right-clicking a style in the Quick Style gallery (or clicking the arrow to the right of a style name in the Styles task pane) and choosing Modify.

Applying a Template to an Existing Document

When you create a document based on a template, the new document begins as a copy of the template, incorporating all its text, graphics, macros, and AutoCorrect entries—as well as its styles.

For details about selecting a template when you create a new document, see "Using Templates to Streamline Document Creation" on page 97.

You can apply a template to an existing document if, for example, you want to use the styles from the template. Note, however, that when you apply a template this way, you don't get its text, graphics, and page layout. But if your goal is to pick up styles, follow these steps:

1. Add the Templates button to the Quick Access Toolbar. (For details, see "Customizing the Quick Access Toolbar" on page 62.) Alternatively, display the Developer tab. (See "Personalizing the Ribbon" on page 57.)

2. Click the Templates button (or the Developer tab) and then click Document Template. The Templates And Add-Ins dialog box appears.

3. On the Templates tab, click Attach. Browse to the template you want to apply, and then click Open. Back in the Templates And Add-Ins dialog box, click OK.

If you want to use other template elements—its page layout and graphics, for example—a better approach is to create a new document based on the template. Copy all the text from your current document and paste it into the new document.

Saving and Modifying Templates

When you make changes to a style, those changes are stored in the current document and affect all instances of the style in the document. When you want those changes to be copied to the template from which the document was created (so that the changes affect documents created from the template in the future), you must take an extra step. For each style that you want to store in the template, open the Create New Style From Formatting dialog box (shown earlier in Figure 7-15) or the nearly identical Modify Style dialog box. Be sure that New Documents Based On This Template is selected, and then click OK. When you close the document, Word asks if you want to save any unsaved changes, and also asks if you want to save changes to the template. Click Save.

INSIDE OUT   Make changes to the Normal style

You can quickly change the font and paragraph style for the Normal style—the template style used for paragraphs to which no other style has been applied—without digging down to the Modify Style dialog box. Simply open the Font dialog box or Paragraph dialog box (easiest way: click the dialog box launcher in the Font or Paragraph group on the Home tab), make your changes, and click Set As Default.

To incorporate the currently selected style set and theme selection into the template, on the Home tab, click Change Styles, Set As Default For *TemplateName* Template. Doing so includes these styles and settings in the template and also uses them as the defaults when you create a new document based on the template.

Adding Pictures and Graphics

In many cases, a Word document consists of much more than just words. Pictures, clip art, line drawings, charts, screenshots, and other types of graphics can visually enhance nearly any document. SmartArt graphics combine text and graphics to produce compelling charts and presentations.

The techniques for creating, inserting, resizing, rotating, and formatting each of these graphical object types are the same in Word as they are in other Office programs. We describe these object types and the techniques for using them in Chapter 6, "Working with Graphics and Pictures."

Although the object types are consistent throughout Office, Word offers unique ways to position such graphics within a document. Word uses one of two basic methods to position a graphic:

- **In line with text**   In-line graphics are treated as part of the document's text stream. They maintain their position between the characters or paragraphs where they are inserted, and they move to the right or down with each character or line you insert before them.

- **With text wrapping**   Word offers several text-wrapping variants, which we explore next. In each of these variants, a graphic's horizontal and vertical position is specified relative to the page, margins, or other landmark. The graphic moves automatically only if the landmark to which it's tied moves.

TROUBLESHOOTING

A graphic is cropped to just one line high

You might find that after you insert a picture or other graphic, it's severely cropped, so that only the bottom of the picture appears. This happens when an in-line graphic is placed in a paragraph that has fixed line spacing. You can fix the problem—and show the entire picture—in either of two ways.

- Change the text wrapping to an option other than In Line With Text.

- Change the line spacing for the paragraph to a setting other than Exactly.

For the simplest placement options, select a graphic and, on the Page Layout tab, click Position. A gallery appears, and Live Preview shows the effect of each gallery option as you hover the mouse pointer over it. Options in the Position gallery let you place a graphic at any margin or centered between the margins.

To more precisely control the positioning of a picture or graphic in Word, you use the Wrap Text option. You can get to Wrap Text by selecting the object and then clicking the Page Layout tab; Wrap Text is in the Arrange group. (You'll also find Wrap Text in the Arrange group on the Format tab under Picture Tools or Drawing Tools.) Alternatively, right-click an object to display a menu that includes Wrap Text.

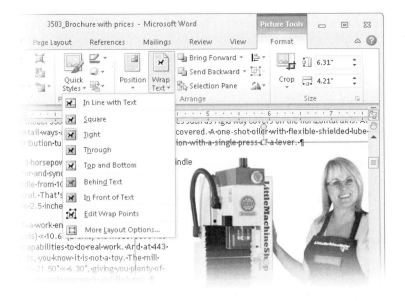

Clicking More Layout Options opens the Layout dialog box, shown in Figure 7-16, in which you can specify additional wrapping parameters, such as whether text wraps on both sides of the graphic or only one side, and the distance between the wrapped text and the graphic.

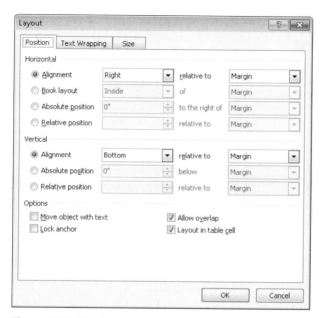

Figure 7-16 The Position tab allows you to place the graphic at an absolute position or relative to various document landmarks, such as a margin, the edge of the page, or a paragraph.

You'll sometimes want to wrap text around an irregular shape, such as the picture shown in Figure 7-17. You do this with the Edit Wrap Points command on the Wrap Text menu. Hold down Ctrl and click on the red outline to create a wrap point, which you can then drag into position. To remove a wrap point, Ctrl+click it again.

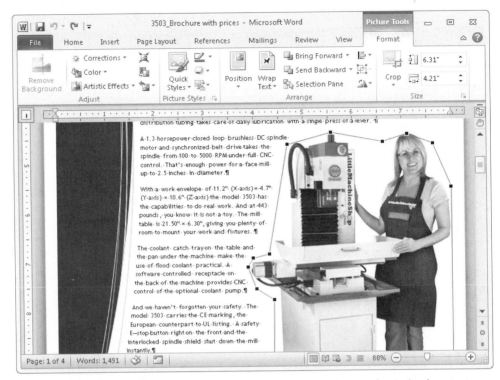

Figure 7-17 The picture is a rectangular image, but wrap points let you determine how text wraps around a graphic, regardless of the graphic's actual shape. We also used wrap points to set the curved left margin in this document.

Working with Bulleted and Numbered Lists

A common element in Word documents is a list. Bulleted lists are typically used when the order of the items is unimportant, whereas numbered lists are often used for procedural steps or in legal documents where each section can be identified by its number.

For simple bulleted and numbered lists, Word formats the paragraphs automatically as you type. Begin a paragraph with an asterisk followed by a space, for example, and Word removes the asterisk and applies an appropriate style that includes a bullet character and is indented properly. A similar conversion occurs when you begin a paragraph by typing the number 1 followed by a period and tab. The AutoFormat process continues when you press Enter twice after the last list item: Word removes the extra paragraph and reverts to the Normal paragraph style for subsequent paragraphs.

To apply standard list formats to existing paragraphs, select the paragraphs and then select the Bullets tool or Numbering tool in the Paragraph group on the Home tab. Click the arrows on the right side of these tools to expose additional options, such as different bullet characters or different numbering styles, as shown in Figure 7-18.

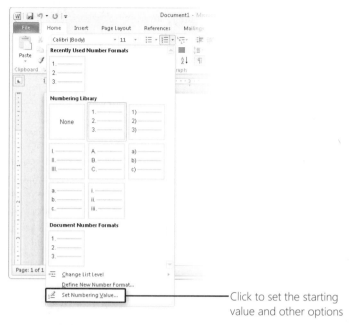

Click to set the starting value and other options

Figure 7-18 If you don't like any of the numbering styles in the library, click Define New Number Format.

Numbered lists are renumbered automatically as you add and remove paragraphs. Ordinarily, numbering restarts at 1 following an unnumbered paragraph. If you want to continue numbering from the previous list, right-click the incorrect number 1 paragraph and choose Continue Numbering. Conversely, you can begin numbering anew at any point by right-clicking and choosing Restart At 1.

To create a list within a list, press Tab at the beginning of a list paragraph. Word further indents the paragraph and applies a different bullet character or numbering style. (For example, if your top-level list is numbered 1, 2, 3, and so on, Word numbers the next level as a, b, c.... If you don't like this standard convention, click the Bullets or Numbering tool and select a different style.) Word restarts numbering for a lower-level list after each higher-level list.

For additional options for multilevel numbered lists, click Multilevel List, the tool to the right of Numbering in the Paragraph group on the Home tab. Here you can make settings that aren't available in the standard Define New Number Format dialog box, and you can make settings for each level (up to nine levels deep) without leaving the dialog box.

INSIDE OUT   Use SmartArt to create compelling lists

To create bulleted lists that are more visually interesting, take a look at SmartArt graphics, which combine lists with chartlike graphics. For more information, see "Adding SmartArt to Documents" on page 180.

One Other Type of Numbering: Line Numbers

Some documents must have line numbers printed in the margin of each page. This feature, which is unrelated to the numbered lists described on the preceding pages, is widely used in legal documents. To add line numbers to a document, on the Page Layout tab, click Line Numbers (in the Page Setup group) to see a menu of numbering options. For additional options (the ability to set the starting number, increment, and distance from the text), click Line Numbering Options. On the Layout tab of the Page Setup dialog box that appears, click Line Numbers.

Checking Grammar and Spelling

Office 2010 has a spelling checker that, for the most part, works the same in all Office programs. For details about its use, see "Checking Spelling" on page 139. As we noted in that section, however, Word also incorporates tools for checking grammar and style into the spelling checker.

Grammatical errors that Word detects are marked in your document with a squiggly green underline. As with spelling errors (which are marked with a squiggly red underline), you can right-click the offending phrase or sentence to see a list of proposed corrections from which you can choose, along with links to more information about the error. Results of the grammar review also appear when you check spelling throughout a document by clicking Spelling & Grammar on the Review tab (or by pressing this option's shortcut key, F7).

Correct grammar is somewhat subjective, and you might want to limit the items that Word flags for review or customize the rules to your personal style guidelines. For example, while there is consensus on proper subject/verb agreement, grammar nitpickers still debate the serial comma. To change how the grammar review works, click File, Options. On the Proofing tab, scroll down to When Correcting Spelling And Grammar In Word. First, decide whether you want Word to check for stylistic faux pas (such as passive sentences) in addition to grammar; next to Writing Style, select Grammar Only or Grammar & Style. Then click Settings to examine the available grammar options.

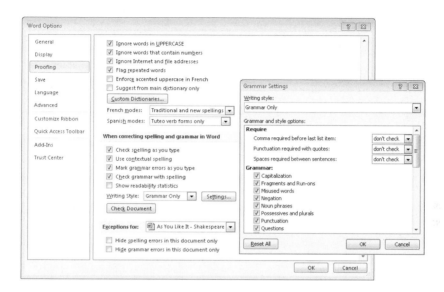

The options you set here apply to all documents you open in Word.

After you close Grammar Settings, you can click Check Document (or Recheck Document, if you've already performed a spelling and grammar review) to proof your document using your new settings.

CHAPTER 8

Working with Complex Documents

W ORD is a workhorse that excels at producing documents with complex layouts, such as newsletters, brochures, and other multicolumn designs. Word also has the features to manage extremely long documents, such as reports, scripts, and books. (You shouldn't be surprised to learn that the manuscript for this book was prepared using Word 2010.)

In this chapter, we focus on tasks that are usually associated with complex or long documents, including outlining, inserting cross-references, and creating tables of contents and indexes. We also explain how to use sections both to break up long documents and to create complex layouts. And we show how to create and format tables, which can be useful in documents of any complexity or length.

Using Outlines to Plan, Organize, and Edit Documents

Writing a well-organized long document usually starts with an outline of topics, headings, and notes. With Outline view, Word provides a work environment that is ideal for planning a document before you begin writing and is also useful for reviewing and organizing your document as writing progresses. In Outline view, you can hide some or all of the body text, allowing you to concentrate solely on the headings.

For details about switching views, see "Working in an Appropriate Document View" on page 193.

In Outline view, paragraphs that have a heading style appear in outline form, with each successive heading level indented a bit more from the left margin, as shown in Figure 8-1. When you work in Outline view, only the document's text appears; graphics are hidden. Although text formatting remains intact, paragraph spacing and indents follow outline style. (If you want to suppress text formatting so that it's easier to focus on the outline's content, clear Show Text Formatting on the Outlining tab.)

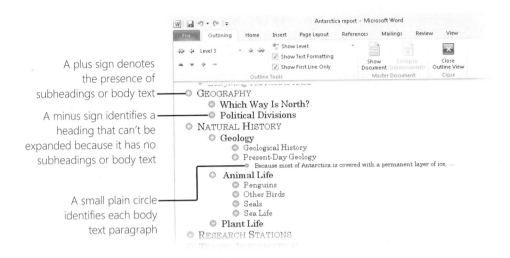

A plus sign denotes the presence of subheadings or body text

A minus sign identifies a heading that can't be expanded because it has no subheadings or body text

A small plain circle identifies each body text paragraph

Figure 8-1 In Outline view, the Outlining tab appears to the right of the File tab.

The outline feature uses heading styles to determine outline levels. In the style sets that are part of each template included with Word 2010, these heading styles are called Heading 1, Heading 2, Heading 3, and so on. (Any paragraph or paragraph style can be modified so that it appears in the outline hierarchy. You do that in the Paragraph dialog box, where you'll find Outline Level under General on the Indents And Spacing tab.) For more information about paragraph styles, see "Formatting Paragraphs" on page 219.

Tools on the Outlining tab make it easy to promote, demote, and view different outline levels:

- The Outline Level box (shown as Level 3 in Figure 8-1) sets the heading level for the current selection.

- The left and right arrows on either side of the Outline Level box promote or demote the selection by one level. For example, if the current selection is formatted as Heading 2, clicking the right arrow demotes it to Heading 3.

- The double left arrow promotes the selection to a top-level heading, Heading 1.

- The double right arrow demotes the selection to body text, applying Normal style.

- The Move Up and Move Down arrows move the selection within the outline. (This tool moves up or down one entry with each click. To move a selection a greater distance, you'll find it easier to drag an outline marker—the circle at the left end of each heading or paragraph. Doing so moves all subheadings and body text as well as the selected heading.)

- The Expand (plus sign) tool expands the selection to show its subheadings or body text.

- The Collapse (minus sign) tool hides subheadings or body text below the selected heading.

- Show Level collapses and/or expands all headings to show the level you select and all higher-level headings.

When you're typing in Outline view, you can use the usual keyboard shortcuts for applying styles (including Ctrl+Alt+1 for Heading 1 and Ctrl+Shift+N for Normal), but you might find it easier to use Tab and Shift+Tab to set heading levels. Indeed, most of the work you do through the Outlining tab can be performed with keyboard shortcuts, which are listed in Table 8-1.

Table 8-1 Keyboard Shortcuts for Working with Outlines

Action	Keyboard Shortcut
Switch to Outline view	Ctrl+Alt+O
Show Level 1 headings only	Alt+Shift+1
Show headings to Level 2	Alt+Shift+2
Show headings to Level 3	Alt+Shift+3
Show headings to Level 4	Alt+Shift+4
Show headings to Level 5	Alt+Shift+5
Show headings to Level 6	Alt+Shift+6
Show headings to Level 7	Alt+Shift+7
Show headings to Level 8	Alt+Shift+8
Show headings to Level 9	Alt+Shift+9
Promote by one level	Shift+Tab or Alt+Shift+Left Arrow
Demote by one level	Tab or Alt+Shift+Right Arrow
Expand a collapsed outline	Alt+Shift+Plus sign
Collapse an expanded outline	Alt+Shift+Minus sign
Move up	Alt+Shift+Up Arrow

Navigating in Long Documents

Outline view also provides a method for jumping directly to a particular part of a document. When you exit Outline view and return to Print Layout view, you'll find that the insertion point or selection remains in the same heading and that the heading is near the top of the screen.

Chapter 8

While that's convenient if you happen to be working in Outline view, there's no reason to switch to Outline view to jump to a heading. A much better tool for that purpose is the Navigation pane. (For details, see "Navigating Within a Document" on page 203.)

Notice that the Navigation pane has many of the capabilities of Outline view. It shows a hierarchically organized outline of your document headings. You can selectively expand and collapse the hierarchy by clicking the triangle next to a heading name. And, just as you can in Outline view, you can drag headings up or down within the Navigation pane to reorganize your document; all subheadings and body text move with the heading you move.

Other outlining features are exposed when you right-click a heading in the Navigation pane, as shown here.

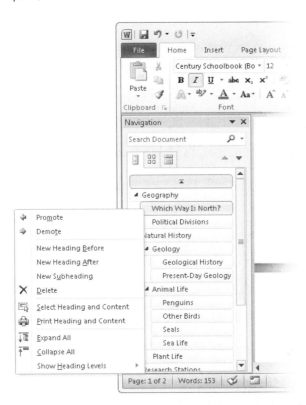

Formatting Columns and Sections

Word uses *sections* to enable the independent formatting of parts of a document that have a different page layout. A section break separates each part that has different page margins, different orientation, a different column layout, or even different headers and footers.

Within a section, you can have different headers and footers for odd pages, even pages, and the first page of a section. And those headers can include variable text, such as the text of the most recent heading. But if you want to change static text or the layout of the header or footer—or if you want a first-page header to appear, say, on the first page of a new chapter in your document—you must insert a section break.

For more information about headers and footers, see "Adding Headers, Footers, and Page Numbers" on page 222.

To insert a section break, place the insertion point where you want the break to go, click the Page Layout tab, and click Breaks (in the Page Setup group). As shown in Figure 8-2, you can choose a continuous break (one that begins the new section immediately below the break without beginning a new page) or a break that starts the new section on a new page. If you want to start on a new page, you must choose whether you want to begin on the next page (regardless of whether it's odd or even), the next even page, or the next odd page. The last two options, which are often used in book layouts (for example, in this book each chapter begins on an odd-numbered page), insert an extra blank page if necessary.

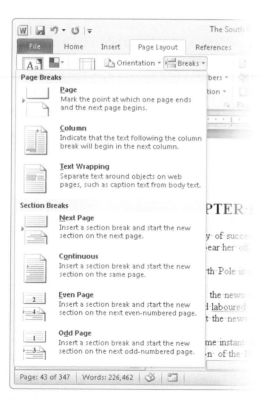

Figure 8-2 Any of the last four options on the Breaks menu inserts a section break.

With section breaks in place, page layout changes you make with options in the Page Setup group on the Page Layout tab apply by default to the current section only (the one that contains the insertion point or selection). To change the margins, orientation, paper size, or column layout for more than one section, select all or parts of the sections you want to format before you apply the format. Alternatively, click the dialog box launcher in the Page Setup group. At the bottom of each tab in the Page Setup dialog box, you'll see options similar to the ones shown here that let you specify the scope of your formatting change. You'll find options like these on the Page Border tab of the Borders And Shading dialog box as well.

When you insert a section break, the new section inherits the page layout settings of the section that follows the break. If no section breaks exist when you insert the first one, the new section inherits the document's settings. Much as paragraph formatting is associated with the paragraph mark at the paragraph's end, section formatting is associated with the section mark at the end of a section. Understanding that little factoid makes it easier to anticipate what happens if you delete a section mark—the new, combined section uses the settings of what was its second section.

INSIDE OUT   Copy section formatting

Understand too that you can copy a section mark; when you paste it elsewhere, the section that it completes has the same page settings as the section from which it was copied.

Creating a Multicolumn Layout

Word can format text in columns, which flow text in such a way that when the bottom of a column is reached, the text continues at the top of the next column, similar to the way newspapers (remember those?) look. Aside from its visual appeal, a multicolumn layout has an important practical benefit: shorter line lengths are easier to read, particularly in smaller point sizes.

To format your document so that it has more than one column, click the Page Layout tab, click Columns (in the Page Setup group), and select a number of columns.

It's a rare document that is formatted using a multicolumn layout throughout, however. A more likely scenario is to have a heading or picture that spans the full page width, with multiple columns below. Figure 8-3 shows an example.

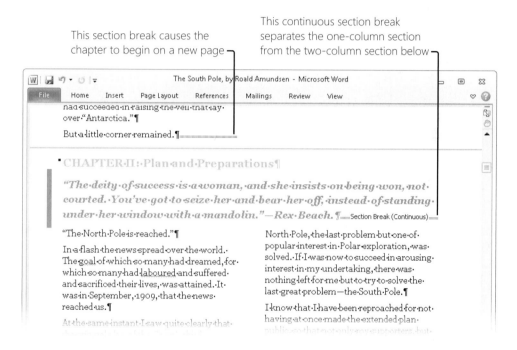

Figure 8-3 It's easier to work with sections and columns when formatting symbols are displayed.

To set up a document like this, follow these steps:

1. If formatting symbols are not displayed, press Ctrl+* or click Show/Hide ¶ on the Home tab.

2. Place the insertion point where you want the multicolumn layout to begin, and then click Page Layout, Breaks, Continuous to insert a section break.

3. Place the insertion point where you want the multicolumn layout to end, and then insert another section break.

4. Click somewhere between the two section marks, and then click Page Layout, Columns. If the basic options on the Columns menu don't suit you, click More Columns to display the Columns dialog box.

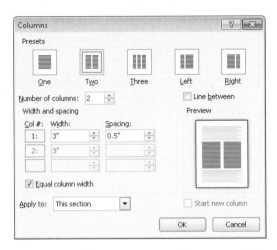

Here you can format as many columns as will fit on the page (the minimum column width is 0.5 inch), and you can set the amount of space between each one. By clearing Equal Column Width, you can set the column width and the spacing independently for each column.

In a multicolumn layout, you can insert a manual column break by choosing Column on the Breaks menu (shown earlier in Figure 8-2) or by using its keyboard shortcut, Ctrl+Shift+Enter.

INSIDE OUT   Balance columns on the last page

Ordinarily, on the last page of a multicolumn layout (or the last page of a multicolumn section followed by a section break that starts a new page), text tends to end up on the left side of the page. That's because Word flows text in the usual way: it doesn't begin a new column until the current column is filled all the way to the bottom.

Your document will look more professional if the last page flows text in all columns to an equal depth. Forcing that to happen is easy: insert a continuous section break at the end of the multicolumn text. (If you already have a new-page section break, as shown in Figure 8-3, this means you'll end up with two consecutive section breaks.)

Working with Tables

Tables, of course, are ideal for tabular data—text or numbers in a gridlike layout of rows and columns, such as the list of keyboard shortcuts shown earlier in Table 8-1. But resourceful Word users find many other uses for tables. For example, when you want to have headings in the left column that align with text in the right column, use a table. Such a layout is used in documents such as resumes and in forms such as the fax cover sheet created by the Origin Fax template. Figure 8-4 shows this template, which is one of the samples included with Word 2010.

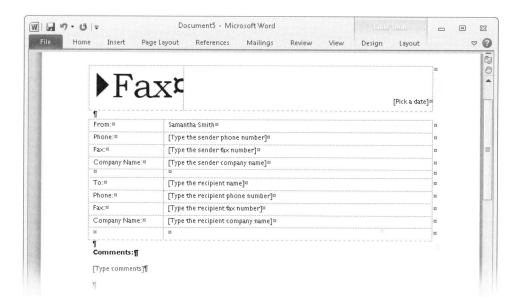

Figure 8-4 This template uses two tables to align text. The gridlines in these tables do not print.

Creating a Table

Word provides several ways to add a table to your document:

- **Insert Table**   Using either a quick-entry gallery or a dialog box, you can insert an empty grid into your document.

- **Draw Table**   You can use a mouse or a stylus to sketch out a table layout, which Word converts to carefully aligned columns and rows.

- **Convert Text To Table**   If you have existing document text with some sort of separator between column data (a paragraph mark or a tab, space, or other character), Word can create a table and place the text in table cells.

- **Quick Tables**   Word includes a gallery of predesigned tables that you can insert. You can add your own tables to the gallery.

Using the Insert Table Command

To add a table to a document, place the insertion point where you want the table to go, and then on the Insert tab, click Table. Now you're faced with a choice. If your table won't exceed 10 columns in width or 8 rows, point to the grid that appears, as shown here.

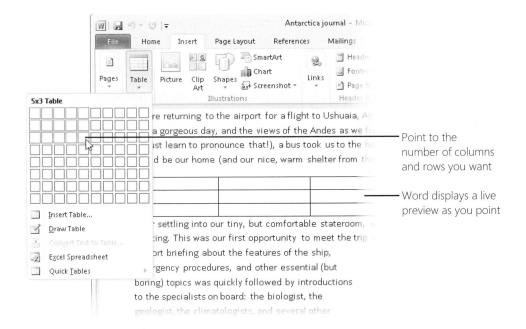

Point to the number of columns and rows you want

Word displays a live preview as you point

You can always add more columns or rows later (see "Adding and Removing Rows and Columns" on page 266), but if you want to start out with more (up to 63 columns and 32,767 rows) or want to set other table options, click Insert Table on the menu to open the dialog box shown next.

Under AutoFit Behavior, you have three options for controlling column width:

- **Fixed Column Width**   Sets each column to the width you specify. If you leave it set to Auto, Word evenly divides the space between the left and right page margins by the number of columns. If you subsequently add or remove columns and the width is set to Auto, Word readjusts the column widths to fit the space.

- **AutoFit To Contents**   Adjusts the column widths as you enter information to get the best fit for each column—"best" meaning that Word expands each column to accommodate each cell's contents in the fewest number of lines without going beyond the page margins.

- **AutoFit To Window**   Evenly divides the space between margins by the number of columns—just like choosing the first option with the width set to Auto.

You can select an AutoFit option any time after you insert a table by clicking in the table and then clicking AutoFit in the Cell Size group on the Layout tab under Table Tools.

INSIDE OUT   Change the default number of columns and rows

If you often create tables with the same number of columns or rows, you can change the default values in the Insert Table dialog box. Specify the values, and then select Remember Dimensions For New Tables before you click OK.

Drawing a Table

This method is the best one for drawing complex tables, such as tables with a cell that spans several columns or rows, or tables that have a different number of cells in each row. To draw a table, on the Insert tab click Table, Draw Table. The mouse pointer becomes a pencil. Drag diagonally to draw a rectangle that defines the outer boundaries of the table. Then draw horizontal and vertical lines within that rectangle to create rows, columns, and cells. You can also draw diagonal lines within a cell, as shown here.

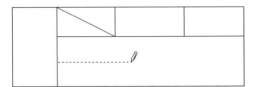

To exit drawing mode, click anywhere (in a table cell or outside the table) and begin typing, or simply press Esc. To resume drawing, click in the table, click the Design tab under Table Tools, and click Draw Table in the Draw Borders group.

To erase a line, click Eraser (on the Design tab under Table Tools), and then click the line you want to erase.

Using tools in the Draw Borders group on the Design tab, you can specify the style, weight, and color of lines you draw. You can make your selections before you draw or, to change an existing line, make your selections and click the line while in drawing mode.

Converting Text to a Table

Word can take text that's in a standard data format and place it in a table. Begin by entering the data, inserting a separator character after each data item (that is, each item you want to go into a table cell), and pressing Enter each time you want to start a new table row. You can use any character as a separator, but commas, spaces, or tabs are the most commonly used. The only limitation is that the separator character can't be part of the data you want to include in the table.

With your data in place, select the text, and then click Insert, Table, Convert Text To Table. In the dialog box that appears (shown in Figure 8-5), Word shows its best guess at which separator character is in use and how many columns and rows will appear in the table. You can, of course, override those guesses.

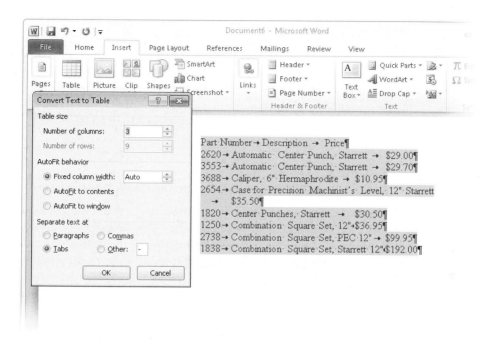

Figure 8-5 Because formatting characters are displayed here, you can see that we used tabs as the separator character.

TROUBLESHOOTING

Comma-separated values files don't convert properly

A widely used data interchange format is a comma-separated values file, or CSV file. A CSV file is a plain-text file that uses a comma to separate each item in a row of data and a paragraph mark at the end of each row. So far, perfect for conversion.

Problems arise when a data item that's intended to go in a single cell contains a comma. Programs that create CSV files deal with this situation by enclosing the item in quotation marks. Unfortunately, Word doesn't recognize this convention, so it ends up splitting data at every comma (and erroneously preserving the quotation marks, to boot).

You can work around this problem in either of two ways. If possible, use a different separator character in your data file; many programs can produce a tab-separated values file as an alternative to CSV. If that's not possible, open the file in Excel, which properly handles quotation marks. You can then use Excel to save the file as a tab-delimited file, or simply copy the data from Excel and paste it into your Word document.

Using Quick Tables

Word includes a gallery of tables that are already formatted and even filled with data. These include several calendar layouts as well as various data tables. Although the data is unlikely to be useful to you, Quick Tables provide handy templates that take care of the layout and formatting tasks, leaving you only the job of filling in the data. To view the gallery and insert a Quick Table, on the Insert tab click Table, Quick Tables.

INSIDE OUT   Add your own tables to the Quick Tables gallery

After you lay out and format a table to perfection, you might want to reuse it (albeit with different data) elsewhere. To add it to the Quick Tables gallery, select the table and then click Insert, Table, Quick Tables. At the bottom of the gallery, click Save Selection To Quick Tables Gallery. In the dialog box that appears, you can give this new building block a name and modify other details—or you can simply click OK.

Working with Table Data

You enter and edit data within a table in much the same way as you do elsewhere in a document. A table cell can contain any amount of text. It can also include pictures and graphics; you can even insert another table within a table cell.

Just as it does in normal text, pressing Enter in a table cell inserts a paragraph mark. To move to another cell, press Tab or Shift+Tab. Pressing Tab moves to the next cell to the right or, at the end of a row, to the first cell in the next row. Shift+Tab moves in the opposite direction. If you press Tab in the table's last cell (the one in the lower right corner), Word appends a new row that's formatted the same as the current last row. Table 8-2 shows other keyboard shortcuts you can use for moving within a table.

Table 8-2 **Keyboard Shortcuts for Moving in Tables**

Action	Keyboard Shortcut
To next or previous cell in a row	Tab or Shift+Tab
To first or last cell in a row	Alt+Home or Alt+End
To first or last cell in a column	Alt+Page Up or Alt+Page Down
To previous or next row	Up Arrow or Down Arrow
Move current row up or down by one row	Alt+Shift+Up Arrow or Alt+Shift+Down Arrow

> **Note**
>
> To insert a tab character in a table cell, press Ctrl+Tab.

Selecting Table Data

To select text within a cell, you use the usual Office and Word techniques. (See "Entering and Selecting Text" on page 107 and "Making Your Documents Look Good" on page 214.)

To select one or more table cells, you can use tools on the Layout tab under Table Tools. Click Select in the Table group, and then you can choose to select the current cell, column, or row—or the entire table. To select the entire table, you can also use the Alt+Shift+5 keyboard shortcut. (You must use the 5 on the numeric keypad.)

You can also use the mouse to select a cell (click in the cell's left margin), a row (click to the left of a row), or a column (click at the top of a column). You'll know you're in the right place when the mouse pointer changes to an arrow (a small black arrow to select a cell or column, or a white arrow for a row). Drag to extend the selection to include multiple cells, rows, or columns. To select the entire table, point to the upper left corner of the table and click when the mouse pointer appears as a four-headed arrow. If you have trouble getting the mouse pointer in the precise location for making a selection, an alternative is to right-click and choose Select; a submenu appears with Cell, Column, Row, and Table commands.

Sorting Table Data

You can sort rows of data according to the content of the cells in a column. You can, in fact, perform a multilevel sort on up to three columns. For example, if you have a directory of names and addresses, you might want to organize the list alphabetically by name within each town. To do that, you sort on postal code, then by last name, and then by first name.

To sort data in a table, click in the table. (Be sure the insertion point is in the table and that nothing is selected.) Then click the Layout tab (under Table Tools) and click Sort in the Data group. The Sort dialog box appears, as shown in Figure 8-6.

If the first row of your table contains descriptive titles instead of data, select Header Row. Then choose the column (or columns) by which you want to sort. Indicate the type of data in each column (text, numbers, or dates) and the sort order to use.

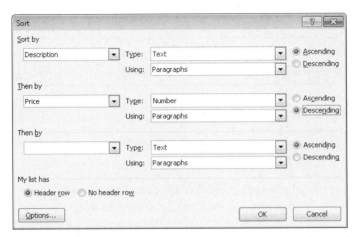

Figure 8-6 This sort groups all items with the same description, and within each group sorts by price, from highest to lowest.

Using Formulas in Tables

Within a Word table cell you can use a small subset of Excel functions for performing numeric calculations. Word identifies cells in a table in the same way that Excel does: a letter/number combination that specifies the column and row, beginning with cell A1 in the upper left corner of the table.

To enter a formula at the insertion point, on the Layout tab (under Table Tools), click Formula in the Data group. The Formula dialog box appears, as shown in Figure 8-7.

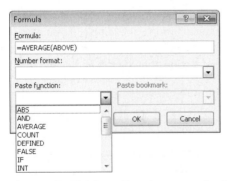

Figure 8-7 Click Paste Function to see the full list of available functions.

Just as you do when entering a formula in Excel, begin your entry in the Formula box with an equal sign. You can then use cell and range references, constants, mathematical operators, and functions from the Paste Function list to complete the formula. For more information, see "Using Formulas and Functions" on page 356.

Word has four range names that you won't find in Excel: ABOVE, BELOW, LEFT, and RIGHT. With these ranges, you can create a formula that includes all the cells in the direction you specify. For example, to display the total of the values in a column, in a row at the bottom of the column you would insert the formula =SUM(ABOVE).

INSIDE OUT   Use an Excel table for more demanding calculations

As noted, the formula capabilities of Word don't compare favorably with those of Excel. If you need text functions, date calculations, or more advanced mathematical calculations, you need to use Excel. That doesn't mean that you can't include the data and the resulting calculations in your Word document, however.

You insert an Excel worksheet into your document in much the same way you insert a table: on the Insert tab, click Table, Excel Spreadsheet. While you work in the Excel spreadsheet, you have the full capabilities of that program. In fact, the ribbon changes to show the same tabs and tools you see in Excel.

To include more or fewer Excel columns and rows in your Word document, drag the borders of the Excel object. When you click outside the worksheet, the Excel interface (such as row and column headings) disappears, and the Word ribbon returns. Double-click in the worksheet to resume editing in Excel.

Formatting a Table

The table you get when you use the Insert Table or Convert Text To Table command is not much to look at: a simple grid of thin black lines, with text aligned at the top and left of each cell. With a few simple commands on the Design and Layout tabs under Table Tools (see Figure 8-8), you can quickly spruce up the table's appearance.

Chapter 8

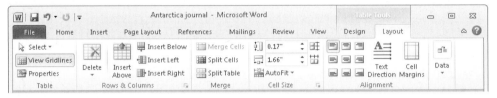

Figure 8-8 These tabs appear under Table Tools whenever the insertion point or selection is in a table.

Aligning Text

When a cell is wider or taller than its contents, where should the text go within that space? You'll probably want ordinary text to be left and top aligned, but you might want to set column headings so that they're centered and bottom aligned. You might want a column of numbers to be right aligned.

To get any of these permutations (or others), select the cells you want to align. Then, in the Alignment group on the Layout tab (see Figure 8-8), select one of the nine options (every combination of left, center, and right; and top, middle, and bottom).

Note that you can use paragraph formatting and styles within a table cell, which allows you to set other alignment options, such as paragraph indents, hanging indents, bullet lists, and so on.

Rotating Text

To rotate text in the selected cells 90 degrees in either direction, click Text Direction (in the Alignment group on the Layout tab).

Rotating text to a nonperpendicular angle is not so easy. You can select the text to rotate (but not the entire cell), convert it to WordArt (click Insert, WordArt), and then rotate the WordArt object. (For details, see "Applying Text Effects with WordArt" on page 182 and "Resizing and Rotating Graphics and Pictures" on page 157.) Alternatively, insert an Excel worksheet in your document, and use Excel to rotate the text in selected cells to any angle.

Adding Borders and Shading

To apply background shading to one or more cells, select the parts of the table you want to shade. On the Design tab (see Figure 8-8), click Shading (in the Table Styles group) and select a color.

To apply a border, first select the line type, weight, and color in the Draw Borders group on the Design tab. Then click the arrow next to Borders (in the Table Styles group) to display a gallery of locations to which you can apply the border. Your gallery choice becomes the default, so you can apply the same border (for example, a border around the outside of the selection) to another selection simply by clicking Borders without opening its gallery.

The Borders And Shading dialog box from earlier Word versions is available in Word 2010; click Design, Borders, Borders And Shading, or more simply, right-click the table and choose Borders And Shading. For tables and cells, the only feature the dialog box provides that isn't available on the Design tab is the ability to apply some unappealing patterns as shading.

Applying Styles

The quickest way to dress up your table is to use a style. On the Layout tab (see Figure 8-8), click the More button by the Table Styles gallery to see nearly 100 colorful table styles from which you can choose.

Check boxes in the Table Style Options group on the Layout tab determine which parts of a style are applied:

- Select Header Row if the first row of your table has column titles. Similarly, select First Column if the first column contains row titles.

- Select Total Row if you want a specially formatted row at the bottom of the table—one that is typically used for numeric totals or summary data. Last Column serves a similar purpose for the rightmost column.

- Select Banded Rows or Banded Columns if you want to use bands of alternating colors to make your table easier to read.

To customize the table style currently in use, open the Table Styles gallery and click Modify Table Style. In the Modify Style dialog box, shown next, you can change any component of the style—fonts, borders, shading, alignment, banding, and so on—for the entire table or independently for each part of the style (such as the header row or last column).

For more information about customizing styles, see "Creating a New Style" on page 233.

Changing the Table Layout

Not surprisingly, you'll find tools for modifying a table's layout—the number of rows and columns—on the Layout tab under Table Tools. See Figure 8-8.

Adjusting Column Widths and Row Heights

Using options in the Cell Size group on the Layout tab, you can set the height of the selected rows and the width of the selected columns. You might find it easier to adjust the size directly. Position the mouse pointer on a table gridline, where it becomes a two-headed arrow around a separation line. At that point, you can drag to resize the row or column.

INSIDE OUT   Resize a single column

When you drag the border between columns to the left, the column on the left side of the border gets narrower and the column on the right gets wider; the opposite happens when you drag to the right. To resize only the column on the left without affecting the column on the right, hold Shift as you drag.

Setting column widths using these methods specifies a precise dimension for each column. To set widths automatically, choose one of the AutoFit options (for details, see "Using the Insert Table Command" on page 254). Another option is to click Distribute Columns, which divides the space evenly among the selected columns. In this case, Word specifies the width as a percentage of the total table size.

For additional control over column widths, click the arrow in the lower right corner of the Cell Size group to open the Table Properties dialog box, shown in Figure 8-9. On the Column tab, you can specify the width for each column as an absolute dimension or a percentage of the total. On the Row tab, you can set the row height to an exact dimension, or you can select At Least, which allows the row to grow to accommodate its content.

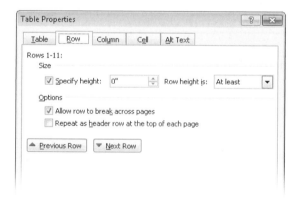

Figure 8-9 You can cycle through your entire table by clicking Previous Row and Next Row (or comparable buttons on the Column tab).

INSIDE OUT   Resize columns and rows using the ruler

Another way to adjust widths and heights is by dragging the column and row separators on the ruler. But here's a neat trick: Hold down Alt as you drag, and Word shows precise measurements of each column or row in the ruler.

Adding and Removing Rows and Columns

Tools for adding or removing rows or columns are in the Rows & Columns group on the Layout tab. You'll find similar options on the menu that appears when you right-click in a table.

If you click Delete, Delete Cells, a dialog box appears, as shown here. You must tell Word whether to move the remaining cells in the row to the left, or to move the remaining cells in the column up.

Merging and Splitting Table Cells

In its Merge group, the Layout tab includes a tool for merging selected cells into a single cell and another tool for splitting selected cells into the number of columns and rows that you specify.

When you merge two or more cells into one, the content of all the original cells is preserved in the new, single cell. Text that was once separated into individual cells is now placed in separate paragraphs in a single cell.

As an alternative to the Merge Cells and Split Cells tools, you can perform these tasks with the Eraser and Draw Table tools on the Design tab. Click Eraser and then click the border between two cells to merge them. Click Draw Table and draw a line in a cell to split it in two.

Positioning a Table

In much the same way that a picture or other graphic can be positioned in the normal flow of text (in line) or placed on the page so that text wraps around it, you can specify text wrapping options for a table. To control a table's position on the page, on the Layout tab click Properties in the Table group. In the Table Properties dialog box, shown in Figure 8-10, click the Table tab, where you can set alignment options and set an indent from the left margin.

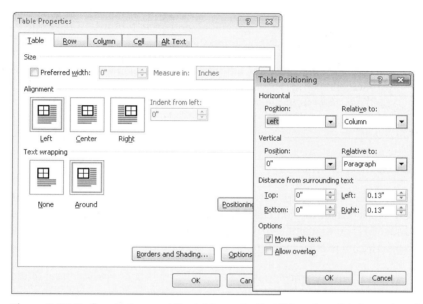

Figure 8-10 To flow text around the table, under Text Wrapping click Around, and then click Positioning to specify placement options.

As an alternative to the dialog box routine, point to the upper left corner of the table. When the mouse pointer turns into a four-headed arrow, drag the table to the position you want. To adjust text wrapping options, you'll need to visit the Table Positioning dialog box.

Working with Tables That Span a Page Break

Two issues come into play when a table goes beyond the end of a page:

- Should rows be allowed to break across pages, or should the contents of each row be kept intact?

- Do you want to repeat one or more rows as column titles at the top of each page?

You'll find settings for both options on the Row tab of the Table Properties dialog box, shown earlier in Figure 8-9.

INSIDE OUT · Insert a paragraph at the top of a page

In a document that begins with a table, if you press Ctrl+Home to go to the beginning of the document and then begin typing, your text goes into the first cell, not in a new paragraph. Solving this problem requires creative use of Split Table, a tool in the Merge group on the Layout tab. As you might guess, that tool splits a table into two tables, with an empty paragraph separating them.

To insert an empty paragraph before the table, place the insertion point in the table's first row, and then click Split Table. Alternatively, you can use the keyboard shortcut for Split Table, Ctrl+Shift+Enter.

Deleting a Table

If you select one or more cells in a table—or even the entire table—and press the Delete key, Word deletes the contents of the selected cells, but leaves the table grid intact. Depending on what you're trying to do, you might consider this to be a feature; after all, it makes it easy to clear the contents of a table or form so that you can reuse it.

If you're intent on removing the table as well as its contents, you have three options:

- On the Layout tab under Table Tools, click Delete (in the Rows & Columns group), Delete Table.

- Select all cells in the table and then cut the selection to the Clipboard. (Note that doing so replaces the current Clipboard content.)

- Extend the selection so that it includes the table and at least one character outside the table, and then press Delete.

Inserting References to Other Parts of a Document

Cross-references are a common part of many document types, including legal documents (which often refer to other sections by paragraph number) and books like this one (which includes numerous page number references to other sections of the book).

Cross-references update automatically when the document content changes. For example, if edits to your document change the page number on which a referenced heading falls, a reference like "see 'Summing It All Up' on page 47" gets the correct page number. And if you change the text of the heading, all references to it update as well. Similarly, if you use captions to number and identify figures or tables, the numbers update automatically when you add, remove, or reorder the numbered items.

Defining Reference Targets

You can insert references to a variety of document elements, as listed next. Notes in the following list explain how to ensure that Word recognizes each reference target as such.

- **Numbered Item** To use a numbered item as a target, apply a numbered list style. (For details, see "Working with Bulleted and Numbered Lists" on page 240.)

- **Heading** To refer to a heading, you must apply a heading style to the heading paragraph. (For details, see "Applying Styles" on page 226.)

- **Bookmark** A bookmark can serve as a browse target as well as a cross-reference target, making it useful for returning to a specific document location. To insert a bookmark, first place the insertion point where you want to place a bookmark, or select the text you want to use as a bookmark. Then click the Insert tab and click Bookmark (in the Links group). In the Bookmark dialog box, type a name for your bookmark; the name can contain letters, numbers, and underscore characters, but it can't contain spaces or other punctuation.

> ### Working with Bookmarks
>
> To jump to a bookmark you've defined, press Ctrl+G to open the Go To dialog box, select Bookmark, select the bookmark name, and then click Go To. (For details about other ways to browse by bookmark, see "Navigating Within a Document" on page 203.)
>
> You can make your bookmarks visible. Click File, Options to open the Word Options dialog box. Click Advanced, and then, under Show Document Content, select Show Bookmarks. A bookmark set to a single point appears as an I-beam; bookmarked text appears between colored square brackets. The bookmark indicators are not included when you print a document.

- **Footnote**   A footnote consists of a footnote reference (a superscript number or symbol in the document text) and a note at the bottom of a page; footnotes are typically used to include explanatory notes or bibliographic citations. To use a footnote as a cross-reference target, you must create it using the Insert Footnote tool, which you can find in the Footnotes group on the References tab.

- **Endnote**   Endnotes are similar in form and function to footnotes, except the notes appear at the end of the document. To use an endnote as a cross-reference target, create it with the Insert Endnote tool, also in the Footnotes group on the References tab.

- **Equation**   To refer to a numbered equation, add a caption that includes a {SEQ Equation} field code, as explained in the following section.

- **Figure**   To refer to a numbered figure, add a caption that includes a {SEQ Figure} field code, as explained in the following section.

- **Table**   To refer to a numbered table, add a caption that includes a {SEQ Table} field code, as explained in the following section.

Creating Captions for Equations, Figures, and Tables

In this book, figures and tables are identified by a sequential number and caption. This common arrangement is easy to create in Word. To create a caption, follow these steps:

1. Select the item for which you want a caption—an equation created with Insert Equation, a picture or graphic, or a table. (In fact, you can apply a caption to *anything* in a document; there's nothing magical about equations, figures, and tables. It's just that Word has predefined caption handling for these common document elements.)

2. On the References tab, click Insert Caption (in the Captions group). The Caption dialog box appears.

Be sure to add a space after the number before you begin typing your caption text

3. Under Options, select the label and position you want to use. If you're not satisfied with the label options, click New Label and define your own.

4. In the Caption box, append your caption text to the label and number that appears.

INSIDE OUT   Use field codes to insert captions

The Insert Caption tool provides a convenient way to insert a caption, but you might find it easier to type captions directly into your document. The cross-reference feature in Word (described in the next section) relies on the presence of a field code to identify equations, figures, and tables. Specifically, any paragraph that includes a {SEQ Figure} field code is assumed to be a figure caption, which can serve as a cross-reference target. Equations and tables are identified by {SEQ Equation} and {SEQ Table} codes, respectively.

To insert a field code at the insertion point, press Ctrl+F9. Then type the field code text between the braces that appear. Before you finish your document, you need to press Alt+F9 to display the field code results instead of the field codes, and you'll need to press F9 to update the fields. Although these extra steps might seem burdensome, typists who don't like to interrupt their typing by reaching for the mouse might find this method to be easier in the long run, especially if tasked with inserting many captions. For more information about working with field codes, see "Using Fields to Automate Documents" on page 333.

As you'll see in the next section, a reference to one of these items can include the entire caption (the entire paragraph that contains the {SEQ} field code), only the label and number (everything in the paragraph before the {SEQ} code and the field code result), or only the caption text (everything in the paragraph after the {SEQ} code).

Inserting a Reference

With your cross-reference targets properly formatted and captioned, as described in the preceding sections, you're ready to insert a reference. To do so, follow these steps:

1. Click Cross-Reference, a tool you'll find in the Links group on the Insert tab *and* in the Captions group on the References tab. Clicking the tool in either ribbon location opens the Cross-Reference dialog box, which is shown in Figure 8-11.

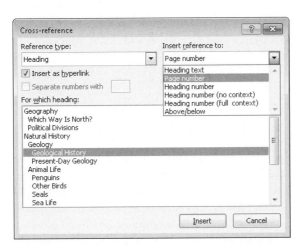

Figure 8-11 The bottom of the dialog box is populated with a list of the document's headings, bookmarks, figures, or other reference targets, based on your selection under Reference Type.

2. Select a Reference Type (Numbered Item, Heading, Bookmark, Footnote, Endnote, Equation, Figure, or Table). When you make a selection here, Word displays the available cross-reference targets in the main part of the dialog box and includes appropriate options under Insert Reference To.

3. Select a cross-reference target.

4. Select an option under Insert Reference To.

Some reference types include references to two types of numbers: No Context and Full Context. This distinction applies to multilevel lists. Full Context includes the complete path to the referenced item, such as 2.a.ii or 507(a)(4), whereas No Context includes only the number of the nested item—using the preceding examples, ii or (4).

The Above/Below option inserts only the word *above* or *below* depending on the position of the target relative to the inserted reference. In many cases the reference and its target are separated by several pages, making "above" and "below" less helpful to a reader. A more elegant solution is to select Page Number under Insert Reference To and also select Include Above/Below (not visible in Figure 8-11). This way, Word inserts "above" or "below," as appropriate, if the reference and target are on the same page; if they're on different pages, Word instead inserts "on page *xx*," where *xx* is the page number.

5. If you want the cross-reference to be a hyperlink to the target, select Insert As Hyperlink. When you create a cross-reference this way, clicking the cross-reference jumps to the target. This works in Word and, if you save the document as a web page, in a web browser. (For other ways to insert hyperlinks, see "Entering Hyperlinks" on page 119.)

6. Click Insert. The dialog box remains open, allowing you to move the insertion point in the document and insert another cross-reference without repeating the first several steps of this procedure. Click Close when you're through inserting cross-references.

Creating Tables of Contents and Indexes

A common feature of long documents is a table of contents, which typically lists all the headings in the document in the order in which they appear, along with the page number each appears on. Bookending many long documents is an index, which lists topics in alphabetical order, with page numbers.

Inserting a Table of Contents

To insert a table of contents in a document, place the insertion point where you want it to go. Then click the References tab and click Table Of Contents. The small gallery that appears has, by default, two viable options (Automatic Table 1 and Automatic Table 2) and one (Manual Table) that's more trouble than it's worth. Automatic Table 1 and Automatic Table 2 are identical except for the title ("Table of Contents" versus "Contents"), which is ordinary text that you can easily edit to your liking. Select one of these options, and Word inserts a table similar to the one shown in Figure 8-12. The built-in automatic options include heading levels 1 through 3 in the table of contents.

The table of contents doesn't update automatically as you make changes to your document. To make it reflect the current document content, click Update Table (in the toolbar shown in Figure 8-12 or in the Table Of Contents group on the References tab). You're then given a choice of updating page numbers only (this option is faster, but it doesn't take into account headings that have been added, removed, moved, or edited) or rebuilding the table from scratch.

If this predefined table of contents doesn't suit your fancy, define your own parameters. Below the Table Of Contents gallery, click Insert Table Of Contents, which opens the Table Of Contents dialog box, shown in Figure 8-13.

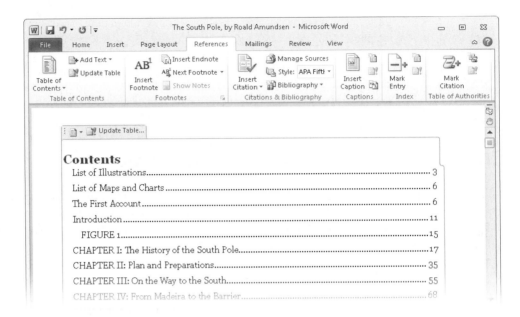

Figure 8-12 When you click inside the table of contents, a frame appears around the table, and a small toolbar appears at the top.

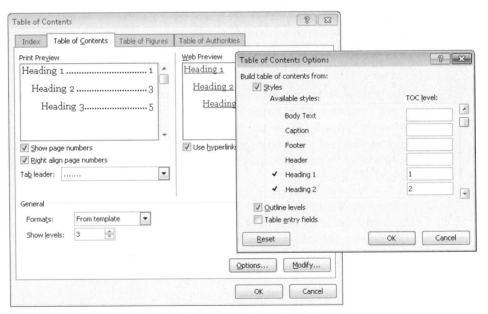

Figure 8-13 Options in the Formats box under General include designs that complement certain style sets.

Here you can specify how many heading levels to include, among other options. To include paragraphs that use styles other than the built-in Heading 1, Heading 2, and so on, click Options. In the Table Of Contents Options dialog box, you can specify each style you want to include and which contents level to assign it.

As shown in Figure 8-13, Word builds a table of contents using up to three different input types: styles (that is, each paragraph that has a particular style applied), outline levels (paragraphs that have an outline level assigned that's within the Show Levels range in the Table Of Contents dialog box), and table entry fields.

These last two options provide alternative ways to include in the table of contents items that wouldn't otherwise be included. To include a paragraph, you can click Add Text (in the Table Of Contents group on the References tab) and select a level; doing so sets an outline level for that paragraph without affecting the underlying style. Alternatively, you can use {TC} field codes to mark table of contents entries, although this method is more complex.

Preparing and Inserting an Index

Unlike a table of contents, which practically creates itself as long as you have consistently applied styles in your document, creating an index—especially a good index—requires a lot of planning and coding before Word can compile it. It's essentially a two-step process: First you mark the items to be indexed in the document text. When that's done, you generate the index.

Marking Index Entries

Identifying the places in a document that should be mentioned in the index, figuring out which alternative terms to use, and marking those terms can be tedious. Depending on the type of document, a good index often has half a dozen or more index entries on each page.

To mark an index entry, select the word or phrase you want to use as an index term, and then click Mark Entry, in the Index group on the References page. The Mark Index Entry dialog box appears, as shown in Figure 8-14. (You can also display this dialog box by using its keyboard shortcut, Alt+Shift+X.)

When you click Mark or Mark All to mark an index entry, Word inserts an {XE} field code. Because this field code is normally hidden, Word turns on the display of hidden text, allowing you to see and edit the field codes directly. Click Show/Hide ¶ (in the Paragraph group on the Home tab) or press Ctrl+* after you've seen enough.

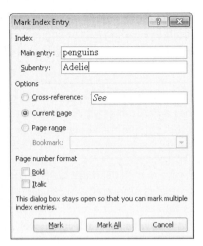

Figure 8-14 Clicking Mark All marks all occurrences of the selected word or phrase in the document.

INSIDE OUT Create multilevel indexes

You might notice in the {XE} field codes that Word inserts that the main entry is separated from the subentry by a colon. For example, the code generated by the text shown in Figure 8-14 looks like this: { XE "penguins:Adelie" }

You can use colons to create multilevel indexes—up to seven levels deep, in fact. You can enter text for additional levels in the field code, of course. But you can also enter it in the Mark Index Entry dialog box, even though it has spaces only for the first two levels. The trick is simple: In either the Main Entry or Subentry box, insert the text for each level, using a colon to separate them. For example, you could type **penguins:Adelie:mating habits** to add a third level.

Generating the Index

After the hard work of marking entries is out of the way, the remaining task is easy. Place the insertion point where you want the index to go, and then on the References tab, click Insert Index (in the Index group). A dialog box like the one shown in Figure 8-15 appears.

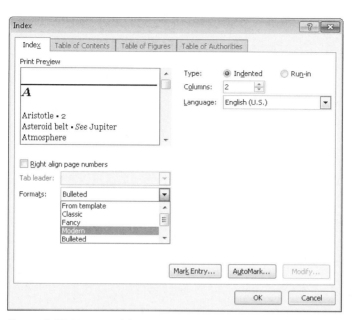

Figure 8-15 You can pick up styles and layout from the current template or use one of the built-in style sets. A sample index in the Print Preview box shows you what to expect.

Your options in the Index dialog box are few. You can choose between Indented (each index entry starts on a new line, indented appropriately to indicate the level) or Run-In (subentries run together in paragraph style) types, and you can specify the number of columns in the page layout.

The alluring AutoMark button deserves some explanation. This feature uses a separate document (called an AutoMark file or, more generically, a concordance file) that contains the terms you want to mark in the document. The AutoMark file is a Word document that contains a two-column table. The left column contains each term you want to search for in the document ("Adelie," for example) and the right column contains the index entry you want to make at each occurrence of the search term (such as "penguins:Adelie"). Invoking AutoMark searches the current document for all occurrences of the terms and inserts the corresponding index entries. While this concept sounds tempting, in practice it generally doesn't produce a useful index.

If you make edits to your document after inserting an index, you need to update the index. To do that, click in the index and then click Update Index (in the Index group on the References tab). Easier yet, click in the index and press F9, the keyboard shortcut to update fields; the index itself is created by an {INDEX} field.

Reviewing and Sharing Documents

U NLESS you use Word to record your deepest secrets in a personal diary, your documents are made to be shared with others. In this chapter we discuss two facets of
document sharing: working with other contributors to improve a document, and
preparing a document to be safely shared with users at large.

Whether you're writing a sales proposal or the great American novel, you probably don't
work alone. Coworkers, managers, editors, proofreaders, and others are likely to have suggestions for improving your document. Your cohorts can make their suggestions directly
in your Word document, and you can then review them and decide whether to accept or
reject them. In the following sections we describe comments and tracked changes, two
features for providing document feedback. We also introduce new features in Word 2010
that allow multiple authors to work on a document simultaneously.

We then discuss methods for sharing a document with others. You want to be certain that
a document doesn't include information that it shouldn't, and you might want to prevent
others from making changes to the document. We wrap up the chapter with a discussion of
a specific type of document you can share: a fill-in-the-blanks form.

Using Review Comments in a Document

A time-honored way to provide comments to a document author is to write notes in
the margin or even to attach a sticky note. Word includes a feature that emulates both
methods. By default, a comment appears on a colored background in the document's right
margin—much like a sticky note.

INSIDE OUT **Make changes directly in the document**

Comments are great for making suggestions, asking questions, or explaining an edit. But when you want to make corrections to a document, don't use comments; transcribing those comments into the document creates more work later. Instead, turn on change tracking and make changes directly in the document. For details, see "Tracking and Highlighting Changes Made to a Document" on page 285.

Inserting a Comment

To insert a comment, begin by selecting the text you want to highlight or place the insertion point at the item you're commenting on. Then click the Review tab and click New Comment; alternatively, press the command's keyboard shortcut, Ctrl+Alt+M. As shown in Figure 9-1, a panel appears in the right margin. Type your comment in the panel.

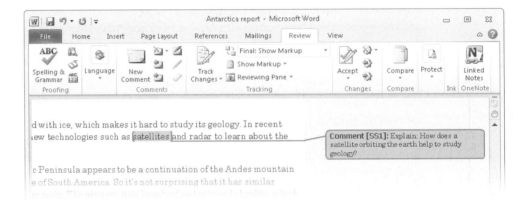

Figure 9-1 Word inserts the commenter's initials and a sequential number at the beginning of the comment.

As comments are added and removed, the sequential number that accompanies each one updates automatically so that comments are always numbered in order from the beginning of the document and no numbers are skipped.

If your computer supports pen input, you can write your comments if you prefer. Select the document text to highlight, and then tap Ink Comment (in the Comments group on the

Review tab). As with typed comments, Word inserts the commenter's initials and a comment number, but the panel displays ruled lines in the writing area, as shown in Figure 9-2. Although this method is sometimes more convenient, particularly if you're editing while on the go, it has a drawback: Word doesn't attempt to recognize handwriting, which means that handwritten text won't be included in search results. If you expect to search your document for text contained in comments, you're better off using an input method that converts handwriting to text, such as the Tablet PC Input Panel included with some versions of Windows.

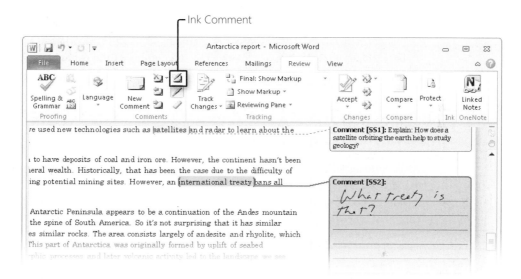

Figure 9-2 Word expands the handwriting input area if needed. When you're finished writing, Word removes the lines and unused space.

By default, for each person who reviews a document, a different color is used for the highlighted text and the comment panel. Along with the initials at the beginning of each comment and the reviewer's full name, which appears in the Reviewing pane, this makes it easy to see who made each comment. If you want to select a specific color for your comments rather than letting Word assign one, click the arrow below Track Changes (in the Tracking group on the Review tab) and select Change Tracking Options. In the Track Changes Options dialog box, select a color next to Comments. (For more information about this dialog box, see "Setting Options for Tracking Changes" on page 290.) Your existing comments as well as any new ones you create appear in the color you select.

You can also change your initials and your full name to better identify comments you make. Click the button under Track Changes and then click Change User Name, which opens the Word Options dialog box, in which you can enter these identifiers. Note that any existing comments retain the initials and user name that was in effect when the comment was created; you can't update them.

INSIDE OUT   Comment on a comment

Note that you can select any text to comment on it—including text in an existing comment. When you do that, the new comment appears below the original, and the number includes an R (for "reply") followed by the number of the comment to which you're replying.

Reviewing Comments

When a document contains one or more comments, three tools in the Comments group on the Review tab become available: Delete, Previous, and Next. Instead of tediously paging through a document in search of comments, you can skip instantly to the next or previous comment by clicking one of these buttons.

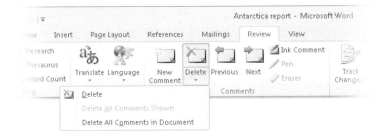

You can also browse by comment using any of these navigation tools:

- **Navigation pane**   Click the arrow at the right side of the search box, click Comments, and then choose the name of the reviewer whose comments you want to see or choose All Reviewers. Then click the arrow buttons to the right of the tabs to jump to the next or previous search result.

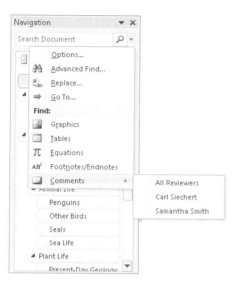

- **Go To command**   Press Ctrl+G and select Comment under Go To What. You can jump to the previous or next comment by a particular reviewer, or you can enter a number to jump directly to a specific comment.

- **Browse tool**   Press Ctrl+Alt+Home or click Select Browse Object (the round button near the bottom of the vertical scroll bar) and click Browse By Comment. You can then jump to the previous or next comment by pressing Ctrl+Page Down or Ctrl+Page Up, or by clicking the button above or below Select Browse Object.

For more information about these browse methods, see "Navigating Within a Document" on page 203.

Comments also appear in the Reviewing pane, which you display by clicking Reviewing Pane, a button in the Tracking group on the Review tab. For details about working in the Reviewing pane, see "Reviewing Tracked Changes" on page 287.

Printing Comments

When you print a document that contains comments (or other changes, as described in the following sections), by default Word includes the comments when you print. It does this by reducing the size of each page to create a margin on the right side large enough for the comment balloons, as shown in Figure 9-3.

Figure 9-3 As shown in the preview image, Word prints comment balloons and other markup along the right side of each page.

To print your document without comments, under Settings click Print All Pages. Then click Print Markup to remove the check mark.

You can also choose to print only the comments and tracked changes without printing the entire document. To do that, click Print All Pages and then click List Of Markup.

For more information about printing, see "Printing a Document" on page 327.

If you're not satisfied with the width of the comment area on the right side of each page, return to the Review tab, click the arrow below Track Changes in the Tracking group, and click Change Tracking Options. Near the bottom of the Track Changes Options dialog box, under Balloons, you'll find options for adjusting the page layout and comment appearance.

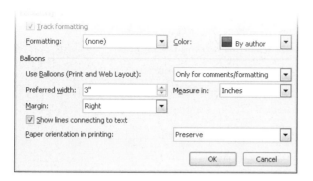

Tracking and Highlighting Changes Made to a Document

Although it's nice to be able to add comments, suggestions, and other notes to a document, sometimes it's easier for an editor or reviewer to simply make changes directly in the document. However, if a reviewer edits your document, you can't easily tell what changes have been made—unless Track Changes is on. To turn it on, click the Review tab and click Track Changes in the Tracking group.

When change tracking is on, you end up with a "redlined" document, so named because it resembles traditional markup done with a red pen. As shown in Figure 9-4, added text appears underlined and deleted text has a strikethrough line through it. These additions and deletions are in color so they're easy to spot, and each reviewer's comments are in a different color, making them easy to differentiate.

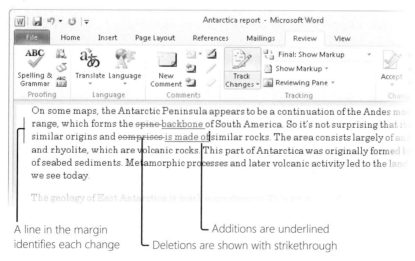

A line in the margin identifies each change

Additions are underlined

Deletions are shown with strikethrough

Figure 9-4 When change tracking is on, the Track Changes button is highlighted.

Chapter 9

Table 9-1 lists some keyboard shortcuts that you might find handy when working with tracked changes.

Table 9-1 **Keyboard Shortcuts for Reviewing Documents**

Action	Keyboard Shortcut
Insert a comment	Ctrl+Alt+M
Turn change tracking on or off	Ctrl+Shift+E
Close the Reviewing pane	Alt+Shift+C

INSIDE OUT Use traditional markup

Some reviewers prefer going old school by using a red pen on printed output. In Word, you can mark up a document this way without even printing it! On a computer with pen support, the Review tab includes a Start Inking tool in the Ink group. Click this tool, and Word displays the Pens tab under Ink Tools, where you can select a pen style and color. You then use the pen to draw directly on the document. (For a list of standard proofreaders' marks, go to *w7io.com/10901*.)

This method provides a handy way to mark up a document when using a keyboard isn't convenient, but it has some disadvantages. First, Word makes no attempt to interpret your scrawl, so it's up to someone else to actually make changes to the document text. And when that happens, another disadvantage becomes apparent: Deleting all the ink marks is a tedious task. Therefore, if you want to employ this method, we recommend that you first turn on change tracking. That way, the ink marks are preserved as a change. Turn off change tracking after you complete the ink markup and before you make changes in the document. After you make the text corrections, you can hide all ink marks by changing the view to Original, or remove them all by rejecting all changes in the document. (These two tasks are described in the following sections.)

Changing View Options

A document that has lots of tracked changes sometimes resembles a graffiti-covered wall and can be challenging to decipher. Changes can also move line breaks and page breaks, and these effects can be difficult to discern when tracked changes are shown. For these reasons, you might want to change the way tracked changes are displayed.

Using options in the Tracking group on the Review tab, you can hide markup altogether, or you can filter the display to show only certain types of changes. Here's how:

- Click Display For Review (the button that shows Final: Show Markup by default), and you can choose to show Final (the document as edited) or Original (the document without changes). Note that you can make changes in Final view and Word continues to track changes, although it doesn't display the markup. However, if you're using Original view and you make a change in the document, Word immediately switches to showing markup.

- To selectively show markup, click Show Markup. On the menu that appears, shown next, you can select which types of markup you want to display and you can select which reviewers' markup to display. The Balloons submenu includes an option—Show Revisions In Balloons—that moves deleted text to a margin balloon instead of using strikethrough text; this option shows final line and page breaks more accurately.

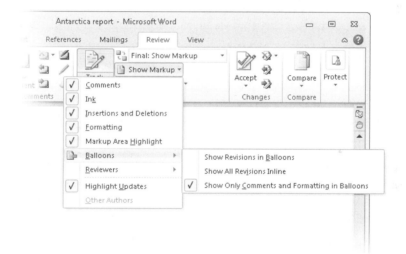

Reviewing Tracked Changes

After one or more reviewers have added their two cents to your writing masterpiece, you'll want to review the changes before committing them. To do that, you use tools in the Changes group on the Review tab.

From the beginning of the document, click Next (or Accept) to jump to the first change or comment. If you agree with the change, click Accept, which removes the markup from the change and advances to the next change. If you don't want to accept the reviewer's change, click Reject, which undoes the change and advances to the next one. Can't decide? Click Next to jump to the next change while leaving the markup in place.

You needn't examine every single change. Click the arrow on the Accept button or the Reject button to display a menu of additional options, most notably the option to accept (or reject) all changes in the document without further review.

Another way to review changes and navigate among them is with the Reviewing pane, which you display by clicking its button in the Tracking group on the Review tab. As shown in Figure 9-5, the Reviewing pane shows the reviewer's name and time of each change. An advantage of the Reviewing pane is that you can search within it to quickly find specific text. You can click a heading in the Reviewing pane (or double-click the revision text) to jump directly to that change or comment in the document. Clicking the Accept, Reject, Previous, or Next button on the Reviewing tab has the same effect whether you're working in the document or the Reviewing pane.

Click to update the revision statistics

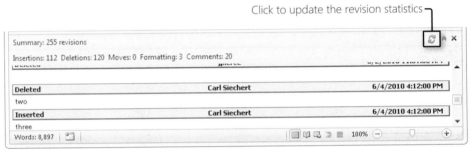

Figure 9-5 The Reviewing pane also includes some interesting statistics at the top.

You'll sometimes want to distribute a document to more than one person for review. After the review copies come back, you're stuck with the unenviable job of merging comments and changes from multiple documents into one. And what if not all the reviewers remember to turn on change tracking? The Combine and Compare tools in the Compare group on the Review tab provide relief for these reviewing headaches.

Both tools use two documents as their input. Compare is designed for comparing a revised document with the original, whereas Combine is intended to merge changes from two different revised documents into one, leaving the tracked changes intact. In practice, the difference between the two tools is slight.

You select the documents to combine or compare in a dialog box similar to the one shown in Figure 9-6.

After you click OK, your documents appear in a multipaned window, as shown in Figure 9-7. The usual collection of Review tab tools for browsing, accepting, and rejecting changes and comments apply here as well.

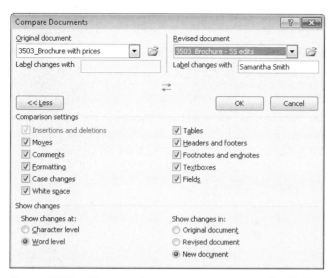

Figure 9-6 You fine-tune the comparison operation by clicking More, which exposes the options shown in the bottom part of this dialog box.

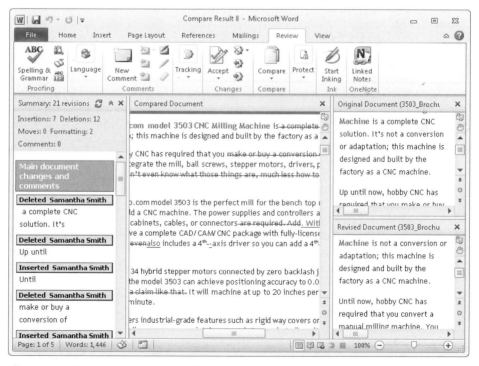

Figure 9-7 The document panes scroll synchronously, making it easy to compare the documents.

Setting Options for Tracking Changes

The default behavior of underlining text additions, striking out deletions, and so on works well for most people—but you're not stuck with it. You can select different ways of marking (bold text for additions, for example), specify which color to use for edits you make, and select which types of changes you want to track. (For example, you might choose not to mark changes to formatting.) You make all these choices in the Track Changes Options dialog box, which is shown in Figure 9-8. To open this dialog box, on the Review tab, click the arrow below Track Changes and then click Change Tracking Options.

Figure 9-8 When By Author appears in a Color box, Word uses a different color for each reviewer's changes.

Another option you might want to set is one that forces reviewers to turn on change tracking. This prevents them from inadvertently making changes to your document that might be difficult to spot when the document comes back to you. To enable this restriction, follow these steps:

1. Click the Review tab and then click Restrict Editing in the Protect group. This opens the Restrict Formatting And Editing pane.

2. Select the check box under Editing Restrictions. Then select either Comments or Tracked Changes (which also allows reviewers to add comments).

3. Click Yes, Start Enforcing Protection.

4. In the Start Enforcing Protection dialog box, enter a password if you want to make it a little harder for a reviewer to remove the protection. For working with trusted associates, leave the password boxes blank. Then click OK.

When you allow only comment editing, reviewers are rebuffed with an error message if they try to make any edits other than inserting a comment or deleting one of their own comments. With editing restrictions set to allow only tracked changes, a reviewer can use any and all tools to edit the document, but all edits are marked as tracked changes, and the reviewer cannot accept or reject changes.

Working Together with Other Authors

A new feature in Word 2010 permits multiple authors to simultaneously edit a document stored in a shared location. The shared location can be a SharePoint site that's running SharePoint Foundation 2010—a setup that's available in many businesses. In addition, hosted SharePoint services are available from many web service providers. Or the shared location can be a Windows Live SkyDrive folder. To use SkyDrive, each user must have a Windows Live ID.

When multiple people open a document for editing, names of the other editors appear on screen, as shown in Figure 9-9. You can see which part of a document another editor is working in, and Word prevents you from making changes to the same place at the same time.

Chapter 9

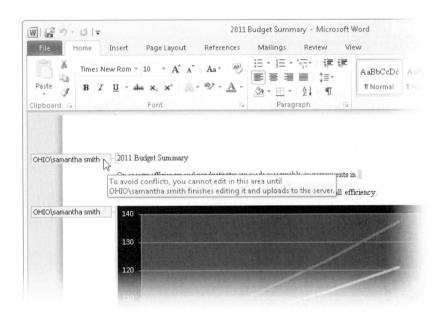

Figure 9-9 Point to an editor's name to display the contact card, which you can click to initiate a conversation.

During a coauthoring session, changes that you and other editors make don't appear on each other's screens in real time; you only get an indication of areas that are locked for editing. To update your document to show changes that others have made, simply save your document. Doing so also makes your changes available to the others, which they'll see the next time they save.

You can see the names of all coauthors currently working on a document by clicking the coauthoring icon on the status bar. You can get more complete information and links by clicking the File tab to open the Info tab in Backstage view, as shown in Figure 9-10.

For more information about coauthoring, see "Simultaneous Editing with Multiple Authors" on page 832.

Figure 9-10 The Info tab shows the status of a coauthored document, and also includes links to others who are currently working on the document.

Preparing a Document for Distribution

Before you share an electronic document with the world, you should review the file to be sure it doesn't contain information that you don't want others to see. You might also want to check for improvements you can make that render the document more accessible to people with disabilities. If you're planning to share with users of earlier versions of Word, you'll want to be sure that they can open the file. (For details, see "Checking for Compatibility with Earlier Office Versions" on page 88.)

You might also want to protect your document from unwanted changes, and you might want to prevent unauthorized users from opening the document. You can also apply a digital signature to a document, which provides assurance to recipients of the document that it came from you and that it hasn't been altered.

You'll find tools for each of these tasks by clicking the File tab to display the Info tab in Backstage view, as shown in Figure 9-11.

Chapter 9

Figure 9-11 Explanatory text under Permissions and Prepare For Sharing highlights potential issues with the current document.

Checking a Document

Several notorious incidents have occurred in which a publicly released Word document disclosed embarrassing information. It doesn't take an Office whiz to discover the name of the document creator and, in fact, it's pretty easy to snoop in a file to find hidden text or even text that has been deleted during editing—especially with documents in the Word 97–2003 Document (.doc) format.

To prevent information in your document from becoming tabloid fodder, on the Info tab in Backstage view click Check For Issues, Inspect Document. Doing so opens the Document Inspector dialog box, in which you select the types of personal information you want to expunge. (For more information about each of these categories, see *w7io.com/10902*.) Make your selections and click Inspect, whereupon you'll see the inspection results, as shown in Figure 9-12.

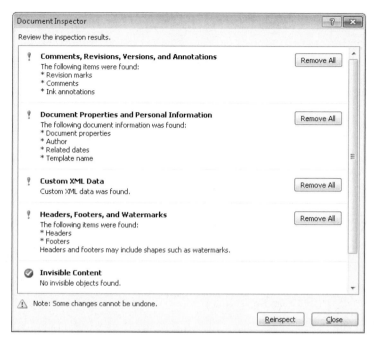

Figure 9-12 Click Remove All for each category to sanitize your document file.

Making a document accessible to the widest group of readers isn't just political correctness; it's smart business. Furthermore, it's required for some business and government documents. Most issues identified make it easier for visually impaired users to read a document. For example, adding alt text to each picture (which text-to-speech software can read aloud) can improve your document's accessibility. If your document contains potential accessibility issues, a notice to that effect appears on the Info tab under Prepare For Sharing. To learn more, click Check For Issues, Check Accessibility. An Accessibility Checker pane then appears next to your document. As you expand and click each item under Errors, Warnings, and Tips, the offending item is selected and explanatory text appears at the bottom of the Accessibility Checker pane.

INSIDE OUT   Save your document before inspecting

Before you summon Document Inspector, save your document. Then use Save As to create a copy for distribution, and perform the inspection on that copy. Some items you remove with Document Inspector can be restored with the Undo command, but many cannot. Unfortunately, there's no obvious way to know which changes can be undone in case you change your mind, so it's best to work on a copy and assume that every removal you make is irreversible.

Protecting a Document

The Protect Document button on the Info tab in Backstage view, shown in Figure 9-13, offers links to several tools you can use to prevent unauthorized changes to your document and to assure document recipients that the document is indeed yours.

Figure 9-13 Text under Permissions summarizes the current protection status.

Options under Protect Document perform the following tasks:

- **Mark As Final**   Choosing this command sets a flag in the file so that it opens in read-only mode. You can't type in the document or edit it in other ways, and most buttons on the ribbon are disabled. This provides adequate protection from inadvertent changes, but it doesn't defend against malicious changes. Anyone can remove the final status by revisiting the Info tab and clicking Mark As Final again or, more simply, clicking Edit Anyway in the message bar that appears, as shown here.

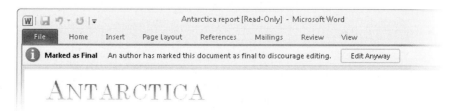

Chapter 9

- **Encrypt With Password** When you choose this command, Word asks you to provide a password, which it then uses as a key for encrypting the document. Thereafter, Word asks for the password each time someone tries to open the document. Be sure you save the password in a safe place because there's no practical way to recover it.

- **Restrict Editing** This command displays the Restrict Formatting And Editing task pane, which you can use to limit formatting changes and edits. For more information, see "Making Global Changes to Your Document" on page 229 and "Setting Options for Tracking Changes" on page 290.

- **Restrict Permission By People** This command uses Information Rights Management (IRM) to keep track of which people are allowed to view or edit a document. If your network doesn't have an IRM server, you can use a free online IRM service from Microsoft. Information about the service and a wizard for setting it up appear when you choose this command and you don't already have an IRM server configured.

  After you configure the IRM service, you can specify which users have Read permission for the document and which ones have Change permission; people who aren't on either list are prevented from opening the document. By clicking More Options in the Permission dialog box, you can set additional restrictions, as shown here.

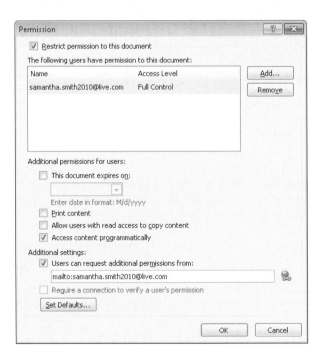

- **Add A Digital Signature**   A digital signature is a code embedded in the document file that ensures that the document came from you (or someone who has access to the private key for your digital ID) and that the document hasn't been altered. In addition, it provides a tamper-proof time stamp for the document. Choose this command to learn about options for obtaining a digital ID if you don't have one already.

Saving a Document in a Shared Location

You can share a document by distributing copies via e-mail or on removable media. By sharing in these ways, however, you end up with multiple copies that can quickly get out of sync with each other. A better way to share a document so that multiple authors can use it is to store the document in a shared location.

If you have multiple user accounts on your computer, you can use the Public Documents folder. All accounts on your computer have full access to documents in that folder, and you don't need to do anything special to set up sharing.

For sharing documents over a network connection, you must store the document in a shared folder. Depending on how your network is set up, the shared folder can be on your computer, on another user's computer, or on a network server drive. The steps for sharing a folder in each of these configurations vary widely depending on the type of network you have, which operating system is in use on the sharing computer and the computers that need to access it, and other factors. Suffice to say, setting up a shared network folder is beyond the scope of this book. But after you (or a network administrator) have gotten past that hurdle, saving and opening documents in a shared network folder from within Word is as simple as using a folder on your computer. The difference is that other users on your network can also use the documents you save this way.

Windows Live SkyDrive offers cloud-based storage (that is, storage on a server that you access via the internet), which has several advantages. You can access your documents from any computer that has an Internet connection. If you choose to share a folder on your SkyDrive with other users, they too can access your documents from any Internet-connected computer. With SkyDrive, you can choose to share a folder (and the documents it contains) with everyone in the world, only with people you specify, or with no one else. (There is, of course, a significant disadvantage: unless you also save a copy locally, your document is available only when you have a working Internet connection.)

To save a document to a SkyDrive folder, click File. On the Save & Send tab, click Save To Web. If you don't have a Windows Live ID (the only prerequisite for using SkyDrive) or if you're not signed in, links on the right side of the window invite you to sign up for an account or sign in using your existing account.

Chapter 9

While you're signed in, the Save & Send tab shows your SkyDrive folders, as shown in Figure 9-14. Select a folder (or click New to create a new one) and then click Save As.

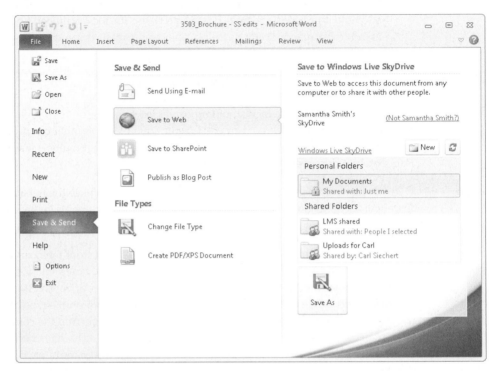

Figure 9-14 Folders that others share with you and folders that you share with others both appear under Shared Folders.

To open a document that you've saved on SkyDrive, click File and then check the list on the Recent tab. If the document has rolled off the list of recent documents (or if you want to open a document for the first time on a different computer), you must use your web browser to view your SkyDrive and open the document from there. This shortcoming—the inability to access SkyDrive through the Open dialog box in Word—will undoubtedly be addressed soon, perhaps even by the time you read this. For updated information about Office Web Apps and SkyDrive, visit *w7io.com/12401*.

For more information about using SkyDrive, see "Storing and Using Office Documents on Windows Live SkyDrive" on page 842.

Creating and Working with Forms

Another type of document collaboration is to use a form. Similar to a printed form on which someone provides information with pen and ink while not modifying the base form, a form in Word can enable users to fill in requested information using Word. Such a form has several advantages over its paper counterparts:

- For each field you can provide instructions and guidance to assist the person filling out the form.

- You can use specialized controls that make filling out forms faster. For example, a date picker content control displays a calendar on which the user can click a date. List box controls offer a list of choices from which the user can select.

- You can place limitations on certain types of form controls (such as allowing the entry of numbers only).

- The completed form is not only neater in appearance, but with some programming expertise, you can extract data from the completed form and add it to a database or a different document or application.

If you've used any of the sample templates furnished with Word 2010, you've probably seen the light-blue frames that surround certain text-entry areas and contain an explanation of what to enter to replace the placeholder text. Those framed areas are called *content controls*, and it turns out that they're perfect for data-entry fields in forms as well as other types of documents.

Creating a Form Template

To make a form, you can start with a new, blank document. But why reinvent the wheel? You might find a form template on Office.com that does what you need or, at the very least, provides a starting point for customizing your own forms. Click File, New and then explore the choices under Office.com Templates. A good place to start, naturally, is by clicking Forms, but you might also want to use the search box to locate an appropriate template.

Before you get into the nitty-gritty of entering form fields, create the document's static elements—items such as your company logo, form title, tables, and field labels. Use standard editing techniques; there's nothing special about a form document.

Save your work as a Word template. For the greatest convenience, save it in your template files folder (by default, %AppData%\Microsoft\Templates). That way you can fill out the form by choosing File, New, My Templates.

INSIDE OUT   **Use a table for laying out the form**

For many types of forms, a table provides the best way to lay out form data. Even if you omit the table gridlines, a table simplifies alignment of fields. For details, see "Working with Tables" on page 253.

Adding Form Fields

To insert form fields (which are also known as *controls*), you use the Developer tab on the ribbon, which is shown in Figure 9-15. This tab isn't displayed by default. If it's not shown on your computer, follow these steps to display it:

1. Click File, Options to open the Word Options dialog box.

2. In Word Options, click Customize Ribbon.

3. Under Main Tabs, select Developer.

Figure 9-15 Form-related features are in the Controls group on the Developer tab.

Before you begin inserting fields and modifying their properties, click Design Mode.

Click in your document where you want to insert a form field, and then in the Controls group on the Developer tab, click the type of control you want to use. Your choices include:

- **Rich Text Content Control**   Use for text entry when you want to allow formatted text, such as bold and italic.

- **Plain Text Content Control**   Use for unformatted text. By default, this type of control allows only a single paragraph, but you can override this limitation by changing a property setting.

- **Picture Content Control**   Allows the user to insert a picture.

- **Building Block Gallery Content Control**   This control lets the user select a building block. This is useful for inserting various blocks of boilerplate text. To create building blocks that can be selected with this type of control, select the document text you want to use. On the Insert tab, in the Text group, click Quick Parts. Then click Save Selection To Quick Part Gallery and complete the dialog box that appears.

- **Drop-Down List Content Control**   Use for a list of options from which the user can select.

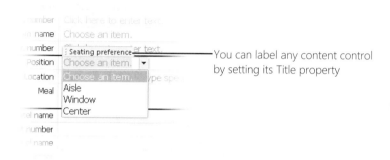

You can label any content control by setting its Title property

- **Combo Box Content Control**   Like a drop-down list, a combo box includes a list of options. Alternatively, a user can enter text.

- **Date Picker Content Control**   When the user clicks this control, a calendar appears so the user can select a date. Properties for this type of control let you specify how the date is formatted.

- **Check Box Content Control**   Use this type of control for yes/no–style choices.

- **Legacy Tools**   Legacy tools are vestiges of earlier Word versions—but there's no reason you can't use them in a Word 2010 form. Some of them duplicate the functionality of the Word 2010 content controls, although the appearance is somewhat different. Some allow data-entry restrictions not available in the content controls.

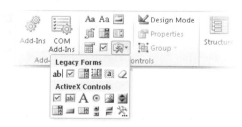

> **Note**
>
> In Compatibility Mode, you can't use any of the Word 2010 content controls. That leaves you with two choices:
>
> - If everyone who will use the form has Word 2010, convert the document to remove Compatibility Mode. Click File to open Backstage view, and next to Compatibility Mode on the Info tab, click Convert.
>
> - If you want to retain Compatibility Mode so that users of earlier Word versions can use your form, use only legacy controls. In the Controls group on the Developer tab, click Legacy Tools to display a gallery of available controls.

After you insert one or more controls, you can examine and set its properties. Click the control and then click Properties (also in the Controls group on the Developer tab). The properties dialog box for some types of controls is quite simple, whereas others have a few more options. Figure 9-16 shows the properties dialog box for a drop-down list content control.

Figure 9-16 Add, remove, and reorder items for a drop-down list or combo box in its properties dialog box.

The Title property is a good place to provide user assistance. Use the small title bar that appears when the user clicks the content control (not in Design mode) to identify what should go in the control. Unfortunately, however, that title bar does not appear if the document is restricted to prevent editing, as described in the following section.

INSIDE OUT   Convert content controls to text

In some situations you might want to remove a content control but preserve its contents. Doing so in a protected form, for example, prevents subsequent changes to a form entry. If you use the sample templates included with Word—many of which are loaded with content controls—you might want to remove them just to tidy up your document.

Conversion is easy: Right-click anywhere within the content control and choose Remove Content Control. Don't worry. The contents remain in the document.

On the other hand, you might want to prevent a user from removing a content control. That's easy too. In the properties dialog box for the control (such as the one shown in Figure 9-16), under Locking, select Content Control Cannot Be Deleted.

You can provide more guidance by changing the default text that appears in the content control (usually "Click here to enter text" or "Choose an item"). To enter something more descriptive or instructive, be sure you're in Design mode. Then simply click in the control and edit the text. The text you enter remains visible regardless of editing restriction settings, and disappears only when someone replaces it with form data.

When you're finished inserting content controls, modifying their properties, and adding instructional text, exit Design mode by clicking the Design Mode button.

Protecting and Using the Form

The last step before you save the form template and begin using it is to protect it by imposing restrictions on editing. Doing so prevents users from modifying any part of the document except those parts within a control. It also makes filling out the form easier because a user can select or edit only the form fields.

To protect a form, on the Developer tab (or Review tab) in the Protect group, click Restrict Editing. The Restrict Formatting And Editing task pane appears. Under Editing Restrictions, select the check box and then select Filling In Forms. Click Yes, Start Enforcing Protection and enter a password if you want to prevent others from removing this restriction. (If you use a password, be sure you keep it in a safe place so you don't lock yourself out!)

Your form template is finished. Save it in a place where those who are going to fill out the form can get to it.

When it comes time to fill out the form, create a document based on the template. If you store the template file in your templates folder, click File, New, My Templates, and then double-click the name of your template. If the template file is in a shared location so that others can get to it, browse to it in Windows Explorer and double-click it.

Because editing restrictions are in place, when you click in the document, Word selects the nearest form control instead of placing the insertion point where you click, as shown in Figure 9-17. Moving between form fields and entering text in them is much like working in a table. Press Tab to move to the next field or press Shift+Tab to move to the previous field. To enter a tab character in a field, press Ctrl+Tab.

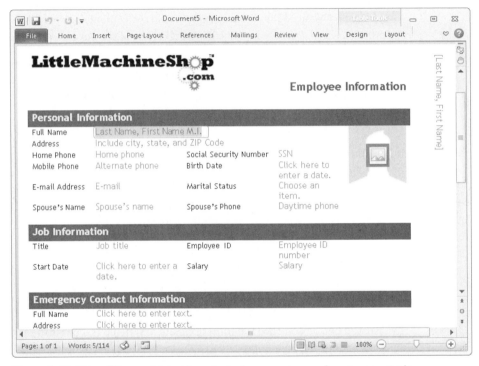

Figure 9-17 This editing-restricted form includes many types of content controls.

INSIDE OUT   Enter a date

You can click the arrow on the right side of a date picker content control to display a calendar, and then click a date in the calendar to enter it. If the date you want is more than a few months away, however, scrolling through the calendar is tedious. Instead, click the control and type the date. When you move to the next field, Word formats the date according to the properties set for the date picker content control.

I N the first three chapters of this section about Word, we cover the basic tasks that nearly anyone who uses Word—whether casual user or full-time writer—needs to master to be proficient. We follow a steady progression from simple tasks to complex documents. In this chapter, we dig deeper. The format is a bit more freewheeling, as we cover a range of advanced, but largely unrelated, topics. These are the ones that'll make you go "Wow!"

We look at some advanced text-formatting capabilities that traditionally have been the realm of desktop publishing and high-end typesetting programs. We show how to use Word to manage your blog. Another topic we tackle in this chapter is mail merge, a task that has confounded word-processing users for a long time; we try to bring some clarity to the subject. We also look at building blocks and fields, features that help you to add content to your document and keep it fresh.

Finally, we describe some of our favorite Word tweaks and tips.

Applying Advanced Text-Formatting Capabilities

Earlier in this book, we described how to format text in any Office program (see "Applying Text Formatting" on page 123) and showed additional formatting options and techniques that are unique to Word (see "Formatting Text" on page 216). But we're not done with this subject yet. Word 2010 includes still more options for dressing up the text in your documents. You probably won't use these effects every day, but when you do have occasion to use them, the results can be spectacular.

Applying Shadows, Reflections, and Other Text Effects

Word has several types of effects that can be applied to document text:

- **Outline** effects add a border around each text character in a color, weight, and line style that you select.

- **Fill** effects, including gradients, control the color of characters.

- **Shadow** effects create a three-dimensional look by making the text appear like it is floating in front of the screen or paper.

- **Reflection** effects also provide the appearance of depth by showing a mirror image of the text, as if it's on a reflective surface.

- **Glow** effects add a radiant appearance to each character.

You can combine these effects to create some wonderful results. But don't overdo it; you can also end up with something hideous.

To apply any of these effects except fill color, find the Font group on the Home tab and click Text Effects. A gallery of effects appears, as shown in Figure 10-1. To specify a fill color or to apply a gradient effect to text, click the arrow next to the Font Color button, which is also in the Font group on the Home tab. (If you click the Font Color button, it applies the last color you used or, if you haven't yet used the tool, red.)

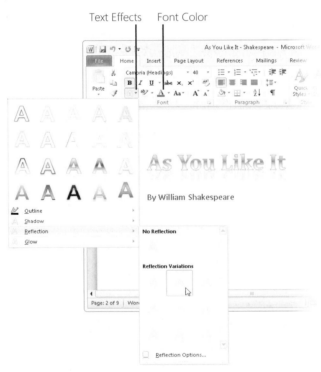

Figure 10-1 As you point to each effect in the gallery, Live Preview shows how it will look.

As an alternative to choosing from the gallery, you can use the Format Text Effects dialog box, which offers more precise control and options not available in the gallery presets. Additional options include gradient fills, gradient lines, shadow colors, and three-dimensional bevel effects. To summon Format Text Effects, which is shown in Figure 10-2, choose the Options command at the bottom of the Shadow, Reflection, or Glow gallery. Or in the Font dialog box, click Text Effects.

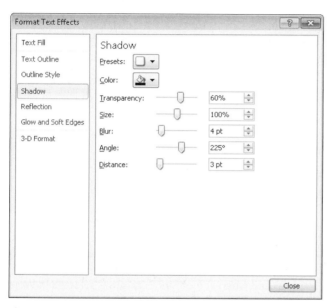

Figure 10-2 For each effect, you might find it easiest to start with a preset and then tweak the settings.

These effects are similar to those available for WordArt; indeed, you can apply any of these effects to text within a WordArt object. However, there are some good reasons to apply text effects to normal document text instead of using WordArt. Document text with effects applied works just like any other document text: you can search for it and check its spelling, for example. In addition, you don't need to mess with positioning and text wrapping because formatted document text flows with other text. On the other hand, WordArt offers some additional effects, such as using a texture as fill. Also, WordArt objects can be inserted in Word, Excel, PowerPoint, and Outlook documents, whereas the text effect techniques described in this section are available only in Word. If you want to reuse your fancy formatted text in another program, use WordArt so you can paste it in the other program. For more information about WordArt, see "Applying Text Effects with WordArt" on page 182.

Text effects can be included in paragraph, character, list, and table styles. For information about working with styles, see "Giving Your Documents a Consistent Appearance" on page 224.

Using Ligatures and Other Fine Typography Effects

Traditional typesetting uses several subtle techniques that make typeset documents look better than anything produced by a word-processing program. These techniques have been used throughout the history of typesetting—in hand-set type, hot metal, phototype-setting, and (more recently) desktop publishing programs. When these techniques are used, graphic designers and typographers can spot the difference at a glance, whereas others might recognize that the text looks better and "more professional," but they can't tell you why. Now, with Word 2010, many of these features are available in word-processing documents, including:

- **Ligatures**   A *ligature* is two or three letters that are combined into a single character because the shapes of the letters are more aesthetically pleasing when combined this way.

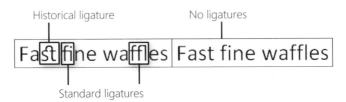

Whether a particular font has ligatures in a particular category (as defined by the OpenType specification) is up to the font's designer, and that decision determines which ligatures are used when any of these options is selected in Word:

- **Standard Only**   Standard ligatures vary by language. In English, common ligatures combine an *f*, *l*, or *i* when it follows an *f*, but other combinations exist in some fonts.

- **Standard And Contextual**   In addition to standard ligatures, this setting includes character combinations that the font designer thinks are appropriate for a particular font, perhaps due to the unusual shapes of some letters.

- **Historical And Discretionary**   Historical ligatures are ones that were once standard (*ct* and *st* combinations, for example, often have a small swash tying the letters together).

- **Number Forms**   *Old-style* numbers have varying heights and are often used when numbers appear within text because the numbers align well with mixed-case text. Modern numbers (called *Lining* in Word) align on the baseline and are of uniform height; these are best for numerical data. Each font has a default setting based on the font's typical usage. For example, the default for Candara, Constantia, and Corbel is old-style, whereas Cambria, Calibri, and Consolas use lining as the default number form.

Old-style 1,987,233 | Lining 1,987,233

- **Number Spacing**   *Proportional* numbers have varying widths; because that generally looks better, proportionally spaced numbers are usually used for numbers within text. *Tabular* numbers all have the same width (more accurately, they all occupy the same space, as the numbers themselves look the same), which is useful for tables of numerical data because the digits align vertically. As with number forms, each font has a default setting. For example, Candara, Constantia, and Corbel default to proportional spacing, whereas Cambria, Calibri, and Consolas use tabular spacing by default.

Proportional   Tabular

171,211,111 | 171,211,111
256,446,398 | 256,446,398

- **Stylistic Sets**   Some fonts include letter combinations with swashes and other flairs that can be used for decorative text in titles and on certificates, for example. Fonts that include stylistic sets often include more than one, with each one identified by an arbitrary number.

Gabriola   Gabriola   Gabriola
stylistic set 1   stylistic set 4   stylistic set 6

We Love Word | We Love Word | We Love Word

Stylistic sets are best reserved for occasional decorative text, such as a title or heading. Getting just the right look often requires much experimentation. You'll sometimes want to apply stylistic sets on a letter-by-letter basis.

These typographical effects are available only with OpenType fonts and, more specifically, only certain OpenType fonts. You're likely to find these features in the newer fonts included with Windows and with Office, including Calibri, Cambria, Constantia, Corbel, and Gabriola.

You apply any of these typographic effects in much the same way as you apply any other text format: you select the text, open the Font dialog box, and apply format settings. Click the arrow in the lower right corner of the Font group on the Home tab or press Ctrl+Shift+F to open the Font dialog box, and then click the Advanced tab, which is shown in Figure 10-3. Make your selections under OpenType Features.

Chapter 10

Select to use stylistic set variants based on surrounding letters or words

Figure 10-3 In lieu of Live Preview showing changes in your document, the Preview box shows the font name or the selected text using the current font settings.

OpenType typographic effects can be included in styles. For information about working with styles, see "Giving Your Documents a Consistent Appearance" on page 224.

INSIDE OUT   Find typographical features in fonts

Unfortunately, there's no easy way to know which typographical effects are available in a particular font. The most reliable method is to simply select some text and try different settings, paying attention to the Preview box in the Font dialog box for clues. You can also find clues in Fonts in Control Panel and by using the Character Map program.

To see whether a font uses old-style or lining numbers by default, double-click the font in Fonts. The number form in the sample text is usually the default for that font. Typically, old-style figures and proportional spacing go hand-in-hand, and lining figures usually default to tabular spacing.

To see which ligatures, if any, are included in a font, open Character Map. Select the font you're interested in, and with Character Set set to Unicode and Group By set to All (or with the Advanced View check box cleared), scroll to the end of the characters. There you'll usually see *fi* and a few other ligatures. In this same area, a collection of swirls and swashes give you an idea about the availability of stylistic sets.

Beginning a Paragraph with a Drop Cap

Another typographic nicety that graphic designers are fond of is a *drop cap*, which is where the first letter or first word of a paragraph is larger than the rest of the text. You can see an example on the first page of each chapter in this book. Creating a drop cap requires not just formatting the letter in a larger font, but also aligning the top of the drop cap with the top of the other paragraph text. (If you simply format the first letter in a larger size, it doesn't "drop.")

Word makes this task easy. Click anywhere in the paragraph (if you want to drop the entire first word, you must select it), click the Insert tab, and in the Text group click Drop Cap. Select a drop cap option, or click Drop Cap Options to specify a font (by default, Word uses the paragraph font) or adjust the size or position using the dialog box shown next.

Understanding Linked Styles

In our earlier discussion of styles (see "Creating a New Style" on page 233), we covered character styles and paragraph styles, which are methods for reusing and consistently applying character formatting and paragraph formatting, respectively.

As you work with styles, you're likely to see another style type: Linked (Paragraph And Character). As the name implies, a linked style incorporates formatting settings for paragraphs (line spacing and indents, for example) *and* for characters (such as font and point size). Confusingly, however, paragraph styles can also incorporate character formats. So what's the point of linked styles?

Linked styles were introduced in Word 2002 (part of Office XP) to enable the use of run-in headings. (A *run-in heading* is one that, instead of being on a line by itself, is immediately followed by paragraph text.) A linked style can be applied to a full paragraph—just like a paragraph style—or it can be applied to a selection of text within a paragraph, much like a character style. Either way, Word recognizes the style's heading level for use in outlines, the Navigation pane, and tables of contents.

In Word 2002 and Word 2003, the default style type for a new style was linked, so when you use templates developed in earlier versions of Word, you're likely to see this type. (In Word 2010, as in Word 2007, new styles are paragraph styles by default.)

Linked styles serve a useful purpose, but they can sometimes cause confusion or annoyance because if text is selected when you apply a linked style, the style is applied only to the selection instead of the entire paragraph. You can avoid the problem in two ways:

- When you create a new style, if you don't plan to use it as a run-in heading, set the style type to Paragraph.

- To work with an existing template that contains linked styles, open the Styles pane (click the arrow in the lower right corner of the Styles group on the Home tab or press Ctrl+Alt+Shift+S), and then select Disable Linked Styles. This setting doesn't actually disable the styles; it merely changes their behavior to work like paragraph styles.

Using Word to Create and Edit Blog Posts

If you maintain a blog, you've probably tried using the web-based interface provided by the blogging service for creating, editing, and posting entries. Many of these interfaces are awful. For users of some popular blogging services, Word 2010 offers a better solution.

With Word, you can create a new post from scratch, or you can publish an existing document to a blog. Word works with most popular blogging services, including SharePoint, WordPress, and TypePad. You create your post using Word's familiar tools, and then with a single click Word publishes it to your blog.

CAUTION

For text-only blogs, Word also works well with other services, including Blogger and Windows Live Spaces. However, its support for publishing pictures to blogs in these services is less satisfactory. If you use one of these blogging services, you might be happier with Windows Live Writer, a free program that's part of Windows Live Essentials. For more information and a download link, visit *explore.live.com*.

To create a new post, click File, New, and then double-click Blog Post. To publish an existing document, open it, and then click File, Save & Send. Under Save & Send, click Publish As Blog Post, and then click the Publish As Blog Post button.

Either way, a new window opens, as shown in Figure 10-4. (The main difference between the two methods is that one includes the content of the currently open document, whereas the other starts with a blank page.) You'll notice some differences from an ordinary document window: a Blog Post tab replaces the Home tab, and most other tabs are missing. (That's because blogs don't support the full range of Word capabilities, so Word doesn't expose the unavailable options.) And a content control at the top of the document commands you to Enter Post Title Here.

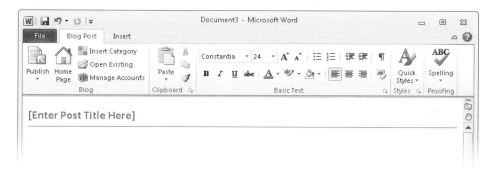

Figure 10-4 The Blog Post tab incorporates features from the standard Home and Review tabs in addition to the blog-specific features in the Blog group.

Managing Blog Accounts

If this is your first time using the blogging feature, Word asks you to register your blog account, as shown in Figure 10-5. Click Register Now to configure Word to work with an existing blog or to set up a new blog. The few steps to register a blog account vary depending on the service, but the onscreen descriptions are reasonably clear and include links to web pages with more details about completing the process. In any case, it takes only a minute or two—but you can postpone the operation if you like by clicking Register Later. If you take that option, you can create, edit, and save blog entries, but you can't post them until you register your account, which you can do at any time.

Figure 10-5 If you choose Register Later, you can initiate the process by clicking Manage Accounts in the Blog group on the Blog Post tab—or simply wait until Word prompts you when you attempt to post an entry.

Chapter 10

TROUBLESHOOTING

Word can't register your blog account

Registration for most blogging services requires you to enter your user name and password (some services use different terms) and then click OK. At that point, you might see an error message that says Word can't register your account. If you're certain that you entered your credentials properly, you might need to make a configuration change using the control panel or dashboard for your blogging service.

For example, with a WordPress blog, you need to open a settings page and enable the XML-RPC publishing protocol. With Windows Live Spaces, you must go to the options page and enable e-mail publishing.

How do you know what settings are required for your service? Start by clicking More Information in the error message that appears in Word, which opens a web page that includes details for configuring some services. If that doesn't help, go to the configuration pages for your blog and look for settings that refer to "remote publishing," "e-mail publishing," "mobile publishing," or similar terms.

To view or modify your blog account settings, or to register another blog, click Manage Accounts in the Blog group on the Blog Post tab.

You can register any number of blog accounts. If you have more than one account registered, a content control titled Account appears in the document window just below the post title. The account identified as the default appears here initially; click the account name to select a different registered account.

To include pictures and other graphics with your blog posts, you need to specify a server for storing pictures. (When a blog entry is posted to a web server, the text—in HTML format—is stored separately from pictures or other images in the post.) During the registration process (or later, by selecting an account in Blog Accounts and clicking Change), click Picture Options. In the Picture Options dialog box, select SharePoint Blog or My Blog Provider, if available. These options store pictures in a designated pictures library associated with your blog account.

TROUBLESHOOTING

Word doesn't recognize your blogging service's picture provider

Unfortunately, Word doesn't recognize the picture-hosting capabilities of some blogging services and instead leaves you with only two choices: None – Don't Upload Pictures (this option is fine if your blog contains only text) and My Own Server.

Don't be dissuaded by the phrase "my own." Although you can use your own web server to host pictures, this is also the option to choose if you plan to use a third-party image provider. Such services are widely available, often at little or no cost to you. Flickr, Photobucket, and Shutterfly are popular services you can use, and a web search for "image hosting service" turns up scores more. To use one of them, select My Own Server in the Picture Options dialog box, and then in the Upload URL box, enter the FTP or HTTP address that the hosting service provides for uploading your pictures. In the Source URL box, enter the HTTP address for viewing your picture collection; Word includes this information in the <img> tag in the blog post.

Unfortunately, you can get into the deep weeds pretty quickly with image providers, which often make it difficult to find the appropriate URLs to use for uploading and viewing. If you run into trouble, we recommend trying Windows Live Writer or—if you're just starting a new blog—switching to a better-supported blogging service, such as WordPress.

Working with Blog Posts

You create and edit your blog post like any other document, albeit with a limited set of tools. The Blog group on the Blog Post tab includes a handful of tools that aren't seen elsewhere in Word:

- **Publish**   When you finish your post, click Publish to upload it to your blog account. Click the arrow below the Publish button to expose a second option: Publish As Draft. This option uploads the post but saves it as a draft instead of publishing it to the publicly available blog. This allows you to review the post and edit it—either in Word or using your blogging service's editing tools—before making it public.

- **Home Page**   Click this button to open your blog's home page in your web browser.

- **Insert Category**   Click this to display a content control below the post title. This content control lets you select a category from a list or type a new one; categorizing your posts makes it easier for viewers to find posts about a particular topic.

Chapter 10

- **Open Existing** Click this button to open a list of posts that have been published on your blog. You can then select a post, download it, edit it, and republish it.

- **Manage Accounts** Click to open Blog Accounts, a dialog box in which you can add, modify, or remove blog accounts, as described in the previous section.

INSIDE OUT Add the Blog template to your Jump List

If you use Windows 7, you can pin the Blog template to the Jump List or Start menu icon for Word, which allows you to start a new blog post directly from your desktop, without even starting Word first.

To set this up, you must have a Word icon pinned to your taskbar, or Word must be on your Start menu, either as a pinned item or in the recently used list. Right-click the Word icon on the taskbar, or click the arrow next to it on the Start menu. If you've recently created a blog post, as described in the preceding sections, a template named Blog should appear under Recent. As shown next, click Pin To This List next to Blog, which ensures that it stays on the list permanently.

Thereafter, when you open the Jump List (from the taskbar icon or the Start menu), you can simply click Blog to open a new blog post window in Word.

When you publish a blog post, it's stored on a web server, but you might also want to save a local copy so that you can work with it when you don't have Internet access. Simply save the file as you would any other document (press Ctrl+S or click File, Save); by default, Word uses its standard .docx file format. Note, however, that after you publish a post to your blog, some formatting is lost, even in your locally saved copy.

INSIDE OUT   Editing your blog's HTML code

Many blog editors—including stand-alone programs and your blogging service's online editing tools—let you switch between a "preview" view (comparable to Print Layout view in Word) and HTML code view. Not Word.

If you need to examine and edit the HTML code, create your post in Word and publish it as a draft. Then use your blogging service's editor to open the draft, where you can tweak away.

Combining Documents and Data with Mail Merge

Mail merge is the process of marrying a document (such as a letter) with data (such as a list of addresses). Although it's typically used for generating form letters and bulk mailings, you can apply mail merge techniques to just about any kind of document and any kind of data. Your data, for example, might include the name of a product a customer has purchased, or the registration number for a seminar attendee, or test scores, or . . . well, you get the idea.

With mail merge features in Word, you can sprinkle data fields throughout a document, you can sort and filter the data, and you can perform conditional merges in which the output depends on information in the data. You're not limited to a single data record per document either; you can use mail merge to create a page of labels (each addressed to a different person) or to print a roster, directory, or catalog (which allows you to format it in far more interesting ways than you could, say, with Excel).

INSIDE OUT   Print a single envelope or label

Merging data from a list is a powerful way to print many envelopes or labels, each addressed to a different person. But often you need just a single envelope or label, which is somewhat difficult to create when starting from a standard blank document. Word has you covered.

Simply click the Mailings tab, and in the Create group click Envelopes or Labels. The dialog box that appears, shown in Figure 10-6, is the same either way; the only difference is which tab is displayed initially.

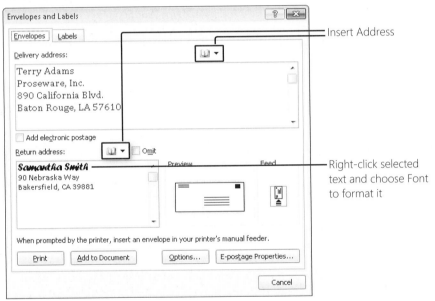

Figure 10-6 On either tab, click Options to select a paper size and type and to set printer options.

Type the addresses (or other information) directly in the dialog box or click Insert Address to select an address from your Outlook contacts. (Bonus tip: If you select text in your document before you click Envelopes or Labels, your selected text appears in the Delivery Address text box.) If you have an account with Stamps.com or another supported electronic postage vendor, you can print a postage "stamp" on your envelope or label.

To complete the task, click Print to send the job to your printer. Alternatively, click Add To Document (Envelopes tab) or New Document (Labels tab) to open the envelope or label in an ordinary Word document window, allowing you to modify it (add a logo, perhaps) or save it for reuse.

Using the Mail Merge Wizard

Word includes a wizard that leads you through the process of selecting data, preparing a document, previewing the merge results, and sending the results to the printer or to a file. To start the wizard, click the Mailings tab, and in the Start Mail Merge group, click Start Mail Merge, Step By Step Mail Merge Wizard. This opens the Mail Merge pane, as shown in Figure 10-7.

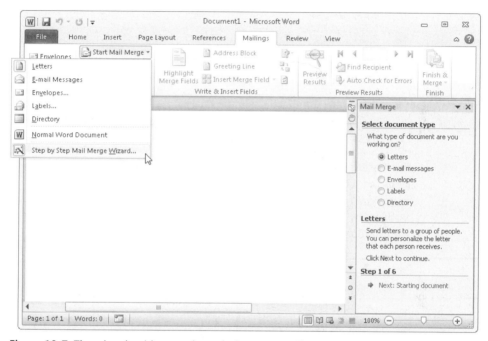

Figure 10-7 The wizard guides you through the process. Choose Step By Step Mail Merge Wizard at any time to display the Mail Merge pane.

The wizard takes you through the following steps:

1. **Select a document type.**   You begin by selecting a document type—letter, e-mail message, envelope, label, or directory. Your choice here affects the layout (the last two choices print multiple records on a single sheet, for example) and the wording that appears in the following steps.

2. **Select a starting document.**   You can use the current document, open a previously saved document, or create a new document based on a template you choose.

Chapter 10

3. **Select data records.**   You can draw data from an existing file or database, from your Outlook contacts, or from a list you type in Word. For more information, see the next section, "Working with Data Files."

4. **Lay out the document.**   In this step, you insert merge fields that link to data in your list. Throughout the process, you can work in the document window to type other information (such as common text that appears in all merged documents), format text, and so on. For more information, see "Inserting Data Fields in a Document" on page 324.

5. **Preview the document.**   Word replaces the field names with actual data from your database. You can page through the data records to verify that the merge works as expected. For more information, see "Previewing the Merged Output" on page 326.

6. **Complete the merge.**   In the final step, you merge the data into the document. You can send the output to a printer, to a new document, or as individual e-mail messages. For more information, see "Completing the Merge" on page 326.

For most users, the wizard is a worthwhile assistant. It ensures that you don't overlook any steps, yet it doesn't get in the way of speed or efficiency, as some wizards do. Nonetheless, as you gain experience you might prefer to use the ribbon tools; you can switch back and forth at any time. Figure 10-8 shows which tools on the Mailings tab correspond to each wizard step.

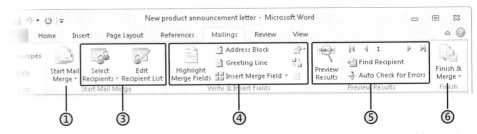

Figure 10-8 Numbers correspond to step numbers in the wizard. (Step 2 is comparable to choosing New or Open from Backstage view.)

Working with Data Files

In the wizard's third step, you connect the document to a data source.

For the simplest data requirements, type the list in Word. In the wizard, click Type A New List. Alternatively, on the Mailings tab, click Select Recipients, Type New List. A dialog box appears in which you can enter your data, as shown in Figure 10-9. After you enter your data and click OK, Word prompts you to save the data as a file, which it saves as an Access database.

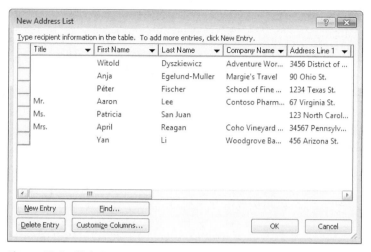

Figure 10-9 Click Customize Columns to add, remove, rename, or reorder columns to better suit your needs.

If the data you need already exists in your Outlook contacts or in a file, select one of those options instead. You can use as a data source any of numerous file types, including an Excel worksheet, a Word document (with data in a table), an Access database, an HTML file (with data in a table), or plain text files in comma-separated values (.csv) or delimited formats. You can also use information in a database that you access with an Open Database Connectivity (ODBC) connector.

> **Note**
>
> Be sure that your data file includes a header record—one that identifies the data field names. If it doesn't, Word uses the data in the first record as a header, which means you get undesirable field names and you lose access to the data in the first record.

After you connect to a data source, you can work with the list data by clicking Edit Recipient List (in the wizard or on the ribbon). The Mail Merge Recipients dialog box appears, as shown in Figure 10-10. Here you can select which records you want to include (select the check box by the ones you want), sort the list (tip: click a column heading to sort instead of clicking Sort), filter the list based on criteria you specify, and make other changes.

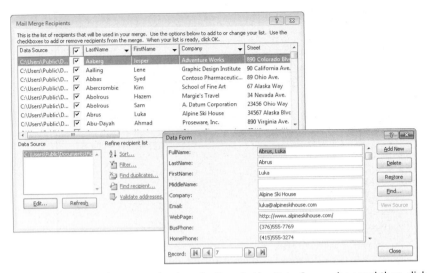

Figure 10-10 To edit a record, select the item in the Data Source box and then click Edit. Any changes you make are stored in the data source.

Inserting Data Fields in a Document

Presumably, in step 2 of the wizard you created the parts of the document that should print with all merged records, such as your logo and company information, the text of the letter, and similar items. This information can find its way into your document from a template, from an existing document, or from edits you make during this session.

With the basics in place, you can then insert data fields—placeholders for data—into appropriate places in your document. Position the insertion point in the document where you want merge data to appear, and then insert fields. You can do this from step 4 of the wizard or by using tools in the Write & Insert Fields group on the Mailings tab.

To insert an individual data field, click More Items (in the wizard) or Insert Merge Field (on the ribbon), and then click the name of the field you want to insert. In the dialog box that appears (see Figure 10-11), you can choose to insert Database Fields (the field list shows the names of the fields in your database) or Address Fields (standard field names for addressing applications).

Note that you can put merge fields anywhere in your document, and you can repeat fields without limitation. For example, you might include in the body of a letter something like "Thanks for purchasing a «ProductName». You might be interested to know that we have a special deal for «ProductName» owners."

Figure 10-11 To correlate the field names in your database with those in the address fields, click Match Fields.

Inserting individual fields can be tedious, so Word includes a couple of "super" fields that you can insert: Address Block and Greeting Line. Click one of these, and a dialog box appears in which you can customize the field output. For example, in the Insert Greeting Line dialog box, shown in Figure 10-12, you can select a default greeting or create your own.

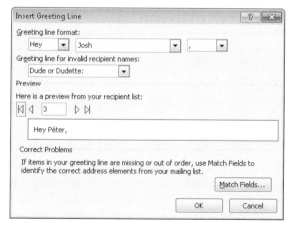

Figure 10-12 The predefined greetings are a bit more traditional than the ones we've typed.

The Address Block and Greeting Line fields have some intelligence built in. For example, if you select Mr. Randall as the greeting line format, each merged record uses the Title field followed by the Last Name field. But what if a record has no entry in the Title field? Word inserts First Name followed by Last Name. And what if a record has no name at all? Word inserts the text in the Greeting Line For Invalid Recipient Names box. The Address

Block field performs similar tricks: it omits blank lines (for example, when a recipient record doesn't have a company name or a second address line) and properly formats addresses.

> **Note**
>
> Although merge field names appear between guillemets (for example, «First_Name»), you can't simply type the symbols and the merge field name. Although you can type your entry using a {MERGEFIELD} field code, the easiest and most reliable way to insert merge fields is with tools on the Mailings tab.

Previewing the Merged Output

In step 5 of the wizard, you can check your work. (As an alternative to using the wizard, click Preview Results on the Mailings tab.) The merge field placeholders are replaced by actual data, and you can click the Next Record and Previous Record buttons to page through the results.

Be on the lookout not just for misplaced fields, but also for missing data and for data that overflows the allotted space. (Perhaps it exceeds the boundaries of a label or adds an extra page to a letter.) When you see errors like this, you can choose to exclude the offending recipient, edit the data, or modify the document or its formatting so that each merged item prints properly.

One option appears in the Preview Results group on the Mailings tab that's not available in the wizard pane: Auto Check For Errors. This review checks spelling and grammar, among other things, and (depending on which option you choose) can also complete the merge.

Completing the Merge

The sixth and final step is to actually perform the merge. Whether you use the wizard or the Finish & Merge tool on the Mailings tab, you can send the merge results to a printer (choose Print Documents) or to a new document (choose Edit Individual Documents). With the latter option, you end up with all the completed documents (letters or whatever) in one humongous document, which opens in a new window. In that document, you can edit individual documents (perhaps to add a personal note) before you print.

Whether you print or merge to a new document, Word first asks which records you want to include. If you want to print a range of records, you need to know the numbers of the first and last records to include; you can determine that information by using tools in the Preview Results group on the Mailings tab.

A third output destination is available by clicking Finish & Merge on the Mailings tab: e-mail. You need to have an e-mail address in each record. In an effort to reduce spam, many Internet service providers limit the number of messages you can send in a given period of time. Therefore, this option is practical only for small distribution lists. (And, of course, you should send e-mail only to those people who want to receive messages from you. Otherwise, you join the ranks of reviled spammers.)

Printing a Document

Many—if not most—Word documents get committed to paper at some point in their life. Printing is a simple task, and is generally the same in all Office programs (and, indeed, in most other programs as well). Click File, Print (or press Ctrl+P), and then click the Print button. A few seconds later, paper comes out of the printer.

But Word has some interesting and unique features related to printing that are easily overlooked. First, as shown in Figure 10-13, the Print tab in Backstage view includes a print preview feature that shows exactly how your document will look when printed. Use the controls at the bottom of the preview pane to page through the document, to zoom in for a closer look, or zoom out for a high-level view. (If you zoom out far enough, Word displays multiple pages.)

The button under Printer shows the status of the current printer and lets you select another. To modify a printer's settings, click Printer Properties.

Chapter 10

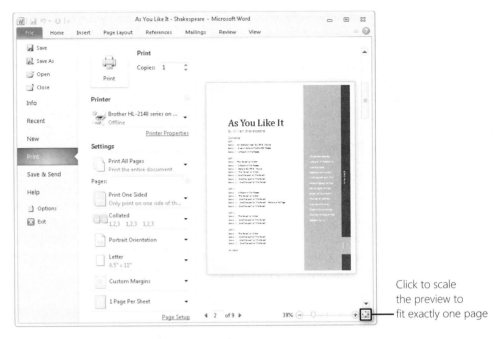

Click to scale
the preview to
fit exactly one page

Figure 10-13 A print preview dominates the right side of the Print tab in Backstage view.

To specify what you want to print, click the first button under Settings. On the menu that appears, shown next, you indicate which part of the document you want to print (all pages, the current selection, the current page, or specific pages). Select Print Markup if you want to show tracked changes, comments, and revision marks. (For details about these features, see "Tracking and Highlighting Changes Made to a Document" on page 285 and "Using Review Comments in a Document" on page 279.)

Options under Document Properties print information *about* your document rather than the document itself.

The button at the bottom of the Print tab offers scaling options. You can print 1, 2, 4, 6, 8, or even 16 document pages on each sheet of paper. Printing reduced size copies this way saves paper and ink when printing proofs, and saves storage space when printing archival copies.

The final option on the scaling menu, Scale To Paper Size, is useful when the paper size in your printer doesn't match the paper size set in the page layout. This commonly occurs, for example, when you receive a document from outside the United States that's designed for A4 paper—and your printer has only letter size paper. When you print the document, leave the page layout unchanged, but set Scale To Paper Size to match the actual paper size in your printer.

Chapter 10

Using Building Blocks

In Word, a *building block* is a stored chunk of content that can be used to quickly enter text and graphics in a document. Word organizes building blocks into galleries of blocks for similar purposes—headers, footers, equations, tables, cover pages, and so on. Dozens of building blocks of various types are included with Word; you can use these as is, modify them, or create your own building blocks. You can download additional building blocks from Office.com.

You insert building blocks into a document by using tools and galleries on the Insert tab. We discuss some of these galleries elsewhere in this book. (See "Adding Headers, Footers, and Page Numbers" on page 222, "Setting Page Layout Options" on page 221, "Using Quick Tables" on page 258, "Entering Mathematical Equations" on page 120, and "Creating Tables of Contents and Indexes" on page 273—as well as the following section, "Using AutoText.")

To view all the available building blocks, click the Insert tab, and in the Text group click Quick Parts, Building Blocks Organizer. The Building Blocks Organizer dialog box, shown in Figure 10-14, lists all building blocks, initially sorted by gallery. (Click a column heading to sort by another field.)

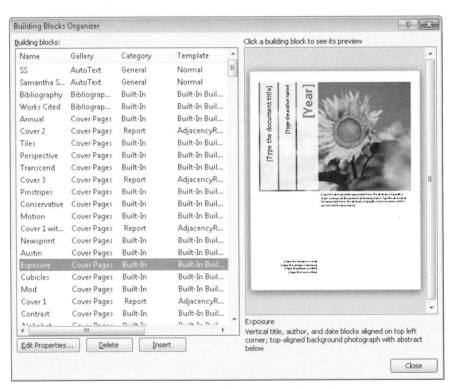

Figure 10-14 Select a building block to see its preview and description.

You can insert a building block directly from Building Blocks Organizer by selecting it and clicking Insert.

Using AutoText

One of the most useful types of building block is called AutoText. AutoText can contain any amount of document content, including formatting. It's typically used for boilerplate text, such as an "about this company" block that must go at the end of each press release, an oft-used disclaimer, or a title block including your logo and address.

To create an AutoText entry, select the content you want to reuse, and then press Alt+F3. (If you can't remember the keyboard shortcut, you can take the lengthier path: Click the Insert tab, and in the Text group click Quick Parts, AutoText, Save Selection To AutoText Gallery.) A dialog box appears, as shown Figure 10-15. Enter a memorable name, which is how you identify the entry when you want to reuse it.

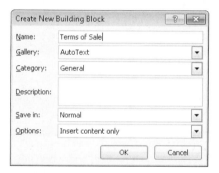

Figure 10-15 AutoText provides an easy way to enter frequently used text and graphics.

To insert your AutoText entry in a document, you can click Quick Parts, AutoText and then click the entry's thumbnail shown in the gallery. But there's a much easier way: Type the name you assigned to the AutoText entry, and then press F3. You don't need to type the entire name; you just need to type enough to uniquely identify it. For example, to enter an entry called Terms of Sale when you have no other AutoText entries that begin with the letter *T*, you could simply type **t** and then press F3. If you also have an entry called Trademark List, you'd need to type (at least) **te** before you press F3.

AutoCorrect provides an alternative way to enter blocks of text. For details, see "Entering Boilerplate and Other Oft-Used Text" on page 116.

Creating Other Types of Building Blocks

The process of creating other types of building blocks is nearly identical to the one just described for AutoText entries. For example, if you want to save a new header in the Header gallery, create and format the header just the way you want it, and then select it. Then, do one of the following to open the Create New Building Block dialog box:

- Click the gallery where you want to add the new entry. For example, to save a new header, click Insert, Header, Save Selection To Header Gallery.

- Click Insert, Quick Parts, Save Selection To Quick Parts Gallery. (Quick Parts is an all-purpose gallery that you might prefer to use simply to differentiate your stored building blocks from the Microsoft-furnished blocks.)

- Press Alt+F3.

Each of these actions opens the Create New Building Block dialog box; the only difference is the selection in the Gallery box, which you can change. Your choice here determines which gallery your building block appears in. Other than maintaining a sense of order, there's no reason you couldn't, for example, put a footer in the Cover Pages gallery. Other fields in Create New Building Block deserve a bit of explanation:

- **Category**   You can create categories within each gallery. Items in a gallery are grouped by their category.

- **Description**   Use this field to enter explanatory text, which appears in a ScreenTip when you hover the mouse pointer over a gallery item and when you view the item in Building Blocks Organizer.

- **Save In**   Specify where you want to save the building block:

  - Select Normal to save the building block in the Normal.dotm global template, which makes it available in all documents.

  - Select the name of the current template to store it in that template, which makes it available in all new documents you create based on the template.

  - Select Building Blocks to save it in Building Blocks.dotx, a template file that's stored in a subfolder of %AppData%\Microsoft\Document Building Blocks. Building blocks you store here are available for all documents you create, but this template isn't easy to share with others.

- **Options**   Specify whether the building block should be placed in a paragraph by itself, on a page by itself, or simply positioned at the insertion point without adding a paragraph or page break when you insert it.

Using Fields to Automate Documents

A *field* is a specialized placeholder for document content. (Word fields are not the same as data merge fields, as discussed earlier in this chapter. In fact, data merge fields are a type of Word field.) Fields can update dynamically, and they can be used for a wide variety of purposes. They can show variable data, such as the name of the document author, the number of pages in a document, or the date the document was last printed. They can be used to generate number sequences or even to perform numeric calculations. You can use fields to include certain text based on conditions you specify. You can use fields to create buttons that run macros or perform other actions, and you can use fields to enable an interactive document (one that asks a question and then enters the answer into the document).

And we're just scratching the surface. There's much more you can do with fields, but detailing it is beyond the scope of this book. What we can do, however, is show you how to work with fields in general. Armed with that knowledge, you should be able to start using fields in your documents.

You've probably already used fields, possibly without knowing it. Many features of Word that we discuss elsewhere in this book (for example, tables of contents, indexes, date and time, and document properties) are implemented with fields, but Word provides an interface that shields you from having to work directly with fields in these cases. Knowing how to work with fields empowers you to tweak those fields in ways that can't be done through the normal user interface.

Working with Field Codes

A field can be represented in either of two ways: a field code (the programming language, if you will) or the field result (the output of the field code as normally displayed or printed in a document). For example, this field code:

```
{Author}
```

might yield this field result:

```
Samantha Smith
```

To switch views between field codes and field results, press Alt+F9. Table 10-1 shows more keyboard shortcuts for working with fields.

A field code looks like ordinary text between curly braces—but there's nothing ordinary about the braces. You must insert them using Ctrl+F9 or with the Field dialog box. The text within those magic braces includes the field name and, in some cases, properties and switches. For example, the field code { SEQ OrderNum \n \#"##0" * MERGEFORMAT } includes the field name (SEQ), a property (OrderNum), and switches (the rest).

Chapter 10

Table 10-1 **Keyboard Shortcuts for Fields**

Action	Keyboard Shortcut
Insert an empty field	Ctrl+F9
Switch views between field codes and field results (all fields)	Alt+F9
Switch views between field codes and field results (selected fields)	Shift+F9
Update selected fields	F9
Go to next or previous field	F11 or Shift+F11
Lock a field to prevent updates	Ctrl+F11
Unlock a field	Ctrl+Shift+F11

Inserting a Field

Before you step up to the big leagues and start entering field codes directly, use the Field dialog box to insert a field. It lists all the available fields, includes a brief description about each one, shows the proper syntax, and provides a method for inserting valid switches. To get there, click the Insert tab, and in the Text group click Quick Parts, Field. Figure 10-16 shows the Field dialog box that appears.

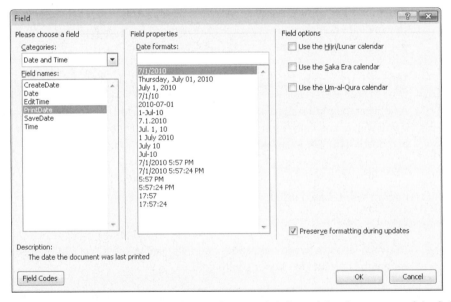

Figure 10-16 A description in the lower left corner briefly explains the purpose of the field selected in the Field Names box.

To narrow your choices a bit, select a category. Then select each field name and view its description to get an idea of what the field is used for. Make selections under Field

Properties and Field Options, and then click Field Codes or the Options button (which appears after you click Field Codes) for assistance in entering other parameters.

There's much to learn about fields, and perhaps we've piqued your interest. If so, you can find additional details about using fields at *w7io.com/11001*, and a detailed reference at *w7io.com/11002*.

Our Favorite Word Tweaks and Tips

We conclude our coverage of Word 2010 with descriptions of some seemingly esoteric customizations, tasks, and features. As it turns out, however, we use them often and it makes our use of Word a tad easier and more enjoyable. Perhaps you'll benefit from their use too. And while some authors wouldn't admit this, we finish off this section with a bit of filler text—but we think you'll like it!

Applying Styles from the Quick Access Toolbar

On the Home tab, right-click an item in the Quick Styles gallery and choose Add Gallery To Quick Access Toolbar. You can now apply gallery styles without displaying the Home tab; simply click the new icon on the Quick Access Toolbar to display the gallery. Note also that when you open the gallery on the Quick Access Toolbar, the dominant style of the current selection is highlighted, making this a handy way to see which styles are currently applied as well as a tool for applying a different style.

INSIDE OUT   **Add any toolbar group to the Quick Access Toolbar**

On the ribbon, a toolbar group is the collection of options between two vertical divider lines. You can add any toolbar group to the Quick Access Toolbar as a gallery-style menu. Right-click the group name and choose Add To Quick Access Toolbar. When you click the new icon on the Quick Access Toolbar, all the tools in the group appear below it.

Customizing the Quick Access Toolbar and the Status Bar

Some of our other favorite additions to the Quick Access Toolbar include the following:

- **Switch Windows**   If you frequently have more than one document window open, this tool makes switching between them quick and easy.

Chapter 10

- **Open Recent File**   This tool is equivalent to clicking File, Recent, saving you one click every time you want to reopen a recent file.

- **New**...   Similarly, this tool saves one click each time you create a new document by jumping directly to the New tab in Backstage view. (Note that the New... command is different from the New command, which opens a new document using the default template.)

- **Navigation Pane**   This tool lets you easily display or hide the Navigation pane.

- **Quick Print**   This tool immediately sends a document to the printer using default settings, thereby reducing three clicks (File, Print, Print) to one.

- **Show All**   When your document isn't laying out the way you expect it to, it's easier to figure out what's going on when you can see paragraph marks, new line characters, tabs, and other nonprinting characters.

- **New Comment**   When collaborating on documents, we often use comments, and this tool saves a trip to the Review tab.

- **AutoCorrect**   If you often add AutoCorrect entries, this tool saves you the drudgery of clicking File, Options, Proofing, AutoCorrect Options.

- **Building Blocks Organizer**   This tool provides an alternative way to insert any type of building block, including AutoText entries.

For details, see "Customizing the Quick Access Toolbar" on page 62.

Because we often use change tracking, we also like to add an item to the status bar. Right-click the status bar and choose Track Changes. You can then click this status item to turn change tracking on or off.

Customizing Backstage View

The Recent tab in Backstage view is a common destination. We're often working on a document for days or weeks at a time, so we start each Word session with a visit to the Recent tab to retrieve documents.

The tab has a few simple, but often overlooked, features for customizing it. First, we select the Quickly Access This Number Of Recent Documents check box at the bottom of the window and select a number of documents that are currently in heavy rotation. This adds those documents to the menu on the left side of the window (between the Close command and Info tab) so they're accessible just by clicking File, regardless of which tab is selected.

We also like to pin certain documents and places so that they stay on the Recent tab permanently. For example, we have a report that we must update monthly; the same document is used regularly but not frequently. During the intervening month, the report usually scrolls off the list if it's not pinned, meaning we have to go hunting for it.

Resetting Word Options

There may come a time when something about Word isn't working the way you want it to, and you just want to restore the default setup. The best way to do that, of course, is to reverse the steps that got you into that situation—but that's not always possible.

If you really get desperate—and if you're willing and able to poke around in the registry and other dark places—check out Microsoft Support article 822005 (*w7io.com/822005*). It can help you to find where deeply hidden settings are stored in the registry and in other files. The article includes instructions for various methods of removing these settings, thereby resetting Word to its default.

CAUTION

The methods described in the support article don't really qualify as a "favorite" tip. Use them only as a last resort, and at your own peril!

Reading Document Text Aloud

It's often useful to have a document read aloud. When you're proofreading text that you've retyped, you can read the original while Word speaks what you typed. And sometimes having something you've written spoken out loud exposes errors that you might miss by staring at the words on the screen or on paper.

Word has a well-hidden Speak command that can assist in these situations. Some very good text-to-speech implementations are available for modern computers; this isn't one of them. The spoken text is unmistakably computer-generated, yet it can be good enough for some purposes.

If you want to try it, you need to dig a bit. Right-click the ribbon and choose Customize The Ribbon. Under Choose Commands From, select Commands Not In The Ribbon. Scroll down to find the Speak command, and add it to the ribbon. (If you don't already have a custom group on the ribbon, you need to create one.) The Review tab is an appropriate location.

For details about adding a command to the ribbon, see "Personalizing the Ribbon" on page 57.

Chapter 10

With the Speak command now ensconced on the ribbon, select some text and click Speak to hear a voice reminiscent of early science fiction movies.

Printing Booklets

Printing a multipage document in booklet form is a difficult task if you do it manually. You need to calculate page sizes and margins, and worst of all, you have to reorder the pages so that they come out in the proper order when the sheets are folded and collated. Fortunately, Word can do all the hard work for you.

> **Note**
>
> You'll have the most success setting up booklet printing if you follow these steps *before* you enter and format the document content.

To set up a document to print as a booklet, follow these steps:

1. On the Page Layout tab, click Margins, Custom Margins.

2. On the Margins tab of the Page Layout dialog box, next to Multiple Pages, select Book Fold.

3. Under Margins, enter dimensions for page margins. Keep in mind that the page size is now one-half of the paper size. (For example, if you're using letter size paper, the new effective page size is 5½ inches by 8½ inches.)

4. If you want to allow additional space along the fold to accommodate a binding, increase the Gutter value.

5. Next to Sheets Per Booklet (under Pages), select the number of pages you want in each booklet. If your document has more pages than the number you select, the document prints as multiple separate booklets.

After you create the document content and you're ready to print your booklet, choose File, Print. Click the second button under Settings, and then select either Print On Both Sides (if your printer can duplex automatically) or Manually Print On Both Sides (if your printer prints on only one side of the sheet).

Generating "Greek" Text

When you work on a design-oriented project in Word, you'll sometimes want to get an idea of how the document will look even before the copy for the document has been written. Graphic designers have long used filler text to show off design concepts without worrying that the client will get bogged down in the content. The technique is sometimes called "greeking"—which is somewhat ironic because the text most commonly used for greeking is in Latin.

That text begins "Lorem ipsum," and it's widely used because it approximates standard English text in word length and letter selection, yet it can't be mistaken for English. To enter that filler text in a document, start a new paragraph, type **=lorem()**, and press Enter. Word replaces this with three paragraphs of filler text.

If you want more or less filler text, insert two parameters within the parentheses: the number of paragraphs and the number of sentences in each paragraph. For example, typing **=lorem(2,4)** generates this text:

Lorem ipsum dolor sit amet, consectetuer adipiscing elit. Maecenas porttitor congue massa. Fusce posuere, magna sed pulvinar ultricies, purus lectus malesuada libero, sit amet commodo magna eros quis urna. Nunc viverra imperdiet enim.

Fusce est. Vivamus a tellus. Pellentesque habitant morbi tristique senectus et netus et malesuada fames ac turpis egestas. Proin pharetra nonummy pede.

Use just a single parenthetical parameter, and Word interprets that as the number of paragraphs you want, with each containing three sentences.

If you'd rather have something that looks more like English, use =rand() or =rand.old() in the same way.

Chapter 10

PERHAPS because of its long association with accountants, Excel has a reputation as staid, even dull. It's the software equivalent of a gray flannel suit. We think that characterization is unfair. Yes, it's true that you can use Excel to count beans and widgets and calculate profits and losses with incredible precision. But you can also use this all-purpose tool for tasks that are completely unrelated to numbers. In the four chapters that begin here, we cover as many of those possibilities as we can.

In this chapter, we cover the nuts and bolts of Excel, with a discussion of what's in a workbook and how to navigate through the multiple dimensions of cells, rows, columns, and worksheets. We also explain how to enter data quickly and accurately.

When you look past the grid-style layout, you can think of Excel as a powerful engine for performing calculations using numbers, dates, and text. The key to making these calculations work for you is understanding how to create formulas using arithmetic, logical, and comparison operators. Most valuable of all is a long list of functions that perform scientific, engineering, and statistical calculations that would take hours to work out manually. We cover the full range of Excel's function library in this chapter.

And finally, we dive into the details of how Excel transforms what you type or paste into what you see on the screen with a look at number formatting.

What's in an Excel Workbook?

The sheer breadth of things you can create using Excel is staggering. Starting from a blank sheet, you can enter simple lists, take inventory of a collection, or prepare a consolidated financial report for a business of any size. With the right formatting, you can produce reports that look like they come from a desktop publishing shop, generate easy-to-read forms, and even construct calendars for use online or on paper. All of these uses start with a workbook, which is the default document format for Excel.

In this section, we assume that you are using the standard Excel 2010 Workbook (.xlsx) format. For a description of other available formats, see Table 4-2, "Supported File Formats in Excel 2010," on page 79.

A workbook consists of one or more worksheets, each of which is made up of a maximum of 16,384 columns and 1,048,576 rows (although it's highly unlikely you'll ever create a worksheet big enough to need all of those theoretically available 17 billion-something cells). At the intersection of each row and column is a cell, which is identified by combining the letter from its column heading and the number from its row heading. Cell A1 is in the top left corner of every worksheet; C11 is the active cell if you move two columns over and 10 rows down; XFD1048576 is in the lower right corner of the sheet. Click in any cell to begin entering text, a number, or a formula that performs a calculation using a worksheet function, with or without references to the contents of other cells. (We discuss formulas in much greater detail later in this chapter.)

Figure 11-1 shows a packing slip created in Excel. An employee who pulls up this template can fill in values in a few cells (or draw them directly from a database with a little programming help) and print out the resulting sheet to include with a shipment. The bold black lines identify the current cell, whose address, G2, appears in the Name box. The formula bar indicates that the cell contains a formula that returns the value of today's date. The formula result (August 15, 2010, in this example) appears in the worksheet.

Excel also allows you to create specialized data structures on a worksheet. You can define a range of cells as a table, for example, which lets you sort, filter, and format data arranged as a list. You can use PivotTables and PivotCharts to slice, filter, and summarize large sets of data. And you can create a chart from data on a worksheet to analyze trends and relationships visually.

For a full discussion of tables and PivotTables, see Chapter 12, "Managing Lists and Data." For more details on how to create and use charts, see Chapter 13, "Charts and Data Analysis."

Although you can put together a workbook using a single worksheet, using multiple worksheets offers some notable advantages, especially in terms of organizing complex collections of data. For a consolidated budget or financial report, you might keep the figures for each department on a separate worksheet. Each department fills in its own numbers using a standard template, and you "roll up" the results into a summary worksheet that uses the same structure to calculate a grand total for each row and column. For a workbook that contains details about a loan, you might keep the summary of interest rates, principal amounts, and payments on one worksheet and display a full amortization table on a separate sheet, where you can view and print it separately. As we discuss elsewhere in this book, you can display charts on their own worksheet, away from potentially distracting source data, and you can reduce complex data sets to easy-to-read summaries by adding a

PivotTable on a separate sheet. You can also use multiple extra worksheets to perform back-of-the-envelope calculations without disturbing a carefully constructed and formatted main worksheet.

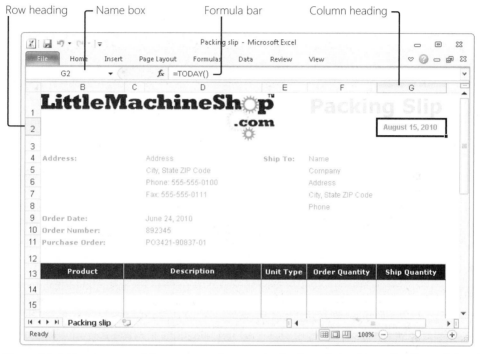

Figure 11-1 The contents of the current cell appear in the formula bar. The cell address, defined by intersecting column and row headings, is called out in the Name box.

INSIDE OUT Change the default number of worksheets

By default, each new blank workbook you create contains three blank worksheets. You might prefer a different number: one, for example, with the option to add extra worksheets manually as needed. To modify this default, open Excel, click File, and then click Options in Backstage view. On the General tab of the Excel Options dialog box, under the When Creating New Workbooks section, adjust the Include This Many Sheets setting. The minimum is 1; the maximum is 255, although we can't imagine why anyone would choose a number that high. Each new sheet increases the size of the resulting workbook file by a trivial amount—approximately 500 bytes per sheet.

To manage worksheets within a workbook, use the controls beneath the worksheet. The current worksheet name is highlighted in bold. From here, you can select one or more worksheets, add a new sheet or delete an existing one, rename a sheet or change the color of its tab, move or copy sheets to the same workbook or a different one, and hide a worksheet. Figure 11-2 identifies these controls.

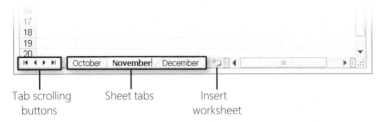

Tab scrolling   Sheet tabs   Insert
buttons   worksheet

Figure 11-2 Use these controls beneath the current worksheet to manage worksheet tabs.

Each worksheet gets its own tab, with the name of the current tab highlighted in bold. If some tabs aren't visible, use the tab scrolling buttons to scroll through the tab list or jump to the first or last tab in the group.

To create a new worksheet, click Insert Worksheet, or use the keyboard shortcut Shift+F11. Newly created worksheets appear to the right of the last tab in the current workbook and get a generic name with a number that is one higher than the most recently used number—Sheet4, Sheet5, and so on. To create a new sheet in a specific location or by using a saved template, right-click the tab to the right of where you want the new tab to appear, and then click Insert on the shortcut menu. From the Insert dialog box (shown here) select Worksheet to create a blank sheet, or choose a previously used template, and then click OK.

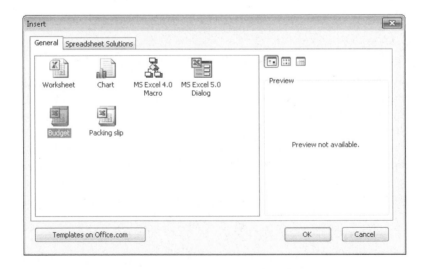

To rename a worksheet, double-click its name on the sheet tab and begin typing. A sheet name can have a maximum of 31 characters and can include spaces, parentheses, and most punctuation marks, with the exception of the following prohibited characters: [ ] / \ ? * : (brackets, slash and backslash, question mark, asterisk, and colon).

CAUTION

Just because you can create a 31-character sheet name doesn't mean you should. The names of worksheets are used in formulas when a referenced cell location is on a sheet other than the one containing the formula. Short, simple, descriptive names work best for this purpose; long, complex sheet names make it difficult to understand the design of a workbook or to debug a formula.

To color-code a worksheet tab (or a group of tabs selected using the standard Ctrl+click method), right-click the selected tab and click Tab Colors. You can choose any standard color or a color from the current theme. Colored tabs are best used sparingly to help visually identify a group of related tabs or to make it easier to spot summary sheets.

To move a worksheet within a workbook, drag the sheet tab left or right. When the black triangular marker is over the location where you want the sheet to appear, release the mouse button. To move a sheet to a different workbook, make sure the destination workbook is open; then right-click the tab you want to move, and click Move Or Copy. In the Move Or Copy dialog box, select the name of the destination workbook from the To Book drop-down list and the tab location from the Before Sheet list, and then click OK.

To copy a worksheet to the same workbook, hold down the Ctrl key and drag the sheet tab left or right. The contents of the copied sheet are identical to the original, and the name is the same except for a numeric suffix. To copy a sheet to another open workbook, follow the same steps as for moving the sheet, but select Create A Copy from the Move Or Copy dialog box before clicking OK.

To hide a worksheet, right-click its tab and select Hide from the shortcut menu. The contents of that sheet are still available for formulas, but they are unavailable for casual inspection. This isn't a security feature—its primary purpose is to remove potentially distracting elements that are necessary for workbook calculations but shouldn't be changed. To see a list of hidden sheets so you can make one or more visible, right-click any sheet tab and click Unhide.

Chapter 11

Navigating in Worksheets and Workbooks

You can plod your way through any worksheet by clicking and typing in individual cells, but worksheets and formulas become much more powerful when you work with multiple cells simultaneously. In Excel's parlance, any selection of two or more cells is a *range*. You can use a range as the argument in a formula and to define data series and labels in charts. You can also enter, edit, and format data in multiple cells simultaneously by selecting a range first. In a budget worksheet, for example, you can select the range containing totals and apply the Currency format to all the cells in that range with a single action.

If you click in any cell and drag in any direction, your selection of adjacent cells is called a *contiguous range*. As you expand your selection, the Name box provides feedback about the size of the range. In this example, the current range consists of 11 rows and 4 columns:

Select All

	A	B	C	D	E
1	InvNum	DateDue	Amount	Status	
2	3235	14-Apr	$167.00	Overdue	
3	3236	21-Apr	$335.00	Overdue	
4	3237	24-May	$267.00	Pending	
5	3238	28-May	$323.00	Pending	
6	3239	26-May	$278.00	Pending	
7	3240	16-May	$217.00	Pending	
8	3241	22-May	$115.00	Pending	
9	3242	1-Jun	$178.00	Pending	
10	3243	15-May	$384.00	Pending	
11	3244	8-May	$268.00	Pending	
12					
13					
14					

11R x 4C   *fx* InvNum

A reference to a contiguous range consists of two cell addresses separated by a colon. The two addresses identify the upper left and lower right corners of the range, respectively. In the previous example, the range address is A1:D11. You can also define a noncontiguous range by holding down the Ctrl key as you select any combination of individual cells and ranges on a single worksheet. You can apply cell formatting to a contiguous or noncontiguous range, and you can use either type of range as the argument in a formula.

One related navigational concept is worth noting here as well. Excel defines the current *region* as the area around the active cell that is enclosed by blank rows and blank columns. If you define a table, for example, Excel expands the default selection to include the current region.

INSIDE OUT   Select rows, columns, and entire sheets

To select an entire row or column, click the row heading or column heading, respectively. To select multiple columns or rows, drag the selection across multiple headings
(or hold down the Ctrl key as you select additional rows or columns). To select all cells
in a worksheet (so that you can apply global formatting, for example), click the unlabeled Select All button in the upper left corner of the sheet, just below the Name box.
To reference a range that includes all the cells in a given row or column, use the row
number or column letter by itself. Thus, a reference to 5:5 means all cells in row 5, and
AC:AE refers to all cells in columns AC, AD, and AE.

Using Cell Addresses and Range Names

The Name box, just to the left of the formula bar (above the current worksheet contents),
shows the address of the active cell. This is true even if the current selection consists of a
range.

You can jump to any cell by entering its address in the Name box and pressing Enter. If you
enter the address of a contiguous range in the Name box (H8:J10, for example), pressing
Enter selects that range and makes the cell in the upper left corner of that range active and
ready to accept input.

The Name box has a much more practical use, however. Excel allows you to assign names
to any cell or range or to a formula or constant. If your worksheet includes a table listing
sales tax rates by state, you can define each rate using a descriptive name: CASalesTaxRate,
AZSalesTaxRate, and so on. You can then use those names in place of the corresponding
cell or range address in formulas. On an invoice worksheet, for example, you can define
Items_Total as the name for the cell that sums up the price of all items in the order and
then use a formula like this one to calculate the sales tax for California residents:

=Items_Total*CASalesTaxRate

That's easier to understand than =D14*E76, isn't it? The advantage of using a range name is
especially apparent when you have to review and revise a worksheet that someone else created (or even one that you created months or years earlier). Think of range names as a part
of the documentation of the logic and structure of a worksheet and workbook.

Excel creates some names automatically—when you define a table or a print range, for
example—but you can also define names manually. The simplest way to define a name is to
select a cell or range, click in the Name box, type a name, and press Enter. For more control

Chapter 11

over the naming process, click the Formulas tab, and then click Define Name from the Defined Names group. That opens the New Name dialog box, shown in Figure 11-3.

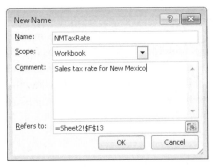

Figure 11-3 Using the Define Name command allows you to add comments to the name you assign to a cell or range.

By default, all names you create use absolute cell references. For an explanation of this type of reference, see "Using Formulas and Functions" on page 356.

The rules for a cell or range name are strict: Names are not case-sensitive. The first character must be a letter, an underscore, or a backslash, and remaining characters (up to a total of 255) can be letters, numbers, periods, and underscore characters. Spaces, punctuation, and other special characters are prohibited. You cannot use any name that could be confused for a cell reference, and you cannot use the single letters C or R (capitals or lowercase).

To pick from a list of all named cells and ranges in the current workbook, even those on different worksheets, click the drop-down arrow to the right of the Name box.

Using Keyboard Shortcuts

For the productivity-obsessed, mouse pointers and scroll bars are like roadblocks and speed bumps. Keyboard shortcuts are almost always faster, and they sometimes offer unique navigation and tricks that aren't available any other way. Excel shares a few keyboard shortcuts with its fellow Office programs, including F2 to make the contents of the current cell available for editing and F4 to repeat the previous action. Ctrl+X, Ctrl+C, and Ctrl+V work for Cut, Copy, and Paste; Ctrl+Alt+V for Paste Special; and Ctrl+Z and Ctrl+Y for Undo and Redo. For formatting, you can count on the old standbys Ctrl+B, Ctrl+I, and Ctrl+U to apply bold, italic, and underline formatting, respectively, to the current selection.

In Table 11-1, we list some useful and unjustly obscure shortcuts available only in Excel.

Table 11-1 **Keyboard Shortcuts Used Only in Excel**

Action	Keyboard Shortcut
Move to beginning of current row	Home
Move to top left corner of current sheet	Ctrl+Home
Move up one window	Page Up
Move down one window	Page Down
Move to next worksheet	Ctrl+Page Up
Move to previous worksheet	Ctrl+Page Down
Expand/collapse the formula bar	Ctrl+Shift+U
Select the current region	Ctrl+Shift+*
Select all cells containing comments	Ctrl+Shift+O
Display the Insert dialog box	Ctrl+Shift+Plus (+)
Display the Delete dialog box	Ctrl+Shift+Minus (–)
Hide selected rows	Ctrl+9
Hide selected columns	Ctrl+0

A few useful keyboard shortcuts require more explanation than we can pack into a table.

In other Office programs, Ctrl+A is the shortcut for Select All. In Excel, however, this keyboard shortcut has at least three separate actions. If the current worksheet contains data, pressing Ctrl+A selects the current region. Press Ctrl+A again to select the entire worksheet. If you select a cell and type an equal sign followed by a function name, pressing Ctrl+A opens the Function Arguments dialog box.

Moving around within a selected range can be tedious, especially when the selection encompasses a long list with boundaries that extend well beyond the edges of the current window. In that case, press Ctrl+period to move the active cell clockwise through the four corners of the selected range, without affecting the selection.

And then there's the End key, which enables a baffling set of navigation shortcuts collectively known as *End Mode*. When you press the End key in Excel, you might miss the small, subtle change along the left side of the status bar at the bottom of the program window, where the words *End Mode* become visible. When this indicator is visible, typical navigation keys temporarily change their behavior in unusual ways.

- Press End and then press any arrow key to move the selection within the current row or column, in the direction of the arrow, to the next cell that contains data, skipping over any blank cells in between. You can accomplish the same movement using the Ctrl+arrow key shortcuts.

Chapter 11

- Press End and then Home to move to the bottom right corner of the portion of the worksheet that contains data—in other words, the cell that is at the intersection of the farthest data-containing row and column in the sheet. So, for example, if the outer reaches of the data in your worksheet (the row farthest from the top and the column farthest from the left) are in cell A277 and Z1, respectively, this shortcut takes you immediately to Z277. The keyboard shortcut Ctrl+End leads to the same destination.

- Press End and then Enter to move to the last cell in the current row, skipping over any blank cells. This End Mode trick has no corresponding Ctrl-key shortcut.

End Mode is enabled only until you press another key. If the next key you press is something other than one of the navigation keys in the previous list, such as a letter or number or function key, Excel turns End Mode off and processes that key press normally. If you accidentally enable End Mode, you can turn it off by pressing End again.

Entering and Filling in Data and Series

For basic data entry tasks, Excel works about as you would expect. Click, type, and press Enter, or use the Clipboard to paste data copied from elsewhere. In this section, we explore a few techniques that are unique (and useful) in Excel.

When designing a worksheet, you might want to enter a constant value (such as 0) or an identical formula in a range of cells. Instead of filling each cell manually, speed things up by selecting the entire range (contiguous or noncontiguous) first. Type the text, value, or formula you want to include in each cell, and then press Ctrl+Enter. When you use this technique to enter a formula into multiple cells, the resulting entry uses relative cell references. If you want one or more references in the formula to use absolute or mixed references, adjust the formula before you press Ctrl+Enter.

For an explanation of the difference between absolute, relative, and mixed references, see "Using Formulas and Functions" on page 356.

To enter today's date into the active cell, press Ctrl+; (semicolon); to enter the current time, press Ctrl+: (colon).

A handful of keyboard shortcuts and mouse tricks allow you to copy data or formulas or fill a series through a range. Filling a range is a very powerful way to quickly build a worksheet, and you can take your pick of menus, keyboard shortcuts, and mouse gestures to accomplish the task.

Consider this scenario. You have a worksheet in which you have set aside column D for the results of this month's sales, which you plan to update daily. You've entered a formula in cell

D2 to track each employee's performance against goal and formatted the cell so it uses the Percentage format. You now want to copy that value and formatting to column D for each of the remaining rows. Here's what this section of the worksheet looks like when we select the range we want to fill.

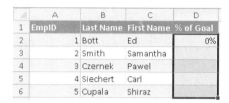

To copy the contents and formatting from the top cell in this range to all other cells, press Ctrl+D. If you prefer a menu-driven approach, click Fill (in the Editing group on the Home tab) and then click Down. If the top cell contains a formula, that formula is copied (with relative references) to the cells in the range below it. If the cell contains text or a number, that entry is copied exactly. If the selection contains more than one column, the contents of the first cell in each column of the range is copied to the cells beneath.

CAUTION

Using any of the Fill options completely replaces the contents of the destination cells. If those cells contain valuable data, you lose that data. To avoid this problem, use Ctrl+click to select the cells whose contents you want to replace and then use the Ctrl+Enter shortcut we discuss earlier in this section to enter the text, constant, or formula into only those selected cells.

A similar technique exists to fill a selection within a row. Enter the value, text, or formula in the first cell, and select the range to the right where you want to fill. Press Ctrl+R, or click Fill (in the Editing group on the Home tab) and then click Right. The Fill menu on the Home tab contains Up and Left options as well; there are no corresponding keyboard shortcuts for those operations.

Even more powerful is the ability to extend a series of numbers, dates, or values. To fill in a series of numbers, enter the first value in the series and then select that cell and the remainder of the range where you want the series to continue. We want to begin a series with the year 1960, so we entered it in cell A2 and selected the balance of the range. Click Fill (in the Editing group on the Home tab) and then click Series to display the dialog box shown in Figure 11-4.

Chapter 11

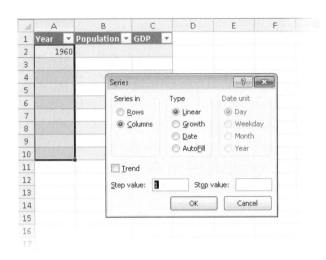

Figure 11-4 Click OK to fill in the values 1960 through 1969 in the selected range. Change the step value to 5 to fill in 1965, 1970, 1975, and so on.

Using the default step value of 1, Excel fills in 1961, 1962, and so on, all the way to 1969 in our selection of 10 cells. If we change that value to 5, each step in the series shifts accordingly, to 1965, 1970, and so on.

Ironically, the Date Unit section of this dialog box is unavailable in the previous figure even though we entered what looks like a date. Why? Because Excel didn't store our entry in date format. To make these options available, we could change the entry in cell A2 to 1/1/1960; if we format that value using the mmm-yyyy format and choose a date unit of Month and a step value of 6, the series will progress through Jul-1960, Jan-1961, Jul-1961, and so on.

We saved our best trick for last, however. All the previous copies and fills can be accomplished just as easily by dragging the fill handle in the lower right corner of a cell or range. Using the fill handle allows you to extend a surprising variety of series, some of which are not available from the Series option on the Fill menu. Besides numeric series, you can extend units of time, including hours of the day (9:00 AM, 10:00 AM, . . .) and days of the week or months of the year, abbreviated (Mon, Tues, . . . and Jan, Feb, . . .) or fully spelled out. As you can see in the folllowing example, the fill handle looks like a thin black cross; as you drag, the border shows you which cells you've selected and a ScreenTip shows what will appear in the cell.

	A	B	C
1	Monday		
2			
3			
4			
5			
6		Friday	
7			
8			
9			

Drag the selection back up (or to the left, if you're working row-wise) to make the AutoFill range smaller. If you continue dragging down past Sunday, the series repeats. Months work the same way.

Excel knows that business runs on quarterly results. If you enter Q1 in a cell and then drag the fill handle down or to the right, Excel smartly assumes you want to continue with Q2, Q3, and Q4 and then start over with Q1. (You can get a similar result if you begin with 1st quarter or Quarter 1.) Excel continues repeating the series in this fashion until you release the mouse button.

If you start with a single cell containing a number and drag the fill handle down, Excel copies the contents of the initial cell into the remainder of the range (1,1,1,1). Hold down Ctrl as you drag the fill handle to change to a series (1,2,3,4). A small plus sign appears alongside the fill handle when it switches to series mode.

You can also fill a series containing text and a number. If you enter District 1 and drag the fill handle down, the series continues with District 2, District 3, and so on.

If you've already filled a range, use the AutoFill menu shown here to switch from Copy Cells to Fill Series or vice versa. You can also copy formatting only or choose Fill Without Formatting to add only the values in your series.

As with so many things in Office, you can also use the right mouse button to good advantage with the fill handle. When you release the mouse button after dragging, Excel displays a shortcut menu showing many of the options from the Series dialog box.

INSIDE OUT   Give Excel some extra clues about your series

For most series, Excel uses the default step value of 1 when you extend the series using the fill handle or the Series dialog box. If you want to use a different series, enter values in two or more cells—enough to make it clear what the series is—and then select both cells and drag the fill handle. If you start with Jan 2011 and Apr 2011, for example, Excel assumes (probably correctly) that you want to continue with July 2011, Oct 2011, and Jan 2012. And you don't have to mess with any dialog boxes to make it so.

For a more detailed of how to use and fine-tune Clipboard options, see "Using the Clipboard with Office Programs" on page 129.

Using Formulas and Functions

If the following section brings up unpleasant memories of high-school algebra assignments and nightmares about trigonometry, we apologize in advance. But we can't talk about Excel without discussing—at great length—its amazing ability to perform calculations. This section is all about formulas, which are equations that Excel uses to perform mathematical and statistical calculations, manipulate text, test logical conditions, look up information in databases, and much more. We promise: there won't be a test.

To begin entering a formula, click in any cell and type an equal sign. Assuming that you follow the correct syntax, Excel evaluates the formula when you press Enter and displays the formula's result in the cell. The formula itself remains visible in the formula bar when you select the cell.

A formula can contain any combination of the following four elements:

- *Constants* are numbers or text values that you enter directly and that remain the same regardless of any ensuing calculations.

- *References* are cell or range addresses that incorporate the contents of the referenced location into the current formula.

- *Functions* are predefined formulas that perform calculations by using specific values, called *arguments*. The syntax of a particular function defines which arguments are required and which are optional. Arguments are enclosed in parentheses after the function name and can consist of constants, references, or other functions. Multiple arguments are separated by commas. A function used as an argument in another function is referred to as a *nested function*. A small number of functions use no arguments. NOW(), TODAY(), and PI(), for example, return the current time, today's date, and the value of pi, respectively.

- *Operators* define the types of calculations performed in a formula: arithmetic, comparisons, text concatenation, and reference. Excel has strict rules on the order in which calculations are performed; you can control the order of calculation by using parentheses.

We define each of these categories in more detail, with examples, in the following section.

Creating and Editing Formulas

The number of things you can do with Excel formulas and functions is literally limitless, especially when you learn to combine functions. We don't, alas, have limitless pages in this section, so we'll be sure we cover the fundamentals thoroughly: how to add a formula to your worksheet, using built-in tools to find the correct syntax for any function and enter its arguments correctly. After we cover that ground, we'll dive into the built-in functions by category, providing examples that we think you're likely to find useful.

Although the examples we show in this section use capital letters, you don't need to wear out the Shift key when you use Excel. You can enter functions, references, and other parts of a formula in lowercase; Excel takes care of converting those elements to the proper case when you enter the formula.

The simplest formulas of all are those that use only constants and simple math operators without references to other cells or functions. The following formula, for example, is perfectly valid:

=2+2

If you're working in Excel, you can use any available cell as a quick-and-dirty calculator—presumably to figure something slightly more complex than 2+2. Just start with an equal sign and use any of the supported arithmetic operators as listed in Table 11-2.

Chapter 11

Table 11-2 **Arithmetic Operators Supported in Excel Formulas**

Operator	Usage
+ (plus sign)	Addition (=14+7, =C4+C5). If one of the values is negative, the result is the same as subtraction.
– (minus sign)	Subtraction (=17–3, =D1–D2) or negation (=–6, =–A7).
* (asterisk)	Multiplication (=3*10, =B5*B6).
/ (forward slash)	Division (=24/8, =B5/C5). The elements on either side of the operator are the dividend and the divisor, respectively. If the divisor evaluates to zero, you get a #DIV/0! error.
% (percent sign)	Percent (=10%, =A1%). The result is the same as dividing the number by 100; typically used with multiplication, as in =10%*42, which results in 4.2
^ (caret)	Exponentiation (=3^2, =C4^D8). Multiplies the number to the left of the operator by itself the number of times specified by the number to the right of the operator

When you use any of the arithmetic operators, the constants, references, functions, or formulas on both sides of the operator must result in values. If your formula is =C4+C5 or =D1*C5 and C5 is a text string, your result is the same: a #VALUE! error.

INSIDE OUT   Keyboard shortcuts for formulas

For touch typists who think moving one's hands away from the keyboard is a surrender to the forces of chaos and anarchy, we offer these productivity-salvaging keyboard shortcuts:

Ctrl+` (The character shown is an accent grave, typically found beneath the tilde at the left of the number row on a standard PC keyboard.) This shortcut alternates between displaying cell values and displaying formulas in the worksheet and offers a useful way to see a worksheet's logic at a glance.

Ctrl+' (The character shown is an apostrophe, typically found to the left of the Enter key on a standard PC keyboard.) Use this shortcut to copy a formula from the cell above into the active cell.

Ctrl+A   Enter an equal sign, followed by any function name, and then press this keyboard shortcut to open the Function Arguments dialog box

Ctrl+Shift+A   Enter an equal sign, followed by any function name, and then press this keyboard shortcut to insert the argument names and parentheses.

The most common of all formulas—so useful it gets its own button on both the Home tab and the Formulas tab in Excel—is AutoSum. If you select a cell (empty or not) and click the AutoSum button, Excel inserts the =SUM formula. If Excel detects numbers in the column above or the row to the left of the active cell (even if some blank cells separate the range from the SUM function), it fills in that range as the argument. You can accept the default argument or adjust it as needed.

Click the AutoSum arrow to choose from a menu of other functions—Average, Count Numbers, Max, and Min—to automatically fill in those functions.

INSIDE OUT   Use names in place of formulas

Although names are most commonly used as cell or range references (as we described earlier in this chapter in "Using Cell Addresses and Range Names" on page 349), you can also assign a name to a formula. The named formula can refer to cells in the current worksheet or workbook, or it can stand on its own. To assign a name to a formula, click the Formulas tab and click Define Name. In the New Name dialog box, enter a name, and then type the formula itself in the Refers To box. For example, you could create the name End_Of_Next_Month and apply it to the formula =EOMONTH(TODAY(),1). That formula checks today's date and then returns the last day of the next month. To use the name as part of a formula, click the Formulas tab, click Use In Formula, and select End_Of_Next_Month from the list of available names.

Making Comparisons

Comparison operators allow you to compare two values and return a logical result of TRUE or FALSE. This type of comparison is usually combined with a logical function such as IF, which allows you to perform one calculation or return a specific value if the result of the logical test is TRUE and do something different if the result is FALSE. Table 11-3 lists all comparison operators that Excel supports.

Table 11-3 **Comparison Operators Supported in Excel Formulas**

Operator	Usage
=	Equal to (A1=B1, C3=0)
>	Greater than (A1>B1, C3>0)
<	Less than (A1<B1)
>=	Greater than or equal to (A1>=B1)
<=	Less than or equal to (A1<=B1)
<>	Not equal to (A1<>B1)

Chapter 11

Comparisons of similar data types work as you would expect. For values—including constants as well as references and formulas that evaluate to values—higher numbers are greater than lower and positive numbers are greater than negative numbers. Dates can be compared to other dates or to numbers. (For the technical reasons, see the discussion of date serial numbers in "Date and Time Functions" on page 368.) Comparing text uses alphabetical order, with letters before numbers and case ignored. (In other words, "District" and "district" are considered equal.)

Concatenating Text

You can combine two or more text values to produce a single text value. What makes this magic possible is the concatenation operator—an ampersand (&). A very common use of this operator is in address lists where first and last names are in separate columns. To combine the names into a single cell, use a formula like the one shown here:

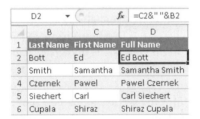

This sample uses two concatenation operators and illustrates that you can insert literal text (like the space between the two names) as long as you enclose it in quotation marks. So, if you have a list of opening and closing dates for a school, with one such date in cell C12, you could convert it to a more readable text value by using the following formula:

="Closing day: "&TEXT(C12,"mmmm dd, yyyy")

The formula grabs the date from the referenced cell, reformats it, and appends the introductory text. Compare the contents of the formula bar to the formula's result, as displayed in bold here:

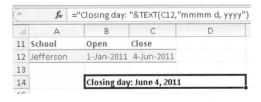

This example also illustrates a requirement for any concatenation operation: to concatenate other data types, such as dates and numbers, you must first convert those values to text. That's why we used the TEXT function in this formula.

For a more detailed discussion of functions used to convert and manipulate text, see "Text Functions" on page 370.

Relative, Absolute, and Mixed References

Any formula can contain references to cells. Excel uses the value stored in the referenced cell to perform any calculations just as though that value had been entered directly in the formula itself. You can combine ranges of cells for calculations by using three reference operators.

The most common is the range operator, which is a : (colon) between two cell addresses. It includes the two referenced cells and all cells in between them. In the formula =SUM(C1:C10), the calculation adds up all values in all cells in the range from C1 to C10.

You can also use a comma as an operator to refer to a discontiguous range. In the formula =SUM(C1,C3,C5-C10), Excel adds all values in cells C1, C3, and C5 through C10.

The most obscure reference operator of all is the rarely seen intersection operator, represented by a space. It returns the values from all cells that are common to the ranges on either side of the space. Thus =SUM(C1:C6 C5:C10) adds the contents of cells C5 and C6, which are the only ones that both ranges have in common.

Unless you specifically choose otherwise, every reference you enter in a worksheet is stored as a relative reference. When you move or copy a relative reference from one cell to another in a worksheet, the reference in the destination cell adjusts to reflect the same relative location. In Figure 11-5, we copied formulas from cell N7 to the corresponding cell in each data-containing row below it. We used the Ctrl+` shortcut to show the formula itself rather than the formula's results, demonstrating how the row number in each reference changes to reflect the correct relative location.

In some cases, you want a reference in a formula to point to the cell even when you copy the formula to a new location. Say you set aside cell A1 as the input cell where you'll enter an assumption, such as the annual inflation rate, for use throughout your worksheet. By trying different values in this cell, you can do what-if exercises with the remainder of the sheet.

To calculate the increase for the value shown in cell D4, you use the formula =D4*(1+A1). So far so good. When you copy the formula for use with D5, D6, and so on, the first reference changes just as you want. But so, unfortunately, does the second reference, so you end up with =D5*(1+A2). Because your assumption is entered only in A1, your formula returns an incorrect (or at least unexpected) result in each of the other cells.

Chapter 11

	A	N
1	**Marketing Budget**	
2	Last updated:	
3		
4		**Total**
5		
6	**Personnel**	
7	Salaries, wages	=SUM(B7:M7)
8	Benefits	=SUM(B8:M8)
9	Payroll taxes	=SUM(B9:M9)
10	Commissions and bonuses	=SUM(B10:M10)
11	**Personnel Total**	**=SUM(B11:M11)**
12		
13	**Market Research**	
14	Primary research	=SUM(B14:M14)
15	Secondary research	=SUM(B15:M15)
16	Library management	=SUM(B16:M16)
17	**Market Research Total**	**=SUM(B17:M17)**
18		
19	**Marketing Communications**	
20	Branding	=SUM(B20:M20)
21	Advertising	=SUM(B21:M21)
22	Web sites	=SUM(B22:M22)

Figure 11-5 When we copied the formula from the top of column N to the cells beneath it, Excel adjusted the references so that they work properly with the data in each row.

The solution is to use an *absolute cell reference,* which is indicated by adding a dollar sign before the column letter and row number in the reference: =D4*(1+A1). When you copy this formula, Excel adjusts the first, relative reference but leaves the absolute reference alone. You can type the dollar signs for an absolute reference directly or click to position the insertion point in the cell reference you want to adjust and then press F4. (To make a range reference absolute, select the entire reference, including the range operator, before pressing F4.)

As we noted earlier in this chapter, named cells and ranges are always treated as absolute references. So, if you select cell A1 and define its name as Inflation_Rate, you can use that name in your formula and copy the formula to other rows and columns without making any adjustments.

Sometimes, a halfway approach is called for, in which either the row or the column reference remains fixed while the other half of the reference address changes. This construction is called a *mixed range,* with a dollar sign in front of either the row or column portion of the reference to indicate that that value should not change. Imagine a sheet where you have department names in column A identifying each row, with month names over each column containing projected spending by that department for the month. In column B, you want to enter a fixed amount for each department, and you want to compare each month's total to that amount. As you copy the formula across each row, you want it to refer to column 2 in each cell. When you copy the formulas to the rows below, you want the row reference to change. Here's how a mixed reference solves that problem:

C7		▾	f_x	=C15*(1+$B7)	

	A	B	C	D
4		**Annual increase**	**Jan**	**Feb**
5				
6	**Personnel**			
7	Salaries, wages	5.6%	10,555	8,444
8	Benefits	5.2%	2,786	2,524
9	Payroll taxes	5.2%	1,052	842
10	Commissions and	5.7%	823	675
11	**Personnel Total**		**$15,216**	**$12,484**

The mixed reference $B7 tells Excel that no matter where you copy the formula, it should always point to the value in column B for the current row. To create a mixed range, type it manually or select the reference and then press F4 multiple times to cycle through each available option.

Controlling the Order of Calculation in a Formula

The order in which Excel performs operations in formulas makes a difference. It's common for formulas to contain multiple operators. Unless you specify a custom order by using parentheses, Excel performs calculations in the following order:

- % (percent)

- ^ (exponentiation)

- * and / (multiplication and division)

- + and – (addition and subtraction)

- & (concatenation)

- =, < and >, <= and >, =, and <> (comparison)

When the same operator is used multiple times in a formula, the calculations are performed in order from left to right.

When you use functions as arguments within functions, you use multiple sets of parentheses to keep things separate. You can nest functions to as many as 64 levels within a formula.

Adding Functions to a Formula

Excel savants who've memorized the syntax of the functions they use regularly can enter a formula as fast as they can type. Start with an equal sign, spell each function name correctly, separate arguments with commas, and make sure every opening parenthesis is matched with a closing parenthesis. As long as you get all those details right, you'll have no problems.

Chapter 11

If you've memorized the syntax for a particular function and the formula is simple enough, manual entry really can be the fastest option. But if you need a little assistance with one or more functions or your typing is less than perfect, Excel has lots of help to offer.

When you're not sure of the name of the function you want to use, click the Insert Function button to the left of the formula bar. That opens the Insert Function dialog box shown in Figure 11-6, where you can enter a search term and click Go or choose a category to filter the list of available functions.

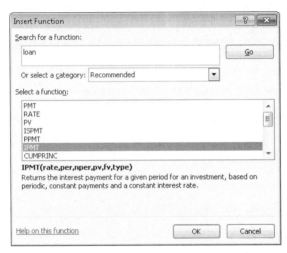

Figure 11-6 Use a search term to filter the list of functions, and then scroll through the Select A Function list to see descriptions and syntax.

After you select a function and click OK, Excel opens the Function Arguments dialog box shown in Figure 11-7, which includes fill-in-the-blank boxes for each argument.

The Function Arguments dialog box contains a wealth of useful information. A bold name means an argument is required. When you click in an input box, the descriptive text changes to help you understand what that argument is for. As you enter arguments, you can see Excel evaluate the results of each one on the right of the input box. The display below the input boxes shows the overall formula result based on all arguments entered so far.

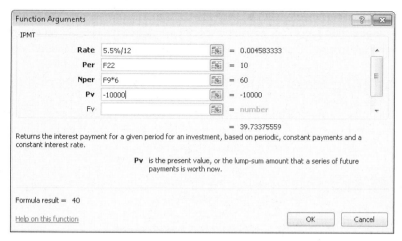

Figure 11-7 The value to the right of each input box shows the actual value that will be used by the formula based on your input. Below that column is the overall result of the formula.

TROUBLESHOOTING

An entry in the Function Arguments box shows as "Invalid"

When you fill in the blanks in the Function Arguments dialog box, you have the option to type a formula containing any combination of constants, operators, cell or range references, or names. If you enter a formula and Excel displays Invalid in bold red letters to its right, check that you got all those elements correct. If the formula is otherwise accurate, you probably added an equal sign at the beginning of the formula. The equal sign is used only at the beginning of a cell, not for formulas used as arguments in a function. Delete the equal sign, and the error should be replaced by a value.

The small button to the right of each input box collapses the dialog box temporarily so you can select a cell or range to insert in that box. After you select an address, click the button to expand the dialog box again.

Even when you type a formula directly in the formula bar (or in the cell itself), you get some help. After you enter an equal sign and begin typing a letter or two, Excel displays a list of all available functions that begin with that combination. As you type, the list narrows further. You can use the down arrow at any time to move through the list, select a function, and then press Tab to add it to the formula bar. When you do, the display beneath the formula bar changes to show arguments for the selected function. In some cases (as in the CONVERT function), one or more arguments might consist of a list of specific options, which are also available from a drop-down list. In this case as well, you can scroll through the list and then press Tab to enter a specific value from that list as an argument. (To see this feature in action, look at the example under "Engineering Functions" on page 374.)

Mastering Excel's Built-in Functions

As we noted in the previous section, Excel divides its hundreds of built-in functions into categories that you can see and explore using the Insert Function dialog box or the Function Library section of the Formulas tab, as shown here.

In this section, we look at some of the most useful options in each category.

Financial Functions

If you work in the accounting department at your business, or if you're involved in the banking or securities industry—or even if you just want to track stocks, bonds, and other financial instruments in your personal portfolio—then the functions in the Financial group will be useful to you.

These functions allow you to take details from a particular transaction or instrument and calculate accrued interest, yields, depreciation, internal rates of return, net present value, and future value for that item. In addition to all-purpose financial functions that can be used with any loan or investment, Excel includes functions that apply to specific classes of securities, such as treasury bills. (See the three functions that begin with TBILL for details.)

One set of financial functions that even nonprofessionals can use is the group of functions associated with loans and interest-bearing accounts of all types. For a mortgage, a consumer loan (such as an automobile loan), or a credit card, for example, you can calculate the monthly payment for a given rate of interest over a specific period of time. Or you can do the calculation from another perspective, figuring the actual interest rate you'll pay given a fixed payment amount over a fixed period. The online help can be confusing because it refers to "an investment," even though that description applies to the lender and not the borrower.

The five functions in this family mix and match the same group of arguments. Here, for example, is the syntax of the PMT function:

PMT(rate,nper,pv,fv,type)

You can use this function to calculate your monthly payment for a car loan or home mortgage. The first three arguments are required. If the interest rate (rate) is expressed in annual terms, you must divide by 12 to calculate a monthly payment. Likewise, you need to express the number of periods (nper) in months—so a 30-year loan is 360 months. Finally, the present value (pv) is the loan amount. Because you're the borrower, it needs to be expressed as a negative number. You can omit the two final arguments: future value (fv) is the amount you'll owe when the loan is paid off, or 0. And the type argument calculates whether you make payments at the beginning or end of the period. (The latter is the default if the argument is omitted.)

Here is the complete formula for a five-year loan of $20,000 at a stated interest rate of 5%:

f_x	=PMT(5%/12,60,-20000)		
D	E	F	G
	$377.42		

And here are two variations on that basic formula, using different functions to solve for a different variable:

- NPER(rate,pmt,pv,fv,type)   Use this formula to calculate how many payments you need to make to fully pay off a credit card balance at a given payment. You can enter the minimum required payment for the pmt argument and then increase the amount to see how quickly extra payments accelerate the payoff. You can perform this what-if analysis in the Function Arguments dialog box, or you can set up input cells for each variable you want to play with and use references to those cells in the formula.

- RATE(nper,pmt,pv,fv,type)   If a loan requires an up-front payment of fees or points, add that amount to the principal amount and plug that into the pv argument. The result tells you how much those fees add to the effective interest rate compared to the stated rate for the loan.

To calculate how much of a specific payment is interest and how much is principal, use the IPMT and PPMT functions, respectively. The syntax for the IPMT function is IPMT(rate,per,nper,pv,fv,type). Enter the payment number (per) to calculate the portion of that payment that is interest. Use the same syntax with the PPMT function (or subtract the result of the IPMT calculation from the result of the PMT calculation) to figure the principal.

Chapter 11

Date and Time Functions

We can think of dozens of reasons to make date calculations in Excel worksheets. You might want to determine a person's age by comparing the person's birth date to today's date. Or perhaps you want to look over a list of invoices and compare invoice date to payment date to determine how long your customers typically take to pay their bills.

To master date calculations, you first have to understand how Excel stores date values. When you enter a date in a recognized format, Excel converts that date to a serial value—a number equal to the number of days after January 1, 1900, which has a serial value of 1. Thus, September 29, 2010, is stored as 40450 and September 29, 2011, is 40815. Not surprisingly, subtracting those two dates, which are exactly one year apart, produces a result of 365.

TROUBLESHOOTING

Dates in a worksheet are off by four years

As we noted at the beginning of this section, Excel 2010 (like all previous versions of Excel developed for Windows) uses a date system based on serial numbers where the start date is January 1, 1900. On a Macintosh, however, date serial numbers begin with January 1, 1904. If you create a worksheet in Excel for Windows and open it in the Mac version of Excel—or vice versa—your dates will look normal because both programs recognize and adjust for the different date formats. However, if you paste a date value from a worksheet created in Excel on a Mac into a new worksheet created in Excel on a Windows PC, your results will be off by approximately four years. The moral? Be very careful when pasting dates between worksheets if you even suspect that your original data might have been created originally on a Mac.

INSIDE OUT   What's the serial number for a given date?

Under most circumstances, Excel handles the work of converting dates to serial values automatically. If you enter 9/29/2011 in a cell, Excel displays it using the default date format in the cell itself and in the formula bar. If you need to know the serial number, you can determine it easily. Select the cell, press Ctrl+1 to open the Format Cells dialog box, and click General. The Sample box shows the serial value. Click OK to change the cell format or click Cancel to return to the worksheet without changing it.

Time values also have a serial number associated with them, measured on a scale that runs from midnight (00:00:00 in hours, minutes, and seconds), to 11:59:59 PM (or 23:59:59, using the 24-hour format). Because the value of a single day is 1, the associated serial values for times run from 0 to 0.999988426, respectively. When you combine date and time into a single serial value, you get a single value that you can use to perform calculations of date and time. The serial value for 11:45 AM on September 29, 2010, is 40450.489583333. If you enter a time without including a date, Excel uses a date serial value of 0. If you then format the cell to show a date (or a combination of date and time), you'll see it listed, nonsensically, as January 0, 1900.

The SECOND, MINUTE, HOUR, DAY, MONTH, and YEAR functions allow you to break out the component parts of a date or time stored as a serial number. Each function takes a single argument and returns the respective parts as a number. Thus, if cell C3 contains the date 29-Sep-2010, the formula =MONTH(C3) returns 9 and DAY(C3) returns 29. To calculate the day of the week, use =WEEKDAY(serial_number,[return_type]), which returns a numeric value indicating the day of the week. If you leave the second argument blank, the result is between 1 and 7, where 1 equals Sunday. If you prefer an alternative numbering system, click the return_type argument and use any of the options shown here:

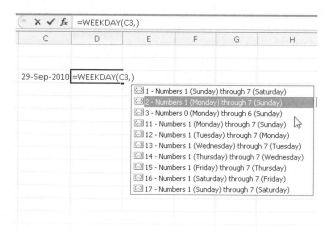

Two date functions are useful in nearly any worksheet. Neither one uses any arguments:

=TODAY() returns today's date

=NOW() returns the current date and time

You can perform date arithmetic by nesting these functions in formulas containing references to other cells containing dates. If cell E17 contains the date when you prepared and sent an invoice that has not yet been paid, you can calculate the number of days since that invoice was sent by using this formula:

=TODAY()−E17

TROUBLESHOOTING

Performing date arithmetic returns a date instead of a number

One quirk of date arithmetic in worksheets is that Excel tries, helpfully, to apply date formats when you use a date function in a formula. If you enter the formula =TODAY()−E17, where E17 is a date 76 days earlier, the result is displayed as April 10, 1900. That's the equivalent date for the serial number 76. The fix? Press Ctrl+Shift+~ (tilde) to apply the General format to the cell.

What if you're using a worksheet that has one or more columns of data containing dates or times formatted as text? If you're unwilling or unable to reformat those cells, use the DATEVALUE or TIMEVALUE functions to do the conversion. If the value is recognizable as a date or time, the respective functions should work properly.

The list of functions under the Date & Time category heading includes a slew of esoteric entries. For example, the DAYS360 function (with European and U.S. options) is used for accounting systems that use a year made up of 12 30-day months. The EOMONTH function helps you calculate the last day of a month that is a specified number of months before or after a target date—a handy trick because Excel can't rely on "30 days has September, April, June, and November" like humans can. If you're doing calculations where the result must be a working day and not a weekend, use the WORKDAY (or WORKDAY.INTL) function.

Text Functions

We confess to having a soft spot for the functions in this category. After all, we're writers and information managers, not accountants, so any tricks that make it easier to manipulate lists and blocks of text are always handy. In fact, we regularly use the functions we discuss in this section, singly or in combination, to split the output from database programs into different fields for use in Excel or Word tables.

The most common way to use the functions in this group is to paste a list from another source into one or more columns in Excel, and then use formulas in adjacent columns to manipulate that text. In this section, we focus strictly on the functions that are most useful for cleaning up and converting text.

The simplest functions are useful for removing unwanted characters from text: CLEAN and TRIM take a single argument (text) and remove nonprintable characters and spaces, respectively, from the string in the referenced location.

If your imported text uses inconsistent or inappropriate case formatting, you can use one of three functions to change it. UPPER, LOWER, and PROPER also use a single text argument. The effect is to change the referenced text to all capitals, all lowercase, or caps for the first letter in each word, respectively. The example shown here illustrates the PROPER function in action, transforming a column of text in all capital letters to easier-to-read initial caps.

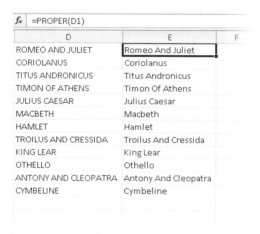

That example also illustrates one of the problems with the PROPER function. It blindly capitalizes every word in the source text, even when those words are articles and conjunctions that shouldn't be capitalized in a title. It also automatically capitalizes the first letter after an apostrophe. That can lead to some inconsistent (and unwanted) results with possessives: FINNEGAN'S WAKE becomes Finnegan'S Wake, for example.

Another group of functions allows you to convert a value to text. This is a necessary step if you have a cell that contains a number and you want to concatenate that number with some text. Here are three useful functions in this group:

- **DOLLAR(number,decimals)**   This function converts a number to text using the $ (dollar) currency format. The second argument is optional; by default, Excel formats the number using two decimal places. If cell B5 contains the value 24.5, the formula =DOLLAR(B5) returns the text string $24.50.

- **FIXED(number,decimals,no_commas)**   Use this function to display a number as text, rounded to a fixed number of decimals. Only the first argument (number) is required. If you omit the decimals argument, Excel displays the result using the default of two decimal places.

- **TEXT(value,format_text)**   When you want to display a number as text using a custom format, use this function. The help text for this function is misleading. You can apply any number format using the same syntax as entries in the Custom category in the Format Cells dialog box. The format string must be enclosed in quotation marks. Thus, if cell B5 contains 24.44, the formula =TEXT(B5,"#,##0_);[Red](#,##0)") returns the text string 24.

If some cells in a column contain text and others contain numbers, you might want to use the T(value) function, which checks the contents of the referenced cell. If the cell contains text, the result of the function is that text; if the cell contains a value, the T function returns an empty text string.

Finally, you can use the VALUE(text) function to convert text to a number. If the text argument can't be evaluated as a number (for example, if it contains even a single letter), the function returns a #VALUE! error.

Logical Functions

The functions in this group are some of the most powerful and useful in Excel. The IF function, for example, allows you to test for a specific condition and then return a result based on the answer to that test. Its syntax is IF(logical_test,value_if_true,value_if_false). In this example, the formula in cell D2 uses a logical test of whether the invoice due date in B2 is less than today's date. If the result is true, it returns the text "Overdue," and if the result is false, it returns "Pending."

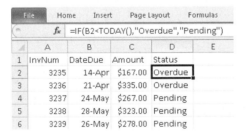

You can combine two or more logical tests, often in conjunction with IF. The AND function returns TRUE if all its arguments are true, and the OR function returns TRUE if any of its arguments are true.

Use the IFERROR function to avoid the possibility that a formula will return an error. Its syntax is IFERROR(value,value_if_error). If you're performing division operations and some cells in the column used for the divisor equal 0, you risk seeing #DIV/0! errors in those cells. To eliminate that possibility, use a formula like this one: =IFERROR(B2/C2,0), which returns 0 in place of any error.

To reverse the logic of any argument, use the NOT function.

Statistical Functions

For students of statistics, the functions in this group are invaluable. If you need to calculate confidence intervals, Poisson distributions, standard deviations, or even the "one-tailed probability of the chi-squared distribution," you've come to the right place. For those of us who aren't math majors, a few functions in this group are still handy for everyday use.

To calculate the arithmetic mean of a set of numbers, use the AVERAGE function. Although you can enter arguments individually, you're most likely to specify part of a row or column as the range to use for this calculation. The AVERAGEIF and AVERAGEIFS functions return the arithmetic mean of all cells that meet criteria you define.

The arithmetic mean is what most nonmathematicians think of when they hear the term *average*. For a slightly different calculation, use the MEDIAN function, which finds the number that is in the middle of a set of numbers.

To find the lowest or highest value in a set or a range, use the MIN or MAX function, respectively. Use the COUNT function to calculate how many numbers are in the referenced range or list of arguments. Four additional functions that begin with COUNT allow you to calculate the number of values (COUNTA), blank cells (COUNTBLANK), or the number of cells that meet a single criterion (COUNTIF) or multiple criteria (COUNTIFS).

Math and Trigonometry Functions

We promised we wouldn't bring up unpleasant memories of math homework, and we'll be true to our word here. If you're a math student or an honest-to-goodness rocket scientist, you'll want to study the entire list of functions in this category. You'll find the usual suspects from trigonometry and math here: sine and cosine and tangent (SIN, COS, TAN), arcsine and arc cosine and arctangent (ASIN, ACOS, and ATAN), and even hyperbolic tangent (TANH) and inverse hyperbolic cosine (ACOSH).

If you're a civilian (mathematically speaking), you'll benefit most from a group of math-oriented functions that all involve rounding numbers.

The ROUND function rounds a number to a specified number of digits. If you have a column full of calculated results and you don't mind permanently converting them to a result that is less accurate than the original, use this function. Its syntax is ROUND(number, num_digits). Two additional functions in the same family allow you to round numbers in a specific direction: ROUNDDOWN and ROUNDUP use the same syntax and round the value specified in the number argument down (toward zero) or up (away from zero).

If the details after the decimal point don't matter, use one of the following functions to round a number to an integer. INT rounds a number down to the nearest integer, EVEN rounds a number up to the nearest even integer, and ODD rounds a number up to the nearest odd integer. All three functions take a single number argument.

And we would be remiss if we left out one of our favorite math functions, which hasn't had much use in the past couple millennia but could be poised for a comeback. If you've been baffled by the intricacies of Roman numerals ("When was that movie copyrighted?"), let Excel help you out. The ROMAN function accepts any Arabic numeral as an argument and converts it to Roman numerals. So, =ROMAN(2011) correctly returns the result MMXI, formatted as text. A second, optional argument lets you choose simpler, more concise formats (MXMIX for 1999 instead of the traditional MCMXCIX, for example), but we prefer the classic display.

Engineering Functions

More than 40 functions are available in this category, and virtually all of them are useful only to professional engineers and engineering students. The single noteworthy exception is the CONVERT function, which allows you to create formulas for translating measurements between different systems. The function's syntax is CONVERT(number,from_unit,to_unit). The second two arguments, which must be enclosed in quotation marks, allow you to specify the type of conversion. To translate gallons to liters, for example, enter a value representing the number of gallons in cell A1, and then enter the following formula in cell B1:

=CONVERT(A1,"gal","l")

When you use the formula helper to enter the arguments for this function, the full list appears for the from_unit argument, with nearly 50 choices available, covering mass, distance, weight, temperature, and other measurement systems. You can convert meters to feet, angstroms to inches, or Atomic mass units to grams, if you're so inclined. After you choose an option for the from_unit argument ("gal" in this example), the options for the to_unit argument are filtered to include only those that are appropriate for the measurement system from which you're converting, as shown next.

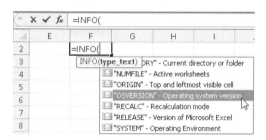

Information Functions

Most of the functions in this group are of interest to advanced worksheet developers. The CELL function, for example, returns information about a cell—its contents, address, and formatting and the workbook in which it's located. The INFO function allows you to determine information about the environment of the system on which the current worksheet is being viewed, including the Windows version and which version of Excel is in use—extremely useful if you're using features that are supported only in Excel 2010, for example.

A long list of functions in this category are logical tests that begin with IS—ISERROR and ISBLANK, for example. Use them to add logic to a formula to suppress error messages, fill blanks with default values, and otherwise prevent you or anyone using a worksheet you design from running into unexpected conditions.

A particularly useful function in this group allows you to return a "Not Applicable" error message. You can use the NA function (which takes no arguments) as an argument with an IF function to add a neat #N/A value instead of an error message when a formula returns a particular result.

Lookup and Reference/Database/Cube Functions

We've combined three categories into one section here, all of them related to managing tables of data in Excel. We discuss the most useful of these functions in more detail in Chapter 12, "Managing Lists and Data."

The functions in the Lookup & Reference category are used with tables created in Excel itself (one exception is the HYPERLINK function). Functions in the Database category all begin with the letter D and are used to perform calculations on the contents of lists or databases on a worksheet.

If you know what Cube functions are, you probably also have a black belt in database management. The seven functions in this group are specifically designed for use with data that comes into Excel via connections to SQL Server Analysis Services or other online analytical processing (OLAP) data sources. These queries are called cubes (or OLAP cubes), which explains the name of the function category.

We cover all types of external data connections in "External Database Connections" on page 391.

> **CAUTION**
>
> The 38 advanced statistical functions listed under the Compatibility category are living on borrowed time. Each one has been replaced in Excel 2010 with a new, rewritten function—faster and more accurate and with a new name. The old GAMMADIST function, for example, has been supplanted in Excel 2010 by the GAMMA.DIST function. The old functions are around only for compatibility with Excel 2007 and earlier versions. If you know that the worksheet you're working with now will be used exclusively with Excel 2010, you should use the new functions. However, if there's any chance that you'll want to share your workbook with someone using an older version of Excel, stick with the functions in the Compatibility category.

Formatting Cells and Ranges

When you enter values, text, or formulas in a cell, Excel applies default formatting to the contents of those cells based on its best guess as to the data type. You can adjust this formatting by using the commands in the Number group on the Home tab, as shown here. A far more extensive set of options is available in the Format Cells dialog box, which opens when you click the dialog box launcher in the lower right corner of the Number group (or right-click any cell or range and choose Format Cells).

The commands in this group allow you to pick from a list of predefined number formats, apply a custom currency style, display a value in Percentage format, show or hide thousands separators (a comma for systems using U.S. regional settings), and increase or decrease the number of visible decimal points.

INSIDE OUT   Create custom formats with cell styles

The Number group on the Home tab mixes commands for predefined number formats and cell styles, which can be used to apply number formats. It also provides access to the Format Cells dialog box, where you can customize formats manually. The three buttons below the Number Format list apply the Currency, Percent, and Comma styles, respectively. (Confusingly, the Currency style actually uses the Accounting number format. Go figure.) You can see these styles in their normal location by expanding the Cell Styles list (from the Styles group on the Home tab) and then looking in the Number Format area.

Normally, clicking the Percent button applies the Percentage format with no decimal places. If you want to replace that default result with one that applies the Percentage format with one decimal place, right-click the Percent style in the Cell Styles list and click Modify. Click the Format button and adjust the value in the Decimal Places box. Save your changes, and the result is complete. You can use this same technique to create additional styles, which you can add to the Quick Access Toolbar or access from the Cell Styles list. Note that this change applies only to the current workbook unless you save these changes to the default workbook template.

If none of the predefined formats work for you, try rolling your own. We explain how to do this in "Creating Custom Cell Formats" on page 459.

It's important to understand that most of the formatting options affect only the display of the data stored in that cell. You can change the number of decimal places and add a currency symbol to a number format, but the underlying data remains unchanged. Likewise, changing the date format for a cell does not change the date serial number displayed in that cell.

If you enter a number or text, Excel applies the General number format. In most cases, this means you see exactly what you typed. If a number you type is too wide to fit in the current cell and the width of the current column has not been manually set, Excel expands the column width to try to accommodate your entry. If you enter a formula, the General format displays up to 11 digits, including the decimal point, rounding the displayed result if necessary to show fewer decimal places than are actually stored for the value.

If you enter a value or a formula whose result won't fit in the defined cell width or that contains more than 12 digits to the left of the decimal place, Excel displays it using scientific notation.

You can override the formatting for any cell by using the short list of available formats in the Number group on the Home tab, as shown here:

Conveniently, this list matches up neatly to the choices in the Number category of the Format Cells dialog box. In some cases, Excel overrides the General number format automatically, based on what you type or paste into a cell. You can manually apply a format at any time.

You can also use any of the keyboard shortcuts shown in Table 11-4 to quickly apply number formatting to the current selection. It's worth noting that all the shortcuts are applied using the Ctrl+Shift keys and the first seven keys in the number row of the standard U.S. keyboard layout.

Table 11-4 **Keyboard Shortcuts for Common Number Formats**

Shortcut	Action
Ctrl+~ (tilde)	Applies the General number format
Ctrl+Shift+1 Ctrl+!	Applies the Number format with two decimal places, a 1000 separator, and a minus sign (–) for negative values
Ctrl+Shift+2 Ctrl+@	Applies the Time format with the hour and minute, followed by AM or PM (11:30 AM)
Ctrl+Shift+3 Ctrl+#	Applies the Date format with the day, month (abbreviated), and year (31-Jan-11)
Ctrl+Shift+4 Ctrl+$	Applies the Currency format with default currency symbol, two decimal places, and negative values in parentheses
Ctrl+Shift+5 Ctrl+%	Applies the Percentage format with no decimal places
Ctrl+Shift+6 Ctrl+^	Applies the Scientific number format with two decimal places

The most useful Excel keyboard shortcut of all, in our opinion, is Ctrl+1. Pressing that combination opens the Format Cells dialog box and selects the Number tab. In the remainder of this section, we look in detail at each of the available formatting options in the Format Cells dialog box.

Number

If you enter a number and use a comma to set off thousands, Excel applies the Number format using the default thousands separator for the region and language as defined in Windows. If the number you enter contains more than two decimal places, Excel stores the exact number you entered but rounds it for display purposes to no more than two decimal places.

Use the Increase Decimal and Decrease Decimal commands (in the Number group on the Home tab) to add or subtract one decimal place at a time from the selection.

To manually set options for the Number format, make a selection and then open the Format Cells dialog box. Figure 11-8 shows which settings are available.

Chapter 11

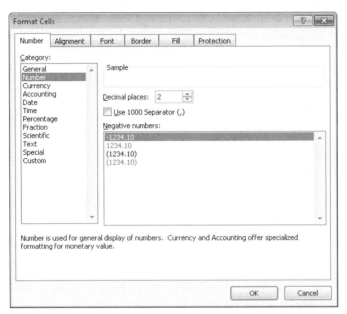

Figure 11-8 In addition to setting the number of decimal places and showing or hiding the 1000 separator, you can choose how negative values are displayed.

Currency and Accounting

Both the Currency and Accounting formats are designed for use with values that represent money. The difference? Currency formats allow you to choose an alternate format for negative numbers (a minus sign, parentheses, or red font formatting). Accounting formats line up decimals and move currency symbols to the left edge of the cell for a neater display in reports. The alignment used in Accounting formats can be hard to read in wide columns that contain small numbers; for readability's sake, choose a Currency format for those situations.

If you enter a number preceded by a dollar sign, Excel applies the Currency format, using the default currency symbol with up to two decimal places, regardless of how many decimal places you enter. Confusingly, when you click the command represented by a dollar sign in the Number group on the Home tab, Excel actually applies the Currency cell style (the Accounting format, with two decimal places). A drop-down list on this command allows you to pick an alternate currency symbol—Euro, pound, and so on.

INSIDE OUT   How to enter alternate currency symbols

Most PC keyboards sold in the United States allow you to enter only a single currency symbol—the dollar sign—directly. To enter a currency symbol that isn't represented on your keyboard, you need to jump through a hoop or two. The simplest option is to click the Insert tab and click Symbol. In the Symbol dialog box, click the Currency Symbols subset, choose a symbol, and then click Insert. If you regularly use one or two alternate symbols and you have a full-size keyboard with a numeric keypad, memorize the ASCII codes for those symbols so you can enter them as needed. To enter the Euro symbol (€), use the numbers on the numeric keypad (not those on the number row at the top of the keyboard) and enter Alt+0128. The British pound symbol (£) is Alt+0163, and the symbol for the Japanese Yen (¥) is Alt+0165. In Excel, you can use the Number tab of the Format Cells dialog box to choose from a list of hundreds of currency symbols when you choose either the Currency or Accounting formats.

Date and Time

When the text or number you enter in a cell matches any of the built-in Windows date formats, Excel converts that entry to a serial number and formats the cell using the closest matching Date format. If the date you enter includes only the month and date, Excel adds the current year.

To choose a custom format, click the Date category in the Format Cells dialog box and choose one of the options in the Type list, as shown on the next page.

The formats at the top of the list, preceded by an asterisk, represent the Short Date and Long Date options as defined in the Region And Language section of Windows Control Panel. You can apply these two formats most quickly by using the Short Date and Long Date choices on the Number Formats list (in the Number group on the Home Tab). If you choose a different format, look at the Sample box above the Type list to see how the current cell contents will be displayed using that format.

When you enter a set of numbers that contain a colon (:) and that can be interpreted as a time, Excel converts your entry to a serial number and applies the default Time format if possible. If the number is followed by a space and A, P, AM, or PM (in caps or lowercase), Excel adds AM or PM to the display format.

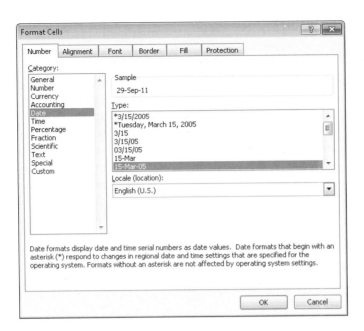

Click the Time category in the Format Cells dialog box to see a list of available formats, as shown here:

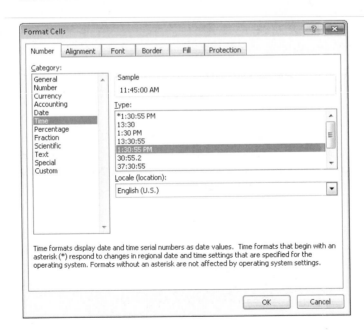

Percentage

When you enter a number that begins or ends with a percent sign, Excel applies the Percentage format, using up to two decimal places. The value you enter in this fashion is divided by 100 for storage. If you enter 5%, Excel stores it as 0.05. When you apply the Percentage format to a number that you previously entered using the General or Number format, Excel multiplies it by 100 for display purposes and adds a percent sign.

Fraction

In sharp contrast to the decimal options available elsewhere, the options in the Fraction category display values using old-style display formats like ½ and ¼. If the number is between 0 and 1, the fraction appears by itself. Excel also supports compound fractions, which include a whole number and a fraction, such as 8½.

To apply a Fraction format automatically when entering data, enter the whole number followed by a space and the fraction. If the number is less than 1, start with 0 and a space, like this: 0 7/16. (If you leave out the zero and space, Excel assumes you mean the date July 16 and will helpfully convert your entry to a date serial number and format.) The value is stored as a decimal, 0.4375 in this example.

For more control over the display of fractions, use the Fraction category in the Format Cells dialog box, as shown here.

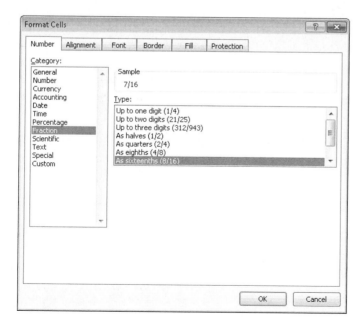

Scientific

Scientific (or exponential) format displays large numbers in a shorthand form—a value, followed by the letter E, a plus or minus sign, and another number. To convert that format to its decimal equivalent, move the decimal point by the number of places that appears after the E—if the value begins with a plus sign, move the decimal point to the right, adding zeroes if necessary; if there's a minus sign, move the decimal point to the left, again adding zeroes as needed. Here are some examples:

- 6.42E+06 is 6,420,000.

- 7.22E-05 is .0000722.

You can enter a number and apply the Scientific format with two decimal places as part of a single action. Just insert the letter E at the appropriate place.

Numbers expressed using the default settings for the Scientific format are rounded for display purposes to a maximum of six significant digits, regardless of the cell's width. To display numbers using more digits of precision, open the Format Cells dialog box, click Scientific in the Category list, and increase the number of decimal places (this value must be between 0 and 30).

Text

When is a number not a number? When you specifically want it to be treated as text. That happens with part numbers and product identifiers, for example, which can contain leading zeroes and aren't typically used in calculations. If you enter a number in a cell, Excel drops the leading zero and aligns it to the right. To display the cell contents exactly as entered (including leading zeroes), you must use the Text format, which is available at the bottom of the Number Format list in the Number group on the Home tab. This category in the Format Cells dialog box has no additional options.

You can apply the Text format automatically by entering an apostrophe before typing the number. The apostrophe is stored with the cell entry but is not displayed. Excel formats the number as text.

Special

The four entries in this category of the Format Cells dialog box (shown here) are useful mostly for address and contact lists created in the United States. They allow you to quickly enter ZIP Codes, phone numbers, and Social Security numbers in any format and without punctuation. Excel handles the work of adding hyphens and splitting the entered values into groups of the correct length.

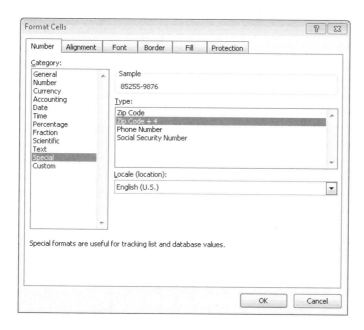

Even if you never use any of these formats, they're worth studying as examples of how to build your own cell formats for automatic formatting, a topic we cover in full in "Creating Custom Cell Formats" on page 459.

CHAPTER 12

Managing Lists and Data

XCEL is no one-trick pony. Yes, the program works wonders with number-crunching tasks, but its rows and columns are also tailor-made for managing data that isn't expressed in numeric formats. With minimal effort, you can keep address lists and membership rosters, track temperatures and rainfall, monitor stock prices, and record your performance in whatever sport or hobby you happen to fancy.

In this chapter, we look at the many options you have for entering and storing data—including tables in Excel worksheets and direct connections to external data sources. We also explain how to sort, filter, cross-tabulate, and summarize that data.

Sorting Out Your Data Management Options

You can create a simple database just by entering data into rows, with or without headings to indicate what's in each column. For example, you can enter a list of names in column A, and then, in column B, enter a phone number alongside each name. As long as that list remains short and simple enough to scan quickly, you don't need to do anything more.

But lists have a way of growing, and even moderately long lists can benefit from sorting, searching, filtering, outlining, and summarizing. Excel provides several options for working with lists and databases of all sizes. Which option you choose depends on where the data is stored and what you want to do with it.

The following sections briefly describe each of your options. You can find more details about each in the remainder of this chapter.

Tables

Microsoft introduced the concept of tables (not to be confused with data tables, which are a rarely used relic of Excel's distant past) in Excel 2007. If you skipped over that version, you have some catching up to do. Tables are roughly equivalent to the feature known as *lists* in Excel 2003, but with more sophisticated formatting options. If you open a worksheet originally created in Excel 2003 that contains one or more lists, you'll need to manually convert those lists to tables.

To turn a range into a table, select the range (or select any cell within the range if the list is in a self-contained region), and then click Table in the Tables group on the Insert tab (or use the keyboard shortcut Ctrl+T or Ctrl+L). You'll see the Create Table dialog box shown in Figure 12-1.

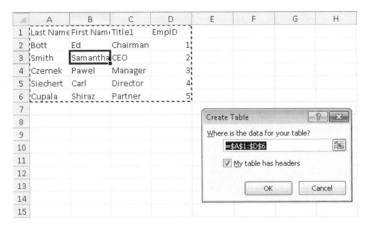

Figure 12-1 Even though we selected only a single cell, Excel expands the selection to include the entire data-containing region, as defined by blank rows and columns.

Had we instead clicked Format As Table, in the Styles group on the Home tab, we would have been required to select a table style before seeing the Create Table dialog box (which in this case is named Format As Table). Using either keyboard shortcut applies the default table style. (We discuss table styles in much greater detail in "Formatting and Using Tables" on page 391.)

Excel correctly detected that this range contains a header row with labels for each column and selected the My Table Has Headers check box. (For the most part, Excel correctly detects the presence of headers, but it can be confused by some configurations, so check this setting before you proceed.) Clicking OK applies the default table style to the range and makes a few other changes. The end result looks like this:

	A	B	C	D
1	Last Name ▼	First Name ▼	Title1 ▼	EmpID ▼
2	Bott	Ed	Chairman	1
3	Smith	Samantha	CEO	2
4	Czernek	Pawel	Manager	3
5	Siechert	Carl	Director	4
6	Cupala	Shiraz	Partner	5

Defining a range as a table makes the following changes, some of which are not immediately apparent. (We explain these changes in more detail in "Formatting and Using Tables" on page 391.)

- Column widths expand as needed to display header text in full. If column headers are not included, Excel adds generic headers—Column1, Column2, and so on.

- A down arrow appears to the right of each column heading, allowing quick sort and filter operations.

- When any cell within the table is selected, a Design tab with customization options appears on the ribbon, under the Table Tools heading.

- A default name is assigned to the table; you can change the name to a more descriptive one by using the Table Name box in the Properties group on the Table Tools Design tab.

- Any cell addresses used in formulas within the table are automatically converted to structured references.

- A triangular handle in the lower right corner of the table allows you to quickly add rows or columns to the table, preserving formatting and copying formulas automatically.

Tables offer a tremendously versatile way to work with large and small amounts of data. In fact, as we explain later in this chapter, a table can serve as the source of data for a PivotTable report, and you can export a table to a SharePoint list or to any of several external data formats.

INSIDE OUT   Don't lose track of headings when you scroll

One of the hidden advantages of creating a table from a range is a small but significant improvement in scrolling. If your list is long enough that scrolling through the list causes the Header row to scroll up and off the screen, Excel has an elegant fix. The headings from the table replace the column headings in the worksheet frame, complete with the arrow that allows you to sort and filter. The effect is similar to what happens if you freeze the top row of the table, but it requires no effort from you beyond creating the table in the first place.

PivotTable Reports

The very concept of a PivotTable report (often called simply a PivotTable) can be daunting if you've never worked with one. But once you discover how quickly and effectively you can use a PivotTable to summarize even the most enormous table, we predict you'll be hooked.

Every PivotTable report starts with source data, which can be stored in a worksheet or drawn from an external database. After you specify a location for the PivotTable (typically a separate worksheet), you lay out the fields to create the report. Figure 12-2 shows a Pivot-Table report that summarizes current inventory by using an Excel table that contains 2,476 rows and 11 columns.

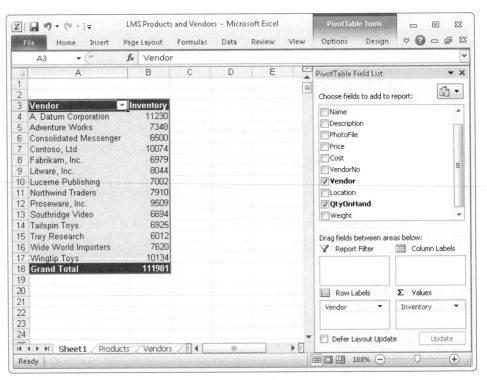

Figure 12-2 The PivotTable report on the left neatly crunches tens of thousands of data points into a simple summary.

PivotTable reports can be used to summarize numeric data by totals and averages or to create reports based on dates. You can show or hide subtotals and details for a group, add filters to extract details for a company or person, and change the format of the report to make it more readable. We explain in detail the techniques for creating, formatting, and working with a PivotTable report in "Using PivotTables" on page 406.

External Database Connections

Data for an Excel table or PivotTable report can come from a variety of sources, including SharePoint lists, external databases in almost any format, other worksheets in other workbooks, and even from web pages. You can make a direct connection to an external data source and then sort, filter, or summarize the data in Excel. You can also extract data from an external source, save it in an intermediate format, and import the data into an Excel worksheet. We describe the most common import/export and data connection strategies in "Importing, Exporting, and Connecting to Data Sources" on page 415.

Formatting and Using Tables

Earlier, we explained how to convert a range into a table. In this section, we dig into the nuances of formatting a table, expanding its size in either direction, and adding totals.

Formatting Tables with Table Styles

Table styles apply formatting—colors, fonts, borders, and shading—to the region that makes up a table. Excel offers a selection of 60 options in the Table Styles gallery, divided into Light, Medium, and Dark groups that correspond to the intensity of the colors used. You can choose from the entire list in either of two ways:

- Click Format As Table in the Styles group on the Home tab. If the current range or region has not already been defined as a table, this option displays the Format As Table dialog box after you make a selection.

- Click the arrow to the right of the Table Styles gallery (or below the Quick Styles button) in the Table Styles group on the Table Tools Design tab.

Figure 12-3 shows the Quick Styles gallery in operation. Note that as you point to an option in the gallery, the formatting in the table changes to preview that selection.

A ScreenTip shows the name of each style. The colors and fonts associated with that style vary depending on the theme used for the current worksheet. If you change the theme, any existing table formats change to pick up the color schemes and fonts from the new theme.

For more on how themes allow you to apply consistent formatting, even in different Office programs, see "Using Office Themes" on page 185.

If you've applied manual formatting to fonts, font colors, cell shading, and so on within a table region, your formatting is preserved when you apply a table style. To clear any manual formatting and use only the formatting specified in the table style, right-click the style from the Table Styles gallery, and then click Apply And Clear Formatting.

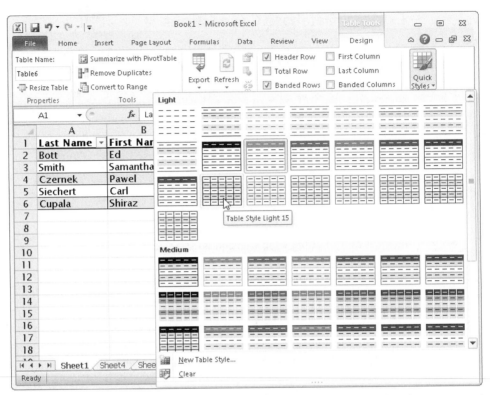

Figure 12-3 Colors and fonts associated with each of these built-in table styles change to match the current theme.

Many of the built-in table styles include formatting that adds shading to alternate rows, which makes reading across wide tables easier. The six check boxes in the Table Style Options group on the Design tab allow you to fine-tune the following format settings:

- **Header Row** Clear this check box to hide all column headings. Doing so also hides the down arrow used to access sort and filter options for each column. Note that Excel remembers the name assigned to any column and continues to use it in structured references within formulas.

- **Total Row** Select this check box to add a row beneath the table, with options to automatically subtotal the contents of one or more columns. If the table contains more than one column, the word *Total* appears in the first column. If you expand the table, this row remains at the bottom of the new range. You can customize the formulas beneath each column by using a drop-down list, as we explain shortly.

- **First Column** Click to apply special formatting to the first column in the table. Use this option to highlight labels that identify each row.

- **Last Column**   Click to apply special formatting to the last column in the table. This option is especially useful if the last column contains totals for each row.

- **Banded Rows**   Apply different background colors for alternating rows to make reading across a wide table easier.

- **Banded Columns**   Apply different background colors for alternating columns.

In effect, these check boxes allow you to provide very specific customizations to the current table style. When you combine those options with the 60 entries in the built-in Table Styles gallery, each of whose color palette and font can in turn be reset using any of 40 built-in themes, you have literally thousands of possible looks to choose from. That's not enough? Then build your own table style by clicking the New Table Style link at the bottom of the Table Styles gallery. Doing so brings up the New Table Quick Style dialog box, where you can set the properties for each part of the table individually.

Starting from scratch to create a custom table style is difficult and potentially confusing. In our experience, you'll find it much simpler to duplicate an existing table style and then modify the style you copied. In the Table Styles gallery, right-click the style you want to use as your starting point, and then click Duplicate. That opens the Modify Table Quick Style dialog box shown here.

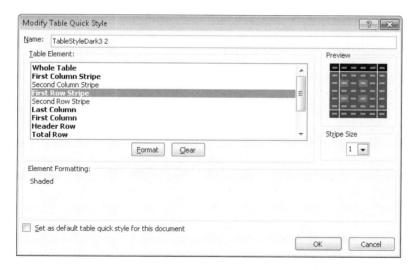

In the Name box, replace the default name with a descriptive name. Then select individual table elements from the list in the center of the dialog box and adjust their definition as needed. Click the Format button to change font style (bold, italic, and so on), cell borders, and shading. The four stripe options allow you to set how many rows are in each stripe that makes up a band. The default is 1, which means that shading alternates from one row to the next. If you choose 2 for First Row Stripe and Second Row Stripe, each band of shading is applied to two rows at a time.

Custom styles appear at the top of the Table Styles Gallery. If you right-click on a saved custom table style, you'll notice that Modify and Delete options are available via the right-click menu; these options cannot be used with predefined table styles.

TROUBLESHOOTING

Fonts and colors in custom table styles behave unexpectedly

Although the Format Cells dialog box for each table element includes a Font tab, most of the options on that tab are unavailable. You can change the font style and color, but the actual font and font size are determined by the current theme. To apply a table font that is not part of the current theme, you must select the entire table and apply the font formatting manually. In addition, if you choose a background or fill color from the selections on the Fill tab, these colors change when you change the theme. To apply a specific color to part of the table and ensure that the color remains unchanged when the theme changes, you must use the More Colors option and define that color manually.

Expanding (or Shrinking) a Table

Although you can define a table by selecting a range of any size, the most common and useful scenario defines a table using the current region, which is demarcated by blank cells (or the worksheet's edge) on the top, bottom, and sides. To add a row to the table, click in the cell in the lower right corner of the table range (if your table has a Total row, use the row above it), and then press Tab. Excel adds a new row using the colors, fonts, and shading from the current table style and moves the active cell to the first column in the newly created row. If your table includes a Total row, it shifts down to accommodate the new row as well.

To expand a table manually, look in the lower right corner of the table for a small triangular handle. Make sure that that cell is not selected, and then aim the mouse pointer at the handle until the pointer turns into a two-sided diagonal arrow. Drag down to add rows to the table, shifting the Total row down if necessary. Drag the handle to the right to add one or more columns (each new column gets a generic heading that you can change later when you're ready to enter data).

You can also drag the table sizing handle up or to the left to remove rows or columns from the defined table range. Any data currently contained in those cells remains.

CAUTION

If your table contains a Total row and you move the sizing handle up to remove rows that currently contain data, you create a circular reference. To avoid this, first delete (or move) the contents of any cells that you plan to remove from the table range.

You can add a reference to any table by using its name, as defined in the Table Name box in the Properties group on the Design tab. The range defined by this name automatically expands when you add rows or columns to the table. (It does not, however, include the Header and Total rows.) If you use the current table as the basis for a PivotTable, any new rows or columns you create are automatically available for use in the PivotTable. Likewise, when you use data from rows or columns in a table to define data series, labels, or other elements in a chart, those elements are automatically updated when you expand the table.

Adding Totals and Formulas to a Table

When you create a table, Excel allows you to perform a few tricks with formulas that aren't available within a normal range. The most obvious is the Total row, which you can use to quickly add summaries of table data. As we explained earlier in this chapter, you can manually enable the Total row by selecting its check box in the Table Styles Options group on the Design tab.

Figure 12-4 shows the Total row for a table containing sales results. Note that Excel automatically added a formula that totals the rightmost column in the table.

	A	B	C
1	Date	Orders	Sales
2	5/7/2010	947	$4,927.18
3	5/6/2010	1062	$5,608.73
4	5/5/2010	680	$8,941.10
5	5/4/2010	659	$3,738.04
6	5/3/2010	494	$9,628.65
7	4/30/2010	605	$6,196.69
8	4/29/2010	606	$9,806.37
9	4/28/2010	634	$7,081.43
10	4/27/2010	745	$9,481.18
11	4/26/2010	565	$9,320.09
12	4/23/2010	533	$4,736.82
13	4/22/2010	604	$5,996.56
14	4/21/2010	572	$2,225.66
15	Total		$87,688.50

Figure 12-4 Excel uses its own internal logic to decide which columns are summarized in the Total row. You can add or change these formulas with a few clicks.

Chapter 12

Although the result is functionally the same as if you had clicked the Sum button, the formula itself uses the SUBTOTAL function instead. You can add a summary formula to any cell in the Total row or change the results for an existing formula by selecting a cell and clicking the arrow just to its right, as shown here:

C15			f_x	=SUBTOTAL(109,[Sales])	
	A	B	C	D	E
1	Date	Orders	Sales		
11	4/26/2010	565	$9,320.09		
12	4/23/2010	533	$4,736.82		
13	4/22/2010	604	$5,996.56		
14	4/21/2010	572	$2,225.66		
15	Total	670	$87,688.50		
16			None		
17			Average		
18			Count		
			Count Numbers		
19			Max		
20			Min		
21			Sum		
			StdDev		
22			Var		
			More Functions...		

As you can see, we added a formula at the bottom of column B that displays the average number of orders per day, and we're about to change the formula beneath column C so that it shows an average instead of a sum. If you look in the formula bar, you can see the syntax of the SUBTOTAL function used for these calculations.

What if you want to create a calculated column that displays totals, averages, or other summaries on a per-row basis? Excel can do that automatically. In the previous example, click any cell in any column to the right of the table range and begin entering a formula. In this worksheet, the number of orders for each day is in column B and the total sales for each day is in column C, so we can click in D2, type an equal sign, click C2, type a slash (/), and click B2. As soon as we press Enter, Excel creates a new column using the current table format and copies the formula we just typed to every cell in that column, as shown in Figure 12-5.

INSIDE OUT   Take control of calculated columns

If you create a formula to the right of the current table and you don't want it to be copied to other cells in the column, use the options on the AutoCorrect menu to immediately undo the calculated column. To prevent Excel from automatically adding new rows or columns to a table, click File, click Options, and then click AutoCorrect Options on the Proofing tab. On the AutoFormat As You Type tab, under the Apply As You Work heading, clear Include New Rows And Columns In Table.

	D2	▾	f_x =[@Sales]/[@Orders]	

⊿	A	B	C	D
1	Date ▾	Orders ▾	Sales ▾	Column1 ▾
2	5/7/2010	947	$4,927.18	$5.20
3	5/6/2010	1062	$5,608.73	$5.28
4	5/5/2010	680	$8,941.10	$13.16
5	5/4/2010	659	$3,738.04	$5.67
6	5/3/2010	494	$9,628.65	$19.50
7	4/30/2010	605	$6,196.69	$10.25
8	4/29/2010	606	$9,806.37	$16.18
9	4/28/2010	634	$7,081.43	$11.17
10	4/27/2010	745	$9,481.18	$12.72
11	4/26/2010	565	$9,320.09	$16.50
12	4/23/2010	533	$4,736.82	$8.89
13	4/22/2010	604	$5,996.56	$9.94
14	4/21/2010	572	$2,225.66	$3.89
15	Total	670	$87,688.50	

Figure 12-5 When we added a formula to cell D2, Excel automatically added a column to the table and copied that formula to every cell in the column.

The new column includes a generic heading that you'll probably want to replace with a descriptive heading, and you might also want to insert a formula in the Total row, but Excel does all the work of creating the calculated column.

If you look carefully at the formula bar in Figure 12-5, you'll see that the formulas Excel creates include some unusual cell references. These are called *structured references,* which are designed to make it easy to automatically copy formulas as you add new rows. They're created automatically when you click to select cell references for use in a formula; you can choose to use standard references instead by simply typing the cell address. Brackets indicate a column heading name and an @ sign indicates the current row. The # sign is used with one of four keywords to refer to specific parts of the table: #All, #Data, #Headers, or #Totals.

Sorting, Filtering, and Outlining Data

In this section we discuss how to create order out of even the most chaotic worksheet data. You can enter or import that data in any order or even at random. Once it's arranged in rows and columns, you can rearrange it as needed. You can sort by numbers, text, or dates. You can also reduce clutter by filtering a list to show only data that matches conditions you define. We also briefly discuss the old-school outlining options that survive in Excel for compatibility reasons.

Sorting a Range, Region, or Table

You can sort a range, region, or table by using values from one or more columns. That's true regardless of the data type. In a membership roster, for example, you can sort the list in alphabetical order using the Last Name column, or by date, oldest to youngest, using the Birthday column, or by number if you're using the Donations column to track progress in a fundraising drive.

To sort the current region, click a single cell in the column you want to sort by and then click Sort & Filter in the Editing group on the Home tab. The choices at the top of the list vary slightly depending on the data type. For text, Sort A To Z and Sort Z To A are available, as shown here. For dates, the choice is Sort Oldest To Newest and Sort Newest To Oldest. For numbers, the choices are Sort Smallest To Largest and Sort Largest To Smallest.

If you prefer to sort the current column with a single click, use the commands in the Sort & Filter group on the Data tab, as shown here. This group includes a pair of buttons that allow you to sort in ascending or descending order, just as you can with the Sort & Filter menu. (The Sort button opens the Custom Sort dialog box, which we discuss shortly.)

If the active cell is in a table, you get yet another set of sort and filter menus to work with. Click the arrow to the right of a column heading to see a menu like the one shown next. The sort options are identical to those on the Sort & Filter menu; the real difference is the greatly expanded filter options, which we'll get to later in this section.

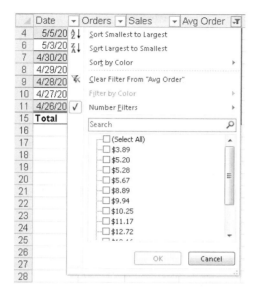

To sort by multiple columns, click Sort on the Data tab; or click Sort & Filter on the Home Tab and then click Custom Sort; or right-click a cell in the table or range, click Sort, and then click Custom Sort.

Any of those roads take you to the Sort dialog box, shown in Figure 12-6. In operation, it's pretty straightforward and easy to figure out. You build a list of sort levels, each based on a column, and then define the sort order for each level.

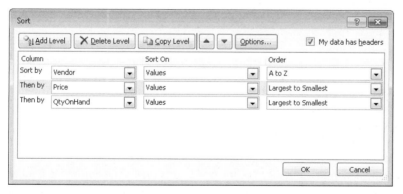

Figure 12-6 Create as many custom Sort By conditions as you need to arrange your list. Use the up and down arrow buttons to change their order.

INSIDE OUT Create a custom column to preserve original sort order

Is the original order of your data important? If so, then make sure you can return to that order easily. For off-the-cuff tasks, you can simply copy a range to a new worksheet, sort and filter as needed, and then delete the copy when you're done. To ensure that you can always return to the original order of a range or table, even if it's sorted accidentally, add a new column (with a descriptive heading like Original_Order) and fill it with numbers that indicate the current order—starting with 1 for the first row and increasing by 1 for each additional row. With this column in place, you can always re-sort the table or range by this column to display its original state.

Most of the time, you'll kick off a sort operation after selecting a single cell or an entire region or table. If you sort part of a region or a table without touching other rows and columns around it, the result can be mismatched data. For example, if you select a group of names from a roster but don't include other columns, the order of names would change but the birthday previously associated with each name would remain in its old row. To prevent that sort of error, Excel displays this warning dialog box:

Excel sorts dates, times, and numbers exactly as you would expect, depending on the sort order you select—Newest To Oldest, Smallest To Largest, and so on. The rules for text are slightly more complicated. For A to Z (ascending) sorts, numbers come first, then most punctuation characters, and then letters in ascending (A–Z) order. The sort is not case-sensitive, so capital letters and lowercase letters are considered the same for sorting purposes. Apostrophes and hyphens are typically ignored except when two strings of text are otherwise identical; in that case, the one that contains the additional punctuation follows the one without. The precise order for punctuation places the space character first, then uses the same numbering as the Unicode character set to determine the order of additional nonalphabetic characters.

You can also sort by a custom series, such as the January through December and Sunday through Monday series that are defined in Excel by default. For more details, see "Entering and Sorting Data with Custom Series" on page 483.

Filtering Data in a Table

As a list gets longer and longer, it becomes more difficult to see patterns associated with subsets of that data. That's when filtering the list becomes useful, hiding rows except those that match criteria you specify. If you're analyzing data from a dozen schools, stores, or customers, each with a unique identifier in a common column, you can filter the worksheet to show only the names you select from that column. You can filter on numbers and dates as well. For example, to create a filtered list of products that are out of stock (or nearly so), you can include only rows where the value in the QtyOnHand column is below 3.

If the number of choices in a column is limited, or if you know exactly which names or values you want to include, the simplest option is to click the arrow to the right of the column heading and pick from the list at the bottom of the menu, as shown in Figure 12-7.

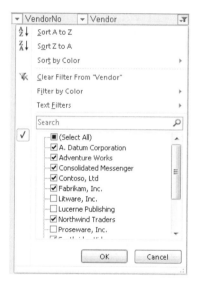

Figure 12-7 To create a completely custom filter, select items in the list at the bottom of this menu, which contains all values found in that column.

The values in this list are drawn from the contents of the current column. Clear the Select All check box at the top of the list to clear all items, after which you can select a few specific items from the list. Click Select All again to reselect all items. When you have a mix of manually selected and cleared check boxes, the Select All box is a solid square as in the previous figure.

If the list of items is too long to be easily manageable, use the search box on the menu to restrict the list of items to those that match whatever you type. Whatever text you enter doesn't have to be a complete word or phrase, and the search results find any match regardless of whether it's at the beginning, middle, or end of a cell's contents. Thus, entering *dat* returns A. Datum Corporation and Consolidated Messenger.

CAUTION

The option to filter by selecting from a list is limited to the first 10,000 items in a list. In the case of a particularly long list in which a single column has many unique values, you see a warning message beneath the list that reads Not All Items Showing. Try using thesearch box to reduce the number of unique items, or choose a different filtering method.

For dates that range over a long period of time, Excel automatically collapses the choices in the filter list, allowing you to choose entire years or to expand the list to include months or even days within a year. Here, for example, we started with a list of stock prices and exchange statistics that includes data from every workday for 75 years. By typing March in the search box, we filtered the list to show only the dates from that month,

If our goal is just to compare data from the month of March for the past five years, we can click Select All Search Results to clear the current list, then manually include 2010, 2009, and so on. Or we can manually choose certain years. When the selection is complete, click Add Current Selection To Filter, and click OK.

In addition to item-by-item filtering, you can create a custom filter for any column to show or hide rows in the list according to the criteria you specify. The exact set of options depends on the data type. The menu option above the search box reads Text Filters, Number Filters, or Date Filters, depending on the contents of the current column.

Options on the Text Filters menu all lead to the Custom AutoFilter dialog box, where you can define one or two criteria for your filter. You can base criteria on the exact cell contents (Equals, Does Not Equal) or on what the cell begins with or contains. This example finds all rows where the contents of the Vendor column begin with B, C, D, or E.

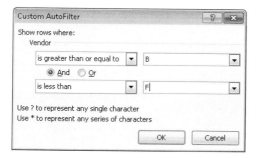

For a column that contains numbers, most of the options on the Number Filters menu lead to the same Custom AutoFilter dialog box. The menu contains three additional choices that work only with numbers. The Above Average and Below Average options work as expected, instantly filtering the list to show only those items that are above or below the arithmetic mean. The other choice, Top Ten, is misleadingly named. It opens the Top 10 AutoFilter dialog box, with Top 10 Items selected by default. However, you can select any number between 1 and 500; you can choose to show the Top or Bottom entries that match that value; and you can change Items to Percent. In this example, we've filtered the list to show only those records with values in the bottom 20 percent.

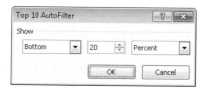

The options on the Date Filters menu are probably the most extensive. You can quickly define a range of dates, choose relative dates (Yesterday, This Quarter), or create a custom filter. Figure 12-8 provides one example of the full range of options.

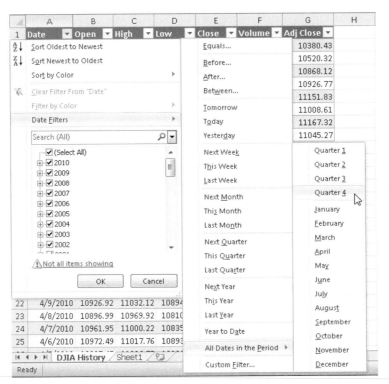

Figure 12-8 Use the Date Filters menu to choose from this extensive list of AutoFilter options when the current column contains mostly dates.

If you choose the Custom Filter option, the dialog box resembles the one available for text and numbers, with the small but crucial difference that it includes calendar controls to use when you are picking dates.

Outlining Data

From its very earliest days, Excel has included features that enable you to subtotal groups of data in lists and then collapse the subtotals into outline form to summarize it. To use this procedure, you must have your data arranged in a list and sorted by the column you want to summarize. You then add formulas (typically using the SUBTOTAL function) to summarize by group. The Subtotal button, in the Outline group on the Data tab, provides a way to create these formulas automatically, as shown in Figure 12-9.

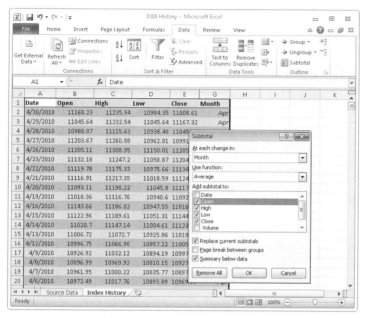

Figure 12-9 The outline functions available in Excel require painstaking setup. In most cases a PivotTable is a better choice.

In the Subtotal dialog box, choose a column in the first list (At Each Change In) to specify where each subtotal goes. Then pick a function (Sum, Average, and so on) and the columns for which you want to create that subtotal. Click OK to create the Subtotal rows and add outline controls in a pane to the left of the row headings. Use those controls to collapse and expand the outline as shown here.

		B	C	D	E	G
	1	Open	High	Low	Close	Month
+	23	11,044	11,133	10,961	11,052	Apr Average
+	47	10,654	10,741	10,602	10,678	Mar Average
+	67	10,199	10,291	10,106	10,215	Feb Average
+	87	10,490	10,581	10,368	10,471	Jan Average
−	88	10,610	10,700	10,525	10,618	Grand Average

E87 ▼ *fx* =SUBTOTAL(1,E68:E86)

The Subtotal command automatically adds the titles beneath the Month column in this example, and you can see one of the SUBTOTAL formulas in the formula bar.

This method of summarizing a worksheet requires painstaking setup, and it severely limits your ability to rearrange data after you complete the setup. In most cases, you can create the same sort of summary with a PivotTable report. As we explain in the next section, PivotTables are easier to set up, allow more flexibility in terms of output, and don't require changes to the structure of the original data source.

Chapter 12

Using PivotTables

The more data you have, the more a PivotTable report can help you make sense of that data. PivotTables allow you to quickly filter, summarize, and group data just by dragging fields around on the screen and picking from lists. One of the most interesting options allows you to move rows to columns (and vice versa); this capability, formally known as *pivoting*, is what gives the feature its name.

In this section, we explain how to create a PivotTable, how to customize its layout, and how to create compelling and visually attractive reports.

Creating a PivotTable

Every PivotTable starts with a data source. Although that source can be external, the most common scenario (and the one we cover in this book) uses source data stored in a range or table on an Excel worksheet. The source data must be organized in columns, each containing a separate data point, with no summaries. The order of rows and columns doesn't matter. Headings aren't required either, although we strongly recommend using descriptive headings—trying to create a PivotTable using generic headings (Column1, Column2, and so on) is a painful process.

To begin, click a single cell in the source data range or table (or select the entire range) and then click PivotTable in the Tables group on the Insert tab. That opens the Create PivotTable dialog box shown in Figure 12-10.

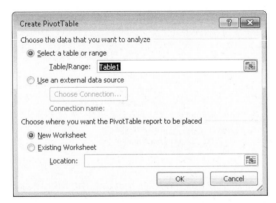

Figure 12-10 The default options shown here position your PivotTable on a new worksheet within the same workbook.

The first pair of options allows you to change the data source if necessary. The options at the bottom of the dialog box allow you to select a specific location for the PivotTable. For most circumstances, we recommend choosing the default options. Keeping a PivotTable on its own page offers the most flexibility and minimizes the likelihood that it will inadvertently interfere with the contents of an existing worksheet.

After your PivotTable is created, you'll see a blank layout like the one shown in Figure 12-11. On the right side is the PivotTable Field List pane, whose contents mirror the headings in your source data table or range. Two new tabs are also visible at the end of the ribbon, under the PivotTable Tools heading.

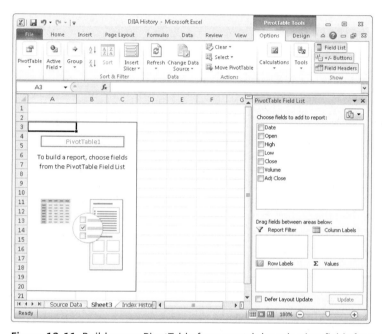

Figure 12-11 Build a new PivotTable from scratch by selecting fields from the list on the right and adding each one as row or column labels, values, or filters.

As you click to select fields from the list in the top of the pane, Excel adds each selected field to one of the four sections in the bottom of the pane. The program makes its best guess as to which field goes where, although you can override the default section assignment for any field by dragging it to a different box. Excel also assigns a default calculation type to the value fields. You can accept the defaults or tweak these settings, as we explain shortly. Figure 12-12 shows a simple PivotTable that starts with 1,095 data points (one for each day of the year for each of three weather stations) and summarizes it into monthly average precipitation amounts arranged by location.

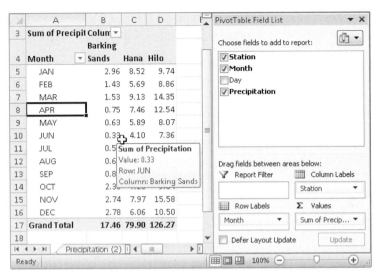

Figure 12-12 Aiming the mouse pointer at a data point in the values section displays a Screen-Tip with additional information.

Swap the row and column labels to get a completely different summary of the same data. When we drag the Station field to the Row Labels section and move the Month field to the Column Labels section, this result allows us to focus on totals by month instead of by location:

	A	B	C	D	E	F	G	H	I	J	K	L	M
1	Day	(All) ▼											
2													
3	Total Rainfall												
4		JAN	FEB	MAR	APR	MAY	JUN	JUL	AUG	SEP	OCT	NOV	DEC
5	Hilo	9.74	8.86	14.35	12.54	8.07	7.36	10.71	9.78	9.14	9.64	15.58	10.50
6	Hana	8.52	5.69	9.13	7.46	5.89	4.10	5.91	5.79	6.12	7.26	7.97	6.06
7	Barking Sands	2.96	1.43	1.53	0.75	0.63	0.33	0.50	0.62	0.84	2.35	2.74	2.78
8	Grand Total	21.22	15.98	25.01	20.75	14.59	11.79	17.12	16.19	16.10	19.25	26.29	19.34

For this iteration, we also added the Day field to the Report Filter section (above the rest of the report). To make the PivotTable more readable, we changed the name of the value field (displayed in the upper left corner of the table) and hid the drop-down lists for filtering rows and columns by clicking the Field Headers button in the Show group on the PivotTable Tools Options tab.

You might also want or need to make some basic adjustments to field settings. To change settings for the active field, use the Field Settings button in the Active Field group on the Options tab. Or click the field button in the Values section of the PivotTable Fields List pane and then click Value Field Settings to display the dialog box shown next.

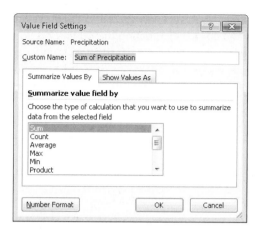

The default name for that field reflects the type of calculation. You can change it to a more descriptive name, such "Total Rainfall" in place of "Sum of Precipitation." You can also choose a different calculation. So, from a list of individual sales, you could choose the Sales_Amount field and click Count to calculate how many transactions each sales person had during a comparable period. Or choose Sum or Average to calculate the total sales amount or the average sale per transaction, respectively.

Click the Number Format button to display the Format Cells dialog box, with only the Number tab available. You can apply any number or date format, set the number of decimal places, and specify whether you want to use a thousands separator. This dialog box is available for value fields only.

The corresponding option for fields in the Filter, Row Labels, and Column Labels sections is Field Settings. The contents of the Field Settings dialog box are significantly different from those available for value fields, as shown here. We look at these options in more detail in the next section.

INSIDE OUT   Customize the PivotTable Field List pane

In the upper right corner of the PivotTable Field List pane is a small, unlabeled button with an arrow to its right (see Figure 12-13). Clicking that button reveals a menu of five alternative arrangements of the two sections. You can arrange fields and areas side by side or show only one section while hiding the other. For most simple PivotTables, the default layout is good enough. Consider changing the layout if you have a complex data source with many fields.

If you add multiple fields in the Row Labels section, you can create an outline view of your data that can be expanded and collapsed. Creating this outline lets you roll up large amounts of data into easy-to-digest subtotals or expand the details under any of those levels. In Figure 12-13, for example, we've added three fields to the Row Labels section and made sure that the +/− buttons are visible (you'll find this option in the Show group on the Options tab under PivotTable Tools).

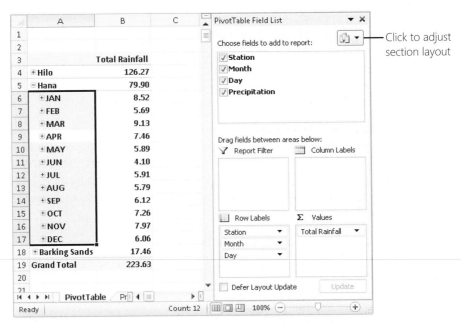

Figure 12-13 Use the +/− buttons to the left of each heading to expand or collapse the data beneath that heading. This arrangement shows subtotals by month for the Hana station only.

Customizing a PivotTable Layout

After you've arranged fields on the PivotTable page, you're ready to tweak the display so it's even more readable. If you don't like the default sort order for rows, for example, you can change it. Right-click any individual row or column label and click Sort to see options for that field. From that shortcut menu, you can sort in ascending or descending order. Click More Sort Options if you want the option to sort by a different field. In the following example, you could see all 12 months, arranged in descending order by Total Rainfall, so that the months go from wettest to driest by row.

If you want to see data in a specific order that defies being expressed as a formula, try moving individual items manually. Make sure Manual (You Can Drag Items To Rearrange Them) is selected in the Sort dialog box for the row or column label field. Then right-click the item you want to move and click Move to see a menu like the one shown here. You can move individual items up or down (left or right if you're working with columns) or to the beginning or end of the current set of row or column labels. You can also move a column field to a row or vice versa.

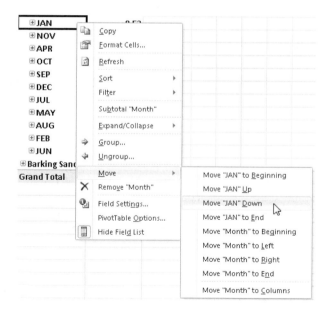

TROUBLESHOOTING

When you refresh the PivotTable, you lose your custom sort order

For row and column labels, the default settings have the AutoSort option enabled. That means you can manually move rows and columns, but as soon as you refresh the Pivot-Table, the sort order pops back to its normal settings. Disabling this behavior requires that you find a well-hidden setting and change it. Right-click the field you want to manually reorder, click Sort, and then click More Sort Options. Click the More Options button (we warned you it was deeply buried) and then clear the check box under AutoSort.

You can also filter data in a PivotTable in a variety of ways. The most formal is to add a field to the Report Filters section of the PivotTable layout. This allows you to reuse the current data arrangement with specific entries in that field. To see the list unfiltered, choose All Items from that list.

To filter a PivotTable on an ad-hoc basis, use the field header. (If this drop-down list isn't visible, click the Field Headers button in the Show group on the Options tab for the Pivot-Table.) The filter options are very similar to those we described earlier in this chapter for ordinary tables and ranges. (See "Filtering Data in a Table" on page 401.) You can show or hide specific entries in a list of values or labels or use the search box to find entries that match the text, numbers, or dates you supply.

To quickly filter a list to show or hide items you specify or one or more items from that field, right-click, click Filter, and then click either Keep Only Selected Items or Hide Selected Items.

Grouping and ungrouping data in a PivotTable provides a dramatic way to zoom in on complex data sets with minimal effort. The source data for the PivotTable in Figure 12-14, for example, includes more than 20,000 separate data points listing activity on a major stock exchange for every trading day for more than 80 years. We added the Date field to the Row Labels section, right-clicked an individual date under that column heading, and then clicked Group on the shortcut menu. Note that we were able to both filter the PivotTable (using the Starting At and Ending At boxes under the Auto heading) and group it by quarters and years with a few clicks.

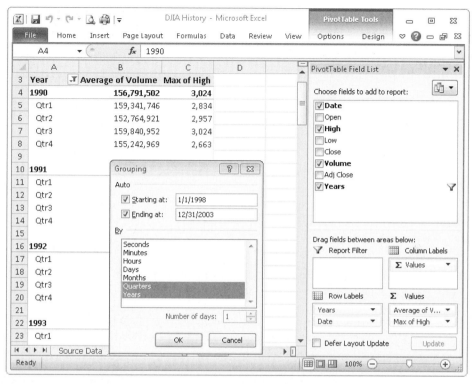

Figure 12-14 Use the Grouping dialog box to collapse and subtotal large amounts of time-based data into slices—by year and by quarter, in this example.

If you look carefully at Figure 12-14, you'll notice that Excel worked its magic by creating a new calculated field called Years (it's at the bottom of the field list, with a filter icon to its right). The Ungroup menu lets you clear the current grouping arrangement and start over.

Changing the Format of a PivotTable

The Design tab contains a full range of options for customizing the look and feel of a Pivot-Table report. It's visible at the right side of the ribbon, under the PivotTable Tools heading, whenever the active cell is in a PivotTable.

The options in the Layout group allow you to quickly show or hide subtotals and grand totals. You can show subtotals at the top or bottom of a group and calculate grand totals for rows or columns or both.

The Report Layout command offers three alternatives for arranging the rows in your report, as shown here:

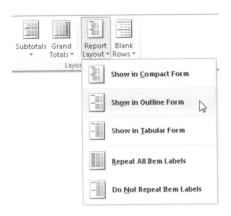

- **Compact Form**   This display option has the least amount of clutter. Multiple levels under a main heading are indented.

- **Outline Form**   Each row label gets its own field header. Each main grouping is on its own row, with secondary groupings in new rows beneath it in a column to the right of the previous level. Subtotals can appear at the top or bottom of each group.

- **Tabular Form**   All data is in a grid, with no indenting. Secondary levels of grouping begin in additional columns to the right of the main heading. In this format, subtotals appear only at the bottom of each group, even if you choose the Show All Subtotals At Top Of Group option.

Figure 12-15 shows the results for each option.

As with ordinary tables, you can apply styles to PivotTables, using the PivotTable Styles gallery. The procedures for creating, modifying, and applying styles are identical, so we won't repeat them here. (See "Formatting Tables with Table Styles" on page 391.) The gallery is much larger, however, with 84 default styles to choose from instead of the 60 selections in the Table Styles gallery.

You'll see the reason for the difference when you duplicate and customize a PivotTable style. In the Modify PivotTable Quick Style dialog box, you'll find 25 individual options for a PivotTable style; that's nearly double the number of options in a regular table style, reflecting the need for separate formats to cover subtotals and grand totals, header cells, subheadings, and other features found only in PivotTables.

Year	Average of Volume	Max of High
1995	**344,039,127**	**5,267**
Qtr1	332,855,714	4,214
Qtr2	339,724,127	4,614
Qtr3	341,134,286	4,839
Qtr4	362,442,381	5,267
1996	**409,580,472**	**6,624**
Qtr1	427,543,968	5,756

Compact Form

Years	Date	Average of Volume	Max of High
1995		**344,039,127**	**5,267**
	Qtr1	332,855,714	4,214
	Qtr2	339,724,127	4,614
	Qtr3	341,134,286	4,839
	Qtr4	362,442,381	5,267
1996		**409,580,472**	**6,624**
	Qtr1	427,543,968	5,756

Outline Form

Years	Date	Average of Volume	Max of High
1995	Qtr1	332,855,714	4,214
	Qtr2	339,724,127	4,614
	Qtr3	341,134,286	4,839
	Qtr4	362,442,381	5,267
1995 Total		**344,039,127**	**5,267**
1996	Qtr1	427,543,968	5,756

Tabular Form

Figure 12-15 The same PivotTable report displayed in three different formats.

Importing, Exporting, and Connecting to Data Sources

Typing data by hand is one way to create a range or table in Excel. If the original data is stored in another program or data file format, it's much easier to import it into Excel. As an added benefit, you get the assurance that the imported data is accurate, avoiding the significant possibility of errors introduced when you rekey data.

The process works in reverse as well. If you have painstakingly entered and edited data in an Excel table or range, it's a straightforward process to export that data, in whole or in part, to another file format for use in another program.

We start with the process of importing data. If you want to import the new data into a completely new workbook, start with the Open dialog box (click File, then Open, or press Ctrl+O). Choose the appropriate file format from the drop-down menu, locate the file containing the data to be imported, and click Open. What happens next depends on the original data format.

The most likely candidate for a successful import is a Comma Separated Values (CSV) file, which represents the universal data interchange format. Fields are separated by commas (and enclosed in quotation marks if necessary), with each record delimited by a carriage return. Excel imports the entire file as a range, with each record in a single row and each field in a single column.

For other data formats, you might be prompted for additional information. For example, opening a Microsoft Access database file (*.mdb) results in a prompt like the one shown here:

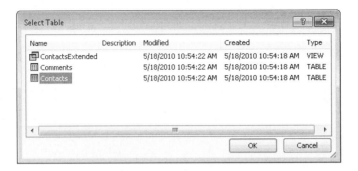

Access databases typically contain multiple tables, but Excel can import only one at a time. Select the Access table and click OK to see it in an Excel worksheet.

For more control over importing data, open an existing workbook (or create a new one), click to select the cell where you want the data to be imported, and then use the options in the Get External Data group on the Data tab. In the case of a text file (including files in CSV format), click From Text, select the file from the Import Text File dialog box, and then click Import. That opens the Text Import Wizard, shown in Figure 12-16.

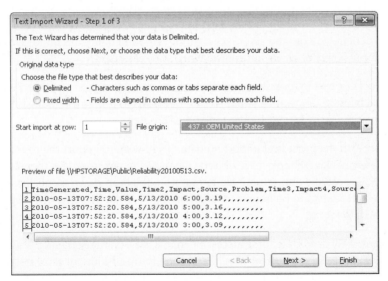

Figure 12-16 The three-step Text Import Wizard lets you fine-tune how data from a text file is broken into rows and columns.

Excel makes its best guesses about the proper way to import your data. It's not infallible, however, so at each step of the process you can override its decisions. For example, if you're importing data that contains no delimiters but is arranged in a fixed grid where each field occupies the same number of spaces, you can choose Fixed Width and try your luck.

The second step of the Text Import Wizard, shown here, allows you to specify a delimiter character. Tab is selected by default. In this example, we had to select Comma before the breaks between fields were recognized.

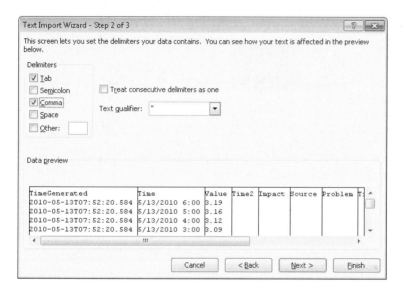

The Data Preview pane at the bottom of the dialog box shows the data as it will appear in your worksheet. It's worth scrolling through the preview to quickly verify that your data will be imported correctly. If you see a potential problem, you can go back and correct the import file in a text editor and try again.

The final step of the wizard allows you to assign cell formats to individual columns and to skip columns you don't want to import. Click to select a column from the list in the preview pane (hold down the Ctrl key and click to select multiple columns), and then choose a format for the selected columns. Click Do Not Import Column (Skip), if you want Excel to ignore the contents of the selected columns.

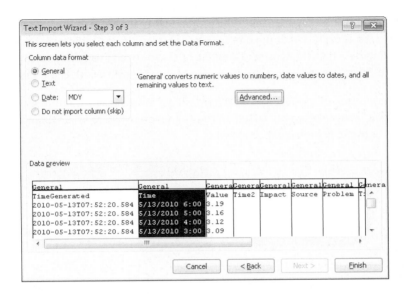

After you click Finish, the wizard allows you to choose an alternate location for the data import. Click OK to complete the import.

By default, when you import data, Excel creates a persistent connection to the data file. For some operations, that's a great time-saver. If your corporate database spits out an updated version of a text file every day in a consistent location, you can click Refresh All in the Connections group on the Data tab to add the most recent data to the table you've imported. Likewise, you can use Access forms to keep a database up to date and then perform analysis on the most recent version of the data in Excel.

But what if you intended for the import to be a one-time operation? In that case, click in the imported table or range, and then click Connections in the Connections group on the Data tab. That opens the Workbook Connections dialog box shown in Figure 12-17. Select the connection you just created, and click Remove to break it.

Export operations are far simpler. Click any cell in the database range or table—or select a specific range if you want to export only a portion of the data. Then click File, click Save As, and choose the appropriate format. If you pick CSV (Comma Delimited), you can count on the data being usable with any other data-management tool.

For tables, you'll find an Export option on the Design tab under Table Tools. This menu allows you to save your data as a SharePoint list. For details, see "Creating, Viewing, and Editing SharePoint Lists" on page 873.

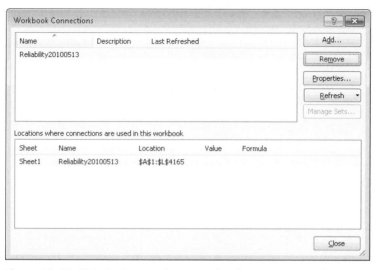

Figure 12-17 Click the Remove button to break a connection after importing external data into a worksheet.

Charts and Data Analysis

Pictures tell stories. You can drone on and on and on about the meaning of statistics and the hidden patterns behind seemingly random measurements. Or you can turn a collection of data into an elegant, information-based graphic and let *it* do the talking. Using a well-designed chart, you can communicate a situation or a series of events in seconds, with only a few well-chosen words required.

Building a visually compelling, information-rich chart from a series of numbers and dates is part science, part art. The science involves recognizing which series of data on a worksheet represent the patterns you're trying to describe. The art is in arranging and fine-tuning the colors, shading, shapes, labels, and other pieces of your chart so that they tell the story most effectively.

In this chapter, we look at Excel's extraordinarily versatile charting engine and explain how to bring numbers to life in chart form. We also look at conditional formatting—a series of features that add color, text formatting, and other changes to individual pieces of data according to conditions you define. And finally, we explain the ins and out of sparklines, a new feature in Excel 2010 that allows you to add tiny trend lines directly to your source data to tell a small part of the story without using a full-size chart.

Using Charts to Visualize Data

The process of building a chart doesn't have to be linear. After you get a few basic design decisions out of the way, you can revisit and refine the chart's layout, formatting, and style options as needed, in any order, trying out alternatives until you're satisfied. If the iterative process turns out a collection of settings you're especially pleased with, or if you want to share your handiwork with other people, you can save the current settings as a chart template and apply all those settings with a single click.

The first, most important step in building a great chart is matching the data you want to chart with the right chart type. As we demonstrate with examples later in this chapter, you can plot your data using one chart type and then change to a different chart type to tell a completely different story using the same data. (See "Choosing the Right Chart Type" on page 429 for more details.) Start by selecting the data to be charted (including column and row labels if you want them to be used as chart labels). The available chart types are listed in the Charts group on the Insert tab, as shown here.

Clicking a specific chart type reveals a menu of subtypes for that category, arranged in subcategories as shown here. To continue, you must select one of the available options. (Don't worry: if you change your mind, you can switch to a different chart type and subtype at any time.)

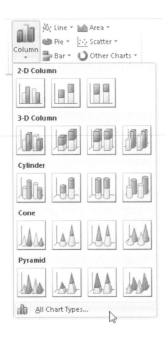

Excel builds and displays the chart immediately, using source data you selected earlier (or the current region, if you didn't make a selection first). If the data isn't appropriate for the chart type you select, you might see an error message, which you must resolve before you can continue. If your original data selection doesn't result in the chart you were expecting, you can modify the data selection or change the chart design as needed.

For details on how to change the source data for a chart, see "Linking Worksheet Data to Chart Elements" on page 439.

To learn more about fine-tuning the look and feel of a chart, see "Advanced Chart Formatting Options" on page 442.

One final option allows you to change the location of a chart. Click Move Chart (the right-most command on the Design tab) to see the dialog box shown here. You can position the chart on its own sheet or as an object that floats on a worksheet—typically the same one containing your source data.

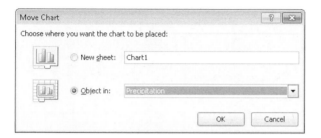

INSIDE OUT   Change a chart's location to suit the task at hand.

It's perfectly acceptable to move a chart to make it easier to work with. As you change the data in a table, for example, you might want to see your changes reflected in real time in a linked chart. In that scenario, move the chart to the current worksheet and position the chart object alongside the data you're entering or editing. When you've polished the chart to perfection, move it to its own chart sheet and give the sheet a descriptive name. That makes finding the chart easier so you can use it in a Word document or a PowerPoint presentation later.

Turning Data into a Chart

In this whirlwind tour of the charting features in Excel, we focus on the nuts and bolts of actually building a chart. If you're looking for detailed explanations of the concepts behind turning information into graphics, we highly recommend starting with Edward Tufte's seminal work on the subject (see *www.edwardtufte.com*). And because space is limited, we can only dive just below the surface in showing you the many options available when you create and customize Excel charts. For a much more complete picture, we recommend *Microsoft Excel 2010 Inside Out,* by our colleagues Mark Dodge and Craig Stinson (Microsoft Press, 2010).

With that disclaimer out of the way, we ask you to look at the simple line chart shown in Figure 13-1, which illustrates the most common chart elements.

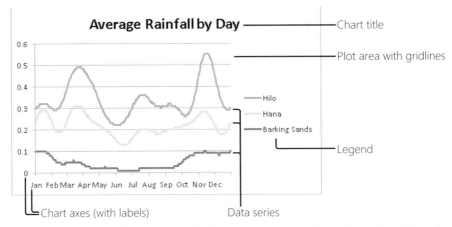

Figure 13-1 This simple line chart includes several common elements—a chart title, a legend, and two axes.

With a little more data and a few more clicks, we could make this chart much more complicated, although that would defeat its purpose. The following list describes the main chart elements available to you in Excel, with specific references to the examples used in Figure 13-1.

- **Data series and plot area** Each series of data appears within the plot area, represented as a line, column, bar, or pie slice, depending on the chart type. You can use a unique color in the plot area (as in Figure 13-1) to make it stand out from the chart background. 3-D charts have a wall, a floor, and rotation options as well.

- **Axes and Gridlines** Column, bar, and line charts typically plot data along two axes. Figure 13-1, for example, shows time along the horizontal axis and rainfall (measured in inches) along the vertical axes. A depth axis is available for 3-D charts. Gridlines help you compare the values in a data series to the values on an axis.

- **Titles** If you choose to use a chart title, you can overlay the title on the chart itself or allow the title to sit above the chart. In addition, you can add a title to any axis to help explain the data plotted along that axis. Figure 13-1, for example, might be easier to follow if the vertical axis had "Daily rainfall (inches)" as a title.

- **Legend**   This optional element functions as a key to the data series, typically providing labels next to the color or shape used for the corresponding data series.

- **Labels**   You can add labels beneath axes to indicate what each step along the axis represents. On the horizontal axis in Figure 13-1, we used month abbreviations (Jan, Feb, Mar) to show a full year's worth of data. You can also add data labels to a data series to indicate the actual values represented by plot points.

After you create a chart, you can change its fundamental organization, layout, style, and location at any time. All the tools you need are on the Design tab, the first of three custom tabs that appear under the Chart Tools heading, as shown in Figure 13-2.

Figure 13-2 Using the commands on this tab, you can change chart type, select different source data, adjust the layout and style, and move the chart.

Once you've settled on the right chart type and selected the correct data, you can add or remove elements so that the chart tells your story most effectively. The Quick Layouts gallery (in the Chart Layouts group) is especially helpful for this task. The choices available are specific to the chart type and subtype you've chosen. Each layout includes a different arrangement of titles, legends, and other chart elements, depicted as a thumbnail graphic that offers a rough preview of the final result. If you choose a line chart with data markers, for example, the Quick Layout gallery includes the 12 options shown here.

Don't look to the ScreenTips for assistance on figuring out what is in each layout, though. When you move the mouse pointer over each layout, you'll see only the generic names Layout 1, Layout 2, and so on.

Whether you start with a default layout or use one of the Quick Layout options, you can add, remove, and change the position and formatting of most elements to make the chart easier to read and understand. Most of the tools you need are on the Layout tab, which appears under the Chart Tools heading only when you click to select a chart. Figure 13-3 shows this tab in action.

Figure 13-3 The Current Selection group at the left tells you which chart element is available for immediate formatting. Other commands allow you to select different parts of the chart.

INSIDE OUT   Use the arrow keys to select individual elements easily

Trying to hit a specific chart element with a mouse pointer can be a frustrating experience even if you have a steady hand and a sharp eye. The easier alternative is to use the arrow keys. Click inside the chart borders (but away from axes, titles, legends, and the like) to select the Chart Area, which is the first entry in the Chart Elements list in the Current Selection group on the Layout tab. Now use the Up and Down Arrow keys to move through the list, to the plot area, individual data series, axes, and so on. Use the Left and Right Arrow keys to move through individual items in a series, a legend, or another element made up of multiple data points. If the legend is selected, press the Right Arrow key to select the first entry in the list, and keep pressing to move through the entire legend.

Most of the commands on the Layout tab lead to additional menus that present the most common formatting options. On the Gridlines menu, for example, you decide whether gridlines are visible for each of the major axes; you can hide gridlines completely, show only major or minor gridlines, or show both major and minor gridlines. Use the options on the

Legend menu, shown next, to position a legend above, below, or on either side of the chart or within the chart itself—or to remove a legend from the chart.

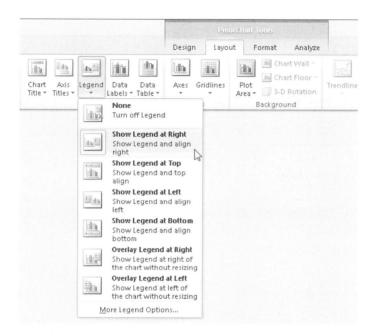

If the predefined options don't match your needs exactly, click the link at the bottom of the menu to open a dialog box containing a full range of options. From the Axis menu, for example, you can set a value-based axis to show numbers in thousands, millions, billions, or a logarithmic scale. If that's not enough, click More Primary Vertical Axis Options to see the dialog box shown next.

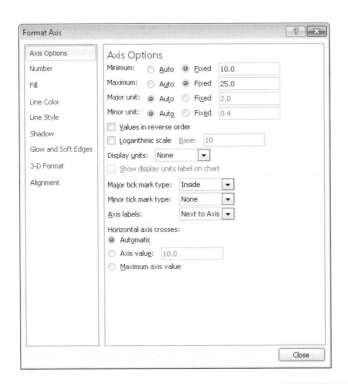

If the data source for your chart is a PivotTable, the result is a PivotChart. What's the difference? The most noticeable change from a regular chart is the addition of field buttons, which you can use to filter data just as in a PivotTable. When you click to select any part of a PivotChart, Excel displays a group of custom tabs under the PivotChart Tools heading. As Figure 13-4 shows, the first three tabs are identical to the Chart Tools tabs you use with a regular chart. The Analyze tab includes a Field Buttons menu that allows you to show or hide specific types of field buttons.

When you filter data using field buttons in a PivotChart, your changes are immediately reflected in the underlying PivotTable. All other procedures for formatting a PivotChart and changing its layout are similar to the techniques used with a regular chart.

For a detailed discussion of how to create and manipulate PivotTables, see "Using PivotTables" on page 406.

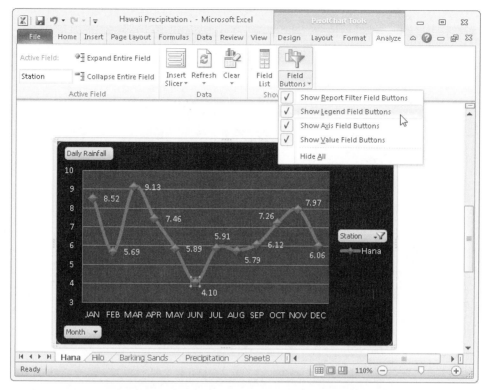

Figure 13-4 Use the field buttons on a PivotChart to filter the data from the linked PivotTable. The icon to the right of the Station field indicates that we've filtered that field.

Choosing the Right Chart Type

As we noted earlier, you must select a chart type and subtype to create a chart initially, but you can switch to a different subtype or even choose a completely different chart type later. Click to select any part of the chart, and then click the Change Chart Type command on the Design tab to open the dialog box shown in Figure 13-5.

Column Charts

Column charts are tailor-made for side-by-side comparisons, especially over time. Available subtypes include clustered columns, stacked columns, and 100% stacked columns, with and without 3-D effects. Figure 13-6, for example, shows a clustered column chart that offers a simple comparison of revenues in four regions over four years. It's easy to see at a glance that revenues in the North and East regions have been flat or down slightly over time, while the South and West regions have grown impressively.

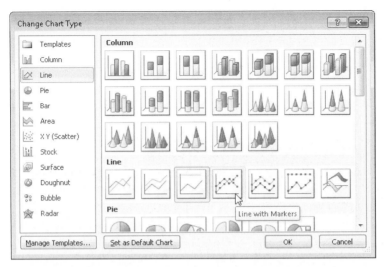

Figure 13-5 You can change the chart type at any time. The selection of subtypes available in each category on the left is identical to those in the Charts group on the Insert tab.

Region	2007	2008	2009	2010
North	581	519	465	499
East	842	835	757	754
South	524	765	842	884
West	579	682	828	863

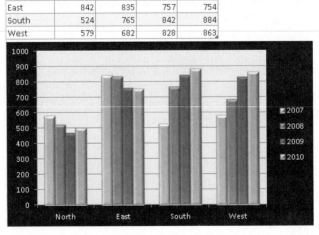

Figure 13-6 Column charts make it possible to compare data points side by side. This clustered column chart shows trends over time for four regions.

INSIDE OUT   Swap the axes to tell a different story

Sometimes all you need is a slightly different angle to see a completely different picture. Clicking the Switch Row/Column button, in the Data group on the Design tab, is
a particularly effective way of looking at column charts from a different perspective.
The command name is misleading: what it really does is swap the data series associated
with the horizontal and vertical axes. The column chart in Figure 13-6 on the previous page, for example, looks at four regions over time, emphasizing the trend for each
region. If you click Switch Row/Column, the data series that make up the clustered columns are swapped, and you get the revised chart shown here:

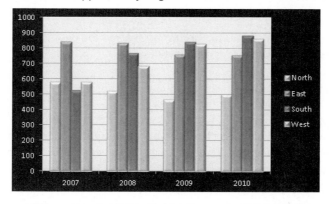

At first glance, the chart looks similar to the earlier arrangement. But the story it tells
is different, emphasizing differences over time, with one region dominating in the first
year, but with a much narrower gap between the leaders just three years later. Which
arrangement you choose depends on which story you want to communicate.

The other main variation in this chart type is the stacked column chart, which combines
data from different series into a single column that emphasizes the relationship of individual items to the total. If your data series includes several similar totals and you want
to emphasize a percentage change in one or more individual components, use a 100%
stacked chart, as shown in Figure 13-7.

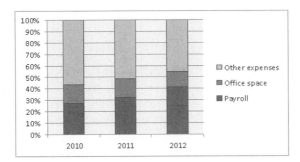

Figure 13-7 Use a 100% stacked column chart when you want to emphasize the percentage changes between parts of a total over time.

For column charts, most of the 3-D subtypes apply visual effects only. The exception is the 3-D Column subtype, which uses the horizontal axis and the depth axis to compare series and categories equally, with values on the vertical axis.

Line Charts

Use a line chart when you want to plot data over time (or along ordered categories) to show trends on a continuous scale: revenues by quarter, economic growth by year or decade, rainfall or high and low temperature by month, and so on. The horizontal axis should be divided into equal units, with no gaps. Figure 13-8, for example, shows a month's worth of daily high and low temperatures plotted on a line graph

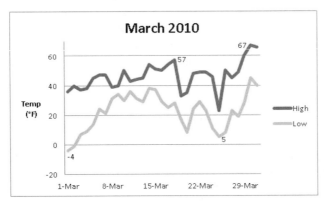

Figure 13-8 Because this line graph has 31 separate data points on each line, we've chosen not to use data markers.

Each of the 2-D subtypes in the Line Chart category includes options to show lines with or without data markers. If the number of data points on the category axis is relatively small, let Excel automatically add markers to show the exact location of each point. That makes it easier to find the value associated with each entry on the horizontal axis. You can custom-ize the color and shape of each marker, and those customizations appear automatically in the legend, as in this example.

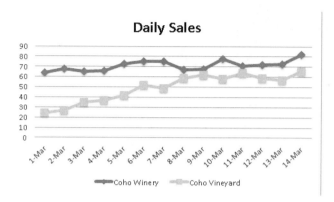

INSIDE OUT   Add data labels selectively

Adding data labels to every point in a series can sometimes lead to information over-load. The alternative is to add data labels to specific data points. Click to select the data series, and you'll see a selection marker over every point in the series. Click any individual data point to select just that point. Now you can show or hide the label for that point alone. Use the options on the Data Labels menu, in the Labels group on the Layout tab, to choose a position for the label, or drag it manually. In Figure 13-8, we used a total of four data labels to identify the two peaks and two valleys on the indi-vidual lines.

Pie Charts

If the data you want to plot is in a single row or column, it just might fit in a pie chart. Each pie chart consists of a single data series. Each data point is a slice proportional in size to the other items in the series, adding up to 100%. Pie charts work best when you have a small number of data points, six or seven at most, and no slice is too close to 0. (Negative num-bers aren't allowed in a pie chart.)

The Data Labels option on the Layout tab allows you to position the data labels (try the Best Fit option). To customize the data displayed—to show percentages instead of values or vice versa—click More Data Label Options, which opens the Format Data Labels dialog box with the Label Options tab selected, as shown in Figure 13-9.

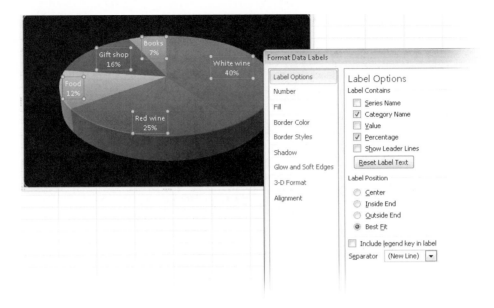

Figure 13-9 Options in this dialog box allow you to specify which values are automatically displayed as part of data labels.

You can emphasize one or more slices of a pie chart by "exploding" it from the rest of the chart. Select a slice and drag it away from the pie. (This option is especially dramatic if you've chosen a 3-D chart type.) If you select the entire series—in other words, every slice of the pie—and drag out, you'll end up with an exploded pie chart, as shown here. This option is especially useful when you want to talk about each data point separately in order of size.

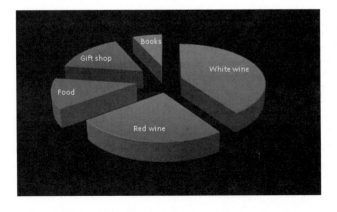

Two of the advanced pie chart subtypes are surprisingly useful when you want to tell a story within a story. It's also a good way to create a readable chart when you have a dozen or more data points. The Pie Of Pie and Bar Of Pie subtypes let you combine two or more slices into a single slice called Other, with those data points plotted in a second pie or bar chart. Figure 13-10 shows the Bar Of Pie chart subtype.

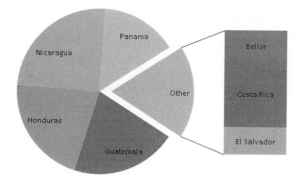

Figure 13-10 You define which values go in the bar chart on the right by setting a condition—in this example, all values less than 12 percent.

The options for the second chart are well hidden on the Series Options tab of the Format Data Series dialog box. Click the chart, select the series from the drop-down list at the far left of the Layout tab, and then click Format Selection. Use the sliders under the Gap Width and Second Plot Size headings to adjust the distance between the two charts and change their size relative to each other. The Split Series By options at the top of the dialog box allow you to define which pieces of the original pie are broken out into the second chart.

Bar Charts

A bar chart is, in its simplest form, a column chart turned on its side, with the values on the horizontal axis and categories on the vertical axis. Bar charts are ideal for differentiating winners and losers—or at least those who are in the lead for now. Bar charts work equally well for presenting results of speed tests and for pointing out who's in a front in a fundraising competition. In Figure 13-11, for example, we could have just as easily plotted this data as a column chart, but the long school names would have been awkward to position along the horizontal axis and look more natural and readable here.

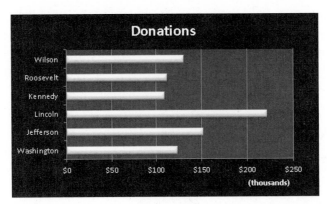

Figure 13-11 Bar charts work especially well when the category names are long, as in this example. The horizontal arrangement makes the current leader easy to identify.

Area Charts

Area charts show the magnitude of change in a data set over time and thus offer a good way to show changes in the relative contributions of different parts of a group. In their plainest form, 2-D and 3-D area charts are like line charts, except that the value between the data point and the next lowest point on another series (or the lowest point on the axis) is filled in with color.

A stacked area chart like the one shown in Figure 13-12 adds all the values together so that the highest point on the chart for each point on the horizontal axis represents the total for that point.

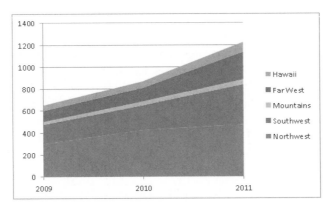

Figure 13-12 Use a stacked area chart to pile each data series on top of the one before it and show its contribution to the total.

Scatter (XY) Charts

Scatter charts (also known as XY charts) are fascinating, versatile, and often misunderstood. A scatter chart is made up of two numeric data series, plotted in pairs on the horizontal and vertical axes (which are also known respectively as the x-axis and y-axis, thus explaining the origin of the XY name). You can use a scatter chart in place of a line chart when data points on the horizontal access aren't linear; the visual result is similar, but without the distortion caused by irregular spacing of data points. One common use of a scatter chart is to identify clusters of similar data in a nonlinear set. In Figure 13-13, for example, we've created this chart type by plotting survey data for 16 companies, with customer satisfaction ratings on the vertical axis and price (from high to low) on the horizontal axis.

Figure 13-13 Each dot represents a pair of survey results for a company. From this data, we can conclude that consumers are less satisfied with the high-priced options in our data series.

You'll notice in this scatter chart that we deliberately hid the values on both axes. The numbers themselves can be on any scale you create. It's the position of the data in this chart that matters most. The data points in the top right quadrant represent the best combination of value and customer satisfaction.

To divide the graph into quadrants, we used the Data Series Options dialog box to define the Major Gridline interval for each axis as equal to exactly half the distance between the lowest and highest points on that axis (50 on a scale of 0 to 100). From the Gridlines menu on the Layout tab, we made Major Gridlines visible on both the horizontal and vertical axis, resulting in a neatly divided rectangle.

You can add smooth lines or straight lines to a scatter chart, with or without markers for each data point. The Scatter With Smooth Lines chart type can produce interesting results when you're trying to show a pattern in data that is not uniformly distributed.

Stock Charts

Analyzing trends in the markets for stocks, bonds, and other securities is one of the most popular uses for Excel charts. So popular, in fact, that stock charts get their own category in the Chart Types list. The four available layout options enable you to plot the movement of stock prices on a daily basis, using a single line to indicate high, low, and closing prices. Opening prices and trading volume are optional data series.

Building a stock chart requires that you arrange your data in a specific order. If you try to create a stock chart using an incorrect arrangement of data, you're greeted with a helpful message like the one shown here. (The exact content of the message varies, depending on the chart subtype you've selected.)

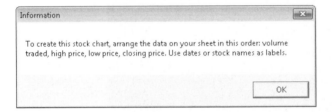

Figure 13-14 shows a stock chart that depicts high, low, and closing prices over a three-month period. We added three text boxes (using the Text Box command in the Insert group on the Layout tab) to call attention to specific sections of the chart for the accompanying commentary.

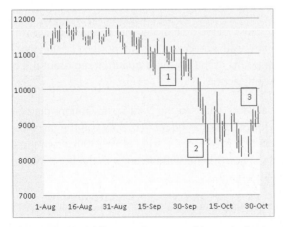

Figure 13-14 Adding text boxes on this stock chart makes it easier to point to specific locations on the chart when describing the gyrations of the market in the accompanying text.

Other Chart Types

You'll find a total of five chart types under the Other category (in the Charts group on the Insert tab). We've already discussed stock charts, which are genuinely useful. It's much more difficult to make a compelling case for the other four chart types, so we'll simply list them here and offer a brief description.

Surface charts are made up of two data series containing numeric data and resemble a topographic map. If you can envision a rubber sheet stretched over a 3-D column chart, you have a pretty good idea of what a 3-D surface chart looks like.

Doughnut charts are similar to pie charts but can contain multiple data series, with one series inside the "doughnut hole" of the next. Excel's Help system notes that doughnut charts are "hard to read" and suggests stacked column or stacked bar charts as alternatives.

Bubble charts resemble scatter (XY) charts with an extra dimension that turns plot points into bubbles of varying sizes. As in a scatter chart, the values in the x and y series plot the location of each data point. The third value determines the bubble size.

Radar charts plot data in a circular arrangement, where one set of numeric values starts at the center of the chart and a second set of ordered values (typically time) is plotted around the outside of the circle.

Linking Worksheet Data to Chart Elements

The elements that make up a chart are, in most cases, linked directly to data within a worksheet. Series names typically come from the label attached to the column or row that provides the data series values. Axis labels and legends are also derived from source data. If you change any of the data points in the source data, the corresponding chart element is updated immediately.

You can view and edit the source data for a chart by clicking anywhere in the chart and then clicking Select Data, in the Data group on the Design tab. Figure 13-15 shows this dialog box for a chart whose data source consists of three rows (each treated as a separate data series) and three columns (each treated as a separate category).

In this example, the source data (as identified in the Chart Data Range box) is a single contiguous range. If your chart consists of selected rows or columns from a larger range or table, you'll see each range listed separately, with commas separating the multiple ranges.

The labels above the two main boxes in the Select Data Source dialog box do not change with the chart type, which can lead to some confusing results. For example, in a pie chart, the values in the Horizontal (Category) Axis Labels box define each slice of the pie and are used for the legend, while the values in the Legend Entries (Series) box contain the values that are plotted in the chart and are *not* in the legend.

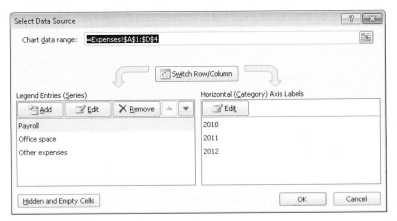

Figure 13-15 You can edit the source data for any series or rearrange the order of series and categories in this dialog box.

When you open the Select Data Source dialog box, it positions itself so that the upper left corner of the chart's data range is visible.

To edit an individual data series, select it in the Legend Entries (Series) list and then click the Edit button. The Edit Series dialog box, shown here, shows you which cell is being picked up as the series name and which range is the data series. In both cases, you can see the current values to the right of the Collapse Dialog button and the equal sign.

> **Note**
>
> **If the series you select is part of a scatter (XY) chart, the Edit Series dialog box contains separate boxes for Series X Values and Series Y Values.**

The Add button opens the same Edit Series dialog box, with no data source selected. Click to fill in the Series Name and Series Values boxes with valid ranges and then click OK to add the new series to your chart. The Remove button completely removes the selected data series from the chart. Use the Move Up and Move Down arrows (to the right of the Remove button) to change the order of the selected data series in the list. (You cannot change the order of categories here—do that by using the Axis Options tab in the Format Axis dialog box.)

TROUBLESHOOTING

Some of your data series are missing or contain incorrect values

In some cases—notably when using stock charts—Excel warns you if the data you've selected is inappropriate for the chart type. But in other cases it blithely allows you to continue without a hint that anything is wrong. A pie chart, for example, can display one and only one data series—a single row with multiple columns, or a single column with multiple rows. But if you select two or more rows from a table, Excel adds the selected data as individual data series but plots the pie chart using only the first series in the list. Likewise, a scatter chart requires exactly two numeric series. If either series contains any text values, they are plotted as zeros and distort the chart. If the results are not what you expect, verify that the number of series and their respective data types are supported by the chart type you've selected.

With a chart that is embedded on the same sheet as the source data, you can edit chart data directly, using color-coded handles that surround the corresponding source data. If you click to select the entire chart, selection handles appear around all values listed in the Chart Data Range box. If you click to select a data series in the chart, the handles appear around the source cells and ranges associated with that series. Figure 13-16, for example, shows the result when we select the third and final series in a clustered column chart.

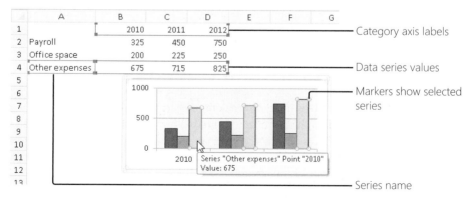

Figure 13-16 The ScreenTip confirms the name of the selected series, and the color-coded selection boxes show the series name and values and category axis labels.

The green box indicates the data series names, the blue box indicates the series values (points to be plotted in the chart), and the purple box identifies category axis labels.

If you use a table as the source data for your chart, adding a new row or column automatically extends the corresponding series in the linked chart. If your data source is a simple range, you have to add new data manually. To do so, enter your data first, including the column or row heading, and then click the chart to expose the color-coded handles. Drag the corner of the range containing the series values so that it includes your new row or column, and then drag the series name or category axis label, as needed, to include the newly added cell.

If you find it easier to use the Clipboard, you can add a new row or column to your data source (or select an existing range that isn't currently part of the chart), copy it to the Clipboard, and then click to select the chart and paste the Clipboard contents. Be sure to include the cell that includes the series name or category axis label, if appropriate.

You can also use the sizing handles to reduce the number of series or data points. For example, if you have a column chart that includes 12 months' worth of results but you want to show only the last three months, drag the corresponding selections in the data source to make them smaller, using just the data you want to include.

INSIDE OUT   No more data limits

Previous versions of Excel imposed strict limits on the number of data points you could include per data series and per chart. With Excel 2010, those limits are completely removed. You can now include as many data points as your PC's memory can accommodate. That's good news for scientists and engineers who want to visualize very large sets of data. However, this change doesn't repeal the most fundamental principle of turning information into graphics: KISS (Keep It Simple, Stupid).

Advanced Chart Formatting Options

Most of the work that goes into making a chart look clear and readable involves the fundamentals of formatting—fonts that are big enough to read at the selected sizes, and complementary colors and backgrounds that enhance rather than distract from the chart itself. These options take advantage of tools, techniques, and themes that are common to all Office programs. If you select an individual chart element and then click Format Selection, for example, you'll see a dialog box with tabs that are appropriate for that element. The selection might include fill, line, and border colors and shadows and glows, in addition to options that are appropriate to the current selection.

Each chart type has a different set of options for handling series and elements that are unique to that chart type. For example, you can use the options on the Marker Line Style tab for a line chart with data markers for extremely fine control over the appearance of those lines.

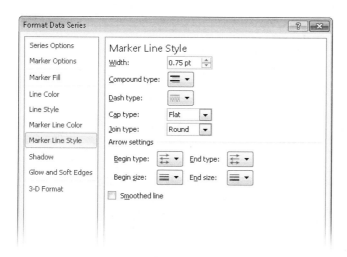

To fine-tune the arrangement of points in an individual data series, use the Series Options page in the Format Data Series dialog box. The specific options vary by chart type. In line and area charts, for example, you can plot individual series on a secondary axis—in that configuration the primary vertical axis remains on the left and a second set of numbers appears on the right. This allows you to plot two data series on the same chart and show the relationship between them even when the scale is dramatically different for each one. With bar and column charts, you can set the overlap between series (columns) and the gap between groups. Figure 13-17 shows the options for a clustered column chart. We changed the default Series Overlap setting from 0% (each column butts up directly against the one next to it) to –10%, which leaves a slight gap between columns in each cluster. We also reduced the default gap between clusters so that it's exactly equal to the width of one column.

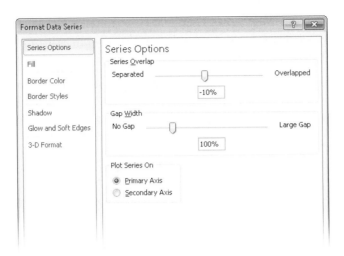

Figure 13-17 The Series Options tab allows you to position chart elements for maximum readability. Options vary by chart type.

Highlighting Trends and Variations in Data

Tables filled with data can be a river of black and white. Charts sometimes lack nuance. Are there intermediate ways to spot patterns and identify anomalies while still maintaining a full view of the data in a table? Indeed there are.

You can help your audience (and yourself) make more sense of data by using conditional formatting to highlight values that meet criteria you define. You can also add minigraphs called *sparklines* to a table to highlight trends within a row or column. In this section, we explain how to take advantage of both of these features.

Using Conditional Formatting to Highlight Cells Based on Their Content

The idea behind conditional formatting is simple: You want a table or a range of data to be able to tell you instantly whether there are any values that demand your immediate attention, or whether there are any patterns that might not be apparent from the raw data. You start by selecting a range of data—an entire table, a column or row containing grand totals, or a subset of data representing groups whose performance you want to examine more closely. Then you define conditions for Excel to test against the values in those cells. Is a particular value greater than or less than a specific amount? Is it in the top (or bottom) of all values in the range? Does it contain a specific word or string of text or fall within a range of dates?

Based on the results of those tests, Excel applies special formatting (typically colors and borders) to each cell that satisfies a particular condition. You can combine multiple rules in the same selection, highlighting values in the top 20 percent in bold green text on a light green background, with values in the bottom 20 percent displayed in bold red italics on a light red background, as shown in Figure 13-18.

	B	C	E	F	G
1	Company	North	Southwest	Midwest	Northwest
2	A. Datum Corporation	199	391	223	*126*
3	Adventure Works	177	407	*159*	459
4	Contoso, Ltd	163	187	198	284
5	Consolidated Messenger	*116*	380	*139*	459
6	Fabrikam, Inc.	*88*	179	250	364
7	Litware, Inc.	199	289	234	305
8	Lucerne Publishing	204	358	174	*89*
9	Northwind Traders	*130*	323	293	256
10	Proseware, Inc.	213	209	*161*	387
11	Southridge Video	207	221	235	428
12	Tailspin Toys	*122*	236	172	393
13	Trey Research	205	*161*	257	253
14	Wide World Importers	*138*	213	460	444
15	Wingtip Toys	193	177	*131*	217

Figure 13-18 The bold italic values here use dark red on a light red background, while bold values are highlighted in green. These two rules make it easier to spot high and low values.

You can apply color scales to an entire range using a gradient of two or three colors—moving from red to yellow to green as the values in the selection go from low to high. You can also add small data bars to a range to visually depict the values in each cell, as shown here.

	B	C	E	F	G
1	Company	North	Southwest	Midwest	Northwest
2	A. Datum Corporation	199	391	223	126
3	Adventure Works	177	407	159	459
4	Contoso, Ltd	163	187	198	284
5	Consolidated Messenger	116	380	139	459
6	Fabrikam, Inc.	88	179	250	364
7	Litware, Inc.	199	289	234	305
8	Lucerne Publishing	204	358	174	89
9	Northwind Traders	130	323	293	256
10	Proseware, Inc.	213	209	161	387
11	Southridge Video	207	221	235	428
12	Tailspin Toys	122	236	172	393
13	Trey Research	205	161	257	253
14	Wide World Importers	138	213	460	444
15	Wingtip Toys	193	177	131	217

To get started, select a range of data and then click Conditional Formatting in the Styles group on the Home tab. That displays the Conditional Formatting menu:

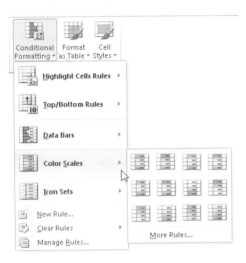

Each of the five main choices on this menu provides access to a range of preset rules. The More Rules option at the bottom of each of the submenus allows you to create custom choices that vary from the preset configurations. The following list describes what you'll find in each of the five main choices:

- **Highlight Cells Rules**   Each of the seven preset options opens a dialog box that lets you construct a formula using a comparison operator (greater than, less than, equal to, and so on) along with a value or cell reference to compare with each cell's contents. Excel fills in values using its internal algorithms; you can change those values or point to a cell reference. The box on the right allows you to choose the formatting to be applied to cells matching your specified conditions.

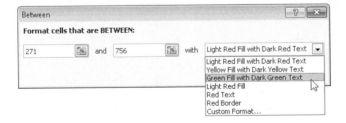

- **Top/Bottom Rules**   The input dialog box that opens when you select any of the choices on this menu also allows you to create a rule on the fly. Don't be misled by the number 10 in the Top 10% and similar options. You can change that value or percentage to a different number if you prefer.

- **Data Bars**   This option adds a small bar (a longer bar equals a higher value) to each selected data cell, using one of a half-dozen solid or gradient options. These bars show up as a live preview in the selected data so you can see the effect before you make it final. Note the ScreenTip, which explains, tersely, what the thumbnail represents.

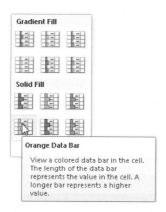

- **Color Scales**   This option applies colored cell backgrounds to the selected range by using two or three colors in a range that is defined by the data itself. The Green-Yellow-Red option, for example, uses green for the lowest values, red for the highest, and yellow for everything in between. The actual number of shades used is much more than two or three, with darker shades representing the extremes of higher and lower values.

- **Icon Sets**   This is the most visually diverse (and potentially cringe-inducing) of all the preset conditional formatting options. You can choose from arrows, circles and other shapes, flags, and rating scales made up of stars and clocks and bars, like the ones shown here.

If none of the preset options match your needs, you can create custom rules from scratch. In some cases, you might start with a preset rule and then, after applying it to the selection, modify the rule. If you click More Rules at the bottom of any of the Conditional Formatting menu options, you get the New Formatting Rule dialog box. If you've already defined rules and want to adjust them, click Conditional Formatting (in the Styles group on the Home tab) and then click Manage Rules. That opens the Conditional Formatting Rules Manager dialog box, shown in Figure 13-19.

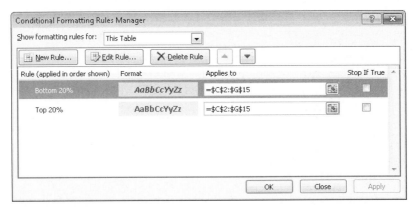

Figure 13-19 You can expand or restrict the display of rules here by using the drop-down list at the top of the dialog box.

To edit an existing rule, select its entry in the Conditional Formatting Rules Manager dialog box and click Edit Rule. The exact options you see here vary, depending on the type of rule you originally created. In the example shown here, we tweaked an Icon Set rule so that it hides the underlying value and shows only the icon. We also adjusted the rules for each icon from their default percentages to a purely numeric scheme.

TROUBLESHOOTING

Conditional formats don't behave as expected.

If the formats you see in a table aren't displayed as you expected, you should check several possible causes. If you experimented with multiple rules, it's possible that you left an old set of rules in place and added a new, conflicting rule that applies to the same data. To check for this possibility, open the Conditional Formatting Rules Manager dialog box and choose This Worksheet from the Show Formatting Rules For list. If you see an old, unnecessary rule, select it and click Delete Rule. It's also possible you have a conflict between multiple rules, with the rule at the top of the list applying one set of formatting that is then overruled by a later rule. If you want the first rule to take primacy, select the Stop If True check box after that rule. Finally, check the numbers used as triggers within each rule. Excel applies some default settings when you create the rule. If your data has changed since then, you might need to tweak the rules accordingly.

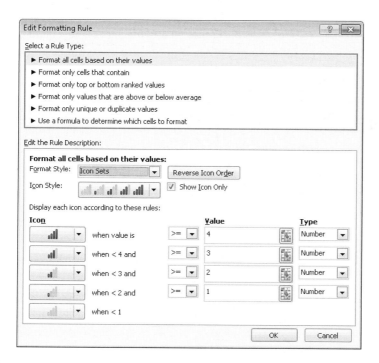

If you experiment a little too much with conditional formatting rules and want to get a fresh start, click Clear Rules from the Conditional Formatting menu. You can erase the rules from a selection, an entire sheet, a table, or a PivotTable.

Using Sparklines to Visualize Trends Within a Range

If you think of sparklines as tiny charts that fit in a single cell, you won't be too far from the truth. This feature, new in Excel 2010, enables you to visualize a data series in a single cell. This example shows quarterly results over a period of several years, with a sparkline at the end of each row that shows the up and down gyrations over each year.

Year	Qtr1	Qtr2	Qtr3	Qtr4	Trend
1990	2,834	2,957	3,024	2,663	
1991	3,018	3,057	3,069	3,205	
1992	3,318	3,435	3,415	3,365	
1993	3,497	3,582	3,682	3,819	
1994	4,003	3,840	3,973	3,958	
1995	4,214	4,614	4,839	5,267	
1996	5,756	5,833	5,952	6,624	

Sparklines come in three varieties: line and column correspond to their full-size brethren, while win/loss shows an up or down marker depending on whether the associated data is positive (win) or negative (loss).

To add a sparkline in a single cell, select the cell and then click Line, Column, or Win/Loss from the Sparklines group on the Insert tab. You can also insert multiple sparklines by selecting a range in a column or row and then defining the corresponding data area in the Create Sparklines dialog box.

To change an existing sparkline, use the Design tab under the Sparkline Tools heading (it's only visible when you select one or more cells containing a sparkline). Figure 13-20 shows the commands available on this tab.

Figure 13-20 As with a full-size chart, you can use commands on this specialized tab to change the style of a sparkline, add data markers, and edit the source data.

Most of the options on the Design tab are self-explanatory. One that deserves special attention is the Axis command, which allows you to customize how each axis in the mini-chart is treated. Normally, each sparkline is treated as an independent series, with values charted using only the data in its source data range. If you want Excel to chart multiple sparklines using the same range of values, click Axis, and then change the selections under Vertical Axis Minimum Value Options and Vertical Axis Maximum Value Options to Same For All Sparklines.

N this chapter, we look at Excel's more advanced features, including a few tricks that make managing large, complicated workbooks easier. We explain how to hide rows and columns, arrange worksheet tabs and windows, and split worksheets into multiple panes so you can scroll without losing your place.

For formatting fanatics, we offer a collection of expert techniques to help you save and reuse custom number formats, cell styles, and workbook themes. If you're trying to extract the useful parts of big blobs of imported text, you'll appreciate our instructions on how to transform and manipulate text with the help of the Clipboard and some arcane but extremely useful functions. We also show you how to prevent data-entry errors.

Finally, we examine some of our favorite Excel tweaks, including how to replace the default workbook template and how to automatically enter custom lists into a worksheet.

Customizing the Worksheet View

During the design and construction stages of any workbook, you probably want ready access to all of Excel's tools. But after construction is complete and you no longer need those tools, it's sometimes useful to hide them so you have more room to view charts, tables, and other worksheet contents. On the View tab, in the Show group, you'll find check boxes that allow you to temporarily remove any (or all) of four prominent features from the Excel interface:

Clear the Gridlines option to remove the lines that define the edges of rows and columns and thus separate cells from each other. Clear the Headings check box to remove the labels above columns and to the left of rows. These two settings are saved on a per-worksheet basis. Clear the Formula Bar check box to hide the formula bar, the Insert Function button, and the Name box. The latter setting is saved with the current workbook and affects all worksheets. The Ruler check box is available only in specialized views, as we explain in the Troubleshooting note later in this section.

You'll find a few extra settings in the Excel Options dialog box. Click the File tab, click Options, and then click the Advanced tab. Scroll down to the Display section, where you'll find the two groups shown here.

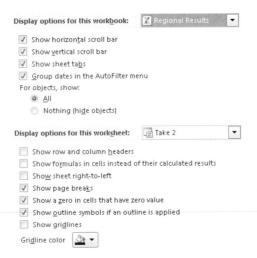

If you're obsessed with the idea of a clutter-free screen, you can clear the first three check boxes in the top group to hide the scroll bars and sheet tabs for the current worksheet. If you also double-click the current tab to hide the ribbon and leave only the tab names, you can create a view that will satisfy even the most diehard minimalist.

TROUBLESHOOTING

Excel won't allow you to remove the ruler

For most worksheet views, the Ruler check box (in the Show group on the View tab) is selected, and the option to remove the check mark is dimmed and unavailable. What's the problem? Check your view. The ruler isn't needed in Normal view, and thus it's not available to hide. It's only visible in Page Layout and Page Break Preview modes, where it's shown by default. Switch to either of those views to clear the Ruler check box.

The commands in the Zoom group on the View tab allow you to change the on-screen size of the worksheet contents. Click Zoom to open a dialog box where you can choose from five predefined magnification levels or enter a custom value. At zoom levels of 39 percent or less, gridlines are automatically hidden.

INSIDE OUT Choose the right Zoom tools for maximum flexibility

Although you can open the Zoom dialog box and pick a magnification level, we recommend using the Zoom slider, on the status bar in the lower right corner of the program window, instead. Drag the slider left or right to make the window magnification larger or smaller in 6 percent increments (these steps are much finer when you move below 100%). Each click of the plus or minus button on either side of the slider increases the window magnification to the next multiple of 10 and then increases in 10 percent increments. To zoom up and down in 15 percent increments, hold down the Ctrl key as you roll the mouse wheel.

For any worksheet, the zoom scale ranges from a low of 10 percent (a bird's-eye view) to a high of 400 percent (an extreme close-up). By contrast, the Zoom dialog box offers only a single larger-than-normal setting (200%) and three evenly spaced smaller levels (25, 50, and 75 percent). Double-click the current Zoom percentage (to the left of the slider) to open the Zoom dialog box. The fastest way to return to normal magnification at any time is to click the 100% command in the Show group on the View tab.

The Zoom To Selection option lets you change the worksheet's magnification so that it shows the entire contents of the current selection, increasing or decreasing the width and height of the worksheet window as needed. This setting is saved as a custom magnification level; it applies to the current worksheet only and is not dynamic. If you change the size of the worksheet window or hide user interface elements, the magnification level remains the same percentage; after you make this type of change, you can resize the window manually by clicking the Zoom To Selection command again.

Hiding Rows and Columns

Some worksheet data is required for calculations but isn't necessary for display purposes and might even be distracting in its raw form. For those occasions, you can hide one or more rows or columns. Click any cell within the row or column you want to hide (or click the heading to select the entire row or column). Then, in the Cells group on the Home tab, click Format, click Hide & Unhide, and then click Hide Rows or Hide Columns. As an alternative, you can right-click any heading and click Hide. You can also hide a column by dragging the right edge of the column heading to the left until its width is 0; to hide a row, drag the bottom edge of the row heading up until it disappears.

To make a hidden column or row visible, select cells on either side of the hidden column or above and below the hidden row, click Format on the Home tab, click Hide & Unhide, and then click Unhide Columns or Unhide Rows, as needed. If you want to unhide a single row or column without disturbing its hidden neighbors, click in the Name box, enter a cell address located in the hidden row or column, press Enter, and then use the Unhide Rows or Unhide Columns option from the Hide & Unhide menu. This technique is especially useful when the first row or column is hidden: type A1 in the Name box to jump to that location and unhide it.

Arranging Worksheet Windows

When you're creating a new worksheet, there's a good chance that you'll want to reuse data from another worksheet, in the same workbook or in a different workbook file. The tedious way is to click back and forth between the two maximized windows, copying, switching windows, pasting, and repeating those steps until everything's just right. The faster way—assuming your PC display is big enough—is to arrange the windows next to each other. You can then navigate through each one independently, comparing similar sections and editing or copying data to your heart's content.

Excel's tools for managing worksheet windows are slightly different from those in Word and PowerPoint. The most noteworthy difference is that individual workbook files can be displayed side by side in a single Excel program window, sharing the ribbon, Quick Access Toolbar, status bar, and other common interface elements.

All the controls you need are located on the View tab, in the Window group, as shown here:

If you have two or more workbooks open already and you want to rearrange them in the current Excel program window, click Arrange All. That opens the dialog box shown here, which gives you four options (plus a check box we'll discuss shortly):

INSIDE OUT   Open a workbook in a separate process? Not so fast . . .

When you create a new workbook or open a previously saved workbook in Excel, the new workbook file runs in the same Excel.exe process as the one you started with. That makes it possible for you to arrange separate workbooks within the same program window. If you're running Windows 7, you can open a new instance of Excel in a separate process by holding down the Shift key as you click the Excel icon on the taskbar. That opens a new, blank workbook. It looks just like the other workbooks you've already opened, and you can switch to it with Alt+Tab or by pointing to the Excel taskbar button and clicking its preview. But if you look on the Processes tab in Task Manager, you'll see a second instance of Excel.exe. And if you click Switch Windows (on the View tab) in the workbook you just opened, you'll see that the newly created process doesn't see any of your existing workbook windows. If you like to arrange windows for easier working, that alone is reason to avoid this technique.

The Tiled option arranges workbooks most efficiently, with the currently selected workbook on the left and additional workbooks stacked up in a checkerboard pattern. If you have three (or more) open workbooks to arrange, this is your best choice. The Horizontal and Vertical options arrange all open workbooks from top to bottom or side by side, respectively. Confusingly, the View Side By Side button in the Window group arranges two worksheet windows one over the other (not side by side). If you have three or more workbooks open, you're prompted to choose which one you want to compare with the current workbook.

What if you want to see two tabs from the same worksheet side by side? Start by clicking the workbook you want to see in a second window, and then click New Window on the View tab. That opens a second view of the current workbook and worksheet, appending a colon and a number to each window. (Each window contains the same file. Any changes you make in either window are reflected immediately in the other window.) If you use the Arrange All button, each instance is treated like any other open workbook. To ignore all other workbooks and just arrange multiple copies of the current window, click Arrange All, select Windows Of Active Workbook, and then click OK.

INSIDE OUT Find worksheet tabs without scrolling

If you create a workbook with a large number of worksheets, you have to scroll one tab at a time to see each sheet name. This technique is especially tedious if you used the Tiled or Vertical options to arrange windows and thereby cut your worksheet to half (or less) of its normal width. The secret solution? Right-click any of the four scroll buttons to the left of the sheet tabs to display a menu containing the names of all worksheets in the current workbook. Click any name to jump straight to that worksheet.

Splitting, Freezing, and Locking Panes

You don't need to open a second window to compare two different parts of the same document. Instead, you can split the screen—vertically, horizontally, or both. Each split screen region scrolls independently, allowing you to compare a block of data in rows 2 through 5 with the contents of rows 2002 through 2005.

To split the current worksheet, use either of the two split boxes. One is located at the top of the vertical scroll bar, the other at the right of the horizontal scroll bar. Click either split box, and drag the two-headed split pointer toward the center of the worksheet, as shown in Figure 14-1.

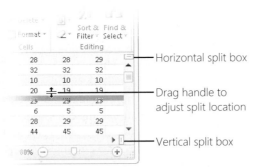

Figure 14-1 When you drag the split pointer, it automatically snaps to the nearest row or column border. Release the mouse button to position the split bar at the current location.

Once the split bar is in place, you can scroll each pane independently and edit cell contents or formatting in either location. Click and drag the split bar to change its location. Double-click the split bar to remove it and return to a normal, single-pane worksheet window.

In some worksheet designs, you might want to lock specific rows or columns into position so that they are always visible as you scroll through the data in the worksheet. This configuration is especially useful when your data range is taller or wider than the visible poriton of the screen and you want to keep labels visible as you move through the worksheet. In this example, we froze Columns A and B into position. As we scroll to the right, the intervening columns disappear temporarily (see how the column headings jump from B to Q?), but the row labels remain visible so we don't lose our place.

Freezing panes properly takes a little bit of practice and a trip to the Freeze Panes menu on the View tab. If your labels are in the top row or first column only, the procedure is simple: click Freeze Panes and then click either Freeze Top Row or Freeze First Column. The new configuration takes effect immediately regardless of which cell is currently selected.

To freeze multiple rows and/or columns, you must first select the cell that is immediately below and to the right of the rows and columns you want to freeze. Pick a cell in the first row if you want to freeze only columns, or pick a cell in the first column if you want to freeze only rows. To freeze columns A and B as we did, click to select cell C1 and then click Freeze Panes. To freeze column A and rows 1 and 2, select cell B3 first.

To restore normal worksheet scrolling, click the Freeze Panes menu again and choose the first option, Unfreeze Panes.

Chapter 14

Advanced Worksheet Formatting

A few chapters back, we went through the most useful of Excel's formatting options (for a refresher, see "Formatting Cells and Ranges" on page 376). In this section, we dig into some lesser-known but useful formatting tools and techniques. You're most likely to find them in one of two places: on the Home tab or in the Format Cells dialog box. (It's worth mentioning again that you can summon this dialog box with the keyboard shortcut Ctrl+1, which every Excel user should memorize.)

On the Home tab, the Borders button is almost lost (and perhaps just a little out of place) among the more familiar options in the Fonts group. Click it to open the menu shown in Figure 14-2.

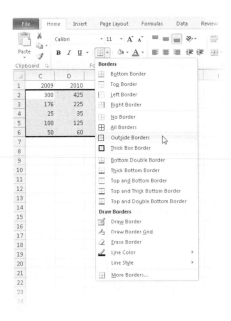

Figure 14-2 You can apply the simplest borders using the choices on the Borders menu. For more intricate projects, try drawing the borders instead.

Whatever option you click on the Borders menu applies to the current selection. Click All Borders, for example, to add black gridlines around and between all cells. This effect works best on small ranges. The Top And Double Bottom Border option is traditionally used to set off the Grand Totals row on a financial worksheet. Click No Border to remove all borders from the current range.

If you want to vary the thickness or color of the borders, use the options under Draw Borders to point and click your way through the process. The Line Color menu lets you choose colors from the current theme (the best choice, as we explain later in this section), and the Line Style menu gives you a dozen border styles, including dots, dashes, thin lines, and thick lines. The More Borders option at the bottom of the menu opens the Border tab in the Format Cells dialog box, which adds one extra line weight and the option to add diagonal lines through a cell.

The Alignment group on the Home tab contains another, equally well-hidden button that contains the orientation options shown here.

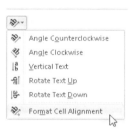

That last option leads to the Alignment tab of the Format Cells dialog box, which offers finer-grain control at angles besides 45 and 90 degrees.

Creating Custom Cell Formats

In our earlier discussion of the built-in categories on the Number tab of the Format Cells dialog box, we left out the very last one: Custom. If none of the ready-made date, decimal, or number formats are exactly what you need for a particular range, you can create a custom format here. You can specify how positive and negative numbers are formatted, create your own date and time formats, and control the number of decimal places and significant digits that appear for each value.

INSIDE OUT   Reuse custom number formats

Excel saves custom number formats on a per-workbook basis, which allows you to use them on any worksheet in that workbook. To copy a custom number format to another workbook by using the Clipboard, first select a cell containing the custom format in the current worksheet and copy it to the Clipboard; then, in the new workbook, click Paste, Paste Special on the Home tab (or press Ctrl+Alt+V) and choose Formats. To make a custom number format available for all workbooks you create, add it to the default workbook template. (See "Changing Default Formatting for a New Workbook" on page 478.)

You needn't start with a blank slate when creating custom formats. Select the Custom category to display a long list of ready-made formats, including some you won't find in other categories. In general, it's easier to start with a format that's close to the one you want than to start from scratch. The Type box includes the codes for the format you previously chose in one of the other categories. In Figure 14-3, for example, we started in the Currency category, changed the currency symbol to the U.K. pound, and then flipped to the Custom tab to review and edit the code for that format.

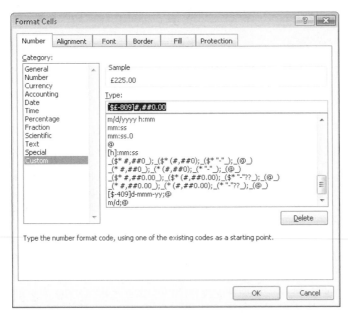

Figure 14-3 Edit the contents of the Type box to add a new custom format. The list below it contains all available custom formats. Note the Sample box, which previews the custom format.

Custom formats use codes that define how to display digits, decimal places, dates, times, and currency symbols.

Each custom format can include up to four groups of these codes, separated by semicolons. The four groups define, in order, the display formats for positive numbers, negative numbers, zero values, and text. If you enter only one section, that format applies to all numbers you enter. If you enter two sections, the first set of codes applies to positive numbers and zero values and the second to negative numbers. If you want to skip a format option (specifying formats only for positive numbers and zero values, for example), insert a semicolon for each skipped section.

To specify a color for any section, enclose the name of one of the following eight permitted colors in brackets: black, green, white, blue, magenta, yellow, cyan, red. The color must be the first format code in the section. Thus, [Blue]#,##0;[Red]#,##0;[Black]0 displays positive values as blue, negative values as red, and zero values as black.

The remaining codes available for custom formats divide neatly into four categories.

Number Format Codes

0 Digit placeholder. Displays zero if the number has fewer digits than placeholders. The format 0.00 displays 2.30 if you enter 2.3. For numbers that are less than 1, it includes a 0 to the left of the decimal point.

Significant digit placeholder. Using the format #.## displays all significant (nonzero) digits to the left of the decimal point and rounds to two digits on the right of the decimal point. Thus, if you enter 0.42, this format displays .42 in the cell, with nothing to the left of the decimal point.

? Align decimals. This digit placeholder works like the # placeholder but aligns decimal points.

Two punctuation marks are useful in custom number formats. Use a period (.) to indicate the position of the decimal point. The comma (,) has two roles. Used with placeholders on either side, it displays the thousands separator: #,###. Adding one or more commas after a custom format scales the number by 1,000 for each comma; to round large numbers (like 42,420,000) by a factor of 1 million, enter this format:

#0.0,," million"

As we explain a bit later, the text in quotation marks appears alongside the result. Thus, this format displays *42.4 million* in the cell, but the value is still stored as a number for calculation.

Date/Time Format Codes

A custom date or time format allows you to create special date formats that aren't included in any of Excel's ready-made selections. You can combine years, months, and days in any order and keep track of elapsed time as well for recording timesheets in Excel format.

d, dd, m, mm Day or month in numeric format. The two-digit varieties add leading zeroes (mm/dd/yy looks like 05/01/11).

ddd, mmm, dddd, mmmm Day or month in text format. Use ddd or mmm for abbreviations such as Mon or Sep; use dddd and mmmm for the fully spelled out day of the week or month.

Chapter 14

mmmmm Displays the first letter of the month. Most useful in chart axes where you can easily differentiate between January, June, and July, or between March and May, by position.

yy, yyyy Year, in two-digit or four-digit format

h, hh, m, mm, s, ss Hours, minutes, or seconds. Use a two-digit format to add a leading zero when necessary. To display time with extra precision, add a decimal point and extra digits: h:mm:ss.00.

[h], [m], [s] Show elapsed time (rather than time of day) in hours, minutes, or seconds. Use this type of format when you're performing calculations using times. On a worksheet where you enter start and finish times for a worker's shift, this format allows you to show the total time for payroll calculations.

A/P, AM/PM Show the AM/PM indicator. If you omit this code, Excel uses 24-hour time format: 18:15 instead of 6:15 PM.

Text Format Codes

To display text in a cell that contains numbers, Excel includes a selection of special format codes. Use this type of format to add a word or phrase, such as *YTD* to indicate year-to-date totals or *shortage* after a negative number. You must enclose the text in quotation marks. The format changes the displayed results but does not alter the contents of the cell. As a result, formulas that reference that cell continue to work.

Remember to add a space inside the quotation marks to separate the text from the numeric value, as in this example:

$0.00" Profit";[Red] $0.00" Loss"

A positive value appears in the default text color, like so: *$150.00 Profit*. Negative values appear in red, with the word *Loss* appended.

You can add the space character, a plus or minus sign, an apostrophe, open and close parentheses, and any of the following special characters without enclosing them in double quotation marks:

$ / : ^ ! & ~ { } = < >

In addition, you can use any currency sign, including $. To enter alternative symbols, use the Symbol command on the Insert tab, or hold down the Alt key in combination with numeric codes from the numeric keypad: ¢ (Alt+0162), £ (Alt+0163), € (Alt+0128), and ¥ (Alt+0165), for example.

A handful of additional formatting codes apply special treatment to text. Use an asterisk (*) followed by a character to fill the cell with that character. Use *- in the third position of a custom format to replace zero values with a line of hyphens, for example.

The underscore (_) followed by a character adds a space the width of that character. Several built-in formats use this code with open and close parentheses to ensure that positive and negative values line up properly.

Use a backslash (\) to display the character that immediately follows the backslash.

The at sign (@) is used only in the fourth (text) section in a custom format and controls the formatting of any text you enter. If you include a text section without the @ character, Excel hides any text in the cell.

Conditions

You can also use conditions as part of custom number formats. Conditions use comparison operators and are contained in brackets as part of a format definition. To see an example, click the Special category, click the Phone Number format, and then click Custom to display the following code:

[<=9999999]###-####;(###) ###-####

If you enter a number of seven or fewer digits in a cell that uses this format, Excel treats it as a local phone number and adds a hyphen where the prefix appears. If you enter a number with eight or more digits, the final seven digits are formatted as a local phone number, and everything preceding that value is enclosed in parentheses.

Creating Custom Cell Styles

If you regularly apply special formatting to cells and ranges, you can avoid the need to repeat the formatting steps by creating a custom cell style. Excel includes a categorized selection of cell styles as part of a default installation, which you can view by clicking Cell Styles on the Home tab to display the Cell Styles gallery. Any custom styles you create appear in a new group at the top of the list, as shown next.

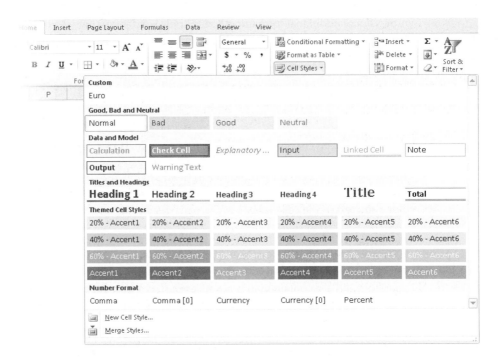

A custom style can include any or all of six formats. In the example shown here, we created a simple cell format that applies the Currency format using the Euro symbol to the active cell or range. It also changes any existing font formatting to use the Body style as set by the current theme. Because we cleared the other check boxes before saving the style, other existing formatting—including alignment, borders, and fill colors—is unchanged.

Finding, Editing, Moving, and Copying Data

Much of the work of building a workbook involves moving data between cells, ranges, and worksheets. For everyday cutting, copying, and pasting, the Clipboard is more than sufficient, especially when you discover some of the lesser-known options in the Paste Special menu and the Find And Replace dialog box.

For an overview of common cut, copy, and paste techniques, see "Using the Clipboard with Office Programs" on page 129. For a discussion of common search and replace tools, see "Finding and Replacing Text and Formatting" on page 136.

INSIDE OUT   Quickly copy the cell above

To copy the contents of the cell above the active cell, press Ctrl+' (single quote). If the cell from which you're copying contains a formula, this shortcut copies that formula. To copy the value from the cell above, press Ctrl+Shift+" (double quote). If the cell above contains a formula, the copy in the active cell consists of the text or value that is the result of that formula.

Knowing a few keyboard shortcuts can save you some time. Ctrl+F (or Shift+F5) opens the Find And Replace dialog box with the Find tab selected. Ctrl+H displays the same dialog box with the Replace tab selected instead. You can close the Find And Replace dialog box and repeat the last Find by pressing Shift+F4. That obscure shortcut is worth memorizing if you regularly search through long tables where the search results might return hundreds of rows.

To learn about an expert tool that lets you find and select in ways that aren't possible with the Find And Replace dialog box, see "Navigating with the Go To Dialog Box" on page 481.

Using the Clipboard to Transform Data

You can use the Paste Special dialog box in Excel, shown next, to perform some interesting and useful on-the-fly transformations. Under the Paste heading, for example, you'll find a Values And Number Formats option that allows you to paste the results of a range full of formulas into a new location.

The choices under the Operation category offer some interesting ways to perform mathematical operations on a cell or range using the contents of the Clipboard. Let's say you have a worksheet containing a year's worth of daily temperature data. You discover that for a two-week period in June, the thermometer was off, giving results 3 degrees lower than they should have been.

The fix? In a blank cell, enter the number you want to use as a constant—in this case, 3. Select that cell and press Ctrl+C to copy its contents to the Clipboard. Now select the cells in the 14 rows containing the incorrect temperature data, click the arrow under Paste, and click Paste Special. Click Add and then click OK. The content on the Clipboard (3) is added to the contents of all cells in the current selection.

You can use this same technique to apply an across-the-board 5 percent price hike to a list of prices. Enter 1.05 in a blank cell and copy it to the Clipboard. Then select all the prices to be adjusted and use the Multiply option in the Paste Special dialog box.

The last check box, Transpose, is our favorite. Want to convert all your rows to columns or vice versa? Select a range and use this option, with or without any of the choices above it.

Pasting Text and Formats into Multiple Worksheets

Entering data into multiple worksheets simultaneously is a useful trick when you're building a complex workbook. If you have many individual worksheets that share a common structure, you can enter text and format those common ranges without a lot of repetitive work.

You can select multiple worksheets one at a time by Ctrl+clicking each sheet tab, or use Shift+click to select a contiguous group of tabs.

If more than one sheet is selected, the bracketed text [Group] appears after the file name in the title bar. Any text you enter in the current cell appears in all matching cells on grouped worksheets. Any formatting you apply to the active sheet, including column widths and cell formats, is also applied to the same location in each grouped worksheet. Obviously, you wouldn't use this technique to enter data, but it's ideal for copying row labels and column headings.

Neither Paste nor Paste Special works with grouped worksheets. When you paste, the Clipboard contents appear only in the active sheet. But you can do the job with one extra step. Copy the Clipboard contents to the current sheet, and then select the cell or range you just copied. Now click Fill (in the Editing group on the Home tab), and then click Across Worksheets. Although you don't have all the Paste Special options, the Fill Across Worksheets dialog box, shown here, gives you the choice of pasting contents, formats, or both.

Manipulating Text with Functions

Data can come from the strangest of places, and it sometimes lands in your worksheet as long strings of text instead of neatly divided chunks of data. In many cases, you can parse the data at the same time you add it to your worksheet. (We describe these techniques in more detail in "Importing, Exporting, and Connecting to Data Sources" on page 415.)

In this section, we introduce you to some functions specifically designed to help you break text strings into smaller pieces and assemble pieces of text into bigger ones.

For a refresher course on this category of functions, see "Text Functions" on page 370.

You can combine text using no functions at all with the & operator. If column A is filled with first names and column B with matching last names, you can use the formula =A1&" "&A2 (note the space inside the quotation marks) to combine each pair into a full name in column C, with first and last name separated by a space. You can also use the CONCATENATE function, which combines two or more pieces of text into a single text string. The arguments for this function are separated by commas and can contain literal text (enclosed in quotation marks), cell references, and CHAR functions such as CHAR(10), which inserts a line break at the current location. (The single argument for the CHAR function is an ASCII code, which specifies the character to be inserted by the function; in this case, 10 is the ASCII code for a carriage return character.)

If you have a column of data that is arranged in a predictable fashion, you can extract data from it by using any of the following three functions:

=LEFT(text,num_chars) grabs a specific number of characters from the left side of a text value. If cell A1 contains the string LMSA10042, the formula =LEFT(A1,3) returns LMS. The RIGHT function has a similar syntax, taking characters from the end of the specified text. Use the MID function to return a specific number of characters starting from a specific position. In the previous example, =MID(A1,3,4) takes four characters, starting from the third character in the string: SA10.

In some cases you have to combine multiple functions to accomplish a goal. Here's how you can find the location of a specific string in a cell and then extract all or part of that string. For this example, we want to search for the string "SA10". We can use either of two functions. FIND and SEARCH perform similar jobs, with one difference: FIND is case-sensitive and SEARCH is not. To search for the position in a string of text where SA10 begins, use =SEARCH("SA10",A1). The result is 3 in our example. Now combine that with the MID function and you can extract 6 characters from the point where that string begins:

=MID(A1, SEARCH("SA10",A1),6)

The LEN function returns the length of a text string. In our previous example, we can use =LEN(A1) to determine the length of the text in cell A1, which is 9 characters.

Printing a Worksheet

Most Excel workbooks are designed to be viewed, edited, and shared on a screen rather than on printed pages. When you do need to add an Excel chart or table to a report, you'll get best results by copying and pasting it into a Word document, where you have a full range of tools for setting up pages and margins to match the paper size in your printer.

But there are times when you indeed want to print a worksheet (or even an entire workbook) so that you can study it offline or share it with others in a meeting. For those occasions, you need to do some extra work before clicking the Print button to ensure that your free-flowing worksheet doesn't break at awkward locations.

Adjusting Print Settings

The print features in Excel 2010 are radically different from those in earlier versions, thanks to Backstage view. If you upgraded from Excel 2003, you'll also find a new Page Layout view (introduced in Excel 2007) that allows you to edit your workbook in a view that mimics the printed page, complete with headers, footers, and margins. If you're planning to print just part of a worksheet, start by selecting that portion; then click File and click Print to gain access to print settings and a live preview pane, as shown in Figure 14-4.

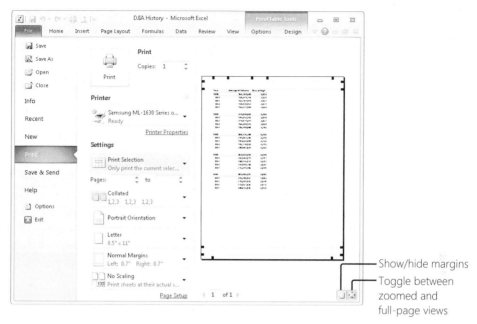

— Show/hide margins

— Toggle between zoomed and full-page views

Figure 14-4 You can handle virtually all print setup options in Backstage view. You can't, however, change headers and footers or adjust page breaks.

INSIDE OUT   Pick the right shortcuts for printing

If you regularly print worksheets, you might want to add a shortcut to the Quick Access Toolbar. Click the arrow to the right of the toolbar, and you'll see two shortcuts available from the Customize Quick Access Toolbar menu. Which should you choose? We don't recommend the Quick Print button. Although the name is tempting, the result might be an unwelcome surprise. Unless you have specifically defined a print area, Quick Print sends the entire current worksheet to the default printer, beginning with cell A1 and extending down and to the right, to the furthest area that contains data or formatting. The better choice is the Print Preview And Print button, which takes you to the Print tab in Backstage view. There, you can double-check all settings, look at the preview to ensure it's laid out the way you want, and click Print when you're ready. Yes, it's one extra click, but it can save you half a ream of wasted paper over time, not to mention avoiding the need to reprint the job the right way. Oh, and regardless of what's on the Quick Access Toolbar, you can always press Ctrl+P to jump straight to the Print tab in Backstage view.

INSIDE OUT
Make a printout fit in a specific number of pages

If you want your printed worksheet to fit in a specific number of pages, Excel can calculate the scaling percentage for you. From the Print tab in Backstage view, click the current scaling option and then click Custom Scaling Options. On the Page tab of the Page Setup dialog box, click Fit To. Pick two numbers if you know exactly how many pages you want to use. (Leave one number blank if you don't want Excel to automatically scale in that dimension.) Click OK to save your settings, check the preview to verify that your worksheet's print settings are correct, and then click Print.

The controls under the Print and Printer headings are pretty self-explanatory. Be sure the right printer is selected, adjust the number of copies to print if you need more than one, and then click the big Print button. The choices under the Settings heading deserve a little more explanation:

- **What to print**   The preset options allow you to print the current selection, print the active sheets (select multiple tabs if you want to print more than one), or print the entire workbook.

- **Collated?**   The default option prints multiple copies in complete sets, one after the other. Choose Uncollated if you want to print all copies of page 1, then all copies of page 2, and so on.

- **Orientation**   Portrait Orientation is the best choice for lists and summary pages that are formatted like a Word document. Annual budgets and other financial reports that tend to be wide, with long row labels and grand total columns or notes, are typically more readable when you switch to Landscape Orientation.

- **Paper size**   The default size is dictated by your country setting; in the U.S., that's Letter (8.5"x11"). You can choose from a fairly long list of preset sizes, including the European A4 standard, or click More Paper Sizes to choose from a potentially longer list.

- **Margins**   The default Normal setting adds 0.75" at the top and bottom and 0.7" on either side, with an extra 0.3 inch for a page footer and header. You can choose from Wide and Narrow options to add or tighten white space around the printed content on the page. If none of those settings are exactly right, click Custom Margins to tweak all four sides, adjust the depth of the Header and Footer areas, and center the content on the page, as shown next.

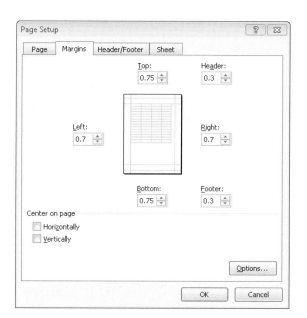

- **Scaling**   Normally, Excel applies no scaling, printing your worksheet at 100 percent of the sizes specified for fonts, graphic objects, row widths, and column heights. You can adjust the scaling to force your printout to fit on a single page, or to shrink the printout so that all rows or columns fit on the page. These options work best for printouts that are just a little bit too large. If you scale the size too small, you'll end up with an economical printout that can only be read with a magnifying glass.

Defining a Print Area

For worksheets that you update and print out regularly, you can define a print area that includes just the portions you want to print. You might choose to exclude the assumptions and data sections of your budget worksheet, for example, and print just the summary sections for handout at your executive briefings.

Start by selecting the print range. If you select a noncontiguous range, be aware that each section prints on a separate page. On the Page Layout tab, in the Page Setup group, click Print Area and then click Set Print Area. Excel creates a named range called Print_Area on the current worksheet. If that all sounds too complicated, you can accomplish the same outcome by making a selection, clicking in the Name box, and then typing Print_Area as the range name. (Don't forget the underscore.)

Each worksheet gets its own Print_Area range. If you select Print Entire Workbook in the Print Settings section in Backstage view, you can preview or print the defined print area on all worksheets in the current workbook.

CAUTION !

When you define a print area, Excel saves its exact location as a named range. If you add rows or columns to the print area later, the named range is *not* updated. You need to clear and then redefine the print area to include the newly created data.

To delete the named Print_Area range on the current sheet and start over, click the Clear Print Area option on the Print Area menu on the Page Layout tab.

Adjusting Page Breaks

When you print a worksheet, Excel automatically (and mechanically) inserts page breaks at the point where each page runs out of printable area. For large, complex worksheets that span multiple pages, you can and should position page breaks by hand. The easiest way to do this is to click the Page Break Preview button (in the Workbook Views group on the View tab). Excel displays dashed blue lines to indicate its automatic page breaks, with oversize page numbers to show the order in which pages will be printed.

In Page Break Preview, dashed lines indicate automatic page breaks inserted by Excel; solid lines represent manual page breaks. To adjust page breaks in this view, point to the thick line between two pages and drag it in any direction. To adjust the print area, drag the solid lines on any edge of the print area; cells that are not in the print area appear gray. Figure 14-5 shows one worksheet after some manual adjustments.

Page Break Preview works best if you start at the top of the worksheet and work in the order it will print—normally from top to bottom and left to right, unless you used the Page Setup dialog box to specify a different order. Move page breaks up or to the left only; moving them down or to the right can cause unpredictable results if you drag past the size of the page as defined by the paper size.

You can also add page breaks manually. Select the cell below and to the right of the cell that you want to print in the lower right corner of a particular page. Click Breaks (in the Page Setup group on the Page Layout tab), and then click Insert Page Break. To add a horizontal page break, select any cell in column A; to add a vertical page break, select any cell in row 1. To remove the page break, select the same cell, go back to the Breaks command, and click Remove Page Break.

To remove all manual page breaks from the current worksheet, click Reset All Page Breaks on the Breaks menu.

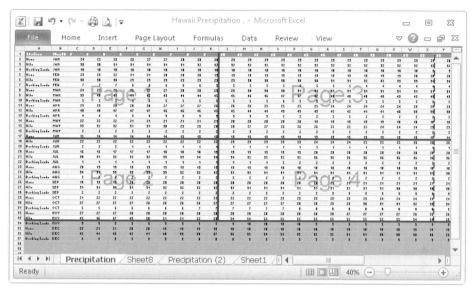

Figure 14-5 The solid lines indicate manual page breaks. The dashed line (on the far right of the worksheet) was set automatically by Excel.

INSIDE OUT   Add extras to your printout

The Page Layout tab includes a wide range of options that allow you to change the margins, orientation, paper size, and other settings that overlap with those on the Print tab in Backstage view. A handful are unique. The most likely options you'll want to change here are potentially confusing. For example, in the Sheet Options section, you'll find View and Print options for Gridlines and Headings, which let you control the on-screen and printed settings separately:

Gridlines For final output, consider hiding gridlines and using borders to set off data areas.

Row and column headings Most of the time you want to hide these portions of the worksheet structure. The exception is when you want to print out your worksheet so you can study its structure. Showing headings allows you to quickly locate cell addresses for editing.

Print Titles This option is in the Page Setup section of the Page Layout tab. If your worksheet data spans multiple pages, specify that you want column and row labels to appear on every page of your printout. Identify the headings using cell addresses in the Rows To Repeat At Top Of Each Page or Columns To Repeat At Left Of Each Page boxes.

Chapter 14

Using Data Validation to Control Data Entry

Some worksheets are designed for repeated use, with specific cells designated for data input and others used for formulas that transform those data points into meaningful results. The danger of such a design, of course, is that you (or someone using a worksheet you designed) might accidentally enter inappropriate data in an input cell. The result can be summed up in four words: "Garbage in, garbage out."

The cure is to assign a data-validation rule to one or more of those input cells so that they accept only the proper type of data or values in a specific range. Using validation rules, you can restrict entries to those that match a list of approved items (budget categories or department names, for example) and even attach a drop-down list from which items are picked. That strategy eliminates the possibility that someone will misspell an entry and inadvertently mess up a report based on that data.

Each data-validation rule is made up of three parts that correspond neatly to the tabs of the Data Validation dialog box. The Settings tab defines the criteria for valid input data; the Input Message tab allows you to create an optional message that provides helpful information when the cell is selected; and the Error Alert tab specifies what a user sees when she tries to enter invalid data.

To get started, first select the cell or range for which you want to restrict data entry, click Data Validation (in the Data Tools group of the Data tab), and define your rule using the options on the Settings tab. Figure 14-6 shows this dialog box after we filled in the validation criteria Excel will use when deciding whether to accept or reject specific input values. Choose a value from the Allow list to restrict data entry to a specific data type and then use additional criteria to define acceptable values.

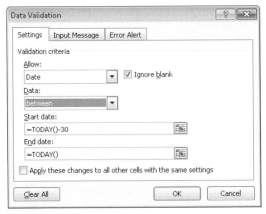

Figure 14-6 The validation criteria defined here use formulas to restrict allowed input to dates that are between the current date and 30 days ago. Any other input will be rejected.

The exact choices available on the Settings tab vary depending on the data type you select from the Allow list. For most data types, you select an operator from the Data list (Between, Less Than Or Equal To, and so on) and then fill in values or formulas that the input data is compared with. In this example, we chose Date as the data type and Between as the operator, adding formulas in the Start Date and End Date boxes that reject any date that is in the future or is more than 30 days earlier than the current date.

The following list summarizes what you can do with each of the options available when you click Allow:

- **Any Value**   Ironically, this default setting does not allow any restrictions on allowed input data. Its purpose is to allow you to display pop-up help text by filling in the boxes on the Input Message tab.

- **Whole Number**   This data type requires numeric input and rejects any value that contains a decimal point, even if the decimal point is followed by a 0.

- **Decimal**   This setting allows any numeric input, with or without a decimal point, provided it meets the other criteria you establish.

- **List**   When you choose this option from the Allow list, any values entered in the input cells must match an item in the list. For a short list, click in the Source box and enter the items directly, separated by commas, as shown here. (Note that list items are case sensitive; if you include *Northwest* as a term, it is allowed only with an initial capital *N*.) Alternatively, you can click the Collapse Dialog button to the right of the Source box and enter the address or name of a range that contains the list of allowed values. If you want users to be able to pick from a list containing these values, select the In-Cell Dropdown check box.

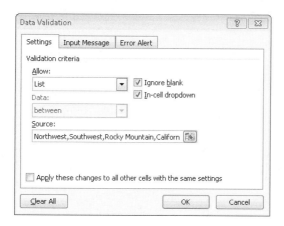

Chapter 14

- **Date**   When this option is selected, Excel will accept input only in a recognizable date format. You must choose an operator and a date or range against which to compare input cells. To allow any date but disallow text or numeric input, choose Greater Than Or Equal To from the Data list and enter 1/1/1900 in the Start Date box.

- **Time**   Your choices here are similar to those provided by the Date option, except that the values entered for Start Time or End Time or both must be in a recognizable time format. If you choose Less Than Or Equal To from the Data list and enter 18:00 in the End Time box, Excel will accept 3:32 PM or 14:32:21 but will reject 8:00 PM.

- **Text Length**   Use this option with comments fields to prevent long-winded entries or to insist on a minimum number of characters.

- **Custom**   When you choose this option, you must enter a formula that returns a logical TRUE or FALSE. This option is most useful when the current input cell is part of a calculation and you want to allow or restrict input based on that calculation. Thus, if you have a formula in cell E5 that sums the values of the four cells above it, you can choose Custom from the Allow list and then enter =E$5 < 100 as the validation criteria for E1 through E4. You can enter any value under 100 in any of those four cells, but if the running total exceeds 100, your input will be rejected.

Use the Input Message tab of the Data Validation dialog box to define a helpful message that appears when you select a cell. The message appears in a pop-up window, with a title in bold and the input message text beneath it. The text you enter here helps prevent confusion by making it clear exactly what type of input is allowed.

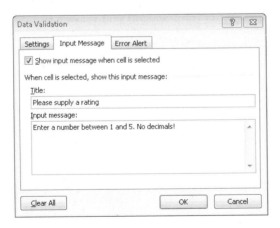

And here's what that input message looks like in a worksheet window.

Finally, use the Error Alert tab to specify what should happen when you (or someone else using a worksheet you created) enters invalid data. You can replace the generic and unhelpful error message with one that offers advice on how to correct the input. If the data type is wrong or the value is outside a permitted range, you can refuse to accept the input at all. For values that are outside the normal range, you can display an error alert that forces you to double-check the value to be sure your finger didn't slip and add an extra zero, converting $40 into $400.

On the Error Alert tab, choose one of three options from the Style box:

- **Stop** produces a dialog box with a red X and Retry/Cancel/Help buttons; the user cannot save the invalid entry.

- **Warning** displays a dialog box that lets you accept the data despite the warning.

- **Information** displays a message but accepts the data as soon as you click OK.

As with the Input Message tab, you need to enter a title and text. In both cases, the Title box accepts up to 32 characters, and the message can be up to 255 characters. Here's an error alert message under construction:

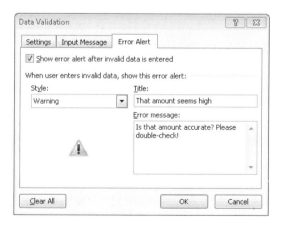

And here's what the Warning dialog box looks like when it's triggered by an attempt to enter an invalid value. Note that the text you enter in the Title box appears in the title bar.

To remove data validation rules, open the Data Validation dialog box, and click Clear All.

TROUBLESHOOTING

Your worksheet contains invalid data

Data-validation rules prevent users from typing invalid data. Unfortunately, users can enter data that fails the validation criteria by pasting it from the Clipboard or by entering a formula whose result is invalid. In addition, data validation rules are not applied retroactively to existing cell contents.

To find cells containing invalid data on the current worksheet, click the arrow to the right of the Data Validation command on the Data tab and click Circle Invalid Data. Excel draws a bright red oval around any value that fails a validation rule. Edit those cells so that they pass validation and then try again. To remove the red ovals, choose Clear Validation Circles from the same menu.

Our Favorite Excel Tweaks and Tips

This section covers a grab bag of interesting tips and techniques that go well beyond the basics but can improve your productivity tremendously.

Changing Default Formatting for a New Workbook

When you create a new workbook without using a template (by starting a new instance of Excel or pressing Ctrl+N, for example), Excel uses the default workbook settings. That defines the number of worksheets, the default font and font size, and so on. To customize these defaults, open the Excel Options dialog box and adjust the options under the When Creating New Workbooks heading on the General tab, as shown next.

When creating new workbooks

Use this font:	Body Font ▾
Font size:	11 ▾
Default view for new sheets:	Normal View ▾
Include this many sheets:	3 ▴▾

The most useful options here are the ability to change the default number of worksheets and the option to change the default font size. In the Use This Font box, you'll see that Excel uses Body Font as the default selection. Although you can choose a specific font, we recommend keeping this setting, which allows you to change fonts on the fly by applying a different theme.

You can also replace the normal workbook template with a custom design that includes graphics, title pages, and other elements (including cell contents and formatting) that you would normally need to add manually. Before you begin customizing your default template, you need to create the special folder Excel uses for this purpose. In Windows Explorer, type the following (including the percent signs): %AppData%\Microsoft\Excel. That opens a folder within the roaming profile for your user account. If the XLStart folder does not exist, click New Folder to create it, being sure to replace the suggested name with XLStart.

Now open Excel and customize the existing default workbook to include whatever content and formatting you want to see in each new workbook. When you're finished, click File, click Save As, use the name Book (with no file extension), and choose one of the following template formats from the Save As Type list.

- **Excel Template**   This is the default format for Excel 2010. Choose it if you know that all your colleagues are able to open and edit workbooks saved in this format.

- **Excel Macro-Enabled Template**   Choose this option if your default workbook contains macros or if you expect to create macros in new workbooks you create later.

- **Excel 97-2003 Template**   Use this format if you want all new workbooks to be readable without modification by colleagues who are using older versions of Excel. Note that any features that are specific to Excel 2007 or Excel 2010 will not be saved in this format.

Don't click Save yet! When you choose any of the template formats, Excel proposes saving your new template in the Microsoft\Templates subfolder of your roaming user profile. That's fine for templates you want to choose from the New tab in Backstage view. But to save the default workbook template you need to choose the XLStart folder you just created. After selecting that location, click Save. Close the template and press Ctrl+N to confirm that the changes you made are being included in new workbooks.

Creating Links Between Workbooks and Worksheets

Cell and range references can point to a location on the same worksheet, on a different sheet, or in a different workbook. The most common use of links is to refer to a cell within a formula, but you can also use links (formally known as *external references*) as a way to consolidate information from multiple workbooks into a single location. For example, if you collect identically formatted workbooks from different departments, you can create a new workbook, design a summary sheet, and fill the new sheet with links to the totals row from each individual department's sheet. When you update the data in the departmental work-books, your summary sheet is automatically updated in real time.

As a security precaution, Excel blocks automatic updates of links to external files. When you open a workbook containing external links for the first time, you see the Security Warning bar shown here.

After you click Enable Content, you're given another choice via this dialog box, which appears regardless of whether the external workbook is currently open or not:

If you click Update and the workbook that contains the linked data is available, Excel refreshes the data on your worksheet automatically. (This is true even if the workbook file is not open; Excel retrieves the data in the background.) Click Don't Update if you know that the linked workbook is unavailable (because you're not connected to the network, for example.)

To add an external reference, copy it from the original location, and then use the Paste Link option (on the Paste Special menu) to insert it in the destination workbook. The syntax for the external reference contains the name of the worksheet format, the file location, the workbook name, and the tab name, with the last three elements separated by exclamation points, as in this example:

=Excel.Sheet.12|'D:\Budget\Results 2010.xlsx'!'!Marketing_Detail!R44C2'

Creating links between workbooks requires a high level of discipline and consistency in file naming and locations. If you move or delete a workbook that contains source data for links in another workbook, you risk breaking the links and orphaning your data.

To see and edit all external links in the current workbook, click File to open Backstage view. On the Info tab, in the lower right corner, click Edit Links To Files. That opens a dialog box that allows you to update values, change the source of the linked data, open the source workbook, or change the Startup Prompt behavior.

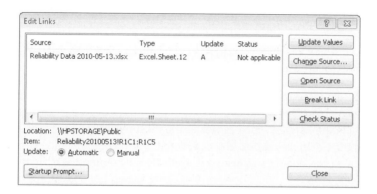

In some cases, you might want to convert the data in your workbook to its current values so that it is no longer dependent on the linked workbooks. That might be your preferred strategy if your fiscal year has ended and the departmental worksheets are final and no longer need updating. In that case, click Break Link to permanently convert any formulas and external references to their current values. As a stern warning sensibly advises, you should make a backup copy before taking this irrevocable action.

Navigating with the Go To Dialog Box

Most of the time, you use scroll bars and keyboard shortcuts to navigate through a workbook. You can use the Name box to jump to named ranges, tables, and charts in the current workbook. A well-hidden Excel feature called the Go To dialog box gives you a list that includes the same options as the Name box as well as a history of cells and ranges you've selected recently. To open this dialog box, click Find & Select (in the Editing group on the Home tab) and then click Go To, or use either of the keyboard shortcuts, F5 or Ctrl+G. The Go To dialog box, shown in Figure 14-7, contains a list of recent destinations.

Figure 14-7 Use the Go To dialog box to jump to a named range or to the cell or range that was selected before the last Go To operation.

In most cases, it's easier to use the Name box to move between named ranges. So why use the Go To dialog box? One advantage is that it keeps track of recent cell addresses you enter directly in the Reference box as well as the most recent cell or range. If you jump to a table from the Go To dialog box, you can jump back to your previous selection by using the Go To dialog box again. (This history is available only during the current session. If you close and reopen the workbook, opening the Go To dialog box shows only named ranges and objects.)

The Go To Special dialog box, available from the Find & Select menu or by clicking the Special button in the Go To dialog box, offers a range of esoteric but occasionally useful options, as shown here.

Make a selection first (or select a single cell within a table to use the entire table as the target). Then open the Go To Special dialog box, select a category, and click OK. This option is most useful when you want to edit, format, or otherwise work with a group of cells that have common characteristics. For example, you can click Blanks to find all blank cells in a range and replace their contents with an error-checking formula or a default value. You can also find only cells that contain constants or formulas (with options to refine the latter selection to show only formulas that produce numbers, text, or logical results).

One especially useful expert trick you can perform with this dialog box is to copy data from a range that includes one or more hidden columns or rows. Normally, copying the current selection also copies hidden cells, which can lead to unexpected results. Select the range you want to copy, open the Go To Special dialog box, choose Visible Cells Only, and click OK. When you paste the Clipboard contents into the destination cells, you'll see exactly what you copied and nothing extra.

Entering and Sorting Data with Custom Series

Several chapters ago, we explained how to automatically fill a range with a series of numbers or dates or with a repeated block of text values. You can also fill in dates using months or days of the week (in full or abbreviated) and then sort on those dates, with Jan and Feb coming before Mar and Apr instead of being sorted alphabetically: Apr, Feb, Jan, Mar. (If you need a refresher course, see "Entering and Filling in Data and Series" on page 352.)

You can add your own custom lists to the collection, specifying the members of the list and their sort order. You can create a list from any text-based values: department names, budget categories, countries, geographical regions, and suppliers, to name just a few examples. Custom lists are stored in the Windows registry and are available for filling in data by row or column and for sorting data in any workbook. You can add as many custom lists as you need, entering them directly or copying them from an existing worksheet.

You can view and edit existing custom lists or create new ones by using an obscure dialog box. Click File, click Options, select the Advanced tab, and scroll nearly to the bottom. Under the General heading, click Edit Custom Lists. That opens the Custom Lists dialog box shown in Figure 14-8.

To create a custom list that includes only a few items, select New List from the Custom Lists box on the left and then type the list directly in the List Entries box, pressing Enter after each entry. Click Add when you're finished. To remove an existing list, select its entry in the Custom Lists box and click Delete.

To create a custom list from a worksheet range, first make sure the range is arranged in the exact order you want to use for your new custom list. Then click New List, click in the Import List From Cells box, select the range in the worksheet, and click Import.

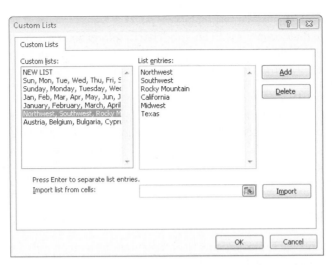

Figure 14-8 For short lists, click in the List Entries box and type entries in order, pressing Enter at the end of each one. Use the Import button to copy longer lists from a worksheet range.

To fill in a custom data series, type any entry from the list in a cell and use the fill handle in the lower right corner to fill the range you select with the remainder of the list. To sort using a custom list, follow the procedure in "Sorting a Range, Region, or Table" on page 398. In the Sort dialog box, select Custom List from the drop-down Order list, choose the custom list you want to use, and click OK. This example sorts a table by values in the Region column, using our custom list of regions as the sort order.

Generating Random Numbers

When you're building a worksheet, it sometimes helps to be able to plug in sample data to verify that your formulas work properly with a wide range of input values. You could just type some numbers into the cells, but it's easier to let Excel fill in some realistic data for you. The secret is to use either of the following two functions:

- =RAND() uses no parameters and returns a random number between 0 and 1, carried to 14 decimal places

- =RANDBETWEEN(bottom,top) requires two parameters, which can be constants or cell references; it returns whole numbers that are greater than or equal to *bottom* and less than or equal to *top*.

Using either of these functions can require a little ingenuity and a combination of other functions. If you're building a worksheet to analyze sales at a restaurant or retail store, you might want a large collection of data to simulate a series of typical sales. If the minimum transaction is $25.00 and the maximum is $150.00, neither function alone will work. RAND returns results that are well outside the range you're looking for, while RANDBETWEEN returns only whole numbers instead of the dollars-and-cents data you need. The solution? Combine the two functions in a single formula you can use in the range containing sales amounts:

=RANDBETWEEN(25,150)+ROUND(RAND(),2)

The first function generates a random whole number between 25 and 150, inclusive. The second function generates a number between 0 and 1 and rounds it to two decimal places. The combination equals a perfect mix of dollars and cents.

Chapter 14

PART 4

OneNote

MICROSOFT'S OneNote is more than seven years old, and yet for many (if not most) Office users it's a complete unknown. That's understandable: After all, in Office 2003 and Office 2007, OneNote was included only in a couple of Office editions, but in Office 2010, OneNote is elevated to marquee status and is part of every edition.

So what is OneNote exactly? In this case, the program's metaphor is absolutely accurate. OneNote really is a digital replacement for a traditional loose-leaf notebook in which you can save class notes, academic research, meeting minutes, or just about anything else you might be tempted to put on a piece of paper. You can type, write, paste, print, snip, clip, and send just about anything to OneNote, which saves each item on a page in a section of a notebook. You can move the pieces around on the page, format text and resize pictures, and arrange text into tidy outlines and lists.

Did we mention that OneNote notebooks are infinitely expandable? You can add new pages and sections, organize pages and subpages, and create as many new notebooks as you can fit in your default storage location. Personal notebooks are stored on your hard drive; you can share and sync notebooks using Windows Live SkyDrive (or, on a home or business network, in a shared folder or SharePoint site).

Even if you already know OneNote well from an earlier version, you'll want to read this chapter carefully. Office 2010 includes some significant new features and capabilities, as well as a new file format.

For more details on the Office 2010 file format and potential issues, see "Choosing the Right OneNote File Format" on page 494.

What's in a OneNote Notebook?

The basic organizational unit of OneNote is the notebook. When you create a new notebook or open a saved one, its icon and name appear in the Navigation bar on the left of the OneNote window, with the hierarchy of sections (and, optionally, section groups) shown in an indented list below the notebook icon and in tabs along the top of the contents pane. Selecting a section displays its contents in the page tabs bar on the right. Selecting a page from that list displays it in the contents pane. To begin adding your own notes, pictures, and web clippings, you can rename the default section and page or start adding new sections and pages of your own.

Figure 15-1 shows an open notebook containing five sections, with five pages in the open section.

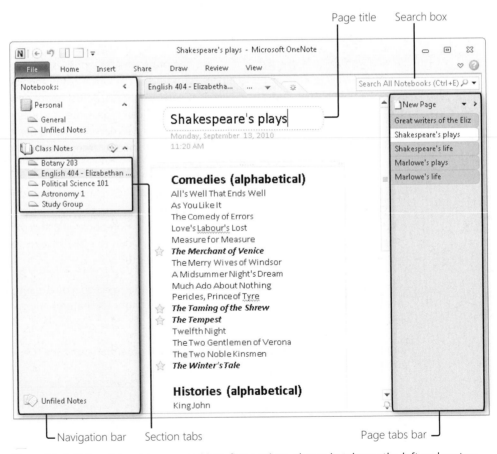

Figure 15-1 This notebook is arranged into five sections, shown in tabs on the left and on top; select a page from the current section using the list on the right.

You can organize your notes in ways that are much more sophisticated than the simple Class Notes notebook shown here. For example, as your collection of notes grows in size and complexity, you can combine sections into section groups and gather a group of related pages together as subpages; although the previous OneNote version also allowed you to create subpages, OneNote 2010 is the first that allows you to collapse them under a parent page. You can also create clickable links that open other OneNote pages, Office documents, Outlook items, or web pages.

For more on how to manage section groups and subpages, see "Expert Organizational Techniques" on page 542. You'll find details on how to link pages to one another and to external content in "Using Links for Quick Connections" on page 530.

OneNote notebooks are automatically included in the Windows Search index. As a notebook grows in size (and especially when you use multiple notebooks), search becomes not just handy but essential. For the best results, use the search box above the page tabs bar.

You'll find full details on how to use the OneNote search box in "Smart Search Strategies" on page 534.

There's no limit on the type of information you can save in a notebook. A partial list of common tasks and activities includes the following:

- Taking notes during classroom lectures and lab sessions

- Organizing online research

- Recording the minutes of a meeting

- Planning a family reunion or vacation

- Creating to-do lists for short-term tasks and long-term goals

- Organizing manuals and warranty information for household appliances

Or anything that strikes your fancy, really.

There's no right or wrong way to build a notebook or to organize its parts. Your personal preferences dictate how you can manage and use notebooks.

Creating and Opening OneNote Files

One striking difference between OneNote and other Office programs is the absence of a Save button or menu. OneNote does indeed store its work in files, but it handles virtually all of the management tasks for those files in the background. Except in rare circumstances, you should never need to directly manipulate OneNote files.

Chapter 15

To create a new notebook, click File, and then click New. Follow the three-step process shown in Figure 15-2 to choose where you want the notebook files stored, and then click Create Notebook to create the new notebook files and begin working immediately.

Figure 15-2 The name you enter in step 2 here is used as the display name for your new notebook and as the name of the new folder where its files are stored.

In this chapter, we assume you're creating and storing the new notebook locally (choose My Computer in step 1). The default location for all new notebooks is the OneNote Notebooks subfolder in the Documents folder of your user profile. You can specify an alternative location in the Location box.

The text you enter in the Name box under New Notebook is used as both the folder name and the display name shown in the OneNote Navigation bar. After you create a notebook, you can change its display name at any time without affecting the original folder name. To do so, right-click the notebook name in the Navigation bar and click Rename. That opens a dialog box like the one shown in Figure 15-3, which also allows you to change the location or format of the notebook.

Figure 15-3 Changing the display name of a notebook here does not affect the name of the folder where its files are stored.

So what about the files themselves? Each notebook section is saved in its own file, using the default Microsoft OneNote Section format with a file name extension of .one. If you create a OneNote notebook by clicking File and then New in OneNote 2010, the program creates a tiny file with the name Open Notebook; this file is saved in Microsoft OneNote Table Of Contents format, with a file name extension of .onetoc2. Strictly speaking, the Open Notebook file isn't needed. If you point OneNote to a folder filled with OneNote section files, it will ask you if you want to open the folder as a notebook, as shown here.

If you click Yes, OneNote creates a new OneNote Table of Contents file, using the folder name as the notebook display name and populating it with all section files contained within the folder.

INSIDE OUT   What's the right way to move a notebook?

If a notebook is simply a collection of OneNote section files in a folder, you can move the notebook to a new location just by moving its folder, right? Yes you can, and for a file stored on your local hard drive the results will almost certainly be successful. But for a notebook stored in a shared network location, manually moving files incurs the risk that any unsynchronized changes in that notebook will be lost. To avoid that possibility, we encourage using the official method: right-click the notebook name in the Navigation bar, click Properties, and then click Change Location in the Notebook Properties dialog box.

Chapter 15

Choosing the Right OneNote File Format

With OneNote 2010, Microsoft has changed the file format used for OneNote section files. When you create a new notebook in OneNote 2010, your files are automatically saved in the new file format. If you intend to share notebooks with people who are still using OneNote 2007, or if you want to preserve the ability to open those files on another computer using the earlier version of OneNote, you need to explicitly choose the alternative format.

To convert a notebook from OneNote 2007 format to OneNote 2010 format (or vice versa), right-click the notebook icon in the Navigation bar and then click Properties. Click Convert To 2010 or Convert To 2007 (the option for the current format will be unavailable). Note that this conversion can be made only on the entire contents of a notebook. When you make the conversion, the format you choose becomes the new default format for sections within that notebook.

When you move a section from one notebook to another, OneNote automatically converts it to the default format of the destination notebook. If you use Windows Explorer to manually move a section file saved in OneNote 2007 format to a notebook whose default format is OneNote 2010, the older format is preserved, and you see an information bar warning you of potential incompatibilities when you open that section.

If you choose to save a notebook using the older OneNote 2007 file format, the following features are affected:

- The math equations feature is unavailable, and any existing equations are converted to static images.

- Context links (linked notes) and version information are permanently removed.

- Subpages are preserved but can no longer be collapsed in the pages tab list.

- The contents of the OneNote Recycle Bin for that notebook are permanently removed.

In addition, you must use OneNote 2010 format to save a notebook in a Windows Live SkyDrive folder or on a SharePoint site so that you can open and edit the notebook in a web browser using the OneNote Web App.

OneNote 2010 allows you to open a notebook saved in OneNote 2003 format, but that notebook is opened in read-only mode. If you convert a notebook from OneNote 2003 format to either OneNote 2007 or 2010 format, the conversion is permanent and cannot be undone.

You don't need to manually save OneNote files. OneNote automatically saves your work every 30 seconds and when you close a notebook or the program itself. If you've just made a large number of changes and you want to force a save instead of waiting for the next automatic save, press Ctrl+S.

The Save As menu allows you to export or share notebooks, pages, and sections in a variety of formats, as we explain in "Printing, Publishing, and Sharing Notes" on page 566.

Filling a Notebook with Text, Pictures, Clippings, and More

Every time you type, paste, or otherwise insert a new item on a notebook page, OneNote creates a note container for that item. Note containers can hold text, pictures, audio and video clips, handwriting, and clippings from a web page or from the screen. The initial size of the container matches the size of the object you're creating or inserting; if you click and begin typing, a new note container is created immediately and explands in width and depth to accommodate your input.

Note containers are normally invisible. To see the container, move the mouse pointer over its contents, click to select the contents, or position the insertion point within the container. Figure 15-4 shows a note container, with the pointer positioned over the Move handle at the top. Click and drag the handle to move the container and its contents to a new position on the page. Click the Move handle to select the entire container so that you can cut, copy, or delete it and its contents. Click the sizing handle in the upper right corner to make the container wider.

We can't understand why anyone would want to hide note containers permanently, but if you do, there's an option for that: click File, and then click Options. On the Display tab, clear Show Note Containers On Pages.

Chapter 15

INSIDE OUT   Merge or split note containers

If you've typed or pasted text into separate containers on the same page, how do you merge them into a single container? Simple: click the Move handle on the second container to select its entire contents. Then, hold down the Shift key as you drag that container into the first one. When you see the contents of the second container snap into position in the first container, release the Shift key. To split text in a single container into two discrete containers, select the text you want to move into a new container and drag it outside the original container. When you release the mouse button, OneNote creates a new container, which you can then work with independently.

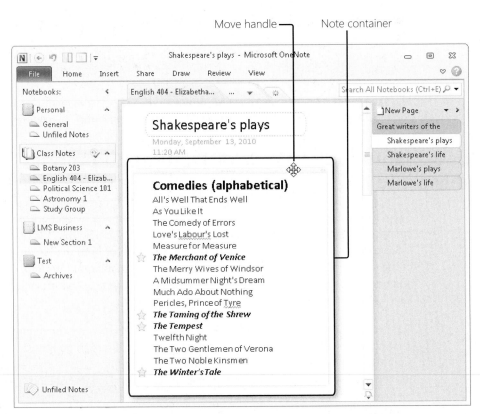

Figure 15-4 Click and drag the Move handle at the top of a note container (shown by the four-headed arrow here) to reposition the container and its contents on the page.

In the remainder of this section, we discuss the specifics of how to work with different types of content that you enter directly or paste from the Clipboard—text, pictures, equations, and ink, for example. But you can also send items directly to OneNote by using the Screen Clipping tool and Send To options in Outlook and Internet Explorer. When you send a web clipping, a screen clipping, or an Outlook item to OneNote, you see a dialog box like the one shown in Figure 15-5. If you choose a section from any open notebook, the item is sent to a new page in that notebook; you can also choose a specific page within a notebook and send the item to that page, where it's placed at the bottom of the page, below any existing content.

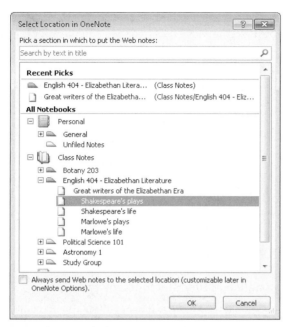

Figure 15-5 When you send an item or a clipping from another program to OneNote, you can specify the destination page or section here.

Text

Entering text from the keyboard is the simplest (and probably the most common) way to fill a notebook. Click to position the insertion point on the page, and start typing. (You can also paste text into a page, with or without formatting.) The text you enter or paste appears in a single note container.

OneNote supports basic outlining functions for text. Press Enter to create a new paragraph, and then change the outline level for that paragraph by pressing Tab (or Shift+Tab to promote a paragraph to a higher level.)

You can move any paragraph up or down or adjust its outline level by dragging it. You can also use keyboard shortcuts: press Alt+Shift and then use the Up or Down Arrow key to move the paragraph up or down in the outline; use Alt+Shift and the Right or Left Arrow key to demote or promote a paragraph in the outline. When you move the mouse pointer over a paragraph, a Move button appears to its left. Move the mouse pointer over the button, and the pointer turns to a four-headed arrow; click to select the entire paragraph and

Chapter 15

move it up, down, left, or right. In the example shown here, the mouse pointer is to the right of "Christopher Marlowe," so the Move button appears to the left of that line.

```
William Shakespeare
Christopher Marlowe
Ben Jonson
Edmund Spenser
John Fletcher
Thomas Kyd
Thomas Middleton
Thomas Nashe
John Webster
John Donne
Philip Sidney
```

INSIDE OUT   Add a date and time stamp to any text

At the top of every notebook page is a title, and beneath the title is a date/time stamp that shows when you created that notebook page. If you use a notebook page to collect random thoughts over a period of weeks or months, you might want to stamp individual note containers with the date and time. The secret? Before you begin typing a new note, right-click at the point where you want the text to appear. At the bottom of the shortcut menu, click the menu option that lists your name and the current date and time. That information appears as the first line in a new note container, ready for you to begin adding your text. To insert just the current date, use the keyboard shortcut Alt+Shift+D. To insert the current time, press Alt+Shift+T. To insert both the date and time (without your name), press Alt+Shift+F.

Lists

You can format any text on a OneNote page as a list using bullets or numbering. List formatting applies to the current paragraph or, if multiple paragraphs are selected, to all paragraphs in the selection. If you've used list formatting in Word or PowerPoint, you already understand the basics. OneNote adds a few twists to simple lists.

To choose a bullet character and immediately apply it to the current paragraph or selection, click the arrow next to the Bullets button (on the Mini toolbar or in the Basic Text group on the Home tab). The selection of characters in the Bullet Library (shown here) is fixed and cannot be customized.

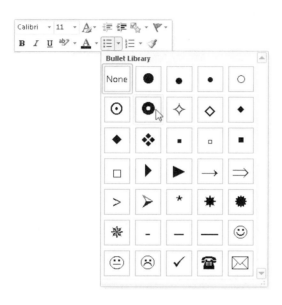

To format the current paragraph or selection with the most recently used bullet character, click the Bullets button or use the Ctrl+period keyboard shortcut. To automatically add a standard bullet character (a big black dot) at the beginning of the current line, enter an asterisk at the beginning of the paragraph.

Numbered lists work in similar fashion. To begin a simple numbered list, start with a number or letter followed by a period, a closing parenthesis, or a hyphen; then press the Spacebar. You can choose from an assortment of ready-made numbering and outline formats using the Numbering Library (shown next), which is available by clicking the arrow to the right of the Numbering button on the Mini toolbar or in the Basic Text group on the Home tab.

Chapter 15

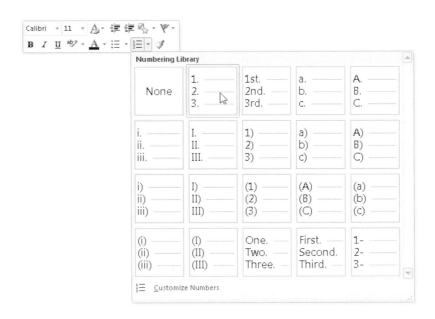

As with automatic list formatting in other Office programs, pressing Enter continues the list formatting in the next paragraph. To end automatic formatting, press Enter twice.

For more details on list-formatting techniques used in Word, see "Working with Bulleted and Numbered Lists" on page 240. For instructions on customizing numbered lists, see "Our Favorite OneNote Tweaks and Tips" on page 572.

Tables

You can add a simple table to any page in OneNote, using its rows and columns to arrange data that doesn't lend itself to simple paragraphs. OneNote tables offer a basic set of features and formatting options, far simpler than those found in Word or PowerPoint. When the insertion point is within a table, OneNote makes a custom Layout tab available, as shown in Figure 15-6. (The same options are also available if you right-click anywhere within the table.)

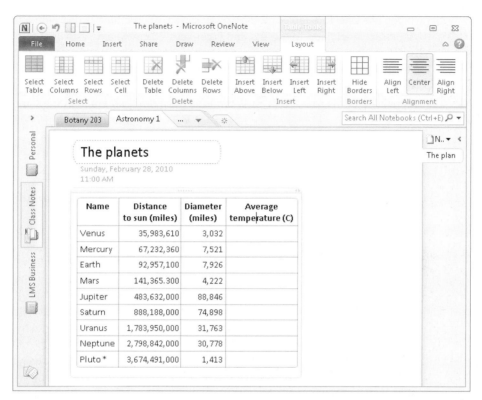

Figure 15-6 The Layout tab allows you to arrange rows, columns, and cells in a OneNote table and align their contents.

To create a table, use any of the following techniques:

- On the Insert tab, click Table and drag the grid to select the number of rows and columns you want.

- Click Insert Table at the bottom of the Table menu and select the number of rows and columns from a dialog box.

- Easiest of all, create a table automatically by typing the text you want to appear in the first cell of the first row, and then press Tab. Continue pressing Tab to create new columns, with or without text, and press Enter to begin a new row.

For more details on how to create and use tables in Word, see "Working with Tables" on page 253.

If you use OneNote tables regularly, you can save some time by learning a few keyboard shortcuts in addition to the Tab and Enter keys. To create a new column to the left or right of the current column, press Ctrl+Alt+E or Ctrl+Alt+R, respectively. To create a new row below the current one, even if the insertion point is in the middle of the row, press Ctrl+Enter. To create a new row above the current one, move the insertion point to the beginning of the row and press Enter. To begin a new paragraph in the same cell, press Alt+Enter.

Pictures

Pictures fit nicely in OneNote pages, either alone or accompanied by text. To add a picture to a OneNote page, you can paste it from the Clipboard or click Picture on the Insert tab and then choose an image file.

What happens next depends on the destination you select. If you choose an empty page as the target for the paste, OneNote drops the picture into a note container, resizing the image if necessary so that its height is under 400 pixels, with the insertion point positioned just below the picture, awaiting your caption. If you insert another picture, it appears in the current note container at the insertion point. However, if you click an empty space, outside a note container, and then insert a picture into a page that already contains at least one item, the pasted picture appears at its original size with no note container. In either case, you can resize the image using handles on the bottom and right sides; use the handle on the lower right corner to preserve the picture's aspect ratio. To resize any image to the full dimensions of the original file, right-click the picture and then click Restore To Original Size.

For a complete picture of how to work with photos and illustrations in Office 2010, see Chapter 6, "Working with Graphics and Pictures."

OneNote treats each picture as if it were a paragraph, so you can move it up and down with text (or other pictures) in a note container. You can also paste or move a picture into a table, as we've done in Figure 15-7. After you insert the first image and resize it to fit the column width and row height, pictures you paste into other cells are scaled accordingly.

OneNote can recognize text in pictures and use that text for searches; we explain how this works in "Our Favorite OneNote Tweaks and Tips" on page 572.

Web Clippings

OneNote and Internet Explorer work exceptionally well together. As you browse, you can collect snippets of text, images, or entire pages for insertion into a notebook page. The mechanics are simple: make a selection (skip this step if you want to save the entire page) and then click the Send To OneNote button on Internet Explorer's Command bar. Alternatively, you can right-click a selection or an entire page and then click Send To OneNote from the bottom of the shortcut menu. Choosing this option opens the Select Location In OneNote dialog box, where you can specify a section or page as the destination.

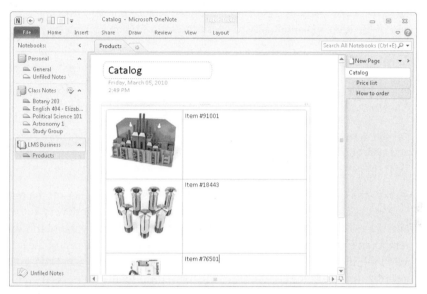

Figure 15-7 You can insert pictures into a table on a OneNote page. After you scale the first image, OneNote handles the remaining images.

TROUBLESHOOTING

A web page doesn't look right when you send it to OneNote

Although the process of sending a web page to OneNote is easy, the results are not always what you'd expect. In particular, heavily formatted web pages often translate poorly onto a OneNote page, with text flowing in an unreadable fashion and tables rearranged haphazardly. If that happens, click the Undo button and try either of these approaches.

- Select the most important portions of the web page and try to send them individually to your OneNote page. You'll lose the overall design, but that might not matter if you're mostly concerned with content.

- Use the Send To OneNote 2010 option on Internet Explorer's Print menu to send the entire page or a selection to OneNote as an image. You lose the ability to copy or edit text on the resulting item, but you are certain to get an accurate (and readable) representation of the page.

If you use a browser other than Internet Explorer, your best option is to select all or part of a web page, copy the selection to the Clipboard, and paste the result into OneNote.

Regardless of the method you choose, OneNote adds a link to the source web page at the end of the item, making it easy to revisit the source when you review your research later.

Screen Clippings

Other Office programs allow you to copy and paste a screen shot from any open window. OneNote offers a more limited Screen Clipping version of that feature.

For full details on how to use screen shots and screen clippings in Office 2010, see "Capturing and Inserting Screenshots" on page 174. To learn how to customize this feature in OneNote, see "Our Favorite OneNote Tweaks and Tips" on page 572.

As with the other Office programs, you can use the ribbon to kick off the process: click Screen Clipping on the Insert tab to select a portion of any window to automatically copy and paste into OneNote at the current insertion point. When you use this option, OneNote temporarily minimizes itself so that you have full access to the rest of the screen; just make sure the window from which you want to clip is visible behind OneNote. Your selection is inserted in the current page at the current insertion point.

Unlike the other Office programs, you can use the Create Screen Clipping keyboard short-cut, Windows logo key+S, to capture a portion of the screen, even if OneNote isn't running. (If OneNote is open, the OneNote window remains visible on the screen, allowing you to capture a clipping from one page and paste it in another.) After you use this option, OneNote displays a variation of the Select Location In OneNote dialog box, shown in Figure 15-8. You can choose a OneNote section or page or use the Copy To Clipboard button to save your selection and use it in another program.

Every screen clipping you add to a page is tagged with the date and time it was taken; if the source is a web page, the tag includes the page name and URL.

Ink

Your keyboard and mouse aren't the only way to put stuff on a OneNote page. The Draw tab includes a full gallery of pens (shown in Figure 15-9) that you can use to draw, write, and highlight information on a page.

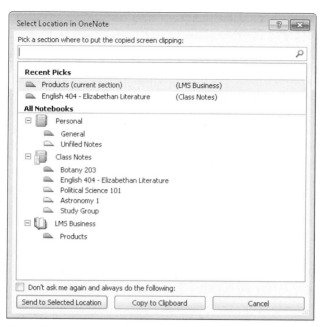

Figure 15-8 Use the Create Screen Clipping shortcut (Windows logo key+S) to copy part of a screen and paste it into OneNote or save it to the Clipboard.

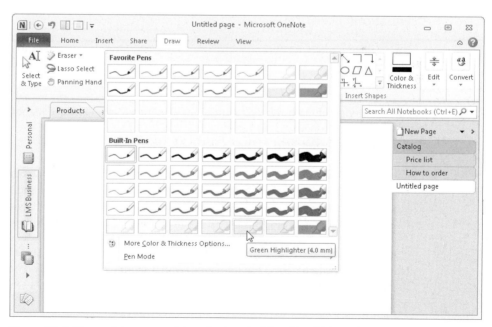

Figure 15-9 Fine-point pens work best for handwriting. The thick markers on the bottom row are ideal for highlighting text.

If none of the built-in pens are quite right, you can customize pens and highlighters, choosing from a variety of colors and thicknesses.

When you select a pen from the Tools group on the Draw tab, the pointer changes to a colored dot or brush whose color and thickness match the pen you selected. Use the pen to draw or write in an unused area of the page, and your ink is captured in a container, where it moves along with any text or graphics in the container. If you use a highlighter, your markup is treated as a discrete drawing and does not move when you move the text. (To highlight text, use the Highlighter button in the Basic Text group on the Home tab, as we describe in "Formatting Text" on page 508.)

To switch from pen mode back to mouse/keyboard interaction, click the Select & Type button at the left of the Draw tab.

If you intend to take handwritten notes or create anything more interesting than stick figures, you'll need a Tablet PC, a touch-enabled PC, or a digitizer and stylus. Although you can add ink using a mouse, the results are rarely satisfactory, especially for handwriting recognition. One noteworthy exception is the set of thick fluorescent-colored highlighters, which work well for marking up printouts.

For more details about how to use ink with Office programs, see "Drawing with Ink" on page 183.

Equations

Engineers and math majors can use the Equation menu on the Insert tab to create valid, editable math equations in OneNote. The tools are identical to those available in other Office applications.

For an overview of math-related features, see "Entering Mathematical Equations" on page 120.

E-Mail Messages and Other Outlook Items

If you use Outlook, you'll find a Send To OneNote button (in the Move group on the Home tab) when you're viewing a mail message in the message list or in a message window. Click that button to send the entire message to OneNote, with the message header (Subject, From, To, and Sent date) in a table and the text of the message itself just below the header.

If you select an Outlook appointment, meeting, task, or contact, you'll see a Linked *Item* Notes button (where *Item* is the item type) with a slightly different button image. Clicking this button allows you to send relevant details from the current item to a OneNote page with a link back to the original item. (If you've already created the item in OneNote, clicking this button returns you to that page.) A Notes section at the bottom of the item allows you to enter additional text. You can use this feature to keep notes about a meeting or to record details of your history with a contact, as shown here.

Bott, Katy

Wednesday, September 29, 2010
3:31 PM

Contact	Bott, Katy
Picture	
E-mail	katy@bott.com
Home Phone	(555) 743-1234

Link to Outlook item

Notes

You can create new linked items in Outlook directly from OneNote as well. We discuss the tight connections between the two programs in "Using OneNote with Outlook" on page 547.

File Attachments

You'll find an Attach File button in the Files group on the Insert tab. When you click that button and select a file from the Browse dialog box, OneNote embeds the selected file and displays its icon and name on the page. The file attachment is an independent copy, not linked to the original file in any way. Changes you make to the original file are not reflected in the OneNote attachment, and vice versa.

Attaching a file to a notebook is a good strategy when you want to preserve the file for historical purposes with your notes, or you want to make sure it's always available with the notebook, even if it's deleted from the file system or e-mail message from which it originated. For a document that you want to continue editing, especially with other members of a team, the preferred strategy is to create a link in OneNote to a file stored in a shared network folder or in Windows Live SkyDrive.

For more details about creating links to files, see "Using Links for Quick Connections" on page 530.

Printouts

During installation, OneNote adds a virtual printer to your Windows Devices And Printers folder. When you choose this "printer" as the output from any program (including a web browser or another Office application), OneNote creates an image of the file as it would appear on paper and inserts that printout on a page you select. You can also create a print-out from a file or use the output from a scanner—both options are available in the Files group on the Insert tab. Use this if you want to preserve the formatting of an original docu-ment or web page.

There's a subtle but significant difference between the two techniques for adding a print-out to a OneNote page. If you use the virtual Send To OneNote 2010 printer, your printout appears on the page you select, without any links to the original document. In addition, you can choose which page (or pages) you want to include on the OneNote page. When you click File Printout on the Insert tab and select the same file, OneNote adds the selected file to the current page as an attachment, with a link to the location of the original docu-ment. It then opens the associated program in the background, creates the printout, and inserts the printout below the file attachment.

Formatting Text

Regardless of its original source, any text on a OneNote page can be formatted using the same tools you use elsewhere in Office. The Basic Text group on the Home tab contains common formatting options, giving you the capability to select a font, change font size and color, and add character attributes such as bold, italic, underline, and strikethrough format-ting. You'll also find the Format Painter button on the Home tab, in the Clipboard group. Most of these options are available on the Mini toolbar as well.

For an overview of common text formatting techniques in Office 2010, see "Applying Text Formatting" on page 123.

As in Word and PowerPoint, you can apply some character formatting without making a selection first. If the insertion point is in a word, for example, and you press Ctrl+B or Ctrl+I (or click the Bold or Italic button), your formatting is applied to the entire word. To apply formatting to a phrase or sentence, you have to select the text first. One formatting shortcut you'll find only in OneNote is a toggle to apply or remove strikeout formatting: Ctrl+hyphen.

The Ctrl+A (Select All) keyboard shortcut works a bit differently in OneNote than it does in the rest of Office. If the insertion point is within a paragraph, pressing Ctrl+A selects the entire paragraph. Press Ctrl+A again to select the entire contents of the current note con-tainer, and press the combination once more to select the contents of all note containers on the current page.

If you've used indenting to create an outline, you can select the current paragraph and all its subordinate paragraphs by using the keyboard shortcut Ctrl+Shift+hyphen.

Unlike previous versions, OneNote 2010 allows you to automatically select from a small group of ready-made styles to apply to text. The list, shown here, includes six heading styles as well as predefined styles for page titles and some common types of body text.

Styles on this list are applied to all text in the current paragraph, regardless of whether any text is selected. In addition, Word users will appreciate that some common style-related keyboard shortcuts work just as well in OneNote. Use Ctrl+Alt+1 through Ctrl+Alt+6 to apply the Heading 1 through Heading 6 styles, and use Ctrl+Shift+N to quickly convert all formatting for the current paragraph to the built-in Normal style.

There's no keyboard shortcut for the built-in Page Title style, but it's worth noting that Ctrl+Shift+T jumps to the page title and selects all text there. You can apply any text formatting to all or part of a page title; if you are unhappy with the results, reapply the Page Title style.

The bad news about OneNote styles is that the formatting associated with this list cannot be customized, nor can you add your own styles to the list.

INSIDE OUT   Apply highlighting quickly

If you want portions of text on a page to stand out, use the Text Highlight Color button to apply a fluorescent yellow background (use the drop-down arrow to choose a different color). You can also use either of two keyboard shortcuts to highlight the current selection using the last color you selected: Ctrl+Alt+H or Ctrl+Shift+H. Note that this highlight applies formatting to the text itself and is not the same as the highlighter pen we describe in "Ink" on page 504. That pen creates a graphic image of the highlighter ink that can be used over a printout, a picture, or text.

Navigating in OneNote

At the beginning of this chapter, we described the basic organization of OneNote, which consists of pages arranged into sections within notebooks. You don't need us to tell you how to use the basic navigation tools—section tabs along the left and top of the page contents, page tabs on the right. In this chapter, we focus on some of the more subtle navigation elements, especially keyboard shortcuts and hidden tricks that you'll value when your collection of notebooks grows too big to simply scan.

The best navigation assistant of all is OneNote's search box, which we discuss in detail in "Smart Search Strategies" on page 534.

INSIDE OUT   Zoom in for a closer look

Most programs in the Office family include a status bar that offers, among other tools, a slider to zoom in on or out from the current page. OneNote lacks a status bar, but that doesn't mean it's lacking in the zoom department. The Zoom group on the View tab includes a list of preset zoom settings that range from 25% to 200%. Alternatively, you can use the Zoom In and Zoom Out buttons, which increase or decrease the zoom level in discrete steps from 11% to 477%. The keyboard equivalents are Ctrl+Alt+plus sign/minus sign (on the numeric keypad) or Ctrl+Alt+Shift+plus sign/hyphen (to the right of the numbers on the main keyboard).

Opening and Moving Between Notebooks

Every open notebook has an entry in the Navigation bar. The icon to the left of the display name provides clues about the notebook's status and its location: a notebook with its covers open indicates which notebook you're currently working with, and separate icons differentiate locally stored notebooks from those that are stored in a shared folder and synced to a local copy.

For more details on how notebook syncing works, see "Sharing and Synchronizing Notebooks" on page 561.

Normally, clicking a section in another notebook replaces the page shown in the contents pane with the most recently opened page in the new section. If you want to open a second notebook without losing your place in the current one, switch to the View tab and click the New Window option on the Window menu (or use the keyboard shortcut Ctrl+M). If you're using Windows 7, you can open a new OneNote window by holding down Shift as you click the OneNote taskbar icon.

If you prefer keyboard navigation to mouse clicks, here's how to switch to a different open notebook. Press Ctrl+G to move the focus to the first open notebook on the Navigation bar. Press Tab to move down the list of open notebooks (use Shift+Tab if you go too far and want to move back). When you see the selection highlight on the notebook you want to open, press Enter.

Working with Sections and Section Groups

OneNote displays the names of all sections for all open notebooks in the Navigation bar. (Click the up arrow to the right of the display name to collapse the list of sections for a notebook; click the down arrow to show the contents of a previously collapsed list.) You can also see a list of section tabs for the current notebook along the top of the contents pane. Click a tab to switch immediately to that section. To move quickly between sections in the current notebook, in order, press Ctrl+Tab (use Ctrl+Shift+Tab to move through the sections in reverse order).

The simplest way to create a new section in the current notebook is to click the Create A New Section button (the asterisk) at the rightmost edge of the section tabs at the top of the contents pane. Alternatively, you can use the Ctrl+T keyboard shortcut. In either case, the new section's default name (New Section 1, for example), is selected so you can start typing immediately to replace it with a descriptive name. To rename a section, double-click its tab and begin typing.

New sections are automatically added to the bottom of the section tabs list. To change the order of sections, drag tabs up or down. You can also drag sections out of one notebook and into another to move them. Hold down the Ctrl key as you drag a section to make a copy in another notebook. If you prefer using dialog boxes for move and copy operations, right-click the section name and choose Move Or Copy from the shortcut menu. Choose a section from the list of open notebooks, as shown in Figure 15-10, and then click Move or Copy to complete the operation.

You can also combine the contents of two sections using the Merge Into Another Section option on the right-click shortcut menu. Choosing this option has the same effect as moving all pages out of the first section and into the second one and then deleting the first section.

Figure 15-10 To move or copy a section, use this dialog box. You might need to click the plus sign to the left of a notebook name to see its list of sections.

If the number of sections within a notebook starts to become unmanageable, the easy solution is to create one or more section groups. The advantage of section groups is that they can be collapsed and expanded in the Navigation bar. Although you can manually adjust the order of section groups by dragging them in the section tabs list, section groups always appear after sections that are not part of a group, as shown here.

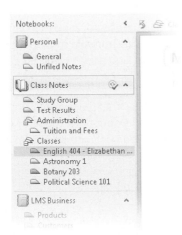

To create a section group, right-click the notebook name and then click New Section Group. Give the new section group a descriptive name and drag sections into it (or create new sections). Note that section groups can be nested within other section groups.

There's nothing magical about section groups. They're actually nothing more than subfolders within the folder that contains the notebook. Creating a section group creates a new subfolder, and moving sections to that section group moves the corresponding OneNote Section files (with the .one file name extension) to that new subfolder.

Working with Pages

The techniques for working with pages are similar to those for working with sections. If you right-click any page name in the page tabs bar, you can use options on the shortcut menu to create a new page, delete the selected page, cut or copy the current page to the Clipboard, or paste a page from the Clipboard to the current section.

To move quickly between pages in the current section, use the keyboard shortcut Ctrl+Page Up (use Ctrl+Page Down to move through all pages in reverse order). To jump to the first or last page in the currently visible set of page tabs, press Alt+Page Up or Alt+Page Down, respectively.

To rename a page, select the page title box and adjust the text there. You cannot directly edit the title text shown on a page tab.

To change the order of pages in a section, drag the page tabs up or down in the page tabs bar, or use the keyboard shortcuts Alt+Shift+Up Arrow/Down Arrow. To move a page to a different section in the same or another notebook, drag the page to the Navigation bar and drop it on a section tab. (Hold down Ctrl while dragging to create a copy and leave the original page intact.) You can also right-click any page and choose Move Or Copy (or use the keyboard shortcut Ctrl+Alt+M) to choose a destination from a dialog box.

Selecting a page involves a few subtle techniques that can be confusing at first. For example, if you click a page tab, the focus shifts to that page, and the insertion point appears on the page at the point where it appeared when you last edited the page. If you're picking up where you left off with a set of meeting minutes or research notes, you can simply start typing. If you click that page icon a second time (or use the Ctrl+Shift+A keyboard shortcut), the entire page is selected, as indicated by a thick blue border around the page in the contents pane. You're then free to cut or copy the page to the Clipboard or press Delete to send it to the OneNote Recycle Bin.

To create a new, blank page, click the New Page button at the top of the page tabs bar, or use the keyboard shortcut Ctrl+N. In either case, your page is added at the end of the current list of page tabs. To add a new page just below a specific page, click its page tab and press Ctrl+Alt+N. To create a new page at a specific location using the mouse, move the mouse pointer up and down the page tabs bar. As you do so, you'll see a small new-page icon and a small black arrow alongside the page tabs bar. When that arrow points to the location where you want to add the new page, as shown here, click the page icon.

Navigating on a page is a straightforward process, with one twist. Although every page has a paper size assigned to it for printing purposes, pages aren't restricted to a fixed size; instead, they expand as needed, in both width and depth, to fit the content you add. If you plan to add a significant amount of new content in a specific location, you can manually add space to a page. Click the Insert Space button at the left of the Insert tab, and then move the mouse pointer over the page. As you move up or down, the pointer changes to a two-headed arrow. When you reach the spot where you want to add space, click and drag in the direction you want. A large blue arrow, similar to the one in Figure 15-11, shows you the dimensions of the new space you're about to add, with a ghosted image of any existing note containers appearing in their new position.

You can also use the Insert Space button to add space at the left side of a page (click in the left margin and drag to the right) or to remove unwanted white space from a page (click and drag up or drag from the right margin to the left).

When editing a page, you can use any of the following shortcuts:

- To scroll up or down in the current page, press Page Up or Page Down.

- To move to the top of the current page, press Ctrl+Home. To move to the bottom of the note container that's lowest on the page, press Ctrl+End.

- To move down the page, from one note container to the next, press Alt+Down Arrow.

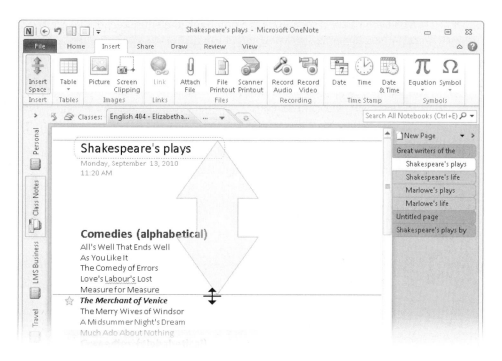

Figure 15-11 Click Insert Space and drag down to add new space above an existing note container.

As in OneNote 2007, you can create subpages that are indented beneath a main page. For notebooks saved in OneNote 2010 format, these subpages are linked to the main page. The group can be collapsed or expanded and can be selected and moved or copied as a group. To create a new subpage below the current page, press Ctrl+Alt+Shift+N

To increase or decrease the indent level of the current page tab (or a group of adjacent page tabs), click and drag right or left, or right-click and use the shortcut menu options Make Subpage and Promote Subpage. You can also use the keyboard shortcuts Ctrl+Alt+] (right bracket) and Ctrl+Alt+[(left bracket) to increase or decrease the indent.

Using the OneNote Recycle Bin

When you delete a page or section from OneNote, the object doesn't actually disappear for good. Instead, OneNote moves the object to that notebook's Recycle Bin. The Recycle Bin, a new feature in OneNote 2010, is stored in a special folder called OneNote_RecycleBin. This folder is added to every notebook you create using the OneNote 2010 file format; if you convert a notebook to OneNote 2007 format, this folder is deleted immediately.

When you delete a section from a notebook, the entire section file is moved to the One-Note_RecycleBin folder. When you delete one or more pages, those pages are moved to the OneNote_DeletedPages file, which is stored in OneNote Section format in the One-Note_RecycleBin folder. To recover deleted pages or sections, right-click the notebook icon in the Navigation bar, and then click Notebook Recycle Bin. In this read-only notebook, you'll see all pages and sections you've deleted in the past 60 days. (An information bar appears at the top of the contents pane to alert you that you're working in the Recycle Bin.)

Figure 15-12 shows the Recycle Bin folder for the Travel notebook. It contains two deleted sections (Czech Republic and Vacation Research) and an indeterminate number of pages in the Deleted Pages section. Note the Read-Only label in the title bar and the information bar that indicates you're working in the Recycle Bin.

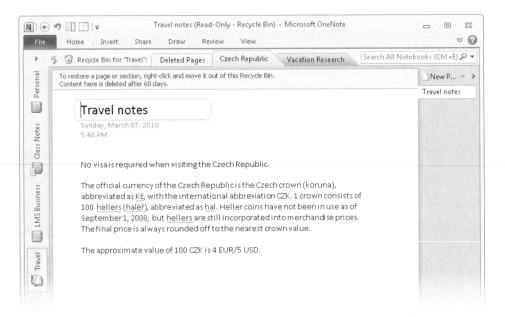

Figure 15-12 To restore a previously deleted section or page, right-click the section tab (above the contents pane) or the page tab, click the Move Or Copy option, and select a destination.

Customizing the Look and Feel of a Notebook Page

By default, every new OneNote page starts out with a bland white background and no adornment. You can change the appearance of a page in a variety of ways—some for purely aesthetic reasons and others, such as rule lines, for practical effect. In this section, we discuss the main customizations you can apply to a page.

OneNote 2010 includes an assortment of templates that incorporate many of the customizations we discuss in this section, and you can save your own templates as well. For details, see "Saving and Using Custom Page Templates" on page 575.

Page Title

The page title box appears at the top of every page in a fixed location, with a date and time stamp below it that (initially, at least) indicates when the page was created. Any text you enter as the title on the page is also used as a label on the page tab.

As far as we've been able to determine, there's no technical limit on the number of characters you can include in a title. From a practical standpoint, however, shorter is better; remember that the main purpose of a title is to provide a label in the page tabs bar.

By default, all page titles are formatted as 17-point Calibri. You can change the font, font size, and color of a title. You can also add hyperlinks, tags, and just about any other type of formatting that's applicable to text. This sort of custom formatting might be useful if you intend to print a notebook page or save it as a PDF file for sharing; just remember that the page tab label does not reflect any formatting.

You can't change the position of the date/time stamp just below the page title, nor can you add your own text to it. You can, however, change the date and time. This option is useful if, for example, you create a page in advance of a meeting so that you can keep minutes and want the date and time stamp to reflect the actual starting time. Click the date field to expose a calendar control (like the one shown here) and choose a date. Click the time stamp and use the clock control to choose a new time. Use the Today button to insert today's date from the calendar. The clock control initially displays the current system time; the list of available alternate times is limited to round values, on the hour and half-hour.

For some pages, such as those that include design sketches or diagrams, you might prefer to have no title. In addition, any Side Notes you create are added to the Unfiled Notes folder with no title. Click Hide Page Title (in the Page Setup group on the View tab) to remove the existing title and date/time stamp and hide the page title box.

Chapter 15

CAUTION

Don't be misled by the wording of the Hide Page Title button. When you click that button, it permanently deletes the current contents of the page title box and replaces the page tab label with the first recognizable text on the page. If you want to keep the page tab label, copy the page title to the top of the page before "hiding" the title.

We discuss the best way to use the Unfiled Notes section in "Expert Organizational Techniques" on page 542.

Page Color

The default background color for every notebook page is white. You can adjust this color to one of 15 pastel alternatives using the Page Color menu on the View tab, as shown here.

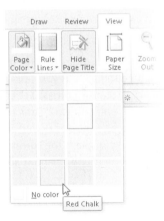

To remove the background color from an existing page, click the No Color button at the bottom of the Page Color menu.

Rule Lines

Adding rules or grid lines to a page can help with a variety of note taking and drawing tasks. To add a default set of rule lines (including a vertical red line in the left margin, just like the one on a yellow legal pad), click the Rule Lines button on the View tab. You can change the default lines by clicking the down arrow and selecting from an assortment of rules and grid sizes on the Rule Lines menu.

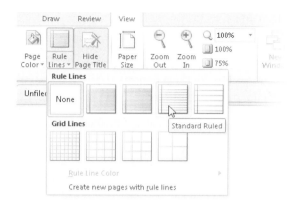

To adjust the color of rule lines from their default light blue to one of 17 alternatives, use the Rule Line Color list on the Rule Lines menu.

You can show or hide rule lines as needed for a specific task. If you're using a Tablet PC to take notes, for example, you might use rule lines to help keep your notes from creeping up or down the page and then hide them for reviewing later. Likewise, you can use grid lines to initially position images on the page. To toggle the display of rule or grid lines using the keyboard, press Ctrl+Shift+R.

If you prefer to use rule lines for all new pages, you can choose a set of rule or grid lines and then set it as the default. The easy way to accomplish this task is to click Create New Pages With Rule Lines at the bottom of the Rule Lines menu. This has the same effect as selecting Create All New Pages With Rule Lines on the Display tab in the OneNote Options dialog box.

Background Image

In addition to background colors, you can choose a single image to use as the background of a page. This option works best with an image that has been specifically created (or edited) for use as a page background. The ideal image has strong elements limited to the top and left margins and soft or faded image elements in the body of the page, where they won't adversely affect readability of the page contents.

For examples of pages that use background images effectively, see the discussion of page templates in "Our Favorite OneNote Tweaks and Tips" on page 572.

To add a background image, first insert the image on the page and position the picture in the upper left corner, making certain it is not enclosed in a note container. Then right-click the image and choose Set Picture As Background. To remove a background image, first clear the Set Picture As Background option, click to select the picture, and then press Delete.

Paper Size and Margins

The Paper Size setting for a default OneNote page is Auto, which means it can expand in any direction with no limits. That's fine if you're planning to use a notebook for strictly digital purposes. However, if you intend to print one or more pages, you'll want to define paper sizes and margins that match the paper and printer you plan to use.

OneNote includes 14 predefined paper sizes as well as a Custom option that allows you to specify your own dimensions. To edit these settings for an existing page, click the Paper Size button on the View tab. That opens the Paper Size pane on the right side of the page. In Figure 15-13, we've used the Index Card setting to mimic a standard 3-by-5-inch index card; to enhance the effect, we've hidden the page title and added rule lines.

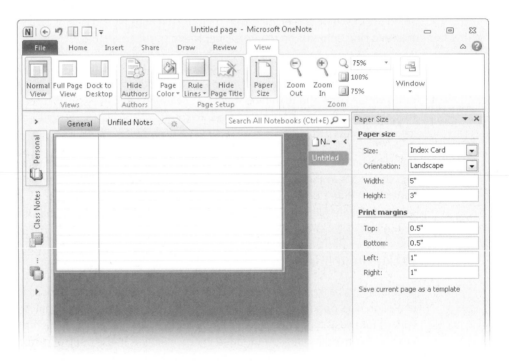

Figure 15-13 These settings allow a OneNote page to mimic a standard 3x5 index card. Save the page as a template to reuse it on new notebook pages.

Personalizing the OneNote Interface

You can customize OneNote's user interface by using the same tools available in the other Office 2010 programs, notably the options to fine-tune the ribbon and the Quick Access Toolbar.

For step-by-step instructions on how to customize these common Office interface features, see "Personalizing the Ribbon" on page 57, and "Customizing the Quick Access Toolbar" on page 62.

The most useful set of personalization options for OneNote reflect the common desire to hide clutter and maximize the workspace as much as possible. This is particularly important when you're typing class notes or meeting minutes on a notebook or netbook, where screen real estate is severely limited. In that scenario, where access to other pages and sections isn't necessary, the quickest path to a clean workspace is the F11 key, which toggles Full Page view (there's also a Full Page View button on the View tab and on the Quick Access Toolbar). In Full Page view, section tabs and page tabs are completely hidden, the ribbon is minimized to just tab headings, and the Quick Access Toolbar remains visible. To toggle back to Normal view, press F11 again. (You can also click the Full Page View button on the Quick Access Toolbar or click the View tab to make its contents visible and then click Normal View.)

For a less drastic solution, you can collapse the Navigation bar and page tabs bar. Click the Collapse Navigation Bar arrow to the right of the Notebooks heading and the matching Collapse Page Tabs arrow to the right of the New Page button above the page tabs bar. With both elements collapsed, the main OneNote window looks like the example shown in Figure 15-14. Note that the section tabs list is invisible and the list of open notebooks is turned on its side. The page tabs bar is still visible, but it's reduced to its absolute minimum width.

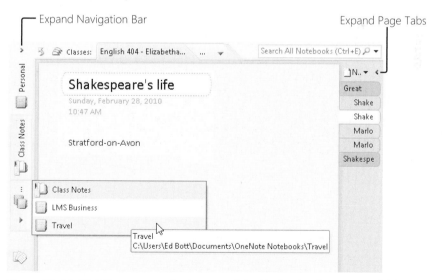

Figure 15-14 Click the arrow at the bottom of the Navigation bar to see additional open notebooks. Use ScreenTips to identify page names and notebook locations.

To restore the Navigation bar and the page tabs bar to their normal widths, click the Expand Navigation Bar shortcut (the arrow just above the first notebook name) and the Expand Page Tabs arrow above the shrunken page tabs bar. In their expanded form, you can adjust the width of either element so that they use less space on a notebook computer or take advantage of the extra desktop real estate on a large monitor. Aim the mouse at the border between either element and the contents pane until the pointer turns into a two-headed arrow, then drag in either direction to widen or narrow the Navigation bar or page tabs bar.

The other personalization options available for the main OneNote interface allow you to change on which side of the screen the Navigation bar, the page tabs bar, and the vertical scroll bar appear. Some OneNote users find it easier to navigate, for example, by moving the page tabs bar to the left side so that the contents of a section appear next to the section tab itself. To adjust this setting, open the OneNote Options dialog box (click File, and then click Options), click the Display tab, and select Page Tabs Appear On The Left.

The other significant personalization option involves the OneNote icon in the notification area. We discuss its settings in more detail in "Customizing the OneNote Taskbar Icon" on page 573.

CHAPTER 16

Tagging, Organizing, and Finding Information

THE more you use OneNote, the bigger your collection of pages and sections and notebooks becomes. And as that collection grows in size and diversity, the challenge of finding something you wrote last month or last year becomes ever more acute. Fortunately, you have a variety of options to help you create order from chaos.

In this chapter we look at the full range of tools, techniques, and strategies you can use to stay organized in OneNote. We start with the powerful Tags feature, which allows you to assign a label and icon to an individual paragraph and then collect similar tags into summary pages and to-do lists. This feature works best when you toss the default tags and create your own.

We fully document OneNote's powerful but occasionally confusing search capabilities, which can be accessed from the Windows search box and in OneNote itself. We also highlight OneNote's many tools for creating links to documents, web pages, and other OneNote pages and sections. That's just one of the strategies you can use to keep from being overwhelmed by a large collection of notebooks.

And finally, we explain how OneNote's Recycle Bin and automatic backup features work, and recommend a few tweaks to ensure that you'll have the best chance of finding a page or a section if you accidentally delete a page containing irreplaceable information.

Using Tags to Highlight Important Notes

You can attach a tag to any paragraph on any page in OneNote. Each tag provides a label (To Do, Important, Remember For Later) and, optionally, a small icon that appears to the left of the paragraph as well as custom font colors and highlighting that are applied to the entire tagged paragraph.

Attaching a tag to a paragraph makes spotting action items easier when you're scanning a page—you just look for the colorful icons or highlighting. But the real value of tags, as we explain later in this section, becomes apparent when you search for tagged items throughout a notebook (or a group of notebooks) and gather them into a single pane. That step makes it easy to find all the to-do items on your list, every snippet of research you've tagged as important, or ideas you've flagged for discussion with your partner.

Figure 16-1 shows a simple list containing six items, three of which have been tagged. The page title has been tagged as well. The Tags Summary pane on the right side of the OneNote window shows the results of a search for tagged items in the current notebook.

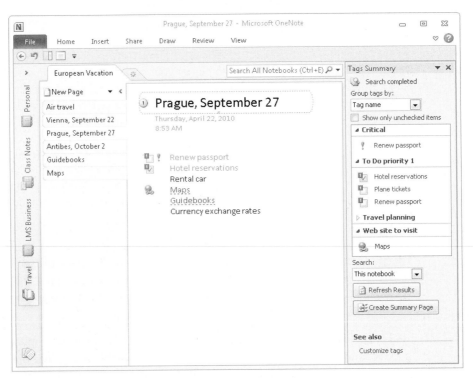

Figure 16-1 The icons to the left of items in this list indicate they've been tagged. The Tags Summary pane on the right includes tags from multiple pages.

For more details on how the Tags Summary pane works, see "Finding Tagged Notes" on page 540.

You'll find a lengthy list of predefined tags, arranged in an arbitrary order, in the Tags group on the Home tab. Only three tags are visible at any one time on the ribbon, with the most recently used tag and its two closest neighbors in this short list. You can scroll through that tiny window to view the entire group, three tags at a time, or click the arrow to reveal the entire list.

Applying and Removing Tags

To apply a tag to a paragraph, click anywhere within the paragraph and then click an entry on the Tags menu. (It doesn't matter whether any text is selected; the tag is applied to the entire paragraph.) You can apply up to nine tags to a single paragraph. For example, you might apply the Critical, To Do, and Project *X* tags to an item so that it appears in your search results if you look for any of those tags. Remember that images live in note containers as paragraphs, so you can tag an image just as easily as a snippet of text.

INSIDE OUT   Use numeric shortcuts for your favorite tags

If you look to the right of the first nine tags on the Tags menu, you'll notice that each is assigned a numeric shortcut, Ctrl+1 through Ctrl+9. To apply one of these nine tags to the current paragraph, press the keyboard shortcut assigned to it.

So how do you change the shortcut for a given tag or assign a shortcut to a tag that currently doesn't have one? The answer is simple, if not exactly intuitive: open the Customize Tags dialog box and use the Move Tag Up and Move Tag Down buttons (indicated by up and down arrows) to move your tags into the correct position. Whichever tag you move to the top of the list is assigned shortcut Ctrl+1, with the tag in the next position getting Ctrl+2, and so on.

You can also access the Tags menu by right-clicking any paragraph and choosing Tag from the shortcut menu. Use the cascading menu to select a specific tag, or click Tag to apply the most recently used tag.

To remove a tag from the current paragraph, click the Remove Tag option at the bottom of the Tags menu, or use the keyboard shortcut Ctrl+0. You can also right-click the tag icon and click Remove Tag on the shortcut menu, or right-click the tagged paragraph and click the Tag option on the shortcut menu. (For a tag that uses a check box, you might have to click twice—once to fill in the check box and again to remove it.)

What happens if you position the insertion point within a tagged paragraph and then click the same tag from the Tags menu? That depends. For most tags, the result is a simple toggle: click once to apply the tag, click again to remove it. But there's a third option for any tag that has a check-box symbol attached to it, such as the default To Do tag. (Because it's at the top of the list, it has the Ctrl+1 keyboard shortcut assigned to it.) If you click the To Do tag or press Ctrl+1, an empty check box appears to the left of the current paragraph.

Click that box to add a check mark to it, which indicates the item is completed, as shown here.

As you'll see later in this chapter, you can distinguish between open and completed tags when using the Find Tags option.

For more on how to find tagged items in OneNote, see "Finding Tagged Notes" on page 540.

The check box in front of a tagged item is a simple toggle that marks the tagged item as open or completed. By contrast, the tag on the Tags menu (and the corresponding keyboard shortcut) are three-way toggles: click once to apply the tag, click again to fill in the check box and mark it as completed, and click once more to remove the tag completely.

Customizing Tags

The standard list of 29 tags that is included with OneNote is interesting, but it's hardly useful. For starters, it includes some items that clearly cry out for customization, like Project A and Project B, not to mention Discuss With <Person A> and Discuss With <Person B> (both of which actually include the angle brackets). Are you really going to use the Movie To See or Remember For Blog tags? And why would you want to tag something as a Phone Number?

No, this built-in list is strictly for illustrative purposes, to give you an idea of things you can do with tags. If you plan to use OneNote seriously, we strongly recommend that you take a few minutes and personalize the list of tags. Get rid of the tags you'll never use, add any custom tags that match your work/study/research habits, and rearrange the order of your tags so that those you use most often have keyboard shortcuts assigned to them. If you need only three tags, that's all you should have.

Your starting point is the Customize Tags dialog box, which is accessible from a link at the bottom of the Tags menu. Figure 16-2 shows the Customize Tags dialog box after adding some new tags and changing the order of existing ones.

To eliminate a tag you have no intention of using, select its entry in the list and click the Remove button (just below the Move Tag Up and Move Tag Down buttons at the right).

Figure 16-2 From this dialog box, you can add or remove a tag, modify an existing tag, and change the order of tags in the list.

To add a custom tag to the list, click New Tag. To change the settings for an existing tag, select its entry in the list and click Modify Tag. The resulting dialog box is nearly identical, with the only difference being the name displayed in the title bar. Figure 16-3 shows the generic Project A tag in the process of being modified.

Figure 16-3 When creating or modifying a tag, you can give it a name and specify how tagged paragraphs appear on the page.

Chapter 16

Every tag consists of four elements, each of which can be customized here:

- **Display name**   This is the name that appears on the Tags menu. It can include any combination of letters, numbers, spaces, and punctuation. For ease of use, we recommend keeping tag names much shorter than their maximum permitted length of 200 characters.

- **Symbol**   This setting defines the small icon that appears to the left of a tagged item. You can choose from the collection of 138 symbols shown here or click None to create a symbol-free tag. All of the symbols in the group of three columns on the left are check boxes that can be marked as open or completed. You cannot assign a custom icon of your own creation.

- **Font color**   Use this optional setting to choose from one of 40 colors that will automatically be applied to all text in a paragraph when this tag is applied to it. The default setting is Automatic.

- **Highlight color**   Use this optional setting, with or without a custom font color, to apply highlight formatting to all text in the tagged paragraph. The 15 color choices match colors available via the Text Highlight Color tool on the Home tab.

CAUTION

When you customize an existing tag, your changes apply only to paragraphs that you tag from that time forward. Existing instances of the tag you just modified are not affected. If you want to sync the old tags with the new ones, you have to do so manually.

Copying Custom Tags to Another Copy of OneNote

Any customizations you make to OneNote tags are saved in your user profile. So, if you use more than one computer (a desktop computer in the office and a portable PC on the road, for example), you need to expend some effort to synchronize your customized tags between the two devices. Unfortunately, OneNote does not include an easy tool for transferring these settings from one PC to another. Instead, you have to choose one of three somewhat clunky options.

The first, most obvious, option is to re-create your customized tags manually. If you use only a handful of custom tags, this option might be the simplest. If your list of custom tags is large, the process will probably be too tedious.

An easier alternative is to copy tags one at a time from your existing OneNote notebooks to your uncustomized copy of OneNote. When you see a tag that was created on another PC and isn't yet on the one you're using now, right-click the tag symbol and choose Add To My Tags, as shown here.

The final and most drastic alternative is to transplant the OneNote preferences file from one computer to another. If the first computer is customized exactly as you like it and the second computer has no special settings you want to keep, this option is appropriate.

INSIDE OUT Use OneNote to keep a record of your custom tags

How do you compare the custom OneNote tags in your office PCs with the ones on your home PC? Take a picture—or more precisely, take a screen clipping. Click the Tags menu to display its contents, and then press Windows logo key+S. Use the Screen Clipping tool to capture a picture of the list, and save the result in a notebook that you can share with the new PC. If you're willing to spend a little more time and energy, make a list of the names of your custom tags, in order, and then apply that tag to each entry in the list. That's what we did to create the list that's shown in the preceding screen shot.

Before you try this, be sure you have up-to-date backups for all your OneNote data files just in case something goes wrong. Be sure that OneNote is closed on both computers, and then follow these steps to copy the customized settings from your customized PC to your new PC:

1. On both computers, open the folder %AppData%\Microsoft\OneNote\14.0 in Windows Explorer. (Enter this exact address, including the percent signs, and Windows automatically expands it to the correct path within your user profile, based on your user name.)

2. On the customized PC, copy the file Preferences.dat to a location that you can access from the new PC—a shared network drive, Windows Live SkyDrive, or a USB flash drive, for example.

3. On the new PC, replace the current copy of Preferences.dat with the file you copied from your other PC.

4. Reopen OneNote, and check to be sure that your custom tags transferred correctly.

If you want to keep your settings for OneNote in sync between two PCs, you can use Windows Live Sync or another similar solution to sync the settings files so that changes on one PC are copied to the other. This solution isn't officially supported.

Using Links for Quick Connections

On any OneNote page, you can create a clickable link that takes you somewhere else. Links can lead to a file (often an Office document, although you can link to other file types as well), to a web page, or to another location in a OneNote notebook.

Some links are created automatically—when you send a web page clipping to OneNote, for example, or when you drag a file icon from Windows Explorer and drop it on a page. You can also paste links from the Clipboard and create links manually.

Creating Links to Web Pages or Files

When you clip something from a web browser and paste it onto a page, OneNote adds a hyperlink to the source page at the bottom of the note container.

If you prefer, you can create a link to a web page manually by using the Link dialog box. If you want to link to existing text or a graphic, make that selection first, or click in an empty place if you plan to add new text for the link. Then, on the Insert tab, click Link (or press Ctrl+K, or use the Link option on the right-click shortcut menu). As Figure 16-4 shows, the Text To Display box holds the link text, and the Address box contains the link location.

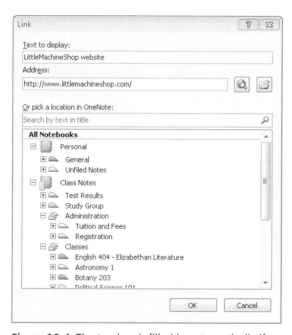

Figure 16-4 The top box is filled in automatically if you select text before creating a link. Use the browser icon to open a browser window, locate a web page, copy its URL from the Address bar, and then return to the Link dialog box and paste the URL into the Address box.

The folder icon, to the far right of the Address box, opens Windows Explorer, where you can select a file from a local or shared folder and fill in the address with the file path. For more options, skip the Link dialog box, and drag a file from Windows Explorer and drop it on the

OneNote page. You'll see a set of options like the ones shown here. Select the top option, Insert A Link To The Original File, to manually create a link to the document.

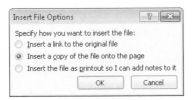

For more on how to manage connections between OneNote and documents you create using Word, Excel, or PowerPoint, see "Linking Notes to Documents and Web Pages" on page 557.

Creating Links to Other Places in OneNote

Being able to jump back and forth between locations in OneNote can be extremely useful for staying organized, especially when you're picky about where you store particular types of data. For example, say your Business notebook contains two sections: a Suppliers section, with a separate page for your notes about every supplier you do business with, and a Complaints section, where you keep notes about your dealings with dissatisfied customers. If a customer complains about a Tailspin Toys product they bought from your shop, you can keep notes in both places, linking the related discussions so that you can quickly cross-reference the discussions later.

The bottom of the Link dialog box (shown earlier in Figure 16-4) lets you link a snippet of text or a graphic to a OneNote location; just choose a notebook, section group, section, or page from the list of OneNote locations.

If you want to create a link to a specific paragraph, use the Clipboard. Right-click the paragraph, click Copy Link To Paragraph, and then paste that link into another page in the same notebook or in another notebook. You can use this technique to copy a link to a single paragraph, an entire notebook, or anything in between. If you right-click a page tab, for example, you can choose Copy Link To Page, as in Figure 16-5.

Section and section group tabs and the notebook icons in the Navigation bar offer corresponding options on their respective shortcut menus. Paste the copied link on any page, and you can click it to jump directly to the linked paragraph, page, section, section group, or notebook.

Editing and Removing Links

To remove a link completely, regardless of what location it points to, just delete the text or graphic containing the link. If you want to leave the text or graphic intact, right-click the link and choose Remove Link from the shortcut menu.

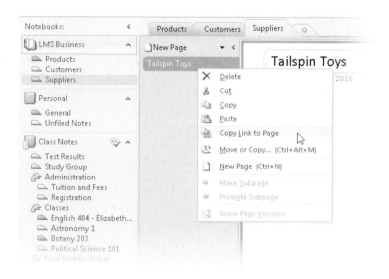

Figure 16-5 Right-click a page tab (as shown here) or a notebook, section, or paragraph to copy a link that can be pasted onto another page.

To change the display text or address of a link, right-click and choose Edit Link. That opens the Link dialog box, where you can change a file location or web address or point to an alternative notebook, section, or page.

Editing a OneNote link isn't recommended. If you choose the Edit Link command for a link that points to a paragraph elsewhere in OneNote, you'll see a complex URL that starts with onenote: and contains a shockingly long collection of alphanumeric characters (collectively known as a globally unique identifier, or GUID) in a strange syntax. Editing that syntax isn't for the faint of heart; you're better off deleting the current link and creating a new one instead.

INSIDE OUT   Build an instant notebook with wiki links

OneNote 2010 supports the same link-creating syntax used in several popular wiki packages. If you enter a pair of left brackets followed by some text and a pair of right brackets, OneNote turns the bracketed text into a link as soon as you type the second right bracket. If the link text matches the name of an existing page or section, the link points to that location. If no existing page or section has that name, OneNote creates a new page in the current section. You can use this technique with a brand new notebook to build a Table of Contents page and fill the notebook full of new blank pages with relevant titles, all ready for you to fill in. Enter a page name in wiki syntax format, press Enter, and repeat.

Chapter 16

Smart Search Strategies

By design, OneNote encourages a kind of willing suspension of organization. The program's breezy, casual, loosely structured interface allows you to add thoughts, save snippets as you work, and create new pages as needed without having to worry too much about where those pages go. You can impose order on this seeming chaos after the fact by using OneNote's many search tools. In this section, we explain how to search for text on a page and how to find words and phrases across sections, within a notebook, or across every open notebook. We also demonstrate how to pull together tagged items into a collection that you can sort, filter, and click to review.

The Fast Search feature in OneNote 2010 is vastly improved over the corresponding capabilities in earlier versions of OneNote. Because it uses the Windows Search index to do the heavy lifting, performance is extremely fast, and search results appear as you type in the search box.

Pages and sections from OneNote appear in the search results when you use the search box on the Start menu (in Windows Vista or Windows 7), but you'll get much better results by searching from within OneNote. You can search on a page, within a section or section group, within a single notebook, or across all open notebooks.

INSIDE OUT Setting up search in Windows XP

OneNote's Fast Search is enabled by default in Windows Vista and Windows 7, which include Windows Search as a feature of the operating system. If you're using Windows XP, you have to jump through one extra hoop, downloading and installing the optional Windows Desktop Search add-on. To get started, click File, then click Options, and then click Install Instant Search from near the bottom of the Display tab.

Searching on a Page

To find a word or phrase on a page, press Ctrl+F, and then begin entering search terms in the search box just above the current page, to the far right of the section tabs. Every match is highlighted in yellow on the page itself. To the left of the search box is a yellow results list that displays the number of matches; click the up and down arrows to scroll through search results on the page (or use the keyboard shortcuts F3 and Shift+F3).

OneNote treats each word you enter as a distinct search term and treats spaces as a logical AND (in other words, all terms must be present on a page to produce a match). Figure 16-6 shows a keyword search that includes results for four words.

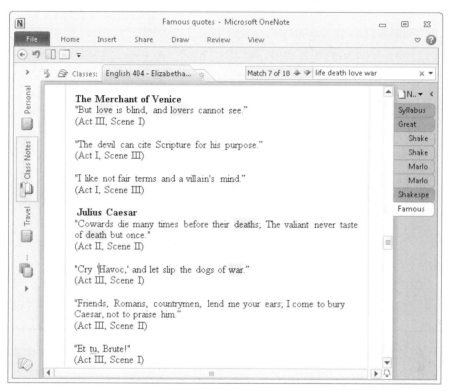

Figure 16-6 OneNote's Fast Search finds any page that contains all of the words you enter in the search box above the page, to the right of the section tabs.

OneNote understands a limited set of Boolean operators to do more complex searches. You can use the operators AND and OR (the capital letters are required) to restrict your search. Our testing with other common Boolean operators, including NOT and NEAR, confirms that they are not supported in OneNote searches.

Place quotation marks around search terms to restrict the results to a specific phrase. In the previous figure, for example, you could enter "love is blind" (with quotation marks included) to return only the text that includes that exact phrase.

Searching by Section or Notebook

To expand your search so that it includes more than the current page, click in the search box (or press Ctrl+E to position the insertion point there) and begin entering search terms. As you type, results appear instantly in a list just below the search box. Figure 16-7 shows the results when we begin typing *shake*.

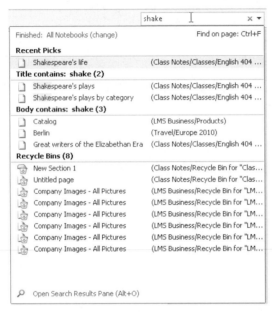

Figure 16-7 If the search term matches the title of a page, section, section group, or notebook, that match is highlighted in this results list.

Some salient characteristics of OneNote's Fast Search are worth noting, especially if you're accustomed to using search in other contexts. For starters, search works only on open notebooks. If you can't see a notebook in the Navigation bar, you can't search its contents.

Search results are grouped, with the pages or sections you've used most recently at the top, followed by results containing the search term in a page or section name, and then by results where the search term appears in the body of a page. At the bottom of the list are pages from the recycle bins for all open notebooks. These groupings cannot be modified.

Search terms are not case-sensitive. You can enter terms using any mix of uppercase and lowercase letters, and the results will be the same. Enclose your search term in quotation marks to search for a phrase, and place AND (in all caps) between two terms to return only pages and sections that include both terms.

If the results aren't what you expected, you can change the scope of the search, increasing or decreasing the amount of ground that OneNote covers while looking for your search terms. If you haven't yet begun your search, click the arrow at the right of the search box to display the list shown here.

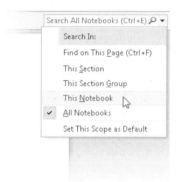

If you're viewing results for a current search and want to expand or restrict the scope of the search, click the link at the top of the results box and then choose a new search scope.

The default scope is Search All Notebooks. To choose a more restrictive setting as the default, choose the search scope you prefer, and then click Set This Scope As Default at the bottom of the list.

When you click a page in the results list, the corresponding notebook, section, or page appears in the OneNote contents pane, allowing you to preview its contents. The results list remains visible if you look but don't click, so you can select another entry from the results list (or use the Up and Down Arrow keys to move through the list) and continue previewing search results. As soon as you click within a page or use the scroll bars to go beyond the preview, however, the results list disappears. (To close the results list immediately, click the X to the right of the search box or press Escape.)

That now-you-see-it-now-you-don't behavior on the part of the results list can be annoying if you have a lengthy list of search results that you want to examine in detail. The solution? Click the Open Search Results Pane link at the bottom of the results list (or press the keyboard shortcut Alt+O). Doing so opens an alternative view of the search results in a pane on the right side of the OneNote program window. Figure 16-8 shows the Search Results pane in action.

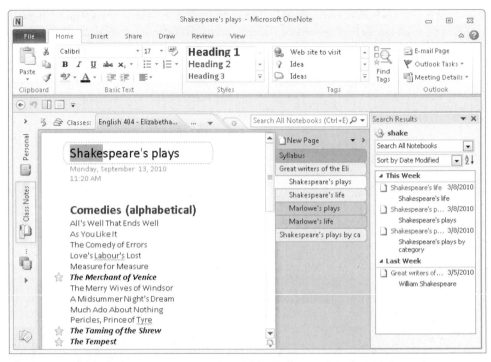

Figure 16-8 The Search Results pane remains visible while you click through its results.

The bold type at the top of the Search Results pane shows the current search term. From this pane, you can do the following:

- **Change the search scope**   You can restrict the scope by section, by section group, or by notebook.

- **Change the sort field**   Instead of the default order, which shows results in reverse order by the date they were last modified, you can choose to sort by section or by title, in alphabetical order.

- **Change sort order**   Click the button to the right of the sort field to toggle between ascending and descending order for the results list.

One thing you can't do with the Search Results pane is change the search term. For that, you have to enter a new search term in the search box (which is pushed to the left by the appearance of the Search Results pane) and then click Open Search Results Pane at the bottom of that new results list.

You can adjust the width of the Search Results pane by dragging its inner edge in either direction. You can also click and drag the title to move the pane to the left side of the OneNote program window, or drag it free of its docked position so that it floats over the page. (If you have a multiple-monitor setup, try dragging the Search Results pane to your secondary monitor, where you can use it to select pages and view them on your primary monitor without any visual distractions.)

INSIDE OUT   Make searches easier by using your own keywords

Although tags are a useful way to associate a note with a project, they're not the only trick available to you. If you're working on multiple projects and you want a quick way to locate all the pages associated with one of those projects, here's a trick that takes advantage of OneNote's search skills. For every page associated with a particular project, embed a unique keyword or code associated only with that project. Be sure you pick a term that you are unlikely to ever use in any other context. (If you're working on your company's annual report for 2011, try a code like ARX2011.) By searching for that unique marker, you can find related pages quickly with just a simple search.

You can switch between searching on the current page and searching in the currently defined search scope at any time by pressing Ctrl+F or Ctrl+E.

Reviewing Recently Modified Pages

Do you use OneNote only on your personal PC, with no shared notebooks? If so, you might miss one of OneNote's most useful search tricks. The Recent Edits menu offers access to a handful of time-based, saved searches that you can use to review the pages you've worked on in recent days, weeks, or months. Confusingly, it's placed on the Share tab, in the Shared Notebooks group. Don't be misled by the location—the choices on the Recent Edits menu let you filter even your personal, locally stored notebooks so that you see only pages that have been recently created or modified. Figure 16-9 shows the contents of a single section filtered to show only pages that were changed yesterday.

The results of the preconfigured searches on the Recent Edits menu show up in the Search Results pane, where you can change their scope and adjust the sort field and sort order.

For more details on the other options in this group, including the Find By Author menu, see "Sharing and Synchronizing Notebooks" on page 561.

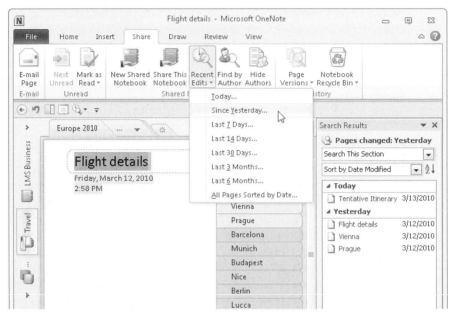

Figure 16-9 Don't be misled by the placement of this menu choice; you can use these saved searches to review your own recent work on a personal notebook as well.

Finding Tagged Notes

If you use tags to mark individual paragraphs for follow-up, then you need to know how to find those tagged items when you need them. Your starting point is the Find Tags button, in the Tags group on the Home tab. Clicking this button shows or hides the Tags Summary pane, shown in Figure 16-10.

In essence, the Find Tags button acts as a saved search that finds all tagged items. The Tags Summary pane offers some options to filter and group its search results; it doesn't offer any way to restrict the summary to only those tags you select, although you can collapse and expand the display of individual tags in the results list. From top to bottom, here's what you can do with the Tags Summary pane:

- **Group Tags By** By default, the results in the Tags Summary pane are grouped by tag name. Use this list to change the grouping to display the results by date, section, page title, or by the note text.

- **Show Only Unchecked Items** Selecting this option filters the list to show only those items that have a check box (such as the built-in To Do tag) and where you haven't clicked the check box to mark an item as completed.

- **Search**   These options filter the search scope (to the current section or notebook, for example) and also offer date-based options, such as Today's Notes or Last Week's Notes.

- **Refresh Results**   The Tags Summary pane remains visible as you work, but its contents don't update automatically. If you're working through your list of tagged items, click this button occasionally so that the list reflects your changes.

- **Create Summary Page**   This option allows you to create a new page in the current section containing copies of all tagged items that are visible in the Tags Summary pane. Use the expand/collapse arrows to the left of each heading in the list of tagged items to control whether the items under that heading appear on the summary page.

Figure 16-10 The Tags Summary pane shows all tagged items in the scope you've selected.

CAUTION !

> When you use the Create Summary Page button, items on the resulting page are identical copies of the originals and include links to the original items. They are not, however, synchronized with those items. If you click the check box next to an item on the summary page to mark it as complete, the original tagged item remains unchecked. Likewise, any notes you add to an original item are not reflected on a summary page you created earlier.

Expert Organizational Techniques

Some people file using meticulously labeled folders. Others use a shoebox. In OneNote, the shoebox is called Unfiled Notes, and it resides at the bottom of the Navigation bar.

When you first set up OneNote, the program creates a single notebook, called Personal, and saves it in the OneNote Notebooks folder in the Documents folder of your user profile. The Personal notebook contains two sections, General and Unfiled Notes. Initially, the Unfiled Notes link at the bottom of the Navigation bar points to its namesake in the Personal notebook. (If you upgrade over OneNote 2007, the default Unfiled Notes location is a section in your default notebooks folder; it is not contained in any notebook.)

INSIDE OUT   Point Unfiled Notes to an alternate section

The Unfiled Notes shortcut doesn't have to point to a section by that name. You can point the Unfiled Notes shortcut to any section in any notebook and use it as a one-click way to jump to that location. To make the change, click File, Options, and then modify the Unfiled Notes Section location on the Save & Backup tab.

So why does Unfiled Notes exist? Its primary purpose is to give you a single destination for screen clippings, printouts, and stuff you collect while browsing web pages or working in Outlook. Rather than specify a destination for each item, you can send them to a new page in Unfiled Notes. That lets you surf, clip, and print without interruption and then sift through your Unfiled Notes section later, at your leisure.

You can customize the destination for all of these Send To options. To do so, click File, click Options, and then adjust the settings on the Send To OneNote tab. By default, each option in this list is initially set to Always Ask Where To Send. Figure 16-11 shows the results after we adjusted the settings.

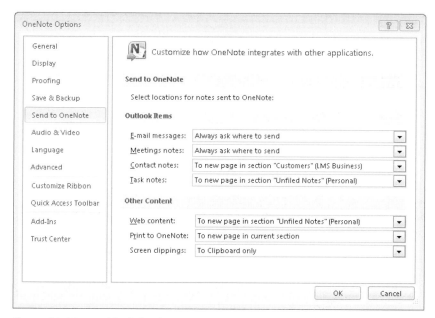

Figure 16-11 Use this dialog box to set default locations for common Send To interactions between other programs and OneNote.

Several of the settings in this dialog box can be set automatically from the Send To Location dialog box.

For details on how web clippings and screen clippings work, see "Using Links for Quick Connections" on page 530. For instructions on how to create links between Outlook items and OneNote, see "Using OneNote with Outlook" on page 547.

Backing Up and Recovering Notebooks

By default, OneNote is configured to create automatic daily backups of every open notebook and to keep the two most recent backup sets for each notebook in a local folder, regardless of the actual location of the notebook itself. You can change the frequency and the number of saved backups, as well as the location of the backup folder. (And yes, the hidden Recycle Bin section for each notebook is backed up as well.) To view the current settings and change them if necessary, click File, and then click Options. Figure 16-12 shows the Save & Backup tab in the OneNote Options dialog box.

Chapter 16

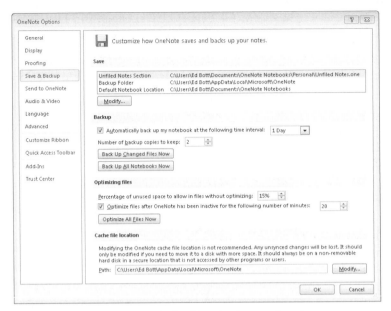

Figure 16-12 Adjust automatic OneNote backup settings here.

If you're paranoid about losing data, you can change the value for Automatically Back Up My Notebook At The Following Time Interval on a sliding scale that starts at 1 minute. At the other extreme, you can set backups to be created as infrequently as every 6 weeks. To disable backup copies completely, clear this check box. You can also set the Number Of Backup Copies To Keep to a value between 0 and 99,999. (You'll want a very large hard drive for the latter setting.)

Backup files are saved in a hidden folder in your local user profile (the %LocalAppData% folder). Fortunately, you don't have to dig to recover a saved backup. Click File, and then click the Open Backups button on the Info tab, as shown next.

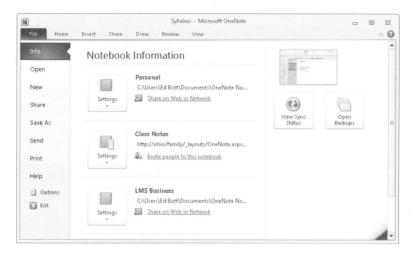

Browse through folders (each one represents a notebook) and subfolders (section groups). The backups themselves are in OneNote Section files, with the extension .one. Each backup has the name of the original section, with the backup date appended to the file name, as shown here.

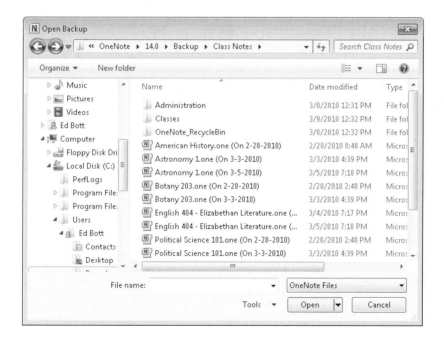

INSIDE OUT
You might have more backups than you think

The default backup settings in OneNote allow you to recover from accidental deletions for up to two days. But what if you discover that the page you desperately need right now went missing last week or last month? If you're using any edition of Windows 7 or the Business or Ultimate editions of Windows Vista, you might be able to locate older backup copies. In Windows Explorer, open your My Documents folder, right-click the OneNote Notebooks folder, and click Restore Previous Versions. Depending on your Windows settings, you might have days' or weeks' worth of previous versions to restore. Ironically, you can even find previous versions of the backups in your Backup folder (%LocalAppData%\Microsoft\OneNote\14.0\Backup). If you use an alternative backup strategy, such as Windows Home Server, be sure to check those backup copies as well.

To restore all or part of a deleted page or section, double-click the backup file and open a read-only copy in OneNote. (The title bar should help you confirm that the section is read-only.) Because the newly opened section is not part of a currently open notebook, it and any other backups you open appear as part of a new Open Section tab at the bottom of the Navigation bar. You can drag sections or pages from the read-only backup to any note-book or section in the Navigation bar to copy them to that location. Alternatively, you can right-click any section tab or page tab in the read-only backup, choose Move Or Copy from the shortcut menu, and select an existing notebook or section as a destination. You can also skim through individual pages and copy text, graphics, or other items from any page to an existing or new notebook.

If you or a co-worker changed part of a page you've been working on, you might be able to recover all or part of the earlier version. See our discussion in "Sharing and Synchronizing Notebooks" on page 561.

OneNote 2010 Inside Out

M ORE than any other member of the Office family, OneNote inspires fierce loyalty among people who use it regularly. In this, our final OneNote chapter, we dive deep into the features and capabilities that make people so passionate about this program—including a few features you might never discover on your own.

We start by exploring the tight connections between OneNote and Outlook. By using these two programs together, you can create a flexible, expandable system to help you manage contacts, tasks, meetings, and other items outside the rigid confines of the Outlook Notes box. We also explain how to link OneNote pages to Word documents and slides in PowerPoint presentations, so that you can keep OneNote's free-form notes and discussions in sync with the more formal output from those programs.

Although it's tempting to think of OneNote as a tool for keeping your personal affairs organized, you needn't limit yourself. In this chapter, we explain how you can share a notebook with other people—or with yourself—on multiple PCs. The synchronization process is as close to magical as it gets. We also cover more traditional options for sharing the contents of a notebook by sending pages (or entire sections) to a printer or publishing them to alternative file formats or blogs.

And finally, we end this chapter with a grab bag of advanced features, including detailed instructions on how to incorporate audio and video recordings into a notebook. Our list of favorite OneNote tweaks includes customizations for the OneNote interface, hints for using OneNote on a Tablet or touch-enabled PC, and step-by-step instructions for saving and reusing custom page templates.

Using OneNote with Outlook

The more you use Outlook, the more likely you are to be frustrated by the limited text box it offers for capturing notes about a contact or a task. And don't get us started about the difficulty of keeping minutes and tracking follow-up tasks from the box at the bottom of a meeting item in an Outlook calendar.

The solution? For contacts, appointments, and meetings, link a OneNote page to the corresponding Outlook item. A button on the Outlook ribbon makes it easy to create the linked page initially, after which you can click a link in either program to move from the item to the OneNote page and vice versa. You can send any task to a OneNote page or, conversely, turn any paragraph on a OneNote page into an Outlook task, complete with a little red flag that allows you to jump to the associated task.

But we start with the simplest and most useful connection of all: sending an e-mail message from Outlook to OneNote.

Sending E-Mail Messages to OneNote

Some e-mail messages are worth saving outside your e-mail store. For a frustration-free vacation, you probably want to save e-mailed confirmations of hotel reservations and e-tickets for plane or train travel. When you purchase software online, the publisher might send license information and product keys that you'll want to keep at hand if you need to reinstall and reactivate the software at a later date. If your research project at school or work includes any interviews conducted via e-mail, you'll want to save that correspondence along with your other notes.

You can send an entire e-mail (with attachments) to a OneNote page with a single click. You can use this technique for simple archiving of important e-mail messages, or you can add those messages to a OneNote page and add notes or other details. In Outlook, you can find a Send To OneNote button (labeled OneNote and located in the Move group on the Home tab) when you're viewing a mail message, either in the message list or in a message window. Click that button, choose a destination in OneNote, and your message appears on the page you selected, as shown in Figure 17-1.

As this example illustrates, the saved message includes essential information from the e-mail header, as well as attachments and the entire message body. Neither OneNote nor Outlook maintains a link between the original message and the saved copy. Changes you make in Outlook (including deleting the message) do not affect the saved copy of the message in OneNote; likewise, when you edit the saved message in OneNote, the original message in Outlook is untouched.

For an in-depth discussion of how to organize e-mail in Outlook, see "Organizing E-Mail Messages" on page 757.

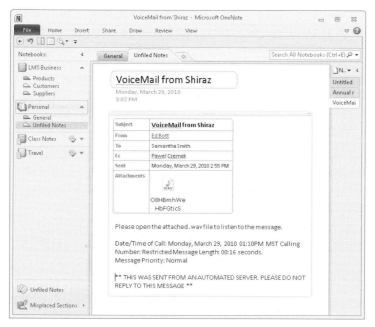

Figure 17-1 Outlook messages that you send to OneNote include attachments. If your voicemail system sends phone messages to e-mail, you can archive them in OneNote.

Linking Outlook Contacts to OneNote Pages

Each entry in your Outlook Contacts folder represents a relationship. You're most likely to open that contact item when you want to make a phone call, send an e-mail message, address an envelope, or perform some other action associated with the person or company whose details are saved there. The relatively small Notes box in a contact item is good for adding little details about a contact ("Met at tradeshow in Scranton, Jan 2009"), but it's a terrible place for keeping detailed records of your interactions with someone. For that, OneNote is a much better choice.

With minimal effort, you can tie an Outlook item and a OneNote page together so that jumping from one location to the other takes a single click. Changes you make in each place are completely independent; the link is simply a navigational aid.

From any Outlook contact item, click the OneNote button. (The ScreenTip identifies this button as Linked Contact Notes. You'll find it in the Actions group on the Home tab, in slightly different locations depending on whether you're viewing a single contact or a selection from the folder view.) If there's no matching page, OneNote creates a new page in the default location for new contact notes or asks you to select a section for the new page. If the linked page already exists, clicking this button opens it and allows you to add new notes or review notes you entered previously. You cannot create a new set of linked contact notes on an existing OneNote page; instead, create a new page and then copy or move the notes from that other page to the newly created page.

For a full discussion of how to work with contacts in Outlook, see "Organizing Your Contacts" on page 715.

For details on how to customize the default locations for saving contacts and other Outlook items in OneNote, see "Printing, Publishing, and Sharing Notes" on page 566.

What appears in OneNote? The name of the Outlook contact becomes the title of a new page in the section you specify. A handful of fields from the contents of the Outlook item are added in a new table at the top of that page, as shown in Figure 17-2.

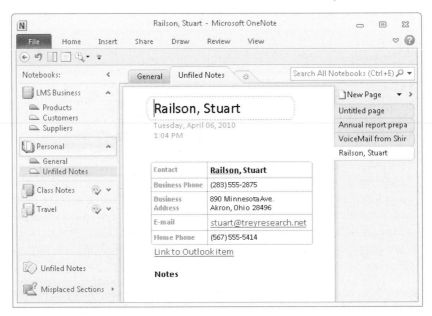

Figure 17-2 If the details you need about a contact aren't in this default set, click Link To Outlook Item and see the full contact item in Outlook.

INSIDE OUT   Link an entire Contacts folder to OneNote

When you select multiple items in an Outlook Contacts folder, clicking the OneNote button creates a new page for any selected contact that does not already have a linked page. It then opens or switches to OneNote and shows you the linked page for the last contact you clicked in the current selection. If you like the idea of linked Contact notes and want to dive right in, open the Contacts folder, press Ctrl+A to select all items, and then click OneNote on the Home tab. When Outlook finishes, you have a single section filled with linked pages, one for each item in your Contacts folder. A big advantage of this strategy is that your entire Contacts folder is available from the search box in OneNote, and you can link other OneNote pages or sections to the page for each contact. The biggest gotcha: you have to remember to manually add or delete the associated OneNote pages each time you add or delete a contact.

TROUBLESHOOTING

Outlook keeps taking you to a deleted OneNote page

When you link an Outlook item to a OneNote page, the link is based on GUIDs in OneNote. That's good news most of the time because you can move a page of contact notes to a new OneNote section without worrying about breaking the link. The link tracking is, perhaps, a little too smart. If you delete a OneNote contact notes page so you can start fresh, OneNote "fixes" the link so it points to the deleted page in the OneNote Recycle Bin. Check the section tabs above the contents pane. If you see that the current page is in the Deleted Pages section, that's what happened to you. The solution is to right-click the page tab and click Delete. That removes the page permanently. Now go back to Outlook, open that contact item, and click the OneNote command on the Home tab. This time you'll get a new page with the correct title and link.

Connecting Appointments and Meetings to OneNote

With Outlook appointments and meetings, you can take your choice of two ways to connect to OneNote. Which option should you choose? That depends. Do you simply want to copy the details of a meeting into a notes page and add some comments? Or do you want to create a link between the Outlook item and the OneNote page?

Adding details from an appointment or a meeting item to a page is simple. Create a new page, or click to position the insertion point on an existing page. Then, in the Outlook group on the Home tab, click Meeting Details. That opens a list showing all appointments on your calendar that are scheduled to start today.

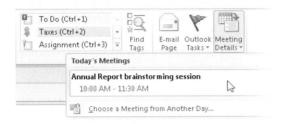

The assumption on this list is that you're preparing to take notes for a meeting that's about to begin. If that's the case, and the meeting is on your calendar, click its entry in the Meeting Details list to add a small table to the current OneNote page, containing the subject, date, time, location, and attendees for the meeting, as drawn from your calendar. Click under the Notes heading to begin adding your own comments.

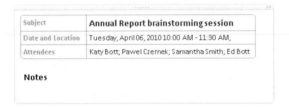

If you want to link a meeting to a OneNote page, make the connection by starting in Outlook. Select the meeting or appointment item in your Calendar, and then click OneNote (you'll find this command in the Actions group on the Meeting or Appointment tab). As is the case with a contact, clicking this button creates a new page, if one does not exist already, or jumps to an existing linked page. The details that are sent to the OneNote page are similar to those you see if you use the Meeting Details menu from OneNote. The difference? Under the meeting details is a generic bit of text: Link To Outlook Item. That hyperlink jumps to the linked appointment or meeting item in Outlook.

INSIDE OUT   Create a custom shortcut to linked Outlook items

When you use the OneNote button to create linked notes for an Outlook contact, appointment, or meeting, the resulting page contains a Link To Outlook Item shortcut. What isn't immediately obvious is that the modest-looking, text-only hyperlink works outside OneNote as well. Right-click the shortcut in OneNote, and click Copy Link. If you paste the copied text into a text editor, you can see the format of the link. It starts with **onenote:outlook?folder=**. That's followed by the name of the folder, typically Contacts or Calendar, and a 48-character GUID that represents the Outlook item. Don't be misled by the unfamiliar syntax; you can use that URL to create a new shortcut in a folder or on the desktop, and Windows will have no problem opening it. In fact, saving that shortcut opens both the OneNote page and the linked Outlook item—opening either or both programs if necessary.

Using Outlook Tasks with OneNote

As far as OneNote is concerned, tasks are different from other Outlook items. In the case of contacts, meetings, and appointments, the idea is to send information from Outlook to OneNote. With tasks, the flow of information moves both ways. You can link an existing task to a OneNote page, just as you can with those other types of items. Unlike with those other item types, however, the process also works in reverse. Using the options on the Outlook Tasks menu, you can create a new Outlook task linked to the current paragraph in OneNote. From that point onward, you can jump directly from a OneNote page to a linked Outlook task and back again.

If an item on your task list represents a big (or even medium-size) project, you might want to create a single task in Outlook to serve as your launching point. You can then break the big project into multiple milestones and add a list of those milestones to your OneNote master page, with each item on that list linked to a separate Outlook task, each with its own start and due dates.

Here's how it works in practice. If you've been put in charge of delivering the company's annual report this year, you might start with a single task called Annual Report, with a start date and due date that represent the timeline of the entire project. Figure 17-3 shows this task.

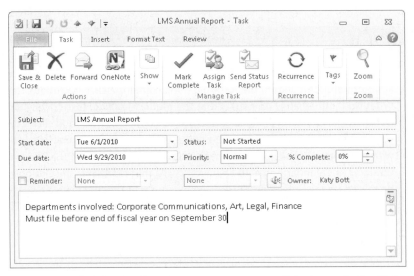

Figure 17-3 Click the OneNote button to create a new linked page in OneNote, with a page title there that matches the Subject here.

After saving the task, click the Send To OneNote button in the Actions group on the Home tab. If you choose a OneNote section, you get a new OneNote page whose title is the same as the text in the Subject field of your new task, and you're taken to the newly created page. Nothing else is copied to OneNote from that task—no body text, no start or due dates, no status or priority indicators.

On the newly created page, begin entering the individual milestones or subtasks you want to track as part of the overall project. Then, for each one, click the Outlook Tasks button (in the Outlook group on OneNote's Home tab) and choose one of the six available flags. Figure 17-4 shows the page after we've created two tasks and while we're in the process of creating a third.

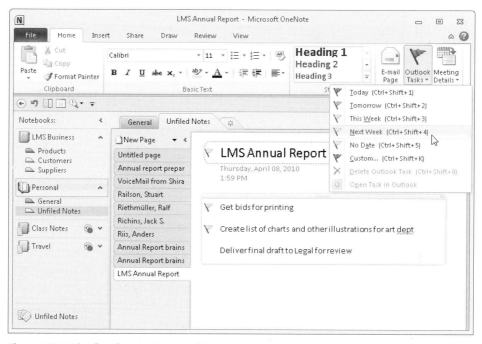

Figure 17-4 The first five options on this menu create and save an Outlook task immediately. The Custom option opens a dialog box where you can choose start and due dates.

Selecting any of the first five options on this menu creates a new task automatically and fills in the due date (or no date) that matches the choice you made from the Outlook Tasks menu. It also sets today as the start date. The sixth option, Custom, opens the Task dialog box for the newly created item so that you can assign specific dates and make any other changes. (And as the text on the menu makes clear, each of these options has an associated keyboard shortcut.)

After the task is created, you can open it by using the Open Task In Outlook option from the bottom of the menu.

Each task you create this way gets a flag icon to the left of the paragraph in OneNote, which in turn links the selected paragraph to the newly created task. When you view the new task in Outlook, as shown next, the contents of the linked paragraph from OneNote appear in the body of the new task, with a Link To Task In OneNote shortcut below the body text. The Subject is limited to 255 characters and is taken from the beginning of the linked paragraph.

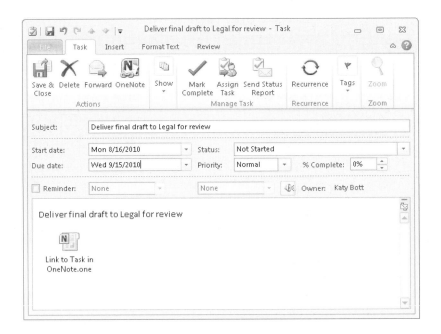

TROUBLESHOOTING

The subject of a linked task doesn't match the note

The options on the Outlook Tasks menu in OneNote are programmed to pick up text from your OneNote paragraph and use that text for the Subject field of any task they create in Outlook. If you select a picture or another nontext item on a OneNote page and then click an option on the Outlook Tasks menu, you can still create a linked task, but the body contains only the link back to the OneNote page, and the Subject reads "[Click the OneNote link in task body for details]." You can and should edit the Subject of the new Outlook task so that it contains descriptive text.

You can also create a task in Outlook and add it to an existing page. To do so, make sure that Always Ask Where To Send is selected as the default location for task notes on the Send To OneNote tab of the OneNote Options dialog box. Then select the specific page where you want the task to be added. The Subject of the task becomes a linked paragraph at the bottom of the page you select.

The Delete Outlook Task option (also available via the keyboard shortcut Ctrl+Alt+0) removes the follow-up flag and deletes the linked task item in Outlook.

For more on how to use and customize OneNote tags, see "Using OneNote with Outlook" on page 547. For more on how to manage tasks and to-do items in Outlook, see "Setting Follow-up Flags and Reminders" on page 771.

Sending a OneNote Page via E-Mail

You can send a OneNote page to an e-mail recipient by clicking the E-Mail Page command in the Outlook group on the Home tab in OneNote (or use the keyboard shortcut, Ctrl+Shift+E). Doing so sends the entire contents of the page, including the title and date/time stamp, to a new message window in Outlook. Add a recipient, change the Subject, edit the body as you see fit, and then click Send.

By default, every page you send this way includes a faint tagline at the end, advertising OneNote. If you prefer a personalized message (or none at all), open the OneNote Options dialog box, click Advanced, and change the text in the Add The Following Signature ... box, under the E-Mail Sent From OneNote heading. (Clear this option to disable the tag-lines completely.) This dialog box also allows you to specify whether you want the e-mail message to include a copy of the page in OneNote format and how you want to handle embedded files on the page.

Linking Notes to Documents and Web Pages

In the previous chapter, we explained how to insert a link to a file or a web page into a OneNote page. (See "Using Links for Quick Connections" on page 530.) That labor-intensive process is suitable for creating one-off links, but it gets tedious and distracting if you're juggling multiple sources. For intensive, heads-down research projects, turn on the Linked Notes feature and let OneNote automatically create those links as you work.

Using Linked Notes takes a little bit of practice; before you begin tinkering with this feature, be sure you have a clear understanding of its requirements and limitations:

- A page containing linked notes must be in a section that is saved in OneNote 2010 Section format. If you see the words *Compatibility Mode* in the OneNote title bar, you cannot use Linked Notes with the current page.

- Linked notes are automatically created and attached to paragraphs in your OneNote page.

- Linked notes work only with web pages viewed in Internet Explorer, documents opened in Word (any format), presentations opened in PowerPoint, and other OneNote pages.

- You can create linked notes only to documents and presentations that have been saved.

When Linked Notes mode is enabled, the OneNote window containing your notes is docked to the side of the screen with a simplified user interface (fewer tabs on the ribbon, and no Navigation bar or page tabs list). A Linked Notes icon appears in the upper left corner of the page.

To begin adding linked notes to the current page, click the Dock To Desktop command on the Quick Access Toolbar (or use the matching keyboard shortcut, Ctrl+Alt+D). You can also begin entering linked notes by clicking the Linked Notes command on the Review tab in Word, PowerPoint, or OneNote, or by clicking the OneNote Linked Notes command on the toolbar in Internet Explorer. If you have previously saved any linked notes using that document, presentation, or web page, OneNote opens the page containing the linked notes and docks it to the side of the screen. If this is the first time you've used Linked Notes mode with this document, presentation, or page, you're prompted to select a location for your notes. You can select a specific page or choose an existing section and allow OneNote to create a new page for your notes.

INSIDE OUT Choose the position of the docked OneNote window

By default, the OneNote window snaps to the right side of the primary monitor. If you prefer it on the left, or if you have multiple monitors and prefer that it be docked on a different display, drag the docked window to the new position. When you reach the edge of any display, the window automatically snaps into the correct position. (If your display resolution has lots of vertical space, you can dock the OneNote window to the top or bottom of any display as well by dragging it to that edge.) To change the width of the docked window (or its height if you docked it to the top or bottom of the display), drag its inside edge to the location. The docked window can use up to half of the available display. OneNote saves the position and width settings in the Windows registry as four values in the key HKCU\Software\Microsoft\Office\14.0\OneNote\Side Note.

With the docked window in place, you're ready to begin taking notes. Open a web page or document in any of the four supported programs, and then click in the OneNote window and begin typing your notes. As soon as you type the first character, OneNote adds a link to the page or document to that paragraph. The link appears as a small program icon to the left of the paragraph. If you point to the icon, as shown in Figure 17-5, a ScreenTip shows a thumbnail image or a snippet of text from the linked page or document.

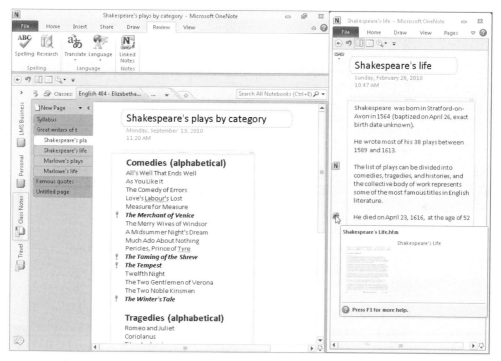

Figure 17-5 The icon to the left of any paragraph indicates that the note is linked to a web page, a document, or another OneNote page.

If you select some text in a document or page and then begin to type a new paragraph in OneNote, the linked note uses your selection as the text associated with that link.

Continue this way, clicking in Internet Explorer, Word, PowerPoint, or a separate (undocked) OneNote window and then entering your comments in a new paragraph that automatically acquires a link to the location you selected. To stop taking notes, undock the OneNote window by clicking the Dock To Desktop command on the Quick Access Toolbar again, or press Ctrl+Alt+D.

As we noted earlier, you can identify a page that contains linked notes by the icon in its upper left corner. If the OneNote window is docked, clicking this icon leads to a menu like the one shown next.

Chapter 17

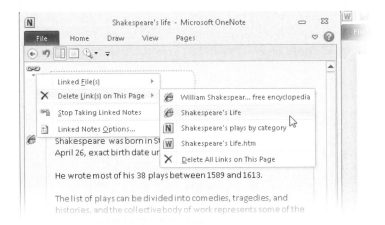

The two options at the top of the menu are available even when the window is undocked. Choices here allow you to find and open any linked documents or pages or delete links to a specific document or page. Click Stop Taking Linked Notes to temporarily disable the creation of automatic links while the page is docked; click Start Taking Linked Notes to resume. Click Linked Notes Options to open the Advanced tab of the OneNote Options dialog box, where you can disable linked-note taking completely and remove all linked notes from all pages in the current notebook.

On a page that contains linked notes, the program icon indicating that a link is present appears when the insertion point is in a linked paragraph or when you move the mouse pointer over such a paragraph. To open the linked page or document, double-click the link icon. To manage the link itself, right-click the icon, which opens the menu shown next.

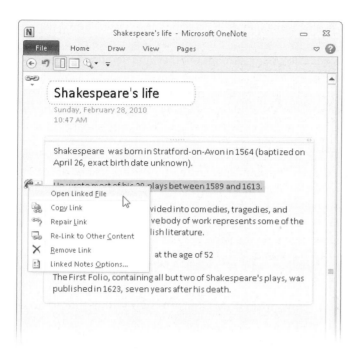

You can use the second and fifth options on this menu to copy a link and paste it into another paragraph on the same page or to remove a link. Both options are available even when the page is undocked and linked-note taking is disabled. The Repair Link option is available only if linked-note taking is enabled and then only if OneNote detects that the current link leads to a document or page that is unavailable (because it has been moved or deleted, for example). The Re-Link To Other Content option is also available only when Linked Notes mode is enabled. To use this option, click the web page, Word document, PowerPoint presentation, or OneNote page you want to set as the new link for the current paragraph, and then immediately right-click the link you want to change.

Sharing and Synchronizing Notebooks

When you work with a notebook stored on your PC—in your personal profile—you and you alone can work with it. But if you save a notebook to a location that is accessible from your local network or over the Internet, you can access its contents remotely from multiple PCs (your desktop PC at the office and a notebook PC, for example). You can also share that notebook with other people if they have access to the location where the remote copy is stored.

Chapter 17

Shared notebooks offer some interesting collaborative possibilities. When we were researching this book, for example, we used a notebook stored on a SharePoint site to effortlessly share our discoveries with one another. And you don't have to be online to collaborate. OneNote keeps a local copy of each shared notebook, allowing you to work with the most recently synchronized version even when you're disconnected from the network. When you reconnect, all of your changes and any changes made by other users are merged so that the shared copy on the network and your local copy are once again identical.

The unusual nature of the OneNote data file format is tailor-made for fast synchronization in the background. Each note container and each page are treated as separate objects, which means that two or more people can add or change notes on the same page at the same time with a minimal risk of collision. In fact, if you open a page in a shared notebook on an active network connection at the same time that a coworker has that page open, you can see her changes appear on the page seconds after she enters them.

INSIDE OUT How often does OneNote sync with a shared notebook?

OneNote has no Save button. Any additions, deletions, or changes you make to a page or section are saved immediately to the local, cached copy of your notebook. This is true even with a notebook that is saved on your PC and not shared with anyone else. (You can view and change the cache location in the OneNote Options dialog box, at the bottom of the Save & Backup tab.) The cached copy of each notebook section is synchronized at regular intervals with the main copy. How regular? That depends on the location of the main copy. For local files, replication takes place every 5 seconds. For notebooks stored on a local network and accessed via UNC shares (*server_name*\ *share_name*), the interval is 30 seconds. Notebooks shared from a SharePoint library or from a web-based connection are synchronized much less frequently—with sync intervals of 10 and 30 minutes, respectively. If you're collaborating with other people on a shared notebook, keep these times in mind to avoid being surprised by changes that appear later than you expect.

If you're creating a new notebook, you can enable shared access from the start by saving it in a network location, on a SharePoint server, or on Windows Live SkyDrive. On the Share tab, click New Shared Notebook (or click New in Backstage view, which leads to the same place). On the New Notebook tab, choose Web (to save the file to Windows Live SkyDrive) or Network (to save to a shared folder or SharePoint site). Give the notebook a name, and then click Create Notebook.

For details of how to create a new notebook, see "Creating and Opening OneNote Files" on page 491.

To make an existing local notebook available for shared access, click Share This Notebook on the Share tab (or click Share in Backstage view, which leads to the same place). On the Share Notebook tab (Figure 17-6), select a notebook and a location, and then click Share Notebook.

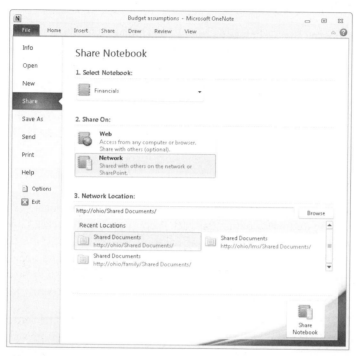

Figure 17-6 Use this dialog box to copy a notebook to a remote location and make it available for sharing.

Doing so copies the local notebook to its new location and begins synchronizing the copy in the local cache to the new location. Note that the files for your original notebook are not disturbed. If you want to delete the files for the original notebook to avoid confusion, you must do so manually using Windows Explorer.

After you use either of these commands from the Share tab, OneNote offers to help you create a link to the new location and send that link via e-mail, as shown here.

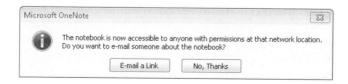

If you click E-Mail A Link, an Outlook message window opens with a link to the location of the notebook you just shared and some boilerplate introductory text. Address the message, personalize the text if you want, and send it.

CAUTION !

> Although you can share a notebook from a local folder (by saving it in the Public Documents folder on your PC, for example), we don't recommend this. If you turn off the PC or allow it to sleep, changes you make won't be available to other PCs that are trying to sync with the shared folder. In the case of a desktop and notebook PC, you have to remember to have both computers turned on and connected to the network before your changes in one location are reflected in the other. If the shared notebook is saved in an always-on location, such as a local file server or a Windows Live SkyDrive folder, this synchronization is much more reliable.

How do you stop sharing a remote notebook and return it to your local PC? Right-click the notebook icon in the Navigation bar, click Properties, and then click Change Location. Choose a local folder in the Choose A Sync Location For This Remote Notebook dialog box and click Select. Doing so copies the notebook to its new location and begins synchronizing the copy in the OneNote cache to the new location. (You can use this same technique to move a shared notebook to a different shared folder.)

It's easy to spot a remote notebook in the Navigation bar. Look for the Sync Status icon to the right of the binder icon and notebook name. It displays one of three status messages: a green check mark when the remote notebook is connected and up-to-date, green spinning arrows when the notebook is in the process of syncing, and a red circle with a slash (the universal No symbol) over the sync icon to indicate that the remote notebook is not available online.

When you click the Sync Status icon, you see the Shared Notebook Synchronization dialog box shown in Figure 17-7.

Normally, OneNote detects when you're connected to a remote notebook and automatically synchronizes its contents at regular intervals. If you make changes while you're disconnected from the network, those changes are synced as soon as you reconnect, with no manual intervention required of you. The Work Offline option allows you to suspend replication even when you're connected to the network, an option you might choose if you want to avoid unnecessary network traffic or distractions from changes made by other users of the shared notebook. To sync manually, use any of the following techniques:

- To manually sync changes for a single notebook, right-click its icon in the Navigation bar and click Sync This Notebook Now (or click to select any section within the notebook and then press Shift+F9). You can also select the notebook in the Shared Notebook Synchronization dialog box and click Sync Selected Notebook.

- To manually sync changes in all remote notebooks, click Sync Now in the Shared Notebook Synchronization dialog box, or press F9.

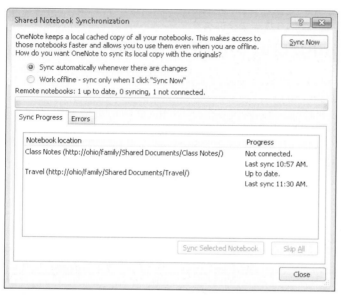

Figure 17-7 By default, all remote notebooks are synchronized automatically. To allow only manual syncing, choose Work Offline.

INSIDE OUT   Keeping prying eyes away from your notebooks

Do some parts of a shared notebook contain sensitive information? You can restrict access to those sections by protecting them with a password. This option is available by right-clicking any section tab and choosing Password Protect This Section. In the Password Protection pane, you can set or remove a password for the current section. After you do that, anyone who wants to view that section (including you!) can only do so after entering the password you create. By default, sections are locked automatically after 10 minutes of inactivity—you can adjust this setting by clicking Password Options at the bottom of the Password Protection pane. Note that the contents of password-protected sections are not available via search unless they are currently unlocked.

Any changes made to a shared notebook are tagged with the author's name and initials, as well as the date and time when the change was made. When changes made by someone else are synced to your copy of a shared notebook, the changed pages and sections are highlighted in bold. Options in the Shared Notebook group on the Share tab allow you to filter the list of recent edits and search for changes by a specific person. If you don't want to be distracted by the tags and highlighting alongside changed items, click the Hide Authors command to suppress them. Click this command again to resume the display of author information.

Printing, Publishing, and Sharing Notes

How do you share information you've captured in OneNote? The right technique depends on how much data you're talking about (a single page, two or three sections, or an entire notebook) and whether you want to preserve the OneNote data file format.

If you want the other person to be able to see your notes directly in OneNote, choose any of the following options:

- Copy the notebook or section to a Windows Live SkyDrive folder and give the other person permission to view or edit the notebook. If the other person has OneNote installed, they can copy pages or sections to a notebook of their own.

- Save the page or a section as a file (in OneNote 2010 Section or OneNote 2007 Section format) and send the saved file as an e-mail attachment. The other person will need to have OneNote installed to open the file locally; as an alternative, they can upload the .one file to their own Windows Live SkyDrive folder and open it using the OneNote Web App.

For a full discussion of how Office Web Apps and Windows Live SkyDrive work together, see Chapter 25, "Using Office in a Web Browser." To learn more about OneNote file formats, see "Creating and Opening OneNote Files" on page 491, and "Which File Formats Does Office 2010 Support?" on page 76.

If remaining true to the OneNote format is not a priority, you have many more options available, including exporting all or part of a notebook to alternative file formats and printing your notebook to distribute in physical form.

In this regard, at least, OneNote retains its idiosyncratic character. Most of the Office programs have a Save & Send option on the File menu in Backstage view. OneNote has separate Save As and Send options there.

The Send option works only with the current page, allowing you to insert its contents into an e-mail message, attach a copy of the page as an attachment to an e-mail message, or send the page contents to a new Word document for editing or to post to a blog. If you make a selection on the current page and then click Send To Word or Send To Blog on the Send tab in Backstage view, OneNote opens a new document in Word and copies only your selection to it.

INSIDE OUT Which file formats does OneNote send?

When you click E-Mail Page As Attachment on the Send tab in Backstage view, a new message window opens in Outlook. It contains not one but two file attachments. The first is in OneNote Section format, with a .one file name extension. This file can be opened only in OneNote. The second attachment is in Microsoft's MHTML format (also known as MIME HTML or Single-File Web Page), with a .mht extension. This file format saves text, formatting, images, and other resources in a single file that can be opened in Internet Explorer and in all modern versions of Microsoft Word and the Word Viewer program. Most alternative browsers (with the exception of Opera) do not allow you to open files saved in MHTML format. You can add support for MHTML files in Firefox and Safari by using an add-on such as UnMHT (*w7io.com/11801*).

The Save As option looks like this:

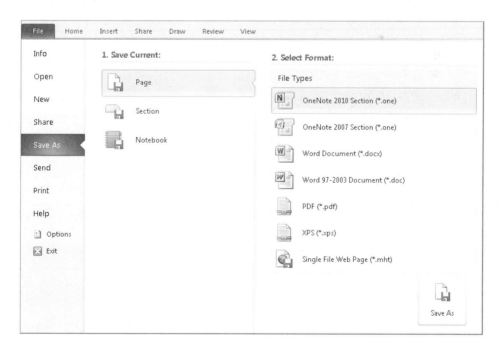

Chapter 17

The format choices available when you select either Page or Section under Save Current are identical. You can choose the OneNote 2007 or OneNote 2010 Section format, Word Document (or the older Word-97-2003 Document) format, PDF, XPS, or a Single-File Web Page format, which opens in Internet Explorer. If you click Notebook, your options shrink to include PDF and XPS formats as well as an oddball format not found elsewhere. The One-Note Package format (with a .onepkg file name extension) can be used to transfer an entire notebook from one PC to another. Although you can also accomplish this goal by copying a folder full of section files, the OneNote Package format has the advantage of residing in a single file. To import a file in this format into OneNote, click File, then click Open. Set the file type to OneNote Single File Package, select the saved file, and click Open.

The Print tab in Backstage view offers a downright spartan set of options for sending all or part of a OneNote section to hard copy. The top choice is Print, which opens the Print dialog box and allows you to select a printer and choose which part of the current section to print. The second option, Print Preview, opens the dialog box shown in Figure 17-8, which provides a thumbnail view of your printed output and allows a number of self-explanatory options.

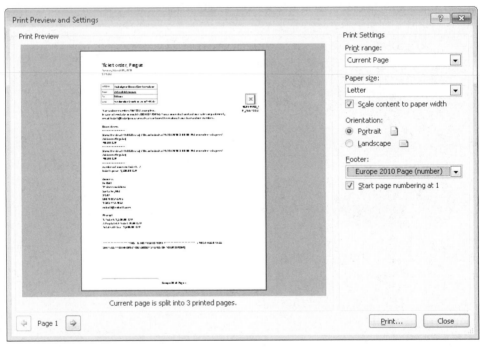

Figure 17-8 Use the options in the Print Range list to expand the printed output to include a group of pages or the entire section.

If you Ctrl+click to select multiple pages first, you can choose to print only those pages. However, the option to print a selection of pages from the current section is not available when you choose Print Preview.

Recording Audio and Video

If you're using OneNote to record the minutes of a meeting, why not literally record the proceedings? OneNote pages aren't just for text and pictures—they can also hold audio and video notes, which in turn are synchronized with the notes you type. Later, when you review your notes, you can add context and fill in any missing pieces by listening to the original remarks. If your PC is equipped with a webcam or other video input source, you can embed video clips (and the accompanying audio track) in a page.

To record an audio or video note, be sure your microphone is properly set up in Windows. Then click Record Audio (or Record Video) on the Insert tab. That opens the Recording tab, shown in Figure 17-9.

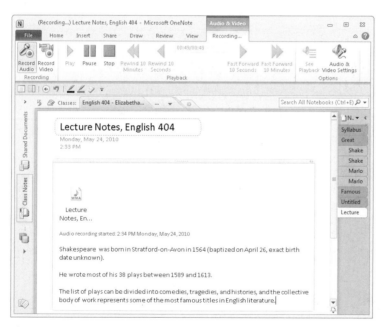

Figure 17-9 You can pause or stop a recording at any time from the Recording tab. The audio or video file itself is embedded in the page, with a time stamp to indicate when it was recorded.

The recording process begins immediately. OneNote adds an embedded icon to the current page, with a date and time stamp beneath it to indicate when the recording began. You can now begin adding notes on that page.

To stop recording temporarily, click Pause. To stop recording and save the file, click Stop. After you click Stop and save an audio or video file, you can no longer add to that file. If you remain on the same page and click Record Audio or Record Video again, OneNote adds a second recording, with its own date/time stamp. Repeat the process and you get a third icon, and a fourth, and a fifth, and so on. Each recording is independent and can be played back separately.

After you begin a recording, you can type notes on the same page that contains the recorded file. OneNote adds a synchronization marker—indicated by a small Play button—at the beginning of each paragraph. Those small markers (visible only when the insertion point is in a paragraph or the mouse pointer passes over a paragraph) are key to effectively using OneNote with audio and video.

You can play back your recording in either of two ways:

- To listen to the complete recording, double-click the file icon that represents the recording. If the See Playback option is selected, OneNote highlights each paragraph in your notes, using the synchronization markers it created during the original recording.

- To play back a selection that corresponds to a specific section within your notes, click in the paragraph and then click the Play button to its left.

Figure 17-10 shows playback in progress. Note that the Playback controls are now enabled, allowing you to skip forward or back, 10 seconds or 10 minutes at a time. (Use the keyboard shortcuts Ctrl+Alt+Y and Ctrl+Alt+U to move 10 seconds backward and forward, respectively.)

You can revise or add to your notes during playback without affecting the synchronization markers. (The noteworthy exception, of course, is that deleting a paragraph deletes the synchronization marker as well.)

To play the file in the default external player for that file type, right-click the file icon and click Open. To save a copy of the recording in its default format, right-click the file icon and click Save As.

Synchronization marker

Figure 17-10 With the See Playback option enabled, OneNote highlights the relevant portion of your notes during playback.

The default format for OneNote audio recordings is Windows Media Audio Voice 9, which records in mono, at a relatively low quality that is more than adequate for voice recordings; for video, OneNote uses Windows Media Video 8 format, at a quality rate determined by your hardware. You can change either of these default settings by clicking Audio & Video Settings on the Playback or Recording tab, which opens the OneNote Options dialog box to the Audio & Video tab, as shown on the next page.

As with all such options, you have to make a trade-off between recording quality and file size. If your goal is to capture details of a professor's notes on a whiteboard or to record a musical performance in stereo, you'll want to choose a higher-quality video profile and/or audio codec. For technical details about the capabilities of each Windows Media Audio and Windows Media Video format, visit *w7io.com/11802*.

Our Favorite OneNote Tweaks and Tips

If you've made it all the way through to the end of our three OneNote chapters, congratulations. You now have a solid grounding in how the program works and how you can integrate OneNote into your workflow. The tips and tweaks included in this section are intended for advanced users like you.

Managing the Recycle Bin and Page Versions

For every notebook that uses the new OneNote 2010 format, OneNote adds a pair of features designed to help you recover quickly and easily when (not if) you accidentally delete valuable content. The Previous Versions feature and the Recycle Bin are not available for notebooks that are saved using the older OneNote 2007 format.

OneNote takes snapshots of every page that is changed by multiple users. You can see alternate versions of the current page by clicking Page Versions in the History group on the Share tab. Options available from the drop-down Page Versions menu allow you to delete all previous versions of pages in the current section, in the section group, or in the notebook.

All deleted pages and sections go to the Recycle Bin by default, allowing you to recover them in case of accidental deletion. You can inspect the contents of the Recycle Bin for any notebook by clicking Notebook Recycle Bin in the History group on the Share tab.

If you'd prefer not to save any previous versions of a page or deleted pages or sections for an individual notebook, click the arrow at the bottom of either command in the History group and then click Disable History For This Notebook.

Customizing the OneNote Taskbar Icon

By default, OneNote adds an icon in the notification area at the right side of the taskbar; this icon is formally known as the Microsoft OneNote Quick Launcher (Onenotem.exe), and it is set to run at startup so that it's available even when OneNote is not running. In Windows 7, this icon is normally hidden. To make it visible full time, you have to click the arrow to the left of the notification area and drag the icon into place with other visible icons in this region. Right-click this icon to display a menu like the one shown here:

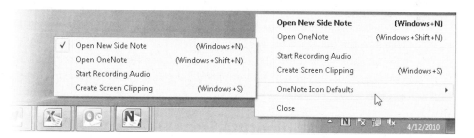

Using the right-click shortcut menu, you can choose any of the four options shown. A simple click of the left button on the OneNote icon performs the default action, which is indicated in bold on the menu. To change the default action, click OneNote Icon Defaults and select a different option. Your current choice is indicated by a check mark.

To remove the OneNote icon temporarily, click Close. To prevent it from restarting, open the OneNote Options dialog box, click the Display tab, and clear the box next to Place OneNote Icon In The Notification Area Of The Taskbar.

Chapter 17

Using Side Notes

What do you do when you want to quickly jot down a thought without covering up what you're working on right now? That's why Side Notes were designed. A Side Note, as shown here, is a small OneNote window, with a lightweight ribbon and no Navigation bars, page tabs, or other user interface elements that aren't directly related to the current note.

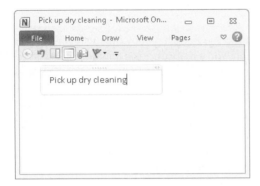

Enter your notes and either leave the window open or close it. The new Side Note is saved in the Unfiled Notes section.

To open a Side Note quickly, regardless of whether OneNote is already running, the One-Note icon (described in the previous section) must be in the notification area. Click that icon or use the keyboard shortcut Windows logo key+N to create the new Side Note.

To pin a Side Note so that it floats above other programs as you work, click Keep On Top on the View tab. To add a page title or move your new Side Note page to a different section, switch to the full OneNote window with its full ribbon and navigation elements by clicking the Full Page View command on the Quick Access Toolbar (or use the keyboard shortcut F11). You cannot return to the simplified Side Note view from the full OneNote program window.

Converting Printouts to Text

When you send a file to OneNote using the Send To OneNote 2010 virtual printer, the program uses its built-in optical character recognition (OCR) features to capture and save any text included as part of that printout. The converted text is also added to the OneNote index, which allows you to locate that printout later using the OneNote search box.

To copy the converted text to another document, right-click the printout and click Copy Text From This Page Of The Printout or Copy Text From All Pages Of The Printout.

Text recognition uses CPU resources; if you're using OneNote on a low-powered PC, you might want to disable this option completely. From the bottom of the Advanced tab in the OneNote Options dialog box, select Disable Text Recognition In Pictures.

To disable text recognition for a specific printout, right-click the printout, click Make Text In Image Searchable, and then click Disabled.

Saving and Using Custom Page Templates

As we noted earlier, you can change fonts, add or hide rule lines, change background colors and graphics, and add boilerplate text to a OneNote page. (All of these formatting options are discussed in "Customizing the Look and Feel of a Notebook Page" on page 516). If you want to reuse a set of such customizations, you can save the result as a Page Template, which then is available for use in the same or any other notebook.

OneNote includes an extensive selection of ready-made templates that you can use with or without additional personalization. To see the full collection, right-click the New Page shortcut at the top of the page tabs list, or click the down arrow to its right, and then click Page Templates. Doing so opens the Page Templates pane shown on the next page.

The ready-made templates are divided into five default categories, which can be expanded or collapsed using the arrows to the left of the category name. Click any template name to use it for the current new page. You can click through any or all the templates to see them previewed on the new page, with each new selection replacing the previous one. If you enter any text on the page, OneNote saves it as a new page, and clicking any template name in the Page Templates pane opens a new page.

The two options on the bottom of the Page Templates pane are worth mastering. Under Choose Default Template, you can select any template to use automatically whenever you create a new page in the current section. If you use the section to take class notes or minutes for a regularly scheduled meeting, using a custom template makes it easier to capture required information in a standard format. In the case of meeting minutes, you can use the E-Mail Page command (in the Outlook group on the Home tab) to send perfectly formatted minutes to other attendees without ever leaving OneNote.

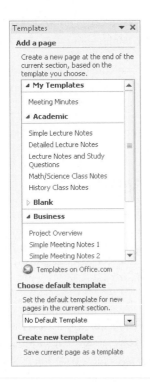

If you've customized the current page, click Save Current Page As A Template to add it to the list. If this is the first custom template you've saved, OneNote creates a new My Templates group at the top of the pane. All custom templates appear in this list.

Inside PowerPoint 2010

E ASY to use, hard to master. That's been the story of PowerPoint since its earliest days. Anyone can create a simple slide show. How hard is it, after all, to double-click the PowerPoint icon and then click and type inside a box that tells you to do just that? But creating an engaging presentation that doesn't lull your audience to sleep takes more than mere pointing, clicking, and typing.

In Microsoft PowerPoint 2010, slides are still the basic building blocks of a presentation. You can still add bullet points, charts, tables, and pictures. You're still presented with the familiar boxes labeled "Click to add text." What's different is the inclusion of more ways to work with rich media, including improved photo editing and the ability to trim a video. There are also new options for sharing your presentation with a wider audience, like the ability to broadcast a presentation on a network via Microsoft SharePoint or over the Internet with your Windows Live account.

Add it all up, and you'll see that the new features in PowerPoint 2010 make it possible for occasional PowerPoint users to go beyond basic slide shows. PowerPoint has evolved into a versatile communication tool that works for a broad range of uses: sharing family vacation photos, creating polished reports for the classroom, or preparing sales and marketing presentations for a business of any size.

In this chapter, we'll whiz through the essential tasks of building a presentation, adding interesting graphical elements to your slides, and customizing the overall design. In the chapters that follow, we'll tackle the tasks of delivering your presentation—in person or over a network.

What's in a PowerPoint Presentation?

Slides. Text. Graphics. Tables. Videos. Charts. Links.

The best PowerPoint presentations include just enough detail to get your point across and the right balance of visual interest to hold someone's attention for the duration. But where do you start? And how do you go from a simple slide with black text on a white background to something with a little more flair?

One effective strategy is to start with a slide (or two), create a rough outline and a basic design, preview and save regularly as you flesh out your ideas, and add audio and video elements as the final step.

Composing a Presentation

Whether you're working on your Senior Year Culminating Project or developing a quarterly snapshot for the board of directors, the bulk of your slide development work is performed in Normal view. In this view, you see each slide individually, with the current slide filling the Slide pane. The Notes pane below the slide allows you to add speaker notes, and the Slides tab on the left provides thumbnails of the current presentation that you can use for navigation. You can add new slides and assign slide layouts as needed.

Figure 18-1 shows a typical slide with text placeholders and an image in Normal view.

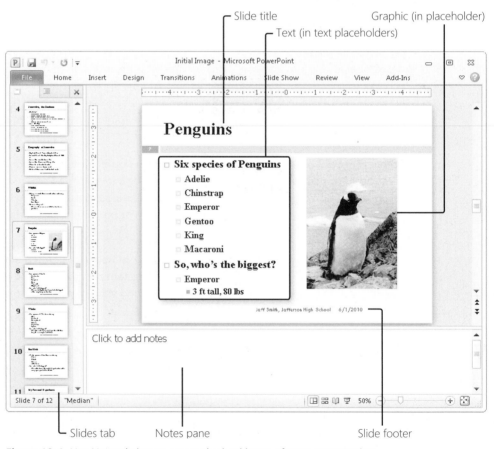

Figure 18-1 Use Normal view to set up the backbone of your presentation.

Slide Basics

Each "page" in a presentation is represented by a slide. Alone, slides can be used to communicate single ideas: a flyer for a garage sale or school play or a company organization chart. By assembling multiple slides and adding transitions and effects, you create a presentation that can be delivered in person or run independently at a trade show kiosk. (Collectively, the slides in a presentation are sometimes called a *deck*.)

To add a slide that uses the default layout, click New Slide in the Slides group on the Home tab, or press Ctrl+M; to choose a slide layout, click the arrow beneath the New Slide command and pick from a menu of predefined slide layouts. (We describe layouts in more detail in the next section.) There's no limit to the number of slides you can add to a presentation, but if your PC has minimal memory and a weak graphics subsystem, you might experience some difficulty running presentations with a large number of slides that contain complex graphics.

Anything you place on a slide is linked to a content placeholder, which is a movable box with dotted borders. Unlike in Word, you can't just click and begin typing at a blank spot on the slide. To add text to a slide, you first have to add a placeholder to the slide layout. To add a table, chart, graphic, or other nontext object, you have to click an icon in the center of the placeholder. A placeholder behaves like other objects: when you select one, additional tabs appear on the ribbon depending on the content type. You can resize a placeholder by dragging a selection handle on any side or corner, or move it by dragging the border.

Because PowerPoint is designed with the idea that most slides are shared on the screen with other users—and that printouts simply position those slides on a piece of paper—there aren't any margins.

Slide Layouts

When you add a new slide to a presentation, it's displayed with its own set of placeholders. Which placeholders you see depends on the slide layout you choose. The first slide in a new presentation typically uses the Title Slide layout, with placeholders for a presentation title and subtitle. If you don't need a title slide for your presentation, you can choose a different layout from the menu under the New Slide command or create a slide using the default Title And Content layout and change it using the Layout menu (also in the Slides group on the Home tab). For example, a PowerPoint file might consist of just one slide, which you'll use as a flyer for information about an upcoming meeting: date, time, location, and description. For this purpose, a title slide won't give you the placeholders you need. But a Two Content or Content With Caption layout might be more appropriate. To change a slide's layout, on the Home tab, click the Layout command, and choose the layout you want to apply to the current slide. Figure 18-2 shows the gallery of layouts on the Layout menu.

This same selection is available on the New Slide menu, which offers a few extra menu options at the bottom.

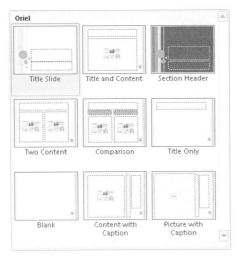

Figure 18-2 Slide layouts determine the location and arrangement of placeholders on a slide. They also reflect the current theme, whose name is shown in bold at the top of the menu.

INSIDE OUT   Copy a group of slides quickly

If you're building a presentation that uses a specific sequence of slide layouts for each of a group of topics, you can streamline the presentation-building process by duplicating those slides for each group. Start by creating the slides for the first group. Then, on the Slides tab, select all the slides in the group, click the arrow beneath the New Slide command on the Home tab, and click Duplicate Selected Slides. Repeat these steps for each topic.

The type of content you plan to use on a slide dictates which layout you should choose. For example, if your presentation is a class report about the Emperor and King penguins, you might use the Comparison layout for a slide showing pictures of each, arranged side by side. Follow that with a pair of slides using the Content With Caption layout, with a picture and details (in bullet format) about each species. Slide layouts are interchangeable; even if you change the layout after you add text, PowerPoint preserves your text within the context of the new layout.

PowerPoint comes with nine standard slide layouts:

- **Title Slide**   The default slide in new presentations that are based on the Blank Presentation template. This layout offers two placeholders: one for the title of the presentation and one for a subtitle (which can be used at formal events to identify the presenter and the session name). Use this layout to create an opening slide for your presentation or to signify the start of a new topic or idea.

- **Title And Content**   This layout is the default when you insert a new slide after a title slide and is one of the most commonly used. It offers two placeholders: one for the title of the slide and one for content. Use this layout when you need to communicate a single idea using a chart or a table, or if you want to build a standard slide with bullet points.

- **Section Header**   The Section Header layout has two text placeholders: one for the presentation title and one for the section title. Use this layout as a low-key alternative to the Title Slide layout when transitioning between presentation topics or introducing new ideas.

- **Two Content**   This layout is similar to the Title And Content layout, but it has a placeholder for the slide title and two placeholders for content. A common use for this layout puts text alongside a graphic or media clip.

- **Comparison**   The Comparison layout looks a lot like the Two Content layout. The difference is that this layout contains placeholders for headings above each of the content placeholders. Use this layout to show how one idea compares with another: before and after, A versus B, and so on.

- **Title Only**   This layout displays just one placeholder for a slide title. Like the Section Header layout, this layout is good to use when a presentation transitions from one topic to another. Another use for this layout is to have full control over content placement, because it gives you nearly a full slide to add your placeholders to.

- **Blank**   This layout doesn't contain any placeholders. Use the options on the Insert tab to populate the slide with the types of placeholders you want, in the exact position you prefer. Use this layout when you need complete control over where placeholders appear on your slide.

- **Content With Caption**   The Content With Caption layout gives you three placeholders to work with: one for the slide title, one for slide text, and one very large placeholder for content of your choice. Use this layout when the inserted content (a chart or table, for example) should be the main focus of the slide, but it needs a title and a few words (a sentence or two at most) for context or introduction.

- **Picture With Caption** This layout gives you three placeholders: one for the slide title, one for slide text, and a large one for a graphic. Use this layout when you have a single image that communicates the main idea of the slide.

The actual position of the placeholders for a particular layout might vary based on the presentation theme. Additionally, the type of layouts available might vary if you create custom slide masters or use a custom template. The layouts listed here are based on the default PowerPoint template.

To learn more about how to create your own custom layouts, see "Saving and Reusing Slides and Themes" on page 654.

Presentation View Options

Although most of your design work is done in Normal view, PowerPoint does have several other views you can choose from, each with its own set of strengths and weaknesses, depending on the task at hand. You can switch between the most useful of these additional views by using the view options on the right side of the status bar at the bottom of the PowerPoint window, as shown in Figure 18-3.

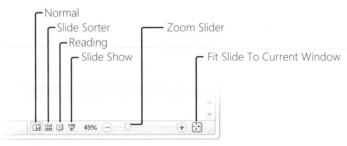

Figure 18-3 Common view options are available at the lower right portion of your window. Additional view options are listed on the View and Slide Show tabs.

You can switch to Normal, Slide Sorter, or Reading view by using commands in the Presentation Views group on the View tab, as shown in Figure 18-4. This group of commands also includes a Notes Page view and is alongside the Master Views group you can use to create new slide layouts.

Figure 18-4 View options not available near the Zoom slider are available on the View tab, including Notes Page view and access to master slide views.

Table 18-1 shows how each view is best used. The sections that follow provide more detail about each view.

Table 18-1 PowerPoint Views at a Glance

View	Best Use
Normal	This is the most common view for working with the overall slide layout and its individual elements. You can edit text, manage placeholders, and set animations and transitions. Normal view is not well suited for tasks that require you to compare the contents or design of the current slide with other slides in the presentation. Use the Slides and Outline tabs to toggle between thumbnails and an outline, which is best suited for viewing and editing slide titles and one set of bulleted text per slide.
Slide Sorter	This view lets you work with the overall slide arrangement within a presentation. You can easily reorganize your slide order, duplicate slides, and transfer slides between presentations. This view doesn't allow any editing of individual slide objects—you can't edit text or change the size and position of placeholders, for example.
Notes Page	Use this view to type and format your speaker notes or presentation handouts within a larger text box. This view is particularly useful because it lets you see exactly how much text fits on a printed page (or on your screen as you're presenting). However, the only text editing you can do in this view is to your notes; it doesn't allow for any text or placeholder editing on the actual slide.
Reading	In Reading view, you can preview your presentation slide by slide in a window. You see exactly what the presentation looks like in Slide Show view, including transitions. You have no access to any editing tools for your slide deck.
Slide Master	Use the large slide master thumbnail at the top of the Slides tab to modify the placeholder layout for the entire slide deck—adding elements that you want to be in the same position and with the same formatting on every slide. Items that appear on a slide because they are part of the slide master can't accidentally be moved during regular slide editing. This view also contains layouts available for the current theme, including custom layouts you create. Edits you make in Slide Master view affect only the current presentation.
Handout Master	In this view, you can set up the exact placement and size of slide images for printed handouts, allowing you to add logos or customize the handouts you share with others. Because this is a master view, you can't edit text or any presentation-specific objects here. Edits you make in Handout Master view affect only the current presentation.
Notes Master	In the Notes Master view, you can change the appearance of Notes Page view on your screen and in printouts. Here, you can modify the size of slide images to allow for more or less room for your notes. Because this is a master view, you can't edit text or presentation-specific objects, and edits you make in Notes Master view affect only the current presentation.

Chapter 18

View	Best Use
Slide Show	Technically, this isn't a view—you actually start, configure, and control a slide show using three groups of commands on the Slide Show tab—but it is most assuredly a full cousin to the options on the View tab. This view gives you the best overall picture of exactly what your audience will see. The slide contents take up your entire screen, and the only way to switch to an alternative view is to click past the last slide in the presentation or press Esc to return to one of the other views. In this view, as with Reading view, you won't have access to deck-editing tools. However, this is a good view to use when you're rehearsing for your upcoming presentation or to record the length of time each slide should be displayed.

Normal View (Slides or Outline)

Most of your initial slide setup and creation is done in Normal view, which is the only view that gives you access to the full set of tools for working with text and placeholder objects on individual slides. Once you begin adding interactivity to a presentation, you can also use this view to see text and animations as well as slide transitions.

In Normal view, the Slides tab is displayed by default in the pane at the left.. Use the Slides tab to navigate between slides. You can also drag slides within this pane to reorder them, or right-click and use shortcut menu commands to copy, delete, and duplicate slides.

Drag the borders between the panes to change the relative size of the pane that contains the Slides and Outline tabs, the Notes pane, and the Slide pane in Normal view.

For more information about working with text and animations, see "Adding Emphasis with Animations" on page 615. For more information on adding slide transitions, see "Using Transitions Between Slides" on page 629.

Click the Outline tab to change the display in the pane on the left and replace the thumbnails with the title and text in each slide's standard placeholders (based on the assigned layout). To see the slide text, click the Outline button in Normal view, as shown in Figure 18-5. Note the subtle change in the tab headings in this figure; when you reduce the width of the pane to the point where there's no longer room for the tab text, you see only buttons.

When you switch from the Slides tab to the Outline tab—or vice versa—the contents of the Slide pane don't change. You can manipulate the slide and bullet hierarchy without cutting and pasting text across multiple placeholders. Just click inside the text in the Outline tab to make your text edits, which appear in the Slide pane as you type.

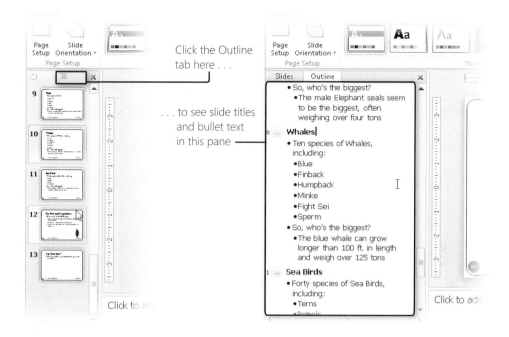

Figure 18-5 Use Outline view to make large text edits.

You can also change the order of slides in the deck from the Outline tab. To move a slide in Outline view, select the small slide icon to the left of any slide title. When the pointer changes to a large, four-headed arrow, click to select the entire slide, and then drag it to the new location in the outline hierarchy. As you drag, the horizontal line indicates the destination for the text you're dragging. Figure 18-6 shows the mouse pointer you see when moving a slide in the Outline tab.

INSIDE OUT   Formatting text using the Outline tab

When working with the Outline tab, you can select multiple bulleted lines at the same time by holding down the Ctrl key as you click to select slide titles or bullets—even those that are not immediately before or after your first selection. Use commands on the Home tab to apply custom formatting to all the items in your selection. You can't reorder noncontiguous bullets in this way, but it does make quick work of what would otherwise be a series of repetitive formatting operations.

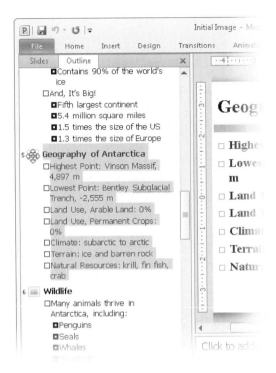

Figure 18-6 Dragging slides in the Outline tab reorders them. If you move the text of one slide directly into the middle of another slide, PowerPoint adjusts the outline hierarchy.

You can select individual bullets in much the same way you select entire slides. This makes fairly quick work of rearranging all your slide-show text. You can also right-click a bullet or slide title in the Outline tab to promote a bullet point to a slide title, to demote a slide title to a bullet point, or to move the current selection up or down.

Slide Sorter View

When you need to work with more slides than you can see in the thumbnails on the Slides tab in Normal view, switch to Slide Sorter view, shown in Figure 18-7. In this view, you work with slides as objects rather than with the individual placeholders.

In Slide Sorter view, you can't edit the text on individual slides or change the placement of content placeholders. You can duplicate one or more slides by selecting them and pressing Ctrl+D. The duplicated slides appear immediately after the last slide in your selection and are selected after being duplicated so that you can drag them to a new location if necessary.

Because this view lets you see so many of the slides in your presentation, it makes quick work of rearranging slides by dragging and dropping. In Slide Sorter view, you can see slide transitions. You can also apply transitions to multiple slides (contiguous or otherwise) or to all slides in the presentation.

You can return to Normal view by double-clicking the thumbnail of the slide you want to edit.

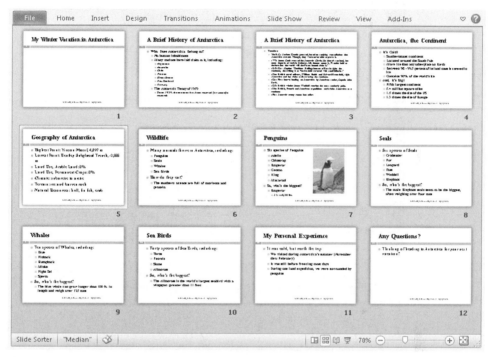

Figure 18-7 Use the Zoom slider to change the size of thumbnails in Slide Sorter view and increase or decrease the number of slides you can see at one time.

Reading View

Reading view, shown in Figure 18-8, lets you see how your slide show looks without having to use Slide Show view. That's invaluable if you need to work with other programs along-side the presentation—for example, if you're writing a script or a supporting document in Word. Because the presentation appears within its own window, you can see exactly what the audience will see without taking up your entire screen.

This is a good view to use to spot obvious problems (like typos and inconsistencies between styles on different slides) and to get a feel for the overall look and feel of each slide. But it's literally read-only: you can't make any changes to text or content.

You can advance through your presentation by using the Next and Previous buttons at the bottom of the window.

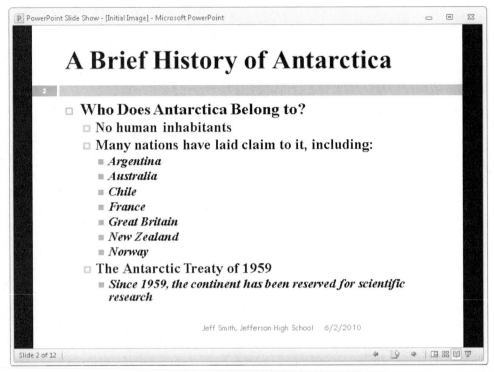

Figure 18-8 In Reading view, you see each slide, absent speaker notes and thumbnails for other slides.

Notes Page View

In Normal view, you get a small window just below the slide where you can add and store presentation notes. Some people use this as a place to keep their presentation script, while others use it to store agenda topics or key points they want to be sure to mention. If you're creating a training presentation, this is also a good place for additional instructions that are simply too long to place directly on the slide.

As shown in Figure 18-9, Notes Page view gives you a larger area to edit the notes that you start in Normal view.

For some presentations, you might want to use Notes Page view to share extended commentary with your audience. This strategy is sensible for a "training the trainers" presentation, for example. If you just want to share your slides in printed form with the audience, you can use handouts, which don't include notes.

For more information on how to format and print handouts, see "Creating Notes and Handouts" on page 642.

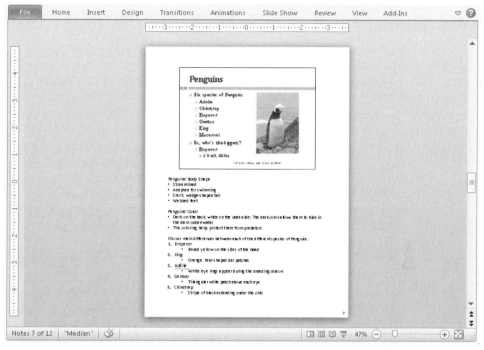

Figure 18-9 See notes you enter in Normal view in a larger window with Notes Page view. Here, you can edit your notes and preview how the page would look if it were printed.

About Master Views

Master views contain all of the behind-the-scenes layout and formatting for the slides your audience sees. This is where the exact positioning of placeholders is defined, as well as the formatting characteristics of the text contained in each. This is also where you can define objects—like a company logo—that appear on every slide.

There are three types of master slides: slide, handout, and notes. The slide master contains master slide templates for each of the slide layouts in your presentation. In Slide Master view, you can rearrange placeholders, insert additional graphics, modify the formatting of text, and insert content placeholders using the available ribbon options.

Figure 18-10 shows Slide Master view.

To change individual slide layouts, click the layout you want to modify in the pane at the left, and then make your adjustment. The changes you make affect only the current presentation.

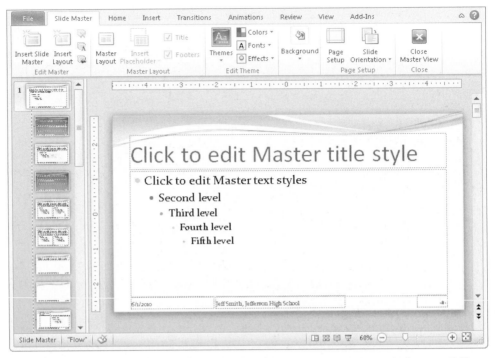

Figure 18-10 Use the option on the View tab to see the slide master. Alternatively, press Shift and click the Normal view button next to the Zoom slider.

Handout Master view is where you customize the handouts you print based on your presentation slides. Using the Handout Master tab, you can define how many slides print on each page, page orientation, slide orientation, and which header and footer elements should print. Then, use the Insert tab to add specific elements—such as company branding or a school mascot.

Notes Master view is where you go to customize how your notes page is viewed and printed. This is a good place to reduce the size of the slide at the top to allow more space for your notes to appear.

For more information on customizing these master views, see "Laying the Groundwork for an Expert Presentation" on page 665.

Slide Show View

This is the view to use when you deliver your presentation in front of an audience. It hides the PowerPoint program window completely and shows your entire presentation, slide by slide, with all animations, transition effects, and timings.

To see your presentation in this view, click the Slide Show button on the status bar (just to the left of the Zoom slider) or press F5. Doing so starts your slide show from the beginning. Alternatively, you can use the From Current Slide or From Beginning commands on the Slide Show tab to choose the starting slide.

For more information on how to navigate in Slide Show view, see "Delivering a Live Presentation" on page 633.

Editing the Presentation Text

Presentations consist of many different elements, but the most common is the basic "Click to add text" variety. But what if you need to add a "Confidential" warning with an embargo date at the top of each slide or type your company's tagline just above each slide's title? In either of these cases, you need to add text in a nonstandard location, outside the familiar boundaries of default layout types. This requires the creation of a text placeholder.

On the Insert tab, click the Text Box option, and then click the slide approximately where you want the text box to be located. The exact location doesn't matter because you can always move it later. Once you type your text, the text box you inserted becomes another placeholder on your slide.

For more information about working with text in PowerPoint, including formatting text, inserting symbols and special characters, checking spelling, and more, see Chapter 5, "Entering, Editing, and Formatting Text."

One of the fastest ways to edit text is to use the Outline tab in Normal view. Modifying slide text in the outline is quicker than adding or removing individual text boxes on the slide itself. In this small pane, press Enter to add new slides or bullet points, press Tab to move the current line to a new, lower level, and use Shift+Tab to promote bullets in the outline hierarchy.

Here's an example where this technique comes in handy. You start with a slide listing five topics you plan to cover in your presentation, each as a bullet point in a text placeholder, and you want to quickly create a new slide for each item in the list. Start by clicking the slide icon to the left of your summary slide, and then press Ctrl+D to duplicate that slide. In the Outline tab, position the insertion point anywhere in the first bullet point on the new slide and press Shift+Tab to turn that bullet into a slide title. Repeat that process for the remaining four bullet points. You now have five new slides ready to fill in. (As one final bit of cleanup, be sure to delete the slide containing the duplicated—and now redundant—title from your original summary slide.)

Using the Enter and Tab keys in the Outline tab, you can quickly build the framework for your entire presentation this way. Remember that this technique is most effective for slides that use a title and a single text box. For more advanced slide layouts that include graphics, media, or multiple text boxes, you need to make adjustments directly on the slide in Normal view.

Basic Slide Guidelines

Once you start placing objects on your slides, it's easy to get carried away. How do you know when enough is enough? That depends on what you're creating. The cardinal rule is to be sure that the end result works for your intended audience. The images, colors, and fonts you use for a school presentation might be inappropriate for a corporate boardroom, for example. Beyond that one overarching rule, it's possible to work with some more general guidelines.

When working with text, bigger is typically better. This is especially true for presentations for which a projector will be used. In this case, you want to ensure that the person sitting in the back row doesn't have to squint. Look at the text sizes for bullet points in one of the built-in themes, and you'll see that they're much bigger than body text in a standard Word document.

Unfortunately, as text size increases, the amount of space on the slide decreases. As a rule, keep slides focused and to the point to minimize the amount of text required. If you plan to present your slide show live, you can and should use short, bulleted text points that help the listener follow along; as the speaker, you can fill in the gaps and avoid the dreaded "Oh no, he's reading his slides" effect. If your presentation will run unattended at a trade show or on the web, you need to be more creative. If the text is too long, consider breaking it up by inserting a video or recorded narration. When in doubt, split the text across two slides with some graphics to add visual interest. Your audience will appreciate the effort.

Starting with an outline allows you to define each slide's main point and see how it fits in the overall theme of your presentation before you get into your design work. Outlines can also help you organize text so that each slide contributes to a consistent flow, with a similar number of bullets per slide and the same basic structure and tone.

If you simply don't know where to start, you can get a little push from the templates Microsoft offers at Office.com. One of our favorites is "Duarte's Five Rules." (To locate this template, click File, click New, type **five rules** in the Office.com Templates box, and click the Start Searching button. Not only is this a highly engaging, self-running presentation, it offers useful tips on how you can create great presentations yourself. As a bonus, it shows some pretty terrific animation effects that will inspire both novice and advanced users.

INSIDE OUT   Maximize your editing space by hiding panes

One of the downsides to working with the Outline tab is the size of the pane on the left, which in its default configuration is just too narrow for serious work. You can drag the divider bar to the right to give yourself some more space. However, when you're making large-scale text edits, you might prefer to hide the Slide pane and allow the outline to use the full PowerPoint window. To do that, hold down Ctrl and Shift and click once on the Slide Sorter view button on the status bar. Hold down Ctrl and Shift and click the Normal view button on the status bar to hide the Slides and Outline tabs and the Notes pane and show just the Slide pane, with full access to all editing tools.

For more information on creating a presentation using an outline, see "Creating a New Presentation" on page 597.

Saving and Sharing a Presentation

Before you share your presentation, you've got to save it. If you even think you might want to add new slides or edit existing ones, you should use the default PowerPoint Presentation format (with a file name extension of .pptx). That's the standard XML-based format for use with PowerPoint 2010 and PowerPoint 2007.

If you need to share your presentation with someone who doesn't have a copy of Power-Point, you have a couple of options. Saving the file in PowerPoint Show format (with a file name extension of .ppsx) allows the presentation to run in slide show view on any computer with the PowerPoint Viewer installed. This free program, which works with Windows XP and later versions, can be downloaded from *w7io.com/11803*.

Or turn your presentation into a PDF format, which can be opened on any computer running any operating system by using Adobe Reader (or a compatible program). Click File, click Save & Send, and then click Create PDF/XPS Document. This file type works especially well when you need to share audience handouts. In PowerPoint 2010, you also have the option of converting your presentation into a video file playable on a DVD, on a web-based service, or in a smaller, portable format.

For a complete list of PowerPoint 2010 supported file types, see Table 4-4, "Supported File Formats in PowerPoint 2010," on page 77. For more information about saving your presentation as a video file, see "Turning Your Presentation into a Video" on page 673.

Compressing Your File

The more graphics and other media you add to your presentation, the larger it gets. That's especially true if you add high-quality video clips. Large files are difficult to share with others via e-mail, and they're a potential hassle for anyone using a slow Internet connection. For presentations that have audio or video clips, use the Compress Media option on the Info tab in Backstage view, shown in Figure 18-11.

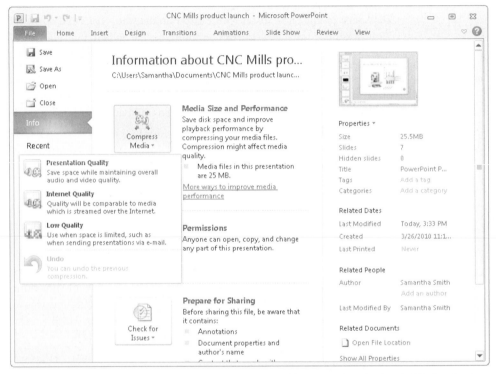

Figure 18-11 Choose compression settings to minimize file size and make it suitable for distribution. This option appears only for presentations that contain audio or video clips.

For a complete list of ways to share your presentation, see "Broadcasting a Presentation" on page 649.

INSIDE OUT   Flatten and compress at the same time

When you're looking to reduce your presentation's file size, another option is to save your file as a picture presentation. This format isn't necessarily designed for compression, but that does seem to be one of its main benefits. First, make a copy of your presentation file—the transformation you're about to perform uses the same file extension as the default format, and you will lose the ability to edit text and graphics individually after this operation is complete.

Click File and then, on the Save & Send tab, click Change File Type. Choose the Power-Point Picture Presentation format to flatten all content on each slide and create a new presentation in which every element—text, charts, lines and borders, media clips, and so on—is converted to a series of pictures and saved as a PowerPoint file. This step is beneficial when you need to share your presentation with others who shouldn't be allowed to copy or change your material. The downsides? The new picture presentation converts all video to images, and you lose your animation effects.

Building a Presentation from Scratch

How you choose to start building your presentation depends ultimately on what information you already have and how much time you can devote to the task. While it's always good if you can start with an idea in mind, it's not a requirement. PowerPoint has plenty of design options to get you started.

Creating a New Presentation

If you've already typed your presentation outline in another program, such as Word, you can import that text into a new PowerPoint file and automatically create slides. You need to be sure that your outline (in Word) has the proper styles applied so that PowerPoint knows how to format the text you're importing.

Figure 18-12 shows a formatted outline in Word.

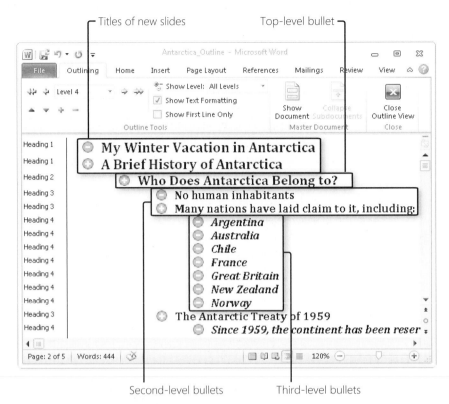

Figure 18-12 Use styles in Word to dictate the flow of text on your PowerPoint slides. Each Heading 1 entry becomes a slide title, with subheadings becoming bullets.

To convert a Word outline to a PowerPoint presentation, choose All Outlines as your file type in the Open dialog box in PowerPoint. When the Word outline is opened, PowerPoint looks for heading styles. For example, text formatted with the Heading 1 style becomes the title of a new slide in PowerPoint.

Figure 18-13 shows the outline in Figure 18-12 converted to a PowerPoint slide.

To learn how to use heading styles in Word, see "Applying Styles" on page 226.

Once your text is in place, you can use the Design tab to apply a theme and quickly enhance how your presentation looks visually.

For more information on themes in Office 2010, see "Using Office Themes" on page 185.

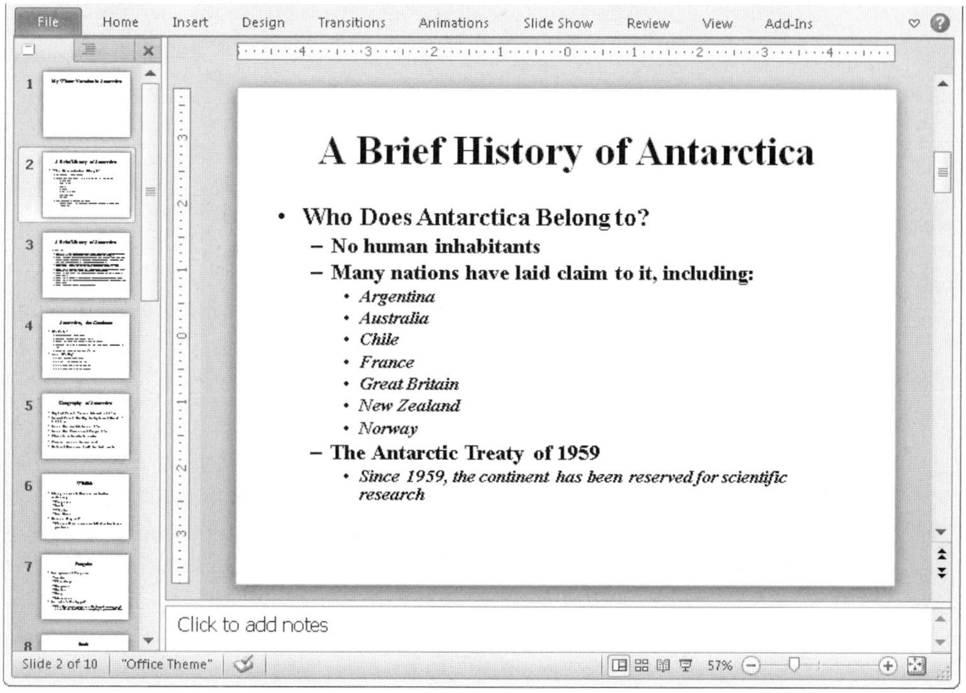

Figure 18-13 Once opened in PowerPoint, Word outlines quickly populate a PowerPoint slide show.

Adding Slides from an Outline

Just as you can start a presentation from a Word outline, you can also use a Word outline to add slides to an existing presentation. This is useful when you've already selected a design in PowerPoint and just need to fill in the text. That way, you don't have to start with a blank presentation.

Start by selecting the slide that will appear before the newly inserted slides. Then, on the Home tab, click the arrow beneath the New Slide command, click Slides From Outline, and pick the Word file containing your outline text.

Using a Template or Design

To save time, create a presentation by using one of the PowerPoint templates that come complete with both design elements and sample text. This approach is useful when you have a standard presentation to deliver, such as one designed to accompany a training class. To create a presentation using a template, click File, click the New tab, and browse through the collection in the Sample Templates folder. You can also select from a much larger selection of templates on Office.com.

Chapter 18

Alternatively, you can create a presentation with the design elements of a template but without the suggested text. To select from all available themes, click the New tab in Backstage view and double-click Themes.

Using Slide Sections

Dividing your presentation into sections allows you to group related sets of slides into logical categories. This feature, which is new in PowerPoint 2010, is useful when you're working with large presentation decks or when you're collaborating with another person and each of you is responsible for a specific set of slides. You can also use sections as you begin a new presentation to organize the larger ideas that you want to communicate.

Sections can be defined in either Slide Sorter view or Normal view. Choose the slide you want to use as the first one in your new section. On the Home tab, in the Slides group, click Section, and then click Add Section. (You can also right-click just before the first slide in a new section and choose Add Section from the shortcut menu.) With the new section created, click Section, click Rename Section, and give the set of slides that follow a meaningful explanation. Figure 18-14 shows several sections in Slide Show view.

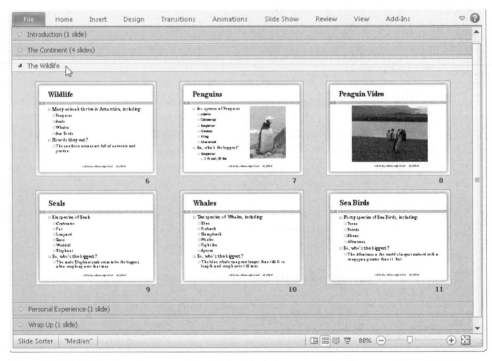

Figure 18-14 Defined sections can be collapsed to narrow your view to a specific set of slides.

From the shortcut menu shown in Figure 18-15, you can move an entire section of slides up or down in the presentation. You can also delete all slides that belong to a section.

Figure 18-15 On the Slides tab in Normal view, right-click any section heading to see the short-cut menu options shown here.

Adding Graphics and Video Clips

Graphics and video clips help you communicate complex ideas in a simple manner. Some-times, one well-placed image or video can tell your entire story, with no bullet points nec-essary. On the downside, adding media to your presentation can significantly increase file size. The trick is to find the right balance.

In PowerPoint, you have more options for what you can include when compared with other Office programs. Of course, you can insert all the standard graphical object types, including pictures, shapes, clip art, SmartArt, and WordArt text effects. This content works the same here as it does elsewhere.

For detailed information on how to add each type of graphical object to your presentation, see Chapter 6, "Working with Graphics and Pictures."

Another new feature in Office 2010 is the option to add a screenshot to a document. This option can be useful in PowerPoint if, for example, you're creating an orientation presenta-tion for new employees. Screenshots can show any other part of what you see on the dis-play: dialog boxes for logging on or connecting to the network, web-based forms for filing out expense reports, filled-in dialog boxes for configuring access to company e-mail, and so on.

Chapter 18

For more information on adding screenshots to your presentation, see "Capturing and Inserting Screenshots" on page 174.

Other content options include tables and charts. In PowerPoint, tables follow the same concept as they do in Word, except, instead of being inserted in line with text (at a paragraph mark), they are stand-alone objects that exist in placeholders and can be resized and moved just like images.

For more information on adding a chart to your presentation, see "Displaying Data Graphically with Charts" on page 179.

Finally, your PowerPoint content can include video and audio, an option not readily available in the other Office programs.

Inserting Graphics

As in other Office programs, you can insert content from the Insert tab. But PowerPoint has something the other programs don't have—layouts. In fact, many of the layouts contain a placeholder for "content." This generic term is used because content can mean any one of six options, including Table, Chart, SmartArt, Picture, ClipArt, or Media Clip.

Figure 18-16 shows the content options displayed inside a content placeholder. To insert a content type, click the associated icon. The three icons in the top row allow you to insert a table, chart, or SmartArt object. The icons in the bottom row are for pictures, clip art, and media clips.

Figure 18-16 Clicking any one of the six content icons is akin to clicking the same option on the Insert tab, only quicker.

In any layout with a content placeholder, you can also insert text by clicking inside the placeholder, away from the content icons.

Working with Graphics

The term "graphics" in PowerPoint encompasses tables, pictures, clip art, screenshots, shapes, SmartArt, and charts—all of which can be inserted from the Insert tab. As you add graphics to your presentation, remember to use Office 2010 tools and image enhancements.

For example, when you have multiple objects on one slide, use the Selection pane (on the Home tab, in the Editing group, click Select, and then click Selection Pane) to work with them. In the Selection pane, you can give each object a descriptive name—like "Penguin Pic" instead of "Content Placeholder 4." This is also a useful place to select an object that is stacked on top of or below another, because it can be difficult to isolate the one object you need to work with.

For details about selecting, positioning, and resizing graphics, see "Working with Drawing Layers in Office Documents" on page 150.

Then, use the new artistic textures to add interest to your images. With Live Preview thumbnails in the gallery, you can see what effect the changes have on your picture before you make your final selection.

In Office 2010, you now have the option to customize any photo by cropping out unneeded elements and removing the photo background altogether.

For information about cropping, color correction, and artistic effects, see "Making Your Pictures Look Great" on page 163.

For keeping multiple objects in order, use the alignment options on the Format contextual tabs. They give you several options for aligning one object on the basis of another object's position. A more visual way to see this alignment is by adding an on-screen grid: select View Gridlines from the Align option on the Format tab.

Enabling the grid adds vertical and horizontal dotted lines to your presentation in Normal view. This way, when you move objects, there's no guesswork as to whether they're lined up with any other object on the slide.

The grid's spacing is set in the Grid And Guides dialog box, shown in Figure 18-17. You can change this setting by selecting Grid Settings from the Align option on the Format tab.

Chapter 18

Figure 18-17 Use the Grid And Guides dialog box to display a grid on the screen. This helps when aligning objects and controls whether you see the smart guides when objects are aligned.

Even without the grid, you'll see smart guides pop up when you move one object within close proximity of another. This is PowerPoint's way of telling you that the object you're moving is aligned with another object already on the slide. These smart guides can be disabled in the Grid And Guides dialog box.

INSIDE OUT   Combining multiple shapes

Combining shapes is based on the principles of Boolean geometry, but don't let that scare you away. This feature is a nice workaround when the Freeform drawing tool just isn't getting you the specific shape you need. Long ago (in PowerPoint 2003, to be specific), the Combine Shapes command was on the default toolbars. In PowerPoint 2010, you have to dig a little for it, but it's still available. Click the arrow at the end of the Quick Access Toolbar, click More Commands, and then choose Commands Not In The Ribbon from the Choose Commands From list. Select Combine Shapes from the list of commands, and then click Add.

This command has four options. Both the Shape Subtract and Shape Intersect options remove portions of selected objects. Where two objects are stacked, Shape Subtract removes the area from the bottom object that the top object covers, while Shape Intersect removes everything except the area where the two objects overlay. The Shape Combine and Shape Union options both unify, or flatten, selected objects. Shape Union merges two objects into one using the outside edge of all selected objects as the basis for the new object. Shape Combine merges the selected objects by cutting out any area where the two selected objects overlap.

Working with Video

Video clips can be embedded in your presentation. Embedding a video clip eliminates the need to send or store additional files with your presentation. But doing so increases your overall presentation's file size, which could lead to performance issues. Another option is to link to a video stored in a generally accessible location (like the Internet or your hard drive).

Inserting Video

To embed a video, click Video on the Insert tab (in the Media group at the right side of the tab), and then click Video From File, as shown in Figure 18-18. Choosing Video From Web Site gives you a dialog box that lets you paste a link to a video stored on a website such as YouTube or Hulu. The Clip Art Video option gives you access to video stored within the Clip Art Gallery.

Figure 18-18 Clicking Video From File allows you to embed a video or create a link to a video stored locally on your computer.

Clicking Video From File doesn't mean you have to embed a video in your presentation. When you select the video in the Insert Video dialog box, click the arrow next to the Insert button and choose Link To File. The video looks like it's embedded, but your presentation file size won't be significantly affected.

You can insert animated GIF files as well as other standard video formats. PowerPoint also supports QuickTime and Flash videos, although playing back either of these formats properly requires that you install separate, stand-alone players for QuickTime and Flash.

Note that when you insert a Flash file, you lose a few key features. For starters, you can't use special effects and fade or trim options on a Flash file. Additionally, you don't have the ability to compress your file size with embedded Flash files as you can with embedded files using video formats such as Windows Media Video or QuickTime.

Editing Video

New in PowerPoint 2010 is the ability for you to make edits to videos that have been embedded in or linked to your presentation. One of the first features you'll notice is the video control panel that shows up at the bottom of inserted videos in both Normal view and Slide Show view. On this panel, you can play or pause your video, jump to a specific section, and adjust the volume. For times when you prefer to not show the video control panel during a presentation, you can remove this panel from Slide Show view by clearing the Show Media Controls check box in the Set Up group on the Slide Show tab.

Unfortunately, you'll often have access to a video that has dead space at the beginning or end or is simply too long for your presentation's needs. For these instances, click Trim Video (in the Editing group on the Playback tab under Video Tools).

Figure 18-19 shows a 24-second video that has been trimmed to just 10 seconds by shaving time off both the front and back of the embedded video.

Figure 18-19 Set your video start and stop times by entering times directly in the boxes or by dragging the start and stop points on the timeline.

Actually, the Playback tab under Video Tools offers several options for controlling how your video appears during your presentation, including fade in and fade out options, playback looping and rewind, and the ability to play the video in full-screen mode. There's also an option that allows you to hide your video in Slide Show view when it isn't playing. The only problem with this option is that if the video playback isn't triggered by an automatic animation, you have no way of accessing the video during your presentation.

Another option on this tab allows you to add *bookmarks*, which are points in your video and audio files that you save for easy access later. Bookmarks allow you to jump to specific audio or video segments within a larger media file and also to start animation effects based on the bookmarked position. To bookmark one or more areas of a video while the video is playing (in Normal view), click Add Bookmark on the Video Tools Playback tab as soon as you reach a spot you want to bookmark.

Bookmarks are noted by small circles that appear on the control panel. To remove a saved bookmark, click it once, and then click Remove Bookmark on the Video Tools Playback tab.

For more information on setting animation effects, see "Adding Emphasis with Animations" on page 615.

Working with Audio

Like video, audio clips can be embedded in your presentation. Although they should be used sparingly, they can be a godsend under certain circumstances, such as when you want to play back the new commercial jingle your company will be using or share a clip from an interview for a report you're presenting at school. Another productive use of recorded audio is adding comments to slides you're reviewing or adding narration for a presentation that might run unattended at a kiosk.

Inserting Audio

In PowerPoint 2010, you can insert audio from a file or from the Clip Art gallery; with the right equipment, you can record audio directly to your computer. To embed audio, click Audio in the Media group on the Insert tab, and choose Audio From File. As with video, clicking Audio From File doesn't necessarily embed the audio file in your presentation. When you select the audio file in the Insert Audio dialog box, click the arrow next to the Insert button and choose Link To File.

To use the Record Audio option, you need to have a microphone set up before you open the PowerPoint program. Then, work with the Record Sound dialog box shown in Figure 18-20.

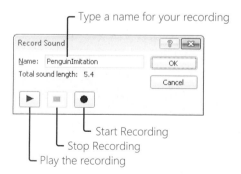

Figure 18-20 You need a microphone or other audio input source to record a narration or other sound file for a presentation.

Another way to add audio to your presentation is to record narration. For details, see "Recording Narration" on page 632.

Editing Audio

The options for editing audio are quite similar to the options available for editing video. In fact, they're even located on nearly the same Playback tab. Just as with video, when you're working with audio, you can add or remove bookmarks, trim audio start and stop points, set fade in and fade out locations, hide the audio during the slide show (just be sure the audio plays on an automatic animation), and loop or rewind the clip.

Customizing Your Presentation's Design

Before you're ready to deliver a presentation, there are some last-minute design changes you can make beyond slide layouts. Design is often the first thing people try to work with in PowerPoint, but it really should be the last. Ideally, you want to get the core of your message down first. The design changes you make will affect much of what you've already entered, but they shouldn't cause you to rework your message. In short, the design should fit your message, not the other way around.

Formatting Text

Formatting PowerPoint text isn't any different from formatting text in a program like Word. You select the text and then use the formatting options on the Home tab or the Mini tool-bar. PowerPoint allows you to format all or just selected pieces of text within a text box.

To format all the text inside an individual placeholder, click once inside the placeholder, and then press Esc. This selects the placeholder as an object. Now, any formatting changes you make affect all the text inside the selected placeholder. Pressing Esc one more time removes the placeholder selection altogether.

For more information about formatting text, see "Applying Text Formatting" on page 123.

Setting Page Layout Options

Because PowerPoint is intended primarily for on-screen use, you'll find very few page setup options. In fact, there are only two of note: Slide Orientation and Headers & Footers.

A slide's orientation can be either portrait or landscape and is defined on the Design tab in the Page Setup group. The option you select affects all slides within the same presentation. In other words, you can't mix slides of different orientations in the same presentation file.

INSIDE OUT   Create a slide show that mixes orientations

You know how we just said you can't mix slides of different orientations in a presentation? That's technically true, but there is a workaround in the event you need to show a few slides in a different orientation from those in the rest of the deck. The trick is to *link* two different slide shows, each created using a different orientation. Create an object on the first slide that you can click while in Slide Show view. With that object selected, click the Action command on the Insert tab. On either tab (Mouse Click or Mouse Over), choose Other PowerPoint Presentation from the Hyperlink To menu. On the last slide of the second presentation, create a similar object with an action that returns to the first presentation, at the slide immediately following the one where you left. (For more on how to create action settings, see "Inserting Action Buttons" on page 675.)

For presentations that will be making their debut on the big screen—or at least in a wide-screen format—you might need to adjust the aspect ratio. For example, you might want to change this setting if you discover that you'll be presenting your senior project on a wide-screen display in the auditorium instead of a standard-definition TV in the teacher's lounge as you originally planned. Most presentations are formatted using a 4:3 aspect ratio, which was originally designed to display well using an 800x600 resolution on an old-school SVGA computer monitor or projector, or a standard-definition TV. On a widescreen display, the aspect ratio is typically 16:9 (for a 1080p or 1080i HDTV with a native resolution of 1920 x 1080) or 16:10 (for computer monitors with a native resolution of 1920 x 1200).

To make this crucial change, use the Page Setup dialog box, which you can access from the Design tab. As shown in Figure 18-21, you can adjust your presentation's aspect ratio using the Slides Sized For list.

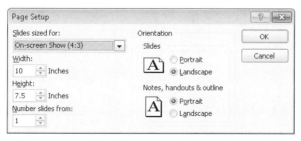

Figure 18-21 Adjust the page size for a printed presentation and the on-screen aspect ratio in the Page Setup dialog.

In this same dialog box, you can adjust the orientation of your slides, notes, and handouts or define a specific width and height.

CAUTION

Adjusting a presentation's aspect ratio after content has been added can wreak havoc. For example, images that looked fine at a 4:3 aspect ratio appear squashed when you switch to 16:9. If possible, determine your final presentation format before graphics and other media are placed on your slides. Otherwise, allow yourself time to modify these items after a new aspect ratio is applied.

An additional page setup option you can use on your slides is headers and footers. These small lines of text help keep you and your audience focused on where you are in the presentation by inserting slide numbers. They can also add the date and time or other custom text that you set.

To customize the header and footer for the current slide and for all slides, click the Header & Footer option on the Insert tab. Use the Header And Footer dialog box, shown in Figure 18-22, to set your preferences. Click Apply to add your settings to the current slide or Apply To All to add your settings to all slides in the presentation.

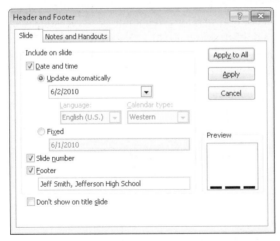

Figure 18-22 Click Apply To All to add the header and footer customization to all slides; select Don't Show On Title Slide to eliminate the customization from any slide formatted with the Title Slide layout.

You can also edit the header and footer at the bottom of Backstage view's Print menu by clicking the Edit Header & Footer link. This brings up the same dialog box shown in Figure 18-22.

Applying Themes

Whether you're designing a presentation for this year's PTA fundraiser or creating a project status report, applying a theme can save you considerable design time. As in other Office programs, themes store related sets of fonts, colors, and graphic effects that affect all slides in a presentation.

But in PowerPoint, themes also bring along background colors and images as well as customized slide layouts. Because of this, themes are ideally suited for on-screen presentations.

The same themes you see in other Office applications on the Page Layout tab are located in PowerPoint on the Design tab. The Themes gallery is shown in Figure 18-23.

Figure 18-23 Themes in PowerPoint provide fonts, colors, and graphic effects, just as in other Office programs. In PowerPoint, they also provide background graphics and slide layouts.

When you hover your mouse over a theme, you'll see the familiar Live Preview functionality, and you have the option to customize and save themes here that become available in your other Office programs. Themes bring a consistent visual look to all of the slides in your PowerPoint deck.

CAUTION

Printing slides with lots of color applied not only takes a ton of ink, but it can make the text difficult to read. The Apex and Elemental themes, for example, are lovely to look at on the screen but can be a muddy mess when printed on a black-and-white printer. To avoid the problem, select Grayscale or Pure Black And White when you print. For details, see "Creating Notes and Handouts" on page 642.

Although applying a theme is fast, the downside is that it affects all slides in a presentation. For an individual slide, one way to get rid of graphics associated with a theme is to use the Hide Background Graphics check box on the Design tab. Selecting this option removes all graphic objects—those that are part of the master slide (including objects you may have added outside the theme), and those that are associated with a theme from the current slide. This setting must be enabled on a slide-by-slide basis, although you can save yourself some time by selecting multiple slides before enabling the option.

For more information on how themes work in Office, see "Using Office Themes" on page 185.

Adding Backgrounds

For more control over the color and design of your slides, you can set your own background, made up of colors, clip art, images, or patterns. One major benefit to defining your own background is that it can be applied to a specific slide and doesn't automatically affect all slides in the presentation.

Backgrounds are customized from the Background Styles option on the Design tab. From this menu, you can customize the background for all slides in your presentation by choosing any of the color styles listed. To add your own images or other design elements (such as a company logo or a corporate sponsor mention), click the Format Background option at the bottom. Figure 18-24 shows the Format Background dialog box you see when you customize a slide's background.

If you insert a file, once the file has been inserted, you'll see a live preview of the image on the current slide behind the Format Background dialog box. Use that preview to customize the offset (under Tiling Options). This helps you place the image in the most appropriate location based on the slide content. Then, for a watermark effect, use the Transparency slider.

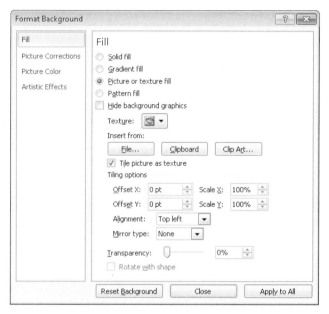

Figure 18-24 Use the Format Background dialog box to specify the type of background you want to create: solid or gradient fill, picture or texture fill, or a pattern.

Clicking Close applies your settings to the current slide. Alternatively, you can click Apply To All to add the custom background to all slides in the presentation. Note that when a custom background is applied to all slides, you lose the Reset Slide Background option at the bottom of the Background Styles menu). To remove the background from all slides, you need to customize another background or choose Style 1 from the Background Styles menu. In this case, selecting a design theme simply overlays the theme on top of the customized background.

For more information on picture corrections, picture color, and artistic effects, see "Making Your Pictures Look Great" on page 163.

Polishing and Delivering a Presentation

I N any of your audiences, it's likely that you'll have a mix of verbal and visual learners, and you want to present to both learning types. That's why you include a blend of text and media in your slides. But even with pictures and graphics, your presentation can still look static.

What on-screen presentations really need is movement. You can add this motion to your presentations in the form of content animation and slide transitions. While activity is good on-screen, it doesn't do much for printouts like audience handouts or speaker notes. These often need some added punch, too.

Then, there's your delivery. Will you deliver to a live audience and be forced to resurrect long-buried opening jokes? Will the presentation run by itself unattended, relying on recorded narration or lots and lots of text to get your message across? Will it be used as a platform to deliver information in a one-on-one setting, like a presentation that new employees must watch before they're given the code to the front door?

In this chapter, we show how you can build on existing presentations to add a level of interactivity through animations and transitions. Then we look at the steps for planning, rehearsing, and delivering a live presentation.

Adding Emphasis with Animations

Consider this scenario: You just spent the better part of the last few days building the basis for your company's new hire orientation. It includes all the pertinent details—like security protocol, holidays and vacation time, and the lowdown on the company big wigs. You even found a few graphics and a design theme that work well with your content. So, what's the problem? All the information is there, but that's it. It's just there. It's boring.

What your presentation lacks you can make up for with a little creativity and some content animation. For example, is it necessary to fill a slide that lists security protocols just with text? Does your audience need to remember all 100 words, or can you summarize it in one really big, animated word supplemented with some audio narration? If you have a bulleted list, does your audience need to see the whole list at the same time, or can you show just one item at a time?

Think outside the box. With animation, you don't need a separate slide each time you want to show something on the screen. You can control which objects appear when and for how long. Objects can have multiple animations assigned to them, each with its own trigger and timing.

Need a Little Inspiration?

Animation is best experienced and not read about; you'll learn more by doing and seeing than by reading. For a little inspiration, view the Five Rules presentation by clicking File, New, Sample Templates, Five Rules, Create.

This presentation was developed to inspire you with some well-placed animation, slide transitions, and narration. After you open it, watch the entire presentation in Slide Show view so you can get the full experience. Then, switch to Normal view and use the techniques in this chapter to see how the dynamic animation and transitions create what looks much more like a video than a presentation.

Adding Animation

When you're ready to add your own animations, use Normal view and the Animations tab, which is shown in Figure 19-1.

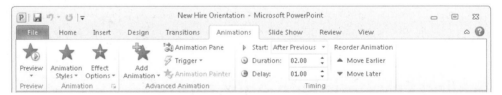

Figure 19-1 From the Animations tab, you can add, remove, and customize animation effects and timing.

Note that animation effects are set in Normal view and seen in Slide Show view. However, there is a Preview option on the Animations tab that lets you see the animation in action while you're working in Normal view.

For more information about working in Normal view, see "Presentation View Options" on page 584. For more information about working in Slide Show view, see "Delivering a Live Presentation" on page 633.

There are several types of animations you can apply to selected objects by using the Add Animation option on the Animations tab, including entrance, emphasis, exit, and motion paths.

- **Entrance** controls how an object first appears on a slide.

- **Emphasis** sets animation on an object already on a slide.

- **Exit** defines how an object leaves a slide.

- **Motion paths** are the most customizable and allow you to define a specific direction or path that an animated object follows. This effect works well for nonstandard motions, such as along a curve.

Using each animation effect or a combination, you can bring life to your slide's objects. You can use animation to stack objects, minimize the amount of text your audience reads at any given time, catch your audience's attention, or mimic a video (as the Five Rules template does). For example, you could use an entrance effect to bring text onto a slide, an emphasis effect to change the color of the text, and then an exit effect to remove it to make room for the next set of text items you'll talk about.

When you click Add Animation, the Animation gallery, shown in Figure 19-2, shows you several available animations.

Although the Animation gallery shows a fairly large list of animations, there are too many to display in one gallery. To see all available animations, you need to select the type of animation you want to apply from the set of More links at the bottom of the gallery. The resulting dialog box lists all available animations for the selected type. If you move the dialog box to the side and then select an effect, you can see a preview of it on the selected object back on the slide. This way, you can still preview the effect before you make your final decision.

Figure 19-2 Set a selected object's animation effect from the Animation gallery. You can assign multiple animations to an object.

Layering Animation Effects

Like we said, animation is best experienced. Toward that end, let's walk through an example to see how animation works. Figure 19-3 shows a slide ready for animation.

Right now, the slide looks like a jumbled mess with all the layered content. That's where animation comes in. We'll use animation to control how and when each of these objects is displayed on the screen and when each leaves. This way, to the viewer, the slide looks like a seamless video. In this example, the slide begins with the text and employee pictures along with prerecorded narration.

For more information about recording narration on a slide, see "Recording Narration" on page 632.

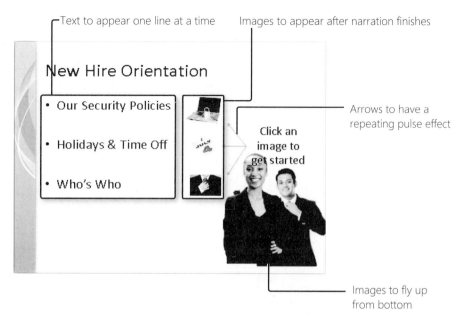

Figure 19-3 Before animation is added and timed, objects on a slide might look like they're sitting on top of one another. Properly orchestrated animation removes this impression in Slide Show view.

The first animation is easy. You select the text box with the bulleted list, click Add Animation on the Animations tab, and select an entrance effect. For this example, we use Zoom. Next we'll add the Fly In entrance effect to the image of the man, and then the woman. The default direction for Fly In is from the bottom of the slide. For our purposes, that works well.

Note that most animations, like Fly In, have their own set of effect options. You have access to the available effects after you apply the animation. You can see an applied animation's effects by clicking Effect Options on the Animations tab. The options vary depending on the animation, but they often include an animation direction. In the case of a text box, you also get the option of animating all the text at once, as one object, or as a paragraph.

INSIDE OUT   Animate a SmartArt object

After you apply an entrance effect to a SmartArt object, you can use the Effect Options menu on the Animations tab to specify whether the object is built all at once or with each element "one by one." Apply the One By One setting to see each bullet or level displayed separately, one at a time.

The next items to appear on the slide are the small images next to each of the bulleted list items. Select all three by using the Ctrl key and then apply the Float In entrance effect. Finally, we need to set the Appear entrance effect for the viewer instructions and the three arrows. A selection technique that works well here is to drag around the objects you want to select, effectively "lassoing" them with your mouse, as shown in Figure 19-4.

Figure 19-4 Only objects that are completely surrounded by your "lasso" are included in the selection. In this figure, only the viewer instructions text box and three arrows are selected. The lasso technique is a good way to select small or layered objects.

Unlike in previous versions of PowerPoint, in PowerPoint 2010, all animations must be added using the Animations tab. Once animations are added, you can display the Animation pane, shown in Figure 19-5, by clicking the Animation Pane option on the Animations tab and then edit animations that have been set up.

INSIDE OUT   Assign names to objects

If you see a list of generic names in the Animation pane, open the Selection And Visibility pane (click the Home tab, and in the Editing group click Select, Selection Pane), and rename your slide objects. For more information on renaming objects using the Selection And Visibility pane, see "Working with Multiple Graphics and Pictures" on page 152.

With the Animation pane, you can reorder your animations, preview them, and modify their timing and effect options. Numbers in the Animation pane correspond to numbers displayed next to the animated object on the slide. You can click a number in either place to highlight the corresponding number in the other, making it easy to find a particular animation in the list or on the slide.

Figure 19-5 Objects are identified in the Animation pane by their assigned name.

TROUBLESHOOTING

Options in the Animation pane are unavailable.

This typically happens when no animation has been assigned. Remember, all animations must be added using the Animations tab. Then you can use the Animation pane to work with existing animations.

It's in the Animation pane that you can remove animations you added by using the Animations tab. To remove an animation, click the arrow next to the animation, and choose Remove from the menu. If you want to change an existing animation to a different animation, you need to use options in the Animation group (click Animation Styles or choose from the gallery), not the Add Animation tool. From there you can change the animation effect that has been applied without needlessly adding additional effects. To fully work with animations, you need to switch back and forth between the Animations tab and the Animation pane.

CAUTION

After an effect has been applied, going back to the Animation gallery to change it applies another animation to the same object. Use the Animation Styles option in the Animation group to modify a selected animation.

Setting Animation Timing

In our example, we've successfully set how each object should appear on the slide. Further, by adding the animations in the order we want them to occur, we saved the step of having to reorder them later (from either the Animations tab or the Animation pane).

By default, each newly added animation is set to appear "on click." But for some animations, it's nice if they simply happen. For instance, for our text placeholder with three bullets, we don't want to have to click to make each new bullet appear. Instead, we can time these bullets so that they enter the slide automatically.

These types of timings can be set for an entire text box, but when the effect option is set to show by paragraph, the text box has a separate animation for each paragraph. This means you have to select all the affected animations before you change the start and duration. You can do that by selecting the entire text box (not just clicking inside it), or by using the Ctrl or Shift keys to select the affected animations in the Animation pane. (You can see how properly naming your slide objects comes in handy.)

On the Animations tab, you work with options in the Timing group, shown in Figure 19-6, to control animation timing. To have selected animations occur automatically, one after another, click the arrow next to the Start option and choose After Previous. Choosing With Previous displays all selected animations on the slide at the same time.

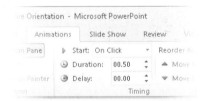

Figure 19-6 Use the Start, Duration, and Delay options on the Animations tab to control when an animation begins and how long it lasts.

The Duration option in the Timing group affects the selected animation and is separate from slide timings. In our three-bullet text placeholder example, the current animation is an entrance effect that displays the text one paragraph at a time and starts with the After Previous setting. So far, so good.

Unfortunately, the default duration is only half a second. PowerPoint divides the duration by the number of objects it needs to display and evenly spaces out the animations. This often means that your text shows up too quickly and doesn't match the pace of your presentation or the slide's background narration. To allow more time between the appearance of each bullet, you can increase the duration.

In addition to adequately spacing out your text displays, another benefit to setting text to be built by paragraphs is that you can insert other objects you want to display in between bullets and then use the Reorder option at the bottom of the Animation pane to adjust the animation sequence. You can use the Move Earlier and Move Later options on the Animations tab to achieve the same effect.

Figure 19-7 shows the sequence in which the animation will appear.

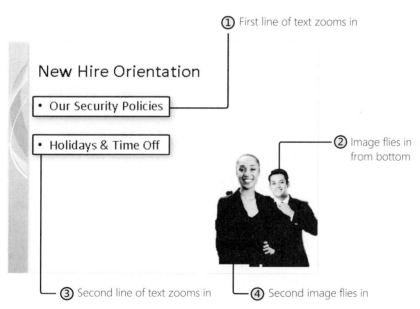

Figure 19-7 You can reorder animations from the Animation pane or in the Timings group on the Animations tab.

One final option related to animation timing is delay. In the Delay box, specify (in seconds) how long the animation should wait before appearing on the slide. A delay is helpful if the narration needs time before the next object appears or if you don't want the presentation to feel rushed. The speed of an animation can evoke a feeling. For example, a fast entrance can convey a sense of urgency, while a slow-moving object can represent a delay or even a feeling of yearning or reminiscence.

To learn more about setting slide timings, see "Planning and Rehearsing a Presentation" on page 631.

In Slide Show view, animations follow either your mouse click or the animation timings that you define. For animations that are set to advance on a mouse click, you can also use the keyboard shortcuts you use to advance to the next slide. For example, pressing Enter triggers the next animation or slide, whichever comes first.

INSIDE OUT   Pull apart clip art, and then animate it

Each clip art object is a set of smaller objects pieced together to make up one graphic. When you apply animation to a clip art illustration, the only option you have is to build it all at once, as one object, unless you take it apart first. Using the Ungroup option on the Format tab under Drawing Tools, you can break up an illustration into smaller segments that you can apply separate animations to and control their appearance on your slides with timings.

For example, when presenting to a group about teamwork, you might talk about how each person is a necessary piece of the teamwork puzzle. A good illustration to use in this case is one that shows several interlocking puzzle pieces. Once the illustration of the puzzle is inserted, ungroup it to make each piece a separate object. Then, add entrance effects to each puzzle piece and set their order and timing. In Slide Show view, your puzzle comes together on the slide while you're talking.

Duplicating Animations with Animation Painter

As you start working with animations, it becomes clear fairly quickly that a lot of customization can be assigned to just one object. Once you animate one object precisely the way you want it—with the right effects, options, and timing—re-creating those steps on a similar object can be time-consuming. In PowerPoint 2010, you can use Animation Painter to copy animations applied to one object to another. It works on animations the same way Format Painter works on formatting.

To use this feature, select an object with an animation assigned, click Animation Painter on the Animations tab, and then click the object you want to copy the animation to.

Animation Painter works well when you're developing complex animations or with objects that contain several animation properties.

INSIDE OUT   Copy animation settings to multiple objects

When you click Animation Painter, it stays active until you click an object. If you need to copy animation from one object to multiple objects, you can keep Animation Painter active until you finish copying.

After you select the object that holds the animation settings you want to copy, double-click the Animation Painter option. Now you can apply the animation settings to as many objects as you need to. When you finish, just click Animation Painter once or press Esc.

Triggering an Animation Effect

For the most part, animations start based on other animations. One follows another, two start at the same time, or they wait for a cue from the presenter. Another way to get an animation effect to start is through a trigger. Separate from the Start option, triggers can be used to display other, hidden objects when the presenter clicks a specific object or reaches a bookmark in a video.

Using a trigger, you can hide a video when it's not playing. You can then set the video's animation trigger to play when another object (such as a picture or a text box) on the slide is clicked. As an example, our new hire presentation has a video related to security. To set the video to play when the security image is clicked, we set the security image as the video's trigger. To accomplish this, insert and select the video. On the Animations tab, click Trigger, On Click Of, Security Image, as shown in Figure 19-8.

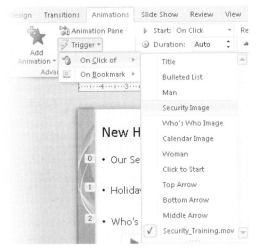

Figure 19-8 Triggers can be used to display hidden objects when another object is clicked or when a bookmark in a playing video is reached.

INSIDE OUT Overlay text on a video with animation

You can use text boxes with animation triggers to overlay text on top of a playing video at defined bookmarks. This works well to create a closed-captioning effect or to highlight specific areas of a video.

To start, create bookmarks for your video at the points when text should appear. Then create a text box, apply entrance and exit animation, and apply a trigger to display the text box at a specified bookmark. As soon as the playing video reaches the bookmark, the text box animation is triggered. If you want to overlay multiple boxes, be sure to set exit animation or define a duration for each text box. Otherwise, you end up with text boxes running over the top of one another.

Setting Additional Effect Options

Each animation has various settings and effects that control how the animation appears. To preview and select these options, select an animation in the Animation pane, and then click Effect Options on the Animations tab. A gallery of effects appears, and as you point to each one, a live preview demonstrates the effect.

However, these galleries don't include all the available effect options. To see additional settings, click the dialog box launcher in the lower right corner of the Animation group on the Animations tab. Alternatively, click the arrow next to any effect in the Animation pane and choose Effect Options from the menu. Either way, a dialog box with two or three tabs (depending on what type of object is selected) opens. In this dialog box, you can get more specific with your effect timing, appearance, and sounds.

For example, most animations are set to happen "fast." They come in. They go out. No muss; no fuss. To make an animation's movement a little slower, click the Timing tab in the effect options dialog box, as shown in Figure 19-9. Next to Duration, select your preferred speed from the list.

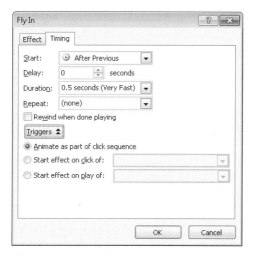

Figure 19-9 The effect options dialog box is different for each type of animation effect.

The Start, Delay, and Triggers options in the effect options dialog box are the same as you see on the ribbon. Two additional options include Repeat and Rewind.

Under the Repeat option, you can select (or type) a specific number of times for the animation to occur, including keeping it going until you click or until the end of the slide is reached. This effect works well if you're animating a ball rolling up or down a hill, but it's often more annoying than effective when you display an object on the screen over and over again.

If you select Rewind When Done Playing, the object returns to its original size and location after an animation is complete. For example, if you use an emphasis animation to increase the size of text, setting it to rewind restores the text to its original size.

CAUTION

When you start customizing animation effects, it's easy to select the wrong type of animation in the Animation pane because they all look alike. You could end up setting the rewind option on a text's entrance effect, which, instead of rewinding the emphasis animation, takes the text off the slide altogether. Pay attention to the icon next to each animation. Green stars indicate entrance effects, yellow stars indicate emphasis effects, and red stars indicate exit effects.

Figure 19-10 shows the Effect tab in the effect options dialog box for a Grow/Shrink emphasis animation.

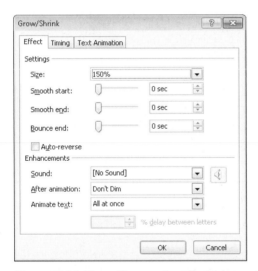

Figure 19-10 The settings on the Effect tab are different for each animation type.

On this tab, you can customize the size and animation of the text. You can also add a sound effect and choose to hide text that has already appeared in the animation. This last option is effective when you're showing a bulleted list and want previous bullets to disappear as each new bullet is displayed.

INSIDE OUT   Use the repeating effect option sparingly

Used improperly, the repeat effect (which you set by making a selection in the Repeat box on the Timing tab of the effect options dialog box) can be more annoying than inspiring. But it can be effective in some situations. In the example we use throughout this chapter, three arrows appear, prompting the viewer to take an action and click a picture. These arrows should remain highlighted until the viewer makes a choice.

To accomplish this, we set the emphasis animation effect on the arrows to Pulse and set the Repeat option to Until Next Click. Then we set the animation start to After Previous so that the emphasis and repeating happen automatically. This way, the arrows quietly draw attention to themselves just enough to catch the viewer's attention.

Using Transitions Between Slides

Animations affect individual objects on a slide; transitions affect how the slides themselves enter the screen in Slide Show view. Like animations, transitions are worthy of their own tab. You can assign a transition to any displayed slide by choosing a transition scheme from the gallery shown in Figure 19-11.

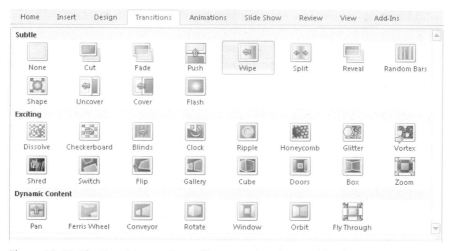

Figure 19-11 The Transitions gallery offers several options and has been relocated to the Transitions tab.

PowerPoint 2010 includes a few new transitions, and several of the standard transitions have been updated to allow slides to enter the screen from any of four directions instead of just two. Note also that a few transitions have been removed from the 2010 version of PowerPoint. However, transitions no longer available in PowerPoint 2010 that have been applied to presentations in an earlier version of PowerPoint still play when the file is viewed in PowerPoint 2010.

Transitions, like animations, are grouped into three categories:

- **Subtle** transitions typically slide in from a set direction; they are quick and barely noticeable by the audience. Use a subtle transition to create a smooth flow from one slide to the next.

- **Exciting** transitions are generally more noticeable to the audience than a subtle transition. They show one slide leaving the presentation view and another coming in. Use an exciting transition to make a more dramatic statement between slides.

- **Dynamic Content** transitions are designed to make your slides look like they are moving through space as one slide leaves and another enters.

Once you select a transition, you'll see a preview in both Normal and Slide Sorter views. If you miss it, click the Preview option on the Transitions tab to see it again. Each transition holds a set of customizable properties that include speed, duration, sound, and—in many cases—direction, shape, and format.

For instance, when you apply the Honeycomb transition, you can modify the default 4.4 seconds that it takes to move from the current slide to the next, but not much else. But when you apply the Shred transition, you can also choose the type of shredding effect you want to see by clicking Effect Options. All of these settings are available on the Transitions tab, shown in Figure 19-12.

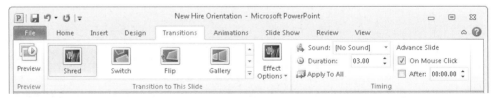

Figure 19-12 Use the Transitions tab to apply and customize transition effects for selected slides. To apply the same transition to all slides in your deck, click the Apply To All option.

Remember, when you apply a transition, it affects only the currently displayed slide (Normal view) or selected slide (Slide Sorter view). You can select multiple slides before you apply your transition settings to affect more than one slide. Press Ctrl as you click to select non-contiguous slides, or press Shift and click to select contiguous slides. You can select multiple slides in Normal view, although you might find this easier in Slide Sorter view.

You can use the Timing options on the Transitions tab to define whether a transition occurs automatically after a set length of time or only when the presenter chooses to advance the slide (on mouse click).

> **Note**
>
> The timing you enter here is independent of the duration you enter on the Animations tab. If the total of the timings you set for animation effects is greater than the slide duration you enter on the Transitions tab, the animation timings take precedence.

To remove a transition already assigned to a slide, choose None at the top of the Transitions gallery.

For more information about working in Normal or Slide Sorter view, see "Presentation View Options" on page 584.

Planning and Rehearsing a Presentation

Preceding every great presentation is usually a lot of practice. The first thing you need to determine is what your primary method of delivery will be. Will this be a self-running presentation set up for individual viewers or for a booth at a conference? Will you be delivering it live before an audience? Will you print your slides? Will your presentation use a combination of these options?

As an example, we'll go back to our new-hire orientation. In most cases, this presentation will be run by a new employee who watches the presentation and occasionally clicks to advance to a new topic. It's unlikely that the slides will be printed because the pertinent information is already contained in the employee handbook.

An automatic presentation like this brings up a few questions: How long will the presentation be? How long should each slide remain on the screen? Will you include audio narration?

Instead of guessing how long each slide should remain on the screen, you can use the Rehearse Timings option on the Slide Show tab to make a practice run through the presentation. As you watch and listen to the presentation in Slide Show view, PowerPoint records the time. Each time you click to move to the next slide, the time the last slide was on the screen is recorded, and that slide's timing is set.

For a presentation that runs automatically, it's a good idea to have someone unfamiliar with the content use rehearsal mode. This way, you can get a true picture of how long someone new to the presentation needs to become familiar with the message on each slide. To start rehearsal mode, click Rehearse Timings on the Slide Show tab. This switches your presentation into Slide Show mode and displays the Recording toolbar, shown in Figure 19-13.

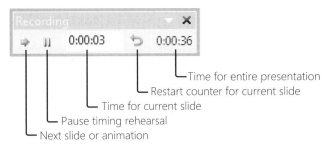

Time for entire presentation
Restart counter for current slide
Time for current slide
Pause timing rehearsal
Next slide or animation

Figure 19-13 Use the Recording toolbar to see how long each slide in your presentation is on the screen. When you finish, you can save or discard the slide timings.

Once you start the rehearsal, go ahead and practice your presentation aloud or have someone else review the content for you. This gives you a good idea of the pacing to use and ensures that each slide is displayed for the right amount of time.

While working in rehearsal mode, you can also pause at any time to make notes, collect your thoughts, or answer your phone. Click Resume Recording in the dialog box that appears after you pause to start again right where you left off. One great benefit to rehearsal is that you get an overall idea of just how long your presentation will last.

You can end rehearsal mode at any time by pressing Esc. It also ends when you reach the last slide in your presentation. In either case, you're given the option of saving the timings recorded in rehearsal mode as the actual timing for each slide.

Recording Narration

Near the Rehearse Timings option on the Slide Show tab is a feature new to PowerPoint 2010, Record Slide Show. This option allows you to set the length of time each slide appears on the screen—like rehearsing timings—and you have the additional options of recording narration and the mouse laser pointer at the same time.

For example, in our new-hire orientation, we could use this option to reduce the amount of text a new employee has to read and supplement what remains with an audio voiceover. The Record Slide Show option offers two choices: you can start the recording from the first slide or from the currently selected slide. Either way, you first need to decide exactly what you will record, as shown in Figure 19-14.

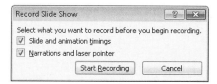

Figure 19-14 When you choose to record a slide show, you can record slide and animation timings, narrations and the mouse laser pointer, or both.

Once the recording starts, you use the Recording toolbar shown earlier in Figure 19-13 as you would when you're running a rehearsal.

When you record audio narration for a self-running presentation (one that runs without a live presenter), the audio adds depth, making the presentation feel more interactive. In addition, recording narration eliminates the need to add a separate audio file to each slide from the Insert tab. (For information about inserting and editing audio on a slide, see "Working with Audio" on page 607.)

Enabling the narration option also records your mouse actions when you enable it as a laser pointer, which is helpful if you plan to point to specific areas on a slide, like the high point on a chart. (For more information about this feature, see "Turning Your Mouse into a Laser Pointer" on page 638.) After you record your slide show, the new slide timings are applied to each slide. You can see them in Slide Sorter view just below each slide thumbnail, or on the Transitions tab in the Timing group.

Note that when you add narration through the Record Slide Show option, a small speaker icon is added to each slide, which indicates that audio narration has been recorded for the slide. In Normal view, you can click that icon to hear or edit the audio. However, the icon does not appear in Slide Show view because the Hide During Show option is enabled by default; you can find this option in the Audio Options group on the Playback tab under Audio Tools.

Delivering a Live Presentation

The animations are in; transitions are set. It's time to actually present this slide show in front of a live audience. It might be to just one new employee, or you might need to present a security briefing to the entire company. Either way, you use the Set Up Show dialog box shown in Figure 19-15 (click Set Up Slide Show on the Slide Show tab to view the dialog box) to define how the presentation will ultimately be delivered.

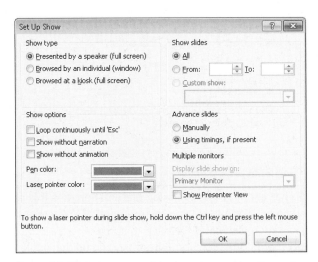

Figure 19-15 Set up your slide show by working through each of the five groups—Show Type, Show Options, Show Slides, Advance Slides, and Multiple Monitors—to define how you'll use this presentation.

Each time you get ready to present, use the Set Up Show dialog box to customize how your presentation will appear. You can make the following settings:

● The three options under Show Type determine the availability of other options in the Set Up Show dialog box. Presented By A Speaker (Full Screen) provides the most options, including Presenter view (if you are using more than one monitor) and the ability to change the annotation pen color. If you select Browsed By An Individual (Window), you lose both of these options. Choosing Browsed At A Kiosk (Full Screen) disables Presenter view and makes the slide show set to loop continuously until you press the Esc key.

● Under Show Options, you specify how the show plays. When Loop Continuously Until 'Esc' is selected, after your slide show reaches the last slide, it starts the presentation again instead of fading to a blank slide. This works well for presentations set to run at trade shows or at the front desk to greet customers as they walk into your office. Another good use of this feature is a presentation for a school science fair project. It cycles through the slide deck until someone tells it to stop.

If you have recorded narration or applied animations, the next two check boxes allow you to disable those features when Slide Show view is activated. Pen Color sets the default pen color for annotations. (This color can be changed during the presentation from the shortcut menu in Slide Show view.) Laser Pointer Color sets the color of your laser pointer when it's activated during a presentation. For more information, see "Turning Your Mouse into a Laser Pointer" on page 638.

- Under Show Slides, you can specify a range of slides that play during the presentation. This option comes in handy when you need to present just a portion of your entire deck. This is a good place to denote a range of slides that make up just one or two sections. Keep in mind, though, that the range of slides must be continuous. Finally, if you have custom shows set up, you can choose the custom show you need to play here. For information about custom shows, see "Creating Custom Slide Shows" on page 657.

- Under Advance Slides, you have the option to use slide timings or not. Slide timings are set manually on the Transitions tab or automatically by using the Rehearse Timings or Record Slide Show options. By selecting Manually, you override all slide timings. This way, the presentation animations and slides advance only on the presenter's cue. For more information on setting slide timings, see "Planning and Rehearsing a Presentation" on page 631.

- Under Multiple Monitors, you specify whether you want to use Presenter view and, if you do, on which monitor Slide Show view should be displayed. With Presenter view, you can show your presentation with speaker notes on a different monitor. For details, see "Working with Presenter View" on page 638.

CAUTION

Before you begin your presentation, check to be sure that the resolution on your computer matches the resolution of the projector. If they don't match, you can run into display issues or your slides might be cropped. You can use the aspect ratio in the Page Setup dialog box to correct this at presentation time, although you should try to verify this setting well before you arrive for your presentation. You can also change the resolution by using options in the Monitors group on the Slide Show tab to match a projector's settings. For more information about setting the aspect ratio, see "Customizing Your Presentation's Design" on page 608.

Navigating in Slide Show View

When working in Slide Show view, you have a fair amount of control over how your slides progress. Ideally, your slides have been created in a logical first, next, last order, but sometimes delivery isn't always as succinct. What are your options? Table 19-1 shows the keyboard shortcuts you can use while delivering a slide show.

Table 19-1 Shortcut Keys for Controlling a Slide Show

Action	Shortcut Key
Go to the next slide	N, Enter, Page Down, Right Arrow, Down Arrow, or Spacebar (also: left mouse click)
Go to the previous slide	P, Page Up, Left Arrow, Up Arrow, Backspace
Go to a specific slide	*number*, Enter
Display a blank, black slide	B or .
Display a blank, white slide	W or ,
Display All Slides dialog box	Ctrl+S

If you need to navigate to a specific slide in Slide Show view, but you don't know the slide number, press Ctrl+S to bring up the All Slides dialog box, shown in Figure 19-16.

Figure 19-16 From the All Slides dialog box, you can select the slide to display by using the presentation's slide titles.

A shortcut menu dedicated to Slide Show view appears when you right-click during a presentation. Its commands allow you to navigate to a specific slide, show a black or white screen, or end the show from any slide, among other options.

> **Note**
>
> To return to the first slide, press and hold the left and right mouse buttons until the first slide appears (about 2 seconds).

Adding Annotations During a Slide Show

During your presentation, you can create on-screen annotations, which is useful for highlighting certain areas of the presentation without altering the content. Annotations turn your mouse pointer into one of three shapes: an arrow, a pen, or a highlighter.

While using Slide Show view, right-click any slide to display the shortcut menu. From there, click Pointer Options, and choose the type of annotation you want. You can also set the ink color and specify whether your pointer is hidden or visible while you're presenting (choose Pointer Options, Arrow Options). Note that you can change the default color of your slide show pen in the Set Up Show dialog box. After selecting Pen or Highlighter, just drag with the left mouse button to draw on your slide.

Each time you advance to the next slide, you need to choose an annotation pointer again. When you reach the end of the presentation (or press Esc to stop), you have the option of saving the annotations or discarding them, as shown in Figure 19-17.

Figure 19-17 Saved annotations are converted into drawing objects and saved on each slide. Once annotations are saved, you can work with them the same way you work with shapes you add in Normal view.

Turning Your Mouse into a Laser Pointer

New in PowerPoint 2010 is the ability to change your mouse pointer into something that resembles a laser pointer. This option works in both Slide Show view and Reading view, and it is probably best used when you're presenting to a large audience, because it allows you to point out something on a slide without drawing on the slide or annotating it.

You need to drive with two hands to show the laser pointer; hold Ctrl and click (and hold) the left mouse button. Once you release the mouse button, your mouse pointer returns to normal. Although this feature works well and does cause your mouse pointer to mimic a laser pointer, it can be cumbersome because it forces you to use the keyboard and the mouse together.

By default, the laser pointer color is red. This can be changed in the Set Up Show dialog box, which you reach by clicking the Set Up Slide Show option on the Slide Show tab.

Working with Presenter View

Consider this scenario: You're standing in front of a large audience getting ready to make your presentation when suddenly you can't remember exactly what you were going to say. What if you forget to mention an important point? And what are all those shortcut key combinations for moving through a presentation? It's a lot to remember.

This is where Presenter view can help. When Presenter view is enabled, you can show your audience the presentation in Slide Show view (on the projector or a second monitor) while you see your slides and notes on your screen, with quick access to annotation tools and slide-show shortcuts. This way, you can refer to your notes while presenting, but the audience never knows the difference—all they see is Slide Show view. To start, you need to have your computer hooked up to a secondary monitor. Then, be sure your system is set up to extend your display to that second monitor. Finally, enable the Use Presenter View option on the Slide Show tab and select the presentation monitor from the Show On list, as shown in Figure 19-18.

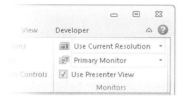

Figure 19-18 When a second monitor is connected to your system, you can enable Presenter View on the Slide Show tab. Be sure to choose the monitor you're sending the presentation to in the box just above the check mark.

After you enable Presenter view, verify that the monitor the audience will see is selected in the Show On list on the Slide Show tab.

> **Note**
>
> You can use at most two monitors for a presentation—one for the audience to see the presentation in Slide Show view and one for you to see Presenter view. If your multi-monitor setup is already configured, all you need to do is select the Use Presenter View option. However, if you're connecting to a second monitor for the first time (perhaps because you're connecting to a projector in a meeting room), PowerPoint notifies you that only one monitor is detected. Click Check in the message box PowerPoint displays, and the Display Settings dialog box appears. In that dialog box, configure the second display (the exact steps vary depending on which version of Windows you have and whether you're using a portable computer) and choose the setting to extend the displays.

Not much happens immediately after you enable Presenter view. You need to start your slide show to see the change. Once started, your presentation is displayed in Slide Show view on the presentation monitor (the one you selected in the drop-down list). Back on your screen, you gain access to the presentation control panel, or Presenter view.

Presenter view is shown in Figure 19-19.

It takes only a few minutes to get accustomed to Presenter view. The large slide you see in the main window is the same slide your audience sees on the presentation screen. That's how you can tell what your audience is viewing. Just to the right is a section that displays your speaker notes. You can drag the divider line between these two sections to customize how large each pane is.

Current slide   Speaker notes

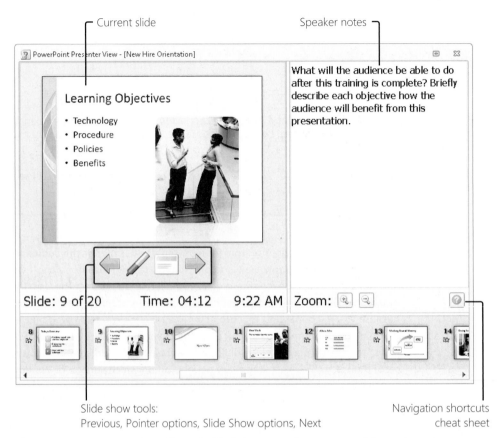

Slide show tools:
Previous, Pointer options, Slide Show options, Next

Navigation shortcuts
cheat sheet

Figure 19-19 Presenter view offers a behind-the-scenes look at your slides and speaker notes and access to slide-show tools.

Just below the slide is a set of control buttons. Use the arrows to move to the next or previous slide in the presentation. When you click the pen, you access the same pointer options you do from the shortcut menu in Slide Show view. The Slide Show button displays the items on the shortcut menu that allow you to move to different slides and sections.

In Presenter view, you can also use the slide thumbnails along the bottom of the window to jump to a slide. This is helpful when you have a particularly interactive audience that forces you to jump through your presentation topics in a nonlinear fashion.

At the bottom of the speaker notes pane, there's a small Help button. When the button is clicked, pertinent slide show keyboard shortcuts are displayed. Just as with the shortcut menus, the audience won't see this Help dialog box pop into view.

INSIDE OUT   Enable a second monitor for Presenter view

If you use Windows 7 or Windows Vista, you can quickly switch between monitor configurations by pressing Windows logo key+P, which opens the window shown next. Use the arrow keys to select the option you want and then press Enter, or simply click an option.

And if you're using a portable computer, you have another interesting option: press Windows logo key+X to open Windows Mobility Center.

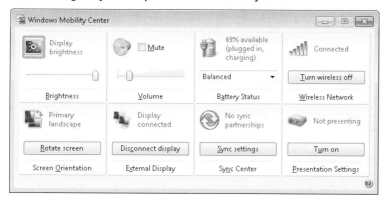

When you turn on presentation settings, power-saving features are disabled so that your computer stays awake. Even better, system notifications are turned off, so your presentation won't be interrupted when someone sends you an instant message or your antivirus program thinks it needs to be updated—*now!*

After your presentation is finished, you can close Presenter view like you close any other window. Then, when you move back to a one-monitor setup, disable Presenter view by clearing the option on the Slide Show tab.

Creating Notes and Handouts

PowerPoint, of course, is designed around presentations that are displayed on a monitor or projector. But you'll sometimes want to print your presentation. Why?

Slides are printed for a number of reasons. They make great notes for the presenter so you don't lose your place mid-presentation. More important, they provide a record that audiences can take home and review.

The print options in PowerPoint are somewhat different from the ones in other Office programs. To see the available options, click File to open Backstage view, and then click Print. You can print each slide on a separate page or squeeze as many as nine slides on each sheet of paper. Click the second button under Settings to display the layout options shown in Figure 19-20.

Figure 19-20 From this menu, you can also add a border around each printed slide by selecting Frame Slides.

The options are separated into two categories: Print Layout and Handouts. The options under Print Layout are generally for the presenter's use. The Notes Pages option prints an image of a slide and the speaker notes for that slide. The Handouts options, as the name suggests, apply to audience handouts. They show just the slides, with blank lines for note taking in some layouts.

Printing Notes

Although the speaker notes are intended for the presenter, that doesn't mean you can't print the notes pages for your audience. It's actually not a bad idea. You can add a lot of formatted content to the speaker notes area, including graphics. But before you print your notes, consider whether Presenter view might work as well. In Presenter view, you still have access to all your speaker notes, but you won't kill a tree printing them.

To print notes pages, from the menu shown in Figure 19-20, select Notes Pages.

To learn how to customize your notes page, see "Customizing Other Masters" on page 669.

Printing Handouts

When you print notes pages, you have only one option. But nine different print layout options are available for handouts. Printed handouts are designed mostly as takeaways for your audience, and the layouts provide varying numbers of slide thumbnails per page.

Figure 19-21 shows the 3 Slides handout layout.

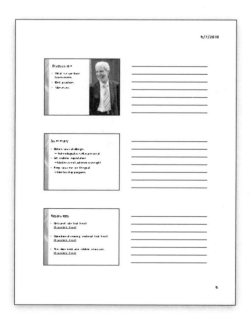

Figure 19-21 The 3 Slides layout also prints a series of blank lines next to each slide thumbnail, providing a handy place for your audience to record handwritten notes during your presentation.

To print handouts, from the menu shown in Figure 19-20, select one of the layouts under Handouts.

Adjusting Color Options

Most presentations contain a lot of color. Color is used not only in graphics, but also in the background color from applied design themes. The problem is that you don't always want to print using that much ink—particularly on a color printer that consumes expensive ink, like a Hummer burning gasoline. You can lower your print costs by not printing in color. You can do that by displaying the Print tab in Backstage view, and then choosing an option from the last button under Settings.

To preserve your color ink, change the print setting to Grayscale or Pure Black And White. Figure 19-22 shows a comparison of the same slide printed in color (it's printed in this book with only black ink, but you can see which colored elements print), grayscale, and pure black and white.

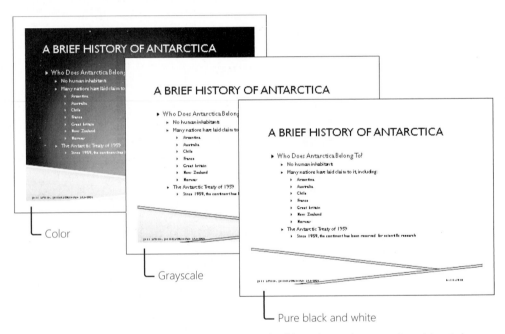

Figure 19-22 Use the Grayscale and Pure Black And White print options to print without showing all of the presentation's design and theme colors and elements.

> **Note**
>
> If the selected printer does not print color, the preview image on the Print tab appears in grayscale even when Color is selected. However, all theme elements and backgrounds are included—much like the "color" image shown in Figure 19-22.

Printing in Grayscale changes theme elements to shades of gray and removes slide backgrounds. Printing in Pure Black And White removes all theme elements and prints slide text in black on a plain, white background. The preview image on the Print tab shows what you can expect to see when the paper comes out of the printer.

INSIDE OUT   Customize color mapping

Some color combinations that look great on a color monitor lack contrast—and therefore legibility—when they're reduced to grayscale or black and white. With a bit of tinkering, you can control how individual colors and objects print when you are not printing in color. To do that, start on the View tab, and in the Color/Grayscale group, click Grayscale or Black And White. That displays a preview image, but unlike the preview on the Print tab in Backstage view, this one is fully editable. A new tab also appears (either Grayscale or Black And White, matching the option you click), as shown in Figure 19-23. You can click an object on a slide and then click the way you want that object to print when you select Grayscale or Pure Black And White on the Print tab.

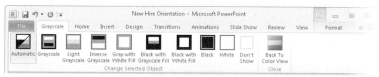

Figure 19-23 Use the Grayscale or Black And White option on the View tab to see how the presentation looks when printed, and to adjust the way colors map to shades of gray.

Editing the Handout Header and Footer

In the same Header And Footer dialog box that you use to set the footer for each slide (for details, see "Setting Page Layout Options" on page 608), a second tab controls the header and footer for your handout pages. You can access the dialog box from the Insert tab or by clicking Edit Header & Footer on the Print tab in Backstage view. Figure 19-24 shows the Notes And Handouts tab in the Header And Footer dialog box.

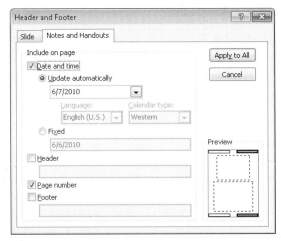

Figure 19-24 Use the Header And Footer dialog box to specify a custom header or footer for each of your printed notes and handout pages.

Unlike settings on the dialog box's Slide tab, the settings you define here are applied to all pages in the printout. You can also add a header to your handouts—a feature that's not available for slides.

Editing Handouts in Word

The limitation of the handout print layouts in PowerPoint is that you can't customize layouts, particularly headers and footers. Although you can create handout masters to meet your needs, a quicker option is to use Microsoft Word. When you export handouts to Word, you have access to all its features, including more control over creating custom headers and footers based on sections. To send your handouts to Word, click the File tab, click Save & Send, and then click Create Handouts. Click the large Create Handouts button that appears, and then choose your preferred page layout from the Send To Microsoft Word dialog box, shown in Figure 19-25.

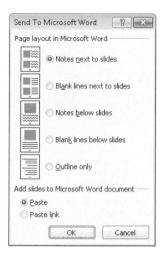

Figure 19-25 When you send your handouts to Word, you get options that differ from the printed handout layouts in PowerPoint.

When you click OK in this dialog box, your selected layout opens as a new document in Word. Note that the changes you make in Word have no impact on the slides in Power-Point. By default, the two files are independent of one another. This means you can't edit your speaker notes in Word and see those changes back in PowerPoint. However, in the Send To Microsoft Word dialog box, if you select Paste Link instead of Paste, you create a connection between your PowerPoint file and the Word document.

CAUTION

Be careful with the Paste Link option. It creates a one-way link between the slides in PowerPoint and the slide images in Word. If you make a change to a slide in Power-Point, the next time you open the Word handout file, you're prompted to update the links, and the slide images are updated. However, if you edit speaker notes in either file, no changes are shared between the two files. You should create a link between Power-Point and Word only for handouts that contain the slide images and not the speaker notes.

For information about creating headers and footers in Word, see "Adding Headers, Footers, and Page Numbers" on page 222. For information about using sections in Word, see "Formatting Columns and Sections" on page 248.

CHAPTER 20

PowerPoint 2010 Inside Out

Microsoft PowerPoint 2010 is a program that you can use to make professional-looking presentations without a lot of effort or experience. Using just the techniques we covered in the previous chapters, you can create presentations that effectively communicate your ideas. Yet there's much more to PowerPoint; in fact, it has spawned a new job title in some companies: Presentation Development Specialist.

In this chapter, we look at ways to save and reuse your work in PowerPoint, including themes, slides, and layouts. We also look at some features usually reserved for the experts, like working with master views and creating custom slide shows. We begin the chapter by describing one of the coolest new features in PowerPoint 2010, the ability to broadcast a presentation over the Internet without requiring any special software on viewers' computers. Later, we cover other methods for sharing your presentations.

Whether you develop presentations professionally or are an occasional PowerPoint user, we think you'll find these features interesting and useful.

Broadcasting a Presentation

With the high cost of travel, more and more people are foregoing face-to-face meetings in favor of working remotely, sometimes with teams located around the world. Many families have members that are scattered far and wide as well. As a result, the need for easier communication is increasing every year. Years ago, businesses began to respond to this need by using clunky video-conferencing systems. The systems worked, but they were expensive. Then came services that allowed you to broadcast your presentations online. They worked, too, but these services were also expensive and most required installation and configuration of software on each participant's computer.

Now there's a better way: You can use the broadcasting feature in PowerPoint 2010 to share presentations with up to 50 coworkers, family, or friends. As the presenter, all you need is PowerPoint 2010 and a Windows Live ID. (Broadcast services other than the default

PowerPoint Broadcast Service might allow more than 50 viewers and might require different logon credentials.) The people you broadcast to view your presentation in their default web browser, so they don't need PowerPoint 2010 or even the free PowerPoint Viewer to see your presentation. They need only an active Internet connection.

For example, you can create a photo album of a recent trip and then send a link via e-mail to your grandmother. All she needs to do is click the link, and your slide show is displayed on her computer in her web browser. You can share the photos while talking to her on the phone about the trip. You can, of course, use a similar approach when making presentations to other audiences; they, too, will appreciate the simplicity.

Sharing a Presentation with Others

In this chapter we describe three different methods for sharing a presentation. Which one you use depends on many factors, including the location and technical acumen of the people you want to share with and whether you want them to be able retain, reuse, and edit your presentation. Table 20-1 summarizes the key differences to help you decide which is the best method for you to use.

Table 20-1 **Methods for Sharing a PowerPoint Presentation**

	Broadcast	Video	CD Package
Viewer requirements	Web browser; availability at broadcast time	Media player	PowerPoint or PowerPoint Viewer
Retains full fidelity	Good	Better	Best
Can be played back any time	No	Yes	Yes
Can be edited by viewer	No	No	Yes

For more information about these methods for sharing a presentation, see "Broadcasting a Presentation" on page 649, "Turning Your Presentation into a Video" on page 663, and "Creating a CD Presentation Package" on page 682.

When you're ready to share your presentation, click the Slide Show tab. In the Start Slide Show group, click Broadcast Slide Show. The dialog box shown in Figure 20-1 appears. By default, PowerPoint uses the PowerPoint Broadcast Service, a free service from Microsoft. If you want to use a different service, such as one hosted by your organization, click Change Broadcast Service. The server for a broadcast site must have Office Web Apps installed, and audience members must be granted access to the site.

Figure 20-1 After you choose a broadcast service, click Start Broadcast to generate a link to your broadcast that you can share with others.

Click Start Broadcast to proceed. If you aren't currently signed in with your Windows Live ID, you're prompted to do so. If you don't have a Windows Live ID, a link takes you to a page where you can establish one.

CAUTION

Even though you sign in to the PowerPoint Broadcast Service with a password, this free service does not use an encrypting Internet protocol, making it theoretically possible for a hacker to view the broadcast. To share presentations securely, you can set up a secure service using SharePoint to broadcast only to people within your organization.

After you click Start Broadcast and sign in, PowerPoint connects to the broadcast service and then displays a dialog box with a link that you can share with others. (See Figure 20-2.) This link is valid only while you are presenting in Slide Show or Presenter view. During that time, anyone who receives the link, either directly from you or from another person, can view your broadcast.

Chapter 20

Figure 20-2 You need a Windows Live ID to start the broadcast, but your viewers need only the link shown in this dialog box and a live Internet connection.

INSIDE OUT Use a URL shortening service

If you send a link via e-mail or as an instant message, it doesn't matter how long or unruly the link is because recipients just need to click it. In some situations, your audience members have to type the URL, however. This is true if you provide the link by phone. A more common scenario is when you're presenting face-to-face to a group, and you want everyone to view the show on their own portable computers—perhaps because no projector is available. In these cases, use a URL-shortening service (such as snurl.com or bit.ly, for example) to trim the link to one that you can easily transmit verbally.

The next step is to click Start Slide Show in the Broadcast Slide Show dialog box. The Broadcast tab appears on the ribbon, as shown in Figure 20-3. (In certain configurations, clicking Start Slide Show starts the presentation in Slide Show view. You can suspend the presentation and view the Broadcast tab by pressing Esc.)

Figure 20-3 Options on the Broadcast tab are similar to those on the Slide Show tab. You can start the presentation from the first or current slide, change the resolution, and enable Presenter view. The Broadcast group includes two buttons: one that shows you the link so you can share it with others (Send Invitations) and one that ends the broadcast.

When you're ready to begin broadcasting your presentation, use the From Beginning or From Current Slide command on the Broadcast tab. At that point, the slide appears in your viewers' browsers. Until you start the broadcast, people who have clicked the link see "Waiting for broadcast to begin . . . " in their browser. You can use either Slide Show or Presenter view to run your show. (For information about Presenter view, see "Working with Presenter View" on page 638.)

> **Note**
>
> Presenter view requires a multimonitor setup. This is true even when you're using your audience members' screens as the presentation monitor. If you want to view your speaker notes and other Presenter view features, you'll need a second monitor (or, at the very least, a second video output). If you're broadcasting from a laptop computer, you might want to print your presentation notes before you begin. For details, see "Creating Notes and Handouts" on page 642.

TROUBLESHOOTING

Your viewers can't see your presentation

If your viewers have trouble seeing your broadcast, verify that they are working with a compatible browser. Although the broadcast feature does offer cross-platform support, it hasn't been fully vetted in all browsers. You can be confident that it works in Internet Explorer 7 and 8; Firefox 3.5 on Windows, Mac, and Linux; and Safari 4 and 5 for Mac.

Chapter 20

When you broadcast, you lose some presentation features that are available when you use traditional presentation methods such as a projector or a second monitor. Although you see the full-featured presentation on your screen, your viewers' experience differs in the following ways:

- Video and audio (including narration) do not play on audience members' computers.

- All transitions are shown as Fade transitions.

- You cannot add annotations or highlighting while broadcasting.

- If you click a link on a slide that opens a website, your viewers don't see the website; their browser continues to show whatever slide is displayed in PowerPoint.

While you're broadcasting, your viewers see only the display from Slide Show view. You can press Esc to exit Slide Show view and go back to Normal view, but your viewers continue to see the last slide that was displayed in Slide Show view. They see this slide until you pick another slide to display or end the broadcast.

Saving and Reusing Slides and Themes

Final slides are often the result of a lot of time and effort. It takes just the right balance of text, graphics, and animation in a slide to make a concept come to life. Whether your slides contain business proposals, training material, research, or something else altogether, you might find yourself gravitating toward a certain "look." One way to reduce development time on future presentations is to reuse slides and elements you've created in the past.

Reusing Slides

While working on a presentation, you can grab slides from a different presentation with the Reuse Slides pane, shown in Figure 20-4. To open it, click the Home tab, click the arrow below New Slide, and click Reuse Slides, an option that appears at the bottom of the New Slide menu. In the Reuse Slides pane, click Browse, Browse File to select the presentation that contains the slides you want to use in the current presentation. You can then click thumbnails of the slides in the presentation you selected to insert them in the open presentation.

CAUTION

When you insert a slide using the Reuse Slides option, it inherits the theme of the last selected slide in the current presentation. If you want the reused slides to retain their original theme, select Keep Source Formatting in the Reuse Slides pane.

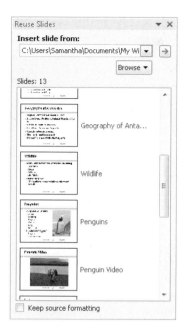

Figure 20-4 Point to any thumbnail in the Reuse Slides pane to see a larger version. Click a thumbnail to insert it in the open presentation.

Another method of copying slides from one presentation to another is to open both files and then use the Arrange All option (in the Window group on the View tab) to position the two windows side by side. Once the presentations are arranged, as shown in Figure 20-5, select the thumbnails for the slides you want in one presentation and drag them to the other presentation.

INSIDE OUT   Reuse slides stored in a Slide Library

Companies running Microsoft SharePoint with Office 2010 can create a repository for slides to be shared among team members with appropriate permissions. This repository is called a Slide Library. Your network administrator (or someone with Design permissions for SharePoint) needs to set this up. To add slides to the Slide Library, click File, Save & Send, Publish Slides. When you save a presentation to the Slide Library, each slide becomes its own file, making it easier to update and reuse the slides in other presentations.

Chapter 20

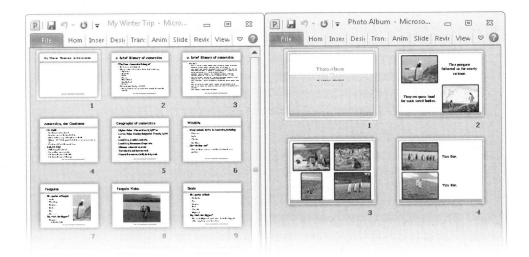

Figure 20-5 By arranging two presentations side by side, you can drag slides from one to the other to copy the slides. The slides take on the formatting of the new presentation unless you choose Keep Source Formatting from the Paste Options button that appears after you copy the slides.

Saving Themes

Office themes are an integral part of PowerPoint—so much so that, unlike in other Office 2010 programs, almost an entire tab (the Design tab) is dedicated to their use. You can also specify a theme when you create a presentation using File, New.

For details, see "Applying Themes" on page 611 and "Creating a New Presentation" on page 597.

Because you can customize themes, they provide an important benefit—branding. Many businesses create their own themes to ensure that the presentations they create match their company image. Typically, this involves choosing a pre-existing theme and then modifying the individual elements—fonts, colors, effects, and backgrounds.

After you have a presentation's theme looking the way you want, save the theme so that you can reuse it in other presentations. From the Themes gallery on the Design tab, choose Save Current Theme. Saved themes show up at the top of the Themes gallery and are available in other Office programs as well.

You can also send your themes to coworkers and friends. By default, themes have the extension .thmx and are stored in %AppData%\Microsoft\Templates\Document Themes. (On a Windows 7 computer with default settings, %AppData% expands to C:\Users\ *username*\AppData\Roaming.)

INSIDE OUT   Copy the design of an existing presentation

You're getting ready to create your new presentation, and you need to apply the same design theme you used on an old presentation. You can picture it, but you just can't remember the theme's name. You could spend your time looking through all the design themes for a match, or you could take the faster route and copy the design theme from a previous presentation.

Open the presentation that contains the theme you want to use and the presentation that you're copying the theme to. Position the presentations side by side by using Arrange All on the View tab. Then select a slide thumbnail (either in Normal view or Slide Sorter view) in the old presentation. Double-click Format Painter (on the Home tab), and then click each slide thumbnail in the new presentation.

For more information about themes in Office 2010, see "Using Office Themes" on page 185. For information about backgrounds, see "Adding Backgrounds" on page 612.

Creating Custom Slide Shows

Custom shows allow you to present a portion of a larger presentation. For example, you might have a 60-slide presentation for new employees that includes a section of 10 slides about the company's security policy. If you receive a request to teach a short seminar about these policies, you can create a custom show using only the relevant slides.

Based on your needs, you create custom shows by hiding selected slides or by setting up a new presentation order for a specific set of slides. Both techniques are equally easy to use. The difference is that when you hide slides, you don't have the option of changing the order the slides are displayed in. When you create a custom show, you do.

Hiding Slides to Create Dynamic Presentations

Hiding slides is a quick way to prevent certain slides from appearing in Slide Show view. When a slide is hidden, it is still visible in any of the editing views (Normal, Slide Sorter, and so on). The only view it isn't displayed in is Slide Show view—unless you explicitly request it.

The ability to display a hidden slide on command is part of what makes this technique so appealing. Hiding slides works well for content that you think might come up during the course of a presentation. It's the equivalent to being over prepared. For example, if you create a slide show to present a thesis, you need to cite your sources, but those citations need to be available only on request. In this case, you could create a slide that contains your citations, mark it as hidden, and display it only if an instructor asks to see your sources.

To hide a slide, select it. Then, on the Slide Show tab, click Hide Slide in the Set Up group. Alternatively, right-click a slide and choose Hide Slide. Figure 20-6 shows three hidden slides in Slide Sorter view.

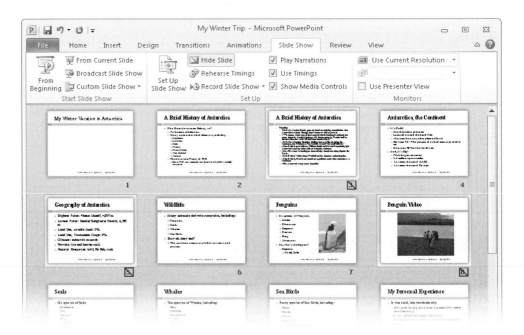

Figure 20-6 Hidden slides remain in the presentation, but they aren't displayed in Slide Show view. In this figure, slides 3, 5, and 8 are hidden, as indicated by the slashed box over their numbers.

Hidden slides let you anticipate audience questions and then stray a little from your agenda if necessary. In Slide Show view, you can display a hidden slide in any of the following ways:

- Type the slide number, and then press Enter.

- Right-click, and then choose Go To Slide. A list of slides in your presentation (including the number and title of each slide) appears. You can identify hidden slides because their numbers are enclosed in parentheses. Click the title of the slide you want to display.

- Press Ctrl+S to display the All Slides dialog box, which includes a similar list of slide numbers and titles. Use the arrow keys to make your selection, and then press Enter.

For more information about keyboard shortcuts you can use in Slide Show view, see "Navigating in Slide Show View" on page 636.

> **Note**
>
> Hidden slides print by default. When you print handouts for a presentation that contains hidden slides, you can prevent the hidden slides from printing by clearing the Print Hidden Slides option on the Print menu, shown here.
>
>

Defining a Custom Show

A custom show offers more flexibility than hiding slides because you can specify which slides are displayed and in what order. This technique is commonly used by presenters with agenda slides. Rather than creating five copies of the same agenda slide to display each time you move to the next agenda item, you can create a custom show that repeats the slide at five specified points. This approach can reduce file bloat by keeping the number of slides in the presentation to a minimum.

You define a custom show by using the Custom Slide Show, Custom Shows command on the Slide Show tab. This command displays the Custom Shows dialog box, where you click New to create a custom show. Custom shows are based only on the open presentation and are set up in the Define Custom Show dialog box, shown in Figure 20-7.

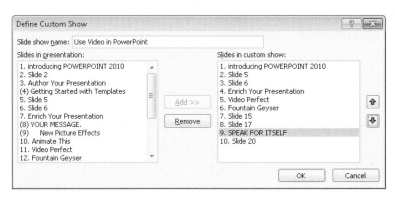

Figure 20-7 In the Define Custom Show dialog box, select slides from the open presentation to appear in the custom show.

When slides are added to a custom show, they are renumbered. For example, in Figure 20-7, the slide titled Enrich Your Presentation is slide 7 in the presentation but slide 4 in the custom show. (One downside here is that you'll have a new set of numbers to remember if you use shortcut keys to navigate to a specific slide during a presentation.)

INSIDE OUT   Defining slides without a title

In the Define Custom Show dialog box, any slide without a title is listed only by slide number. In a large presentation, this makes identifying the content on some of your slides difficult if not impossible. To fix this, add a title to untitled slides by applying a simple layout, such as Title And Content. (If a slide already uses a layout that includes an unused title placeholder, you don't need to change the layout.) Add a title in the title placeholder, and then drag the title off the slide area. The titles don't show up in your presentation, but they give you the background information you need to identify slides in the Define Custom Show dialog box.

Custom slide shows are listed under the Custom Slide Show option on the Slide Show tab. Choosing a custom show launches the presentation in Slide Show view. To edit a custom show or to delete one, you need to go back to the Custom Shows dialog box.

Custom shows are also listed in the Set Up Show dialog box (opened from the Slide Show tab). When you select a custom show in that dialog box, the custom show becomes the default show when the slide show is presented.

> **CAUTION**
>
> When you run a custom show, slides that you didn't include from the complete presentation are not available in Slide Show view. To retain access to slides you might need to refer to, hide the slides instead.

Working Collaboratively on a Presentation

In this digital age, working with a team can present some challenges. In fact, the most challenging task these days seems to be finding a day and time when all team members can meet. If everyone can't meet, you're left to rely on meeting minutes and e-mail comments to get the latest status update. In PowerPoint 2010, you can track team members' suggestions with the Comments feature and then bring two presentations together for comparison as a method of collaborating.

Another way to work collaboratively is for multiple authors to work on a single PowerPoint presentation file simultaneously. For details, see "Working Together with Office 2010" on page 826.

Using Comments

The commenting feature in PowerPoint is limited compared with the review and change-tracking capabilities in Microsoft Word. Nonetheless, you can attach comments to a character, a word, or an entire slide. Comments don't actually change a slide's content; it's best to think of them as notes you would write on a paper to remind you or a team member of edits to make at a later date. For example, a teacher might use comments to highlight areas of improvement before your final presentation or to explain the grade you received. A coworker might use comments to ask you to clarify a point.

You add a comment by clicking New Comment on the Review tab, shown in Figure 20-8. The comment is inserted at the insertion point or the selection; if nothing is selected, the comment appears in the upper left corner of the current slide. Type your comment text, and then click outside the comment box.

Figure 20-8 Click Show Markup to show or hide the comment markers.

Comments are indicated by a small icon that displays the commenter's initials. (The initials and the commenter's name come from settings on the General tab in the Options dialog box.) To display a comment, simply click it. The full comment appears, as shown in Figure 20-9. Alternatively, click Next or Previous on the Review tab to cycle through all comments in your presentation.

Comment indicator

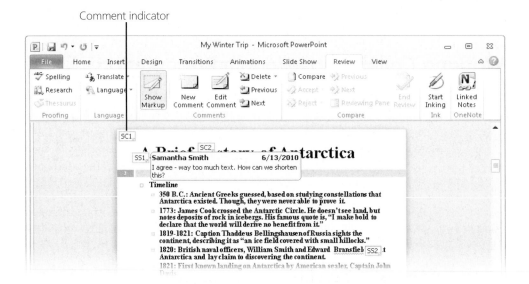

Figure 20-9 You can drag a comment indicator to relocate it on the slide.

TROUBLESHOOTING

Your comments have disappeared

If you know there are comments on a slide, but you don't see the indicators, be sure that Show Markup on the Review tab is enabled. Even when Show Markup is turned off, you can click Next or Previous to view each comment.

When a comment is selected, the Edit Comment option is available. Use this command to change an existing comment. Use the Delete option to remove the selected comment, all comments on the slide, or all comments in the presentation.

Merging and Comparing Presentations

When more than one person works on a version of a presentation, comparing the two versions can be tedious. One way to compare presentations is to stack them side by side by using the Arrange All command on the View tab. Unfortunately, this method forces you to look at each slide and determine where a change was made, if any.

A better alternative is to use the Compare option on the Review tab. Click this option, and then select another version to merge with the open presentation. The second presentation is combined with the first presentation, and changes to text and formatting are highlighted in the Revisions pane, shown in Figure 20-10, along with any comments. (You can hide or display the Revisions pane by clicking Reviewing Pane in the Compare group on the Review tab.)

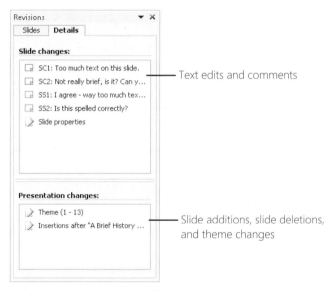

Text edits and comments

Slide additions, slide deletions, and theme changes

Figure 20-10 Comments are listed by reviewer initials on the Details tab in the Revisions pane.

CAUTION

Using the Compare feature does not create a third file, like the comparable feature in Word does. Instead, the second file's differences are merged into the first file. When you click Save, you overwrite the original file. To preserve an unaltered copy of the destination file, use Save As before you start to save a copy under a different file name.

You'll see revision indicators in the Revisions pane and on the slide. Click any of these indicators to see a description of the revision. To accept the revision, select the check box next to it, as shown in Figure 20-11. Alternatively, click Accept in the Compare group on the Review tab.

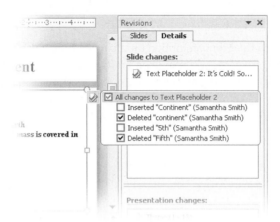

Figure 20-11 Click any revision to see the change in greater detail. The change appears on the slide when you select the check box next to a specific revision.

When you accept a revision, you haven't yet committed to the change. Until you end the review, you can clear the check box or click Reject to undo your acceptance. Note also that the Compare group on the Review tab, shown next, has some additional options that are available during a review. By clicking the arrow next to Accept or Reject, you can accept or reject all revisions for the current slide or all revisions for the entire presentation. If you completely trust (or distrust) your reviewers, these options make quick work of the review process. If you want to take a more methodical approach, click Next or Previous to step through each change.

After you complete your review, click End Review. Doing so stops the review process and closes the Revisions pane, discarding all revisions that you did not accept.

INSIDE OUT   Merge and compare more than two presentations

Unfortunately, the Compare feature allows comparison of only two presentations at a time. However, it's often the case that you have a version for each team member working on the presentation. To merge multiple presentations, you must use the Compare option repeatedly. Open the first presentation and compare it with the second. After you accept or reject each change, end the review. Then click Compare again, and this time choose the third version. Continue this way until you've merged and compared all versions.

Laying the Groundwork for an Expert Presentation

Regardless of your audience or the presentation content, most presentations have one goal in common: a consistent look and feel from slide to slide. Like a professionally decorated room, great presentations give the audience a sense of flow, with harmonious touches that help connect the content on each slide to the greater whole of the presentation.

This consistency is controlled by masters (slide masters, handout masters, and notes masters). You can access each from the Master Views group on the View tab.

Customizing the Slide Master

Slide masters control the layout and formatting of slides in your presentation and are therefore a critical component in achieving a consistent appearance. It's on the slide master where you define the default settings for every slide in the presentation—including the background, colors, fonts, effects, and placeholder sizes and positions. Figure 20-12 shows a typical Slide Master view.

On a slide master, you can add your company logo or a picture of your school mascot. When you create your slides, the image appears in the same location on each slide.

As you can see in Figure 20-12, the Slide Master tab appears when you click Slide Master on the View tab. Use this tab to work with theme settings and to add or remove slide masters or slide layouts. The other tabs (such as Insert, for inserting a logo or another graphic, and Home, for applying text formatting) remain available.

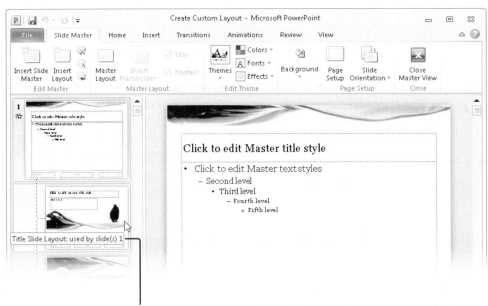

Hover over a master to see which slides in your presentation use that layout

Figure 20-12 Slide Master view shows several layout masters. The top master is the slide master, which holds the design elements for the entire presentation. The indented masters define formatting and design elements for each of the theme's available layouts.

Working with slide masters requires a mild learning curve, which probably stems from having to think of the presentation as one object and not as a collection of individual slides. Once you get past this learning curve, slide masters save you time because changes you make on them affect all slides you add later. For example, you use a slide master to define the theme for the presentation. Of course, you can overwrite these design settings in Normal view; on the slide master you're merely setting the presentation defaults.

Under the slide master, the indented thumbnails show layout variants based on the theme and other characteristics of the slide master. For example, an image you add to the slide master appears on all slides in the presentation, whereas an image you add to a slide layout appears only when that layout is applied to a slide.

CAUTION

If you're thinking about modifying the slide master, do so before you create your presentation slides to ensure that every slide matches the slide master settings. If you edit the slide masters after you've done some editing in the presentation, the new master slide settings might not carry over. Whether the revised slide master settings prevail depends on several conditions that, practically speaking, make it somewhat unpredictable. If you find that your slides aren't using newly applied master slide formats, try using the Reset Slide option on the Home tab in Normal view.

To avoid this problem and make creating presentations easier in the future, make your changes to the slide master and layouts, and then save the presentation as a template.

INSIDE OUT   Use more than one theme in a single presentation

When you apply a design theme to a presentation, it affects all slides. It's the best and worst thing about PowerPoint. What if you want to use two design themes in the same presentation? (Despite the desire for consistency within a presentation, this is not an uncommon requirement. For example, it's useful when you have several topics in your presentation and you want to differentiate each topic, perhaps with a colored bar down the side or "tab" indicators along the top of each slide.)

You can do this with slide masters. Simply add a second slide master to your presentation in Slide Master view. (On the Slide Master tab, click Insert Slide Master.) Apply a different theme to each slide master, or make other changes. Then, in Normal view, apply the layout with the theme you want by choosing it from the gallery that appears when you click New Slide or Slide Layout in the Slides group on the Home tab.

Creating a Custom Layout

Each design theme has its own set of layouts. Some good; some you'll never use. You often end up picking a layout that provides the closest match for what you need and then move things around a bit. Your time might be better spent customizing layouts with placeholders where they'll be used most often.

To create a custom layout, in Slide Master view, click Insert Layout on the Slide Master tab. A basic layout with a title placeholder (and little else) appears. Add placeholders by clicking Insert Placeholder on the Slide Master tab to display the gallery of placeholder types shown in Figure 20-13. Select a placeholder, and then drag on the layout to position it.

Figure 20-13 Add placeholders to custom slide layouts so you can easily insert content when you create a presentation—just as you can with the themes included with PowerPoint.

Unfortunately, PowerPoint doesn't do a great job of naming layouts you create. The first layout you create is named "Custom Layout." Subsequent layouts are assigned names with numbers in front, like "1_Custom Layout."

It's a good idea to give your custom layouts meaningful names while you're still working in Slide Master view. Select a layout thumbnail and click Rename in the Edit Master group on the Slide Master tab. Alternatively, right-click the thumbnail and choose Rename Layout from the shortcut menu. This simple step makes finding the layout you need much easier while you're working in Normal view. (If you still have trouble locating your layouts, consider deleting the default layouts you don't use or using all capital letters when you rename layouts.)

INSIDE OUT ## Use a customized slide master in other presentations

Customizing a slide master takes work, although not nearly as much work as customizing every slide in a deck. The changes you make apply only to the current presentation. To make a customized slide master available for other presentations, save the presentation as a template by clicking File, Save & Send, Change File Type, Template. Then, to use your new template, click File, New, My Templates, and open a new presentation based on the template you created.

Customizing Other Masters

When customizing your presentation masters, you'll probably spend most of your time in Slide Master view. But there are two other master views you can work with: Handout Master and Notes Master.

These views, which are used primarily for printed output, offer fewer options for customization. Unlike with slide masters, you can't add content placeholders to either handouts or notes, but you can add items like headers, footers, page numbers, and slide thumbnails. The available options appear on the tab for each type of master, as shown in Figures 20-14 and 20-15.

Figure 20-14 On the Handout Master tab, you can specify the orientation for printed handouts and for the slides on each handout.

Figure 20-15 On the Notes Master tab, you select which items you want to print on each page.

INSIDE OUT Make More Room for Your Notes

The downside to the notes page is that the slide image takes up nearly half of the printed page. But, if you reduce the size of the slide image (just as you would make any other image smaller), you can increase the size available for your notes. Be careful here. If you later remove and then add the "Body" element back in, it comes back at its default size, and you'll have to resize it again.

For details about printing handouts and notes, see "Creating Notes and Handouts" on page 642.

Creating a Photo Album with PowerPoint

Remember the days when you sat on the living room floor with hundreds of vacation photos in front of you and stuck them, one by one, onto the pages of a bound photo album? Can you still hear the plastic cover peeling back from the glue on the pages? That was back when you had to develop and print photos to see the results of your efforts. You had to print doubles if you wanted to share your photos with others.

Now you can create electronic photo albums that display your pictures much like those old albums did, except they're far easier to share. You can use these electronic albums to document birthday parties and family vacations, but they're not just for personal use. Photo albums also work well to document the progress of a project or to show a sequence of before and after photos.

The Photo Album feature in PowerPoint creates a new presentation that includes the photos you want. Although you can achieve the same results by creating a presentation with File, New, it's quicker and easier with Photo Album. Instead of creating a presentation, inserting a slide for each picture, inserting each picture individually, and then adding titles and captions, the Photo Album feature performs the entire process with a single dialog box, which is shown in Figure 20-16.

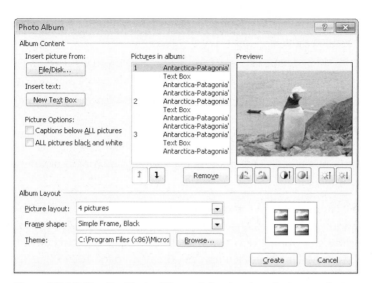

Figure 20-16 Use the Photo Album dialog box to select your photos, retouch them as necessary, and define the slide layout.

To create a Photo Album, follow these steps:

1. On the Insert tab, in the Images group, click Photo Album. The Photo Album dialog box shown in Figure 20-16 appears.

2. Click File/Disk to open the Insert New Pictures dialog box, which is nearly identical to the standard Open dialog box. Select the picture (or pictures) you want, and then click Insert.

INSIDE OUT   Insert pictures the easy way

You can do a couple of things to expedite this step. First, put all the pictures you want to use in a single folder. Second, instead of selecting a single picture file, clicking Insert, and then clicking File/Disk to insert another, select multiple files in the Insert New Pictures dialog box. To do that, click the first picture file, and then Shift+click the last picture file in the sequence to select them all. If the files you want are not contiguous, press Ctrl as you click each file name.

3. Click New Text Box for each text box you want to include. Each text box you insert takes the place of a picture in the layout. You might want one for each picture or one for each slide, for example. (You enter the text for each text box in Normal view after the photo album is created.)

4. Under Album Layout, in the Picture Layout list, select the number of pictures you want on each slide.

   From the Frame Shape list, select the type of frame you want around each picture. (This option isn't available if you choose Fit To Slide as the picture layout.)

   If you want to apply an Office theme, click Browse, select a theme file, and then click Open.

5. Now return to the Pictures In Album list. The numbers identify the slide for each picture or text box. Use the arrow buttons to set the order of pictures and text boxes as you want it.

6. In the Pictures In Album list, select each picture, and then use the tools under the preview image to make corrections to the picture as needed. (More advanced tools are available in Normal view, which appears after the photo album is created. For details, see "Making Your Pictures Look Great" on page 163.)

7. If you want to show the name of each picture file below the picture, select Captions Below All Pictures.

8. Click Create. Your photo album opens in a new PowerPoint window.

Figure 20-17 shows a slide from a photo album. There's nothing special about a presentation created with the Photo Album feature. You can work with the resulting images and text boxes in much the same way you would if you had inserted each individually, you can apply themes, and you can make other changes to your presentation. However, you might find it easier to revisit the Photo Album dialog box to reorder items, adjust the layout, or add more text boxes. To do this, on the Insert tab, click the arrow next to Photo Album, and then click Edit Photo Album.

Figure 20-17 This photo album uses a four-picture layout: two text boxes in between two images.

Turning Your Presentation into a Video

Earlier in this chapter, we explained how to use the broadcast feature to share a presentation with other users. (For details, see "Broadcasting a Presentation" on page 649.) But that doesn't work if your audience isn't available at the time you want to give the presentation, and it doesn't provide them with a copy of the presentation that they can keep to view again.

You can overcome those restrictions by saving your presentation as a video, complete with recorded narration. You can save any type of presentation this way, whether it's a sales presentation you want to send to key prospects or a vacation photo album for your fellow travelers. The resulting video is saved in Windows Media Video (.wmv) format and plays with Windows Media Player (which is included with Windows) or most third-party media player programs. You can burn the resulting file to a DVD, upload it to YouTube or another video-sharing site, or send it via e-mail.

Unlike the broadcast feature, a video incorporates all recorded timings, narrations, annotations, and laser-pointer movements. All transitions play normally, as do embedded audio and video. Because it's a movie, however, you lose any interactive capabilities, such as jumping directly to a particular slide, displaying hidden slides on request, and so on.

To create a video, click File to open Backstage view. On the Save & Send tab, under File Types, click Create A Video. As shown in Figure 20-18, your options are few.

INSIDE OUT   Burn your video to a DVD

If you copy the video file you create to a DVD, the result is a data DVD. A DVD created this way can be played by most computers and by some standard DVD players (such as one you'd connect to a television). To be sure that your video can be played on the widest variety of devices, including standard DVD players, you should make a video DVD.

To do that, you need Windows DVD Maker, a program that's included in most editions of Windows 7 and Windows Vista, or a comparable program from another source. To create a video DVD with Windows DVD Maker, open the program and click Add Items. Browse to the location of the presentation video you created with PowerPoint, select it, and then click Add. Click Next, and then customize the DVD menu if you want to before clicking Burn.

Chapter 20

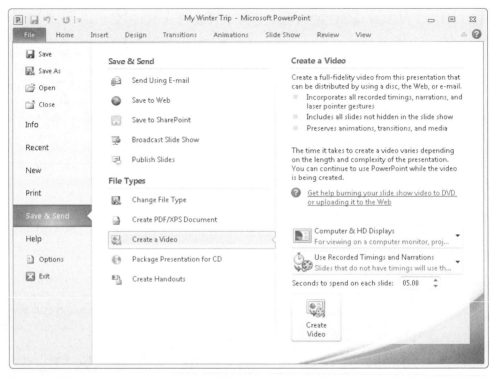

Figure 20-18 Before you click the Create Video button, expand the two menus above the button and set your output options.

In the first menu, you set the size of your video output, choosing between small, medium, and large. In the second, choose whether to include any assigned slide timings or recorded narration in the final video. After you make your selections, click Create Video.

Our Favorite PowerPoint Tweaks and Tips

Up to this point, we've shown you everything you need to know to create some beautiful presentations. Combine this knowledge with some of the graphics techniques discussed earlier in this book, and you're way ahead of the presentation game. But we're not done yet. On the following pages you'll learn about some additional features in PowerPoint 2010 that take your presentations from beautiful to downright stunning.

Inserting Hyperlinks

Adding hyperlinks to a presentation gives you and your viewers a quick way to jump to specific slides or websites. You can also use hyperlinks to launch an e-mail message or create a document. For example, if you're creating a slide deck with information about your company's products, you can lead the viewer to more information by embedding links to your company's website or to another slide with additional information. To create a hyperlink, start by selecting the text or object you're linking from, click the Insert tab, and then click Hyperlink. That opens the Insert Hyperlink dialog, shown in Figure 20-19.

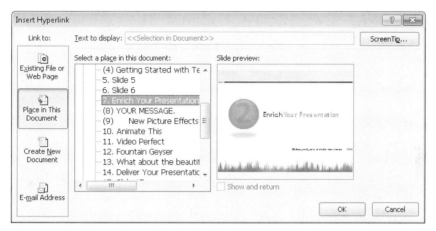

Figure 20-19 If you click Place In This Document, you can create a link to any slide or to any custom show saved as part of the current presentation.

INSIDE OUT   Create a linked custom show

Inserting a link to a custom show allows you to create dynamic agenda slides on which each agenda item is linked to a custom show. You can also incorporate "one-off" custom shows that you can launch via a hyperlink if topics off the agenda come up during the course of the presentation. For more information about custom shows, see "Defining a Custom Show" on page 659.

For more information about inserting hyperlinks, see "Entering Hyperlinks" on page 119.

Inserting Action Buttons

Action buttons are specific shapes with defined hyperlinks that allow you to jump to specific slides in a presentation. In this way, action buttons are similar to hyperlinks—but you can do much more with an action button.

To insert an action button, click the Insert tab, click Shapes (in the Illustrations group), and scroll to the bottom of the Shapes gallery, where you'll find the Action Buttons category.

Click one of these buttons, and then drag to draw it on your slide. The Action Settings dialog box, shown in Figure 20-20, appears.

Figure 20-20 This dialog box appears automatically when you insert an action button. You can display it later by selecting the button (or other object) and clicking Action in the Links group on the Insert tab.

On the Mouse Click tab in the Action Settings dialog box, select the action you want to occur when a viewer clicks the button. Similar settings are available on the Mouse Over tab; these actions take place when a viewer hovers the mouse pointer over the button in Slide Show view.

As shown in Figure 20-20, the list below Hyperlink To offers options similar to those in the Insert Hyperlink dialog box. Other options in the Action Settings dialog box allow you to specify a program to run or a sound to play when the button is clicked.

INSIDE OUT   Apply mouse click and mouse over actions to any object

There's nothing magical about the action button shapes. True, when you insert one on a slide the Action Settings dialog box opens automatically, and each button has a predefined action assigned to it. But actions that take place on mouse click or mouse over can be assigned to any object—other shapes, pictures, or text boxes, for example. Simply select an object, and then click Action in the Links group on the Insert tab to assign an action.

You might find it useful to include action buttons in a self-guided presentation because some people might not know how to navigate between slides in PowerPoint. You can add familiar navigation action buttons to the bottom of every slide to help your viewers move to the first and last slides in the deck as well as to the next and previous slides, as shown in Figure 20-21.

Figure 20-21 Action buttons used for slide navigation are easily spotted in the lower right corner of each slide. After you create the first set, copy the objects and paste them onto the remaining slides—or better yet, add them to the slide master.

Typically, navigation buttons are best when they have been placed on every slide in the presentation. This can create the feeling of consistency for your audience. It's best to pick a location that doesn't interfere with any object on any of the slides. Then, consider creating and placing the action buttons on the slide master. This way, you can be sure they show up on every slide in the same location.

For information about adding elements to the slide master, see "Customizing the Slide Master" on page 665.

INSIDE OUT Use action settings to create hot spots

A hot spot is an area on an image that is linked to another slide or a website. For example, in a group photo, you might define a hot spot around each person that displays that person's contact information when the hot spot is clicked. You could take it a step further by adding the person's name as a ScreenTip.

As another example, on a map of the United States, you could create a hot spot in each time zone; clicking the hot spot takes the viewer to a slide with information about that region of the country, such as a radio or television broadcast schedule. To do that, follow these steps:

1. Insert a shape. For this example, insert a rectangle that's slightly larger than the Central Time zone.

2. To make the hot spot invisible, use options on the Format tab under Drawing Tools to remove both the fill and outline color.

3. Use Edit Shape, Edit Points on the Format tab to set the shape's points to roughly correspond to the time zone borders, as shown here.

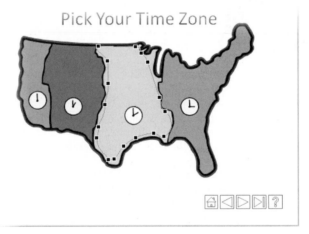

For information about inserting a shape, formatting it, and editing points, see "Adding Shapes and Text Boxes" on page 175.

4. Select the shape, and on the Insert tab, click Action. In the Action Settings dialog box, select Hyperlink To, select Slide, and select the slide about the Central Time zone.

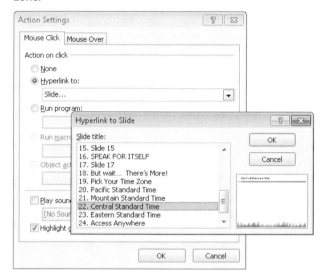

To test your handiwork, open the slide in Slide Show view. You won't be able to see the shape that defines the hot spot area, but when you click it, PowerPoint should jump to the specified slide.

Embedding Fonts in a Presentation File

An issue we often see is presentation text that looks fine until it's displayed on a different computer. This typically happens when the computers you're using don't have the same sets of fonts. A way to prevent text from looking different on other computers is to embed the fonts a presentation uses into the file.

To embed fonts in your presentation, click File, Options. In the PowerPoint Options dialog box, click the Save tab, and select Embed Fonts In The File, as shown in Figure 20-22. Selecting this option embeds each OpenType and TrueType font that's used in the presentation. (Other font types, such as PostScript and printer fonts, can't be embedded.)

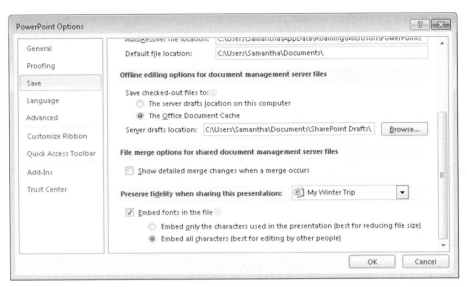

Figure 20-22 Under Embed Fonts In The File, select the first option if the presentation will be viewed on other computers; select the second option if it will be edited on another computer.

CAUTION

Be sure the fonts you plan to embed don't have any license restrictions that might prevent them from being embedded. When embedded, some fonts allow printing and viewing but not editing. Other fonts allow full use when embedded, and still others don't allow embedding at all. To determine whether a particular font can be embedded, open the Fonts folder in Control Panel, right-click the font (an individual font, not a font family), and choose Properties. On the Details tab, check the Font Embeddability property.

Playing Music Behind Your Slides

Some presentations—particularly photo montages—don't require narration and can benefit from a musical accompaniment. You can apply music (or other recorded audio) to a series of slides or to an entire presentation. Along with a snappy Office theme, adding music can really enhance an otherwise snooze-inducing photo album of vacation snapshots.

CAUTION

Although digital rights management (DRM) technologies that prevent copying music tracks are largely disappearing in favor of DRM-free formats like MP3, be aware that most recorded music is protected by copyright. A roomful of lawyers (probably with no two of them agreeing) could explain how copyright law applies to music used in PowerPoint presentations, but understand that legal minefields abound, particularly if your presentation will be posted to the Internet or presented in anything resembling a "public performance."

To set up background music, begin by inserting the audio file on the slide where you want the music to start playing. (On the Insert tab, click Audio, Audio From File.) After inserting the audio object, select it and click the Playback tab under Audio Tools. Select Hide During Show, and then select Play Across Slides in the Start box.

In Slide Show view, the audio starts playing automatically when you display the slide where you inserted the audio file.

INSIDE OUT   Hide the audio icon

If the icon for the audio object gets in your way while you're editing in Normal view, drag it off the slide into the gray area on the side.

Creating a CD Presentation Package

Earlier in this chapter we discussed two ways to share a presentation with others. Broadcasting a presentation requires nothing of the viewers other than an Internet connection—and that they're available when you present your slide deck. Broadcast presentations suffer from some loss of fidelity, and the viewer doesn't get a version of the presentation that can be saved. Saving your presentation as a video overcomes some of those limitations, but the viewer ends up with a copy of the presentation that can be viewed but not edited.

For details about these sharing methods, see "Broadcasting a Presentation" on page 649 and "Turning Your Presentation into a Video" on page 673.

Now we examine a third method for sharing: packaging for CD. With this option, you can save multiple presentations to one location (physical media such as a CD or a shared network location, for example) to share with others. PowerPoint creates a menu of presentations as part of the package, making it easy to select one for viewing. Saving files to a CD package also provides a portable backup of your work; presentations on the CD are saved as standard PowerPoint files. In addition, fonts are embedded and all linked files are included in the package. A CD package works well for turning in a final project to your instructor or sharing a photo album with family members.

Like the other methods, this one has its own drawbacks. First, this feature is intended for distributing final presentations. Therefore, all comments, revisions, and ink annotations are removed from the file before it is copied to the package location. (Oddly, however, you cannot create a package from a presentation that has been marked as final, but you can add a finalized presentation to a package.) Second, because the package contains standard PowerPoint files, package recipients must have PowerPoint or the PowerPoint Viewer (a free program that can be downloaded from Microsoft) installed on their computers. The computers, of course, must be capable of running PowerPoint.

> **Note**
>
> In previous versions of PowerPoint, you could select an option that included a copy of the viewer program with the CD package. This option is not available in PowerPoint 2010. However, the package's menu screen includes a prominent link to the download site for the viewer.

To create a CD package, click File to open Backstage view. On the Save & Send tab, under File Types, click Package Presentation For CD, and then click Package For CD. This opens the Package For CD dialog box, shown in Figure 20-23.

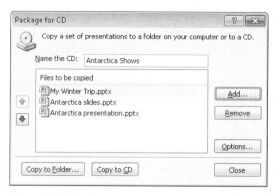

Figure 20-23 Here you can add or remove presentations to include in the package. Use the arrow buttons to determine the order in which the presentations appear on the menu that PowerPoint generates.

The open presentation appears as one of the files to be copied to the CD. Click Add to select additional presentations or other files. You can add files of any type to a CD package. Each file you include gets a link on the menu that PowerPoint creates for the CD package.

Other options you can change here include the CD name. The name you specify is used as the volume name if you copy the files to a CD, so it has a maximum length of 16 characters. (This limitation applies even if you save the package to a folder.) Nonetheless, try to come up with a meaningful name (like "Sales demos" or "SmithFamily2010"), which helps to identify the disc when you examine it in Windows Explorer. The name also appears as the title in the package menu. If you save the package to a folder, PowerPoint proposes to use the CD name as the folder name, although you can override this suggestion.

Click Options to specify whether linked files and embedded fonts should be included in the package. The Options dialog box, shown in Figure 20-24, also includes options to require a password to view or edit the presentations in the package.

Figure 20-24 By default, linked files and embedded fonts are included, and no password protection is applied.

With your options set, click OK to return to the Package For CD dialog box. Insert a blank CD in your writable drive and click Copy To CD. If you'd rather save the package to a hard drive or network drive, click Copy To Folder. PowerPoint copies the requested files and also creates a menu similar to the one shown in Figure 20-25. If AutoRun is enabled on the computer when you insert the CD, the menu appears automatically. If AutoRun is disabled or if you saved the package to a folder, you can display the menu by opening the CD or folder in Windows Explorer, opening the PresentationPackage subfolder, and double-clicking the file named PresentationPackage.html.

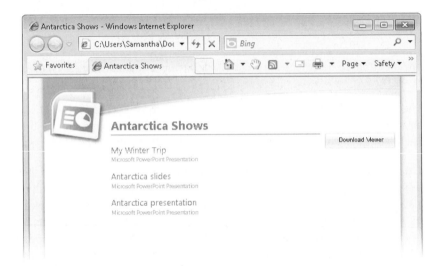

Figure 20-25 The menu is actually a web page with a link to each presentation or other file included in the package.

Creating Custom Bullets

Many of the text placeholders you use in PowerPoint include bullets for bulleted lists. As you can with other Office 2010 programs, you use the Bullets option on the Home tab to select bullet shapes and styles. Office 2010 has a little-known feature that is particularly useful for bullets in PowerPoint presentations: the ability to import your own images. For example, on a corporate presentation, you might use the company logo as a bullet; on a presentation about penguins, you could use a penguin photo as a bullet.

To create your own custom picture bullets, select the lines of text you want to modify and click the arrow next to the Bullets option in the Paragraph group on the Home tab. Click Bullets And Numbering, the command at the bottom of the Bullets gallery. In the Bullets And Numbering dialog box that appears, click Picture. In the Picture Bullet dialog box, click Import. Now you can select any image on your computer and see it dropped back into the Picture Bullet dialog box, as shown in Figure 20-26.

Figure 20-26 You can use any image as a bullet—including one that is decidedly nontraditional.

Click OK, and your new bullet is applied to the selected text on the slide. Notice that your custom bullet now appears in the Bullets gallery, making it easy to apply to other lists.

For something like a corporate logo that you'll want to use in all business presentations, apply your custom bullet on slide layouts within your slide master that include bulleted lists.

Chapter 20

PART 6

Outlook

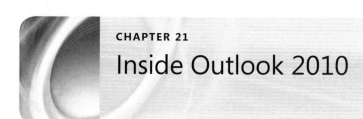

W E saved our three chapters on Outlook 2010 for the end of this book. That decision doesn't imply any judgment as to Outlook's relative worth—rather, it reflects the program's curious place in the Office family. The four programs we covered first—Word, Excel, OneNote, and PowerPoint—are included with every Office edition. Outlook, by contrast, is available only in the business editions of Office 2010.

Outlook is a big, feature-packed program that might be overkill for some people, especially those who don't need to connect to corporate mail servers. If your e-mail needs are met with a personal account or two from your Internet service provider and free webmail services, you might not need or want Outlook. In fact, it's not even an option if you use Office 2010 Home and Student edition.

But if you live and die by e-mail at the office, there's an excellent chance that Outlook is the first Windows application you start up in the morning and the last one you shut down at night. For anyone who needs to manage a high volume of e-mail messages and juggle a crowded calendar, Outlook's rich feature set and extensive customization options are essential. (The list of available features becomes even longer if you connect to Microsoft Exchange Server at work.)

If you're not sure whether Outlook is right for you, we encourage you to read through these three chapters. You might find that the features in Outlook make it worth its learning curve.

What's in an Outlook Profile?

When you start Outlook for the first time after a clean installation of Office 2010, you're prompted to run a startup wizard. The wizard's job is to configure your Outlook profile, which contains two crucial types of information:

- Settings for one or more e-mail accounts—including server names, logon details, e-mail address, and the display name that recipients see on messages you send.

- Where to store your e-mail, contacts, appointments, and other Outlook items on your local PC. Just as in previous versions, Outlook 2010 stores most types of data in local files that use the Outlook Data File format, with the file name extension .pst. If your profile includes one or more accounts that use the Microsoft Exchange ActiveSync protocol, Outlook might use an offline Outlook data file, with the file name extension .ost.

After you finish that startup wizard, you have a single profile that uses the default name, Outlook. For most people, that one profile is sufficient, and they never have to manage that profile or create a new one. If you routinely created multiple profiles with previous Outlook versions, you might find that architectural changes in Outlook 2010 make those extra steps unnecessary. The most important change is the ability to include multiple e-mail accounts from an Exchange server in a single profile—previously, you had to create a new profile for each Exchange account (although you could add other types of e-mail accounts to the same profile).

There are still scenarios where maintaining separate Outlook profiles is necessary, despite the hassle it involves. For example, you might want to maintain a strict separation between one important work e-mail account and your personal e-mail. If those accounts are combined in a single profile, you risk inadvertently sending a personal message from your work account, or vice versa.

To manage existing profiles or create a new one, make sure Outlook is closed, and then open Mail in Control Panel. (Outlook adds this icon to the User Accounts And Family Safety group as part of Office setup.) The Mail Setup dialog box is shown in Figure 21-1.

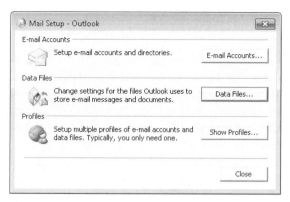

Figure 21-1 The top two choices in this dialog box apply to the default Outlook profile. Click Show Profiles to add, change, or delete a profile.

Clicking E-Mail Accounts or Data Files allows you to change those settings for the default profile. Click Show Profiles to display the profile manager shown in Figure 21-2.

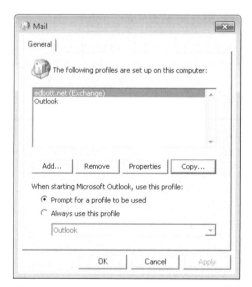

Figure 21-2 Options in this profile manager enable you to specify which profile is used by default or to choose a new profile at startup.

Click Add to kick off a wizard that is virtually identical to the Outlook startup wizard, allowing you to build your new profile by filling in the blanks. The Remove button deletes all settings for the selected profile—irrevocably and immediately. Click Properties to change e-mail account and data file settings for the selected profile without opening Outlook. Click Copy to duplicate the selected profile so that you can experiment with settings while maintaining your option to roll back to the original settings.

CAUTION

Profiles are stored on a per-user basis in the Windows registry, under the key HKCU\ Software\Microsoft\Windows NT\CurrentVersion\Windows Messaging Subsystem\ Profiles. Although it's theoretically possible to make changes to a profile by editing the registry manually, we strongly advise against it. The individual settings are complex and not fully documented, and the risk of unexpected consequences is too high in our opinion. Instead, use the profile manager from Control Panel.

INSIDE OUT   Make it easy to switch between profiles

You cannot switch to a different profile within Outlook. If you maintain two or more Outlook profiles that you use regularly, you can configure Outlook so you have the opportunity to select a profile each time you start up. In the profile manager, under the heading When Starting Microsoft Outlook, Use This Profile, select Prompt For A Profile To Be Used. Click OK, and then restart Outlook to open the Choose Profile dialog box, shown here, where you can select from the Profile Name list or even create a new profile on the fly.

To set the selected profile as the default, click Set As Default Profile at the bottom of the dialog box before clicking OK. If this check box is hidden, click the Options button at the right to reveal the Options section.

Outlook Items

What distinguishes Outlook from other e-mail programs? The biggest difference is the fact that the contents of your data file include so much more than just e-mail messages. The key to mastering Outlook is understanding what's in each item type and how to make different item types work together. (We discuss how these different items are organized into folders later in this chapter. See "Personalizing the Outlook Interface" on page 700.)

The overall view for each item type includes a set of tabs containing commands that are unique to that item type. When you open an individual item, its window includes yet another arrangement of tabs with commands to help you work with that item. The sheer diversity of tabs and commands is one of the key factors that makes Outlook such a challenge to master. In the remainder of this section, we describe each of the major item types in Outlook.

INSIDE OUT   Create a new item from any view

The first icon on the Home tab for every Outlook view allows you to click and begin creating a new item of the type associated with that view. From Mail view, you can click the New E-Mail command; from Calendar view, you get New Appointment and New Meeting; and so on. But what if you're in Tasks view and you want to create a new Contact item? Click New Items, and choose from its menu, which includes options for all available item types. If this is a regular scenario, learn the keyboard shortcuts for creating a new item of each type:

- E-Mail Message   Ctrl+Shift+M

- Appointment   Ctrl+Shift+A

- Meeting   Ctrl+Shift+Q

- Contact   Ctrl+Shift+C

- Task   Ctrl+Shift+K

- Note   Ctrl+Shift+N

E-Mail Messages

Incoming messages open in a window that contains a single tab with commands for acting on that message. For most common actions—responding to the sender, filing the message, tagging it for follow-up, or deleting it—you'll find commands on the Message tab (shown here) to be sufficient.

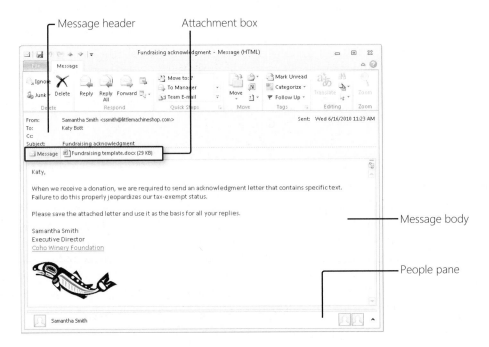

When you're creating a message to send to other recipients, the editing window includes a much richer set of commands. We cover this interface in more detail later in this chapter; see "Creating, Sending, and Receiving Messages" on page 729.

For details on how to preview, open, or save file attachments, see "Working Safely with File Attachments" on page 820. We describe the People pane in more detail in "Using Outlook Social Connector and the People Pane" on page 807.

Appointments

Appointments are items in your Outlook calendar that have a start and end time but don't involve scheduling and coordination with other people or resources. If you select the All Day Event check box, the Start Time and End Time boxes are unavailable and the appointment is listed as an event at the top of the calendar for that day. The Copy To My Calendar button here indicates that this appointment is in a separate calendar that is not the default Outlook calendar.

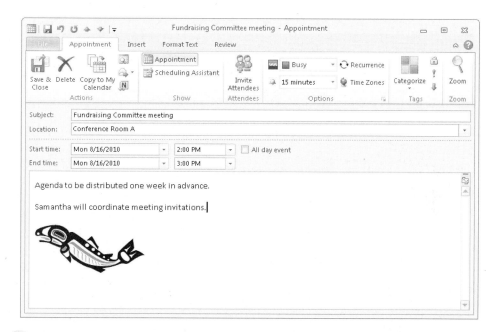

For an overview of how multiple calendars work, see "Sharing and Comparing Calendars" on page 777.

Meetings

In Outlook's specialized definition, a meeting is an appointment that includes invitations to other attendees (sent by e-mail) and, in some organizations, scheduling of resources such as conference rooms that have their own shared calendar. You can turn any appointment into a meeting by clicking the Invite Attendees button. The meeting shown in Figure 21-3, for which invitations have already been sent, contains tools for tracking responses from attendees and finding available meeting rooms.

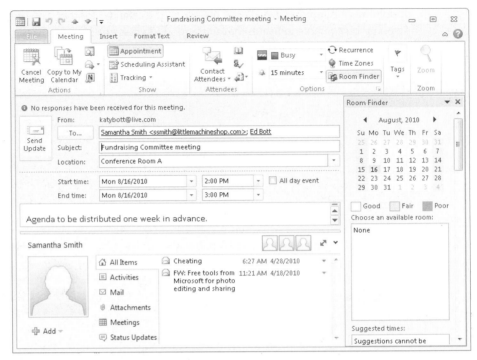

Figure 21-3 Information about invitees and attendees appears on the Meeting tab and in the People pane below the item itself.

For more about how to create and manage appointments and meetings, see "Managing Your Calendar" on page 723.

INSIDE OUT   Meeting requests work with outsiders, too

Outlook's tools for managing meetings work best on corporate networks, where coworkers can use the Scheduling Assistant to pick a time that's most likely to work with everyone's schedule. But even families and one-person shops can use meeting requests to good advantage. Invitees who use Outlook can accept the meeting request, which automatically adds the meeting to their own calendar and sends a response to the meeting organizer. If any invitee needs to make a change to the meeting schedule, they can send an update to the organizer, avoiding scheduling snafus. The key to using meeting requests under these circumstances is for all parties involved to get in the habit of sending responses to meeting requests so that everyone's calendar is properly updated.

Contacts

An Outlook contact can be as simple as the name and e-mail address of a casual acquaintance, or it can contain the equivalent of a full dossier on a working partner or a key customer. Figure 21-4 shows a contact item that's been filled in with an impressive amount of detail.

Send mail ⌐   Double-click to change picture   Business Card view

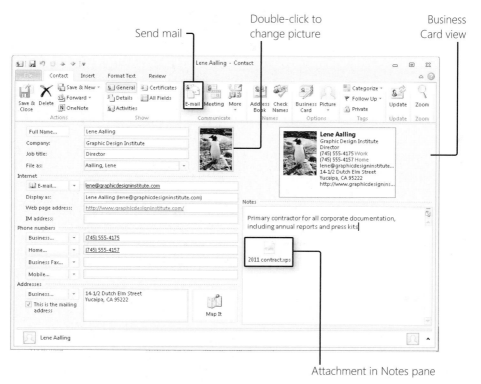

Attachment in Notes pane

Figure 21-4 Adding a picture to a contact item lets you associate a name with a face or a logo or even a company mascot. You can also add attachments in the Notes pane.

You can create contacts directly from incoming mail and also share contacts with other people. It pays to organize large groups of contacts, although the shoebox approach also works, thanks to very effective search tools. Outlook typically displays multiple folders in the Navigation pane, each associated with a different e-mail account or service. In addition, you can create Contact Groups so that you can easily bring together a filtered list of contacts who are related in some way—coworkers, classmates, or customers.

For more on how to create and manage contact items, see "Organizing Your Contacts" on page 715. For more on how address books work, see "Using Address Books and Directory Services" on page 767.

Tasks

If your productivity depends on to-do lists, you'll use Task items frequently. You might never need to open the Tasks folder, however, because all these items are available as you read your e-mail, in the Task List section of the To-Do Bar, to the right of the contents pane. You'll also find a daily task list in Day and Week views of your calendar.

A task, such as the one shown here, can have start dates and due dates, and you can attach reminders to each item as well. As with other Outlook items, you can include a full range of formatting and objects in the notes section, below the header. In the task shown here, we've used a command on the Insert tab to create a table in the notes section.

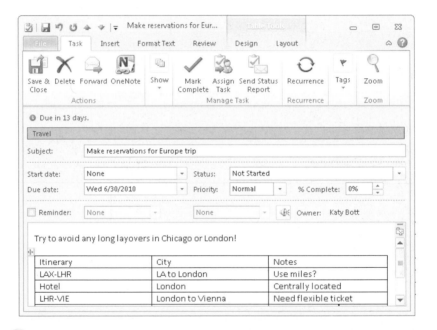

For more on how to attach alarms and deadlines to tasks, see "Setting Follow-up Flags and Reminders" on page 771.

Notes

Items in the Notes folder are unlike any other Outlook item type. Clicking the New Note button on the Home tab opens an editing window that resembles the yellow sticky notes that are ubiquitous in offices. You can type or paste text into a note (including hyperlinks, which are clickable), but you can't format that text directly, nor can you paste any non-text object, such as a picture, into a note.

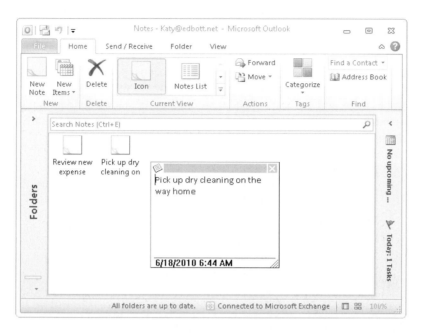

Customization options for the Notes folder are sparse. On the Notes And Journal tab of the Outlook Options dialog box (click File, and then click Options), you can change the default color and size for new notes, as well as select a default typeface and size.

INSIDE OUT   Better options for note-takers

If you like the small, free-form nature of items in the Outlook Notes folder, you have much more interesting alternatives than this frankly limited feature. For starters, consider using OneNote, which allows you to save more types of content on notes. You can open a Side Note with the keyboard shortcut Windows logo key+N and type or paste anything you want. In Windows 7, you can also add the Sticky Notes gadget to the desktop, making similar notes available any time your PC is on, even if Outlook is closed.

Chapter 21

Journal Entries

The Journal folder and its associated content type are relics of bygone Outlook versions, where items of this type tried to maintain connections between related items. This functionality is delivered better and more conveniently in Outlook 2010 using search tools, the Activities page, and the new People pane. The Journal stays around for compatibility reasons, but it's disabled by default, and there are few shortcuts to open it. If you accidentally click the Journal folder in the Folders list, you see this message:

We strongly recommend that you click No at this point, and instead of using the Journal, follow our suggestions in "Using Outlook Social Connector and the People Pane" on page 807.

Personalizing the Outlook Interface

Outlook's user interface is built around a relatively small number of elements, but their arrangement and contents shift dramatically according to the view you choose from the icons at the bottom of the Navigation pane on the left. Each view (Mail, Calendar, Contacts, and so on) has a layout specific to the item type, and you can also control the contents displayed in the center pane by selecting a specific folder to display. The To-Do Bar, on the right in most views, contains a date navigator and a summary of upcoming appointments and tasks.

You can choose from six views, five of which are associated with item types; the sixth shows a list of all folders. The exact content and layout of each view varies. Figure 21-5 shows the Folder List view, which gives you access to the widest range of items without having to change views.

To quickly open any of these views, use this little-known group of Outlook keyboard shortcuts: Ctrl+1 for Mail, Ctrl+2 for Calendar, down to Ctrl+6 for Folder List. A seventh icon, called Shortcuts, allows you to assemble a list of shortcuts to Outlook folders, to folders on a local hard disk or a shared network drive, or to web pages. It's more interesting in theory than it is useful in practice. If you dig deep enough, you'll find an eighth icon, for the Journal folder; it is hidden by default.

Navigation pane ⌐   Contents pane ⌐   ⌐ Reading pane

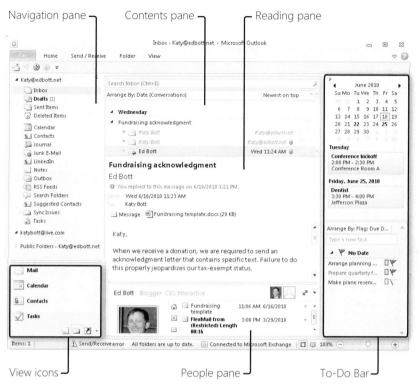

View icons ⌐   People pane ⌐   To-Do Bar ⌐

Figure 21-5 Clicking one of the view icons at the bottom of the Navigation pane changes the layout to the previously saved settings for that view.

You can tweak the arrangement of items in each view by using commands in the Layout group on the View tab, as shown here. Any customizations you make to the layout for a specific view are saved and restored when you return to that view.

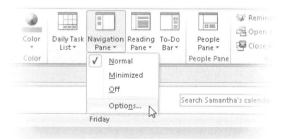

Chapter 21

The default layout for each view is different. Click the Mail view icon, for example, and the Navigation pane displays all available mail folders, with a customizable Favorites list at the top of the pane. We've dragged two folders into the Favorites pane for quicker access in the example shown here.

Customizing the Navigation Pane

In all views, the Navigation pane is visible by default on the left side of the Outlook window. On PCs with a small display size, you can minimize this pane to a slim strip on the left by clicking the arrow in the top right corner of the pane. (You can also use the Minimized option on the Navigation pane menu on the View tab.) This gives you more room for working with the contents of the current folder.

INSIDE OUT
Show just the view icons you need

If screen space is at a premium, you can shrink the list of view icons at the bottom of the Navigation pane to a single row of icons without labels by dragging the bar above the Mail icon down as far as it will go. Dragging this bar up moves icons from the top of the list to their own row, with a label. To remove icons from this group, click the tiny arrow in the lower right corner of the View Icons section to display the Configure Buttons menu shown here. Click Add Or Remove Buttons, and then click any entry in the list to toggle its button off or back on.

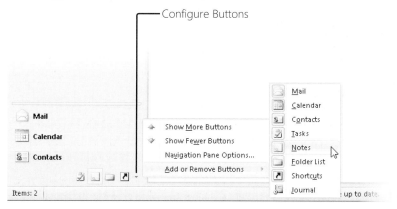

To change the order of view icons, click Navigation Pane Options on the shortcut menu (or click Options on the Navigation Pane menu on the View tab), and then use the Move Up and Move Down buttons in the Navigation Pane Options dialog box.

When the Navigation pane is minimized, the word Folders appears in all views, in bold letters running sideways up the pane; in Mail view only, you can also see the first few choices from the Favorites section. View icons appear at the bottom of the pane, sans labels, unless you hide them completely by dragging the separator line to the very bottom of the window. Click Folders to display a pop-out list of all available folders, as shown next. After you make a selection, the list disappears again.

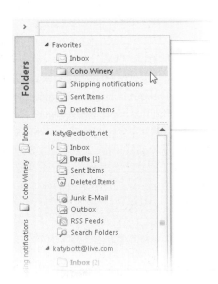

To completely hide the Navigation pane, right-click the minimized pane and select Off from the shortcut menu (or use the equivalent menu command on the View tab). To restore the pane to its full width, click the Expand arrow at the top right corner of the minimized pane, or use the Navigation Pane menu on the View tab.

INSIDE OUT Be more productive with multiple Outlook windows

If you regularly use two or more Outlook views—Mail and Calendar, for example—consider keeping each view open in a separate window. In the Navigation pane, right-click any folder or view icon, and then click Open In New Window. For these secondary windows, such as those for the Contacts or Tasks view, you can make the most economical use of space by hiding the Navigation pane and collapsing the ribbon. This configuration also allows you to arrange windows side by side. That arrangement makes it easy to see openings and conflicts on your calendar as you reply to e-mail messages from clients or customers. It also allows you to drag contacts or e-mail items into your calendar to create appointments.

Organizing the To-Do Bar

On the right side of the Outlook window is the To-Do Bar. It's visible in the default layout for all views except Calendar, and it behaves much like its counterpart on the opposite side of the screen, the Navigation pane.

The To-Do Bar consists of three sections. The Date Navigator, at the top, shows one or more months, with bold numbers indicating days that contain appointments, events, or meetings. Use the arrows alongside the month name to navigate to the previous or next month, or click the month name to select from a list that includes the three months before and after the month you click on. Click a day of the month (or drag to select multiple adjacent days) to switch to Calendar view and display all items from the selected date or dates.

Beneath the Date Navigator is the Appointments section, which shows the next few appointments or meetings on your calendar. And below that section is the Task list, which displays upcoming items from the Tasks folder, in list format. If you have a particularly full calendar and rarely use the Tasks folder, you can allow more room for upcoming appointments by hiding the Task list. In fact, you can display or hide any of the three sections using the To-Do Bar menu on the View tab, as shown here. (The same choices are available as a shortcut menu if you right-click the To-Do Bar.)

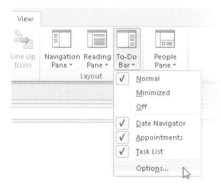

Just as with the Navigation pane, you can use the arrow at the top of the To-Do Bar to minimize it to a thin strip that shows only your next appointment and a summary of your Task list. Click anywhere on the minimized pane to pop out the full To-Do Bar temporarily. After you make a selection or click elsewhere in the Outlook window, the To-Do Bar retreats into hiding again.

For slightly finer-grained control over what appears within each section on the To-Do Bar, click Options on the To-Do Bar menu, which opens this dialog box.

Clear the Show All Day Events check box if you want to show only appointments and meetings with specific start and end times, for example, and not clutter up the Appointments section with labels describing a day's events. You can also hide details of items you mark as Private (using the Show As menu in the Options group on the Meeting tab).

Any changes you make to the To-Do Bar apply immediately and are reflected in all views.

INSIDE OUT Use a widescreen monitor to see extra months

In its default configuration, the To-Do Bar shows a single month in the Date Navigator. If you have a big enough monitor and an active calendar, increase the value in the Number Of Month Rows box to 2, and then drag the inside edge of the To-Do Bar to the left until a second (or third) month appears in each row. This arrangement has the additional advantage of lengthening descriptions of items in the To-Do Bar, making them more readable.

Using the Reading Pane

The Reading pane allows you to click an individual item and preview its contents without having to open that item in its own window. Although it's most obviously useful for reading and replying to e-email messages, you can use this pane in other views as well, and any customizations you make (whether to show or hide the pane and whether to position it at the bottom or the right of the contents pane) are saved for each view independently.

The Reading pane doesn't allow editing, but you can follow hyperlinks, preview attachments, respond to meeting requests, and view important messages in the InfoBar. When you use the Reading pane in Mail view, attachments appear in a bar below the Subject line, where you can preview their contents.

For more on the security implications of attachments, see "Working Safely with File Attachments" on page 820.

Clicking Options on the Reading Pane menu (in the Layout group on the View tab) opens the dialog box shown here, where you can control whether and when new messages are marked as read after you view them in the Reading pane.

Setting Up Mail Accounts

Outlook's prime directive is to manage your e-mail, fetching and processing incoming messages and making sure that messages you compose and send go to their intended recipients. You're prompted to set up the first account by the Outlook startup wizard, which allows you to set up additional accounts at the same time. Afterward, you can add new accounts and reconfigure or remove existing accounts from the Info tab in Backstage view. Click File, and then click Info to display options similar to those shown in Figure 21-6. (The exact choices available depend on the type of e-mail account selected in the list directly under Account Information. We discuss these differences in more detail in the following sections.)

The simplest way to set up a new account is to click Add Account and then enter your display name, your e-mail address, and your password on the Auto Account Setup page of the Add New Account dialog box. Outlook can automatically configure account settings for most Internet-standard e-mail accounts and for well-known web-based mail services. Outlook first tries to make an encrypted connection, and if that fails, it asks for your approval to try an unencrypted connection. Configuration is also automatic with any Microsoft Exchange server that has been configured to use the Autodiscover service.

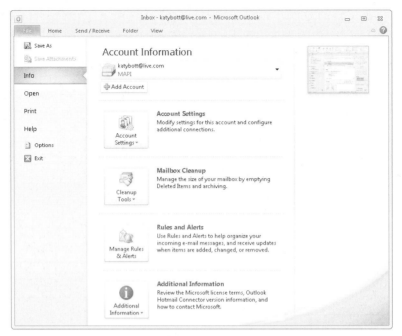

Figure 21-6 The list at the top of this pane shows accounts you've already set up. The options for a Microsoft Exchange account are significantly different from those shown here.

> **Note**
>
> For technical details about the Autodiscover service on Exchange 2010, see the TechNet article at *w7io.com/12101*.

If the automatic configuration fails, you see an error message. If you know the server names and any other nonstandard settings, such as alternate port numbers, you can configure the account manually. Click Back to start over, and then select the Manually Configure Server Settings Or Additional Server Types option. Or, in the dialog box that displays the error message, select Manually Configure Server Settings, and then click Retry.

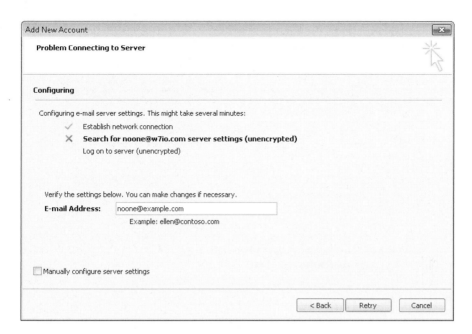

To change the settings for an existing e-mail account, click Account Settings on the Account Settings menu (and no, that's not a typo—the duplicate menu options are by design), select its entry in the accounts list, and then click Change.

Figure 21-7 shows an Outlook profile that contains four accounts. The white check mark in a black circle denotes the default e-mail account, which is used to send newly created messages unless you specify an alternate account. Replies are always sent using the account through which the original message was received, although you can choose a different account if you prefer.

We look at the different options available for each type of mail account in the following sections.

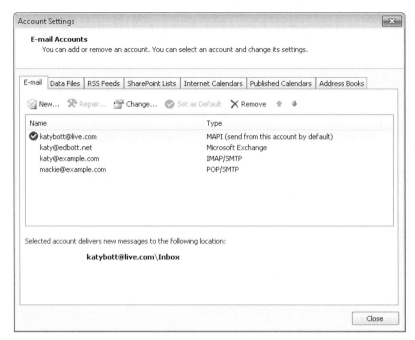

Figure 21-7 Select an account from this list, and then click Change to view and edit its settings.

Using Internet-Standard Mail Servers

Many traditional Internet service providers and web-hosting companies offer subscribers and customers access to e-mail servers that use well-established, even venerated e-mail standards. The most common is the combination of Post Office Protocol (POP or POP3) for receiving messages and Simple Mail Transfer Protocol (SMTP) for sending messages.

Figure 21-8 shows the Internet E-Mail Settings page for POP/SMTP e-mail account.

What you enter in the Your Name box under the User Information heading is what recipients see when you send them an e-mail message. If you have an account that you use only for specific purposes, you might want to add that information as part of the display name. For an account you use exclusively to contact reporters and analysts, for example, you might add (Media Relations) after your name.

The other Internet standard e-mail account type is Internet Mail Access Protocol (IMAP), which is an alternative to the POP standard. On an IMAP server, your messages stay on the server and are synchronized with a local copy. Some ISPs and hosting companies provide IMAP and POP services on the same server; in that case, Outlook's automatic account configuration might choose IMAP when you wanted POP, or vice versa. You can't change the account type after initially configuring an account; instead, choose the manual configuration option and create a new account using the same settings, and then choose the correct entry from the Account Type list. Use your existing Outlook data file as the delivery location. After you verify that the new account works properly and your messages are intact, you can delete the old account.

Figure 21-8 You can change your name or enter new server names after you create an account. The Deliver New Messages To options are available only when you create a new account.

If the esoteric setting you're looking for isn't visible in the Internet E-Mail Settings dialog box, click the More Settings button in the lower right corner. There, you'll find a collection of settings that you might never need; but knowing how to adjust the settings there can fix some of the following types of e-mail glitches:

- If your SMTP server requires that you use a different set of credentials from the ones you use to receive mail, enter this information on the Outgoing Server tab.

- To change the name that identifies the account in the E-Mail Accounts list, click the General tab and enter a name in the Mail Account box. By default, Outlook initially fills this field with the e-mail address for an account, but you might want to replace that with a descriptive account name.

- For IMAP accounts only, use the Deleted Items and Sent Items tabs to control where these items are stored. You can choose folders on the server side or folders in your local Outlook data file.

- If your Internet service provider or network blocks traffic on some network ports, you might need to specify alternative ports to send or receive e-mail. This might happen if your ISP insists that you use its SMTP servers for outgoing messages and blocks traffic on the standard SMTP port 25. If the administrator of your SMTP server has defined an alternate port for either incoming or outgoing messages, you can fill in the correct port numbers on the Advanced tab.

Options on the Advanced tab vary slightly between IMAP and POP accounts, as shown in Figure 21-9.

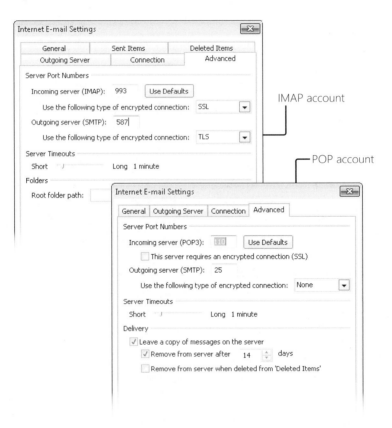

Figure 21-9 The IMAP configuration (left) uses secure connections for incoming and outgoing servers; the POP account (right) uses the standard SMTP port 25, which is blocked by some ISPs.

Configuring Exchange Accounts

If one or more of your e-mail accounts is on a server running Microsoft Exchange, it's almost certain that your account is for business, and a server administrator can provide you with the detailed instructions to connect to that account and begin synchronizing its contents with a local Outlook data file. If the server administrator is sensible enough to have configured the Exchange Autodiscover service, all you need to do is enter your name, your e-mail address, and your password in the Add New Account dialog box. The configuration steps after that are automatic.

INSIDE OUT Let someone else run your Exchange server

Microsoft Exchange Server has earned a reputation over the years as complex and suitable only for use in large enterprise settings. That intimidating image is softening with the steady growth of hosted Exchange services, which allow businesses of any size (even single-person shops) to connect to Exchange servers over the Internet, paying a monthly fee to a service provider that handles the headaches of server administration and backup. You can purchase a hosted Exchange account as part of the Business Productivity Online Suite directly from Microsoft (*microsoftonline.com*) or from a Microsoft partner (*w7io.com/12102*). You can also try third-party partners such as Apptix (*mailstreet.com*) and Intermedia (*intermedia.net*).

If you need to configure settings manually, you have to go through a few dialog boxes to enter server names and your credentials. If you access your e-mail over the Internet (rather than on an internal network), you also need to ensure that Exchange Anywhere (the official name for a secure connection to Exchange using HTTP) is configured properly. Open the Account Settings dialog box for your Exchange account, click Change, and then click More Settings. On the Connection tab, shown next, click Exchange Proxy Settings and fill in the server names and connection details exactly as they're supplied to you by your Exchange server administrator.

Outlook 2010 supports multiple Exchange accounts, all of which can be run in Cached Exchange Mode, in which a copy of your server-based mailbox is maintained locally.

Using Windows Live Hotmail with Outlook

Windows Live Hotmail traces its roots to one of the oldest free web-based e-mail services. Hotmail was founded in 1996 and was purchased by Microsoft in 1997. (Trivia note: The name of the service was originally HoTMaiL, with the capitalized letters HTML providing a clue that, yes, this service runs on the web.) Windows Live Hotmail, the latest version of the service, still runs on the web, but it also hooks up neatly with Outlook with the help of a small add-on called the Outlook Hotmail Connector.

When you first set up an e-mail account, Outlook asks you if you also want to set up a Windows Live Hotmail account. If you say yes, it downloads and installs the Outlook Hotmail Connector and walks you through the configuration process. (To download and install this utility manually, visit *w7io.com/12103*.)

With the help of the connector software, you can synchronize contacts, calendars, rules, and safe/blocked senders lists from your Windows Live Hotmail account to Outlook. It also improves the experience of using your Windows Live Hotmail account so that it works like a traditional e-mail account.

Setting Up a Webmail Account from a Non-Microsoft Service

Microsoft is not the only big company with a free web-based e-mail service. If you set up a new e-mail account using an address (and its associated password) from Google's Gmail (*gmail.com*) or Yahoo Mail (*yahoomail.com*), Outlook automatically configures the correct account settings—using IMAP for Gmail and POP for Yahoo. For other web-based services, you might need to dig to find the correct settings to use. In some cases, you might need to pay for a premium subscription or tweak settings for the account using its web-based administrative interface so that it emulates a POP/SMTP or IMAP account.

Organizing Your Contacts

Your Outlook profile has at least one Contacts folder, and most have several. Your primary Outlook data file is where your local Contacts folder is stored. Each Windows Live Hotmail account you connect to Outlook includes its own Contacts folder, and connections to social media services like LinkedIn also appear as folders in Contacts view. A new feature in Outlook 2010 adds a Suggested Contacts folder for every e-mail account you set up. (We have more on the pros and cons of that feature later in this section.)

Contacts folders typically build up over time. When you meet a new neighbor or acquire a new customer, you probably want to add their e-mail address, phone number, and other details to Outlook. To create a new Contact item from scratch, you click New Contact (on the Home tab in Contacts view) and fill in the blanks. If you've just returned from a trade-show or a sales call with a fistful of business cards, you can enter each new contact's information in a new Contact form, clicking Save & New after each one.

Using Contact Cards for Quick Viewing

You don't need to browse to a Contacts folder or open a Contact item to see details about a person. An alternate view called the *Contact Card* is available from any e-mail message. To see a mini version of this information, point to any name or e-mail address in the header (the From:, To:, or Cc: fields) to pop up the compact version of that person's Contact Card. If that person's name is in a Contacts folder, detailed information (including a photo, if one is available) appears on the Contact Card. If you right-click the name or address in the message header, you see a shortcut menu and the mini Contact Card, as shown next.

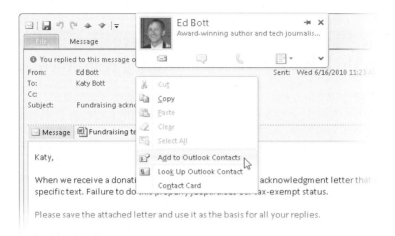

The four icons at the bottom of the mini Contact Card allow you to compose an e-mail message addressed to that contact, send an instant message, make a phone call, or schedule a meeting. (The instant-message features work only if you're signed in to a compatible service, such as Windows Live Messenger, and you can make a phone call only by using Office Communicator on your company network.) You can create a new Contact item for that person and add it to your Contacts folder or look up existing details for the contact by using the menu items at the bottom.

The Send E-Mail icon is especially useful if you're looking at a message and you want to start a completely new conversation. Rather than reply to the original, unrelated message, right-click your recipient's name in the message header, and then click the Send E-Mail icon.

Click the arrow in the lower right corner of the mini Contact Card to display the full Contact Card, which has additional details such as phone numbers. To keep the Contact Card from disappearing as soon as you move the mouse pointer, click the pushpin icon in its upper right corner. That keeps the item visible until you close it.

Browsing the Contents of a Contacts Folder

In Contacts view, the Navigation pane displays a list of all folders containing Contact items. Select a folder from that list to display all its contacts in the contents pane. Figure 21-10 shows a well-stuffed Contacts folder using the default Business Card format.

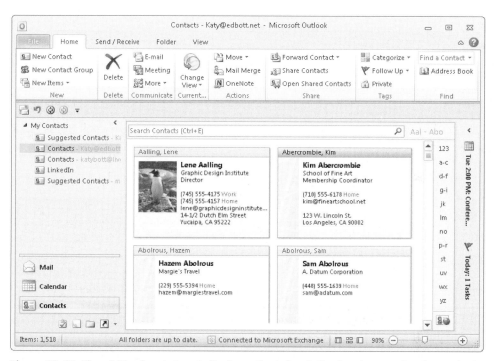

Figure 21-10 The width of each item in Business Card view is fixed and cannot be changed. The more information you fill in for a contact, the more you see on the business card itself.

In both the Navigation pane and individual business cards, note the frequent use of gray text. The e-mail account associated with a Contacts folder appears in a light gray after the folder name, which is in black type. Likewise, the words Home and Work and Mobile appear (in gray) immediately to the right of phone numbers (in black) on a contact's business card. The gray type makes it easier for your eye to focus on the data that matters and tune out the extra details until you need them.

INSIDE OUT Include a title for every contact

Whatever you type in the Full Name field is parsed by Outlook, which usually does a good job of distinguishing first names from last names. If Outlook gets any details wrong, open the item and click the Full Name button, which opens the Check Full Name dialog box shown here:

As you can see, the contents of the Full Name field allow you to specify a title, as well as a middle name or initial and a suffix. A courtesy title is essential if you use a Contacts folder as a mail-merge source and you want to be able to address recipients formally ("Dear Dr. Smith"). The drop-down Title list allows you to choose from some standard options: Mr., Miss, Mrs., Ms., Dr., or Prof. You can skip that step if you enter the title at the beginning of the Full Name field when you create a new Contact item. Thus, when you enter Mr. Jeff Smith, Outlook correctly parses Mr. as a title. Some courtesy titles that aren't in the drop-down Title list work automatically as well. Outlook parses the title correctly if you begin the Full Name field with Monsieur, Madame, or Mademoiselle; Herr, Frau, or Fraulein; Sir or Madame; or Signore, Signora, or Signorina. For unsupported titles, such as Señor, Señora, Lord, and Lady, or for alternate spellings like *Madam*, you can type directly in the Title box.

Changing Display Names and Sort Order

When browsing through contacts, you might notice two separate name fields on each one. In Business Card view, for example, the name at the top of each card is taken from the File As field; by default, this is Last Name, First Name. In bold letters on the card itself is the Full Name field, which normally appears as First (Middle) Last. If you want to change this order for new cards you create, open the Options dialog box (click File, then click Options) and display the Contacts tab, as shown in Figure 21-11.

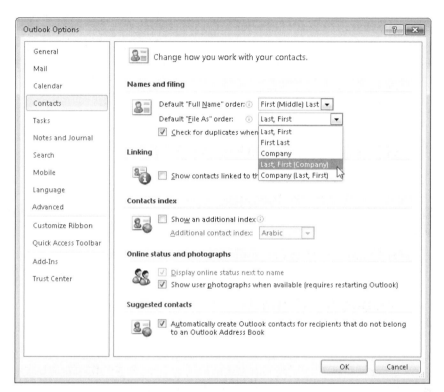

Figure 21-11 Any changes you make in the Names And Filing section apply to new contacts you create but do not affect existing Contact items.

The settings you assign here dictate how these fields are filled in for new Contact items. They don't change existing items. At any time, you can override the current settings in the Names And Filing section. The five default File As choices, as shown here, combine the contact's first, last, and company names. For professional contacts who you don't know well, you might prefer to include the company name as part of the field you see so that you can recognize it quickly when browsing, as shown next.

For a more compact view of a Contacts folder that contains many items, switch to List view, where the Full Name and File As fields have their own columns.

For an explanation of how to customize, save, and switch between views, see "Selecting and Customizing Views in Outlook" on page 753.

Searching for Contacts

If a Contacts folder contains more than a dozen items, it's often easier to search than to browse. The Search Contacts box at the top of the contents pane lets you instantly filter the contents of the current folder. (Press Ctrl+E to move the insertion point directly to this box so you can begin typing.) This is a word-wheel search that responds immediately (or nearly so) as you type. Contacts appear in the list if any part of any field in that item matches the text you type in the search box. So, typing *tra* locates your friend Shirleen H. *Tra*vers and anyone who works at Margie's *Tra*vel.

INSIDE OUT   Search through all Contacts folders at once

The Search Contacts box is the fastest way to find someone if you know which Contacts folder contains the details you want to use. But what if you're not sure which folder the person's contact details are located in? Or what if you created a contact record for a business associate and that person's LinkedIn profile is also available in a Contacts folder? For those occasions, click in the Find A Contact box at the right side of the Home tab in any view, enter part of the person or company name you're looking for, and then press Enter. If Outlook finds one and only one match, it opens that item directly. If it finds more than one match, it displays the Choose Contact dialog box, which lists matching contacts (using the Full Name field) and also shows the source of each one. Select a name, and then click OK to open that contact.

For more on how to use search features throughout Outlook, see "Mastering Outlook Search" on page 741

Creating and Using Contact Groups

If you routinely send e-mail to the same group of people (or schedule meetings with a committee or club), you can avoid the tedium of picking each name individually and create a Contact Group item that includes those names. Open the folder that contains the contacts you want to save as a group, and click New Contact Group on the Home tab. Give the Contact Group a name, and then click Add Members to begin picking from your Contacts folder or another address book. The resulting group appears among the rest of your contacts, with the group name displayed with individual contacts using the File As settings, as shown in Figure 21-12.

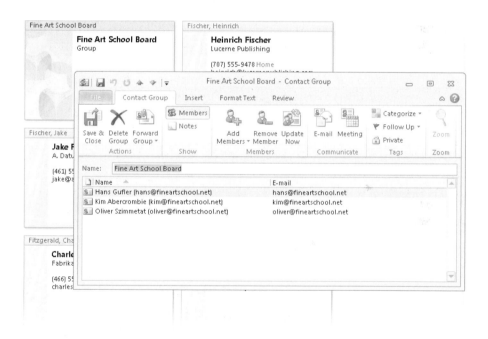

Figure 21-12 Use Contact Groups to make it easier to send e-mail to people working on a project or to schedule a meeting with a board or committee.

Double-click a group to change the group name, add or remove members, or add notes about the group. Use the E-Mail command (in the Communicate group) to address a message to all the members of the group or to prepare meeting invitations that include everyone in the Contact Group.

CAUTION

A Contact Group is not the same as a mailing list (sometimes also called a *discussion list*) managed by an e-mail server. The latter allows you to use a group name (like coho-list@example.com) to send and receive e-mail messages, which are in turn passed on individually to list members, who see only the alias in the To: or From: field. When you use a Contact Group to create a new e-mail message, it initially appears in your message window as a single bold name that matches the Contact Group name. But when you click Send, the group name is immediately replaced with the addresses that it contains. If you enter the group name in the To: field and it contains 37 e-mail addresses, every recipient will see every one of those 37 addresses. If you don't want your recipients to be identified, use the BCC field instead.

Dealing with Duplicate Contacts

If you try to add a new contact with the same name as an existing contact, Outlook intervenes and offers to merge information from the new contact into the existing contact. This works especially well when you get a message from a friend who has updated her e-mail address. Right-click the address in the message header, and click Add To Outlook Contacts. Because a Contact item by that name already exists, you see a dialog box like the one shown here:

INSIDE OUT How to merge two contacts into one

As we note in this section, Outlook intercedes if you try to create a new item with the same name as an existing contact. But how do you force this detection if you accidentally create multiple contact items for the same person under slightly different names? The technique is a little tricky. First, make sure the Full Name field is identical for both contacts. In Contacts view, click to select the Contact item whose e-mail address you want to see as the first one in the merged contact. Press Delete. (Don't worry, this is only a temporary step.) In the Navigation pane, click the Folder List icon, and then click the Deleted Items folder for the Outlook data file that contains the Contacts folder you're working with. Find the freshly deleted Contact item, and press Ctrl+C to copy it to the Clipboard. Now return to the Contacts folder, and press Ctrl+V to create a new item from the contents of the Clipboard. Outlook will offer to merge the two items. If you approve, click Update. This process is surprisingly effective, and it even combines the contents from the Notes field in both items so that you don't lose any important information you inadvertently kept in two places.

Managing Your Calendar

An Outlook calendar can do things that a traditional printed calendar can't. Outlook allows you to keep multiple calendars—so you can keep personal and work-related events firmly separated but combine the two when you're viewing your schedule. You can add follow-up flags and reminders to an appointment, keep perfect track of appointments that recur weekly or monthly, and schedule meetings with coworkers. If you work at a desk, you probably have Outlook open at all times, and your calendar is never more than a few clicks away. If you travel, you can synchronize your Outlook calendar with a smartphone or a portable PC so that any appointment you enter or change in one place shows up in the other.

For more details on how to get Outlook to nag you (in a good way) about what's coming up on your calendar, see "Setting Follow-up Flags and Reminders" on page 771. For an overview of how to sync PCs and devices, see "Receiving and Synchronizing Data" on page 788.

In Calendar view, you see all meetings and appointments (and all-day events). The Date Navigator control (identical to the one found in the To-Do Bar in other views) sits at the top of the Navigation pane, with a list of available calendars just below it. When you select one or more adjacent dates in the Date Navigator, the contents pane shows you meetings and appointments for those dates only, as in Figure 21-13.

Drag to select a group of dates . . .   . . . and see all items for those dates

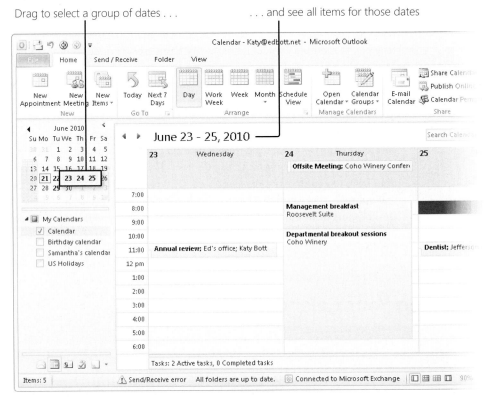

Figure 21-13 Use a command to view your calendar by Day, Work Week, Week, or Month. For a custom view, select multiple days (in this example, three) from the Date Navigator on the left.

The Arrange group on the Home tab contains single-click shortcuts. Day, Week, and Month are straightforward, but the other two selections deserve some extra discussion.

Click Work Week to show a week's worth of events, with all working hours visible and your days off hidden. By default, this view is set for 8:00 AM to 5:00 PM, Monday through Friday. If your hours or workdays are different, you can adjust these settings on the Calendar tab of the Outlook Options dialog box, as shown next.

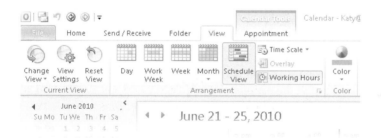

Schedule View (especially with the Work Week option selected), gives you a day-by-day view of your calendar that works by scrolling from left to right. It's most useful when you're comparing your calendar with someone else's in search of free time for a meeting or a lunch date.

For a closer look at how to coordinate schedules in Outlook, see "Sharing and Comparing Calendars" on page 777.

In Day or Week views, where appointments and meetings are presented in columns, pressing Home takes you to the beginning of the selected workday, and End jumps to the end of the workday (based on your Work Week settings). Press Ctrl+Home or Ctrl+End to jump to the beginning or end of the day—normally midnight. In any Calendar view, press Alt+Page Down or Alt+Page Up to move to the next or previous month, respectively.

Chapter 21

Creating and Editing Appointments and Meetings

To create a new item from scratch in Calendar view, click the New Appointment or New Meeting command on the Home tab. If the date you want to use is visible in Day or Week view, you can double-click a time to begin creating a new item with that date and start time filled in. Drag to select a time interval, and then right-click to open a form with a non-default end time. To begin creating an all-day event, double-click in the colored bar just between the date heading and the top of your hour-by-hour calendar

INSIDE OUT Turn an e-mail message into an appointment

If you receive an e-mail for which the follow-up action involves scheduling an appointment on your calendar, you can skip the Clipboard and allow Outlook to fill in the Subject and add details. If you don't need to keep the original e-mail message, click Move (in the Move group on the Home tab if you're reading the message in the Reading pane, or on the Message tab if you've opened it in its own window). Click Calendar (if you don't see this option in the list, click Other Folder and select it from the folder list) to copy the subject to a new Appointment item, fill in the details pane with the body text from the message itself, and move the original message to the Deleted Items folder. If you want to keep the original message and create a new Appointment item using the subject and body text, drag the message from the message list and drop it on a date in the Date Navigator at the top of the To-Do Bar. You'll probably want to change the subject of the new appointment, and you might also want to adjust times and trim unwanted information from the details pane. When you're satisfied, click Save & Close.

The New Appointment and New Meeting forms are nearly identical. The difference is the To: box, where you choose attendees for your meeting, and the Send button, which replaces the Save & Close command used with appointments that go on your calendar alone. In fact, you can turn an appointment into a meeting by clicking the Invite Attendees button (in the Attendees group on the Appointment tab); to turn a meeting back into an appointment, click Cancel Invitation (in the Attendees group on the Meeting tab).

For more details on how to send and respond to meeting invitations, see "Working with Meeting Invitations" on page 780.

Most of the fields in either form are self-explanatory, and making best use of them involves common sense. The Subject, for example, can be up to 255 characters long, but shorter is better, especially if you plan to synchronize meetings with your smartphone. The Location list accepts any typed input and allows you to choose from the last 10 locations by clicking the arrow at the right of the list. The Show As settings in the Options group on the Appointment tab are worth noting. You can choose Busy, Free, Tentative, or Out Of Office to add a color-coded strip to the left of each item. If you share a limited view of your calendar with other people, they can check times when you're available without seeing details of your schedule.

You can enter dates in any format that Outlook is able to recognize; in the date box alongside Start Time or End Time, for example, type *aug 9* or *8/9* (U.S. style) to enter the date August 9, with the current year assumed. When you open a new item, Outlook fills in dates from the currently selected day, regardless of which view (Day, Week, Month) you're using. To add a couple of days, a week, or a few months to that date, click in either date box and type *2 days*, *1 week*, or *3 months*. When you move to a new field, Outlook automatically adjusts the date by the amount you specified.

You can also use abbreviations for days of the week (*mon*, *thu*, or *thurs*) and date-related words and phrases (*today, tomorrow, two weeks from yesterday*), with or without the names of holidays (*Thanksgiving, three days after Christmas, Friday before New Year's Eve*).

A few shortcuts are also available for entering times. If you simply type a number without using a colon, Outlook converts it to a time. It usually guesses correctly at AM and PM designations, defaulting to times in your workday if possible. You can override these settings by providing hints: *1015p* becomes 10:15 PM, and *5a* is 5:00 AM.

To understand the intricacies (and possible pitfalls) posed by cross-country and international travel, see "Juggling Multiple Time Zones" on page 810.

Setting Up Recurring Appointments and Events

Any appointment, meeting, or event can be defined as a recurring event that repeats on a schedule you specify. From a new or existing item, click the Recurrence command (in the Options group on the Meeting or Appointment tab) and specify the details of the schedule using the dialog box shown next.

Chapter 21

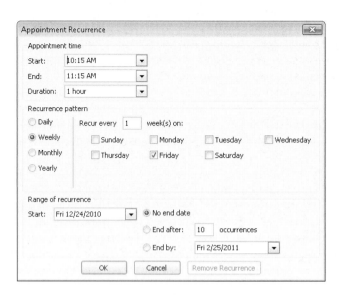

Enter a Start and End time and then select options from the Recurrence Pattern section to define the schedule. If you have a 10:00 AM meeting on the same days every week, select Weekly and click the scheduled days: Tuesday and Thursday, for example. The Range Of Recurrence section allows you to define a series that ends on a specified date or after a certain number of occurrences.

When you double-click an item on your calendar that is part of a recurring series, Outlook asks whether you want to edit the individual occurrence or the series. Choose the former option if you just want to cancel next Tuesday's meeting; use the latter option if the schedule changes to Wednesday and Friday.

For more details about how to view someone else's calendar alongside yours, see "Sharing and Comparing Calendars" on page 777.

Creating, Sending, and Receiving Messages

When you create a new e-mail message or reply to an existing one, Outlook opens a Message window like the one shown here.

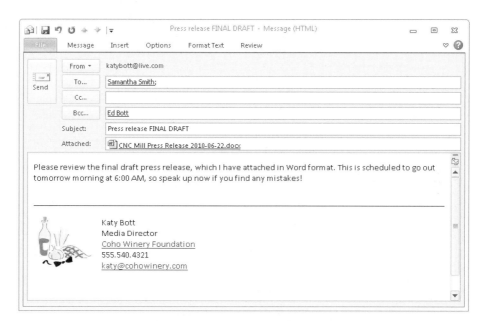

We assume that you've sent and received enough e-mail messages that you can figure out the basics of composing, addressing, and sending a message or reply. In this section, we concentrate on some interesting and useful e-mail options that you're less likely to discover without a determined search.

For starters, there's the BCC box, which is essential when you want to send a copy of a message to someone without alerting the other recipients. The BCC box is normally hidden; to make it available, click the Options tab and then click BCC (in the Show Fields group).

A group of esoteric settings at the far right side of the Options tab (in the More Options group) allow for some interesting treatment of messages you send.

Click Save Sent Item To, and then select an alternative folder from the default Sent Items or click Do Not Save.

Chapter 21

The Delay Delivery and Direct Replies To options open the Properties dialog box shown in Figure 21-14, which is specific to the message you're in the process of composing.

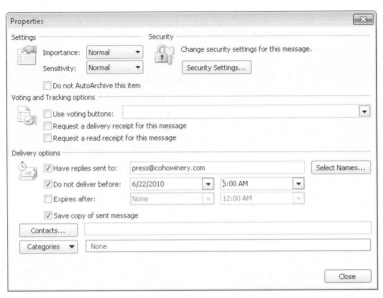

Figure 21-14 The top two settings in the Delivery Options area allow you to specify an alternative Reply To address and delay delivery until a specified date and time.

To delay delivery of your message, select the Do Not Deliver Before check box and enter the date and time when you want the message delivered. Note that your computer must be on (not sleeping or hibernating), and Outlook must be running for the message to be sent. If your computer is off or you've closed Outlook, the message will be sent at the first available opportunity after the specified date and time.

The Have Replies Sent To option allows you to specify an e-mail address that is used when recipients click the Reply button after reading your message. If you're sending out a new press release or sales promotion from your everyday e-mail account, you might want replies to be shunted to a special sales or press alias. That allows a team of people to receive those replies and respond to them promptly, without cluttering your Inbox.

For more on how to avoid errors when addressing e-mail messages, see "Managing Auto-Complete Lists and Suggested Contacts" on page 812.

Choosing the Right Message Format

When you compose a new message, Outlook offers three format choices that dictate how the message appears to recipients. These options are available in the Format group on the Format Text tab.

By default, Outlook sends new messages in HTML format, which allows you to use fonts, text formatting, tables, rules, and graphics in much the way you would create a web page. If you're sending messages from an account on a Microsoft Exchange server to other recipients with mailboxes on the same server, your message is sent in Rich Text format, which enables some advanced features that apply only to Exchange users. This format also allows a broad range of text and graphic formatting options.

The Plain Text format strips away all formatting and leaves behind only text. If you've added bold or italic formatting for emphasis, it will be lost. Recipients will see your message using their default font. Any graphics embedded in the message body are stripped out as well (pictures and documents attached to a message as files are handled properly).

When you reply to a message, Outlook tries to match the format of the message you received. So if a correspondent sends you a message in Plain Text format, your reply will be in Plain Text format as well.

Adding and Editing E-Mail Signatures

A signature can add crucial contact details, branding, or a whimsical touch to any message. Typing your name, title, and phone number at the end of every message is a tedious process, and you risk making an embarrassing error if you do this often enough. A much better option is to create and save one or more signatures, any of which can be associated with new messages or replies sent from a specific e-mail account. A signature can include formatted text, hyperlinks, graphics, and HTML markup.

To create a new signature, click the New E-Mail command or open an existing message window. From the Include group on the Message tab, click Signature and then click Signatures. That opens the Signatures And Stationery dialog box. Click New, and give your signature a name (you can change it later). Click in the Edit Signature box, and then enter the text you want to use for your signature, using the formatting tools to adjust fonts and font sizes, change alignment, and insert graphics and hyperlinks. (You can also paste formatted text and graphics into this box.)

Although the built-in signature editor offers a reasonable set of tools, it lacks some capabilities, including the capability to insert tables, horizontal rules, and clip art. All of these capabilities are present in the Outlook e-mail message editor. If you want any of these items to be part of a signature—or if you've already created a signature manually and want to save it as a named signature—select the signature block from the message editor, copy it to the Clipboard, and then open the Signatures And Stationery dialog box and paste your work into the Edit Signature box. Figure 21-15 shows a signature we created using a horizontal rule to set it off from the message text. The clip art is in one cell of a table (with hidden borders), with contact information in a cell to its right. A signature this complex cannot be created directly in the Edit Signature box.

Chapter 21

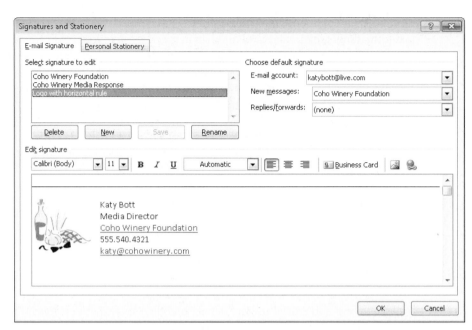

Figure 21-15 Use different signatures for different types of e-mail. This signature, composed in a message window, includes a rule, some clip art, and a hidden table.

To insert a signature from your collection into a message you're composing, click Signature, and then choose the name of the saved signature. To switch to a different signature, right-click the signature block in the message body and choose an alternative from the list of saved signatures.

CHAPTER 22

Organizing Outlook Information

O UTLOOK can store an astonishing amount of data on your behalf. But all that information—e-mail messages, contact details, reminders of upcoming appointments—is just wasted disk space if you can't reliably find it when you need it.

In this chapter, we explore your strategies for filing and finding Outlook items. We start with the basics of items and folders, which superficially resemble their counterparts in the Windows file system but work in significantly different ways. We spend the greatest part of this chapter on Outlook's Instant Search feature; its seemingly simple interface hides a tremendous amount of power that helps you find what you're looking for, even when your filing system is the digital equivalent of a shoebox. We also explain the intricacies of views, which allow you to sort, filter, and arrange the contents of a folder so that you can scan its contents quickly and efficiently.

Finally, we help you make the most of a pair of features that let you harness Outlook to manage incoming e-mail automatically. Rules have been part of Outlook for several versions; Outlook 2010 adds Quick Steps, which allow you to save a sequence of actions and apply those saved actions in order to one or more items with a single click.

Managing Outlook Data Files and Folders

Every Outlook profile contains at least one Outlook data file. In some configurations, that one file might be enough to handle all your Outlook data; more complicated profiles with multiple e-mail accounts might have their data stored in several different files, some of which are local copies of your mailbox on a server. Each data file appears as a separate node in the Navigation pane, with a list of default folders beneath it, in a hierarchy that you can expand or collapse with a click of the plus/minus sign to the left of the file or folder icon. You can add folders and subfolders within any of those nodes.

Managing Data Files

Outlook generally does a good job of insulating you from the need to manage how and where your data files are stored. But on those rare occasions when you need to trouble-shoot problems with a data file or export information, you need to know a few technical and logistic details.

For starters, as we explained in Chapter 21, "Inside Outlook 2010," Outlook stores your data using two different file formats. When you use Windows Explorer, both formats are identi-fied in the Type column as Outlook Data File. The only way to tell which file is local (with a .pst file name extension) as opposed to offline (.ost) is to look at the file name extension or the file icon. An offline file has a double-headed blue arrow beneath it, as shown here, indi-cating that it's a synchronized or cached copy of content that is stored on a server.

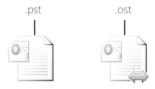

Outlook creates a new, primary data file (what used to be called a Personal Folders file) when you set up a new profile using an Internet-standard e-mail account. It also creates a new data file when you add an account to your profile (although you can override this decision in some cases, as we explain shortly). Archiving a mailbox creates a .pst file that is not associated with an e-mail account, and you can manually create a .pst file at any time, an option that is most useful if you want to manually archive Outlook data or copy a subset of a data file for use on another PC.

To see all data files in use in your current profile, click File, and on the Info tab in Backstage view click Account Settings (on the Account Settings menu). Click the Data Files tab to reveal a list like the one shown in Figure 22-1.

Why would you want to work directly with an Outlook data file in Windows Explorer? That option comes in handy if you're copying a .pst file for use on another PC or backing up an important data file. Select an entry from the list on the Data Files tab, and then click Open File Location to display that file in Windows Explorer. An even faster route is to right-click the name of the data file in the Navigation pane (in Mail or Folder List view) and then click Open File Location.

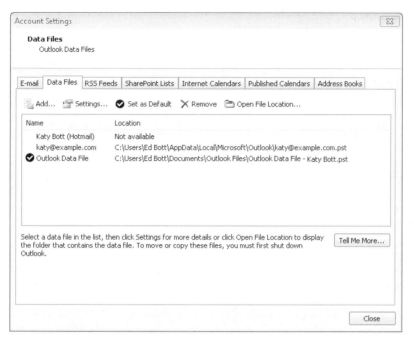

Figure 22-1 View details about all data files in your profile here. Your options vary depending on what type of e-mail account is associated with the data file.

CAUTION

Before you can copy, move, rename, or delete an Outlook data file that is part of the current profile, you must close Outlook completely.

What you can do with each data file depends on the type of e-mail account it's associated with, which also defines its format. The following list summarizes the rules:

- **POP/SMTP** If this is the first account you create in an Outlook profile and you use the Auto Account Setup option, Outlook creates a .pst file with the same name as your e-mail account—katy@example.com.pst, for example—and delivers your incoming mail there. If you add a POP account to an existing Outlook profile, the default setting creates a new .pst file (also named after the e-mail account) to which all mail from that account is delivered. You can override this setting and have messages delivered to an existing .pst file by manually configuring the new e-mail account and then choosing Existing Outlook Data File in the Add New Account dialog box.

- **IMAP** When the first account you create in an Outlook profile is an IMAP account, you end up with two Outlook data files. One, called Outlook.pst and identified in the Navigation pane as Outlook Data File, is your primary Outlook data file and holds your contacts, calendar, and other items that aren't e-mail messages. The other is named after (and associated with) your e-mail account and contains local e-mail folders whose contents are synchronized with your mail server. When you synchronize e-mail with your IMAP server, all new mail is delivered to this second data file.

- **Microsoft Exchange** An Exchange account running in cached mode has its own offline data file (.ost), which is synchronized with the Exchange server and normally contains a full set of folders for all item types.

- **Windows Live Hotmail** Using the Outlook Hotmail Connector creates an offline data file (.ost) that is synchronized with the Windows Live Hotmail service so that local folders are available via the web and vice versa.

For more details about getting started with each type of e-mail account, see "Setting Up Mail Accounts" on page 707.

You can change the name that appears in the Navigation pane for a .pst file associated with a POP account—but not any other type of account—by right-clicking the file name in the Navigation pane and clicking Data File Properties. This displays the Outlook Today dialog box, which shows the display name for the account.

Although it looks like you can just click and type to change the name displayed at the top of the General tab, that doesn't work. Instead, click the Advanced button to open the Outlook Data File dialog box. The Name box here allows editing.

Edit this text to change the display name in the Navigation pane

In previous Outlook versions, all Outlook data files were stored in a hidden subfolder of the logged-on user's profile. That occasionally led to data disasters when a Windows user backed up all the visible folders in their user profile and completely missed their irreplaceable Outlook data file. That possibility is less likely in Outlook 2010, which stores local .pst files in a new Outlook Files subfolder it creates in your Documents folder. If you back up the entire Documents folder, your Outlook data is backed up along with it.

Offline copies of server-based accounts are still stored in the hidden recesses of your user profile. That's by design, because the preferred method of restoring a backup copy of your data from an Exchange, Windows Live Hotmail, or IMAP account is to download and sync a new copy from the server itself.

If you've used Outlook long enough, you probably remember a time when 2 GB was a hard-and-fast limitation on file size for an Outlook data file. Thankfully, that has not been an issue for several versions now. It's still a good practice to keep Outlook files down to manageable sizes for the sake of performance and maintenance, but if you're willing to accept those potential risks, Outlook allows you to fill up a data file that's as large as your server administrator and your hard disk allow.

Chapter 22

TROUBLESHOOTING

Outlook says your Hotmail data file is unavailable

In the list of data files for your Outlook profile, you can see the file name and location of each folder associated with a POP, an IMAP, or an Exchange account. But under the Location heading next to the entry for any Windows Live Hotmail account you see the words *Not Available*. That's a fib—or at least it's not the complete truth. Your Hotmail items are in an Outlook .ost file in a hidden subfolder within your user profile. If you've configured an Exchange account, you'll find the Hotmail files right alongside their Exchange cousins in that folder. Consider it a friendly message from Outlook that it really *really* doesn't want you messing with those files. If you absolutely must inspect that data file in its original location, just type %LocalAppData%\Microsoft\Outlook in the Address bar of Windows Explorer and look for a file name that includes your Hotmail or Windows Live user name followed by an underscore and the word *hotmail* or *live*.

Using and Managing Folders

As we noted in the previous section, Outlook creates a data file with a set of default folders for every e-mail account you configure. If this is your default Outlook e-mail folder for an Internet-standard e-mail account, the local data file includes folders for all supported Outlook data types. If you add a second POP account, that account gets a separate data file with a set of folders limited to mail items. Figure 22-2 shows a profile with two POP accounts configured.

Outlook 2010, in a change from previous editions, groups the most important e-mail folders at the top of the folder list for each data file. Technically, the only mail folder you need for a POP account is Inbox, which is where Outlook delivers messages. The other mail-related folders—Sent Items and Deleted Items, for example—are created locally to handle your outgoing and deleted messages, junk mail, and so on.

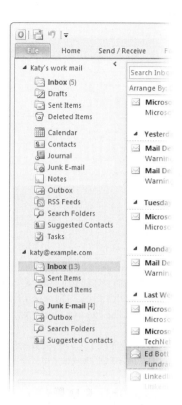

Figure 22-2 This profile is configured for two Internet-standard POP accounts. Note that the second account has only mail-related folders.

For a local Outlook data file (.pst) associated with an Internet-standard e-mail account, you can add new folders and subfolders to any location in the Navigation pane, with the exception of the Calendar. To create a new folder in the Inbox, right-click the Inbox icon and click New Folder. To create a new top-level folder at the same level as the Inbox, right-click the icon for the data file itself. The Create New Folder dialog box shown next lets you add a descriptive name, specify the type of items the folder contains, and choose a location.

Chapter 22

The assortment of default folders for an Exchange Server or a Windows Live Hotmail account differs slightly. In addition, any third-party services you add to Outlook via the Outlook Social Connector might add their own folders for storing contacts and news feeds.

You can copy, move, rename, or delete any folder you create; to do so, use the commands in the Actions group on the Folder tab. You cannot move or delete default folders (deleting the Inbox would make it impossible for new messages to be delivered), nor can you add subfolders in a Windows Live Hotmail account. In the latter case, you can create folders at the same level as the Inbox.

TROUBLESHOOTING

Folders for an IMAP account aren't in the Navigation pane

When you add an IMAP account to an Outlook profile, you might see only an Inbox folder under its heading in the Navigation pane, and trying to send or delete a message results in an error complaining that the Sent Items or Deleted Items folder doesn't exist. This can happen if the account is new and those folders have not been created on the server yet. The simplest workaround is to use a web-based interface to create and send a message and to delete at least one message. That creates the necessary folders. Then return to Outlook, right-click the account icon in the Navigation pane, and choose IMAP Folders. Click Query to display a list of all available folders, which should now include the previously missing special folders, available for you to subscribe to.

Mastering Outlook Search

Outlook's Instant Search lives up to its name. On modern hardware (not expensive, just reasonably up to date), Outlook should be able to locate a message, a contact name, or an appointment instantly, or very nearly so, even with large Outlook data files.

The secret of this search engine's success is that it works with Windows Search, which is included with Windows 7 and Windows Vista Service Pack 2. (For earlier versions of Windows Vista or Windows XP Service Pack 3, you must manually install Windows Search 4.0. Outlook includes a shortcut to help automate this process; click File, click Options, and look for a Search Engine Upgrade button on the Search tab of the Options dialog box.)

You'll find a search box above the contents pane in all Outlook views—above the message list in Mail view. Click in the search box (or press Ctrl+E) and begin typing to kick off a search. Figure 22-3 shows results from a simple keyword search, where we typed the letters *fun*.

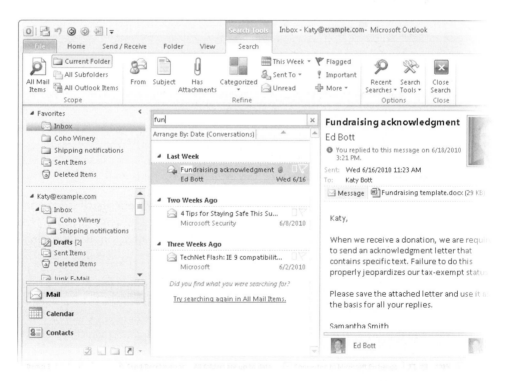

Figure 22-3 The search box is available in all Outlook views—it's just above the message list here. And the custom Search Tools tab appears as soon as you click in that box.

Chapter 22

Because this is a word-wheel (or "search as you type") search, the results of your search appear instantly (there's that word again), and any matches are highlighted in yellow. In this example, typing the letters *fun* filters the list to show messages that contain the words *fun, fundraising,* and *fundamentals.* Continue typing to filter the list even further.

To clear a search and restore the full view of all items in the current folder, click the X to the right of the search box, or just press Esc.

As soon as you click in the search box, Outlook displays the Search tab (under the orange Search Tools heading). Use its commands and options to change the scope of the search—so that it looks in subfolders of the current folder or in other folders that contain items of the same type, for example—or to refine a search with additional filters so that it returns a reasonable number of results.

The exact options available on the Search tab vary depending on the item type for the current folder. Figure 22-4, for example, shows what you see when you click in the search box in Calendar view.

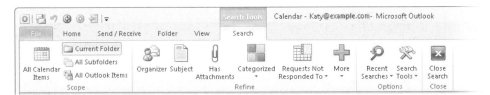

Figure 22-4 You can refine any search by using options on the Search tab. Choose an option in the Scope group to expand or narrow which folders and items are searched.

Changing the Scope of a Search

When you type in the search box, Outlook compares your search string against the contents of the current folder. Thus, if you're viewing the contents of your Inbox, anything you type in the search box returns results that match messages in the Inbox, but not in other folders or subfolders.

If your search results are in list form, you'll find an inviting link at the bottom of the list that reads Try Searching Again In All Mail Items. (If you're searching for a different item type, this link might be different—All Calendar Items, for example.) That link has the same effect as the first command in the Scope group on the Search tab, which includes three additional options for changing where Outlook searches:

- **Current Folder** This option is normally selected when you click in the search box—unless you change the default using the steps we describe in this section.

- **All Subfolders** If you've created subfolders within your Inbox, their contents are not normally searched. Click this option to change the current scope so that it includes all subfolders of the current folder.

- **All Outlook Items** Use this option when you want to find every Outlook item that contains your search term in any of its main fields (names, addresses, subject, and message body, for example).

If your e-mail is organized into many folders (or if you use multiple mailboxes), you might prefer to set the default search scope to include all folders. You'll find this setting on the Search tab in the Outlook Options dialog box (click File and then click Options). Change the first setting under the Results heading to All Folders to always start with an expanded search.

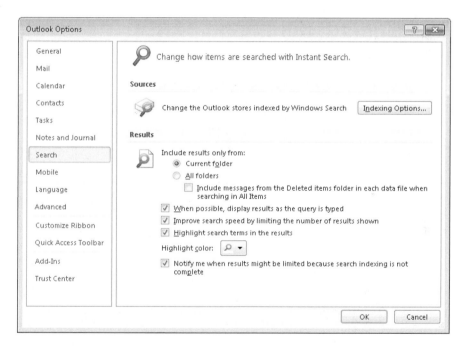

Note that when you choose this option the light gray text in the empty search box changes to read Search All Mail Items (Ctrl+E).

For more on how to create and configure rules that move incoming messages into folders automatically based on their contents or the sender's name, see "Using Rules to Manage Messages Automatically" on page 762.

Adding Criteria to a Search

If you simply begin typing in the search box, Outlook returns an item in the results list if your search text matches any of the main fields in that item: sender or recipient name, subject, body, and so on. Partial matches succeed if the search text appears at the beginning of a word in an item, but not if it's in the middle of a word. So, searching for *ed* turns up e-mail messages sent or received by Ed Bott but not those from Ted Bremer, as well as those containing the word *editor* in the message body but not those containing *shipped*. If your search term contains two or more words separated by spaces, Outlook treats each word as a separate search term and returns only results that contain all of the terms in your list. To find a phrase, enclose it in quotation marks.

If you want to search only within a specific field, use the options in the Refine group on the Search tab. As we noted earlier, the available options are different depending on the item type you're currently viewing, and they represent a subset of all the properties available for that item type. In some cases you can choose from a drop-down list, such as the Search For Mail By Received Date list, as shown here.

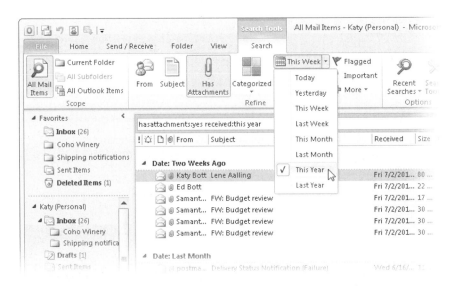

If the exact field you're looking for isn't in the Refine group, click More to see a list of all available search properties. This list also includes the top options that are highlighted in the Refine group. This is not just a duplication of what you can do with the main options on the Refine tab—instead, selecting one of these options adds it as a fill-in-the-blanks field or list just below the search box. This creates a custom search form like the one shown in Figure 22-5, which is ideal for filtering a Contacts folder filled with many items. In this example, we filtered the list to include only contacts whose names start with *A* and whose company name includes the word *fine*.

Figure 22-5 Adding search fields to an Outlook view creates the equivalent of a custom search form. This arrangement of fields is still there when you return to this view, even if you restart Outlook.

Search fields you add this way remain in place and are available the next time you search for that item type. You can have separate arrangements of search fields—essentially custom search forms—for each item type.

The techniques we've described so far represent ways to automatically build a search query in the search box by using keywords and criteria that can be combined for extremely fine-grained results. In the next section, we look more closely at the syntax for this powerful feature.

Building Search Queries with Keywords

The Instant Search query syntax isn't particularly difficult to master. Each individual element in a query consists of a keyword that defines which field to search, followed by a colon and (optionally) an operator (an equal sign or greater than/less than sign), followed by criteria that define what to search for. Some keywords use text strings as criteria, others accept dates (or text that represents specific date ranges, such as *next week*), and still others use a simple yes/no syntax. You can combine multiple keyword/criteria pairs to build refined searches that zero in on exactly what you're looking for. This, for example, is a search query that finds all messages in the currently defined search scope that were received in the current month, have one or more file attachments, and contain the word *confirmation* in the message body:

```
hasattachment:yes received:this month contents:=confirmation
```

Note the use of the equal sign, which specifies that the exact text must be used for the comparison; without that equal sign, the result would return any word that begins with that text (both *confirmation* and *confirmations*). In this example, each keyword/criteria combination is separated from its neighbors by a space, which functions the same as the Boolean operator AND. (Outlook is smart enough to ignore the space in *this month* and treat it as the criteria for the *received* keyword.) You can also use OR and NOT as operators, with or without parentheses. The following example returns messages sent in March or April of the current year, from any sender whose name or e-mail address includes a word that starts with Carl or Ed, unless the subject contains the word *confirmation* or *confirmations*.

```
from:(Carl OR Ed) sent:March OR April NOT subject:confirmation
```

For all these Boolean operators, you must use capital letters. If you enter *and, or,* or *not* in lowercase letters, the search engine treats them as normal text.

For date ranges, numbers, or text, you can use the equal sign (=), greater than sign (>), or less than sign (<). Use these operators in combination to specify a range of dates:

```
sent:>=1/1/2011 <3/15/2011
```

In the case of text, a minus sign has the same effect as the NOT operator. So, *–confirmation* returns a match for anything in the current view that doesn't contain *confirmation* in the subject, body, or message header.

You have a surprising amount of flexibility when entering dates as criteria. You can enter a specific date in any format that Outlook recognizes (based on the Windows regional settings). So, in the United States, you can type 29-Sep, 9/29, or Sep 29, and Outlook will recognize that specific date. You can type a day of the week, fully spelled out or abbreviated (*thursday* works, as does *thu* or *thur*); a month, with or without a year, abbreviated or spelled out (*feb* or *February*); or a year (*sent:2010*).

The following date-related words and phrases also work with any keyword that uses dates for its criteria:

- *yesterday*

- *today*

- *tomorrow*

- *last week*, *last month*, or *last year*

- *this week*, *this month*, or *this year*

- *next week*, *next month*, or *next year*

INSIDE OUT   Outlook's search syntax works in Windows, too

One very good reason to learn the fundamentals of how to build an Instant Search advanced query is that much of the syntax can be used in the Windows search box as well, to return results even if Outlook isn't running. You can enter an Outlook search query directly into the Start menu's search box, and your results will appear in the Start menu, or you can type the query in the search box in the top right corner of Windows Explorer to return the results in that window. For example, on a Friday afternoon you might use this query to show you a list of all Outlook items that you've flagged for follow-up next week:

```
followupflag:followup flag due:next week
```

Now, remembering that exact syntax is a challenge, and manually typing it into the Start menu's search box without errors is hardly a time-saver. Instead, build the search in Outlook, and then copy the syntax from Outlook's search box and paste it into the search box in Windows Explorer. After verifying that the results are what you expect, click Save Search on the Windows Explorer toolbar. Give the search a descriptive name (Items Due For Follow-up Next Week), and click OK. You can now rerun that search any time by going to the Searches folder in your user profile. For even faster access, drag the shortcut for a saved search into the Favorites list at the top of the Navigation pane in Windows Explorer.

In all, Outlook supports well over 100 search keywords, most of them specific to one or two item types. We cover most of these keywords in the series of tables that begins on the next page. In each table, the Property column describes what you see when you choose from the More menu in the Refine group on the Search tab. The Keyword Syntax column lists the actual keyword and the criteria it accepts.

We start with five universal keywords, which are available for any type of item in any view. Table 22-1 lists these all-purpose keywords and the type of criteria they accept (italics mean you can enter your own criteria as long as your input matches the specified data type).

Table 22-1 **Search Keywords That Can Be Used with All Outlook Item Types**

Property	Keyword Syntax
Body	contents:*text*
Categories	category:*text*
In Folder	folder:*text*
Modified	datemodified:*date*
Subject	subject:*text*

In the case of the *category* keyword, it's usually easier to use the Categorized menu in the Refine group on the Search tab, which contains a dynamic list of all categories in use. The most common use for the *folder* keyword is to restrict a search to a specific location; for best results, use an equal sign: *folder:="Inbox"*.

Table 22-2 lists search keywords that are designed primarily for use with e-mail items (and, in Calendar view, with meeting requests.)

Table 22-2 **Search Keywords for Use with E-Mail and Attachments**

Property	Keyword Syntax
From, To	from:*text*, to:*text*
Received, Sent	received:*date*, sent:*date*
Bcc, Cc	bcc:*text*, cc:*text*
Message Size	messagesize:*number*
Flag Status	followupflag:Unflagged/Completed/Followup flag
Attachments	hasattachments:Yes/No
Attachment Contains	attachment:*text*
Read	read:Yes/No
Expiration Date	expires:*date*
Importance	importance:Low/Normal/High
Sensitivity	sensitivity:Normal/Personal/Private/Confidential

Most of the keywords and criteria in Table 22-2 are fairly self-explanatory. The *messagesize* keyword is useful if you're interested in quickly whittling down the size of your Inbox by moving or deleting messages with large attachments. For the criteria, you can use K or KB and M or MB to specify kilobytes and megabytes, respectively. For keywords that recognize a finite set of values as criteria, you must enter the full text: *importance:high*. Upper/lower-case is ignored.

INSIDE OUT   Keep the message, ditch the attachment

In some cases, you might want to keep an e-mail message that contains important information, but do you really need its big, bulky file attachment in your Outlook data file? If you no longer need the attachment, or if you've saved it to a local drive or a shared network folder, you can remove it without disturbing the message. In the Reading pane or the message window, click the attachment to display it in the preview pane, and then use the Remove Attachment command on the Attachment tab; if you want to save a single file or all attachments before removing them, use the Save As or Save All Attachments command.

If you're looking for personal details about one or more people, use any of the keywords in Table 22-3.

Table 22-3 Search Keywords for Locating Personal Information About Contacts

Property	Keyword Syntax
First Name	contactfirstname:*text*
Last Name	contactlastname:*text*
Full Name	fullname:*text*
Title	personaltitle:*text*
Job Title	jobtitle:*text*
Company, Department	company:*text*, department:*text*
E-Mail	emailaddresses:*text*
IM Address	imaddress:*text*
Web Page	webpage:*text*

The distinction between Title and Job Title is worth noting, and easier to understand if you look at the keyword and not just its name on the Search menu. Title (which uses the *personaltitle* keyword) refers to Mr., Mrs. Dr., and other honorifics, while Job Title (which uses the *jobtitle* keyword) is associated with the Job Title field just below Company on the main contact form.

To search for details about an address or phone number of a contact or group of contacts, use any of the keywords in Table 22-4.

Table 22-4 Search Keywords for Locating Address Information from Contact Items

Property	Keyword Syntax
Home Address	homeaddress:*text*
Business Address	businessaddress:*text*
Other Address	otheraddress:*text*
Mailing Address	mailingaddress:*text*
Street Address	street:*text*
PO Box	pobox:*text*
City	city:*text*
State	stateorprovince:*text*
ZIP/Postal Code	postalcode:*text*
Primary Phone	primaryphone:*number*
Business Phone	businessphone:*number*
Home Phone	homephone:*number*
Mobile Phone	mobilephone:*number*

For address-related searches, one small keyword oddity is worth noting. In an Outlook Contact item, you can enter up to three separate addresses per contact: Home, Business, and Other. Pick one of these three addresses, and then click the This Is The Mailing Address check box to set that entry as the contact's mailing address. For search purposes, Outlook uses only the address designated as the mailing address with the Street Address, City, State, PO Box, and ZIP/Postal Code fields. The Primary Phone field is normally blank. To specify a number here, you must click the arrow to the left of a phone number in a Contact item and choose Primary from the drop-down list.

Table 22-5 lists search keywords for use with meetings and appointments, and Table 22-6 contains keywords associated with tasks.

Table 22-5 Search Keywords for Use with Calendar Items

Property	Keyword Syntax
Start, End	start:*date*, end:*date*
Show Time As	showtimeas:Free/Tentative/Busy/Out of Office
Location	meetinglocation:*text*
Meeting Status	meetingstatus:Meeting organizer/Tentatively accepted/ Accepted/Declined/Not yet responded
Organizer	organizer:*text*
Recurring	isrecurring:Yes/No
Required Attendees, Optional Attendees	requiredattendees:*text*, optionalattendees:*text*
Resources	resources:*text*

Table 22-6 **Search Keywords for Use with Tasks**

Property	Keyword Syntax
Complete	iscompleted:Yes/No
Date Completed	completed:*date*
Due Date	due:*date*
Owner	taskowner:*text*
Priority	priority:Low/Normal/High
Reminder Time	remindertime:*date*
Start Date	start:*date*
Status	status:Not Started/In Progress/Completed/Waiting On Someone Else/Deferred

Because you can create a task from an e-mail message, several of the keywords primarily associated with task properties (Due Date and Start Date) are also available with searches in e-mail.

Creating and Using Search Folders

Search folders resemble subfolders but are actually virtual folders. Their contents are assembled dynamically from messages in one or more folders that match conditions you specify. Search folders work on the contents of a single data file only and are saved with that data file.

The Search Folders link for an Outlook data file appears in the Navigation pane at the bottom of the folder hierarchy for that file. Initially, the Search Folders node is empty. On the Folder tab, click New Search Folder to display the dialog box shown here.

The New Search Folder dialog box contains 13 default options that you can use to create useful search folders. If you use rules to automatically sort incoming messages into folders according to their sender or their content, for example, you can and should use the Unread Mail search folder to see all unread messages in a single view, grouped by folder.

INSIDE OUT   Make a search folder a favorite

You can add search folders to the Favorites list at the top of the Navigation pane in Mail view. That's an excellent spot for the Unread Mail search folder. It's also a good location for custom search folders, such as those that show you all mail you received today or this week, or all messages that are flagged for follow-up and are due (or overdue) today.

These ready-made search folders offer limited customization options. If you click Mail From Specific People, for example, you're prompted to choose one or more names from your Address Book (you can also enter a domain name or an e-mail address manually in the From box). For a more comprehensive set of tools for creating a finely tuned search folder, click Create A Custom Search Folder at the bottom of the list in the New Search Folder dialog box, and then click Choose. That opens the Custom Search Folder dialog box shown here.

Give the search folder a short, descriptive name, click Browse to select which folders to search, and then click Criteria to open the Search Folder Criteria dialog box, where you can select criteria using form fields. On the Messages tab, for example, the Time box allows you to choose Sent or Received and then choose from a list that includes Yesterday, Today, In The Last 7 Days, Last Week, This Week, Last Month, and This Month. These dates are always relative to the current date, so a search folder that uses Sent In The Last 7 Days as one of its search criteria always shows exactly one week's worth of e-mail, up to and including the current day. Use this search folder in combination with the search box to quickly find a recent message that contains a particular word or phrase.

INSIDE OUT   Don't overlook simple Find and Filter options for e-mail

You don't need to dive into search tools to perform some simple search tasks. In the message list, you can right-click any item and choose Find Related, which displays a menu of two choices: Messages In This Conversation and Messages From Sender. (The same options are also available if you open a message in its own window; use the Related menu in the Editing group on the Home tab.) You can also refine which items are shown in the current e-mail folder by using the Filter E-Mail menu, in the Find group on the Home tab. Choices here allow you to show messages that meet a certain condition and hide all others. For example, you can choose Unread to filter out messages you've already opened or previewed, or refine the list by date—Today, Yesterday, This Week, and so on.

Selecting and Customizing Views in Outlook

Each folder in Outlook has a standard view that defines the arrangement and format of items and the layout of navigation elements. From any folder, you can click the View tab to choose a different predefined view, tweak the currently applied view, or create and save a custom view.

In previous editions of Outlook, custom views represented an essential way to organize your data—in fact, many of the options we talk about here were on the Organize menu in previous editions. In Outlook 2010, you can accomplish most of those same organizational goals much more directly by using Instant Search tools and filters.

Creating and Saving Custom Views

We think that most Outlook users will choose a standard view for each folder and then stick with it rather than invest a great deal of time creating and managing custom views. If you need a fresh view of your Contacts folder, you can change the sorting and grouping of data temporarily—to group your Contacts folder by company, for example, so you can see how many of your contacts work at each one. If you find yourself using that view regularly, you can save it as a custom view.

The view options we discuss in this section work with all Outlook item types. In most cases, you'll find the options on the View tab, where the exact choices vary by folder. If you click Change View, you see a list of all the predefined views for folders of the current item type. Figure 22-6 shows this menu for the Contacts folder, where you can choose one of four predefined views (including the default Business Card view) or a saved custom view, as we've done here.

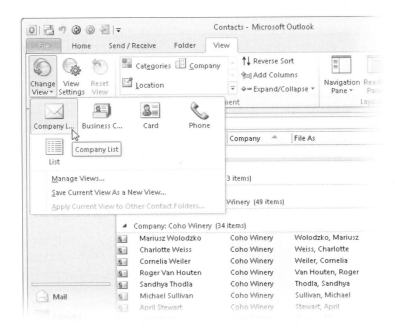

Figure 22-6 This custom view of the Contacts folder starts with Outlook's List view, but it groups items by Company so we can see colleagues and coworkers together in this list.

In this example, we created a new view called Company List. We started by clicking Change View and then clicking List, which displays all contacts in a single table with column headings—choosing a Table view for any item type makes grouping possible. Next, we right-clicked the Company heading and clicked Group By This Field, as shown here.

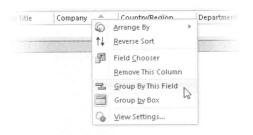

Finally, we clicked Change View again and clicked Save Current View As A New View, which adds it to the menu of defined views.

For views of Mail folders, the predefined views are Compact, Single, and Preview, which define how many lines are used in the message list. Use the options in the Arrangement group on the View tab to change the sort order. The Show In Groups option (selected here) is available for all item types, but only in Table views such as the three message views used to display e-mail.

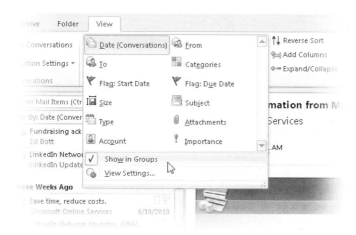

To restore the default sort/group orders, click Reset View (in the Current View group on the View tab).

Viewing E-Mail Conversations

One setting on the View tab in Mail folders deserves some special discussion. If the Show As Conversations check box (in the Conversations group) is selected, Outlook automatically pulls together messages and replies (even, in some cases, when those messages are in other folders) and displays them in a threaded view, with the most recent message at the top. Any conversation that includes even a single unread message has a bold heading in the message list, as shown next.

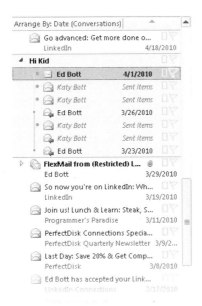

In our experience, most people learn to love conversations—eventually. But the initial view can be confusing if you're used to a purely chronological order for your Inbox. If you don't like Conversation view, you can turn it off by clearing the Show As Conversations check box.

If you occasionally feel overwhelmed by work-related e-mail, we can suggest two good reasons to persevere through the Conversation view learning curve. Both of them are in the Delete group on the Home tab.

Click Clean Up, and then click Clean Up Conversation to remove what Outlook identifies as redundant messages in a conversation. That minimizes clutter in your Inbox, but it also runs the risk of deleting an important message that was mistakenly tagged as redundant. To lessen that risk, you can adjust the Conversation Clean Up options (click File, then click Options, and look about halfway down the Mail tab).

Conversation Clean Up

Cleaned-up items will go to this folder: [   ] [Browse...]

Messages moved by Clean Up will go to their account's Deleted Items.

- [ ] When cleaning sub-folders, recreate the folder hierarchy in the destination folder
- [ ] Don't move unread messages
- [x] Don't move categorized messages
- [x] Don't move flagged messages
- [x] Don't move digitally-signed messages
- [x] When a reply modifies a message, don't move the original

If you prefer to be able to recover cleaned-up messages, click the Browse button and select a backup folder where you want the cleaned-up messages to be preserved.

TROUBLESHOOTING

Some of your conversations are broken

Conversation view in Outlook 2010 is based on properties that are defined as part of an Internet standard. The behavior differs in Outlook depending on what e-mail server (or service) delivered a particular message to your Inbox. Here's a quick summary:

For Internet Mail (POP and IMAP), Outlook 2010 attempts to build a Conversation-ID property based on the SMTP Message-ID property. If the References field contains a message ID (indicating that the message is a reply in a thread), this property is based on the first message ID in the References field. Most PC-based mail clients support this behavior; however, some webmail clients mangle the References field and thus cause Outlook to treat replies as new threads.

With Exchange Server 2007 and earlier, Outlook 2010 behaves as prior versions of Outlook would have, using the PR-Conversation-Topic property to group the mail (this property is most often equivalent to the subject). In this configuration, you will likely see conversations grouped by subject only.

An Exchange Server 2010 server looks at the Message-ID, References, and In-Reply-To properties to set or fix an appropriate Conversation-ID on incoming messages. If Outlook 2010 sees that a conversation is being tracked and tagged by an Exchange Server 2010 server, it uses that information.

If you see unusual or apparently broken strings of conversations in your Inbox, the most likely cause is a quirky e-mail server somewhere in the chain of messages. It might take some advanced testing and troubleshooting to figure out which sender is to blame, and fixing the problem might not be possible, especially if you don't have direct control over that server's configuration. In that case, your best option is to turn off conversation tracking for that view.

Chapter 22

Organizing E-Mail Messages

Left to its own devices, e-mail has a way of taking over your Inbox and then taking over your life. If you receive 200 e-mails a day and you spend 10 seconds just scanning each one (forget about thoughtfully reading them), you've lost a half-hour each day. Gaining back control requires that you develop a system for processing your e-mail, and your secret weapons are a pair of Outlook features that we explain in detail in this section.

- Quick Steps are customizable shortcuts that enable you to perform a series of actions with one click, such as moving an incoming message to a folder or replying to a message with boilerplate text and then archiving the message immediately.

- Rules let you define actions that happen automatically when you receive or send a message, based on conditions you specify. You can use rules to automatically file incoming messages from mailing lists into folders or forward messages to a coworker based on their subject or body.

In both cases, a small investment of up-front effort provides a large payoff later, allowing you to sweep away clutter quickly so you can spend your time dealing with the messages that really matter.

Configuring Quick Steps

Quick Steps are new in Outlook 2010. You can think of each Quick Step as a shortcut that allows you to perform multiple actions by clicking a button. With the help of a Quick Step, for example, you can reply to an incoming message, flag the message for follow-up in a week, and then move it to a folder, all with one click. Creating a Quick Step requires no programming skill. Quick Steps work with e-mail messages only, in any folder.

A default installation of Outlook includes an assortment of Quick Step shortcuts (in the Quick Steps group on the Home tab) to get you started. In addition, you'll find a half-dozen ready-made options (and one Custom choice) on the New Quick Step shortcut menu shown here.

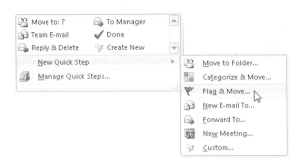

Most of these default Quick Steps are only partially constructed and require some additional setup on your part. If you click Flag & Move, for example, you see a First Time Setup dialog box like the one shown in Figure 22-7. Replace the generic text in the Name box with a more descriptive label and choose options for each of the items in the Actions list, as we've done here, to customize it for your use.

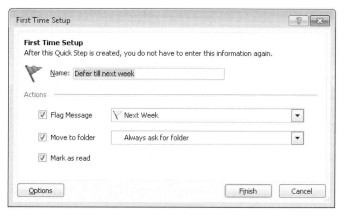

Figure 22-7 This simple Quick Step shortcut flags the currently selected item (or items) for follow-up next week and then allows you to move it to a folder of your choosing.

TROUBLESHOOTING

Quick Steps you created don't appear on the Home tab

Each Outlook data file has its own collection of Quick Steps. If your profile contains multiple e-mail accounts, the choices available in the Quick Steps group on the Home tab change depending on the account you're working with. If you created a Quick Step for your primary POP account and you want to use the same actions with your Windows Live Hotmail account, you need to create a duplicate Quick Step.

Most of the default Quick Step options are easy to figure out from the name. The To Manager and Team E-Mail Quick Steps are most useful if you're connected to a Microsoft Exchange server, in which case Outlook is able to retrieve the necessary information automatically from the global address list; if you use another type of mail server, you can delete these shortcuts or configure them manually.

The most interesting Quick Steps are the ones you build from scratch. You can start with the Create New button in the Quick Steps gallery, or click the Custom option at the bottom of the New Quick Step menu. That brings up the Edit Quick Step dialog box, which is divided into three parts:

- **Name** This box contains a generic description (My Quick Step initially). Change this to a short, descriptive name. Remember that only the first 15 characters are visible in the Quick Steps gallery on the Home tab, so choose a name accordingly.

- **Actions**   You create the first action by choosing from a drop-down list that contains 25 choices in six categories. Some actions are straightforward: Mark As Read and Create A Task With Text Of Message, for example, do exactly what their names say. Other actions, such as Categorize Message, include additional options. Click Add Action and repeat the previous process for the second action, and so on, until you've built the entire sequence of actions for the Quick Step. (You can include up to 12 actions in a single Quick Step, although we find it difficult to imagine any plausible scenario where you would need that many actions.)

- **Optional**   You can assign numeric shortcuts to up to nine Quick Steps, using Ctrl+Shift in combination with the numbers 1 through 9. You can also add descriptive text that appears in a ScreenTip when you hover the mouse pointer over the Quick Step button.

Figure 22-8 shows a simple Quick Step under construction. Its list of actions starts by creating an appointment from the message text, then marking it read, and finally deleting the message.

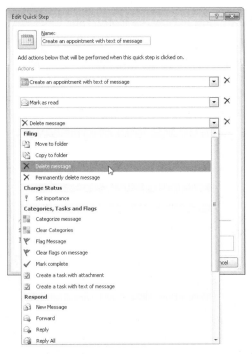

Figure 22-8   Starting from a blank Quick Step, build a sequence of actions by choosing from the categorized list shown here.

Quick Steps can be an incredible time-saver if you have a sales or support job that involves "canned" responses to e-mail requests. Choose the Reply action and click Show Options to see the full dialog box shown in Figure 22-9. We've filled in the body of the message in the Text box and also set a follow-up flag for Next Week. In this case, we haven't selected the Automatically Send After 1 Minute Delay option; leaving this check box clear allows us to personalize the message or tweak the boilerplate text to make the reply seem more personal.

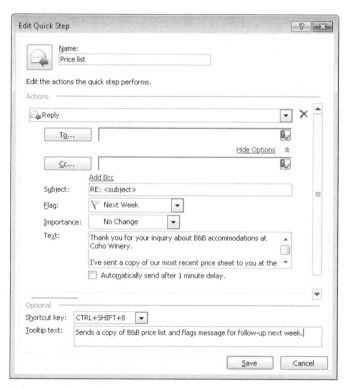

Figure 22-9 Use the Reply action to create one-click responses to routine e-mail requests.

Outlook Quick Steps don't allow you to connect to other Office programs, so you can't send an e-mail message to OneNote or Word as part of the sequence of actions in a Quick Step.

To edit an existing Quick Step, right-click its button on the Home tab, and then click the Edit command at the top of the shortcut menu. From this same menu, you can also duplicate or delete the Quick Step you're pointing to or open the Manage Quick Steps dialog box shown next.

INSIDE OUT Organize Quick Steps for easy access

If you use Quick Steps extensively, you'll want to think carefully about how you organize your collection. Each new Quick Step moves to the top position in the Quick Steps group on the Home tab, where buttons appear in columns of three. Depending on the width of the Outlook window, you might see as few as three or as many as a dozen individual Quick Steps on the Home tab itself. The others are in the gallery, available with a click of the More arrow in the lower right corner of the Quick Steps list. Use the Manage Quick Steps dialog box to change the order of items in the list so that the ones always visible on the Home tab—and thus truly a single click away—are at the top of the list, with names that make it easy to see exactly what each one does. And if you bristle at the thought of having to switch back to the Home tab to get to your Quick Steps gallery, right-click the Quick Steps group label, and then click Add To Quick Access Toolbar. Click the lightning-bolt button to choose a Quick Step without having to use the ribbon.

Using Rules to Manage Messages Automatically

Where Quick Steps are manual, rules are fully automatic. Most rules are designed to check incoming messages to see whether they meet specific conditions and, if they do, automatically take a defined action, such as moving those messages to another folder. Rules can also help you file outgoing messages, and you can create "housekeeping" rules to periodically sweep your Inbox or archive folders of clutter.

The most common use of rules is to move low-priority messages out of your Inbox as soon as they arrive, filing them in their own folders (but leaving them marked unread) so you can read them at your convenience. This is a great way to handle newsletters, messages from busy mailing lists, or sales pitches from online vendors.

INSIDE OUT   Take advantage of the Unread Mail search folder

If you use rules to sort incoming mail into folders based on its priority, you might only want to monitor your Inbox during the workday, leaving low-priority messages for when you're free to think about things other than work. To gather all your new messages into a single view, use the Unread Mail search folder. (See "Creating and Using Search Folders" on page 751 for details on how to create it.) Arrange this view by folder, and you can quickly scan what's new by folder. If a particular low-priority folder is full and your time is in short supply, just mark all messages in that folder as read and move on.

The simplest way to create a new rule is to start with an existing message that matches the conditions you want to use. On the Home tab, in the Move group, click Rules. That displays a short menu like the one shown here.

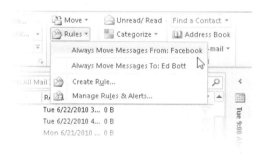

The option to move messages from the sender is always available. If the message was sent to an e-mail address other than the one associated with the current data file, that option is available here. That allows you to quickly create a rule to handle messages sent to a mailing list that you belong to.

If one of the options here will do the trick—if you always want notifications from Facebook to go into your Facebook folder, for example—then click that option and choose a destination folder (or create a new folder) in the Rules And Alerts dialog box. Outlook immediately creates the rule and runs it against the contents of the current folder, moving other messages that match your condition to the folder you just specified.

What if the condition you want to use as the trigger for your rule isn't on the short menu? In that case, click Create Rule, which opens the dialog box shown here. It offers a slightly expanded set of actions and conditions. Choose at least one condition from the top half of the Create Rule dialog box and at least one action from the bottom half, click OK, and you're done.

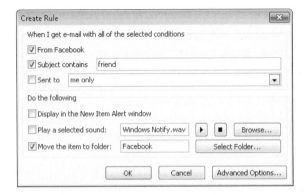

In this example, the original message subject was long ("Samantha Smith has confirmed you as a friend on Facebook") and too specific to identify similar new messages. So we trimmed away the unnecessary parts and selected the top two check boxes. Now, any message that arrives from Facebook and contains the word *friend* will be automatically moved to its own folder.

You can use the options in the Create Rule dialog box to highlight important messages as well. If you want to be sure you see a message from your boss as soon as it arrives, select the Display In The New Item Alert Window option. That option pops up a message box like the one shown here, which remains visible until you dismiss the alert window.

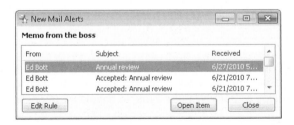

For full access to all the capabilities of Outlook's rules engine, click the Advanced Options button at the bottom of the Create Rule dialog box. That opens the Rules Wizard, where you can build your rule by clicking through its four somewhat cluttered pages. On each page, you select from a list of options in the top of the page and view a rule description in the box at the bottom. When a condition or action requires additional details, click the blue link in the description box at the bottom to fill in those details.

First, you select the conditions to check for. The list of more than 30 options here is impressive; for example, if you want to define special treatment for any messages sent by anyone in your organization, you can use the With Specific Words In The Sender's Address condition and specify your company's domain.

Next, you specify the actions to perform, as shown in Figure 22-10.

Figure 22-10 For conditions or actions that require input from you, click the "specified" link in the box at the bottom and fill in text, a date range, folder name, or other necessary details.

On the third page, you specify any exceptions to the rule—for example, you might want to automatically file any messages sent to a particular mailing list unless they're also specifically addressed to you.

The wizard's final page allows you to specify a name for the new rule and gives you one last chance to review its conditions before enabling it and, optionally, running it on the contents of the Inbox.

CAUTION

The Permanently Delete It action is a powerful alternative to the more conventional Delete It action. Maybe too powerful, in fact. What's the difference? Delete It moves the targeted messages to the Deleted Items folder; Permanently Delete It bypasses that safety net and removes the selected message or messages completely, with no option of recovery. We strongly recommend against using the Permanently Delete It action with rules that apply to incoming messages because of the risk that you will inadvertently delete an important message. Instead, use this action with clean-up rules that you run manually after making a good backup of your data files.

To manage rules you've already set up, or to create a new rule based on a template, click Rules (in the Move group on the Home tab), and then click Manage Rules & Alerts. That opens the Rules And Alerts dialog box shown here, which lists the rules you previously created.

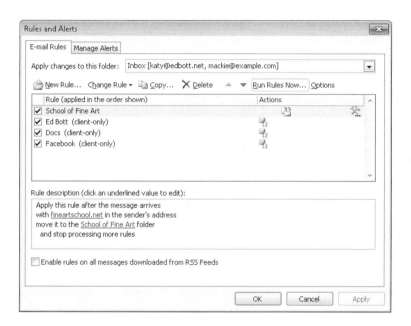

The New Rule button offers a set of templates before proceeding to the full-blown Rules Wizard. Click Change Rule to choose from a group of options for editing the currently selected rule. The Move Up and Move Down arrows (just to the left of Run Rules Now) are so subtle that you might miss them. But these options are extremely important for ensuring that your most important rules run first. If you have created a rule that trumps all others—such as one that flags messages from your manager as High importance if they contain any of the words *urgent, now,* or *important*—you want it to run first, and you don't want the same message to be processed by another, lower-priority rule. For best results, move the primary rule to the top of the list and make sure it includes Stop Processing More Rules as its final action.

Using Address Books and Directory Services

The most important thing to know about the Outlook Address Book is that it doesn't exist. Oh, it looks real enough, and you can get to it from just about anywhere in Outlook. In each of the main Outlook views (the ones represented by buttons at the bottom of the

Navigation pane), you'll find an Address Book button in the Find group on the Home tab. You can also open the Address Book with its Outlook keyboard shortcut, Ctrl+Shift+B (to memorize this one, just think of B for Address _Book_).

You'll find that same Address Book button in the Names box on the Message tab when you create a new e-mail message, in the Names group on the Contact tab when you create a new Contact item, and in the Attendees group on the Meeting tab in a Meeting request. In any new message window, you can click To, Cc, or Bcc to display the Address Book as well.

So with all those ways to open a window whose name is indeed Address Book, why do we insist that the Address Book doesn't exist? Because its contents come from elsewhere, and the Address Book is just a tiny shell that provides an alternative means of getting to those names, addresses, and other details. If you think of it as Address Book view, you're getting closer to understanding how it works.

When you open the Address Book from a new message window, Outlook opens a dialog box like the one shown in Figure 22-11. That's a search box in the top left, with a drop-down list of Address Book data sources to its right. A table-style view of the currently selected data source is displayed in the large contents pane. Select any name and click To, Cc, or Bcc to add it to the list of recipients for the message you're creating.

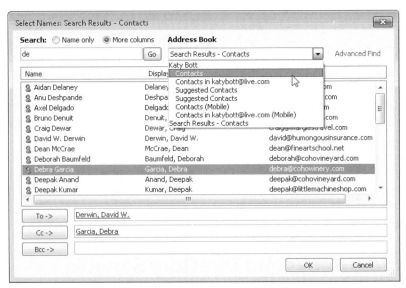

Figure 22-11 Filter the Address Book contents using the search box on the left, as we've done here, and change its data source by picking a different entry from the Address Book list.

The Address Book search box behaves oddly and inconsistently. When the Name Only option is selected, whatever you type in the search box is treated as if it were an index word, and Outlook jumps to the nearest entry that matches what you typed. If you type *Damien,* but there's no one by that name in your Address Book, the selection jumps to the first name after that entry alphabetically—in this case, probably *Dan* or *Dana* or *David.* All other names remain in the Address Book window, and you can scroll up or down at will.

On the other hand, when you select More Columns, Outlook clears the contents pane immediately and awaits your instructions. Type a search term, and then click Go to filter the list to entries that contain any word that *begins with* your search term.

If you open the Address Book from the main Outlook window, you lose the address field buttons at the bottom but gain some interesting opportunities to tweak the Address Book. For example, click Tools and then Options to reveal this dialog box, where you can use the option at the bottom to make sure you see the right names and e-mail addresses when you open the Address Book.

Your Outlook profile includes at least one and possibly many more sources, which can be selected from the drop-down Address Book list. That selection controls what's displayed in the contents pane beneath it, and it also determines the search scope of anything you search for here.

Your primary Outlook data file contains a Contacts folder that is available as an address book. So do connections to Windows Live Hotmail accounts. Connections to a Microsoft Exchange server give you access to that server's global address list and to your private address list. If you use the Outlook Social Connector to add a service like LinkedIn to your profile, the LinkedIn address book shows as a data source here as well.

INSIDE OUT Customizing the contents of the Address Book list

If you find that one or more of the entries in your Address Book list is irrelevant—if you never use the Suggested Contacts folder for your Windows Live Hotmail account, for example—you can remove it from the Address Book list using one of two well-hidden settings.

The first is available when you right-click on any folder under the My Contacts heading in Contacts view and then click Properties. Click the Outlook Address Book tab, as shown here, and clear the Show This Folder As An E-Mail Address Book option.

The less obvious route is to use the Address Books tab of the Account Settings dialog box. (Click File, and on the Info tab click Account Settings and then Account Settings.) Select Outlook Address Book from the list and click Change. That opens the Microsoft Outlook Address Book dialog box shown here and moves you into the very elite circle of people who have actually seen this very obscure dialog box.

If this seems like the long way around, you're right—except that this dialog box offers an option you won't find elsewhere. Use the Show Names By option at the bottom to change the filing order. For a personal or family address book you might prefer the default First Last order, but for a work account you'll probably prefer the File As option, which lets you scroll through the Address Book by last name.

Outlook 2010 Inside Out

WHAT'S on your to-do list today? If you use Outlook 2010, the answer can be just a click away. In this chapter, we explain how you can flag e-mail messages, contacts, and tasks for follow-up so that they appear as prioritized to-do items in any view. We also show how to set reminders so that you're less likely to miss important appointments or tasks and how to coordinate multiple calendars—yours and others.

For the most part, receiving new e-mail messages and synchronizing data with servers is an automatic process in Outlook 2010, but there are circumstances under which it makes sense to tinker with send/receive schedules, as we explain here. We also cover the essentials of importing, exporting, and archiving your Outlook data.

In Outlook 2010, two features allow you to bring data from the web directly into Outlook. If a website provides an RSS feed, you can link that feed to an Outlook folder and read each item as if it were an individual e-mail message. You can also use a new Outlook 2010 feature called the Outlook Social Connector to get a quick look at what your friends and associates are up to on social networks such as LinkedIn and Facebook.

Setting Follow-up Flags and Reminders

All Outlook items are not created equal. For those that deserve a little extra attention, click Follow Up, which is available in the Tags group on the Home tab for an e-mail message or a contact item. (For tasks, the Follow Up options get their own group on the Home tab, and Calendar items don't need flags because they have their own region at the top of the To-Do Bar.) Clicking Follow Up allows you to add an item to the To-Do list and, optionally, set its Due Date field using any of the half-dozen options at the top of the menu, as shown here.

Choosing Today or Tomorrow has an obvious effect on the Due Date field. If you choose This Week or Next Week, Outlook sets the Due Date field to the last day of your work week—Friday, unless you change this default. These options have an unexpected effect if you work on a Saturday, which Outlook considers the last day of the week. In that case, clicking This Week on the Follow Up menu sets the due date to Friday of the current week—in other words, yesterday.

TROUBLESHOOTING

The Follow Up menu shows only a single choice

What type of e-mail account are you working with? Outlook displays the full range of Flag options on messages from a POP account, as well as those from a Windows Live Hotmail account or one on a Microsoft Exchange server. The one exception is an IMAP account, including those on Google's Gmail service. For messages associated with an IMAP account, Outlook supports only the most basic form of flagging: click Flag Message from the Follow Up menu to add the item to your To-Do list, and click Clear Flag to remove the item from that list. The Mark Complete option is unavailable, as are the date-related options in the Follow Up group on the Task List tab. Fortunately, there is a workaround. Move or copy the message from the folder in the data file associated with your IMAP account to your primary Outlook data file. The same e-mail message, stored in this alternative location, supports all Flag options.

A flag consists of four properties, including a Reminder date and time. You can see (and change) any of these four settings in the Custom dialog box. If you click the Custom option on the Follow Up menu, Outlook opens this dialog box without changing any settings. If you click Add Reminder, Outlook opens the Custom dialog box and selects the Reminder check box, if necessary. Reminders are tremendously useful if you want Outlook to nag you when an item is due (or overdue) for follow-up. You can also change the text that appears in the Reminders window. Figure 23-1 shows a to-do item under construction.

Figure 23-1 Click the Reminder check box and set the exact date and time when you want Outlook to nag you about the current flagged item.

The four properties of a flag that you can edit are as follows:

- **Flag To** The default text is *Follow up*, and for most items this will probably work fine. Choose one of the other options in this list or enter your own text if you want a more detailed description of why you flagged an item. This text appears at the beginning of the InfoBar at the top of any flagged item and at the top of the Reminders window for the selected item. For a flagged Contact item, you might choose Call or Send E-Mail as the Flag To text.

- **Start Date** Outlook fills in this field using a default value if you use one of the ready-made options on the Follow Up menu. Use this field for a rudimentary form of project management. If you estimate that a project will take two weeks, you can fill in a start date based on the due date. If you make use of this field, click the Arrange By heading in the Task list (at the bottom of the To-Do Bar) to change the grouping to Start Date or back to Due Date.

- **Due Date** This field is filled in automatically when you choose Today, Tomorrow, This Week, or Next Week. As with the other date-related fields in this dialog box, you can use a calendar control to pick a date. In the Custom dialog box, click the arrow to the right of the Due Date field to display the date picker. Use the Today button to fill in today's date, or click None to remove the due date.

- **Reminder**   When you select this check box, you can enter an exact date and time when you want Outlook to pop up a Reminders window with a link to your flagged item and play an accompanying sound. For the date field, click the down arrow and use the familiar date picker. For the time field, you can pick from the drop-down list, with intervals at round half-hour increments (10:00 AM, 5:30 PM), or you can type an exact time (4:55 PM).

INSIDE OUT   What makes Calendar reminders different?

The Reminders window shows flagged items and upcoming appointments and meetings. Reminders for Calendar items work differently than their counterparts on flagged messages, contacts, and tasks. To set a reminder directly for any Calendar item, use the drop-down Reminder list in the Options group on the Appointment or Meeting tab. Unlike flagged items, for which you can specify the exact time when you want Outlook to pop up a reminder, Calendar items only allow reminders that are relative to the start time of the meeting or appointment. You can choose a reminder time from this list—15 Minutes, 3 Days, or 1 Week, for example. You can type your own values in this list as well, provided that you use the proper relative format. So, you can enter 45 Minutes or 5 Days, even though neither option is on the default menu, but you can't use a specific date and time for the reminder on a Calendar item. If you try to enter a specific date or time, Outlook simply ignores your input.

When Outlook is running, it keeps track of reminders you set previously. If Outlook is running when the reminder time rolls around, it opens a Reminders window, like the one shown in Figure 23-2. (If your PC is turned off or Outlook is not running at the specified time, you see the missed reminders the next time you start Outlook.)

When you see a reminder, you can click Dismiss to clear the reminder for that item and ensure that you don't see it again; click Dismiss All to do the same with every item in the Reminders window. If you want to deal with a reminder later, select the item, pick a time from the list at the bottom of the dialog box, and then click the Snooze button.

Flagging an item creates a to-do item, which appears in the Task list at the bottom of the To-Do Bar. You can also see the full list from the Tasks folder (click To-Do List in the Navigation pane) and in the Daily Task list at the bottom of daily or weekly Calendar views.

For a refresher course on how the To-Do Bar fits with the rest of the Outlook interface, see "Organizing the To-Do Bar" on page 705.

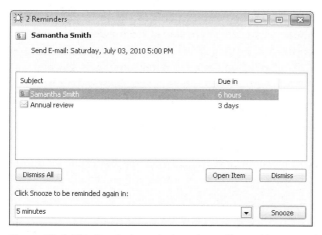

Figure 23-2 The Reminders window shows flagged items, such as this Contact item, alongside appointments and meetings. Note our custom Flag To text: Send E-Mail instead of Follow Up.

INSIDE OUT   Drag items to the To-Do Bar to flag them

If you want to flag more than a few items at once, skip the Follow Up menu and drag them to the Task list section of the To-Do Bar instead. Note that the Task list must be arranged by Start Date or Due Date for this procedure to work. Drop one or more items onto the list under a date heading to create new to-do items using that date.

When you click to select a flagged item in the Task list, Outlook displays the Task List tab shown here. (Note that the Follow Up group and the Mark Complete command in the Manage Task group are not shown for flagged messages from IMAP mail accounts, including Google's Gmail.)

Most of the commands on this tab are also available from the shortcut menu when you right-click a flagged item. You can mark the item complete, change the follow-up date, and change the grouping for the list by clicking a field in the Arrangement group.

Chapter 23

It's important to note a distinction between items on the To-Do list and those in the Tasks folder. To-Do list items are created by flagging a message, a contact, or a task, and they retain the properties and content of the original item type. If you click a flagged e-mail message in the To-Do list, you open that message. Tasks, by contrast, are a distinct Outlook item type, with the same four properties as a flagged item, as well as a few extras, such as Status, Priority, and % Complete. Tasks also have their own notes and accept file attachments.

One of most interesting options you have with a task—not available for flagged items—is the ability to specify a recurrence pattern. If you are responsible for distributing a status report at the end of every workweek, for example, you can create a new task (Distribute Status Report) and click the Recurrence button to display the dialog box shown in Figure 23-3.

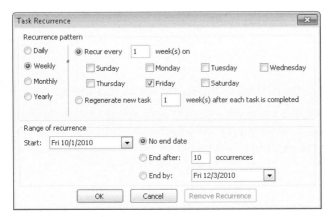

Figure 23-3 You can set a recurring task so that it shows up on your task list on the same day each week or month, or regenerate a new task whenever you mark the current task as complete.

Recurring tasks behave a lot like their Calendar counterparts (see "Setting Up Recurring Appointments and Events" on page 727), with the noteworthy exception of the Regenerate New Task option. This option allows you to schedule a new task at a set interval after the completion of the previous one. You might use this if you want to be reminded to check in with a customer if 30 days go by since your last phone conversation. Create a recurring task (Call Samantha), choose Monthly under Recurrence Pattern, and then select Regenerate New Task 1 Month(s) After Each Task Is Completed. After each phone call, add your call notes to the task and click Mark Complete. That creates a new copy of the task, with a new due date. All your notes remain in the item as well, with a separator line above the old notes. The previous task stays in the list, with a strikethrough to indicate it's complete.

INSIDE OUT   ## Add reminders to flagged items automatically

By default, flagging an item adds it to the To-Do list with a due date that matches the Follow Up menu option you click. But it doesn't add a reminder—you have to do that manually. To change the default settings so that every flagged item gets a reminder, open the Outlook Options dialog box (click File, Options). On the Tasks tab, select Set Reminders On Tasks With Due Dates. By default, Outlook sets the reminder date to the same date as the due date and the time to 8:00 AM. You can change this time using the drop-down Default Reminder Time list. In the same dialog box, you can also change the color for overdue tasks (the default is red) and completed tasks (gray).

The absolute fastest way to flag an e-mail message for follow-up is to click the flag icon at the right of its entry in the message list. By default, this has the same effect as clicking Today on the Follow Up menu. To change this default, click Follow Up, then click Set Quick Click, and choose an alternative from the list, as shown here.

If you use OneNote, don't overlook that program's strong connections to Outlook, including the ability to link OneNote pages and paragraphs to Outlook tasks. We explain this feature in full in "Using OneNote with Outlook" on page 547.

Sharing and Comparing Calendars

How many individual calendars are available when you switch to Calendar view? In the Navigation pane, under the My Calendars heading, you'll find your main Outlook calendar and separate calendars for birthdays and holidays. If you have linked a Windows Live Hotmail account to your Outlook profile, its calendar shows up here as well. And as we explain later in this section, you can also open shared calendars from other users, if they've given you permission.

INSIDE OUT Add holidays to your default calendar

Items on the Holiday calendar are specific to your country and are not included as part of your default calendar. To add items from the Holiday calendar to your current calendar, open Outlook's Options dialog box and click the Calendar tab. Under the Calendar Options heading, click Add Holidays, select your region, and click OK.

Arranging Multiple Calendars

The initial challenge with multiple calendars—whether they're yours alone or shared with others—is comparing them effectively. Fortunately, Outlook includes several tools to help you arrange multiple calendars on the screen, side by side or overlaid in a single display.

Say you have your calendar in an Exchange account at the office and a friend's shared personal calendar in Windows Live. How do you see them together? Start by clicking the check box to the left of each calendar in the Navigation pane. That displays the two calendars side by side, as shown here.

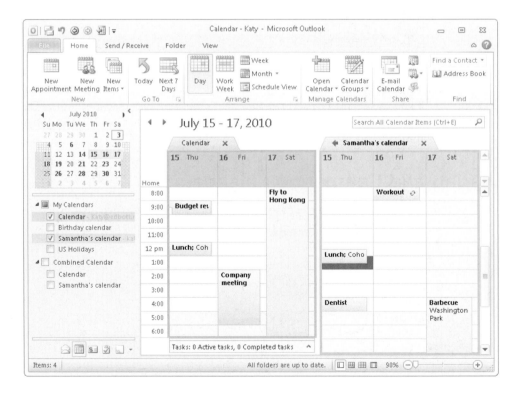

The side-by-side calendars scroll up, down, and from side to side in unison. If you click a single date or drag to select a range of dates (as we've done here), those dates are displayed in both places. Likewise, any commands in the Arrange group apply to both calendars simultaneously.

INSIDE OUT   Change a calendar's background color

In Outlook, each calendar is color-coded, with the color band in the Navigation pane matching the background color for the corresponding calendar. If you find that one of these automatically applied colors makes the calendar hard to read, it's easy enough to change the color. On the View tab, click Color, and then choose one of 15 pastel alternatives. This option can be especially helpful when you're overlaying two calendars and you want a more obvious visual contrast between items from the different calendars.

Side-by-side displays are fine for a quick comparison, but if you really want a unified display, click the View tab and then click Overlay (in the Arrangement group). Figure 23-4 shows the same calendars as before, this time as an overlay.

CAUTION

When you select or open a meeting or an appointment from a calendar that is not your default calendar, you see a Copy To My Calendar command on the Appointment or Meeting tab. That option does exactly what it says—copying all details from the original item to a new item in your default calendar. It does not create a link between the two items, however. If the original item is in a calendar under someone else's control, you run the risk that he or she will change the date, time, location, or other important details in the original item, leaving you with an incorrect, outdated item. In general, you should only copy items to your calendar when you control both the source and the destination calendars. If you do copy an appointment from another calendar, we recommend that you make a note in the new copy that includes the source of the appointment details, the date it was copied, and (if possible) a link to the original calendar item.

If you find yourself regularly referring to the same group of calendars, you can cut a few clicks out of the process of arranging them. Click to select the calendars you want to save as a group, and then click Calendar Groups, Save As New Calendar Group (in the Manage Calendars group on the Home tab). Your new group appears as its own node in the Navigation pane. Click the check box to the left of the Calendar Group name to display all its members in the current window.

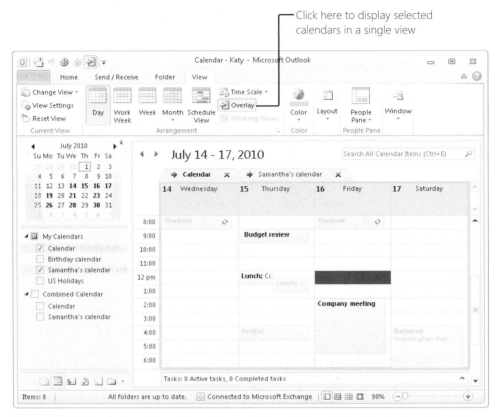

Click here to display selected calendars in a single view

Figure 23-4 Color coding helps distinguish appointments from different calendars. The bold type on appointments indicates that those are part of the currently selected calendar.

Working with Meeting Invitations

Meetings closely resemble appointments, with the crucial difference that they involve invitations sent via e-mail. (To see what one of these invitations looks like, see "Meetings" on page 695.)

Your experience depends on how your e-mail environment is set up. In a corporate setting, where everyone involved has an account available in the Microsoft Exchange Server global address list, you are typically able to view free and busy times for others in your group. When creating or viewing a meeting request in that environment, you can click Scheduling Assistant (in the Show group on the Meeting tab) to see the shared calendar. A Room Finder pane on the right lets you see which conference rooms are available, and suggested meeting times appear at the bottom of that pane, based on the free times for members of your Attendees list.

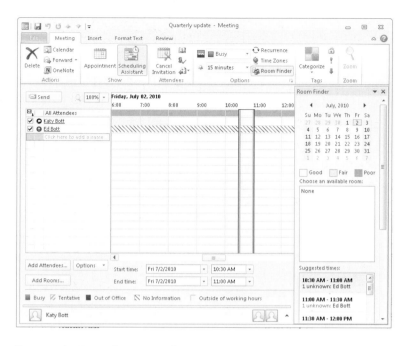

But you don't need to use Exchange to turn appointments into meetings. If you create a meeting request and send it to potential attendees, they receive a meeting request that superficially resembles an e-mail message. A closer look reveals a few twists, as shown in Figure 23-5.

If you and your fellow attendees are on the same Exchange-based mail setup, the server handles the work of coordinating who has accepted and who has declined and who has yet to respond. If you're using Internet-standard mail, it's important to send a response, so that the meeting organizer doesn't have to manually follow up with you. When you click Accept, Tentative, or Decline, you can choose whether to send a response immediately or to edit the response first. After you send the response, Outlook updates your calendar and moves the meeting request to the Deleted Items folder.

And what if the recipient isn't using Outlook? You still might be able to coordinate your meeting, depending on the calendar system he or she uses. If your recipient an Outlook meeting request in the web version of Windows Live Hotmail, for example, Windows Live offers the same Accept/Tentative/Decline options. Gmail accounts that have been connected to a Google calendar offer a similar Yes/Maybe/No option. In both cases, the meeting organizer gets a proper response and the appointment is updated accordingly.

Chapter 23

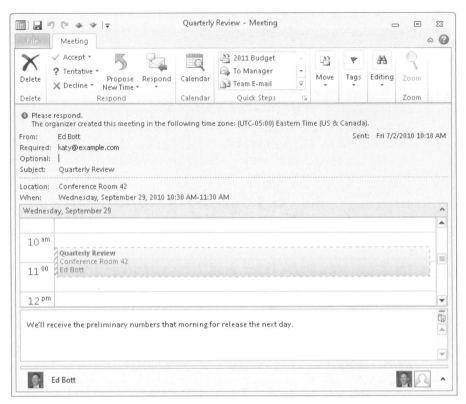

Figure 23-5 Options in the Respond group allow you to accept, decline, or suggest a new time. The body shows the proposed meeting time in your calendar, to help identify conflicts.

Sharing Contact and Calendar Items via E-Mail

You have information in Outlook, and you want to send it to someone else, without a lot of tedious cut-and-paste work.

If the items in question are contacts or appointments, you're in luck. Outlook allows you to share those types of information with anyone, as Outlook items or in one of two Internet-standard formats specifically designed for data interchange.

Both of these standard formats consist of simple text files, with a syntax that any compatible program can decode. For sharing Contact items, Outlook uses the vCard format, which creates a file with the .vcf file name extension. For Calendar items, Outlook uses the iCalendar format, with the .ics file name extension. (For more details about the vCard format in Outlook, see the Microsoft Knowledge Base article at *w7io.com/290840*.) An older format for exchanging appointments, vCalendar, is no longer used.

Why would you want to send someone else an item from your Contacts folder? The most common situation, we suspect, is sending your personal or work-related contact information to someone else via e-mail, just as you would hand them your business card if you were to meet at a trade show.

That scenario is so common, in fact, that Outlook's designers devised a Business Card format specifically to address it. The Business Card format allows you to pick and choose information from your own Contact item, spruce it up with a picture and (optionally) a custom background color, and arrange the information on the card so it's easy to read. To design your own business card, start by opening your own contact record (if it doesn't exist, create a new one for yourself), and then click Business Card in the Options group on the Contact tab (or double-click the default business card, in the upper right quadrant of the Contact item). That opens the Edit Business Card dialog box, shown in Figure 23-6.

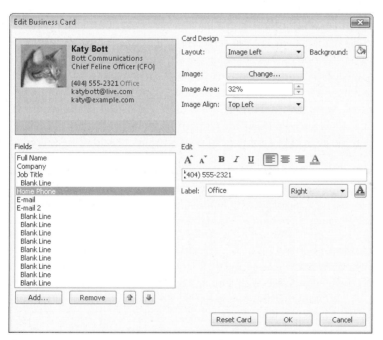

Figure 23-6 Information you add as a label here goes on your business card but isn't stored in the corresponding fields in the Outlook Contact item.

You build the business card line by line, clicking the Add button to choose fields from your Contact item and clicking the Move Field Up and Move Field Down arrows to position each line just so. You can edit each line on the business card (and provide labels to distinguish different types of phone numbers and addresses) in the Edit box on the right, where you can also choose fonts, adjust font sizes and colors, and specify alignment options. Use the options in the upper right corner to choose a photograph, position it on the card, and provide a complementary background color. When you're finished, click OK to save the Business Card layout and its data as part of the Contact item.

The beauty of the Business Card format is that it allows you total control over what personal information you disclose about yourself. The underlying Contact item might include all sorts of personal information (like your home address and details about your spouse and family) that you would never willingly share. By creating a business card, you get to choose exactly what goes on the card.

To send contact information via e-mail, start in the Contacts folder by selecting one or more items and then clicking Forward Contact (in the Share group on the Home tab), or open the contact in its own window and click Forward (in the Actions group on the Contact tab). You have three e-mail options in all:

- **As A Business Card**   The resulting e-mail message contains an embedded image of the card (in JPEG format) and a file attachment in the standard vCard format, with a .vcf file name extension. You can edit the message subject or text before sending. If you receive one of these messages in Outlook, you can right-click the business card image and click Add To Outlook Contacts. Or, as an alternative, double-click to open the item in an Outlook Contact window, where you can add your own notes or edit existing fields before clicking Save & Close. If a recipient opens a message containing a vCard file on a PC where Outlook is not installed, they have to add the contact using the instructions for their e-mail software or another registered vCard handler.

- **As An Outlook Contact**   The resulting e-mail message contains a blank body and an attachment that contains the full Outlook item, with a .msg file name extension. As long as the recipient has Outlook installed, he or she can double-click to open the contact, make any changes or additions, and then click Save & Close.

- **In Internet Format (vCard)**   This option is available only if you open a Contact item in its own window (click Forward, in the Actions group on the Contact tab). It opens a new e-mail message with a blank body and with the current contact attached as a vCard file. Note that this file contains all available fields from the contact item, not just those shown in the business card.

Unless you sign up for a third-party Outlook add-in that allows you to send Simple Message Service (SMS) text messages to phones, you can ignore the Forward As Text Message and Forward As Multimedia Message options.

To share details of appointments in your Outlook Calendar, the procedure is similar to what you do with a contact. Click the arrow to the right of the Forward command (in the Actions group on the Appointment tab) and then click Forward or Forward As iCalendar. (For meeting requests, you should have the meeting organizer add the recipient to the meeting rather than forward someone else's meeting request details.)

Both options send the item as an attachment to an e-mail message. The Forward command sends your appointment in Outlook item format (with a .msg file name extension). If the recipient has Outlook installed, she can double-click the attachment (or open it in the preview pane) and then click Copy To My Calendar. Use the Forward As iCalendar option whenever you are not certain whether the recipient has Outlook installed.

Sharing a Calendar via E-Mail or the Web

In the previous section, we discussed how to send details of a single appointment as an attachment to an e-mail message. But what do you do if you want to share details of a week or a month's worth of appointments when those details are part of a local calendar? This scenario has a variety of uses besides the obvious ability to share your personal calendar. For example, if you're the secretary of a committee planning a major fundraising event, you have meetings, rehearsals, and the event itself to coordinate with other committee members. By creating a new Outlook calendar (click Open Calendar, Create New Blank Calendar in the Manage Calendars group on the Home tab), you can manage the committee's schedule in its own dedicated calendar and send updates as needed to committee members via e-mail.

The simple (but effective) option is to allow Outlook to copy the details of those appointments to an iCalendar file and send that file as an e-mail attachment to one or more recipients. Start by opening the calendar whose details you want to share. Click E-Mail Calendar, in the Share group on the Home tab. That opens a dialog box like the one shown in Figure 23-7, where you can specify the range of dates and other options for the calendar you're about to send via e-mail.

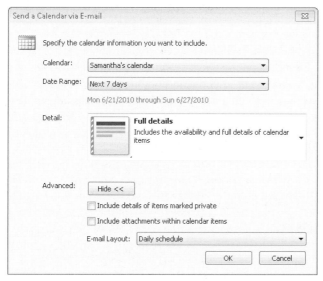

Figure 23-7 The Date Range option allows you to choose a predefined range of dates (a week, a month, and so on) or to specify a custom start and end date for a calendar to be sent via e-mail.

In the Send A Calendar Via E-Mail dialog box, use the Date Range option to choose which dates should be on your shared calendar, and then pick an option from the Detail box to choose how much information to include in each item on the shared calendar. If you're updating a colleague on where you'll be during a week-long business trip, you might choose Next 7 Days and Limited Details. For a custom calendar you've created for your fundraising committee, you would probably select Whole Calendar and Full Details.

When you click OK, Outlook prepares an e-mail message that matches the specifications you just entered. The attached iCalendar file allows your recipients to import the calendar into their PC-based calendar program if they choose, but they don't need to take that extra step. The e-mail message itself contains all the details they need.

INSIDE OUT   Use the web instead

If you're sharing a calendar with a group, it might make more sense to start with a web-based calendar instead, using Windows Live Hotmail or a similar online service. From your free Windows Live Hotmail account, open your calendar and click Add A New Calendar. You can give the calendar a descriptive name, edit sharing permissions to allow access by a small trusted group or the public, and send a link to the shared calendar via e-mail. This option might require a little more work on the recipients' part, but it also allows you to share the work of managing the shared calendar.

Sharing a calendar as an e-mail attachment is a one-way process, and it doesn't create links between the appointments on your local calendar and those on the copy you've sent out via e-mail. If you change the details of next Tuesday's meeting, you need to send another e-mail to alert every attendee. As an alternative, you can share your local calendar via the Microsoft Outlook Calendar Sharing Service. This free service, hosted at Office.com, allows you to publish details about your calendar and update them at regular intervals. You can then set permissions that allow other people to share the details of your calendar. This option is especially useful if you and a business partner work in different offices and you want to be able to see each other's schedules at a glance so that you can arrange conference calls and meetings with a minimum of fuss.

To get started, you must have a Windows Live ID. Open your Outlook Calendar, click Publish Online (in the Share group on the Home tab), and then click Publish to Office.com. After you sign in, you see the dialog box shown next. (If this is the first time you've used this feature, you need to accept a license agreement.)

Adjust the options as shown here to change the date range and the amount of detail available to other people. When you click OK, you're prompted to sign in to the Microsoft Outlook Calendar Sharing Service using your Windows Live ID. After you accept the license agreement, your calendar is updated at Office.com.

By default, the Outlook Calendar Sharing Service updates your calendar automatically, at intervals specified by the server. To modify these options, click the Advanced button in the Publish Calendar To Office.com dialog box:

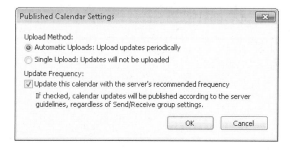

The final step of this initial setup process allows you to send invitations to your shared calendar via e-mail. Recipients must have a Windows Live account associated with the e-mail address to which you send the invitation. After setup is complete, you can send additional invitations by clicking Publish Online and choosing Share Published Calendar. (This option is available only if you have already published a calendar to Office.com.)

To remove calendar-sharing permissions for one or more persons on your list, click Change Sharing Permissions. To stop sharing the Calendar completely and remove it from the web-based service, click Remove From Server.

Although the Outlook Calendar Sharing Service is designed to work with Office, it can also be used with other calendar services, such as Google Calendar. For an extensive overview of the different techniques available for Google Calendar, see "Transfer Calendars Between Outlook and Google Calendar" at *w7io.com/12301*.

Receiving and Synchronizing Data

If you have a fast, always-on Internet connection, sending and receiving e-mail probably isn't something you think about often. Outlook automatically connects to your outgoing mail server and sends messages as soon as you click the Send button. It retrieves messages from POP and IMAP servers every 30 minutes when you're online. It synchronizes mail, calendar, and contact folders in Microsoft Exchange accounts as they arrive, using the Exchange ActiveSync protocol. As of summer 2010, Windows Live Hotmail accounts use the Exchange ActiveSync protocol as well, which means that mail, contact, and calendar items sync to your Windows Live account on the web and in Outlook almost instantly.

You might choose to adjust these settings if you use a POP or IMAP account and you want notification of new mail more often than every 30 minutes. You also might choose to tweak settings here if you're traveling and have limited Internet access. If your Internet access plan charges by the minute and/or by the byte, you can modify your settings to minimize the amount of data exchange and temporarily suspend send/receive operations for nonessential accounts.

You'll find options for sending, receiving, and synchronizing everything in your Outlook profile on the Send/Receive tab, which is just to the right of the Home tab in every Outlook view, as shown here.

The commands in the Send & Receive group work with all accounts. Send/Receive All Folders connects to each POP, IMAP, and Windows Live Hotmail account, one after the other, without regard to the schedule defined for those accounts. It sends any messages in the Outbox and picks up any newly arrived messages from the server. (For POP and IMAP accounts only, this command is also on the Home tab, at the far right.) The keyboard shortcut for Send/Receive All Folders is F9.

The Send/Receive Groups menu allows you to perform a send/receive operation for a single account. It's also where you can define global settings for automatic send/receive/synchronize operations and where you can set up groups. Click Define Send/Receive Groups to display the dialog box shown in Figure 23-8.

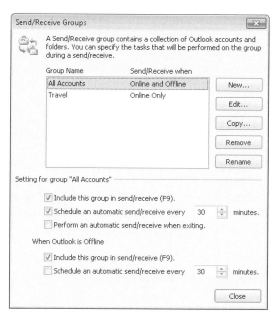

Figure 23-8 In a default Outlook installation, the All Accounts group defines send/receive settings for all accounts. You can change global defaults or create new groups here.

INSIDE OUT   Understanding Outlook's unconventional keyboard shortcuts

Despite the fact that it's been a full-fledged member of the Office family since 1997, Outlook has never fit in with its Office-mates when it comes to keyboard shortcuts. In Word, Excel, and the other Office programs, for example, Ctrl+F allows you to search the current document, worksheet, or presentation. In Outlook, that keyboard shortcut forwards the current message, and you need to remember that F4 opens the Find dialog box to search within the contents of an e-mail message. Ctrl+Z is Undo in Outlook, just as in other Office programs, but Ctrl+Y isn't Redo—instead, it opens the Go To Folder dialog box. Outlook's approach to keyboard shortcuts is so quirky, in fact, that we recommend not bothering with them at all. If you're a keyboard diehard, you can find all of Outlook's oddball shortcuts in a single (very long) page, available via Outlook Help or online at *w7io.com/12304*.

Normally, Outlook shows a progress dialog box as the send/receive operation is under way. If you want to check the results of the most recent send/receive operation, click Show Progress to display this dialog box. The Errors tab displays any messages that indicate a failure to connect or to receive or send messages.

Chapter 23

By default, Outlook creates a single All Accounts group with separate settings for online and offline use. The Schedule An Automatic Send/Receive Every *nn* Minutes option is set to an initial default of 30 minutes. To change this automatic send/receive interval for all POP and IMAP accounts, enter a different value here. To apply different default settings for different accounts, you need to create multiple send/receive groups. Click the New button to create a new group and give it a name of your choosing. For each account whose settings you want to control via the new group, click Include The Selected Account In This Group. Then click Edit for the All Accounts profile, select those same accounts, and clear the check box. You can now select each group in turn and adjust the settings below the group list, as needed.

The Edit button provides access to an almost overwhelming assortment of options, which differ by account type. Figure 23-9, for example, shows settings for a Microsoft Exchange account.

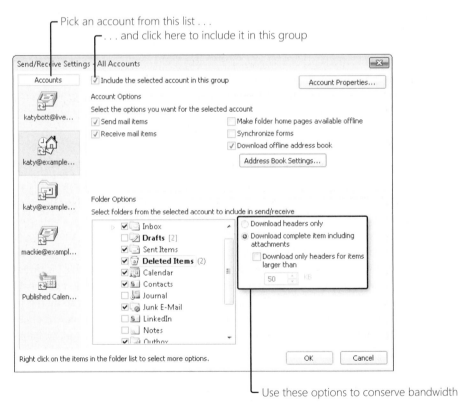

Figure 23-9 Click an account in the list on the left to see its options on the right. If Internet access is expensive or very slow, consider downloading only message headers.

TROUBLESHOOTING

Some folders aren't synchronized with your Exchange server

That might be by design. Drafts, RSS Feeds, contact folders from third-party services, and a handful of other folders in your offline data file aren't synced by default with the Exchange server. That's a precautionary measure intended to prevent you from inadvertently exceeding storage limits imposed by your mail server's administrator. You can manually include or exclude folders for an Exchange account by opening the Send/Receive Settings dialog box, clicking the Exchange account icon, and selecting or clearing folders in the list under the Folder Options heading.

Settings for other types of accounts vary depending on the account type. POP accounts, for example, handle e-mail, and that's all. A POP server is designed to receive incoming e-mail addressed to you and hold it for your pickup. It isn't equipped to keep track of contacts or your calendar or to store messages in folders. Normally, when you connect to a POP server, any waiting messages are downloaded to your Outlook Inbox and then deleted from the server. For a POP server, as with any account, you can choose to download headers only for the Inbox folder, or to download full messages that are smaller than a specified size and download only headers for messages above that size. In this example, we've configured the account to download full message bodies if the message size is 50 KB or less. For messages above that size, Outlook downloads headers only. That saves you from wasting time or money downloading a large file attachment on a slow, expensive connection.

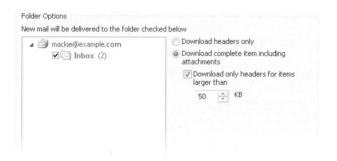

After you download headers to your account, you can go through and mark the ones you want to download in full, leaving the others unmarked. To accomplish this task, use the Mark To Download and Process Marked Headers commands on the Send/Receive tab.

IMAP accounts are also intended for e-mail only. The key difference from POP accounts is that messages are stored on the server, organized in folders you create. When you connect with Outlook, you synchronize a local copy. Configuring an IMAP account requires a visit to two different locations. The first is the IMAP Folders dialog box, where you can specify which server folders are synchronized with your local copy. Right-click the top-level icon for the IMAP account in the Navigation pane and click IMAP Folders on the shortcut menu.

From the Send/Receive Settings dialog box, select the IMAP account and look at its settings on the right. To manage bandwidth by downloading headers instead of full messages, click Receive Mail Items and choose either Download Headers For Subscribed Folders or Use The Custom Behavior Defined Below. The latter option makes the Folder Options section available for defining which folders you want downloaded as headers only.

Synchronizing with a Windows Live Hotmail account requires no special settings. The only available setting in the Folder Options section allows you to download headers only for messages in your Inbox.

Importing and Exporting Outlook Data

You can drag any Outlook item into a folder in Windows Explorer (or onto your desktop) to save it as an individual item that you can open later in Outlook. Use this technique to share individual items between different Outlook profiles (even on different PCs). Drag a group of messages or contacts to a folder on a USB key, for example, and you can open that same folder on another PC and drag the saved items directly into an Outlook folder on that computer.

To copy a large number of messages, contacts, appointments, or tasks to or from Outlook, use the Import And Export Wizard. The path to this utility is confusing (a rare user-interface mistake on Microsoft's part). Click File, then click the Open tab, and finally click Import. Although that sequence of commands doesn't include the word *export* anywhere in its buttons or descriptions, it opens the Import And Export Wizard, shown here:

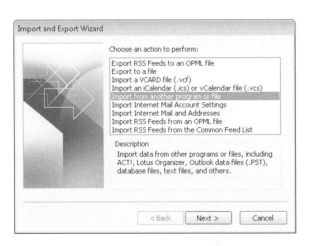

Three of the options shown here (one export, two import) are used with Outlook's collection of RSS feeds. (For more details, see "Reading RSS Feeds in Outlook" on page 803.) Another two options deal with the standard Contact and Calendar formats we discussed earlier in this chapter (see "Sharing Contact and Calendar Items via E-Mail" on page 782).

The two options that begin with Import Internet Mail are more specialized and far less useful than they might appear at first glance. These import tools do not work with data files; the program from which you want to import data must be installed on the same PC that's running Outlook 2010. You can import account settings, messages, and address books from PCs on which you are currently using an ancient version of the third-party Eudora program, Outlook Express (Windows XP only), or Windows Mail (Windows Vista only). You cannot import settings from Windows Live Mail.

That leaves the two generic options, Export To A File and Import From Another Program Or File, which we describe in more detail in the balance of this section.

Select Export To A File and then click Next to show a list of available file types to use for your exported data, as shown here.

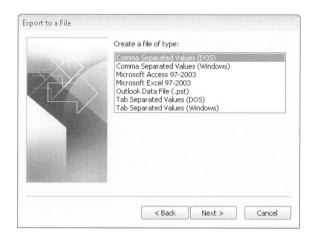

Which file format should you choose? That depends on the destination and its import capabilities. Comma Separated Values (Windows) is usually the best choice when transferring data to a program other than Outlook. The Outlook Data File (.pst) format is an interesting choice if you're exporting data to share with another Outlook user (or with a different Outlook profile on a different PC). We explain why this format is so useful in the example that follows.

Click Next to move to the next step of the wizard, where you select the folder from which you plan to export data. The exact options available here depend on the output file type you previously selected. Because we're exporting to a .pst file, we have the option to export only a portion of the folder's contents by clicking the Filter button and filling in criteria using the Filter dialog box. Figure 23-10 shows the settings we used to export only Contact items where the Company field includes *Coho*.

Chapter 23

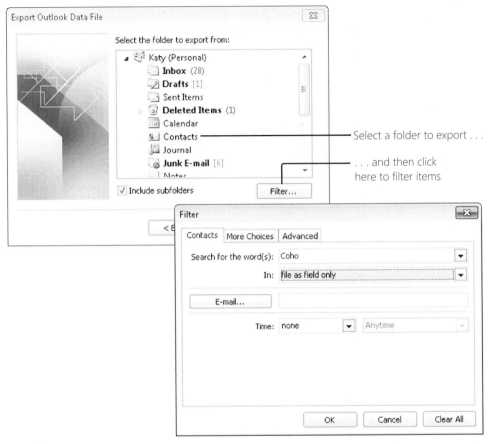

Select a folder to export . . .

. . . and then click here to filter items

Figure 23-10 Use the check box beneath the folder list to include subfolders in your export. Click Filter to refine the list of what gets exported—by company name in this example.

INSIDE OUT   How effective is Outlook's password protection?

If you choose Outlook Data File (.pst) as the export file type, you're offered the option to create a password with which to protect the file. This option provides only a basic level of security, mostly intended to prevent a casual snoop from peeking at the contents of the file. A determined data thief would have no problem blowing past that password by using one of the many password-cracking tools available on the Internet. So add a password if you feel like it, but don't expect it to offer real protection for sensitive data. If you can't remember the password for an Outlook data file, we recommend NirSoft's free PstPassword utility to help recover it. Details are at *w7io.com/12305*.

Click Next, and then choose a location for the exported items. If the file name you specify already exists, the items you export are added to the file.

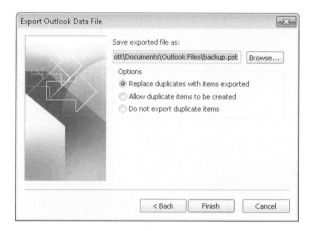

To import saved data from a file into Outlook, you go through a similar process. Select Import From Another Program Or File and then click Next to display the list of supported file types shown here. Note that this list includes the same core file formats as the Export A File equivalent, as well as a few very old third-party contact management programs.

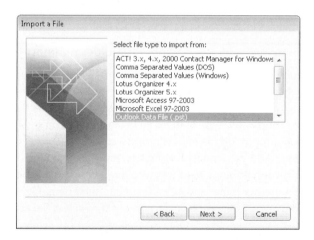

Click Next to browse for the file and choose how you want to handle duplicates. Then click Next to fine-tune your import. Figure 23-11 shows the contents of the Outlook data file we created earlier, which contains a filtered collection of Contact items.

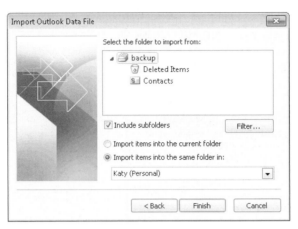

Figure 23-11 Importing information from a .pst file is a straightforward process. Pick the folder to import from, select a destination folder, and then click Finish.

Had we chosen to import a comma-separated values file, we would have had to deal with one additional step: mapping the values in the original file to the fields in the destination folder. If the source data comes from Outlook, this mapping should be perfect. If the source data is from another program, you'll need to drag field names out of the From pane and drop them onto field names in the To pane to set up the correct mapping.

INSIDE OUT   When in doubt, use a temporary folder for imports

Importing large amounts of information incorrectly can make a complete mess of an Outlook folder. If you have even the slightest doubt about the import process, try importing your data to a temporary folder as an intermediate step. Start by creating a new, empty folder to contain the type of items you're importing (on the Folder tab, click New Folder). Then go through the import process, selecting your new, empty folder as the destination. After the import is complete, inspect the folder's contents carefully. If you're satisfied that things went well, you have two choices: you can drag the items out of the temporary folder and move them into their permanent destination, or you can run the import operation again, and this time select the actual destination folder. In either case, when the import is complete, you can safely delete the temporary folder.

Archiving Outlook Data

Without regular pruning, Outlook data files have a way of growing to gargantuan proportions. Keeping a data file lean improves performance and also makes it easier to perform backups and other maintenance tasks.

Outlook 2010 provides a helpful assortment of tools you can use to clean up a single folder or an entire data file manually. For quick access to this toolkit, click File, select a mailbox from the list beneath the Account Information heading, and then click Cleanup Tools on the Info tab to display the menu shown in Figure 23-12.

Figure 23-12 To manage the size of your Outlook mailbox, start by selecting an account from the list at the top of this page, and then click Cleanup Tools.

Note that if you're connected to an Exchange server and your server administrator has restricted the size of your mailbox, you'll see a bar beneath the Mailbox Cleanup heading (to the right of the Cleanup Tools button) that shows how much of your quota is in use and how much remains available.

Click Mailbox Cleanup to open the dialog box shown in Figure 23-13, which provides centralized access to information about the contents of the currently selected mailbox as well as a variety of management tools.

Figure 23-13 Use the options shown here to gather information about the contents of the current mailbox and manually archive or delete items.

CAUTION

If you configure your Outlook profile with multiple e-mail accounts, make sure you select the right account before opening the Mailbox Cleanup dialog box. The options shown here apply to that account only. If you use the AutoArchive option, you can move or permanently delete data in that file. When in doubt, double-check!

The Mailbox Cleanup tools are divided into five groups, each with at least one button:

- **Mailbox size**   Click to open the Folder Size dialog box, which gives you a bird's-eye view of how much space each folder is occupying in the current data file. For Microsoft Exchange accounts, this dialog box includes a second tab (Server Data) that lets you see how much of your server quota is in use.

- **Find**   Choose either of the Find Items options and select settings to archive items based on their age or size. Then click Find to open the Advanced Find dialog box with those settings entered on the Advanced tab, and click Find Now to run the search.

- **AutoArchive**   Clicking this button immediately begins moving and deleting items from the current account, based on your AutoArchive settings, which we describe in more detail later in this section.

- **Deleted Items folder**   Click View Deleted Items Size to see just how much space is being used by items you previously sent to the trash, or click Empty to immediately and permanently remove the contents of the Deleted Items folder.

- **Conflicts**   This section is available only with Microsoft Exchange accounts. (It's not available for other account types.) It shows the size of the Conflicts folder, which contains items that the server was unable to synchronize properly. To view the items in this folder, switch to Folder List view and look under the Sync Issues folder.

Quick Cleanup Techniques

Outlook's Delete command moves items to the Deleted Items folder rather than permanently erasing them. That configuration is a useful safety net, allowing you to easily recover items you delete by accident. However, it can also result in an overstuffed data file. To clear the contents of the Deleted Items folder immediately, select an account from the list at the top of the Info tab and then click Empty Deleted Items Folder on the Cleanup Tools menu. Note that you must perform this operation separately for each account. If you want Outlook to automatically perform this housekeeping task for all accounts, click File, Options, click the Advanced tab, and select Empty Deleted Items Folders When Exiting Outlook (this option is under the Outlook Start And Exit heading).

The other major source of bloat in Outlook data files is messages that contain large attachments, such as movie files, PowerPoint presentations, and high-resolution images. Use the Find button in the Mailbox Cleanup dialog box in combination with the Find Items Larger Than *nn* Kilobytes option to manage this; to limit the results to messages larger than about 2 MB in size, for example, use a setting of 2000. In the Advanced Find dialog box, you can choose to delete messages you no longer need and move others to an archive file. Be sure to empty the Deleted Items folder after performing this type of maintenance operation!

Archiving Messages Manually

An Outlook archive file is an Outlook data file (with a. pst extension) that is created specifically to store items you want to move out of the file associated with an e-mail account. By default, when you use one of Outlook's archive options, it creates a file named Archive.pst and stores it in the Outlook Files subfolder of your Documents folder. (You can change the name and location of this file when you create it.) When you perform an archive operation, Outlook opens the archive data file and displays it in the Navigation pane, where it gets its own Archives node. It remains open until you explicitly close it by right-clicking the Archives heading in the Navigation pane and clicking Close "Archives" on the shortcut menu.

Is one archive file enough? If your e-mail load is light (or if you're scrupulous about deleting most messages), you can probably get by for years with a single archive file. In this configuration, you can keep messages in your main mailbox for a standard time—six months or a year—and then periodically move messages older than that to your archive file. If you receive a large volume of e-mail and need to archive messages for legal or business reasons, you might choose a different archive strategy, with separate data files for each year.

Although Outlook includes options to automatically archive messages, you can perform these tasks manually as well. Just drag items or folders out of your main data file and drop them into the corresponding folders in your archive file.

To archive a single folder, click Archive (the last option on the Cleanup Tools menu). Doing so opens this dialog box.

Select a folder from the list, choose a date to use as the cutoff point, and select an archive file as the destination. If the file you choose doesn't exist, Outlook creates it; if the file exists, your archived items are added to that file's contents.

This archiving option works with a single folder and all of its subfolders—you can't cherry-pick multiple folders or subfolders for archiving (although you can archive all folders in a single data file by clicking the top-level folder). Items from the selected folder go to the same location in the archive folder and are deleted from the original file.

INSIDE OUT   For safety's sake, copy (don't move) important items

You can't move system folders, such as the Inbox, and you shouldn't move folders that you intend to keep using. For example, you might have created a subfolder under your Inbox that contains all incoming orders, using a rule to move incoming orders to this folder. A month or two into the new year, you want to archive last year's orders. But your Orders folder already contains some e-mail from this year that shouldn't be moved. The alternative? Copy the Orders folder to your archive file, and check to be sure all the messages survived the trip. Then use Instant Search to clean up each copy. In the newly added folder in your archive data file, type **Received:this year** in the search box to find all messages in that folder that are from the current year and don't yet belong in the archives. Delete them. In the Orders folder, do the same thing, except with **Received:last year**.

When you click OK, the Archive dialog box closes, and you might be momentarily lulled into thinking that nothing's happening. Look closer, and you'll see that Outlook is busy doing your bidding. For starters, look just to the left of the zoom controls in the status bar, where a small message advises you of the progress of your archiving operations, with a bright red X you can click to cancel the archiving. In the Navigation pane, you'll see the Archives folder. Click to open that file, and you can see its contents change as items are moved from the original data file into their corresponding archive folders and subfolders.

Automatic Archive Options

If you prefer not to be bothered by manual maintenance tasks, you can have Outlook do the work of archiving old items for you automatically on a schedule you determine. Auto-Archive settings are fully customizable on a per-folder basis. You can use default settings for all folders or customize settings for each one individually. Select any folder in the Navigation pane and then click AutoArchive Settings (in the Properties group on the Folder tab) to display the dialog box shown in Figure 23-14.

Setting custom AutoArchive options is especially useful for folders containing messages that you don't need to archive, such as daily e-mail updates from a newspaper or sales pitches from online merchants. For those folders, consider setting the Permanently Delete Old Items option.

Chapter 23

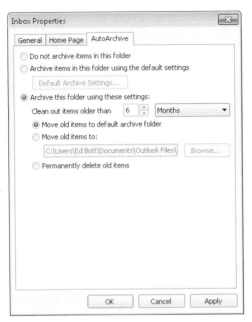

Figure 23-14 Use the bottom set of options in this dialog box to fine-tune what Outlook does with that folder's contents when you use the AutoArchive feature.

CAUTION

"Permanently Delete" means just that. If you set this option for a folder, its contents will be vaporized when you run AutoArchive. The only way to recover those deleted messages is from a backup copy of the Outlook data file. Use this option on folders that you know for certain contain only nonessential messages.

By default, AutoArchive options clean out items older than six months. If you want to be more or less aggressive than that with your archiving strategy, you can change this setting for all folders in one operation. Start by selecting Archive Items In This Folder Using The Default Settings, and then click the Default Archive Settings button to display the dialog box shown next.

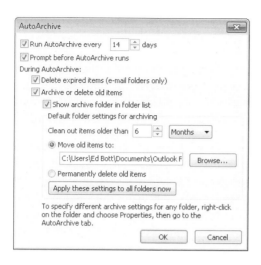

Note that all options here appear dimmed and are unavailable unless you select the Run AutoArchive Every *nn* Days check box. After you do that, you can change the settings under the During AutoArchive heading and then click Apply These Settings To All Folders Now. When that operation is complete, you can leave the Run AutoArchive Every *nn* Days option selected (choosing a different interval if necessary), or clear it and click OK. To perform a manual AutoArchive operation using the current settings, click Archive on the Cleanup Tools menu, select Archive All Folders According To Their AutoArchive Settings, and click OK.

Reading RSS Feeds in Outlook

Outlook 2010 does more than just e-mail. It also allows you to subscribe to RSS feeds, which provide summaries or the full text of web pages. (Technically, RSS is short for Really Simple Syndication, but we've never heard anyone use that high-falutin' name in years. It's just RSS.)

An RSS feed is an index file representing the contents of a website, typically updated every time a new page or post is added to that site. The feed file is written in XML and saved at a specific address. Your favorite news and shopping sites almost certainly have RSS feeds associated with them. You can follow someone on Twitter by using the RSS feed for their Twitter account. SharePoint and Windows Live SkyDrive folders have RSS feeds associated with them, so you can be notified almost immediately when a file is added in one of those locations.

In Outlook, each feed you subscribe to gets its own subfolder under the RSS Feeds heading in the Navigation pane. Each item in the feed is treated as a separate message, which you can flag, forward, and delete. You can't reply to an RSS feed item; they're not e-mail messages.

The advantage of using Outlook to subscribe to RSS feeds is that it delivers the items to you in a familiar place, alongside your other Outlook data. You don't need to open a separate program or use a web browser. Items are fully searchable as well, which makes it a great way to keep a searchable index of posts from particularly interesting or useful websites.

You can add a website directly to Outlook by copying the URL for its RSS feed. Right-click the RSS Feeds icon in the Navigation pane, click Add A New RSS Feed, and paste the copied URL into the New RSS Feed box. An even easier solution is to subscribe to the feed using Internet Explorer and then configure Outlook so it shares the Windows Common Feed List. From Internet Explorer, visit the page to which you want to subscribe and look for the RSS icon on the Command bar to take on an orange glow, indicating that the site has one or more RSS feeds.

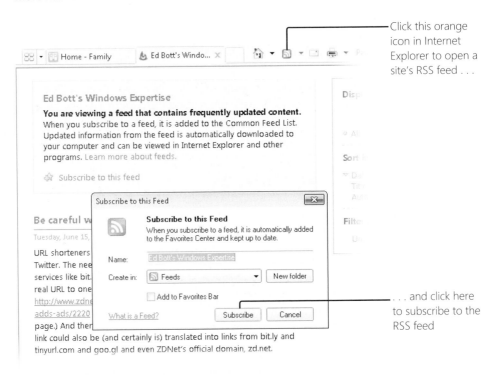

Click this orange icon in Internet Explorer to open a site's RSS feed . . .

. . . and click here to subscribe to the RSS feed

> **Note**
>
> For a technical overview of RSS in Windows, see the MSDN article "Introducing the Windows RSS platform" at *w7io.com/12302*.

To link the Common Feed List to Outlook, open the Advanced tab of the Outlook Options dialog box (File, Options). Under the RSS Feeds heading, select Synchronize RSS Feeds To The Common Feed List (CFL) In Windows.

To see a list of all RSS feeds to which you're currently subscribed, click File, and on the Info Tab click Account Settings, Account Settings. Click the RSS Feeds tab to see a list like the one shown in Figure 23-15.

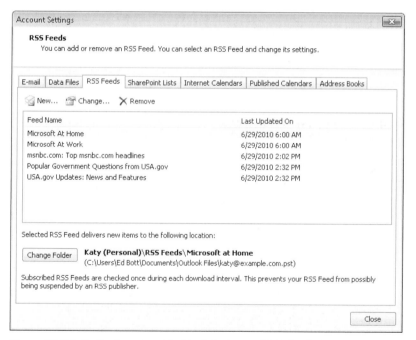

Figure 23-15 Outlook starts with this default set of RSS feeds for your region of the world. Remove the ones you don't want to follow and then add your own.

TROUBLESHOOTING

RSS feeds from the Common Feed List don't appear in Outlook

We've seen this happen ourselves. One easy fix is to restart Outlook, which also refreshes the Common Feed List as part of its startup tasks. A less intrusive method is to click File, Open, Import. In the Import And Export Wizard, choose Import RSS Feeds From The Common Feed List and click Next. That opens a dialog box showing all available items from the Common Feed List. Select the ones you want to add and finish the wizard. The missing feeds should now be present and accounted for.

To tweak settings for an individual feed, click its entry in the RSS Feeds list, and then click Change. That opens the RSS Feed Options dialog box, shown here.

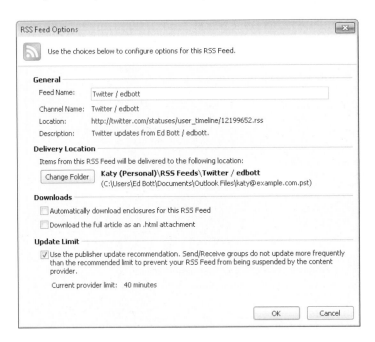

One useful option here is the Change Folder button, where you can choose which Outlook folder to use as the delivery location. This option allows you to consolidate multiple related feeds into a single folder so you can scan them all at once. The two options under the Downloads heading let you automatically download enclosures (such as podcast files) or the entire web page as a self-contained HTML page.

INSIDE OUT   **Share RSS feeds with other people**

When you view a folder containing RSS feed items, a new RSS group appears on the Home tab. Share This Feed is the most interesting command in this group. It opens a new e-mail message with the details of the RSS feed embedded in it, along with some descriptive text and a link to the feed URL. If another Outlook user shares an RSS feed with you, look for a link at the top of the message that allows you to add the feed to Outlook with one click.

Using Outlook Social Connector and the People Pane

At the bottom of every e-mail message and contact item is a resizable pane whose purpose is to display information about the person (or persons) associated with that item. The People pane displays contact information about each person, including his or her picture, if it's available. In a series of tabs to the right of the picture are lists of e-mail messages, Calendar items, file attachments, and other Outlook items associated with that person. Each link is a live link to the item, so if you receive an e-mail message from Ed Bott, you can quickly scroll through all messages you've received from him previously and open any that look interesting.

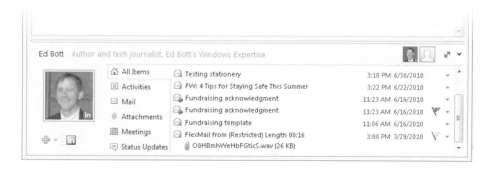

Using a feature new in Outlook 2010, called the Outlook Social Connector, you can expand the range of information in the People pane so that it also includes status updates, comments, and messages from social networks. (This feature was still under development at the time we wrote this chapter, so you'll want to read the latest updates from Microsoft, available at *w7io.com/12306*.) The good news is that this is an Outlook add-on that can be upgraded without a lot of fuss.

Connecting to a specific social network requires you to install a small helper program for that network. When you do, the network is added to the list of available networks, which you can access from the People pane for any contact. You can also click the View tab and then click People Pane, Account Settings. That opens the dialog box shown in Figure 23-16.

Figure 23-16 Each social network you add to Outlook is available from this dialog box, where you enter your credentials so that Outlook can receive updates for that account.

Our Favorite Outlook Tweaks and Tips

In this section, we include some of our favorite little tweaks for Outlook, ones that don't fit anywhere else but are too good and useful not to mention.

Changing Default Formatting for New E-Mail Messages

When you create, reply to, or forward an e-mail message, any text you enter uses the default font of 11-point Calibri. You can choose a different font and font size, change the font's color, and pick a style such as bold or italic. You can also choose different settings for messages you create and for replies and forwards.

Click File, Options. On the Mail tab, click the Stationery And Fonts button to bring up the Signatures And Stationery dialog box, shown in Figure 23-17.

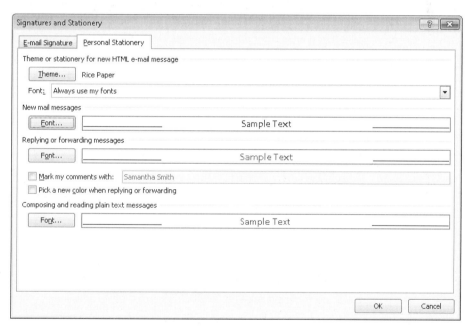

Figure 23-17 If you don't like Outlook's default typeface selections for outgoing HTML-formatted messages, you can change them here.

If you click Theme, you can choose one of the Office-wide themes, which includes body and heading fonts as well as background images, colors, and horizontal rules (but not custom bullet characters). If you prefer your own fonts, you can choose Always Use My Fonts in the Theme Or Stationery For New HTML E-Mail Message section (or use no theme). If you don't use a theme, click the Font button beneath New Mail Messages and Replying Or Forwarding Messages to choose fonts, sizes, and colors for each of those settings.

INSIDE OUT Choose the right font for your outgoing messages

It's worth making an effort to choose fonts that your recipients can view. If you choose an obscure font, your outgoing messages will look just fine on your PC, but there's no telling what your recipients will see—their PCs will substitute another font when necessary that might or might not have the same visual appeal of your choice.

The best solution is to use any of the fonts in Microsoft's ClearType Font Collection, the six font families designed for and included with Windows Vista and Windows 7. (For more details, see *w7io.com/12303*.) The list includes all weights of Constantia, Corbel, Calibri, Cambria, Candara, and Consolas. (We think Candara is especially attractive for e-mail.) If you encounter a friend or coworker who can't see these fonts correctly, they're probably using an old version of Windows and don't have a modern version of Office installed. Suggest that they install one of the free Office viewer programs for Office 2007 or later, all of which include these font families.

Attaching Pictures to Contact Records

Attaching pictures to contact records is amusing and potentially even emotional (especially for friends and family), but it also has its practical uses. If you're meeting a coworker for the first time, you can send the other person an Outlook business card containing your picture. Any pictures you add to Outlook items can be synced to your phone, as well. Choose Picture, Add Picture from the Options group on the Contact tab. If the Contact item already has a picture associated with it, you'll find Change Picture and Remove Picture options here. If you need to crop the picture, do so before adding it to Outlook, which doesn't use the picture editing tools available in other Office 2010 programs.

Juggling Multiple Time Zones

When you create or edit an appointment or a meeting, you have the option to specify a time zone for both the Start Time and End Time fields. This feature was introduced in Outlook 2007, and it solves a longstanding headache caused when you and Outlook travel across the country or around the world.

What's the problem? Consider this scenario. You're leaving Los Angeles on Friday and fly-ing to Sydney, Australia. Your flight leaves at 10:30 PM, and you arrive Down Under at 6:30 AM on Sunday. You have a handful of meetings during the day on Tuesday. When you enter times, Outlook assumes that the time you specify is in the current time zone. So, when you change time zones on your portable PC, the times displayed in Outlook change as well. If you were in Los Angeles and entered details for an appointment on Tuesday at 10 AM, changing the time zone on your PC would change the starting time of that appointment—making you late by 18 hours.

The solution is to click the Time Zones command on the Appointment or Meeting tab and then select the correct time zone for both the start time and end time. That allows your Sydney appointment to be displayed correctly when you change the time on your PC.

Having multiple time zones in your Outlook calendar solves that problem but causes another one, as you have to continually guess about which time zone you're currently showing. To add a label to the time list on the left of the Calendar window, open the Outlook Options dialog box, click the Calendar tab, and enter descriptive text in the Label box.

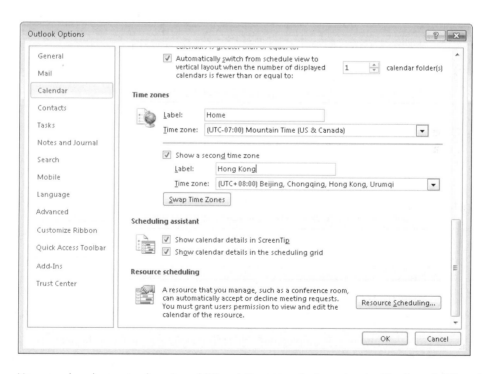

You can also choose to show an additional time zone in the calendar. That's useful if you're traveling, and also if you work with people in different parts of the world. Seeing both time zones allows you to tell at a glance whether you're trying to call a business in Moscow at midnight or Hong Kong at 3:00 AM, when no one's there to take the call.

Managing Auto-Complete Lists and Suggested Contacts

If you've used Outlook for any length of time, you've probably seen its Auto-Complete feature at work. When you click and start typing in an address field for a new e-mail message, a list of suggested names and e-mail addresses appears below the field. You can click to accept one of these Auto-Complete suggestions.

Auto-Complete causes problems when you inadvertently select an incorrect address that was saved as a potential shortcut for you, or when a frequent correspondent changes e-mail addresses, making your saved Auto-Complete entry for his or her name incorrect.

Fixing a single incorrect Auto-Complete entry is easy: start typing until you see the incorrect entry and then click the X at the end of the list item. That deletes it immediately.

In previous Outlook versions, the Auto-Complete list was saved in a file on your PC, with the file name extension .nk2. In Outlook 2010, these entries are now saved in your Outlook data file (or, for Microsoft Exchange Server accounts, in your mailbox on the server, which allows the same list to appear on any computer where you use Outlook with that account).

To clear the Auto-Complete list and start over, open the Options dialog box (File, Options), click the Mail tab, and click Empty Auto-Complete List, under the Send Messages heading. To stop Outlook from suggesting names in this way, clear the Use Auto-Complete List To Suggest Names When Typing In The To, Cc, And Bcc Lines box in the same location.

The Auto-Complete list also draws names from the Suggested Contacts folder for an account. This feature, new in Outlook 2010, adds a Contact item to this folder any time you respond to an e-mail message whose sender is not in an Outlook address book. You can drag a Contact item from the Suggested Contacts folder to your main Contacts folder and fill in extra details if you discover an important contact here. If your work requires lots of e-mail messages to strangers, this feature might be more confusing than helpful. In that case, you can disable this behavior by opening the Outlook Options dialog box, clicking the Contacts tab, and clearing the option under the Suggested Contacts heading.

Repairing a Damaged Data File

If you suspect that your Outlook data file is damaged—if your profile refuses to open or you notice some items are displaying incorrectly—you might be able to repair it by using the Inbox Repair Tool, Scanpst.exe. Close Outlook, and then open Windows Explorer and browse to the Program Files\Microsoft Office\Office14 folder on your system drive (usually C). If you're using a 64-bit Windows version and 32-bit Office, this folder is in Program Files (x86).

Double-click Scanpst.exe to open the Microsoft Outlook Inbox Repair Tool and browse for the file you want to diagnose. The scan operation takes a few minutes. If it finds errors, it displays them here and offers the option to repair the file.

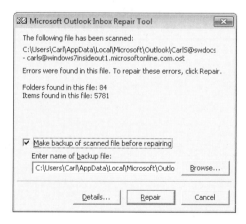

The Make Backup Of Scanned File Before Repairing option is selected by default. If you know you have a good backup of the file, you can safely clear this check box and save a few seconds. But if you're not sure, take advantage of the opportunity to make a backup here. The repair operation can be destructive.

Security, Sharing, and Collaboration

Among the signature features of Office 2010 are the capabilities it provides to help you work together with others on documents or projects. Traditionally, coauthoring has been a sequential process: you make edits to a document and send it via e-mail to the next person, who then does the same. That process—with some improvements—is still the most common way to share documents. The goal remains the same as always: to create a final document that incorporates the work (or at least the approval) of several people.

A centrally managed SharePoint 2010 environment enables storage and workflow scenarios for groups of knowledge workers, and we touch on some of those settings in this chapter and in Chapter 26, "Working with SharePoint 2010." For example, you and your coworkers or friends can simultaneously edit a document that's stored in a shared location, such as a SharePoint library. SharePoint isn't for everyone, however, and Office 2010 has other sharing and collaboration options that don't rely on SharePoint.

The ability to share documents doesn't come without risk, however. The minute you start passing data around over a network and accepting documents from others, you expose your computer to potential malware. If the person who shares a document with you isn't careful about computer security, you could pay the price for that person's carelessness. Even riskier are documents from unknown sources; perhaps that amusing article making the rounds via e-mail includes a virus that isn't funny at all. Fortunately, Office 2010 includes several built-in protections against these risks, and we begin this chapter with a discussion of the security features in Office 2010.

How Office 2010 Protects You

In the wild and woolly past, Word documents (and, to a lesser extent, documents from other Office programs that include a macro language) were sometimes used by malicious hackers to spread viruses and other malware. This came about largely because of the macro capabilities of Word and users' naiveté about the potential dangers. Macros are a form of programming used for document automation that allow a document to perform actions similar to executable programs; most users didn't realize that documents had macro capabilities, let alone a macro's power.

With earlier versions of Office, the mere act of opening a document could trigger a macro to run. The Melissa virus, which spread quickly in 1999, worked this way. An unsuspecting user would open an infected Word document that was received as an e-mail attachment. A macro would run that would send a message with the infected document to contacts in the user's address book.

Other risks arose from the use of ActiveX controls (another type of program) embedded in documents.

Although Office documents still support the use of macros and ActiveX controls (topics beyond the scope of this book), features in newer versions of Office greatly mitigate the risks associated with them. Office settings are secure by default, meaning that you must take positive steps to enable macros, ActiveX, or other technologies that have the potential of doing harm—as well as working to your benefit.

By default, Office prompts you and requests your permission whenever a document uses macros or ActiveX controls. In addition, *Protected View*—a feature-restricted read-only mode—prevents documents of unknown provenance from doing any harm.

Office has other, less apparent, protections in place as well. For example, Data Execution Prevention disables add-ins that work in ways that can lead to a crash or might be a sign of a program trying to do some harm.

What You Can and Can't Do in Protected View

The most visible sign of Office security is Protected View. You can view a document open in Protected View, but as you click the various tabs on the ribbon, you'll see that most editing functions are disabled. Printing is also disabled. Office displays several prominent indications to let you know that Protected View is in effect, as shown in Figure 24-1.

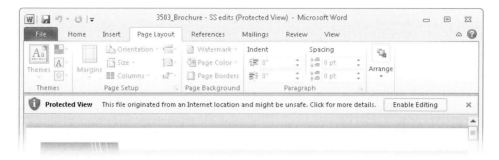

Figure 24-1 Office lets you know about Protected View with text appended to the file name in the window caption, disabled tools on the ribbon, and, most prominently, a yellow or red message bar below the ribbon.

A document opens in Protected View for any of several reasons, including:

- The file originated from an Internet location. Because the Internet is the source of most viruses and other malware, Office invokes Protected View whenever you open a document directly from an Internet location or when you open a document that was downloaded from the Internet.

- The file was received as an e-mail attachment and the sender has not been identified as safe.

- The file is stored in an unsafe location, such as the Temporary Internet Files folder.

- The file is blocked by File Block, a feature that causes documents from older versions of Office (by default, documents from Word 95 and earlier and from Excel 4 and earlier) to open in Protected View. The code used to open and save these outdated file types has security vulnerabilities.

- The file is corrupt. Office validates each file when it opens it; files that fail validation open in Protected View.

In Protected View, all the tools for viewing, searching, reviewing, and navigating within a document are available. However, you cannot edit, print, or save a document in Protected View.

If you trust the source of the document and are confident that it's safe, you can exit Protected View, thereby enabling the full panoply of Office tools and features. To exit Protected View when a yellow message bar appears, simply click Enable Editing in the message bar. Alternatively, click the File tab and click Enable Editing on the Info tab, shown in Figure 24-2. (You can also exit Protected View from the Save or Print tabs in Backstage view.)

Chapter 24

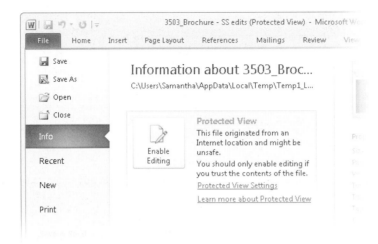

Figure 24-2 You can open the Protected View tab in Trust Center by clicking Protected View Settings.

If the Protected View message bar is red—which indicates a more severe risk—you must go to Backstage view to exit Protected View.

For information about modifying Protected View and File Block settings, see "Fine-Tuning Security Settings" on page 823.

Working Safely with File Attachments

E-mail has long been a vector for many viruses and other malware because malicious hackers realized that it's an efficient way to distribute infected files to unsuspecting users. And in the early anything-goes days, Outlook did little to prevent the spread of malicious files.

The biggest risk with e-mail is file attachments because an attached file can be just about anything, including a malicious program. Another risk comes from HTML-formatted messages that contain damaging scripts. In the past, simply viewing one of these messages—even in the Reading pane—could cause the script to run and do its dirty deed.

Outlook 2010 mitigates the risks in several ways.

- Junk mail filters automatically remove many problem messages from your Inbox. (In addition, spam and virus filters on your mail server and an antivirus program on your computer remove most other dangerous messages or attachments. These components are not part of Office.)

- Outlook prevents you from opening attachments of the types commonly used as malware. Attached executable files, including .exe, .com, .bat, and .vbs files, are blocked altogether. When you open other attachment types, including .doc, .xls, and .ppt, Outlook displays a warning message, giving you a chance to consider whether you trust the source or to first save the file so you can scan it for viruses.

- Viewing messages in the Reading pane is safe because in Outlook 2010, scripts don't run and attachments don't open in the Reading pane.

INSIDE OUT   Send blocked attachments

Outlook prevents you from attaching potentially dangerous files to messages you send. This sometimes annoying feature serves two purposes: It prevents malware from surreptitiously using Outlook to send dangerous attachments without your knowledge, and it also forces you to pause and think about what you're sending. (In all likelihood, the recipient won't be able to access an executable file even if Outlook allows you to send it. The e-mail system at the receiving end would block it anyway.)

If you must send an executable file, several workarounds are possible. The easiest is to put the blocked file into a ZIP archive and then attach the resulting .zip file. Outlook and most other e-mail programs do not block ZIP archives. Another alternative to consider: upload the file to a shared server. Windows Live SkyDrive works well for this purpose, and numerous other services are also available, usually at no charge.

Inspecting and Removing Personal and Confidential Information

Another threat to your security comes from hackers who pore through your document files to glean bits of information about you. Although the information that Office stores in a document is generally pretty innocuous—items such as your name, the amount of time spent editing a document, and so on—you might not want it revealed, perhaps for competitive reasons. Hackers who know their way inside a document file might find other interesting tidbits.

Word, Excel, and PowerPoint have a feature that examines a document to find and (optionally) delete any personal information stored in the file. To use it, click the File menu to open Backstage view. On the Info tab, click Check For Issues, Inspect Document. Figure 24-3 shows the Document Inspector dialog box for PowerPoint.

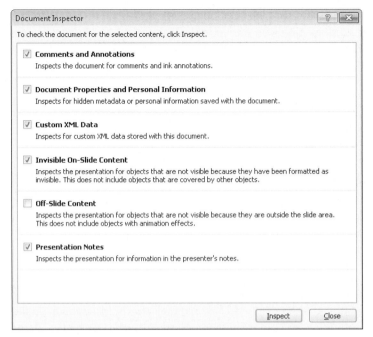

Figure 24-3 The document inspector feature in Word and Excel looks for comparable items.

For more information about options under Check For Issues in Word, see "Checking a Document" on page 294.

INSIDE OUT   Protect documents from unwanted access or copying

Office also includes tools for protecting your documents from snooping and for ensuring that your document has not been altered. With Word, Excel, and PowerPoint, you can encrypt a document so that it can be opened only by someone who knows the password, and you can configure permissions (enforced by an Information Rights Management server) so that only people you authorize can view or edit a document. You can also apply a digital signature that people can use to verify who created the document and confirm that it hasn't been changed since the signature was applied.

For more information about these options, see "Protecting a Document" on page 296.

Fine-Tuning Security Settings

As with so many activities in computing (and in life generally), there's a tradeoff between security and convenience. You could lock down your computer and Office so that they're perfectly safe—but you wouldn't be able to share usable documents or get anything done. On the other hand, you could throw caution to the wind; you wouldn't be slowed down by extra clicks to clear warning messages, so you could work quickly and efficiently—until the first malware strikes. The trick, of course, is to find the proper balance between security (annoyance and inefficiency) and convenience (danger).

We find that the default settings for Office straddle the line nicely, but if you want to make adjustments to the security settings, you need to visit the Trust Center. To get there, click File, Options. Click the Trust Center tab, and then click Trust Center Settings.

Tabs in the Trust Center dialog box, shown in Figure 24-4, provide access to settings for managing various security risks.

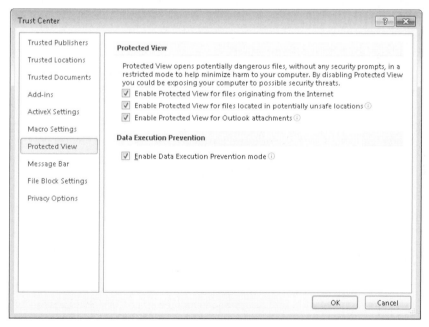

Figure 24-4 You can go directly to this tab (without going through Options) by clicking the Protected View Settings link shown in Figure 24-2.

If you must work with files from old versions of Office, take a look at the File Block Settings tab, shown in Figure 24-5. Each file type that does not have a check mark can be opened and saved normally. A check box in the Open column causes the file to open according to the setting at the bottom of the dialog box (in Protected View by default). A check box in the Save column prevents you from saving the file in its original format; you must save it as another supported file type. (For information about supported file types, see "Which File Formats Does Office 2010 Support?" on page 76.)

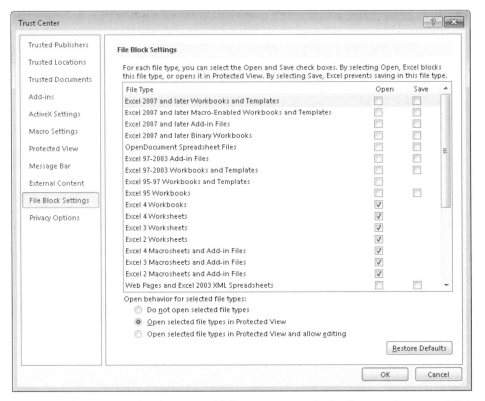

Figure 24-5 Opening and saving some old file types uses code that has security vulnerabilities that a hacker could exploit; File Block limits or prevents access to these files.

Managing Add-Ins

An add-in is a supplemental program, often created by a developer other than Microsoft, that plugs into Office to add features or capabilities. The Trust Center has an Add-Ins tab, which is where you can place restrictions on which types of add-ins can run. However, this isn't the place to manage individual add-ins.

To do that, click File, Options, and then click Add-Ins. As shown here, Office displays a list of installed add-ins (many of which are provided with Office), including those that are installed but not currently active.

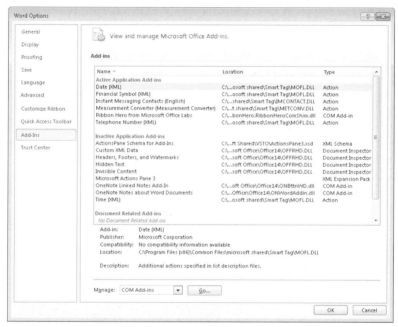

To remove or disable an installed add-in, in the Manage box select COM Add-Ins and click Go to display the COM Add-Ins dialog box, shown in Figure 24-6.

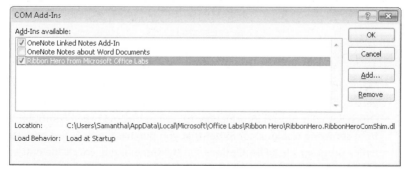

Figure 24-6 Clear a check box to unload an active add-in.

INSIDE OUT   Use an add-in to learn about Office

One of the add-ins listed in Figure 24-6 is Ribbon Hero, which is a program that makes a game out of learning how to use Office. It's especially instructive for users migrating from Office 2003 or other earlier versions that don't have a ribbon interface, but it's helpful for anyone who wants to learn how to use various features in Office. With Ribbon Hero, which was created as a project of Microsoft Office Labs, you can gain experience with add-ins as well as learn about Office features. Download Ribbon Hero from *w7io.com/12402*.

Working Together with Office 2010

Working on a document, worksheet, presentation, or notebook of substantial size or significance is seldom a solo effort. Each Office program includes features for collaborating with other authors and editors to create a final product. Although the overarching purpose of these features is the same in each program, the implementation varies a bit among the programs. This variation can be attributed partly to the different nature of the document types and partly to historical differences between programs with separate origins.

In the early days of computing, one person might create a document and pass it to another, who then made edits and corrections. However, there was no way to know who did what. Hence, the common collaborative tool of the day was marking up a printout rather than making edits directly in the file. Collaboration features in Office let many people work on the final product, while still keeping track of each person's contributions.

In the following pages, we discuss methods for collaborating asynchronously—that is, in a sequential fashion in which one person works on a document and then passes it to the next person to make changes. Then, in the next section, "Simultaneous Editing with Multiple Authors," we explain new features in Office 2010 for real-time coauthoring.

INSIDE OUT   Be sure your user name is correct

Many Office collaboration features rely on the user name and initials to identify the person making a change to a document. For the benefit of your coauthors, be sure that Office has your proper information. (It's often incorrect on a computer that you inherit from someone else or a computer that you purchase with Office preinstalled.) In any Office program, click File, Options. On the General tab, check the entries in the User Name and Initials boxes.

Inserting Comments for Review

A comment added to a document provides a way to offer an explanatory note or a suggestion, or to pose a question to the author. The process for adding a comment is the same in Word, Excel, and PowerPoint: Select the item you want to comment on, click the Review tab, and in the Comments group click New Comment. Figure 24-7 shows a comment that has been added to an Excel worksheet.

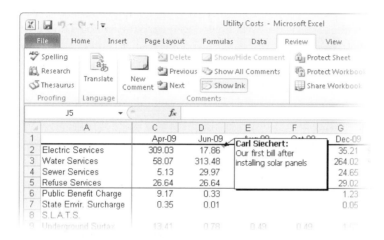

Figure 24-7 In Excel, a small red triangle in the upper right corner of a cell indicates that a comment is attached. Point to the cell to display the comment.

In PowerPoint, a small colored box with the commenter's initials indicates the presence of a comment; point to the box to view the comment. In Word, comments appear in the margin when you use Print Layout view; unlike in Excel and PowerPoint, in Word, you don't need to point at an indicator to display a comment.

For details about inserting, reviewing, and printing comments in Word, see "Using Review Comments in a Document" on page 279. For information about comments in PowerPoint, see "Using Comments" on page 661.

Tracking Changes to Documents

Comments replace the functionality of sticky notes applied to document printouts. Like applying a sticky note, adding a comment to a document file can provide some useful guidance, but it doesn't actually get the document any closer to completion. To do that, contributors must make their edits and corrections in the document.

This is an area in which each Office program works quite differently.

Chapter 24

In Word, the process begins when you click Track Changes in the Tracking group on the Review tab. With change tracking enabled, every addition or deletion is recorded in the document. By default, each addition is shown in a distinctive color and underlined, and each deletion is shown in color and with a strikethrough line. Each item that's moved is also clearly identified. A different color for each contributor helps you to see at a glance who made each change. (A heavily edited document can be hard to follow. Fortunately, you can suppress all the markup so that only the latest version shows.)

As shown in Figure 24-8, ScreenTips, marginal notes, and the Reviewing pane provide additional details about each edit, allowing you to retrace the entire editing history. Tools on the Review tab make quick work of reviewing and then accepting or rejecting each change. Among the Office programs, Word offers the best tools for tracking changes.

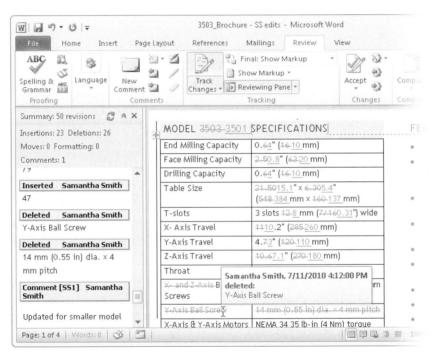

Figure 24-8 When you point to an edit, Word displays a ScreenTip that shows who made the change and when.

For complete details about change tracking in Word, see "Tracking and Highlighting Changes Made to a Document" on page 285.

In Excel, the process of tracking changes begins in the same way: on the Review tab, click Track Changes, Highlight Changes. This step opens the Highlight Changes dialog box, as shown in Figure 24-9.

Figure 24-9 In Excel, you choose which changes (determined by when they're made, who makes them, and in which part of the worksheet they appear) are tracked.

Enabling change tracking in Excel also shares the workbook, which allows multiple users to work on it simultaneously. (For others to work on it, the workbook must be stored in a shared network location, and permissions must be set appropriately. For more information about workbook sharing, see "Sharing Documents on a Network" on page 832.) Even if you're tracking only your own changes, workbook sharing must be enabled to record changes.

CAUTION

Excel does not track certain types of changes, such as formatting changes, worksheet additions and deletions, and hiding or unhiding rows or columns. (Of course, changes that don't meet the criteria you set in the Highlight Changes dialog box are not tracked either.) Therefore, change tracking is not an adequate alternative to the Undo command, nor is it a substitute for a backup. If you need to see an original, unaltered version of your workbook, be sure to save a backup copy before you begin making changes.

Note also that Excel doesn't keep change history forever; by default, it discards records of changes after 30 days to keep the change log from becoming too large. To adjust this default lifespan, on the Review tab click Share Workbook, click the Advanced tab, and enter a value under Track Changes.

With change tracking enabled, each time a change is made that meets the criteria set in the Highlight Changes dialog box, Excel identifies the changed cell with a thin border and a triangle in the upper left corner. Point to the cell to see details of the change, as shown next.

Chapter 24

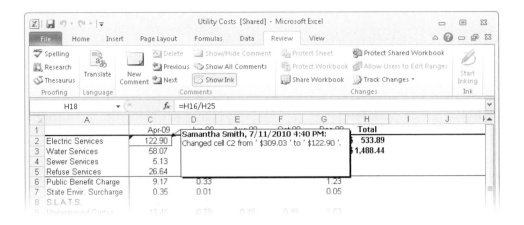

If you select List Changes On A New Sheet in the Highlight Changes dialog box, Excel adds a worksheet called History to the workbook. (Although you can make this selection before or after you begin tracking changes, the History sheet is updated only when you save the workbook.) The History sheet keeps a record of each change, including the date and time of the change, who made it, and exactly what changed.

TROUBLESHOOTING

The History worksheet disappears

As noted, the History worksheet is updated only when you save. But in a perverse irony, Excel hides the History sheet when you save. To make it reappear, click Track Changes, Highlight Changes, select List Changes On A New Sheet, and then click OK.

To review the changes made to a workbook, on the Review tab click Track Changes, Accept/ Reject Changes. Excel asks which changes you'd like to review, as shown in Figure 24-10.

Figure 24-10 In the When box, Not Yet Reviewed refers to changes that have been neither accepted nor rejected.

After you make your selections in the dialog box shown in Figure 24-10 and click OK, Excel then displays each matching change.

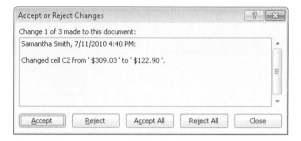

> When you turn off change tracking by clearing the first check box in the Highlight Changes dialog box, Excel accepts all unreviewed changes and then discards the entire change history. If you want to keep a record of the changes, copy the History sheet to another workbook or print it before you turn off change tracking.

PowerPoint doesn't have a feature for tracking changes within a single presentation file. However, you can use its compare feature to note the differences between two versions of a presentation file. For more information, see the following section.

Comparing Versions

Adding comments and tracking changes allow team members to make changes to a document in a way that works toward the goal of producing a final version and provides accountability. For a variety of reasons, however, it's sometimes impossible for contributors to work on the same document.

In these situations, your best option is to take the copy of the file that another contributor has been working on and compare it with your own copy. This process, while not as smooth as those described in the preceding and following sections, provides a form of after-the-fact version control.

In Word, you access the Compare Documents feature using tools in the Compare group on the Review tab. For details, see "Reviewing Tracked Changes" on page 287.

The comparable feature in PowerPoint is also found in the Compare group on the Review tab—although the implementation of the feature is quite different from the one in Word. For details, see "Merging and Comparing Presentations" on page 663.

Simultaneous Editing with Multiple Authors

Up to this point, we've talked about the techniques for collaborating on documents the traditional way—sharing them via e-mail or opening them from a shared network folder. That process is asynchronous, with each collaborator making his or her changes and then routing the document to the next person on the list.

But what if your deadline is more urgent and you can't afford the luxury of waiting for each member of the team to finish his or her contribution before the next person begins? For those scenarios, you can use a handful of Office 2010 features that allow two or more people to work on the same document at the same time. The level of support for this type of editing varies by program, and in this section we cover the different techniques required by each of the three main Office programs. (We do not discuss Outlook, which is not designed for collaboration, and OneNote's unique data file structure allows anyone to work on any notebook from any location at any time.)

For more on how OneNote supports collaboration, see "Sharing and Synchronizing Notebooks" on page 561.

Sharing Documents on a Network

All of the main Office programs have well-established procedures for preventing conflicts when two people try to open a document from a shared network folder at the same time. This process is complicated significantly by the introduction of Office Web Apps.

> ### Note
>
> At the time we wrote this chapter (summer 2010), Microsoft had announced its intention to enable simultaneous editing capabilities for Word and PowerPoint documents shared on Windows Live SkyDrive, but that capability was not yet enabled. As a result, our coverage of this feature is incomplete. For the most recent information on this topic, see our online update at *w7io.com/12401*.

We start with Excel, which offers the richest set of simultaneous editing features in the Office family. Consider this scenario: a coworker opens a workbook in Excel (the full program, not the Excel Web App) from a shared network folder. If you try to open the same workbook, you see this error:

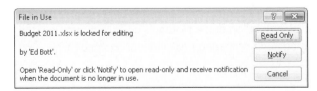

If you only want to peek at the file without changing its contents, click the Read Only button to open a local copy. Although you can make changes to this file, you cannot save those changes using the original file name and location.

If you're willing to wait, click Notify. When the person who is currently editing the workbook saves his changes and closes that Excel window, you see the following notification:

Click Read-Write to replace your read-only copy with the most recently saved changes and begin editing the workbook. If you made any changes to the read-only copy, you have to save those changes in a separate file or discard them before opening the network file.

For shared network files, Word and PowerPoint offer a similar sequence of permission dialog boxes, although the exact wording varies. For a Word document, you can choose the option to receive a notification when the locked document is available for editing. For a PowerPoint presentation, your only option is to open a read-only copy. The bottom line for all three programs is simple: the first person who opens a document, workbook, or presentation from a shared network location in the full Office program has complete control over that file. Others who want to work on that file have to wait their turn.

For Excel (but not for Word or PowerPoint), the first person who opens a workbook from a network folder can explicitly enable that workbook for sharing. On the Review tab, click Share Workbook (in the Changes group). That opens the Share Workbook dialog box, where you can click Allow Changes By More Than One User At The Same Time. With this option enabled, you and your coworkers can open the shared workbook and make changes at the same time. The Share Workbook dialog box shows who is currently editing the workbook, as shown in Figure 24-11.

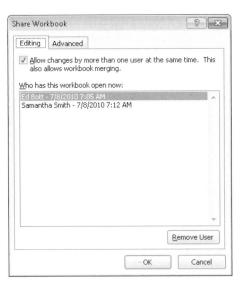

Figure 24-11 Select the check box at the top of this dialog box to allow more than one person to edit a workbook at the same time.

With this option enabled, the title bar changes to include the word *Shared* (in brackets). By default, any changes made by other people appear in your workbook when you save it. (To change this option so that Excel automatically incorporates revisions made by other people, click the Advanced tab in the Share Workbook dialog box and specify how often you want Excel to check for changes, under the Update Changes heading.)

TROUBLESHOOTING

You are unable to share a workbook

The most common cause of this error is that your workbook includes a range that has been formatted as an Excel table. Excel cannot share a workbook that has data arranged in this fashion. To resolve the error and enable sharing, convert the table to a range by clicking anywhere in the table and then clicking Convert To Range (in the Tools group on the Table Tools Design tab).

If you and your coworkers have divided responsibilities so that you're each working on different areas within the workbook, your saved changes will merge smoothly. If you inadvertently try to edit the same cell on the same worksheet, Excel will warn the person who tries to save the conflicting change and offer to resolve the conflicts, as shown next.

Sharing Documents from a SharePoint Site

If you and your colleagues have access to a Windows server running SharePoint 2010, your collaboration options are greatly enhanced. The most significant change with Word and PowerPoint is that multiple people can open the same file at the same time, without error messages and with no requirement to explicitly enable sharing. Ironically, you cannot open an Excel workbook from a SharePoint site, even after you click the Share Workbook button. You must open that workbook from a traditional network share.

When you first open a document or presentation that other people are currently editing, you see a balloon notification in the status bar for that program. The balloon goes away after a few seconds, but the status bar maintains a count of how many people have the current document open. Click that indicator to see a list of names, as shown here.

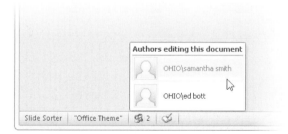

Any changes you make are initially saved locally in the Office document cache. When you save your changes, Word and PowerPoint send XML messages containing information about those changes to the SharePoint server, which then notifies the other users who have that file open.

For more on how Word handles shared documents, see "Working Together with Other Authors" on page 291. For details about collaborating on PowerPoint presentations, see "Working Collaboratively on a Presentation" on page 661. For an overview of SharePoint collaboration, see "How SharePoint and Office Work Together" on page 864.

Chapter 24

Using Office in a Web Browser

O PENING and saving documents used to be simple. You selected a local hard disk (or a shared network drive) as the destination, and you used folders to keep things organized. If you wanted to take a file to another location, you used removable storage, such as a USB flash drive or a writable CD. And if you forgot to bring the file with you, well, you were out of luck.

Today, thanks to the practically omnipresent Internet, you have options that don't tie you down to a physical location. You can save any file online (in the "cloud," as it's generically known) using a variety of free and paid services. With most cloud-based services, you can designate those files as private, share them with specific people or groups, or make them available to the public. You can retrieve your saved files from anywhere—as long as you have an Internet connection and access to a web browser.

Simultaneous with the release of Office 2010, Microsoft has introduced some significant upgrades to its cloud-computing infrastructure specifically designed to help Office users be more productive. The most useful is Microsoft's free Windows Live SkyDrive service, which lets you upload Office documents (and other files as well) into virtual folders. You (or anyone to whom you grant permission) can view and edit those files directly in a web browser by using Office Web Apps. The same features are available if you have access to a properly configured Windows server running SharePoint 2010 and the Office Web Apps add-in.

Connecting to the cloud in this way makes it possible to collaborate with friends, coworkers, and classmates. It also guarantees that you'll have access to important documents, even if you're using a borrowed computer that doesn't have Office installed. In this chapter, we discuss how to use SkyDrive and other cloud-based features with Office 2010; we also explain the limitations of Office Web Apps.

What Can You Do with Office on the Web?

With previous editions of Office, you could share a document with friends or colleagues, but they needed their own copy of Office to edit the contents of the file, and even viewing a document required installing software. Microsoft's new cloud-based services make that extra layer of software unnecessary. Word documents, Excel workbooks, PowerPoint presentations, and OneNote notebooks can all be viewed and edited directly in a browser window, with no additional software required. In fact, if you store your documents in locations that support Office Web Apps, you can grant access to those documents to anyone you choose, and they in turn can view and edit those documents in their browser window using Office Web Apps.

Most remarkably, Office Web Apps work with a variety of browsers and operating systems, even those not made by Microsoft. The official list of supported browsers at the time we wrote this includes the following:

- Internet Explorer 7 and later on Windows

- Safari 4 and later on Mac OS X

- Firefox 3.5 and later on Windows, Mac OS X, and Linux

Microsoft describes Office Web Apps collectively as "online companions" to the corresponding programs that are part of the Office family, and that's an accurate description. Even though you can accomplish some impressive tasks with Office Web Apps, they have nowhere near the power or flexibility of the full programs.

Figure 25-1 shows a Word document open in Internet Explorer using the Microsoft Word Web App running on Windows Live SkyDrive. The font formatting, graphics, and layout are indistinguishable from the same document opened in the full Word 2010 program.

INSIDE OUT   Make the browser go away

In Word, PowerPoint, and OneNote, you might not notice the unobtrusive button just above the document window on the far right. But click the Pop-Out button, and the current document pops out into its own window, with the viewing and editing menus from the web app but minus toolbars, tabs, and other pieces of the browser itself. The advantage of this separate window is that you get more space to view or edit the document. The disadvantage is that you lose some of the useful navigation features of the browser.

Figure 25-1 In Office Web Apps, even complex formatting like the border on this photo displays correctly when viewed in a browser.

In this "viewer" mode of Word-as-a-web-app, the page's appearance is virtually identical to the document as it was created in the full-strength Word program. The display fidelity is very high: You can see page borders, paragraph breaks, and accurate font formatting. Even complex layout elements like the tilted border and shadow around the accompanying photo appear where the document author placed them. Anyone who uses a browser to open this document can read it with full fidelity. The other Office Web Apps offer similar fidelity in rendering worksheets, presentations, and OneNote pages.

For more on how to lay out graphics in Office documents, see Chapter 6, "Working with Graphics and Pictures."

Although the document looks identical in both places, the web app itself has some significant differences from the corresponding full program. For starters, you'll notice the Address bar, which contains a URL pointing to the file location. You can see the status bar at the bottom, which lets you know whether you're running in Protected Mode in Internet Explorer.

When you use an Office Web App as a viewer, the menu bar is stripped to its essentials. Figure 25-2 shows the Excel Web App in action on a SharePoint site, with its abbreviated File menu (note that there's no Info pane, as there is in the full program) and a mere four buttons.

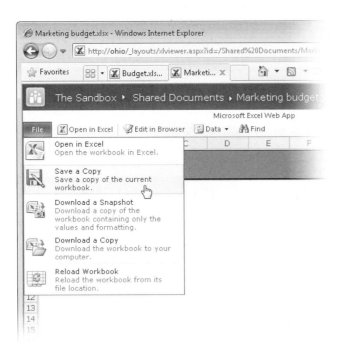

Figure 25-2 In viewer mode, your choices are limited, especially in comparison to the corresponding full program.

In this mode, you can save a copy, refresh the data, or reload the workbook to incorporate recent changes. But if you want to actually change the contents of the document, you need to open it in editing mode. For each of the four programs available as a web app, you have a choice of two editing options:

- **Open In <*Program*>**   Loads the current document in the full Office program associated with the document type, where *<Program>* is Word, Excel, PowerPoint, or OneNote. Use this option when you want access to the full editing capabilities of the program. You'll see an error message if you click this button on a computer that doesn't have a compatible version of the corresponding Office program installed, or if you use a web browser that doesn't directly support opening documents.

- **Edit In Browser**   Opens the document in Editing view within the browser. Your editing options are greatly limited compared to the full program, as even a cursory inspection of the stripped-down ribbon will confirm.

  Figure 25-3, for example, shows a workbook that has been opened for editing in the Excel Web App. What you see on the Home tab represents just about everything you can do with a worksheet using the web app (the Insert tab contains only two commands).

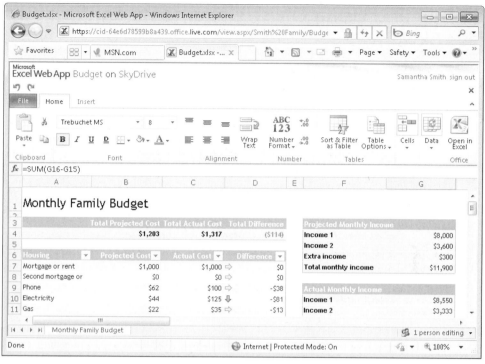

Figure 25-3 The set of features available in the Excel Web App represents only a small percentage of those available in the full program.

As we noted earlier, Microsoft describes Office Web Apps as "online companions to Microsoft Word, Excel, PowerPoint, and OneNote, enabling people to access and do light editing or sharing of Office documents from virtually anywhere." To use Office Web Apps, you need to store your document in a compatible shared location:

- The Windows Live SkyDrive service (*w7io.com/12701*) is free for anyone with a Windows Live ID. It offers 25 GB of storage, with a maximum per-file size of 50 MB. We explain how to use and customize SkyDrive more fully in the next section.

- Microsoft SharePoint Foundation 2010 and Microsoft SharePoint Server 2010 (*w7io.com/12702*) run on the Windows Server platform. On corporate networks, Office Web Apps can be installed as part of SharePoint and made available to customers who are licensed for Office 2010 through a volume licensing program. Microsoft has also announced that SharePoint 2010 and Office Web Apps will be available as hosted solutions from a variety of third-party suppliers, making them available to small businesses and individuals.

For a more detailed discussion of how SharePoint and Office work together, see Chapter 26, "Working with SharePoint 2010."

Storing and Using Office Documents on Windows Live SkyDrive

Microsoft launched its SkyDrive service, which is part of the Windows Live family, in 2007. Today it's available worldwide, offering 25 GB of online storage to anyone with a free Windows Live ID. You can store any file on SkyDrive, but our focus in this chapter is on documents saved in one of the four Office 2010 formats that work with Office Web Apps.

One challenge we face in documenting a web-based service like SkyDrive is that the service can change at any time. By adding or changing bits on its web servers, Microsoft can make new features available, increase the amount of available storage, change the user interface, or even rename the service (that already happened once, in 2007, when Microsoft changed the name of the service from Windows Live Folders to Windows Live SkyDrive). We fully expect that the SkyDrive user interface will change significantly over time, so in this section we've avoided detailed descriptions and step-by-step procedures in favor of more global instructions.

To begin using SkyDrive with Office, sign in at *live.com* with your Windows Live ID and click Office (to the right of the Windows Live logo at the top of the page). That takes you directly to an Office-specific view of your SkyDrive contents, with recent documents highlighted at the top of the contents pane and specific folders in the bar on the left. Figure 25-4 shows one such SkyDrive account, with three custom folders in addition to the default selection.

Creating New Folders

SkyDrive categorizes your online files based on the three available folder types—Documents, Favorites, and Photos—which in turn can contain folders and subfolders. The Documents category is most relevant for Office users. When you sign in to SkyDrive for the first time, you'll find a private My Documents folder there, along with a Public folder where you can make files available to everyone.

That's a fine start, but if you plan to use Office Web Apps, especially with other people, you should create some custom folders to help keep things organized. You'll find a New menu near the top of every SkyDrive page, with Folder available as the last option. This menu is available in custom SkyDrive folders you create, allowing you to create subfolders within a folder.

The biggest advantage of creating folders and subfolders is that it gives you the ability to apply custom permissions to each one, and part of the process of creating a new folder involves assigning permissions to it. You'll find more details on this subject in "Setting Permissions" on page 844.

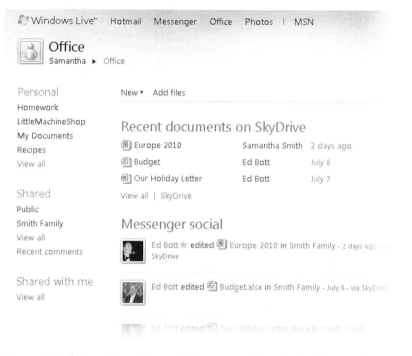

Figure 25-4 This page provides an Office-centric view of what's in your SkyDrive storage. To see its full contents, click SkyDrive below the Recent Documents list, or point to the Windows Live logo and click SkyDrive on the menu.

Uploading One or More Files

The Office Web Apps included with SkyDrive contain only a subset of the features of the full Office programs. If you have Office 2010 installed on your PC, you'll find it much faster and easier to create files using those full programs. Then, when you've completed your draft, you can upload the file to a SkyDrive folder. If you want to make a group of documents (or an entire subfolder) available on SkyDrive, you can install an uploader control that allows you to drag files from Windows Explorer to an Internet Explorer window for uploading.

TROUBLESHOOTING

The option to upload multiple files isn't available

The multiple-file uploader option for SkyDrive is available only with Internet Explorer. If you're using another browser, your upload options are limited to the standard upload page, where you can select files one at a time and upload them in batches of five or fewer. To speed things up, use Internet Explorer to perform the upload task, and then return to your SkyDrive folder using your default browser.

Creating a New File

Although SkyDrive works best as a way to view documents created in the corresponding full Office programs and make minor changes to them, you can navigate to a SkyDrive folder and create a new document in that folder using any of the four supported Office 2010 formats. In the design we looked at, the New menu is available in any SkyDrive folder, below the folder name and the breadcrumb-style navigation bar, as shown here. On the main Office page (but not in folders or subfolders), you can create a document by clicking one of the four icons under the Create A New Online Document heading.

When you choose one of these options, you must enter a file name and then click Save. Your new file opens immediately in the associated Office Web App for editing. Word requires you to click a button on the File menu to save changes; this step is not necessary with the other three Office Web Apps, which save changes automatically as you work.

Setting Permissions

SkyDrive allows you to set custom permissions for each folder located in the top level of your SkyDrive collection. These settings apply to all files and subfolders within that folder. You cannot change permissions for a subfolder; it inherits the permissions assigned to its parent folder.

When you create a new top-level folder, part of the setup process involves assigning default permissions. After you enter a folder name, you can see its default permissions at the bottom of the new, empty folder. Click Share, Edit Permissions and choose one of the five options on the Who Can Access This slider, as shown next.

Chapter 25

Windows Live™   Hotmail   Messenger   Office   Photos | MSN

Edit permissions for LittleMachineShop
Samantha ▸ Office ▸ LittleMachineShop ▸ Edit permissions

You're sharing this folder. Clear these settings

Who can access this

- Everyone (public)
- My friends and their friends   Can view files
- Friends (2)   Can view files   ▾
- Some friends (1)   Can add, edit details, and delete files ▾
- Just me

Sharing this with Friends, My friends and their friends, or Everyone (public) may also publish updates to some connected services you have set up.

Add specific people
Enter a name or an e-mail address: Select from your contact list

katybott@live.com

Save   Cancel

The options shown here apply permissions as follows:

- **Everyone (Public)**   Use this setting to make the contents of the folder available to anyone who has the URL for the SkyDrive folder. If you assign permissions to this group, the Can View Files setting is selected automatically and cannot be changed. As a result, visitors can read but not edit files in this folder unless they are part of another group to which you assign editing permissions.

- **My Friends And Their Friends**   This option allows anyone who is connected to a friend of yours (via Windows Live or another social service) to view files in this folder. The Can View Files permission cannot be changed.

- **Friends**   This option includes every member of your Windows Live contacts list and, possibly, other connected services. The default permission is Can View Files (read-only). You can change this setting to allow anyone on your friends list to add, edit details, or delete files.

- **Some Friends**   Choose this option if you have used the Limited Access option for one or more individuals among your Windows Live contacts and you want to block access to those individuals.

- **Just Me** Using this default setting, the folder is not shared. You and you alone have complete access to view and edit files in this folder and any subfolders contained within it.

If you want to assign permissions to individual people or groups of people (categories), you can add their names or e-mail addresses in the Add Additional People box at the bottom of the page.

After you create a folder, you can adjust the permissions assigned to it at any time by opening that folder, clicking Share, and clicking Edit Permissions.

To remove all permissions and stop sharing a SkyDrive folder (in other words, to return it to the default Just Me setting), click Clear These Settings at the top of the Edit Permissions page.

To see your full collection of SkyDrive files—Office documents, favorites, and photos—click the SkyDrive link or visit *skydrive.live.com* and sign in with your Windows Live ID. The full SkyDrive view, shown in Figure 25-5, adds small overlays to the folder icons to indicate private, public, and shared folders.

Figure 25-5 From your SkyDrive page, you can see permissions for each folder at a glance. Icons here indicate that the Recipes folder is private and the Smith Family folder is shared.

Sharing Files and Folders with Other People

Setting permissions properly allows you to grant other people access to a shared SkyDrive folder. But that's only half the job. The other, crucial step is helping your invited guests find the shared files so that they can view, comment on, and (if permitted) change those files.

If another person on your Windows Live contacts list has shared one or more SkyDrive folders with you, you can browse the contents of those shared folders by clicking Office at the top of your Windows Live home page. Click any of the View All links on the left side of the page to see a full list, sorted by contact name, of all shared folders to which you have been granted permission, either as an individual or as a member of a group.

There's an easier option to ensure that friends and coworkers have quick access to files you've chosen to share with them. From SkyDrive, you can send a link to a shared folder or to an individual file that is not stored in a folder (in other words, if it's in the root of your SkyDrive). Click Share, and then click Send A Link. You can enter an e-mail address, select any existing category from your contacts list, or begin typing the name of a person from your contacts list to choose their name from a list, as shown next.

Continue adding the names of individuals and groups until the list is complete. You have the option to enter a personalized message before you click Send.

To send a link that is accessible to anyone, regardless of whether they've logged on with a Windows Live ID, clear the Require Recipients To Sign In With Windows Live ID box. To copy a link to a specific file so that you can paste it into an e-mail or instant message window, first be sure that you've granted permission to the person to whom you're sending the link. Next, open the SkyDrive folder, click More, Properties, and copy the full link from the Web Address box on the right side of the window, as shown next. (You might see an advertisement between the file name and its properties.)

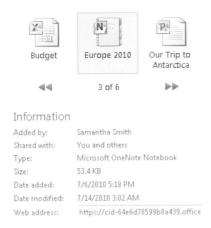

Managing Files and Folders in SkyDrive

At the time we wrote this chapter, Microsoft had not announced any way to access the contents of your Windows Live SkyDrive storage from Windows Explorer or from a Windows common dialog box. We expect that missing piece to appear someday, perhaps even by the time you read this. In the meantime (and even afterward) you can open your SkyDrive folder in any supported web browser and move, copy, rename, and delete files to your heart's content.

CAUTION

> SkyDrive has no Recycle Bin. When you delete a folder, it disappears immediately and permanently, along with its contents. If you're trying to delete a file, make sure you select the file first and don't accidentally delete a folder.

Clicking the Properties option on the More menu opens a page with a single large folder icon, the folder name, and a place where you can add a description of the folder. On the right side, under the Information heading, is a box like the one shown here in Figure 25-6.

Information
Shared with: People with a link
Keep until: Deleted
Type: Documents
Size: 2.1 MB
Web address: https://cid-fea7e5b2229991d8.office-

Figure 25-6 Use the top three links to change permissions, expiration date, or folder type, respectively, in a SkyDrive folder.

The Shared With field tells you who the folder is shared with. The Type field lists which of three folder types is assigned to the folder. The Information box also lists the cumulative size of all files in this folder and provides an easy-to-copy link to the folder's full web address.

INSIDE OUT   Decoding and managing SkyDrive URLs

The web address associated with a SkyDrive folder is long and complex—too complex to memorize, in fact. The key to your account is a unique identifier consisting of the letters *cid* followed by a hyphen and 16 alphanumeric characters. That unique ID string is followed by the skydrive.live.com or office.live.com domain. The SkyDrive URL for the test account used in this chapter is *http://cid-64e6d78599b8a439.office.live.com*. What you see when you open that address in your web browser depends on your Windows Live ID. If you're not logged on to Windows Live at all, you see only the default Public folder and any additional folders that have been created with public permissions. If you are logged on to Windows Live and you're the owner of the account, you see all folders and have full access to their contents and settings. If you're viewing someone else's SkyDrive and are logged on to Windows Live, you see the Public folders and any additional folders to which you've been granted permission.

The portion of the address that follows the domain name opens specific views of Sky-Drive folders and files. The summary.aspx page for your account, for example, shows folders you've accessed recently, a history of other SkyDrive accounts you've accessed, and recent activity from other people in your network. The home.aspx page (available by clicking All Folders in the sidebar on the left), shows all available folders in your account and allows you to create new folders and add files. URLs for folders and files use syntax based on the folder or file name. A document you open in Editing view from a SkyDrive folder will contain an embedded link to *officeapps.live.com*. (You can see this link if you view the source code for the page or if you click the Pop-Out button to open the document in a new window.)

Because all these locations are defined by standard web addresses, you can save any SkyDrive location as a favorite in Internet Explorer (or as a bookmark in other browsers). That includes your SkyDrive summary and home pages, as well as the locations of your Public folder and even individual files. If you plan to use the Public folder regularly, consider using a free URL-shortening service such as tinyurl.com to create an alias that's easier to remember than the long and daunting formal address.

TROUBLESHOOTING

A custom folder is assigned to the wrong folder type

When you create a new folder, SkyDrive assigns a folder type automatically based on the type of files you add to the folder initially. If you create one or more custom folders and plan for each to contain a mix of documents and photos, you might need to override this automatic setting. To do so, open the folder, click More, and then click Properties. Under the Information box on the right side of the page, you'll see a value to the right of Type. Click that value to open a settings page where you can choose a different folder type: Documents instead of Photos, for example. Click Save to apply the change.

Saving Files to SkyDrive from Office Programs

When you create a new Office document, you can save it directly to a Windows Live SkyDrive folder. The secret is to avoid the Save command and instead click File, Save & Send. Then click Save To Web, sign in if necessary using your Windows Live ID, and browse through your SkyDrive folders. (In OneNote, this option is available by clicking Web on the New tab, but only when you first create a notebook). Figure 25-7 shows our SkyDrive account as viewed through Word.

Figure 25-7 This page in Backstage view is the only built-in way to access your SkyDrive folders from an Office program.

Click a SkyDrive folder, then click Save As to open a conventional Windows Save As dialog box where you can enter a file name. If you want to add a new folder, click New; that opens the Create A Folder page in your web browser. You can also click the Windows Live SkyDrive link to view your SkyDrive account in your default web browser and perform management tasks such as renaming a folder or changing permissions. Come back to this page and click Refresh to see your changes and pick a folder.

Officially, there's no way to open a file from a Windows Live SkyDrive folder in an Office program. But if you've already used Backstage view to save a file to a SkyDrive folder, you inadvertently created a secret shortcut. In Backstage view, click Recent and look at the Recent Places list. You should see shortcuts to recently used SkyDrive folders there. Click the pushpin icon to the right of any such folder to pin it to the top of the list, where you can browse and open files from a Windows Open dialog box.

Synchronizing Office Files with SkyDrive

When you open a file in one of the full Office 2010 programs from a SkyDrive folder (using the Open In *<Program>* menu option), you can make changes to that file if the folder permissions allow you full access. You can't save the file directly, however. Instead, Office 2010 uses its own Upload Manager to synchronize your local changes with the file on the remote server. (If the document type supports simultaneous editing by multiple users, this synchronization process also merges their changes into your local copy.) This comes in especially handy if you open a file from SkyDrive on your notebook and then lose the connection to the network. While offline, you can continue to work on the file, and your changes are cached locally when you save. An Upload Pending message in the status bar indicates that your changes have not been saved to SkyDrive yet.

> **Files you open from a SkyDrive folder are not automatically available for editing. For details on how to enable editing, see "What You Can and Can't Do in Protected View" on page 818.**

If you click File and open the Info tab, you'll see a message like the one shown next, alerting you that the server is unavailable.

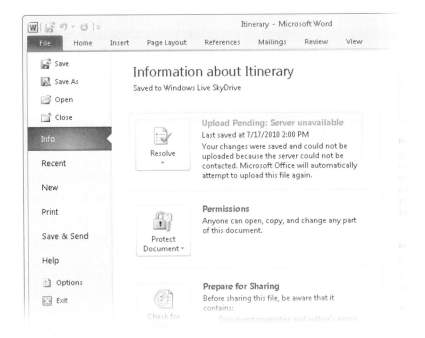

You can use the Resolve button to discard your changes or open the Microsoft Office Upload Center, shown in Figure 25-8. The Actions menu allows you to visit the associated server to troubleshoot, save a local copy of the file, and discard a cached copy.

Figure 25-8 Files that have been changed but not synchronized with SkyDrive appear here. Use the Actions menu to save a local copy and cancel the upload.

The Upload Center works with SharePoint servers as well, as we discuss in "How SharePoint and Office Work Together" on page 864.

What You Can and Can't Do with Office Web Apps

At the beginning of this chapter, we described the basic workings of Office Web Apps. In this section, we take a closer look at the features available in the Editing view for each of the four available programs. Our list of supported and unsupported features is not comprehensive, but it does give a good picture of what you can expect from each web app.

INSIDE OUT   Use Silverlight to improve the performance of Office apps

Silverlight is a free plug-in designed to improve the experience of using rich applications and media in a web browser. It is currently available for Internet Explorer, Safari, and Mozilla Firefox. When you use an Office Web App in a browser that does not have the Silverlight plug-in installed, you might be prompted to install it. Should you do so? If you're using the Word or PowerPoint Web App, the answer is absolutely yes. With those two programs, you'll see pages load faster and animations appear smoother. Silverlight provides improved text fidelity and more accurate searches in the Word Web App, and allows slides in your PowerPoint presentation to scale with the browser. The plug-in has no effect on Excel or OneNote. For more information about Silverlight, see *w7io.com/12703*.

When you open a Word document, a PowerPoint presentation, or a OneNote notebook or section using the associated Office Web App, your file opens by default in Reading view. Click Edit In Browser to switch to Editing view. In each of these three programs, you'll find a View tab that allows you to switch back to Reading view. When you open an Excel workbook for editing in the browser, you'll notice that the View tab is missing. To switch back to Reading view, click the browser's Refresh button.

CAUTION

Each of the Office Web Apps offers a subset of the features available in the corresponding full program. In theory, any of the features and formatting in a document that are not supported in a web app are preserved when you edit and save a document using the less capable browser-based version. In practice, you might find that seemingly minor changes made using the Word or PowerPoint Web App can affect formatting in unexpected ways. If you intend to do anything more than the simplest edits using a web app, we recommend that you make a backup copy first and check each set of changes carefully in the viewer portion of the web app.

Word

When you use the Word Web App, your editing options are adequate for simple documents. Using commands on the Home tab, you can tinker with text formatting, including fonts and font sizes, text highlighting using a virtual marker in yellow or any of 14 other colors, and paragraph alignment. You can apply styles from a list of standard styles as well as those that you add to the current document using the full Word program. You can also see most pictures, although any special effects or custom layout options do not render correctly in Word's Editing view.

The Word Web App doesn't offer advanced formatting options, and if a document originally created in the full Word program contains certain types of formatting, you are likely to encounter pages that don't render properly. Figure 25-9 illustrates a document where some formatting is missing in Editing view, with bracketed placeholders marking their position on the page.

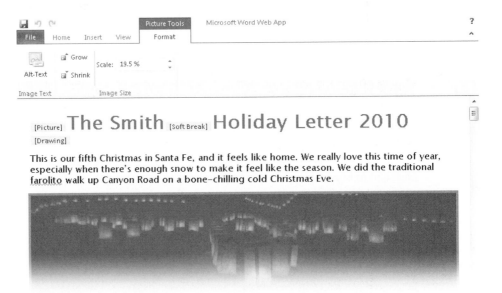

Figure 25-9 The bracketed placeholders indicate formatting that was added in the full Word program but can't be changed in the Word Web App.

You'll quickly hit a brick wall if you try to do any sophisticated formatting. You can't add a manual page break, paragraph break, or section break, for example. You can't attach a template to a document, nor can you create new styles or change existing styles. If your document includes a header or footer, you will see it in Reading view but not in Editing view.

If you look carefully at the previous figure, you'll notice that a picture is selected and a Picture Tools tab is visible on the ribbon. It's remarkably short of editing and effects options, especially when compared to the range of tools you get with the full Word program. You'll find similarly limited capabilities for tables: you can create simple grids and format the text within cells, but you can't apply table styles.

Excel

In Editing view, Excel follows the same keep-it-simple philosophy as Word. The Home tab contains most basic formatting options to help you change fonts, font sizes, and text attributes. You can adjust the alignment of cells and ranges and insert or delete cells, rows, and columns. Moving the mouse pointer over a cell reveals its full contents in a ScreenTip. When viewing a list, you can sort and filter using controls like the one shown in Figure 25-10.

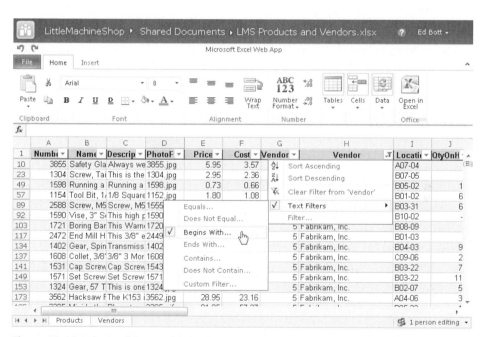

Figure 25-10 When editing a table in the Excel Web App, you can sort and filter using this drop-down menu.

So what's missing when you edit a workbook in your browser? Most advanced formatting, for starters, including table styles, conditional formatting, and styles. You can choose from a list of 10 predefined formats (in addition to the General format) to apply to a cell but cannot create or modify custom formats.

If your workbook contains PivotTables, you can view their contents as simple lists using the last saved arrangement of data. The Excel Web App has no tools for modifying or filtering a PivotTable, although you can refresh the connection to an external data source to update the current display.

Charts are visible in Editing view but appear as simple graphic elements. The Excel Web App includes no tools for creating, formatting, or editing charts.

The File menu for the Excel Web App contains a menu option to save a local copy of the workbook, but it also includes a Download A Snapshot menu choice. This option saves a local copy of the file that contains only the values and formatting from the original workbook. It replaces formulas with their results, converts PivotTables to static lists, and breaks the links between chart data and the ranges that contain the original source data. The snapshot is in Excel format, so it opens in your local copy of Excel.

PowerPoint

Unlike Word and Excel, the PowerPoint Web App includes three views. In Reading view, you'll see a Start Slide Show button on the PowerPoint Web App menu; in Editing view, this option exists on the View tab, as shown here.

In Reading and Slide Show views, with Silverlight installed, the presentation automatically resizes to fit the browser window. You can show or hide the Notes pane in Reading view, and animations work as expected, using the timings and settings you define in the full PowerPoint program. Slide transitions, on the other hand, are stripped to a generic fade effect regardless of the defined transition.

In Editing view, you can perform most basic presentation tasks. You can add and delete slides, hide a slide, or change the order of existing slides by dragging thumbnails in the pane on the left. All layouts in the current presentation, including custom layouts added from a template, are available for your use.

You can add pictures and SmartArt to a slide in the PowerPoint Web App, but you can't add charts, videos, clip art, or tables. After you choose a picture to insert into a slide, the Picture Tools Format tab appears, offering a full range of effects in the Picture Styles group, as shown in Figure 25-11.

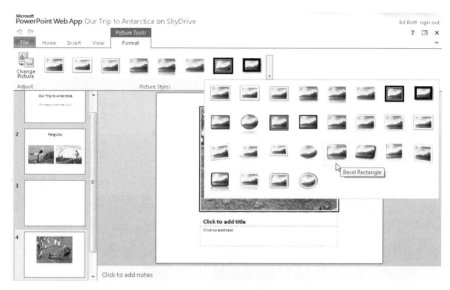

Figure 25-11 When adding or editing a picture in the PowerPoint Web App, you can choose from the full range of effects,

The picture itself is fixed in size, adapting its dimensions to the placeholder. To crop the image, change its borders, or add effects, you need to open the presentation in PowerPoint. If you use the full PowerPoint program to apply custom attributes (reflections and shadows, for example) to pictures or text, those effects are preserved if you change the picture or edit the text in the PowerPoint Web App.

Advanced design tools, such as those used to apply a custom theme, transitions, or animations, are not available in the PowerPoint Web App.

OneNote

OneNote differs substantially from its fellow Office programs, so it should not be surprising that the OneNote Web App also differs in some significant ways from its fellow web apps. You can switch between Reading view and Editing view in the OneNote Web App just as you can in Word and PowerPoint. But OneNote's Editing view offers a handful of tricks you won't find in those other programs, especially when you use the right mouse button.

In Editing view, you can directly enter text and insert pictures into pages. You can delete pages and delete or rename sections from the Navigation bar on the left using right-click shortcut menus. You can add pages by clicking the New Page icon on the right of each section heading. Unlike the full program, where sections and pages appear in separate panes, their contents are combined in the browser view. You can collapse and expand the list of pages under any section by clicking the section heading.

The list of basic styles and tags is available from menus on the Home tab, and you can add tags to any paragraph or picture, as shown in Figure 25-12.

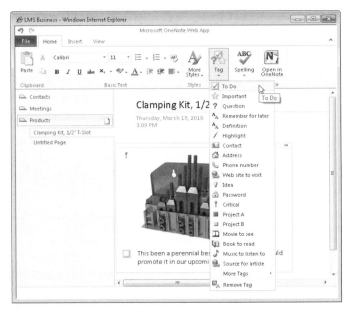

Figure 25-12 Tags available in the OneNote Web App lack some attributes such as the yellow highlighting applied to paragraphs with the To Do tag.

If you've customized the list of OneNote tags, you might find it frustrating that your changes are not available to the browser-based version of OneNote. The list includes only standard tags. It does not allow you to add custom tags, even if they have already been used in the current notebook.

The OneNote Web App lacks the explicit links to Outlook found in the full program. It also lacks drawing tools and the ability to record audio or video clips. In short, it's an excellent way to review your existing notes and to allow you and your collaborators to jot down text or insert graphics when you're away from your main PC. But it's no substitute for the full program.

CHAPTER 26

Working with SharePoint 2010

Microsoft officially describes SharePoint as an "integrated suite of server capabilities that can help improve organizational effectiveness by providing comprehensive content management and enterprise search, accelerating shared business processes, and facilitating information-sharing across boundaries for better business insight."

That's quite a mouthful. In simpler terms, having access to a SharePoint server means you and your coworkers can collaborate on projects, share document libraries, participate in threaded discussions, build lists and group calendars, and even publish a blog. You can do all this in a web browser, using Office programs (and Office Web Apps) to create, edit, share, and manage content along the way. And you don't need to be in a big business, either (although it helps).

The greatest strength of SharePoint is that anyone with the right permissions can build a new site or customize an existing one with no more than a few clicks. The sheer variety of sites and elements that you can create is impressive. With relatively little work (and a not-too-steep learning curve), you can build a custom SharePoint site around a document, a project, or a team and then use it for a week or a year (or more). And you're not limited to the ready-made templates, either—a large and active developer community specializes in building add-ons and custom SharePoint sites.

We'll leave it to others to write a book—maybe even a whole series—that explains how to set up SharePoint and use it to its full potential. In this chapter, our focus is on the strong connections between the 2010 versions of SharePoint and Office and how you can combine the strengths of each platform to get more work done. We assume that SharePoint 2010 is already installed, configured, and available on your network. We also assume that you're using Office 2010. If your network includes older versions of SharePoint or Office, your experience will be very different from what we describe here.

What's in a SharePoint Site or Workspace?

When someone on your team sends you a link to a new SharePoint site, what are you likely to see when you visit? In this section we look at the building blocks of SharePoint itself, as viewed through a browser window. Our examples are simple, and they're mostly based on templates and Web Parts available through a default SharePoint Foundation installation. In an enterprise that has made a large investment in SharePoint development, you can expect to see much richer and more interactive designs.

INSIDE OUT SharePoint isn't just for big businesses

In earlier generations, SharePoint was mostly adopted by large enterprises that had the IT staff to set up and maintain SharePoint servers. Today, thanks to fast, always-on Internet connections, you can let someone else do all that setup and mainte-nance. SharePoint Online is available as a hosted service from Microsoft Online (*w7io.com/12801*), by itself or as part of the Business Productivity Online Suite (with Microsoft Exchange Online, Microsoft Office Live Meeting, and Microsoft Office Com-munications Online). These services are available for as few as five users, at prices that we believe most businesses will find very reasonable. Third parties also provide SharePoint as a hosted service—enter the term "hosted Sharepoint" into your favorite search engine and you'll find dozens of leads to follow.

If you have a server running Windows Server 2008 or later, you can install the free SharePoint Foundation release (formerly known as Windows SharePoint Services) and begin building SharePoint sites on your own local network. You'll find detailed instruc-tions at *w7io.com/12802*.

During the course of writing and researching this book, we used an earlier version of SharePoint on Microsoft Online, running SharePoint 2010 on our own on-premises servers. The difference was startling. If you're currently using Office 2010 with an older version of SharePoint, we recommend signing up for a trial account with a hosted ser-vice provider so that you can see what you're missing.

Figure 26-1 shows a SharePoint site we built for LittleMachineShop.com. The home page includes a custom logo, lists of announcements and shared documents, and a sidebar with links to other site elements, such as a group calendar and a tasks list.

Tab bar

Quick
Launch
pane

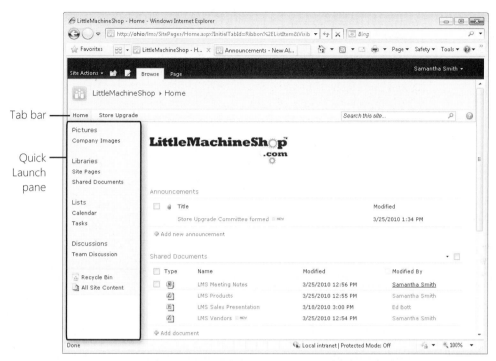

Figure 26-1 This SharePoint site layout has a ribbon, a tab bar to switch between sites, a Quick Launch pane on the left, and content under a company logo. It took just a few minutes to build.

SharePoint Users, Groups, and Permissions

The name of the currently logged-on user appears in the upper right corner of the site window. Permissions that an administrator assigns to your account, either individually or by adding you to a group, dictate what you can do on that site. Figure 26-2 shows the permissions assigned by default to the Home Members group.

The simplest and quickest way to create a new site is to sign in using an account that has Full Control permissions (the default setting if your account has been assigned to the Owners group for your site). Click Site Actions (at the left side of the ribbon) to display the menu shown on the bottom of the next page.

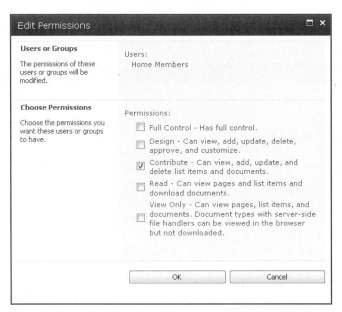

Figure 26-2 If your user account is assigned to the Home Members group, you have the Contribute permissions listed above.

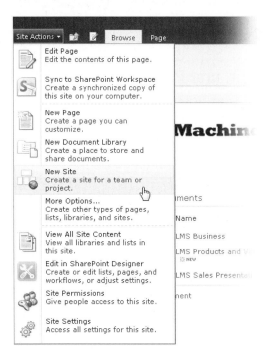

It's worth taking a minute to study the contents of the Site Actions menu. If you sign in with an account that has Contribute permissions, you see only the top three choices and View All Site Content. If your account is part of the built-in Viewers group, you have only Read permissions, and you don't see the Edit Page and New Page options on this menu. When your account has Full Control permissions, however, you can change the site's design, create new lists and libraries, adjust site permissions, and tweak site settings.

Creating a New SharePoint Site

You can create dozens, even hundreds or thousands, of separate sites on a single Share-Point server. A new site can be completely independent or it can be a child of the current one, with navigation links that take you back to the parent site. This latter organization is handy if you and your immediate coworkers have your own site for departmental announcements, contacts, tasks, and shared documents. Within that site, you can create individual sites for projects, committees, wikis, or documents like annual reports—anything that involves multiple people. An administrator or site owner can create a site and make anyone an owner of the new site. As an owner, you can create additional sites under your site's hierarchy.

To create a site, click the New Site choice on the Site Actions menu. That opens the Create dialog box, which offers a selection of site templates like the ones shown in Figure 26-3.

Figure 26-3 The default selection of sites and workspaces includes templates for different types of meetings and documents, a team site, and even a blog.

Whether you start with the Blank Site template or one that's partially built, you can flesh out your SharePoint site by adding and customizing the following types of elements:

- **Libraries**   These are online repositories for documents, forms, pictures, or wiki pages. We cover libraries and their interaction with Office programs in much more detail in "Creating and Using SharePoint Libraries" on page 869.

- **Pages**   A page can contain text, images, links to wiki pages, and ready-made Web Parts. We explain the essentials of creating and using pages in "Creating and Editing SharePoint Pages" on page 875.

- **Lists**   Don't be fooled by the name. Yes, lists can consist of column headings and rows filled with data, but they can also appear in SharePoint as calendars, issue-tracking databases, and threaded discussion forums. Learn more in "Creating, Viewing, and Editing SharePoint Lists" on page 873.

How SharePoint and Office Work Together

Up to this point we've been talking about SharePoint mostly as it appears through a browser window. But you can interact with documents in a SharePoint library directly through the Open and Save As dialog boxes in Office 2010 programs.

To connect to a SharePoint site from Word, Excel, PowerPoint, or OneNote, click File, then click Open. Enter or paste the URL of the site in the address bar (or in the File Name box) and press Enter. If your credentials pass muster, you'll see a dialog box like the one shown in Figure 26-4.

INSIDE OUT   Create simple shortcuts to SharePoint servers

Typing a URL is a tedious way to get to a SharePoint site or document library, especially if the site has a long, hard-to-memorize address. For faster access, add a shortcut to Windows Explorer so that you can get to your site quickly. In Windows Vista or Windows 7, open Windows Explorer and click Computer in the Navigation pane. Right-click the empty space at the bottom of the contents pane, and then click Add A Network Location. Follow the prompts: click Choose A Custom Network Location, enter or paste the URL of the server or site (in the format *http://server_name/site_name*), and give the shortcut a descriptive name. You can now browse to this location by clicking the Computer icon and double-clicking the shortcut you just created. You can also populate the Favorites list at the top of the Navigation pane in Windows Explorer with shortcuts to sites, document libraries, pages, and other locations within a SharePoint site. Start by browsing from the Computer window, and then drag the folder or page icon from the address bar or the contents pane to the Favorites list.

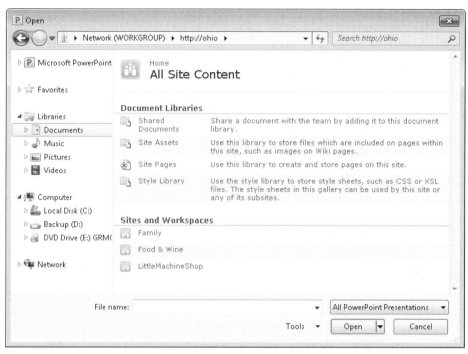

Figure 26-4 To browse files and folders on a SharePoint site, enter the site's URL in the address bar of the Open dialog box.

After you open a file from a SharePoint library (and, if necessary, enable it for editing, click File and check the Info tab. Options available to you depend partly on the settings for the library, partly on the procedures you and your coworkers have agreed to follow, and partly on your preferences.

If you want exclusive access to a document so that you and you alone can make changes to it, you need to check it out of the library. After you've saved your changes, you can check it back in and allow other people to see what you've done and make their own changes if they want to.

The Check Out option is available on the Info tab for Excel, Word, and PowerPoint; click the Manage Versions button to see a menu like the one shown next. (The equivalent menu for Word includes an option to compare major versions.)

Other users on the network are able to open a checked-out document in read-only mode, but they can make changes only by saving it under a new name or waiting until the document is available for editing again. When you have a document checked out, this button appears at the top of the Info pane:

Click Check In, and you're given an opportunity to add comments to describe your changes; if the document library is set up to save versions, your comments are saved as part of the version history. If you don't want your changes to be saved in the SharePoint library, you have two options. Click the Discard Check Out button to close the document and remove the checked-out designation; any changes you made since the last save are lost. As an alternative, click File, Save As, and save the document under a new name. As part of the save, you can discard the check-out.

In some cases, you might not need or want to limit editing on a document. If you and a group of coworkers have divvied up responsibilities for a big document that's due tomorrow, your only hope of finishing on time is to work on the file at the same time. When two or more people are editing the same document in Word, Excel, or PowerPoint, the top of the Info pane shows details like those in Figure 26-5.

INSIDE OUT
Synchronizing local files with a SharePoint site

If your organization makes extensive use of SharePoint, you should take a close look at Microsoft SharePoint Workspace 2010. This utility, included with Office 2010 Professional Plus, is the successor to Groove Workspace from earlier Office editions. It allows you to create an offline replica of libraries and lists (including tasks and discussions) from a SharePoint site. You can search, view, and edit documents and lists offline; when you reconnect to the network, SharePoint Workspace handles the work of syncing your changes and those made by others. You'll find SharePoint Workspace in the Microsoft Office folder on the All Programs menu.

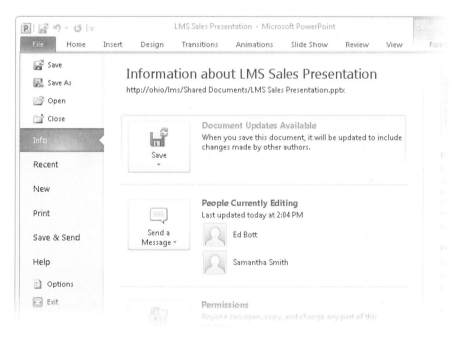

Figure 26-5 When two or more people are simultaneously editing a document stored in a SharePoint library, details appear at the top of the Info pane,

Changes to the current document made by other people are not automatically displayed in your document as you work—that would be distracting, to say the least. Instead, the Share-Point server sends periodic notifications that other people have made changes to the document. You can see these notifications on the status bar and in the Info pane. Those changes are downloaded and merged into your document when you click Save.

> For more details about how to use document-sharing features, with or without SharePoint, see "Working Together with Office 2010" on page 826 and "Simultaneous Editing with Multiple Authors" on page 832.

Customizing a SharePoint Site

The template you select when you create a SharePoint site dictates what elements are initially included as part of that site and how they are laid out. But as a site owner you can change both the layout and the selection of elements at any time to change the site's look and feel. In this section, we provide an overview of the basic techniques for customizing a SharePoint site, along with specifics about the site elements that are most useful with Office 2010.

The key to customizing any SharePoint site is the ribbon, which displays custom tabs containing editing tools for the selected page, list, library, or Web Part. Figure 26-6 shows the custom tabs available when we selected a Web Part containing an Announcements list on the home page of our LittleMachineShop site.

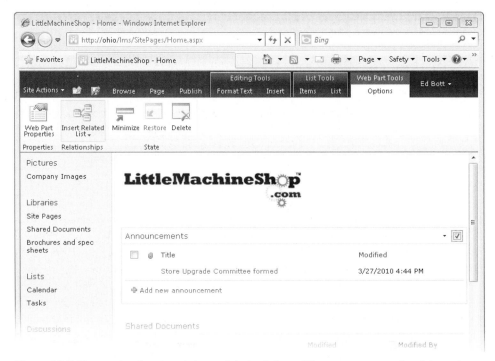

Figure 26-6 These sets of custom tabs contain tools for editing pages, managing lists, and customizing the placement of Web Parts on a page.

Creating and Using SharePoint Libraries

Libraries are literally folders on a server. In the case of a document library, SharePoint adds to those folders the ability to easily adjust permissions, track versions, and allow documents to be checked out for exclusive access. This type of library is so useful that New Document Library gets its own place of honor on the Site Actions menu. But SharePoint actually offers the option to create four different types of libraries. From the Site Actions menu, click More Options, and then click Library in the Create dialog box. The full list of available library types includes the following:

- **Document Library**   This type of library can store any file. You can enable versioning and customize the library so that adding a new document uses a specific document template. In the remainder of this section, we focus mostly on this type of library.

- **Form Library**   Items in this type of folder allow users to create reports or orders by using forms created by an XML editor such as Microsoft InfoPath. We do not cover form libraries or InfoPath in this book.

- **Picture Library**   The default view for this type of library consists of thumbnails; menu choices include options to upload and download pictures, insert an image into a document or an e-mail message, or view pictures as a slide show.

- **Wiki Page Library**   A wiki library consists of web pages that any user can edit. It grows in free-form fashion as users create new pages and link them to existing pages. Wikis are ideal for collecting and organizing knowledge—using notes from customer support representatives, for example, to build a troubleshooting knowledge base.

INSIDE OUT   Use wiki-style links to create new pages instantly

The beauty of a wiki library is that you don't need to explicitly create and link new pages. Instead, you can create them on the fly using a well-established wiki-link format. (The same format is supported in OneNote pages.) Creating a wiki library adds an entry to the Quick Launch pane on the left of the browser window and creates a Home page and a second page called How To Use This Library. To edit the Home page, click the Edit button at the top of the page, to the left of the Browse tab. You can replace the existing text with an introduction of your own and create links in the format [[*page_name*]], where *page_name* is the title of the page you want to link to. If the linked page doesn't exist, clicking the link creates a new page with that title and immediately opens it for editing. You can add links on any page and create a link back to the Home page by entering **[[Home]]**.

As we mentioned earlier, a library is at its heart just a folder on a SharePoint server. Its contents can appear in multiple places on a site, on its own page, or as a Web Part alongside other content on a page. (See Figure 26-1 at the beginning of this chapter for an example of the latter layout.) Unless you change the default setting, each new library gets a link in the Quick Launch pane on the left. Figure 26-7 shows the contents of a document library we created for the LittleMachineShop site.

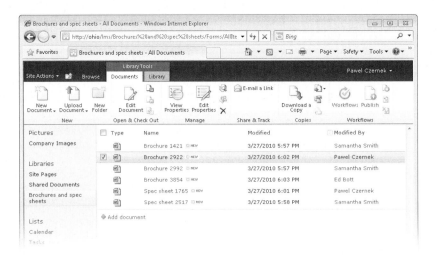

Figure 26-7 When you display the contents of a document library, these two custom Library Tools tabs appear on the ribbon.

Managing Files in a Document Library

Commands on the Documents tab provide access to basic file-management tasks. Using the commands in the New group, for example, you can create a document and begin editing it immediately. You can also upload documents or create subfolders.

To use commands that apply to individual documents, you first have to select at least one document by clicking the check box to the left of the document name. (In the previous figure, the check mark means we've selected the file Brochure 2922.) You can edit the selected document, check it out for exclusive access, edit its properties (including file name and title), or delete the document. For a more focused list of commands that apply to a specific file, click the arrow to the right of the document name and choose from the menu shown next.

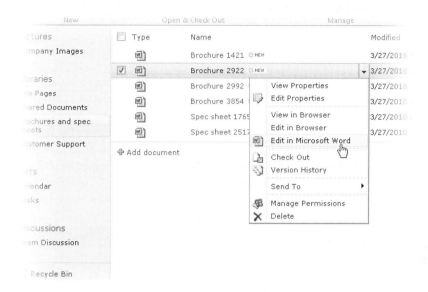

Changing Settings for a Document Library

The Library tab, shown in Figure 26-8, contains commands that allow you to change settings for the current library.

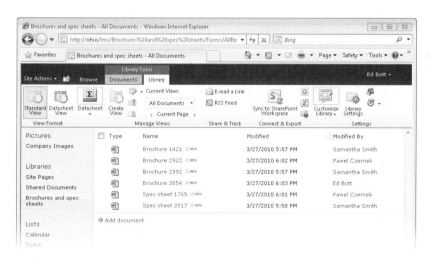

Figure 26-8 Commands on this tab allow you to change the view of the current library. Click Library Settings to set global preferences.

In the Manage Views group are commands that allow you to add or remove columns from the current view, change the sort order and grouping, and filter the library's contents. You can also use these settings to create multiple custom views to make navigation easier in a crowded document library.

The Library Settings button leads to a dialog box that is packed with options to change the appearance and behavior of the current library. For example, you can edit the library's title and description and customize whether it gets a link on the Quick Launch pane. For some document libraries, you might want to ensure that clicking New Document always creates a specific document type. Figure 26-9 shows the Advanced Settings dialog box (available from Library Settings) for our Brochures And Spec Sheets folder. To allow would-be contributors to start with a standard Word document, enter the URL of a previously created Word template or click Edit Template to add customizations to the default template.

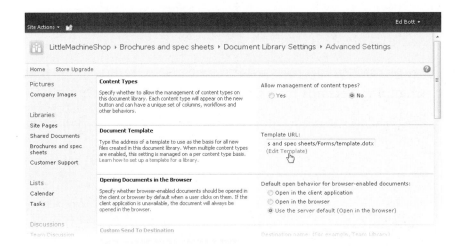

Figure 26-9 Customizing a document template allows every new document in a library to start with a standard look and feel.

> To learn more about how templates work with each of the Office programs, see "Using Templates to Streamline Document Creation" on page 97.

Other options available in the Library Settings dialog box allow you to enable or disable versioning, change which columns are visible, set custom permissions for the library, and define RSS settings to alert you when changes are made to the library's contents.

> For more on how to use RSS feeds as an alert system, see "Using Notifications and Feeds to Track SharePoint Activity" on page 880.

Creating, Viewing, and Editing SharePoint Lists

The generic term *list* covers a surprisingly broad swath in SharePoint. Calendars are stored in lists, as are contacts, tasks, links, and announcements. When creating a new list, you can choose from a full selection of ready-made list types or create your own from scratch. To start, click the Site Actions menu, click More Options, and then, under Filter By, choose List. The full selection of items includes the handful shown here.

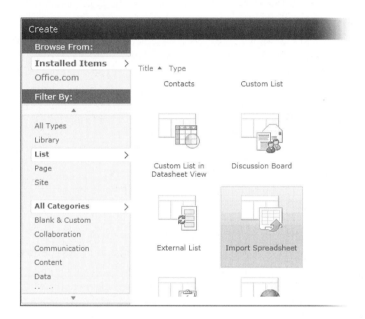

If none of the default list types are suitable, you can create your own by choosing one of the Custom List options, or you can connect to an external list, such as a query on a database server. The Import Spreadsheet option allows you to take a list you created in Excel and import its contents into your SharePoint site. Click Import Spreadsheet, click Create, and enter a name and description for the new list. Specify the location of the Excel file containing your existing list, and click Import. Your workbook opens in Excel, and you see the dialog box shown in Figure 26-10.

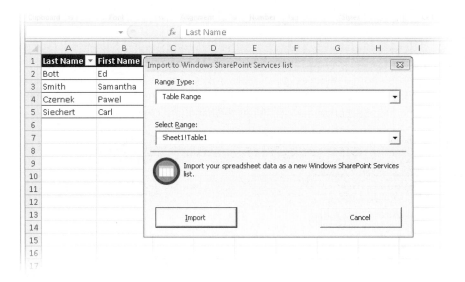

Figure 26-10 Importing an Excel table into SharePoint as a list allows you to share its contents with a larger group. The new list is not linked to the original workbook.

Importing an Excel table into a SharePoint list using the technique we just described is a one-way operation. Changes you make in the Excel workbook are not reflected in the SharePoint list, and vice versa. If you perform the operation in the opposite direction, however, you can create a persistent link between a SharePoint list and an Excel workbook. From the SharePoint list, click the List tab (under the List Tools heading) and click Export To Excel from the Connect & Export group. That saves the list properties in Microsoft Excel Web Query File format, with an .iqy file name extension. Open that file in Excel, and the resulting workbook includes a live connection to the SharePoint list, as shown in Figure 26-11.

The Refresh command, on the Table Tools Design tab, allows you to update the contents of the linked Excel table based on the most recent entries in the underlying SharePoint list. You can also create PivotTable reports from the data. To break the link between the worksheet table and the SharePoint list, click Convert To Range or click Unlink.

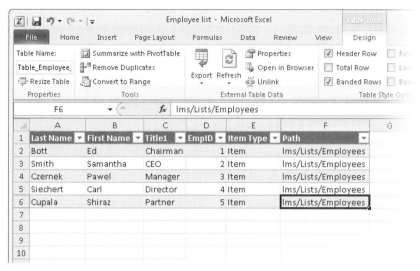

Figure 26-11 Any changes you make in the underlying SharePoint list are reflected in the copy saved here. Click Refresh to update data, or click Open In Browser to see the list in SharePoint.

As we mentioned at the beginning of this section, calendars, tasks, and threaded discussions in SharePoint are also lists. It makes little sense to import these types of data into Excel, but there are obvious benefits in being able to connect this type of data to Outlook. We explain how SharePoint and Outlook work together in "Connecting Lists, Calendars, and Discussions to Outlook" on page 877.

Creating and Editing SharePoint Pages

Pages on a SharePoint site are HTML documents that can be edited directly by using the Web Edit controls in SharePoint. Most common site templates include a Home page. If your permissions allow it, you can also create a new page using the Site Actions menu. Use the Page tab, shown in Figure 26-12, to see what options are available for that page.

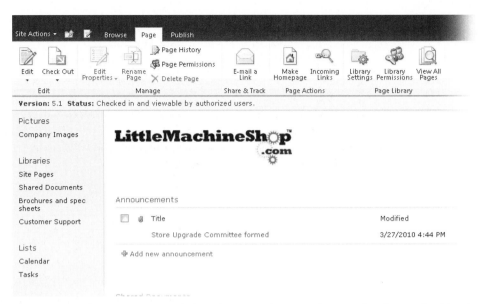

Figure 26-12 The status message below the Page tab means this page has been edited but is not yet published. To commit the changes, use the Publish tab.

From the Page tab, you can click Edit to see a full list of layout, markup, and formatting options. Commands on the Editing Tools tabs allow you to change the layout of the page (number of columns, header and footer, and so on), apply styles, insert pictures, add Web Parts such as lists, and edit the HTML code for the page directly. If versioning is enabled, you can click Page History to see previous versions of the page, as shown here.

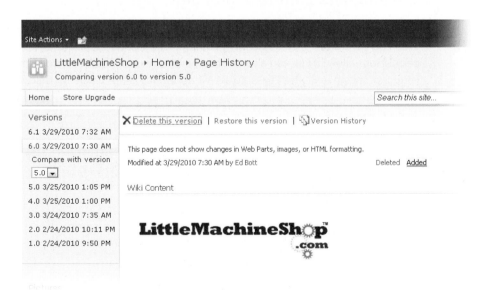

INSIDE OUT   Build more sophisticated pages

The browser-based page editor is fine for creating quick SharePoint pages from build-ing blocks, and it might even be good enough for entire sites. But if you want to exten-sively customize the look and feel of pages or add workflow features and connections to external data, you need to leave the browser. For those tasks, use the free SharePoint Designer, a stand-alone program that resembles the other members of the Office fam-ily and allows you to create rich SharePoint sites offline and deploy them as packages. For more information, visit *w7io.com/12803*.

Connecting Lists, Calendars, and Discussions to Outlook

It's easy enough to work with individual documents using the programs associated with those documents. But how do you keep track of calendars, tasks, and threaded discussions without constantly checking your web browser to see what's changed? The easiest way to manage this type of data is by connecting it to Outlook.

In fact, virtually every part of a SharePoint site can be connected to Outlook, which allows new and changed items to appear in your Outlook window. Calendars appear in the Calen-dar pane in Outlook, under the Other Calendars heading. Tasks are added to the Tasks pane in Outlook. Document Libraries and threaded discussions appear under a SharePoint Lists heading in the Mail pane of Outlook. Figure 26-13, for example, shows a SharePoint team calendar as viewed in a web browser.

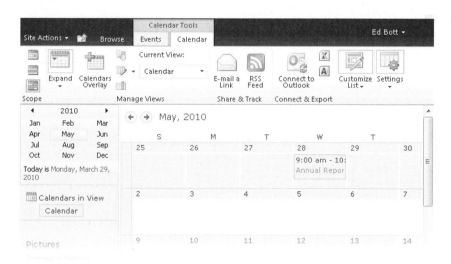

Figure 26-13 The browser-based view of a calendar is adequate but doesn't offer an easy way to compare events with those on your personal calendar.

After connecting this calendar to Outlook, you can view its contents using the familiar Outlook calendar tools and views. In particular, you can view the team calendar from the SharePoint site alongside your personal calendar to quickly spot potential conflicts, as shown here.

Viewing discussions is also simpler in Outlook. Figure 26-14 shows a single conversation (in flat, not threaded, view) from the Team Discussion list on our LittleMachineShop SharePoint site.

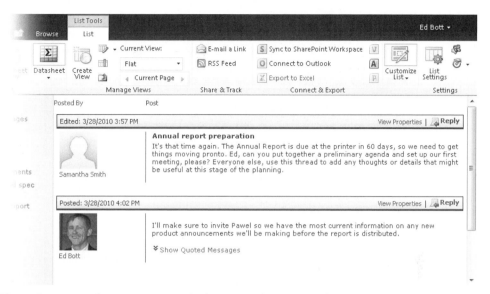

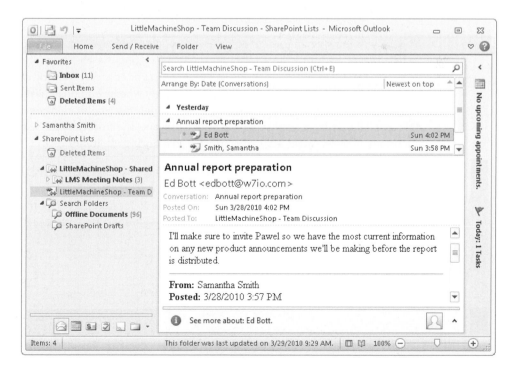

Figure 26-14 Use the Connect To Outlook command to capture these threaded discussions in Outlook and avoid the need for a trip to the browser.

After connecting the discussion group to Outlook, you can view and participate in the same discussions using its entry in the SharePoint Lists group in the Navigation pane, shown here.

To connect a SharePoint list or library to Outlook, open the calendar, discussion list, or other page, and then find the Connect To Outlook command, which is part of the Connect & Export group. For a calendar, this command is on the Calendar tab, under Calendar Tools. For tasks and discussions, the command is on the List tab. For a document library, look on the Library tab.

Clicking this button displays a consent dialog box like the one shown here.

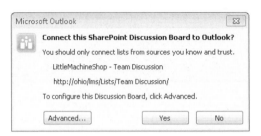

Under the hood, this command creates a web query using the stssync protocol and sends it to Outlook, which breaks the query into its component parts and begins syncing data between Outlook and SharePoint. It's important to note that this is a true synchronization. Any changes you make in either place are reflected in the other.

Using Notifications and Feeds to Track SharePoint Activity

How do you know when something has been added or changed on a SharePoint site? For some projects, you might be able to get by just by visiting the site in your browser once or twice a week. For others, that option isn't practical or efficient. For projects on a tight deadline, you might want to be notified immediately whenever a document is changed or added. For long-term projects, where changes happen rarely and are never on a predictable schedule, a timely notification via e-mail prevents the frustration of discovering an important addition weeks after it was posted to a document library.

SharePoint supports two types of notifications. The first is an Alert, which can be set for many types of individual SharePoint items: a Word document or Excel workbook in a document library, an event on a team calendar, or any task, for example. Click the check box to the left of the item in the library, and then click View Properties. That opens a properties dialog box like the one shown next.

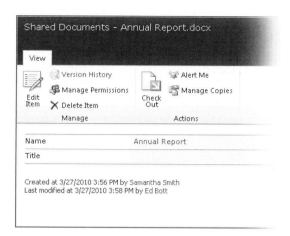

Click Alert Me to open a New Alert dialog box for that item. To keep track of all activities associated with a document library or list, your entry point is slightly different. In the SharePoint main window, click the arrow to the right of your user name (in the upper right corner) and then click My Settings. Click My Alerts, and then click Add Alert. That option displays a list of all lists and libraries that support alerts. Select the location for which you want to create an e-mail alert, as we've done here, and then click Next to proceed to the New Alert dialog box.

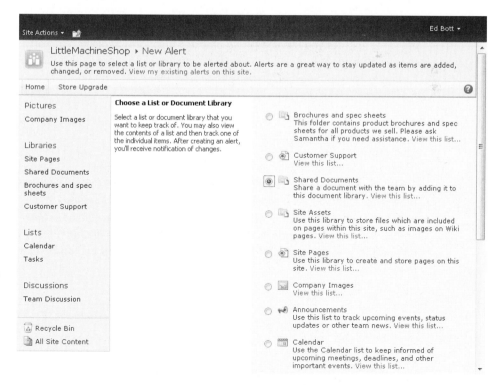

Your options vary slightly depending on whether you've chosen an individual item or a list. For an individual item, your options are as shown in Figure 26-15.

Delivery Method

Specify how you want the alerts delivered.

Send me alerts by:

- ● E-mail   edbott@w7io.com
- ○ Text Message (SMS) [   ]
  - ☐ Send URL in text message (SMS)

Send Alerts for These Changes

Specify whether to filter alerts based on specific criteria. You may also restrict your alerts to only include items that show in a particular view.

Send me an alert when:

- ● Anything changes
- ○ Someone else changes a document
- ○ Someone else changes a document created by me
- ○ Someone else changes a document last modified by me

When to Send Alerts

Specify how frequently you want to be alerted. (mobile alert is only available for immediately send)

- ○ Send notification immediately
- ● Send a daily summary
- ○ Send a weekly summary

Time:

[Monday ▼] [9:00 AM ▼]

Figure 26-15 Using the settings shown here, you can cut down on e-mail volume by tailoring the scope and frequency of alerts.

For time-sensitive, high-priority projects, you might want to receive notifications immediately. For libraries you use in high-volume, lower-priority projects, you can ask SharePoint to roll notifications into daily or weekly summaries. In the previous figure, for example, we configured a summary alert to be sent daily at 9:00 A.M., with notifications of everything that happened the previous day.

To create additional alerts for other lists or libraries, repeat the preceding process, starting with the My Alerts dialog box.

If you want alerts to appear somewhere other than your e-mail inbox, you can use RSS feeds, the details of which can be read in any compatible RSS client (including any web browser or Outlook). To subscribe to the feed for a list or library, click the RSS Feed command on the List or Library tab. That opens the feed for the current page in the browser and allows you to subscribe to the feed in Internet Explorer or Outlook. If you prefer a different RSS reader, copy the URL from the browser window and paste it into your feed reader.

For more details on how to add an RSS feed to Outlook, see "Reading RSS Feeds in Outlook" on page 803.

To customize the contents of the RSS feed, click List Settings (or Library Settings), and then click RSS Settings under the Communications heading. The extensive list of options here allows you to choose exactly which fields the feed will include, whether it contains links to enclosures and attachments, and whether long fields (over 256 characters) will be truncated for efficiency.

Index to Troubleshooting Topics

Program / Feature	Description	Page
Pictures and graphics	Grouped objects remain grouped after you choose Ungroup	162
Pictures and graphics	Changes to pictures can't be undone, or edits disappear	171
Pictures and graphics	Text or graphics get clipped	221
Pictures and graphics	A graphic is cropped to just one line high	238
PowerPoint	Options in the Animation pane are unavailable	621
PowerPoint	Your viewers can't see your presentation	653
PowerPoint	Your comments have disappeared	662
Windows Live SkyDrive	The option to upload multiple files isn't available	843
Windows Live SkyDrive	A custom folder is assigned the wrong folder type	850
Word	Comma-separated values files don't convert properly	257
Word	Word can't register your blog account	316
Word	Word doesn't recognize your blogging service's picture provider	317

Index

Symbols and Numbers

& (ampersands), 360, 400, 467–468
* (asterisks), 211, 358, 463
@ (at signs), 397
\ (backslashes), 463
[ ] (brackets), 397, 463, 854
^ (carets), 358
, (commas), 361, 461
: (colons), 276, 361, 381, 745
$ (dollar signs), 361–363
= (equal signs), 359, 745
/ (forward slashes), 358
> (greater than operators), 359, 745
>= (greater than or equal to operators), 359
- (hyphens), 400
< (less than or equal to operators), 359, 745
<= (less than, equal signs), 359
<> (not equal operators), 359
% (percent signs), 358
. (periods), 461
+ (plus signs), 358
# (pound signs), 397
" (quotation marks), 462–463, 535, 536
? (question marks), 211
_ (underscores), 463
3-D effects in charts, 429, 432, 436, 439
3-D graphic rotation, 167–168, 178
32-bit and 64-bit editions, 22–23, 39
100% stacked column charts, 429, 431–432

A

Above Average filtering, 403
ABOVE range (Word table formulas), 261
absolute references in worksheets, 361–363
.accdb or .accde file extensions, 80
accelerator keys, 72. *See also* keyboard shortcuts
accepting
   changes to files, 287–289, 664, 830–831
   meetings, 781
Access databases, 416
access to files, restrictions, 46, 298. *See also* permissions
accessibility issues, 295

account setup for Outlook, 707
accounting worksheet cell format, 380–381
.acl file extension, 118
ACOS worksheet function, 373
ACOSH worksheet function, 373
action buttons (presentations), 675–679
actions, Quick Step, 760, 761
activating Office, 35–37
active worksheets, printing, 470
ActiveX controls, 818
Add A Digital Signature option, 299
Add New Account dialog box, 707
add-ins
   managing, 53
   preventing harm from, 818
   security settings, 825
   Silverlight, 853
   Windows Desktop Search, 534
Add-Ins tab, 53
Address Book, 767–770
address searches, 750
administrators for SharePoint sites, 863
Adobe Acrobat, 595
Adobe Reader, 595
Advanced Settings dialog box (SharePoint), 872
Advanced tab (Backstage view), 69
Advanced tab (ribbon), 70
advancing slides, 635
agenda slides, 675
alerts. *See also* notifications
   e-mail messages, 764
   SharePoint activities, 880–882
aligning
   Excel cell text, 459
   graphic objects, 155–156
   numbers in Word documents, 311
   objects on presentation slides, 603
   shapes, 176
   text formatting, 125, 126
   text in Word tables, 262
   Word tables, 267
all caps text, 217
All Slides dialog box, 636

T

About the Authors

Ed Bott is an award-winning author and technology journalist who has been researching and writing about Windows and PC technology, in print and on the Internet, for nearly two decades, with no intention of stopping anytime soon. He has written more than 25 books, all on Windows and Office. His books have been translated into dozens of languages and distributed worldwide. You can read Ed's latest opinions and hands-on advice at Ed Bott's Microsoft Report on ZDNet (*www.zdnet.com/blog/bott)* and Ed Bott's Windows Expertise (*edbott.com/weblog)*. Ed and his wife, Judy, live in northern New Mexico, in a house full of very lucky pets—Katy the cat, who was plucked from a shelter in the Puget Sound area in 1997, and Mackie and Lucy, who were adopted with the help of English Springer Rescue America (*springerrescue.org)*. All three make cameo appearances in this book.

Carl Siechert began his writing career at age eight as editor of the *Mesita Road News*, a neighborhood newsletter that reached a peak worldwide circulation of 43 during its eight-year run. Following several years as an estimator and production manager in a commercial printing business, Carl returned to writing with the formation of Siechert & Wood Professional Documentation, a Pasadena, California, firm that specializes in writing and producing product documentation for the personal computer industry. Carl is a coauthor of more than 20 books, covering operating systems from MS-DOS 3.0 to Windows 7 and productivity applications from Microsoft Works 3 to Office 2010. In a convergence of new and old technology, Carl's company now operates a popular website for hobby machinists, *littlemachineshop.com*. Carl hiked the Pacific Crest Trail from Mexico to Canada in 1977 and would rather be hiking right now. He and his wife, Jan, live in Southern California.

What do you think of this book?

We want to hear from you!

To participate in a brief online survey, please visit:

microsoft.com/learning/booksurvey

Tell us how well this book meets your needs—what works effectively, and what we can do better. Your feedback will help us continually improve our books and learning resources for you.

Thank you in advance for your input!